Between Public and Private

Readings and Cases on Canada's Mixed Economy

Edited by

Diane Jurkowski
George Eaton

Captus Press

Between Public and Private: Readings and Cases on Canada's Mixed
Economy

National Library of Canada Cataloguing in Publication

Between public and private : readings and cases on Canada's
mixed economy / edited by Diane Jurkowski and George Eaton.

Includes bibliographical references.
ISBN 1-55322-059-5

    1. Industrial policy—Canada. 2. Industrial policy—Canada—Case studies.
I. Jurkowski, Diane II. Eaton, George E.

HD3616.C32B48 2003   38.971   C2003-905101-3

Captus Press Inc.
Mail: Units 14–15
          1600 Steeles Avenue West
          Concord, Ontario
          L4K 4M2
Telephone: (416) 736–5537
Fax: (416) 736–5793
Email: info@captus.com
Internet: www.captus.com

Canadä We acknowledge the financial support of the Government
of Canada through the Book Publishing Industry Development Program (BPIDP) for our publishing activities.

0 9 8 7 6 5 4 3 2
Printed in Canada

Table of Contents

Preface

Diane Jurkowski

This is the first edition of *Between Public and Private: Readings and Cases on Canada's Mixed Economy*. The purpose of this book is to give students a better understanding of the relationships between business and government.

Every day we hear and read news reports about the status of the economy, the risk of trade wars and the implications of globalization. In Canada, these events have resulted in increasingly important relationships between business and government. The practices of business and the affairs of government are woven together. To many contemporary Canadian experts, such as business strategists, economists and government leaders this relationship is fraught with red tape, regulation, bureaucracy, inefficiency and non-necessity. But the reality is that business and government are constantly in consultation and discussion on governing policy instruments. Government influences the behaviour of individuals, groups and businesses in society. Business influences monetary and fiscal policies of government as well. Business interest groups are constantly lobbying government to protect their interests and ameliorate their demands, especially in the quest for profitability of business interests.

Even before Confederation, the scope and nature of relationships between business and government in Canada were well established. These associations can often be characterized as a love-hate relationship. On the one hand, business views government as intrusive when it regulates and taxes. There is the question to what extent is government intervention essential. On the other hand, when government embarks upon protectionist policies, this may be viewed more favourably by indigenous industry sectors. The questions that are asked

Diane Jurkowski

relate to whether government over steps moral or ethical boundaries in attempting to accommodate business and are there sacred rights and freedoms of business that transcends ethical considerations. The question that we ask ourselves as citizens is does government reserve the right to protect its citizens and consumers against the seemingly natural activities of business.

I would like to acknowledge the support and encouragement of Professor Randy Hoffman who has given me wonderful opportunities to pursue my interests in business and government activities. My appreciation is expressed to my co-editor, Dr. George Eaton and the contributors who answered the call to submit articles for discussion. My thanks are also expressed to Dr. Len Karakowsky who is a wealth of good counsel. I thank Pauline Lai, Jennifer Wong and the staff of Captus Press Inc. for their assistance in realizing the publication of the book. I always had the dedication of my son, David Jurkowski as my research assistant. I owe a great deal to students and colleagues at York University for their participation in courses that I have taught.

Introduction to Part I

The Structure of the Canadian Government

The first part of this book is to familiarize the reader with the nature of the Canadian government.

The first article, "Liberal Democracy and Its Ideological Underpinnings: From Laissez-faire to the Welfare State and Beyond?", traces the evolution of political and economic ideologies to the relationships between business and government. It establishes the reasons for the interventionist role of government that will be further explored in the second part of the book.

The second article, entitled "Introduction to Legal Studies", establishes the legal and constitutional framework of Canada. Laws serve a variety of functions as formal legal rules and actions intended to control and guide behaviour in society. Laws also become an expression of the relationships in society. The origins of law are presented to provide an overview of the Canadian context of civil and common law systems. The frameworks of the written and unwritten constitution are presented to provide an overview of the Canadian Constitution Act.

The third and fourth articles, entitled "Summary of Constitutional Events" and "The Constitutional Timeline of Canada", are intended to present a background to the study of constitutional events that have shaped Canada's concerns about the evolutionary and constitutional development of Canada and the relationships between federal and provincial jurisdictions. The exclusion of Quebec from the final agreement on the Constitution Act of 1982 has resulted in constitutional attempts to remedy the fact that Quebec considered itself excluded from Confederation and sought sovereignty. Provinces made strong statements about equality among provinces and equal powers, though recognizing the unique character of Quebec's language, culture and civil law tradition within Confederation.

The fifth article, entitled "Understanding the Canadian Parliamentary Government", examines the two usages of the term public administration. It presents the machinery of how Parliamentary governmental powers are allocated to establish the legislative and executive decision making of Parliament and the judicial and legal services.

The title of the sixth article, "The Case for a 'Triple E' Senate", refers to explaining the arguments for reforming the Canadian Senate and making it "equal, elected and effective". The revised Senate would have special responsibility to articulate provincial and regional interests. Such responsibility would be regarded as a constitutional safeguard, though the House of Commons' would retain its present dominance in Parliament.

The seventh, eighth and ninth articles present an understanding of how public service often operates. "Public Administration and Business Administration" compares and contrasts the management of government. It examines the general nature of administration generally, and relates it to the generic concepts of management, administration and linkage to politics as a prelude to examining differences between public administration and business administration. It examines the differences in conditions of employment in both sectors and then proceeds to evaluate five selected differences between public administration and business administration. Finally, it examines challenges presented by the new public administration of reinventing government or the business models. "Public Sector Restructuring: Eight Minor Details" suggests the development of the New Public Management was incorrectly focussed on customer service. Broader issues of public policy reform are addressing the fundamental policy issues that are of real concern. Eight principles are essential to the effective provision of public service. "A Comparison of Public and Private Sector Restructuring: Their Impact on Job Satisfaction" presents that the spread of restructuring practices to the public sector is based on a major assumption, which has, to a large extent, gone unchallenged. The authors' research findings indicate that downsizing, one of the key tools used in implementing the New Public Management, is often poorly applied in the public sectors. They argue that downsizing may in fact be an inappropriate tool in many public sector situations.

The tenth article, entitled "Role of Interest Groups in Influencing Public Policy in Canada", describes and discusses some of the important aspects of the role of interest groups and their ability to influence the public policy process in Canada. Business managers and citizens need to understand how interest groups operate in the political arena and the policy making process. Interest groups make an effort to influence the public policy process. Many groups obtain direct financial assistance from government and individual business firms obtain indirect assistance because of their expenditures on government relations. A number of interest groups seek to influence the behaviour of business firms as well as government. Interest groups perform important functions in a democratic society by lobbying and involvement in consultations, improving the making and implementing of public policy.

Liberal Democracy and Its Ideological Underpinnings

From Laissez-faire to the Welfare State and Beyond?

George E. Eaton

Introduction

The purpose of this article is to trace the evolution of political and economic ideologies relating to the relationship between private enterprise and the state. Why should it be felt necessary to explain the reasons for the interventionist role of the state or, perhaps, more meaningfully, of the government, more so when the students being taught may have known nothing other than a welfare state that has impinged on their lives and existence from the cradle to the grave? In education, there is compulsory attendance at the primary level and the setting of minimum standards for primary and secondary education. Tertiary education is also largely dependent on public funding. In public health there is extensive regulation and setting of standards, extending even to the preparation and marketing of food and drugs. A form of socialized medicine or health care has come to be regarded as part of the national heritage of Canadians. Economic activities throughout the economy are likewise subject to a variety of regulations in the public interest, including protection of consumers against misrepresentation and fraud or restraining efforts on the part of firms to inhibit competition and/or fix prices. There is regulatory protection of the physical environment in terms of utilization and conservation. Both levels of government — federal and provincial — in response to the imperatives of nation building, have for long, in a variety of ways, assisted natural resource-based industries such as agriculture, mining, oil exploration and refining, petrochemicals, lumbering and fishery. Governments also have been directly involved in the creation and ownership of public or economic enterprises in transportation and communication, petroleum and petrochemicals, public utilities and liquor distribution, to cite a few.

Another major responsibility of government has been to provide a wide range of social services (the so-called safety net) to afford some measure of economic relief for those who are, unwittingly, the casualties of endemic economic instability and occupational hazards, or for those who may be unable to fend for themselves because of disability or old age. Governments also have been charged with responsibility for the regulation of employer-employee and labour-management relations, and to enact and enforce legislation to prevent discrimination in labour markets or in the accessing of public goods and services, on the basis or race, colour, creed, gender or sexual orientation. Finally, in the wake of the Great Depression of 1929, which saw the collapse of the free market system, and the end of World War II, governments, with a great deal of public support, assumed responsibility for influencing, if not managing, the level of economic activity and achieving full employment through fiscal and monetary policies.

The answer usually given to the question posed earlier, as to why it should be considered necessary to explain the reasons for such extensive intervention on the part of the state, is that on the eve of the 21st century, our thinking and attitudes — ideology if you will — are still deeply influenced, if not dominated, by the intellectual or ideological heritage of 18th- and 19th-century industrial capitalism or classical liberalism. Since numerous references have already been made to the state and government and ideology, it may be helpful to provide a brief clarification of these terms.

The State and Government

Over the centuries, many definitions of the state have been put forward by theorists, reflecting, in each case, their discipline orientation or school of thought and the purposes to be served. For instance, for some, the state is a community organized for the purposes of government with the community being the whole body of people, or a nation, who live together within defined territorial boundaries. For others, "association" rather than "community" is the preferred term. Today, probably few political scientists would quarrel with the definition of the state as people living in a specific territory under a common legal and political authority. Often mentioned in the same breath, and considered an essential attribute of the state, is the concept of sovereignty. But, this too, is a concept fraught with ambiguity and troubling implications. The concept of sovereignty originated in the 16th and 17th centuries when European peoples were searching for a secular basis for the political authority of emergent nation states. At best, it can be described as a notion that suggests that there is, embodied within the state, an absolute, autonomous and indivisible power that may be brought to bear, internally, against citizens to ensure the maintenance of social order and, externally, against those who may be perceived to threaten the territorial integrity or national interests of the state. Stated in another way, sovereignty is the monopoly of coercive power wielded by the state, exercised by government as the agent of the state. Government, in turn, is the public administration or machinery, which encompasses the legislature, executive, and judicial structures and processes. It may be noted in passing that the state has served as a crucial myth in struggles for national unity by virtue of being the centre of loyalty for populations or communities. Unhappily, the concept of state and its corollary, sovereignty, have also served as the justification in many countries, for internal repression, external aggression and, indeed, genocide and other crimes against humanity.

In modern democracies, where emphasis is placed on government by consent and under the rule of law, the concept of sovereignty appears to be inconsistent with constitutionalism: that is, a government limited and restrained by checks and balances, including the assertion of political rights and freedoms.

Ideology

Ideology is a much more straightforward concept. It refers to the set of shared values, beliefs and ideas, even perceptions, through which members of a society interpret the reality of their past and present as well as shape their expectations and ambitions for the future. It is ideology that gives us a vision of our society, how it operates, and whether it may be considered good or bad, caring or uncaring.

Political ideology provides us with our view or perspective as to how power is attained and used, while economic ideology, which is probably more important, provides us with our view — both as individuals and as members of a particular socio-economic class — as to how wealth is created and distributed. Thus, its focus is on material possession. Power is to political ideology as material possession is to economic ideology, and they are closely inter-related in that each can be used to influence the other. At any given time, the dominant ideology is the particular set of ideas, beliefs, and values that are most widely held among the populace and that have the greatest impact on social action during that time. Similarly, the counter ideology, or opposing ideology, is the set of ideas and values held by a substantial minority that also may have a not inconsequential impact on social action.

Classical Liberalism and Its Credo

Classical Liberalism took its characteristic form during the 18th and 19th centuries, and gave ideological expression to the profound changes — social, economic and political — engendered by the Industrial Revolution and industrial capitalism. As such it represented a transition in the Western world, though first fully manifested in Great Britain, from a pre-market or typically agrarian handicraft society to a market or urbanized and mechanized society. The transition also was characterized by the appearance of more clearly defined classes and new social philosophies. On the theoretical side, classical liberal thinkers and philosophers were greatly influenced by the methodology or approach of the physical sciences which enjoyed enormous prestige after the publication of the celebrated *Principia* by (Sir) Isaac Newton (1642–1727). He argued that the external world was governed by laws that could be discovered and understood through the application of reason and the scientific method. Both classical economic and political theorists, though dealing with social phenomena that were grounded in the social sciences, sought to emulate the rationalism of the physical sciences and insisted on applying mechanical principles to the science of man and society. It resulted, among other things, in the identification of the natural with the reasonable and in an appeal to nature as the ultimate model of order and regularity. Accordingly, the natural order, with its ordained and immutable laws, was to be preferred over the arbitrary and often irrational societal arrangements contrived by man.

For the purposes of this article, the intellectual heritage or legacy of Classical Liberalism will be examined from two perspectives:

1. as a weapon intended to help in the destruction of an obsolete or constrictive Medieval Order; and
2. as a set of generalizations about man and society and government

Classical liberalism grew out of the dissatisfaction on the part of new and energetic middle classes with a social order that frustrated the achievement of their own social agenda. This class was new and middle in the sense that its members did not come directly from, or belong to, the nobility and landed aristocracy or the clergy, or the peasantry and artisanal classes, all of which constituted the medieval social hierarchy. In contrast with the medieval classes, their forebears, the new middle class wanted an environment that would free production and trade from "unnecessary restraints". They wanted a world in which their characteristic activities, economic transformation, and creating and amassing wealth would be regarded as normal and necessary rather than peripheral and disreputable. They wanted peace, and order over areas large enough to accommodate expanding trade. They wanted social institutions that would dispense with an obsolete and hierarchical structure and a political voice commensurate with the growing economic clout, particularly in determining what social services should be provided by the state and how much they would cost.

Freedom from Unnecessary Restraints

The new entrepreneurial class wanted to free production from the regime of "unnecessary restraints" associated with merchant and commercial capitalism, the very system that they were poised to take to its next and more advanced evolutionary stage: industrial capitalism.

The development of commercial capitalism was made possible by a number of factors, but for the purpose of this article, only a number will be selectively mentioned.

First and foremost was the growth of nation states, which began to emerge after the Protestant Reformation was instigated in 1513. The existence of states claiming the allegiance of populations within areas or physical boundaries controlled by a ruler raised issues of citizenship, and the exercise of power by rulers over citizens or subjects for the purpose of maintaining peace and order. In turn, it led to the articulation of the concept of political sovereignty, the supreme indivisible coercive power within the state, and whether or not it could be restrained or constrained by law, both secular and divine, by custom and tradition or morality, or implied contractual rights. These implied rights might be the result of a series of compacts or social contracts between God and secular ruler (divine right of kings) and/or between God, ruler and subjects or citizens. The issue of political allegiance was compounded by the competing claim of religious allegiance and led to long drawn-out religious warfare, and the necessity of finding a basis for separating or divorcing political allegiance from religious allegiance.

Economic self sufficiency also soon came to be considered an essential attribute of sovereignty, providing the justification for the involvement of the sovereign and state in trade and economic activities. Maritime discoveries, often the result of the quest for gold or other "exotic" commodities (e.g. spices), provided the impetus for an expansion of trade and, incidentally, to the establishment of colonies and colonial empires. Naval and military power were used not only to penetrate and protect markets but also, when conflict erupted, to subjugate and colonize local populations.

The state or sovereign became involved in joint ventures with merchant adventurers, expediently conferring monopoly of trading rights upon joint stock or huge trading companies, the vehicle (and forerunner of the modern corporation) devised to facilitate the sharing of the high risk involved in otherwise very profitable ventures and undertakings, and in so doing, the expansion of foreign trade.

Commercial Capitalism or Mercantilism

Economic historians, both early and modern,[1] have tried to provide a better understanding of the forces at work in the evolution of the feudal and pre-market economic structures into merchant or commercial capitalism, and to make sense of political and economic policies pursued by rulers and statesmen of the time by using mercantilism as a common framework. "Mercantilism" refers somewhat arbitrarily to the period from the 14th to the 17th centuries, and what makes it distinctive is the appearance in a number of Western countries of a set of theories, though not necessarily schools of thought, that explained or underlay the practices of ruling elites over this period of centuries.

The main ideas or themes associated with Mercantilism were the following:

1. Identification of wealth with precious metals. This is often associated with the early phase of mercantilism or Bullionism, coinciding with the search for gold in distant lands. Money was given a definitive force and trade depended on a plentiful supply of it, failing which trade would be sluggish.

2. Attitude to selling — fear of goods. Since the acquisition of wealth was linked to foreign trade, via the route of exchanging goods for precious metals (Bullionism), it was better to sell than to buy; hence, the "beggar thy neighbour" policy in foreign trade. It should be the objective of

trade to achieve a favourable surplus or balance in each area of trade. In the latter stages of mercantilism it was argued that it was a favourable general, and not a particular, balance of trade that should be the calculus of success.

3. Opposition to usury. Traders had great fear of the ability of financiers to charge high rates of interest. This was essentially a conflict between financial capitalism and commercial capitalism.

The political policies associated with the ideas outlined above led to direct control by the state of foreign exchange and the prohibition of the export of bullion. There was also general agreement that the expansion of trade and wealth required intervention by the state and, therefore, strong government was also a necessity. The practical implication was that it was both desirable and legitimate for the state to use economic measures to achieve national unification and national power. State regulation was essential for the widening of the market and the benefits accruing by way of profits could be readily identified with the national good or the strengthening of the power of the kingdom. It was not surprising, therefore, as noted earlier, that monopoly, protection and state regulation, along with state participation in private enterprise, became hallmarks of mercantilism.

Since competitive advantage in trading was also conducive to the amassing of wealth, it was necessary for the state to provide bounties at home to foster production for export, as well as to impose tariffs against foreign goods. Equally important for competitiveness was the necessity for the state to set and keep wages low, which in turn meant the regulation of the prices of basic food crops.

In effect, it would not be too much of an exaggeration to say that mercantilism represented in Great Britain and European countries a form of state capitalism based on an alliance of convenience between authoritarian rulers and private entrepreneurs.

The Enclosure Movement

The Enclosure Movement began in England as early as the 13th century and reached its climax in the late 18th and early 19th centuries. By the end of the period, about 10 million acres, nearly half the arable land of England, had been enclosed. The initial impetus was the monetization of the feudal economy. The cash nexus served to awaken the landed aristocracy to the revenue-generating potential of producing larger cash crops. Sometimes enclosures were designed to expand the scope for improved methods of farming, while at other times its effect was to convert arable land into pasture. The growth of commerce effectively destroyed subsistence farming and made farming both dependent upon, and subservient to, large markets — hence the commercialization of agriculture. As the growth of revenue accelerated the accumulation of commercial capital, the emergent middle class — for reasons of profit, political power and prestige — began investing in land, while the opposite took place with the landed aristocracy. Intermarriages, for much the same reasons, began to forge an alliance between financial and commercial capital and landed interests.

In short, the Enclosure Movement fulfilled two major purposes. First, it facilitated the agricultural revolution, which was a pre-condition for the Industrial Revolution and, second, by dispossessing peasants, it created a rural proletariat, that is, a vast pool of landless peasants, deprived of the traditional means of livelihood, who were thus forced to seek wage and employment and to ultimately join with the other component of the working class created by the industrial revolution: the urban proletariat. The creation of the urban working class was also an evolutionary process. To begin with, under Commercial capitalism, goods and services were produced by skilled artisans, regulated by Guilds, who were responsible for completing the cycle of production. They owned their tools, bought raw materials, owned the products that they sold, and kept the revenues. They were, however, transformed into semi-independent craftsmen when fledgling entrepreneurs and capitalists provided them with the raw materials and paid them to make the product, which was then claimed and resold by these financial intermediaries. The independent craftsmen, while still owning tools and production site, became transformed into part wage earners who were alienated from the final product (The Verlag or Putting Out system). The Industrial Revolution completed the process of alienation by bringing large numbers of workers, no longer owning the means of production, under a single roof — the factory — to be wholly dependent on wages for income. In the process, they became subject to the direction and control of capitalists or owners of the means of production, entitled to appropriate the residual surpluses as profit. The differentiation of classes between owners and employees and between managers and workers, and of wages being a cost to the employer but the sole source of income to the employee, provided the clash of economic interests that led workers to form trade unions and to engage in collective bargaining. Trade unions also became the main vehicle for the politicization of the working classes.

The Protestant Reformation — The Protestant Ethic and Capitalism

The burgeoning middle or capitalist class not only wanted trade and production to be freed from secular and sacred restraints, but they also wanted their characteristic activities — commerce, trade and manufacturing — to be regarded as necessary and legitimate. Throughout the medieval era or Middle Ages, economic activity and economic theorizing were subsumed under the theology of the universal Rome-based Catholic Church. Human beings were deemed to function at two levels of existence — secular and spiritual — with the spiritual being the ultimate and higher purpose. Accordingly, economic activity and, indeed, the amassing of personal wealth were to be subordinate to, and constrained by, the spiritual purpose and, not surprisingly, bound by laws of morality. The Church adhered to the Aristotelian view of money as a standard of value and, therefore, neutral in terms of value creation. Hence, money should not be used to gain advantage. Since money by itself did not create additional value in the reciprocal process of exchange, interest was usurious and, therefore, to be condemned. However, the Church, a very large land holder and, therefore, partly an economic institution, gradually found itself having to legitimize exceptions to usury as, for example, recognizing and compensating lenders for losses due to depreciation of assets because of lack of cash pre-empted by loans or for foregoing investment opportunities (opportunity cost idea). However, trade and commerce were still considered disreputable. The guiding principle in trade and employment relationships was that of "the just price". The just price was that which enabled each of the co-operants — investor, employer and hired help — to live as befitted their stations in life.

The religious sanctions and restraints imposed on economic activity were weakened when Protestant Reformation shattered the central doctrinal authority of the Universal Church. A new perspective on economic activity and wealth creation was provided by Protestant reformers and their sects, most notably Calvinism (John Calvin, 1509–1564), and later, more generally, by Puritanism. Because of the theological importance it attached to predestination, or being chosen to be saved and made part of the "elect", Calvinism sanctified and approved economic activity as an index of spiritual worth. Spiritual worth and material well-being based on dedicated or hard work were not to be considered mutually exclusive but rather one was the corollary of the other. Unlike Catholicism, therefore, Calvinism encouraged wealth seeking and the ethos of a businesslike world. But more important to Calvinism than its creation and accumulation was the use or purpose to which wealth was being put. Above all, wealth should not be used for conspicuous consumption or to emulate the debauched or degenerate lifestyle of the nobility. Calvinism, therefore, promoted and made a virtue of the habit of thrift and of productive investment. Indeed, Max Weber, the German sociologist, considered to be the founder of modern sociology in "The Protestant Sects and the Spirit of Capitalism" and, later, R.H. Tawney in "Religion and the Rise of Capitalism" propounded the thesis, still under debate, that the Protestant Ethic contributed to the rise of a new materialist or gain-centred socio-economic philosophy. Moreover, to the extent that it brought respectability and legitimacy to creating and accumulating wealth, the philosophy gave a strong impetus to the growth of market capitalism and its underlying motivation of personal acquisitiveness.

Classical Liberalism, Individualism and Human Motivation

Individualism — The Religious Contribution

Christianity emphasized the worth of the individual in the sense that all individuals were, and are, created equal in the sight of God. This equality, however, based as it was on faith, served primarily to heighten the individual's moral consciousness within himself as a member of society but it did not guarantee equality within the society. The Protestant Reformation emphasized that salvation was a gift of grace to the individual through revealed truth, and that this personal relationship of the individual to God dispensed with the need for the priest as an intermediary. Thus, the ultimate choice of decisions about right and wrong was the conscience of the individual.

The Protestant Reformation produced a situation where governments differed in the religion they tried to enforce, and in situations of conflict — between majority and minority denominations — it enabled rulers to invoke the practical necessity of citizens or subjects according absolute loyalty and authority to the ruler and to the state; hence, rulers with absolutist tendencies were the main beneficiaries. The issue of political obligation, therefore, became a central concern — the divine right of kings to rule and of the duty to obey the sovereign — or, alternatively, of a right to resist and depose a heretical king. The result was a mixture of political theory and religious belief or theological dogma.

In France the religious wars of 1562–1598, and the threat the wars posed to civilization itself brought home the urgent necessity of separating religious and political obligations. A solution was sought in the revival of the Natural Law Theory. It was a theory that had served the ancient Greeks as a system of universal laws — the ultimate and most reasonable standard of right and wrong — and of the good life according to nature. To the Romans, it likewise served as a universal law that recognized the intrinsic equality of humans, all of whom were endowed with the capacity to reason, and a source of restraint on rulers whose authority proceeded from the people. To the Early Christian Church as well as the Medieval Universal Church, natural laws provided the basis for a system of rational ethics that recognized that human society was governed by a complex of laws: Eternal Law, embodying the reason of God, the Creator; Natural Law, divinely bestowed reason on humans; Divine Law, the basis of revealed truth; and, finally, Human Law or promulgated law. Human Law was the corollary of natural law.

The revival of Natural Law in the Post-Reformation climate of war and internecine conflict, likewise recognized that such law was the dictate of right reason, universal to all peoples whatever their political or religious belief, and would exist even if God did not exist. As such, natural law offered a valid scientific approach to all social disciplines as well as a scientific guide to social conduct and practice, including the issue of political obligation.

Individualism and Human Motivation

The Psychological Egoism of Thomas Hobbes (1588–1679)

The theme of individualism was carried in a much more radical direction by Thomas Hobbes, often considered to be the father of liberalism. Hobbes was concerned with staving off the civil war, which was soon to engulf England from 1642–1688 and pit Protestants (Puritans) against Catholics, and Parliament versus monarch, for supreme control. His first task was to dispose of medieval concepts of natural law and the social contract that, with their mix of political theory and theological dogma, held that the ruler may be above his own laws but subject to God's law and the law of nature. Heavily influenced by the physical sciences, Hobbes' mechanistic view of the universe made for a quick dispatch of the religious element: "All that exists is body — all that occurs is motion". Once a body is put in motion, it goes on and on unless something stops it. Accordingly, God as the first mover could be removed from physics, leaving motion and matter. Religion could, therefore, be relegated to the realm of fiction and could not be the basis either for divine rule or for political or civil resistance. Moreover, just as physical matter may be broken into the smallest particles, atoms, so too could civil society be reduced to its basic elements: namely, individuals who, incidentally, are deemed by Hobbes to have initially existed in a state of nature. The upshot is that government must be based on the science of psychology and politics. Psychologically, man is comprised of two parts — reason and passion, the rational and the irrational. Passion prevailed in the primal (and notional) state of nature, where life is "solitary, poor, nasty and brutish and short". The fear of death thus becomes the basis of civilization, for society is really man writ large. The only rational solution is to create the "Leviathan" (the title of Hobbes' political treatise published in 1651), or sovereign ruler to guarantee peace. If society is thought to be formed on the basis of a social contract, then there must be a sovereign or sovereign power above society to enforce the contract, and the sovereign cannot, therefore, be part of the contract. All social institutions, including the Church, are subordinate to the sovereign, who ultimately is the source of law and morality. The only time that the sovereign ruler may be resisted, and indeed replaced, is if he threatens the physical security of persons, since self-preservation is the first law of nature. The only justification for the existence of the state is the benefits of government under the sovereign, which accrue to individuals. The value of society is thus measured in terms of self-satisfaction or utility that it affords to individualism, most notably peace and security. There is no such thing as the common good. Government is to be judged by its effectiveness. The theory of human motivation is egoism. Man is by nature self-seeking, although his self-interest may be disguised by elaborate subterfuges. The difference between man in the state of nature, where life is uncertain and man in society is that the reckless egoist aware of his capacity for self-destruction yields to the calculating egoist.

Hobbes, the academic philosopher, offended everybody: Parliament, because of the argument that even if government is based on consent, people must in turn consent to absolute and undivided sovereignty; Royalists, because there is no basis to the theory of divine right of kings to rule; common lawyers, because their reliance on custom and precedents is a reflection of stupidity; Christians in general, because actions were mechanically explainable and the free will, therefore, was an illusion; the universities, because their pursuit of scholasticism and dogma-based systems of thought and theories were retarding science.

Possessive Individualism[2] and Constitutionalism — John Locke (1632–1704)

Thomas Hobbes lived through the period of the civil war that saw the execution of a king in 1649, the establishment of a republic (1653–1658), the restoration of the monarchy in 1660 and, finally, a bloodless or palace revolution in 1688, which deposed an actively Roman Catholic regal dynasty and installed a Protestant successor line. The political settlement of the so-called Glorious Revolution produced in 1689 a statutory Bill of Rights that summed up concretely the 17th-century liberal movement. It restored the traditional constitution of vested interests, but the monarchy was now constrained by sovereignty of the electorate, supremacy of law, right to personal liberty, and the legal supremacy of Parliament (the House of Commons), now to be dominated by the new middle class. The theory of divine right of kings was laid to rest.

It was left to John Locke, university teacher and public servant, to interpret the settlement of 1688 and to temper the radical individualism of Hobbes. In so doing, Locke emerged as the leading spokesman for the rising middle class and their political grouping: the Whigs. He became the leading theorist of the Glorious Revolution and the main source of ideas for the American Revolution of 1776 and, probably, the most representative thinker in the Anglo-American political tradition.

Like Hobbes, Locke begins with the presumption of a state of nature in which men are equal and separate units, each one having equal right to do as he pleases. The state of nature is not, however, the state of war postulated by Hobbes, but rather one of peace, goodwill, natural assistance and preservation. Society is formed when men consent to a community or a government and become a corporate body politic. Although he does not use the term, Locke implies that sovereignty inheres in the people at all times. The majority has the right to act as a trustee for the individual, just as the government is a trustee or fiduciary and may be dismissed for breach of trust. Government is not given an independent position because it is not a party to any social contract. The notion of contract is dismissed as being too favourable to government. Why do men consent to community and government? Locke's answer is that, in the state of nature, man has certain inalienable rights, but there is no organization to give them effect. Among these rights are life and liberty, but by far the most important is private property, that with which man has mixed his labour.

While Locke appears, therefore, to be resuscitating the medieval concept of natural law, thereby preserving continuity with the past, he rejects one of its central moral concerns: the common good. Natural law no longer enjoins the common good. Instead, derivative natural rights become a bulwark against interference by the community with individual freedom and private property. Locke's state of nature and of society is, therefore, as egoistic as Hobbes'. The presumption of both men is that individual self-interest is prior, clear and compelling, while that of the community is vague and insubstantial. Individuals have claims against the government but the reverse does not hold. The protection of private property rights is made synonymous with promotion of the common good. Organized society and representative government may be altered, but not individual rights, which are indefeasible. Locke's individualism is very much in agreement with the interests of the class that elevated it to the status of a social philosophy, namely, the middle or capitalist class.

From Possessive Individualism to Hedonism and/or Utilitarianism

After Locke, a period of quiescence ensued as the middle classes consolidated their position in England. Locke's ideas, however, became the inspiration for the revival of political and social theory in France in the 18th century. In his concern to preserve the social fabric, Locke had attempted a synthesis combining the medieval traditions, which embodied the unifying principles of universal Christianity, and universal natural law, on the one hand, with the scientific approach derived from Newtonian physics, on the other. But in France, under the absolutism and decadence exemplified by Louis XIV's long rule, there could be no appeal to traditional rights. Locke's assertion of prior and inalienable rights of individuals became abstract rights of liberty, equality and fraternity and an attack on vested interests in France. Its culmination was the French Revolution of 1789, which resulted, ultimately, in the overthrow of the monarchy, the institution of republicanism and the physical decimation of the nobility and landed aristocracy, which were deemed to be a parasitic and useless class.

The spread of Locke's influence to France was largely the work of philosophers of the French Enlightenment, most notably Montesquieu (1689–1755) and Voltaire, both of whom had visited England and returned to popularize his ideas. In his "Spirit of Law" (1848), Montesquieu concluded that the liberty and freedom enjoyed by Englishmen were due to the separation and balance of power, not between social classes, but between the three branches of government — legislative, executive and judicial. This system of checks and balances, constitutionalism, served to effectively restrain the government. But what Montesquieu had observed was, in fact, not a constitutional separation, but rather a functional separation of power among the three branches. In the British (Westminister) model of parliamentary government, the legislature and executive, if anything, were fused in that there was considerable overlap of functions and personnel between the legislature and the executive. Nevertheless, Montesquieu's interpretation of the doctrine of separation and balance of powers was enshrined in the American Independence Constitution.

For his part, Voltaire, though not interested in popular government, was ardent in his defence of intellectual freedom and insisted on universal religious toleration. Denying the existence of revelation, he advocated the abolition of censorship, separation of Church and state, and a state strong enough, albeit acting under general rules of law, to cope with forces obstructive to social progress and individual liberty. More important, for our purposes, Voltaire and Helvetius (de l'esprit 1758) translated Hobbes' and Locke's egoism into utilitarianism, by substituting a single standard of value: the greatest happiness of the greatest number. The state then becomes a machine for the creation of happiness.

Utilitarianism

The doctrine of utilitarianism returned to England where it was elaborated by jurist Jeremy Bentham (1748–1832), author and classical political economist James S. Mill, and his son John Stuart Mill (1806–1873), political economist and philosopher, to become the school of Philosophical Radicalism, espousing programs of legal, economic and political reforms.

According to Bentham, "nature has placed mankind under the governance of two sovereign masters, pain and pleasure. It is for them alone to point out what we ought to do, as well as to determine what we shall do. On one hand, the standard of right and wrong, and on the other, the chain of causes and effects, are fastened to their house". This hedonistic calculus provides the operating principle for both state and government: namely, to increase pleasure and reduce pain. Since in terms of the calculus of pleasure and pain, each one counts for one and no more, the intervention of the state must be guided by the principle of maximization of the greatest happiness of the greatest number. While the majoritarian principle implied in Bentham's hedonistic calculus logically implied that the state could play a positive role in the conduct of public affairs, nevertheless, to Bentham and followers, legislation was acceptable, though considered an evil designed to reduce worse evils. The immediate beneficial effect of utilitarian liberalism was the reform of British criminal law. Bentham argued that the punishment or pain to be applied in the punishment of crimes or misdemeanour should only proportionately exceed the pleasure or gain derived and, accordingly, the harsh use of penology of the 18th century was uneconomical. Leniency was not only a natural and shrewd calculus but also a humane treatment.

Utilitarianism proved to be a vehicle for radical reform to remove restraints that seemed desirable to the middle class, but as a social philosophy it too had no conception of the common good, a concept viewed with suspicion at the very time that the total welfare of community or nation was becoming more important.

Economic Liberalism or Laissez-faire Capitalism

The Classical School of Political Economy
Exemplified by Adam Smith (1723–1790)
and David Ricardo (1772–1823)

Adam Smith, the first academic economist and founder of the discipline of economics, also drew on the naturalist school of philosophy which, as noted earlier, evolved from the Greco-Roman epochs as a system of universal laws, to a system of rational ethics during the medieval era, to a system of natural rights during the development of liberalism or constitutionalism.

For Smith, human conduct is actuated by six motives — self love, sympathy, desire to be free, sense of propriety, habit of labour and propensity to truck (trade) barter and exchange. Given these springs of conduct, each man is naturally the best judge of his personal interest and should be left free to pursue it. If left to do so, he will contribute unwittingly to the common good. This result is achieved because Providence has made society into a system in which a natural order prevails. In the pursuit of individual self-interest, each one is "led by an invisible hand to promote an end, which was not part of his intention". The invisible hand is the market, guided by the forces of demand — generated by consumers and supply — and the response on the part of producers. Exchange makes possible the simultaneous satisfaction of individual interests and, therefore, there must be no obstacles to trade, which serves to maximize the advantages of division of labour and specialization (productivity). Economic freedom and competition must, therefore, be made to prevail.

The consequences of this belief in a natural order is that government can rarely be more effective than when it is negative or does not interfere. Government incursion in human affairs is generally harmful and, to cite Smith's classic articulation of economic laissez-faire, "Government is best which governs least". The natural balance of motives is seen most effectively at work in economic affairs. In seeking to maximize profits, each person is obliged to co-operate with others, a necessity enhanced by division of labour and specialization. The peculiar strength of Smith's doctrine of laissez-faire was its appeal — being made part of an immutable or unchanging natural order. But Smith's purpose was not just to state an abstract principle, but to destroy the actual conditions — the residual structures and policies of mercantilism — that conflicted with this principle. Thus, if there is room for state action, the principal duty of economic policy must be the preservation of free competition; but beyond that, the functions of government should be limited to (a) defence against foreign aggression, (b) exact administration of justice and (c) undertaking public works that are not profitable to private enterprise.

The impact of Smith's writings was enormous. The new industrial or capitalist class and their economic activities were given the imprint of respectability. Self-interest, the directing principle of everyday business, becomes the central motive of human conduct, and the pursuit of profit is made unselfish. The common good is now identified with a specific activity — the production of goods and services — and a specific motivation, profit making, and the businessman becomes in theory what he is in practice: the leader of the economic and political order. This natural order also implied a harmony of interests of individuals and classes, which could only be disturbed by the acquisition of privilege. Privilege, however, arises from action contrived in defiance of natural law — that is to say, political intervention.

Economic liberalism, therefore, reinforced political liberalism of Locke, reflecting a particular view of society and of the state.

The state is placed partially outside society and partially above society. Government as the agent of the state is needed but primarily for the protection of property and, by extension, of those who have property (the haves) against those who have little or none at all (the have nots). Smith's self interest turns out to be no different from egoism or Locke's "possessive individualism".

Development of Classical Economic Theory

David Ricardo (1772–1823)

Ricardo added intellectual rigour and refinement to Smith's analysis and competitive model of the economy and, in so doing, differentiated between static and dynamic theory. From the static or mechanistic point of view, economic science elucidates that production and exchange are governed by the market mechanism: the price system, which impersonally allocates resources and determines prices. Economic society is composed, on the one hand, of individuals — or consumers seeking to maximize satisfaction of wants and directing production through expenditures — and, on the other hand, of individual producers competing with each other to satisfy these wants. Consumers seek to buy as cheaply as possible, while producers seek to sell for the best price possible, and in the process, an equilibrium or balance is achieved. From the point of view of social dynamics, however, Ricardo points out that economics is the theory of distribution among classes, "the division of the produce of industry among the classes who concur in its formation". These are landlords (rent), capitalists (profits) and workers (wages). Smith's natural order and harmonious relations are deemed to exist in the section of production governed by the natural order, but the distribution among classes opens up the possibility of conflict between classes, an eventuality examined by Ricardo.

What held these incompatible assumptions together was not logic, but the identity of middle-class interests being served.

The Political Creed of Classical Liberalism

The political creed of Classical Liberalism may be summed up by the term "constitutionalism", or limited purpose government; but, even so, further restrained by checks and balances. It reflects an attitude of ambivalence towards the state. At one level of thought, there is near rejection of the state. Society may be a blessing, but government, even in the best state, is a necessary evil. The state is personalized and, as such, can acquire power. Since absolute power corrupts absolutely, that power must be restrained, failing which it may be a threat to the individual and his property. The solution is to restrict the state, the government and its agent, to minimalist functions. Society, state and government are all seen as serving instrumental purposes.

What happens, however, when as a result of the growth of political democracy and the broadened base of citizenship, the social question becomes accommodation of the interest of the working class, the numerically largest class?

While the utilitarian principle of the greatest happiness for the greatest number, which logically translates into the majority rule principle in political decision making, would imply that the state may serve as the instrumentality to create the conditions for realizing the greatest happiness or welfare of the majority, 19th century liberalism also feared mass participation. It reflected a very negative perception of the capacity of the "lower" and largely unpropertied classes to appreciate the values of liberalism.

Challenges to Classical Liberalism: Alternative Ideologies

The Revolt against Reason: Restoration of the Community

In France, the popularization of Locke's liberalism gave rise to an intellectual movement that came to be characterized as the Age of Enlightenment, or the Age of Reason. Its major tenets were a belief in the inevitability of progress to be realized through the application of reason, and a belief in terrestrial happiness. Individualism was exaggerated to the point where it seemed to be destroying society by reducing it to an atomized collection of propertied individuals, demanding rights without corresponding social obligations, elevating reason and frowning upon revelation and spontaneity, and preaching self-interest and decrying love. It seemed as though men were being freed from despotism to be subjugated by a new and callous system.

The Enlightenment produced a dramatic response in the revolt against reason inspired by Jean Jacques Rousseau (1712–1778). In his celebrated work, *The Social Contract* (1762), Rousseau denounced the thinking man as a depraved animal. The worth of society was the worth of common feelings: the affections of family life, joy and beauty. Science was mere idle curiosity and intelligence, to the extent that it undermined reverence and destroyed faith, was dangerous. Rousseau attacked Hobbes' and Locke's conceptions of the utilitarian society and juxtaposed the community as a moralizing force. Accordingly, the fundamental category was man, not citizen. In a famous passage, Rousseau declared: "Man is born free but everywhere he is in chains".

Underlying his theory of the social contract were three propositions: the state as a progressive and moralizing and uplifting force; the state must be based on rational or reasonable will; and the individual surrenders himself to the community of persons that exercises sovereignty, or the general will. Paradoxically, the general will is not quite the same thing as the will of all. While the general will expresses the innate moral capacity of man, and is always right, it could give rise to two possible interpretations: one consistent with the tradition of Liberal Pluralism, that rightness of the general will is the result of rational discussion and negotiations; the other totalitarian, to the extent that differences of opinion, or factionalism of, say, political parties, are inimical to social integration. Rousseau's general will was given practical expression by the French Revolution of 1789, where the individualism of natural law was replaced by a single party that embodied the general will, and ended in dictatorship. Locke's individualism which, in political terms, meant oligarchic rule of the select few and enterprising people who refuse to be submerged in the mass, was now confronted by the sovereignty of mass democracy.

Classical Conservatism
— Edmund Burke (1729–1797)

In England, reaction to the exaggerated individualism of the Enlightenment, as well as the impact of the Industrial Revolution on the rural way of life, and the revolutionary zeal of the French Revolution, led Edmund Burke, a practising politician, to enunciate his view of society and principles of government. It became the statement of Classical Conservatism, the ideology of the agricultural classes.

Exposed to both the possibilities and constraints of nature, it is easy for farmers to conceive of progress in terms of organic growth, a perspective very much at odds with the mechanistic rationalism of the 18th-century philosophers. Conservative thinkers like Burke were able to draw on rural sentiments to develop a doctrine of conservatism and, by inspiring the rural classes to resist the forces of the Enlightenment, aroused an important section of the population to political consciousness.

19

Evolution, not revolution, was Burke's rallying theme. Man is both rational and passionate, and passion needs to be restrained. Man's better self is the product of social discipline, not reason, and societies are held together by traditional morality and force of habit. Hence the need for authority. Only the state has the coercive power to regulate lesser associations. There is nothing inevitable about the progress of civilization, which involves adding precept to precept to precept, and invention to invention. Burke's fear was that a single generation of liberals would undo the work of centuries, and the only defence was a strong, authoritative government backed by state and Church. The state is not, as suggested by liberal theorists, a limited association for limited purposes. Rather, it is an unlimited partnership of successive generations, a balance of vested interests.

The constitution is, therefore, prescriptive and its justification and authority is that it has existed time out of mind. The body politic does not exist to guarantee indefeasible rights of individuals, especially abstract rights, but to preserve the partnership between the living, between the living and the dead, and those yet to be born.

It should be emphasized that Burke was not a democrat. He rejected individual parliamentary representation in favour of representation of interests or classes. Political parties existed to facilitate both representation and government, under the leadership of a public-spirited minority. This was in sharp contrast, therefore, to classical liberals who were preoccupied with individuals and individual mobility. Burke accepted the desirability and necessity of a natural hierarchy of classes within which individuals have assigned roles as befit their stations in life.

The logic of conservative theory, as enunciated by Burke, lay in forging an alliance between the monarchy, the aristocracy and landed interest to deal with the new situations, political and economic, created by the Industrial Revolution. Hence, the social dualism: the preservation of traditional pieties and a strong government.

The Contradictions of Classical Liberalism and the Emergence of Socialism

Classical political economy considered the welfare state to be incompatible with the dynamics of capitalism. According to Smith, the general welfare of society was nothing more than the sum of the welfare of individuals within it. Hence, social welfare would be best served by maximizing the sum of individual welfares. Such maximization likewise could best be realized by permitting individuals, within the legal framework based on freedom of contract, to pursue their own economic interests without any external restraint.

The best mechanism for such economic maximization was a freely competitive market economy, comprised of large numbers of consumers and individual producers, where production was directed solely by the laws of supply and demand: in effect, pre-empting the ability of individual producers or firms to influence output and price.

Smith and his immediate successors did not, however, anticipate some of the many deep-seated economic, political and social changes that would occur in the wake of the Industrial Revolution. They included:

1. long-term decline in agricultural employment and the rural population, both a cause and effect of the Enclosure Movement referred to earlier;
2. extensive urbanization and the growth of large cities, and of urban ways of life, with all the associated problems: health and sanitation, housing, unemployment (a new phenomenon), crime and prostitution;
3. creation of a landless, manual working class concentrated in particular sectors and residential neighbourhoods;
4. changes in the composition of the labour force, occasioned by industrialism, and the need to provide minimum levels of education; fragmentation of tasks and de-skilling of workers caused by mass production techniques, along with the job alienation of workers; and
5. changing patterns of family life and community life as factory employment accentuated the division between working and non-working (dependent) populations, and between home and workplace.

Some of the highly visible social consequences were child labour, exploitation of women, long hours, occupational hazards, illness and accidents. Therefore, by 1840, it had become necessary for state and government to enact factory legislation to deal with these problems.

Earlier, we noted the contradiction inherent in the assumption made by classical political economists that production was the result of interactions between individual consumers and producers, constrained by the impersonal, or self-regulatory price mechanism, or the forces of demand and supply, while the resulting economic pie was shared among classes, leading to the possibility of class conflict and involvement of the state and government. The granting of the right to vote, or suffrage, and the expansion of the enfranchised electorate in successive Reform Acts in Britain in 1832, 1867, 1884 and 1885 served to usher in the era of mass politics, and to give to Bentham's guiding maxim for determination of public policy — the greatest happiness for the greatest number — a practical political significance that he probably did not wish to anticipate: namely, the exercise of power on the basis of majority rule, with each voter counting for one and no more. At the same time, many liberals found themselves still preoccupied with preserving individual values identified with an oligarchic and/or aristocratic social and political order. As they became defenders of the status quo, more radical groups, most notably the socialists, soon took their place as social critics and reformers.

Another apparent contradiction to be resolved by Classical Liberals and latter generations in the liberal tradition arose from the growth of corporate power. The Industrial Revolution and technological innovation increasingly gave rise to large-scale organizations capable of yielding economies of scale and enhancing productive capacity.

The resources from personal, family or partnership sources that were available to the pioneering captains of industry and the Industrial Revolution — the original investors and entrepreneurs — soon proved to be inadequate to meet the growing demand for capital, and prompted a return to the joint-stock company of the mercantilist era. The result was the emergence of the modern corporation, based on shareholding and the concept of limited liability. This large-scale unit of production not only involved systematizing of operations and tasks, but also the creation of large workforces within the ambit of a single establishment or employer. Big business, in effect, begot big unions. But more immediately, how could this unit of production representing a large agglomeration of interests and assets, capable of exercising both political and economic power, be reconciled with the classical competitive model that assumed large numbers of small producers, each individually being incapable of influencing price? This contradiction was resolved by legal ingenuity in creating the legal fiction of corporate personality: the corporation being treated as a person and equal at law to any individual, be it consumer or worker.

Another factor was that while the Industrial Revolution and mechanization in the long run created an expanding demand for labour and new occupational skills, it initially threatened the jobs and living standards of skilled craft workers. In defence, they created trade unions, or workers' organizations, to protect their jobs, wage levels, and living standards. In effect, workers challenged the reality of corporate personality by juxtaposing their own collective personality, to achieve a more effective counterbalance of power through collective bargaining and withholding of labour. They were, however, legally threatened and restricted in their organizational and bargaining efforts by governments wedded to liberal economic doctrines of free trade and freedom of competition, and persecuted and harassed by common law judges — staunch defenders of private property rights — who deemed them to be criminal conspiracies operating in restraint of trade. To ensure survival, the unions turned to political action to remove legal disabilities and achieve a legal framework that would enable them to pursue economic objectives through collective bargaining and industrial action. In the process, they and the broader working class became politicized, gave support to or formed their own political parties and, as a labour movement, articulated a social philosophy and ideology typically identified with socialism.

Socialism: A Radical Working Class Ideology

Unlike classical liberalism and conservatism, which also emerged as protest doctrines, socialism represents a much greater spectrum of views, or factions, and its family tree is quite extensive. Nevertheless, it is still possible to identify a number of underlying and unifying strands of thought.

First, socialists generally repudiate the laissez-faire or negative state and, in particular, the assumption of harmony of interests among different classes. Capitalism — and the term is being used here to indicate an economic system in which the greater part of the means of production is privately owned, and in which economic activity is undertaken with the expectation of profits — is perceived by socialists as a system in which the ruling class extracts wealth from the subordinate classes. Inequality is, therefore, endemic and, consequently, it may be necessary for the state to intervene to harmonize work relations, and to effect a more equitable distribution of income or wealth.

Second, there is a significant role for the state to play in providing relief from the overall exploitative or oppressive nature of capitalism. More significant, this may entail collective action and public ownership of enterprises to ameliorate the conditions of the masses. Public ownership can be undertaken by all levels of government, or through co-operative enterprises.

Third, there is the element of humanism, an optimistic belief in the perfectibility of human beings, given the proper environment and circumstance. A brief description will now be provided of the various strands, or schools of thought, of socialism.

Utopian Socialism

The earliest school of thought, which dates from about 1800, was utopian socialism. Leading protagonists developed their ideas in the early stages of the industrial revolution when there were rapid and disruptive changes, and workers did not yet have the capacity to exercise effective countervailing power in both the political and industrial arenas. Utopian socialists considered the competitive market economy to be unjust and irrelevant. They preached universal brotherly love rather than class struggle, and promoted co-operative communities and co-operative ventures with progressive capitalists.

Christian Socialism

Christian socialism developed in England and Germany after 1848. It appeared after the defeat of radical movements in both countries, and offered workers the consolation of religion to assuage their pain and give hope. The Bible served as the manual of inspiration for employers, workers and political rulers. It revived the medieval concept of a divinely inspired order of mutual love and fellowship, and of property owned by the rich being held in trust for the benefit of all. This movement eschewed violence and class warfare, and advocated reforms through progressive social legislation.

Anarchism

Anarchists, the most prominent of whom were Russian and French, regarded the state as the root of evil, and all forms of government to be oppressive. Human nature was essentially good, if not corrupted by the state and its institutions. The solution lay in a social order based on self-governing groups and voluntary or associative effort. Private property should be abolished, to be replaced by collective ownership of capital by co-operating groups. Production would be carried on within communities under the control of associations of producers, and trade would take place with other communities. In effect, members of this fringe group espoused supremacy of the individual over state and society.

Marxian / Scientific Socialism

Scientific socialism is associated with the writings of Karl Marx (1818–1883) and his associate and collaborator, Frederich Engels (1820–1845), and is the most influential body of socialist thought.

The Marxian system consists of three elements: (a) a dialectical and materialist interpretation of history derived from German classical philosophy; (b) a theory of state and of revolution taken from French revolutionary socialist tradition; and (c) a system of political economy of which the dynamic part is the labour theory of value (first hinted at by Locke, and elaborated on by David Ricardo) and a theory of surplus value, both inspired by the classical school of (British) political economy. The other elements of the system of political economy are a theory of capitalist accumulation, the dynamic aspect of capitalism; a theory of increasing (capital) accumulation; a theory of increasing misery; and a theory of crises. All of these will ensure the overthrow of capitalism because of their inherent contradictions.

Marx argues that in every historical epoch, the prevailing method of production and distribution (economic determinism) creates the social structure of classes (the infrastructure) which, in turn, breeds attitudes, actions and civilizations (the superstructure). In other words, the resultant social organization forms the basis for the legal, political, cultural and intellectual structures. As each socio-economic system develops its productive forces (resources), the relations of production (relationships between groups) become a barrier to further progress. Accordingly, the system has to be revolutionized so that the new productive relations among people permit the higher development of the process of production. There is, then, a cycle of thesis, antithesis (or challenge) and synthesis, the emergence of the new system. The mechanism for overthrowing each system is the class struggle. Thus, slavery, the oldest form of class society, developed its productive capacity to the maximum possible, and gave way to feudalism. In turn, feudalism developed its own dynamics and evolved into capitalism, which created the working class, the class with the historical mission to transform capitalism into socialism.

The state is viewed by Marx as an instrument of coercion used by one class against another. The capitalist state oppresses workers but, in turn, the working class — or proletariat, those who do not own the means of production and must rely on employment income — will overthrow the capitalist, or bourgeois state, and will establish its own dictatorship to destroy the bourgeoisie as a class. Since private property (the Marxian equivalent of sin) is the source of dominion of man over man, and of inequality, private ownership of the means of production must be abolished, and all the means of production owned by the state. Since the members of the society no longer own the means of production, the basis will be laid for a class-less society in the sense that there are only workers of the brain and of the hand, and, therefore, no subordinate class to exploit.

Communism

The next higher stage of society, according to Marxism, is communism, when the state will wither away and, in the absence of antagonistic classes, the government over persons will be replaced by the administration over things such as infrastructure and utility systems. Under communism the transitional socialist slogan, "From each according to his ability to each according to his work" will be succeeded by the communist slogan, "From each according to his ability to each according to his need". The enormous productive capacity of the capitalist system should also be realized before it would be ripe for revolutionary overthrow.

It is instructive that Marx seized upon the inconsistencies of Classical Political Economy to turn them into a radical critique of its economic and political philosophies. Thus, if labour adds value, and it can be shown that capital or machinery is nothing more than canned labour, and that management is but more highly trained labour, it is, then, labour that creates surplus value in excess of what is required to meet the subsistence needs of workers, but that surplus is appropriated by capitalists solely by virtue of ownership of the means of production. Marx also used the classical subsistence theory of wages, which postulated that population increase and resulting competition among workers would ensure that wages, in due course, would return to the subsistence level, a theory later dubbed "the iron law of wages". But for Marx, capital accumulation and technological unemployment would swell the reserve army of the unemployed. The result would be overproduction and underconsumption, thereby increasing impoverishment of workers and generating crisis after crisis, raising the level of militancy on the part of the working class, leading to the inevitable overthrow of capitalism.

Revisionism — Evolutionary or Democratic Socialism

In Germany and England, economic determinism and the methods and analysis of Marxism held great attraction for left-wing theorists and reformers. It seemingly provided the means for a sophisticated theoretical dissection of contemporary society that exposed its evils and offered solutions. The revolutionary solution of Marxism was, however, tempered by the fact that the socialists accepted some of the basic values of liberalism. Thus, for instance, the Fabian Socialists, the intellectual precursors of the socialist British Labour Party that came to power in 1945, abjured class warfare and denied that the state must always be a repressive class institution. Instead they pinned their hopes on education, the electoral process and gaining control of the government by constitutional means.

In relying on the support of trade unions, Parliamentary socialists came to be identified with the social democratic tradition, which placed great emphasis on egalitarianism. They could accept the need for a mixed economy while at the same time seeing a significant role for government, which might involve regulation of monopolies, setting employment standards, providing employment protection, public ownership of public utilities and even ownership of certain strategic enterprises or industries.

For socialists in the social democratic tradition, the ideal became the welfare state that could be compatible either with state capitalism or state socialism. Under state capitalism, the government, as an entrepreneur, owns and operates enterprises on the basis of economic viability in a predominantly capitalist milieu. Under state socialism, again within a capitalistic framework, the government undertakes to own and operate sectors of the economy for overall social benefits, rather than for profit.

Syndicalism

Syndicalism, often lumped with anarchism, was promoted and popularized largely within the labour movements by Georges Sorel (1847–1922). Syndicalists believed that seeking to reform capitalism through parliamentary means would only lead to opportunism to gain political power, and weaken the revolutionary thrust of the working class. Workers should be brought under the organization of one big union, using strikes to foment revolutionary consciousness and militancy. Eventually, the general strike, the workers' revolutionary instrument par excellence, would be used by one big union to overthrow capitalism. In and of itself the act of violence would be creative and provide its own solution. Capitalism having been overthrown, industries would be organized as autonomous units to be managed by workers and linked together in a federation, the administrative centre. Like anarchism, syndicalism also believed in the abolition of private property and the extinction of coercive political government.

Guild Socialism

Advocated by G.D.H. Cole (1889–1959), a professor of Economics at Oxford University, Guild Socialism remained primarily a British movement. Guild Socialists accepted the necessity of the state to serve the general interests of citizens as consumers, but believed that the management of industries should be the prerogative of employees, as producers, organized in industrial guilds. In this concept of "industrial democracy", to be gradually achieved through reform, the antagonism between labour and capital would be muted, producing a society based on a partnership of equals. Producers and consumers would be represented by national associations — the guilds, and the government.

Pseudo Socialism — National Socialism and Fascism

Both the regimes of Adolph Hitler's Nazism (1930s–1945) and Benito Mussolini's Fascism (1930s–1945) represented, in many respects, a revolt against reason. In place of reason, they offered insight. Life controls reason, reason does not control life and, thus, will and action are self-justifying. Nazism classified itself as national socialist: national because nationalism is a sentiment of universal appeal; socialist, so that it could appeal to, as well as neutralize, radical socialists and syndicalists organizations. Emphasis was also placed on co-operative socialism to appeal to small shopkeepers and the lower middle class. Additionally, the waste and friction of the class struggle could be avoided by requiring corporations to make the decisions about the conduct of economic life, and to achieve a more equitable distribution of income between capital and labour and, in so doing, contribute to the advantage of the state or national community. In this context, force could also be used to control dissidents or worker discontent.

Instead of seeing the progression of history and civilization as a struggle between classes, both Nazism and Fascism held that all history could be interpreted as a struggle between races. For Italian Fascism, the national community could be seen as the heir to the Roman Empire. For Nazism, the myth of the folk was substituted for glorification of the historic mission of race, more specifically, the Aryan or culture-creating race, as opposed to lesser breeds of races. Accordingly, every race is under the necessity of suppressing what is foreign or degenerating. The result was encouragement of the preferred population and eugenic legislation. The fears and hatreds of many kinds also were transmuted into fear of a single tangible enemy, the Jews, and resulted in a policy of anti-Semitism and anti-Jewish legislation, as well as physical liquidation of Jews on a massive scale.

The theory of the state under both national socialism and fascism was based on a social hierarchy of the masses, the ruling class and the (maximum) leader. When this theory was operationalized in political terms, it gave rise to totalitarian parties and dictatorship of the right, just as Communism (with a more sophisticated and conceptual framework) gave rise to a totalitarian party and dictatorship of the left.

The Evolution of Classical Liberalism into the 20th Century

From Reform Liberalism to Welfare Capitalism

The major challenge faced by Classical Liberalism, certainly in England during the latter half of the 19th century, was to reconcile the broadening of the scope and role of government, implicit in both the utilitarian, hedonistic calculus and the majoritarian principle, with the elitist concern about the capacity of the newly enfranchised lower classes to appreciate the commitment of Liberalism to liberty and freedom, the sanctity of private property and limited, or restrained, governments.

No one better exemplified this liberal ambivalence than John Stuart Mill, a political economist who was rigorously groomed intellectually from very early childhood by his father James Mill to be the ultimate apostle of utilitarianism. The younger Mill tried to abandon the utilitarian moral value based on the calculus of pleasure and pain, and focussed more on respect for the dignity of the individual. Political and social freedom, in themselves, are the proper condition of Man. The functions of the liberal state in a liberal society are not negative, but positive. There is much that government can do directly and indirectly to help improve the well-being of people. Laissez-faire or "let alone" philosophy was no longer tenable. The best guarantee of a liberal society is an educated society, but only the state and government can put education within the reach of all, even at the primary level. Mill was, however, deeply concerned about the tyranny of the majority. His essay entitled "On Liberty" (1859) is still considered one of the most eloquent defences of free speech. All mankind has no right to silence one dissenter. Liberty is not an individual good but a social good, and without it a good society is impossible. Both society and government must be tolerant. Greatly influenced by Classical Political economist David Ricardo, Mill's contribution lay in eclecticism in theory and compromise in politics.

The attempts to resolve the contradictions in classical liberal theory were taken further by the Oxford Idealists (T.H. Green, B. Bosanquet, and D.G. Ritchie). British philosopher Thomas Hill Green (1836–1882) put forward the so-called "organic liberalism" designed to prevent "hindrance to the good life". The state has a positive role to play in providing the good life for both individual and society. Freedom is as much a social good as it is an individual good, a quality of society as it is of the individual. Liberty exists, therefore, in relation to the common good. Freedom of contract, though desirable, is not an end in itself and must mean freedom to share in increased output. But the burgeoning of power of the employer and of the industrial employee are not equal. The free market is a social institution, not a natural institution, and may require regulation to preserve competition. Green, then, does away with the rigid demarcation between economics and politics.

The notion of the supremacy of Parliament as the sovereign legislative body also brought into question the presumption of inalienable natural rights. The extension of the franchise, or the right to vote, as well as the legal recognition of the right of workers to form trade unions and to bargain collectively within a legally defined institutional framework, represented the triumph of common sense over logic. Individual rights were not derived, and indefeasibly so, from a fictional or natural pristine state of nature, but were political rights conferred by statute, and interpreted and reinforced by the judicial system.

The Great Crisis of Liberalism and Its Transformation into Welfare Capitalism

By the end of the 19th century and early part of the 20th century, Classical economic theory had undergone refinement to the point where a differentiation could be made between the Classical School of economics and its successor, the Neo-Classical School. It reflected, in part, the growing prestige of economics as an academic discipline, and the concern of academic economists to make the discipline more rigorous analytically. In the process, it also became more esoteric and remote from the reality it sought to explain.

The refinement inspired by utilitarianist W.S. Jevons (1835–1882) in England, and carried forward by the so-called Austrian School — Carl Menger (1840–1921) and Leon Walras (1834–1910), among others, and later in England by Alfred Marshall (1842–1924) — gave economic theory a non-utilitarian interpretation by disengaging demand theory from the hedonistic calculus of pleasure and pain, and making value dependent upon utility, an individual subjective factor. Greater emphasis also was placed on making economics as mathematical as the physical sciences, and this was reflected in the concept of the margin or incremental analysis. Thus, a demand curve of an individual consumer could be constructed by utilizing the principle that the consumer would be prepared to pay a high price for an initial unit of a good or service because of scarcity and the correspondingly high level of utility or satisfaction. But, as each additional, incremental or marginal unit is purchased, it will be at a progressively lower unit price because of the law of diminishing marginal utility or satisfaction. Thus, the demand curve for an individual or market can be constructed graphically to reflect these trade-offs, or rate of substitution between satisfaction and dollar expenditures, and generalizations made. For instance, with the assumption of other things being equal, or fixed (such as income or tastes or preferences), the law of demand or general proposition may be stated that at higher prices less will be demanded or bought, and at lower prices more will be demanded or bought.

The same incremental analysis was employed to develop the marginal physical productivity theory, loosely referred to as productivity in popular imagery, to explain both the rational allocation and utilization of factors of production — labour, capital and land — and the determination of prices, or rewards for these factors. The picture of the rational individual carefully and mindfully maximizing utility and adjusting preferences at the margin, much like a householder does in the supermarket, and the profit-maximizing producer doing the same thing in relation to marginal product and marginal cost, conferred a legitimacy on the outcome and facilitated mathematical precision. It mattered little that the theory of consumer demand and the theory of production (marginal physical productivity) rested on rather heroic, or far-fetched assumptions of perfect information on the part of consumers and of workers, of owners of loanable funds (interest), of landlords (rent), and of investors (profit and/or dividends); perfect mobility of factors and homogeneity, or interchangeability of units of inputs, including labour; discreteness and measurability of inputs and outputs; and linearity, or fixed proportionality between inputs and outputs.

The marginal productivity theory also could be utilized to refute the Marxian theory of exploitation. If each factor of production is paid the value of its contribution to the total economic pie, then each share, or slice of the economic pie, is accounted for and there is no surplus or leftover to be wrongly appropriated by capitalists.

Rise of Corporate Civilization and Impact on Market Structures

Even as Neo-Classical economic theory was transforming the competitive model of the economy into a more stylized and abstract model of efficiency central to the teaching of economics as an academic discipline, the transformation of the structures of production in more industrially advanced capitalist economies were moving in the opposite direction. Nowhere was this better exemplified than by the trust and merger movements in the United States of America during the last two decades of the 19th century.

In 1879, Samuel Dodd, a lawyer for the Standard Oil Company, devised the idea of a trust, under which stockholders surrendered shares to the Board of Directors' trust and gave up working control in return for entitlement to profits. As a result, Standard Oil Directors could wield control over all associated companies. By the late 1800s, the new giant corporations financed by great entrepreneurs, the so-called robber barons, had been created in steel, railroads, oil, coke, shoes, tobacco, meat packing and agricultural machinery. The growth in size was made possible by the creation of national markets facilitated by the development of the railroads. However, rapid expansion of the facilities led to overbuilding of capacity, making competition more expensive because of the increase in fixed charges.

When cutthroat competition and price wars threatened bankruptcy, owners agreed that it would make more sense to collaborate than to compete, especially since the merger movements made it easy to arrive administratively at gentlemen's agreements and at pooling of markets. Unlike the Industrial Revolution, where the emphasis was on the engineering function, the new entrepreneurs were industrial and financial strategists. The engineering function of the pioneering captains of industry became the province of salaried production experts. As big capital seemed poised to gobble up small capital (as Marx had predicted by his theories of growing capital accumulation and corporate concentration), there was growing agitation by small businessmen for government intervention to protect them. The result was the Sherman Anti-Trust Act of 1890, which declared trusts illegal. But mergers continued through the use of the holding company, or financial conglomerate, posing what appeared to be the threat of economic feudalism and, once again, as a result of demand for regulation, the Clayton Act of 1914 was passed to prohibit certain forms of price discrimination and mergers by stock acquisitions.

Growth continued, in the process fleshing out characteristics of corporate civilization, including legal personality and the legal fiction of equality at law, notwithstanding the great concentration of economic power; capacity for self-generating growth and continuity; a changing concept of property based on shareholding, or fragmentation of property into pieces of paper and, along with it, dispersal of ownership; separation of ownership from control — the managerial revolution — with use and control passing to professional managers, in effect, from the property system to the power system. This transition was captured in the classic study by A. Berle and G. Means, *The Modern Corporation and Private Property* (1932), and, later, by J.K. Galbraith's *American Capitalism — The Concept of Countervailing Power* (1952).

The Post-World War II Era and the Ascendancy of the Welfare State

The welfare state means different things to different people, depending upon the socio-economic class to which they belong, or the socio-economic states they ascribe to themselves. The dictionary meaning attributed to welfare is "well-being", or the material and social preconditions for well-being. The addition of adjectives immediately gives rise to nuances and differing perceptions. For instance, social welfare introduces the fairly neutral idea of the collective provision, or receipt of welfare or well-being, while economic welfare refers to those forms of welfare, or well-being secured through the market: for example, monetary income and fringe benefits of one kind or another. State welfare refers to state measures for the provision of a wide range of key services such as health, education, housing, income maintenance and personal services. This is often the popular understanding of the welfare state. But, in a broader sense, the term "welfare state" may be used to define a particular form of the state, a distinctive political system of government and a specific type or vision of society. For the purpose of this article, the modern welfare state (modern in the sense of being distinct from earlier forms of, say, the Christian or medieval eras) is one that attempts to provide or to ensure a minimum standard of living to its citizens. To the extent that it represents a logical extension of positive liberalism in the post industrial revolution era, the welfare state of our concern may properly be regarded as welfare capitalism.

The minimum standard of living referred to is not a static one. Under Classical Political economy, as noted earlier, the acceptable minimum standard was defined by the subsistence theory — the wages and means "necessary to enable the labourers, one with another, to subsist and to perpetuate their race, without either increase or diminution" (David Ricardo, 1817, *Principles of Political Economy and Taxation*). For many less developed or developing countries, the minimum standard has been identified with a basic needs approach — adequate housing or shelter, clothing and food. In the industrially advanced capitalist countries, trade unions have redefined minimum living standards to mean decent living standards to reflect the relatively higher living standards obtaining and the fact that once conventional luxuries (such as the automobile) have become conventional necessities. Since wealth and poverty are relative, the minimum standard of living comes down to what is socially accepted in each time span.

To be able to enjoy a minimum standard of living, however perceived, members of society must acquire some means of purchasing power (income), and typically this comes through gainful activity or employment. In the context of the industrially advanced countries, the commitment to try and ensure minimum standards led to a further undertaking, the commitment to full employment.

The concept and implications of full employment were spelled out in a very influential report submitted by Lord William Beveridge to the British Government in 1944, entitled, "Full Employment in a Free Society". The general idea was that every able-bodied and willing worker should be able to find gainful employment, and that unemployment, if experienced, should be reduced to short intervals of standing by (in economic terminology, frictional unemployment) with the certainty of employment before long. Hence, the genesis and purpose of unemployment insurance. The criteria for full employment stipulated by Beveridge included: (a) more vacant jobs than job seekers, in effect, a seller's market from labour's perspective, the implication being that employers competing for scarce labour would put upward pressure on wages; (b) jobs should be productive and progressive, career-oriented and at fair wages; and (c) jobs should be conveniently located, the implication being that it might be necessary for government to direct the location of business establishments and factories.

Influenced by the writings of John Maynard Keynes (of whom more will be said later), Beveridge concluded that since unemployment resulted from a deficiency of total expenditure or aggregate demand in the economy, the state and government had an obligation to maintain expenditures and income (aggregate demand) at the required level, so that all goods and services produced would be purchased. Accordingly, the government should use its budgets to influence the level of activity in the economy, including the private sector. Incidentally, a Full Employment Policy and Commitment was adopted by the United Kingdom Parliament in 1945, and in the United States of America by the Full Employment Act of 1946.

A corollary of a full employment policy is the acquisition of the skills required to fill the wide range of jobs in an ever evolving industrial and technological society, leading to a further directly related commitment of the state to provide minimum levels of education. Whereas investment in physical capital confers upon investors rights of ownership and control, the non-transferability of property rights in the human stock (prohibition of slavery) presumptively inhibits the development of a commercial market for investment in people, as their services can only be hired or rented. Hence, education must be treated primarily as a public good and not as a private good.

A further rationale is that if education is to be treated as a private commodity, one likely consequence is limited accessibility. Thus, the assumption by the state of the responsibility for the education system is the best way of ensuring equality of opportunity for individuals, a necessity acknowledged by John Stuart Mill, often considered a transitional figure in the shift from negative to positive liberalism.

The next commitment of the modern welfare state flows from the concern of individuals, organizations and institutions to realize some form of cushion or protection against insecurity, an insecurity that is endemic to the capitalistic or market economy, which gives rise to recurring cycles of booms and busts. One source of this instability is the dynamic of ever changing expectations of investors regarding the soundness and profitability of investments. Indeed, the market system has built-in mechanisms for transforming mass optimism into mass pessimism, and vice versa. Nowhere is this more evident than in the gyrations of the stock markets, which reflect not only constant revisions of expectations of investors, but also of speculators trying to second-guess markets.

Another source of instability is the savings investment nexus, perhaps the most dynamic element of the capitalist system. Savings represent that portion of income, which is not spent on consumption and, as such, constitutes a withdrawal from the flow of spending. On the other hand, investment, which is fuelled by the availability of savings, adds to the productive capacity and to the flow of spending. The problem is that the decisions to save and the decisions to invest are not necessarily made by the same sets of people. Savings are being made by the millions of householders for reasons of their own, as well as by corporations, also for purposes of their own.

There is really no mechanism of the market that correlates to the decisions to save with decisions to invest, and rarely do planned savings and planned investment expenditures coincide. If savings are unspent, demand for goods and services are correspondingly reduced and, through a ripple effect, there will be a contraction in sales, employment and investment. Thus, the process of recession, if not depression, is set in motion. Conversely, if the economy is operating at near full productive capacity of plant or labour, or both, and producers seek to invest in aggregate more than available supply of savings, there will be bidding up of prices, and an inflationary spiral requiring counteracting remedies to dampen the level of activity.

To mitigate against insecurity occasioned by cyclical unemployment, technological unemployment, impaired health, indigence in old age or loss of savings through bank failures; to mitigate against the gross disparities between rich and poor; and to provide a floor for the incomes of economic casualties such as the disabled, widows and orphans — in sum, to deal with considerations of social justice that are beyond remedy by the impersonal price mechanism, the modern welfare state is led to establish a comprehensive social security system.

Convergence of Forces and Rapid Ascendancy of the Welfare State

The rapid ascendancy of the modern welfare state in the immediate post-World War II era may be attributed to the convergence of a number of factors. Selectively included are (a) the Great Depression, 1929 to the 1930s; (b) changes in market structures and the revision of Neo-Classical Theory; (c) the World Wars and the Cold War; (d) the New Keynesian economics; (e) legal citizenship and egalitarianism; and (f) the preoccupation of emerging nations — less developed countries (LDC's), or the so-called Third World, with economic planning.

The Great Depression

Until the Great Depression, a fundamental premise of Neo-Classical economic theory was that although there might be temporary departures, the basic tendency of the economy was towards employment of all willing and available workers at close to maximum output. In other words, the price mechanism would always tend towards full employment of resources, human and otherwise. This presumption was based on Say's Law, named after the early 19th-century French economist, Jean Baptiste Say, that there would never be any general overproduction or glut of capital. This was because every supply involves a demand, and every demand creates a supply. In other words, production provided the income that purchased that production, so that eventually, what was produced, overall, was purchased. It also assumed that what was saved was invested, and should there be any imbalance or disequilibrium, the price mechanism — via the rise of interest or price of loanable funds — would restore equilibrium. The practical implication of the presumption of full employment of men and resources was that there could be no involuntary unemployment. If unemployment existed, it could only mean that monopolistic forces were at work, such as trade unions through monopolistic bargaining power, maintaining wages above the market determined levels.

However, the Great Depression saw the virtual collapse of the market economy, leaving millions of able-bodied and willing people unable to find employment and, therefore, involuntarily unemployed. It was also apparent that state intervention would be necessary to rejuvenate the economy and, in the United States, it produced a significant shift in economic philosophy in the form of the New Deal of President Franklin D. Roosevelt. This involved, among other things, restructuring of the financial system to prevent a repeat of the speculative excesses that had contributed to the debacle, as well as a significant increase of the level of public expenditures, both to boost job creation and levels of aggregate demand and aggregate expenditure.

Changes in Market Structures and Revisions of Neo-Classical Theory

Reference was made earlier to the rise to prominence, by the end of the 19th century, of large corporations as the major producers of output, and the dominance that they could exercise in and over product markets. The process of adaptation of liberal economic theory to the realities of evolving market structures was hastened by the work of the academic economists working independently in the United States and England. Harvard Professor Edward Chamberlin's book, *The Theory of Monopolistic Competition* (1933), explored a range of markets that were neither purely competitive nor totally monopolistic, but combined elements of both. Professor Joan Robinson of Cambridge University, in *The Economics of Imperfect Competition* (1933), explored much the same ground, but added to the concept of pure monopoly (a single supplier) the concept of monopsony — a single buyer, such as a company town dominated by a single employer or buyer of labour. Subsequent refinements led to the differentiation of five market structures:

1. Perfect competition, the idealized model of perfect economic efficiency based on highly restrictive assumptions.
2. Pure competition with slightly less restrictive assumptions.
3. Monopolistic competition, typified by corner stores, where there are elements of both competition (numerical) and monopoly based on personalized service and product differentiation (qualitative).
4. Oligarchy, or markets characterized by relatively few, very large firms in particular industries (for example, the automobile industry). Here firms have the ability to influence both output and price, and tend to compete for market shares, a process that involves reacting vigilantly to each other's competitive strategies, whether on the basis of manipulation of prices or on product differentiation or both. The sovereignty of the consumer as director of production is also "qualified" by advertising and other forms of consumer motivation.
5. Pure monopoly, where there is a single supplier, the usual case being that of a public utility where the need for regulation to protect consumers is more readily conceded.

World War II and the Ideological Cold War

World War II witnessed the mobilization of enormous resources needed for the successful prosecution of a global conflagration, with much of the same resources being dedicated to mutual destruction. The liberal democratic state was transformed into a constitutional dictatorship with the state and government assuming the power to, among other things, regulate wages and prices and profits; introduce schemes for forced savings; convert a peace-time economy into a war-time economy; pre-empt resources, ban strikes and lock-outs; direct labour, regulate conditions of employment and introduce rationing.

Not only did the conduct of the war result in a tremendous expansion of the influence and activities of the state, but governments indicated that they had both the administrative capacity and capability to manage and/or regulate the economy. As people became accustomed to the idea of change, it became increasingly difficult to sustain the notion that, somehow, the social order was externally or naturally ordained. If anything, it could be made to serve social purposes, not the least of which was the quest for security.

This security consciousness was not confined to citizens as householder and employees. As noted earlier, the development of the concepts of corporate shareholding and limited liability were prompted by considerations of risk sharing and income security. Indeed, as J.K. Galbraith later highlighted in *The New Industrial State* (1967), much of what corporations regarded as planning consisted of minimizing or getting rid of unreliability of markets. By the same token, backward integration to ensure stability of supplies, forward integration to protect consumer markets and horizontal integration (diversification), all may be regarded as efforts aimed at insulating the corporation against insecurity.

Given the incredible amount of planning and direction involved in the mobilization, deployment, and effective utilization of resources for war purposes, it did not seem an unreasonable expectation on the part of the mass of the population that, to the extent permitted within the framework of a peace-time economy, resources could be mobilized and dedicated to achieving full employment, and a social safety net to cushion against exposure to the economic risks associated with the market economy.

The Cold War, reflecting the ideological divide on a worldwide basis between two polarized, competing systems — liberal, pluralist democratic and capitalistic on the one hand, and anti-private enterprise, centrally planned command economy controlled by a communist-totalitarian political regime, on the other, — further extended and perpetuated the intrusion of the state and government into economic decision-making relating to domestic and international trade. Both the economic rationale for trade and the doctrine of free trade were made subordinate to the imperatives of foreign policy and political ideology. Embargoes were placed on movement of physical goods and services, as well as people between countries and regions. The Cold War also influenced the allocation of resources between civilian and military production and priorities, and saw the integration of industrial and military productive facilities into the so-called military-industrial complex.

The Keynesian Revolution and the New Economics

John Maynard Keynes (1883–1946), later Lord Keynes, published his seminal work, *The General Theory of Employment, Interest and Money,* in 1936. It signalled the emergence of the Keynesian school of thought, or the New Economics, which held sway until the mid-1970s. The basic premise of the Keynesian system is that there is a high correlation between national income and employment. National income is, at one and the same time, the total value of a nation's net output of goods and services, the total flow of spending and the total flow of income payments to factors of production. The determinants of income and employment are consumption and investment spending. Consumption is a function of income, and the consumption function indicates the amount spent on consumption at each higher level of income. Above certain thresholds of income, not all income is consumed, leaving a portion to be saved. In effect, what is not consumed is saved, and the marginal prosperity to save is the reciprocal of the marginal prosperity to consume. Thus, if at a certain level of income, 80 percent is being spent on consumption, then the remaining 20 percent is being saved. The other side of the identity equation is investment spending which is influenced by the rate of interest, one determining component of which is people's desire to keep a certain amount of cash on hand, or liquidity preferences, and by the marginal efficiency of capital or expected rate of return (profit).

Using this schema, Keynes challenged some of the most fundamental tenets of Classical and Neo-Classical economic theory. First of all was the assumption based on Say's Law, that the economy always tended towards a state of full employment of men and resources. If so, there could be no involuntary unemployment. Keynes argued that because of the marginal propensity to save, there could be a shortfall or deficiency in aggregate demand, represented by savings, which constitutes a reduction in the circular flow of income. Faced with an inventory of unsold goods and loss of income, producers would cut back on production and employment until an equilibrium was reached. Only, it would be less than full employment; the workers associated with the reduced level of production would remain involuntarily unemployed. To restore full employment levels of income and expenditure, the deficiency of aggregate demand would have to be made good and only the government was in a position to inject and sustain, by appropriate fiscal and monetary policies, the full employment levels of economic activity.

The New Economics clearly envisaged a very expanded role for the state and government in the economy. Compensatory fiscal and monetary policies provided the tools for government to fine tune the economy. If there was a deficiency in the aggregate demand. the level of economic activity could be stimulated by public budgetary expenditures and incentives, including subsidies to the private sector and reduction of personal and corporate income taxes, which would have the effect of increasing disposable income. Monetary policy also could be used to increase the money supply, and thus lower interest rates, thereby stimulating investment and credit-financed consumer expenditures. If, on the other hand, aggregate demand exceeded planned expenditures on goods or services, that is, productive capacity, it would lead to a general rise in prices, or inflation. Compensatory fiscal and monetary policy would again be used, but in the opposite directions, to dampen aggregate demand and investment until a stable and full employment equilibrium was reached.

Citizenship and Mass Participation

In the earlier discussion of Classical Liberalism, it was noted that liberal political theory called for equality before the law, and equality of rights, especially as it related to private property. However, it was not egalitarian in the sense of achieving equality of conditions for all. Equality of opportunity and equality of conditions were confined to the privileged classes. Utilitarianism, with its emphasis on the greatest happiness of the greatest number, hinted at the majoritarian principle but, again, could have no political significance until the franchise was extended.

With the politicization of the working class, including the rural proletariat, the franchise was gradually extended, eventually to include women, so as to be made consistent with the notion of citizenship and the rights of participation, which it conferred. Equality of political rights would then have to mean not only the right to vote, but also the right to run for office and otherwise participate in the political process. Equality of political right thus could not be divorced from equality of conditions. For example, property qualifications could not be accepted if they served to preclude significant segments of the electorate from running for office, or otherwise participating in the political process.

Political equality also leads to the necessity of making decisions within the framework of representative government, and majority rule is the normal working principle in a democracy. It is not surprising, therefore, that as the mass political party developed, both to facilitate participation and promote majority interests, including more broadly defined equality of conditions, that citizenship then comes to be identified with social rights, such as the right to work, the right to social protection when out of work, temporarily or for a prolonged period, and the right of equal access to a range of services deemed to be vital. The public role in economic and social transactions expands correspondingly. Thus, to the extent that democratic institutions are founded on mass democracy, the welfare state is a logical outcome.

The Influence of Third World or Development Economics and State-led Economic Development

The immediate post-World War II era saw the break-up and dismantling of colonial empires and the emergence of a host of new nations — the so-called underdeveloped, or less developed, countries. To most of the nationalist leaders of these countries, capitalism tended to be identified with imperialism, exploitation and underdevelopment; hence the predisposition to be anti-capitalist. More often than not, they turned to socialism, partly because of its appeal as a doctrine of protest, partly because it provided seemingly infallible methods of analysis for diagnosing the causes of underdevelopment and offered solutions for social and economic ills.

Whether inspired by economic philosophy, or by the practical necessity of promoting economic growth, economic planning came to be almost universally viewed as the surest and most direct way to economic progress. Typically also, the offshoot of economic planning was a comprehensive economic plan that spelled out national goals and objectives, as well as specific targets covering all aspects of the national economy, including the private sector. Against this backdrop, the state and government were expected not only to play an active role in promoting economic growth and development, but also in initiating and managing public sector activities, projects, and enterprises.

The preoccupation with the dynamics of growth and development was not just confined to the less developed world. By the 1950s, socio-economic planning had actually begun in Great Britain, France, the Netherlands, Norway and Sweden, and by 1966 14 countries in Western Europe could be said to have development plans. The modern welfare state had achieved its ascendancy.

The Welfare State Under Siege — The Neo-Conservative and Neo-Classical Counter-Revolutions

For 25 years after World War II, it appeared that the welfare state had provided solutions to most, if not all, of the more pressing problems of unregulated capitalism, namely, recurring economic instability due to stop-and-go economies; unemployment induced insecurity of individuals and families; gross disparities in incomes leading to inequality in material conditions; and social costs (diseconomies) of private investment decisions, such as sometimes ruinous exploitation of natural resources, or degradation of the physical environment.

The New Economics, likewise, seemed to offer governments the analytical framework and policy instruments to ward off depressions and to make possible acceptable trade-offs between the goals of full employment, economic growth and price stability. Indeed, to many it seemed that modern capitalism owed its survival to the New Economics.

The quest for equality of material conditions or social justice led to the provision of a wide range of social services, considered to be the core of the welfare state, including health care, unemployment insurance and various forms of income supplementation. It also led to government intervention into the labour markets to mitigate against imperfections such as systemic discrimination on grounds of colour, race, ethnicity, gender, age and disability as well as to redress unequal bargaining power by setting minimum wages and other employment standards or, alternately, by promoting collective bargaining.

The process of transforming laissez-faire capitalism into welfare capitalism involved a very significant expansion of the scope and influence of the public sector. For instance, in Canada, government expenditures on goods and services and transfer payment rose from 28.6 percent of GNP (Gross National Product) in 1947 to 41 percent in 1975, and to 48 percent in 1980. Between 1965 and 1975 most of the spending related to transfer payments, such as unemployment insurance, family allowance and old age security payments.[3] In terms of employment, federal government employees grew from 116,500 in 1946 to 326,000 in 1975. For the same period, total public sector employment, including all levels of government and Crown corporations, grew at an annual rate of almost 7 percent, increasing from slightly over 400,000 employees to more than 2 million, representing 24 percent of total Canadian employment. If we focus more narrowly on goods and services produced as a result of *direct* government activity, the movement in percentage terms is equally impressive, from only 3.7 percent between 1947 and 1951 to 13.9 percent by the mid-1970s and 16 percent by 1980.

In terms of its functions and roles, the state and government could be said to have come full circle. In the 17th and 18th centuries, the government, as the agent of the state, functioned as an instrument of vested interests and of the ruling classes. Its primary role was that of being the guardian and protector of private property. In the 19th century, the rise of mass politics brought an added dimension, the state being protector of the weak against the strong. In the 20th century, both state and government progressively became positive agents of change, promoting economic growth and development and stability along with social justice. Government shifted from being a player in the "passive" (not-for-profit) sectors of the economy, to becoming a player in the "active" (profit-oriented) sectors.

Quite apart from organized ideological resistance, which became more vocal in the 1960s and was given impetus by economic developments in the 1970s, the expanded functions and roles of both state and government gave rise to contradictions that served to bring the welfare state to a situation of crises, fiscal and otherwise.

The potential for fiscal crisis arose from the fact that the role of the state in economic transactions was being expanded while leaving the ownership of productive enterprises primarily in the private sphere. This situation is, of course, compatible with the concept of a mixed economy. Thus, in pursuit of the objective of full employment, private production is supported by public expenditures for highways, airports, research, education of technicians and so on. At the same time the state also tries to meet the social needs not met by the system of private production, such as unemployment insurance, health insurance, old age pensions and other relief payments. There is also the expectation, legitimized by Adam Smith in the *Wealth of Nations,* that the state may properly acquire ownership of economic units, which are essential to the economic system, but are no longer profitable to private owners. It is not surprising, therefore, that state-owned or public enterprises historically have been concentrated in the "passive" sectors of the economy, such as transportation and public utilities, that are involved, as it were, in the "politics of displacement". However, as government responds to problems in the economy, it leads invariably to the enlargement of the size of the public administration in the "non-productive sectors" and, as a corollary, increases the burden of taxation. The welfare state thus increasingly becomes publicly accountable for the performance of the economy, while its resources required for this purpose may be limited. Faced then with the growing responsibility and burden for supportive expenditures for the private sector, as well as growing expenditures for economic justice, and the probability of growing resistance to taxation, particularly on the part of wage earners who bear the burden of taxation in the welfare state, what is the state to do?

Here is the crux of the dilemma of welfare capitalism (or positive liberalism, if you will). The liberal democratic state accepts a system of production for private profit while at the same time absorbing the costs of supporting corporate structures, including the social costs of production for private profit-seeking investors as well as the costs of correcting the injustices to those shuffled out of the production system.

By expanding the size and role of the state, by encouraging the state to move into unprofitable areas of public need while reserving profitable enterprises for the private sector, the welfare state becomes vulnerable to fiscal crises. One pragmatic response is for the state to become more entrepreneurial and to enter into the more "active" sectors of the economy where profits and surpluses are being made, and thus, acquire additional revenue. In this entrepreneurial role, the welfare state also becomes more vulnerable to criticisms that may be more strongly ideologically based. It can, for instance, be argued quite compellingly that the public sector is competing with the private sector, without being subjected to market penalties in the event of unsatisfactory economic performance; that the state, from its privileged position, is competing with the private sector for scarce resources and, indeed, may be "crowding out" the private sector. Hence, the economic playing field is no longer even.

The Ideological Attack on the Welfare State
The New Right and Neo-Conservatism

In the United States, the persistence of inflationary pressures during the 1960s enabled believers in the free enterprise and free market system, somewhat paradoxically labelled neo-conservatives, to sow the seeds of disenchantment with the welfare state. The intellectual centre for this movement was the Chicago School inspired by Professor Milton Friedman, who was awarded the Nobel Prize in 1974 for his contribution to economic theory. Considered one of the most formidable apostles of free enterprise, Friedman was largely regarded as a curiosity during the 1950s and his views were considered extreme. The 1960s, however, provided more fertile ground for his economic philosophy, which was expounded in his book, *Capitalism and Freedom* (1962). He argued passionately that economic freedom was a precondition for political freedom. The best guarantee of economic freedom, however, was the marketplace since it was not under the control of one person or a committee. The transactions of millions of persons are being unconsciously co-ordinated, and while freedom may not be always efficient, in the long run it is the best solution.

Friedman also challenged the widely shared belief of the Keynesian School in the efficacy of fiscal policy in macroeconomic management, or the influencing of the level of economic activity in the economy. He argued that changes in the money supply — hence the "Monetarist School" — caused changes in the level of business activity. He declared that "inflation is everywhere and always a monetary phenomenon". Moreover, expectation played a significant part in inflation in that the expectation, on the part of producers and workers, especially those represented by trade unions, that prices would rise could become a self-fulfilling prophecy. Hence the need to break the cycle of expectations by restricting the money supply and raising interest rates, even if it meant short-term pain — increasing levels of unemployment — for long-term gain, which was economic stability. If expectational inflation were not nipped in the bud, it would become embedded in the fabric of the economy, impairing the efficiency of the market or price mechanism. The preference for monetary policy, as against fiscal policy, also reflected an ideological bias. Fiscal policy allowed the government to play a more active role in the economy, and such intervention was likely to worsen the outcomes, especially since, for every level of income or activity, there was a "natural" rate of unemployment. Monetary policy, on the other hand, fell within the purview of autonomous central banks or equivalents and their operations were more in accord with market forces. The rediscovery and extolling of the virtues of market forces also was abetted by the creation and work of a series of right-wing think-tanks, not just in the United States, but also in Canada and in the United Kingdom. In effect, a new generation of free market and, therefore, politically more conservative economists and practitioners was cultivated and equipped intellectually to propagate neo-conservatism as the counter welfare state ideology. The preoccupation with inflation was further enhanced by the oil crisis that resulted from the politicization of oil by the OPEC Cartel (Organization of Petroleum Exporting Countries), which controlled most of the supply of crude oil in the Middle East as well as internationally. Crude oil prices rose dramatically from US$3 per barrel to US$38 per barrel in a relatively short time, giving rise to external "supply" or price shocks and to severe cost-induced inflation. It also produced a combination of high rates of inflation with high rates of unemployment, the so-called stagflation, which defied the Keynesian post-depression formula of compensatory fiscal and monetary policy.

The 1970s therefore bid farewell to the post-war commitment to full employment. Whereas in the United States unemployment had ranged from 4 to 5 percent during the 1950s and 1960s, by the 1970s it had risen to 7.6 percent.

The election of Republican Ronald Reagan to the Presidency of the United States of America for two terms (1980–1988) provided neo-conservatism with one of its most articulate and powerful protagonists, so much so that his views came to be identified with "Reaganomics". Influenced by Milton Friedman's ideas, Reagan declared that "Government is not the solution. It is the problem". His battle cry resulted in the reduction of government regulations and tax cuts, along with increased military expenditures to beef up national security. Tax cuts fitted into his framework of "supply side" economics, its logic being that those with higher incomes, who also constitute the pool of entrepreneurs or investors, have a greater propensity to save and, therefore, to invest. Accordingly, cutting taxes appropriately would serve to increase the supply of entrepreneurs and resources for investments, thereby stimulating economic progress. In the long run, beneficial effects would "trickle down" to other segments of society.

A similar and perhaps even more powerful neo-conservative ideology emerged in the United Kingdom under the prime ministerial regime of Mrs. Margaret Thatcher (1979–1989) and the Conservative Party. "Thatcherism" rejected the post-World War II consensus or set of shared assumptions within which partisan or competitive policies of "ins and outs" was accommodated.[4]

In terms of domestic politics, the consensus included the commitment to a mixed economy, full employment, consultations with the trade unions, the provision of core welfare services and adjustment to the loss of empire. These were policies that were thought to be administratively manageable, economically affordable and politically acceptable. Thatcher rejected the institutionalized consultation between government and major stakeholders, and attacked consensus as the outcome of shabby compromises. Her conservative manifests included the retrenchment of the welfare state, abandoning the commitment to full employment and letting market forces achieve what might be the appropriate natural levels of unemployment, legal containment of trade unions, deregulation of wage protection afforded by minimum wage legislation, privatization of public enterprises and tax cuts. Thatcher repudiated Edmund Burke's and classical conservatism's conception of society as an organic whole when she declared in

41

1987 that there was no such entity as society-only individuals — men and women — and families.

In Canada, the election of the Progressive Conservative Party for two consecutive terms under the prime ministership of Brian Mulroney (1984–1993) produced a mild flirtation with neo-conservative ideology and policies. Since retrenchment of the welfare state had not been made an election issue, the Conservative government could not claim to have received a mandate to do so. Nevertheless, the Mulroney government did attempt to redefine the universality of social benefits by arguing for selectivity: that scarce resources should be channelled to those in greatest need. The government also expressed concern about the level of unemployment benefits in terms of being both a drain on public resources and impairing labour mobility and labour market efficiency.

There were also proposals to de-index pensions and family allowances. However, having been elected on a centrist mandate within the tradition of brokerage politics in Canada, the government backed off in the face of public opposition and settled for the de-indexing of family allowances. Since Canada had never explicitly committed itself to, or pursued, a policy of full employment, this issue did not become an ideological one. What the Progressive Conservative Party under Mulroney could not achieve by way of retrenchment of the welfare state, certainly as far as social services were concerned, the succeeding Liberal Party regime under Prime Minister Jean Chretien has achieved in part through drastic reductions in public expenditures and transfer payments to the provinces, so as to eliminate the federal government's accumulated budgetary deficits and reduce the public debt.

The electoral adoption and pursuit of an explicit neo-conservative agenda has been more successfully pursued at the provincial level, most notably in Alberta and in Ontario, under the auspices of Progressive Conservative parties. In Ontario, the government, reflecting a radical small business and rural orientation, has embarked upon its "common sense revolution" and has implemented drastic reform of the education system; downsizing of government activities and public sector employment; selective privatization of public enterprises; tightening of conditions for entitlement to income supplements and the imposition of "work fare", a form of compulsory employment for welfare recipients. Labour legislation considered too favourable to trade unions has also been repealed and replaced.

Neo-Conservatism — A Summary of Its Credo

Enough has been said to make it possible to summarize the common themes that constitute the creeds of neo-conservatism.

To begin with, there is the belief that the welfare state has achieved most of its original purposes but that its social programmes are no larger affordable. Neo-conservatives, therefore, challenge the very principle behind the welfare state, that government should assume responsibility for maintaining a decent minimum standard of living for all citizens, particularly when it involves a commitment to full employment, to universal social services and a safety net of income support or maintenance. At the extreme, the New Right are now persuaded that in principle the welfare state is incompatible with economic progress in a capitalist society. Already, the public sector has become too large, claiming too much of resources and is crowding out the private sector. Hence, there must be downsizing of government activity. Since the greater part of the budget of the modern welfare state goes to services and transfer payments, it is these areas — education, social assistance, pensions, health care and unemployment insurance — that must necessarily be targeted for selective reductions in scope and funding or across the board cutbacks. It is for these reasons that the attack against the welfare state has been characterized as a revolt of the rich against the poor. A second belief is that the private sector is over-regulated, thereby raising, unnecessarily, the costs of doing business and being competitive. Hence, the need for "deregulation" or removal of government controls on market activities.

A third policy priority is privatization, or the sale of publicly owned enterprises or Crown corporations, the proceeds of which may or may not be reserved to reduce either budgetary deficits or the public debt. Economic policies also stress the need for balancing the budget and effecting tax cuts.

In terms of purely social policy, Neo-Conservatives may be differentiated from their free market neo-liberal brethren by the importance they attach to preserving traditional values and institutions such as the family. This social perspective implies a number of political positions — opposition to sex education in schools, which may encourage promiscuity (that is, value free sex education), making abortions difficult to obtain; and very strong opposition to, and resentment of, policies of the state (that is, homosexual rights) which may be interpreted as weakening traditional institutions such as marriage and the family.

Neo-Conservatism also adopts a strong anti-crime posture, advocating much harsher penalties for crime, including juvenile crime. As is to be expected with all ideological groupings, Neo-Conservatism is not free from inconsistencies. There is espousal, on the one hand, of the completely free market and, correspondingly, a minimalist role for government but, on the other hand, upholding the necessity for strong government to uphold law and order, and to control markets where necessary. But if society is no longer to be considered an organic polity and a moral socializing force but, rather, as a collection of atomized individuals, and families, then how will traditional values and institutions be preserved? Or, if social services and social relations are to be privatized, how will it be possible to maintain traditional social values and to cultivate caring and humane communities? These are contradictions yet to be resolved.

Neo-Liberalism and Neo-Conservatism

It was noted later, in the latter half of the 19th century, that the need for the state to address unanticipated economic and social problems engendered by the Industrial Revolution led to a softening of laissez into more positive liberalism. As the 20th century unfolded, liberalism became more a frame of mind than a rigid dogma.

In contrast with conservatives, liberals tended to become more hospitable to change, more willing to examine established institutions and practices in the light of new problems and needs. This made them less reverent of the status quo. However, in contrast to revolutionaries or adherents of radical change, liberals tended to be more apprehensive of the consequences of sudden changes and in this context they were, and still are, closer to the conservatives.

In the post-World War II era, positive or reform liberalism could be reconciled with Keynesian or the New Economics, for while it challenged some of the fundamental tenets of classical economics, much of Keynesian analysis still drew on neo-classical economic theory. Thus, while Keynesian policy prescriptions and their implications for the role of the may have represented radical departures, methods and tools of analyses did not represent a break with Neo-Classical tradition. When, in the 1970s, the New Economics fell from favour, it was not too difficult for followers of the Keynesian School to be reconverted to Neo-Classicism.

What makes it possible to speak of neo-liberalism as distinct from neo-conservatism is the newfound reverence of the market since the 1980s. It represents both a reaction and a response to a number of factors, including: disillusionment with the seeming inability of governments to deal with persistent socio-economic problems; doubts about the efficacy of economic regulation; the effective promotion of monetarism and the revival of laissez-faire ideology in the wake of the collapse of the post-World War II Keynesian consensus; the disappointing record of development (centralized) planning and extensive governmental intervention in LDCs or the so-called Third World; and the active promotion of market capitalism by the world's two most powerful international financial agencies — the International Monetary Fund (IMF) and the International Bank for Reconstruction and Development (the World Bank) — both controlled by boards of directors, the majority of whom are neo-classicists or exponents of free enterprise and free markets. The interjection of the development experience of LDCs into the ideological debate in the developed countries about the role of the state warrants some elaboration.

During the 1970s the LDCs with a few notable exceptions (the Newly Industrializing Countries or Asian Tigers) began to experience deterioration in economic performance and living standards. Among the major contributory factors were rising grain prices and the OPEC oil price shocks that impacted very severely on the economies of countries that were wholly dependent on imported oil and petroleum for fuel; and increased reliance on budgetary deficit financing and heavy external borrowing at both concessional and commercial borrowing rates, to avoid self-imposed austerity measures as well as to sustain existing levels of economic activity. The result was accumulation of onerous external debt burdens as well as serious balance-of-payment deficits. These balance-of-payment crises prompted recourse to the IMF for relief and accommodation by way of hard currency (US$) loans to service debts and ease budgetary constraints.

In return for financial assistance, the IMF imposed terms or "conditionalities", essentially macro-stabilization policies, but linked relief measures to Structural Adjustments Programmes (SAPS) administered in tandem by the World Bank. During the 1980s, as world economic recessions further aggravated their precarious conditions, more and more LDCs were effectively placed under the trusteeship of the IMF and World Bank by virtue of having to accept a standard deflationary model.

The IMF stabilization policies and World Bank-administered SAPS had four main objectives: First, curbing inflation through monetary restraint, deficit reduction, controlling wages and dismantling consumer-oriented price controls. Second, fiscal balance by reducing government expenditures, raising taxes and reforming the financial administration system. Third, eliminating current (trading) account deficits by exchanges-control action, invariably devaluing the currency, along with promotion of exports; and fourth, promoting market capitalism through liberalization. The term "liberalization" encompassed a wide range of policies and measures, including deregulation, ostensibly to promote domestic competitive efficiency as well as freer trade externally; limiting the role of the state by divestment and privatization of public enterprises; structural and institutional reforms within the public and private sectors to create a more businesslike environment and the adoption of "market friendly policies" (a World Bank term), so that the private sector could become the engine of job creation and development.

Between 1982 and 1988, the IMF, jointly with the World Bank tested the standard deflationary model in 28 of 32 nations, but at the cost of economic stagnation and rising unemployment and could not claim one success, even where governments followed the prescribed economic medicine and dosage.[5]

The failure of the deflationary models to restore economic vibrancy and the persistence of relatively high levels of unemployment and mass impoverishment in LDCs led both institutions to explore the proposition that the offending cause might be the inability of economies to quickly adapt and adjust to rapidly changing product and market conditions. Thus, more recently the focus has been shifted to the workings of labour markets and the obstacles that may be impairing efficiency in labour market operation or so-called labour market flexibility. Thus, the new concern holds true for both LDCs and developed countries. Indeed, labour market flexibility has emerged as a much more controversial issue in developed countries for two reasons. First, this shift of attention to labour markets is also in harmony with the ideological preference for market-oriented or supply-side economics. Second, the preoccupation with labour market reform is consistent with the realities of the new international economic and trading environment associated with globalization, which will be discussed in the next section. But how did the experience of LDCs become a factor in the neo-classical revolution? According to conservative and free market economists, the lesson to be learned from the LDC development experience was that the poor record of performance and achievements by the LDCs was not so much the result of the dominance and predatory practices of the advanced capitalist world but rather due to too much state intervention: too much regulation, corruption and inefficiency, and stifling of individual initiative. The solution lies in a return to free market capitalism, limiting the role and activities of the state, privatizing state enterprises and downsizing, promoting free trade and exports, and ensuring a market-friendly environment that will attract foreign investment. These things would allow in President Reagan's phrase for "the magic of the marketplace" to unfold. But what if attempts at liberalization do not appear to be paying off? It is, say neo-liberals, because market determination is not being taken far enough. It is this exaggerated belief in the efficacy of free markets, that differentiates neo-liberalism from neo-conservatism. This same exaggerated opinion of the market is also reflected in the "public choice" theory, also known as the new political economy approach. Its premise is that the government can do nothing right because it runs afoul of the dominant human motivation, which is self interest. The result is that government or the public administration itself is torn between, or becomes the captive of, special interests — be they privileged politicians and bureaucrats who run the political system, or business interests, or organized workers and citizens — all of whom are seeking to use the instrumentality of the state to achieve their self-interested purposes. Even worse, the state power exercised by government is used to confiscate private property. The conclusion, therefore, as Adam Smith declared, is that "Government is best which governs least". The resurgence of neo-liberalism was also given a big boost by the collapse and balkanization of the USSR and Eastern Europe at the beginning of the 1990s. With the discrediting of the alternate command model of the economy, the ideal of the free self-regulating market could once more emerge triumphant. For neo-liberals, everything is for sale. All areas of human endeavours and spheres of activities may be treated as markets, including political democracy. The civil bureaucracy can be privatized and services delivered along the lines of the private sector model. Executive agencies or autonomous units can be deemed to enter into implied social contracts or compacts to deliver services not to citizens, but to clients. Market defects, if any, can be remedied by structural incentives rather than by regulation, and decision making can occur on the basis of mathematically determined precision or in accordance with the principle of market equilibrium.

Globalization and Reinforcement of the Neo-Classical Counter Revolution

Global Integration of Production and Internationalization of Capital

"Globalization" is a shorthand term for the forces that are at work, creating a new international economic and trading environment. Its most pronounced features are the global integration of production and internationalization or increased mobility of financial capital. Shared production, technological change and continually falling communication costs have made cross-border transport and trade much more feasible and easier in the closing decades of the 20th century.

This process has been given added momentum by the removal of political barriers. The result has been growing interaction, spatially and otherwise, between countries in various parts of the world seeking to take advantage of new opportunities for trade — opportunities that also have been enhanced by the lowering of tariff and non-tariff barriers. Increasing mobility of capital also has given impetus to a new international division of labour and shared production. Capital flows and foreign investment, in particular, can now respond rapidly to new profit opportunities by shifting production to places where wages are low, relative to potential productivity. The mobility of capital also has been greatly enhanced by electronic information devices that transcend spatial distance, time zones and national boundaries and the real economy of goods and services and the "symbol" (or paper) economy of money, credit and financial capital appear to be diverging rather than being bound together as they were in the past. Indeed, there is the real danger that the symbol or paper economy could replace the real economy as the flywheel. In this environment, national economies, in effect, have become production stations for transnational or multinational corporations (MNCs) and transnational corporate federations, and are increasingly being integrated into expanding international markets. The 350 largest corporations currently control more than 40 percent of world trade and dominate the production, distribution and sale of many goods from LDCs. Equally significant is the fact that almost one quarter of international exchange involves intra-firm MNC sales of intermediate products or equipment from subsidiaries in one country to another.[6] They constitute, therefore, global factories searching for opportunities anywhere in the world, and seeking to take advantage of existing price differentials.

Impact of Globalization

The impact of globalization is perhaps most clearly evident in labour markets, and the result of so-called restructuring of businesses and government units and, indeed, of the economy as a whole. In the corporate sphere, restructuring is reflected in seemingly contradicting tendencies. On the one hand, there is a new wave of corporate concentration and integration (but now, on a grander and even mind-boggling scale both nationally and internationally, through mega amalgamations, and mergers, takeovers and strategic alliances). On the other hand, there is decentralizing and downsizing (retrenchment) as these mega-corporations reconstitute themselves for operational purpose into networks of smaller and often autonomous units.

In the public sector, restructuring has been induced by privatization of public enterprises and some public services, as well as the streamlining of government operations and retrenchment of public servants and government paid employees.

In labour markets, the impact of globalization can be seen in trends in employment and unemployment, composition of employment, structural changes and job creation and in the structure of earnings.

Employment Trends

In both developed countries and LDCs there has been, since the 1970s, a marked disappearance of jobs, especially in manufacturing or the blue-collar workers sector. Already high levels of unemployment, in comparison with the 1950s and 1960s, are being exacerbated by continuing downsizing not necessarily to meet the challenge of increasing competition at regional and international levels, but as the most convenient way of increasing profits and enhancing share values.

Where new jobs are being created, they are predominantly in the services sector or service sub-economy, where women predominate and are more vulnerable, to the extent that they are not readily susceptible to unionization and lack institutional representation to deal with issues such as pay equity and job security.

Furthermore, the bulk of the jobs being created in the collective service sector are so-called non-standard jobs: part-time, self-employment, dependent and independent contractors. An allied development has been the significant increase in both short hours of work and long hours of work. The former is a reflection of the growth in part-time employees, that is those who average 30 or less hours per week; the latter is due to the fact that those who are permanently employed and survive downsizing are expected to make up for those who lost their jobs and end up working longer hours. Polarization of working hours is also associated with polarization of income. Those with adequate or high income are working longer hours to stay where they are, while those with low incomes are trapped in jobs that are not full-time or may not last very long. Not surprisingly, therefore, considerations of equity and amelioration of poverty have emerged as central concerns in reports on labour market reforms issued by the international development agencies.

The new international economic environment has created a new lexicon — "increased competitiveness", "increased productivity" and "increased flexibility". The increased flexibility is now seen as the instrument for achieving greater productivity and competitiveness, and these are to be realized not only by reducing the number of permanent full-time workers to a minimum but, also, by making regular work hours more variable. It means increasing reliance on people whose work can be changed easily, namely, temporary workers and self-employed contractors, including home workers, who usually do not participate in private pension and benefits plans. Thus, everywhere, the once standard eight-hour day and five-day work week are increasingly being pushed to the margin and there is a constant ratcheting effect as enterprises operating on non-standard hours, demand goods and services from those who have not yet made the shift to flexible hours and work operations. What does all this mean for the welfare state under siege? On the grounds of competitiveness, especially in export markets, employers are proclaiming the need for a level playing field: which translated, means securing relief from the payroll costs of the protective shield of the welfare state. This could mean reducing both premiums and levels of coverage and benefits of unemployment insurance, and of health care benefits and accident and occupational hazards compensation. It could also mean lower minimum wage protection and separation (redundancy) costs to facilitate the process of re-engineering and downsizing, completely flexible working hours without prescribed fixed rest days, and recourse to part-time and contract workers without the necessity of paying employment benefits generally accorded to full-time workers.

The Excesses of Globalization and Counter-reaction

In an earlier section of this paper, it was noted that the proponents of laissez-faire political economy did not anticipate all the social and negative consequences that would follow in the wake of the changes wrought by the Industrial Revolution, and the necessity of state intervention and regulation to ameliorate the harmful consequences. The same may be said of the proponents of globalization. There is, for instance, the presumption, reminiscent of the 18th century Age of Enlightenment, of the inevitability of social progress. In this case, it is not reason and the scientific method, but rather the dynamics of globalization and, in particular, the integration of national economies into the new international economic order. This time the catalyst is the new technological and organizational revolution made possible by the information and electronic age.

Another premise, not unlike Say's Law of the Markets, is that while there may be temporary or transitional dislocations, as far as globalization is concerned, the prospect is of ever expanding markets and consumers' demands. To realize, however, the full potential of globalization it is necessary to encourage trade liberalization, a goal that has been vigorously advocated by the IMF, the watchdog of the international financial system and supportive partner the World Bank. But recent experience has demonstrated the lack of preparation of many national economies, more so the LDCs and developing countries, to cope with the consequences of liberalization, especially the exposure of domestic producers to the far more efficiently produced goods and services of the industrially advanced countries; deep currency depreciation and havoc they have wrought in the financial services sector and the economy as a result of rapid influx and outflow of huge sums of money across currencies to take advantage of differences in interest rates. While volatile currency markets may be good for key elements in the national financial community in the short run, such as banks and other financial intermediaries, they may be bad for the national economy, and indeed, the global economy in both the short and the long term.

Since the mid-1990s the stability of an increasingly integrated global economy has been shaken by a series of major financial crises. In 1995, the United States spearheaded an international bail-out of the Mexican economy after the collapse of its currency, and the justification put forward was that the repercussions of not doing so for American and other investors from the advanced countries would be far more severe. In 1998, a similar crisis enveloped the ASEAN-5 (Indonesia, Malaysia, the Philippines, Singapore, Thailand) and South Korea. The ASEAN-5 and South Korea had experienced several decades of outstanding economic performances, and achieved manifold increases in per capita income. In 1996, these NICs in Asia had attracted almost half of total capital inflows to developing countries, nearly $100 billion. They were also touted by the IMF and World Bank and neo-liberals as exemplary models of countries that had achieved economic transformations and take-off through reliance on free markets capitalism. This was, however, a misrepresentation of the development of the countries of this region which had developed both domestic and export output capabilities as a result of extensive state intervention and support. The influx of large capital inflow from the advanced economies and global markets seeking to benefit in the short-run from high yields but risky ventures were to set the stage for the Asian crisis. As a leading IMF executive conceded: "Developments in the advanced economies and global financial markets contributed significantly to the build up of the crisis".[7]

When individual countries began to experience economic imbalance as a result of unsustainable accumulation of short-term financing, markets overreacted by shifting money out, provoking a major upheaval and a domino effect began. To avoid further "contagion", the IMF organized an even more costly international rescue and, again, the major beneficiaries were investors of the most powerful nations. Pressure was also put on the Asian countries to dispose of national assets built up over decades of development, to MNCs at fire sale prices. Whether or not the excesses of globalization may be excused as inescapable consequences of the transition to the new international world order, the harsh fact remains that they have had the effect of impoverishing millions of vulnerable and unprotected workers and peasant farmers in LDCs, and of aggravating unemployment in all countries, whether less developed, developing or developed, as restructuring and retrenchment have become a "contagion" spearheaded by corporate mega-corporations.

Unemployment, once seen as part of the problem of unregulated capitalism, has now become part of the solution to retrenchment and possible dismantling of the welfare state. Relatively high levels of unemployment are now considered as natural and inevitable and a necessary price to pay both to contain inflation and to discipline trade unions. Faced with permanent loss of traditional blue-collar workers through restructuring and downsizing and the difficulty of organizing the fastest growing element of the labour force, the part-timers, unions have been constrained to give priority to bargaining for job security rather than wage increases.

As labour markets have become increasingly laissez-faire, income inequality has worsened. Universally, the top 20 percent income earners have increased their share of income at the expense of the lower-income strata. The situation in the United States, the world's most powerful economy and leader of the neo-classical counter revolution, has been described as follows: "During the quarter-century between 1947 and 1973, the economy both grew faster than in our era, and produced an earnings distribution that gradually became more equal. Median family income adjusted for inflation, slightly more than doubled. The bottom 20 percent of households, however, realized income gains of 138 percent, while the top 20 percent gained 99 percent. These trends reversed after 1973. In the period between 1979 and 1993, the top 20 percent gained 18 percent, while the bottom 60 percent actually lost real income and the poorest 20 percent lost most income of all — an average of 15 percent of an already inadequate wage".[8]

Even more dramatic is the disparity between the compensation of executive management and their employees. In the United States in 1997, the average raise of the blue-collar worker was 2.6 percent. CEO (Chief Executive Officers) compensation was 13 times higher. Whereas the average raise of white collar workers for the same year was 3.8 percent, that of CEOs was over nine times higher. The average CEO or boss earned 326 times what a factory worker did. In Canada, CEOs of the 255 largest companies listed with the Toronto Stock Exchange received in 1996 an 11 percent increase in compensation over 1995, whereas the average employee earned a 2.8 percent increase.

From Laissez-faire to the Welfare State and Beyond?

Together, capitalism and liberalism have shown great resilience. Capitalism's enduring pre-eminence as an economic system cannot, on the basis of historical development, be divorced from timely intervention on the part of the state and government. The Great Depression brought unregulated market capitalism to its knees and was resuscitated under the mantle of welfare or regulated capitalism. The period of the ascendancy of the Welfare State — the decades of the 1950s through the 1970s — was one of relative prosperity for the industrially advanced countries and some developing countries. It also witnessed the reassertion of the sense of community, which has characterized most of human history. The ascendancy of the Welfare State has been challenged, and effectively so, by the Neo-classical counter-revolution, based on a coalition of neo-conservatism and neo-liberalism. Whether the retrenchment so far effected will be made irreversible remains to be seen. The core services of the welfare state and, indeed, the entire public sector, including support for the poor and protection of labour rights, are being re-evaluated and reshaped, on the basis of markets and efficiency models, ostensibly to lessen the dependency of the disadvantaged and poor on welfare assistance. Renewal of faith in idealized market structures has prompted stripping away community and government safeguards against market abuse and imperfections. Unfettered markets are considered to be of the essence of human liberty and as noted elsewhere, if markets, with their presumed capacity for mathematical-like precision in decision-making are not optimizing, it means that they are not sufficiently market-like.

But the Neo-classical counter-revolution could soon find itself on trial at the polls and in the halls of government. Growth in world output during the decade of the 1990s, the decade of liberalization, amounted to 2 percent per annum, compared to about 3 percent per annum during the turbulent decade of the 1980s. Societies characterized by great disparities in income between the social classes are susceptible to conflict and violence. Democracy is a child of peace and cannot live apart from its mother.

It is instructive that the World Bank in its "1999/2000 World Development Report" has found it timely to outline its own "Comprehensive Development Framework", which appears to be a repudiation of its previous commitment to economic fundamentalism of unfettered markets. "Fifty years of development have yielded four critical lessons. First, macroeconomic stability is an essential prerequisite for achieving growth needed for development. Second, growth does not trickle down; development must address human needs directly. Third, no one policy will trigger development; a comprehensive approach is needed. Fourth, institutions matter; sustained development should be rooted in processes that are socially inclusive and responsive to changing circumstances". We must, cautions the World Bank, "step beyond debates over the role of governments and markets, recognizing that they need to complement each other and put to rest any claims that any particular policy intervention is the magic formula that will inspire development in all times and places". For the World Bank, it may well be that the chickens are coming home to roost.

Even more timely and compelling are the concerns about globalization voiced by the United Nations Development Programme (UNDP) in the "Human Development Report, 1999", incidentally, the tenth Anniversary Report. In the overview, appropriately entitled, "Globalization with a human face," it is acknowledged that while globalization offers great opportunities for human advances, the opportunities and benefits need to be shared much more widely. As it is, globalization is creating new threats to human security. More to the point, as far as this article is concerned, are the observations that "Competitive markets may be the best guarantee of efficiency, but not necessarily of equity. Liberalization and privatization can be a step to competitive markets — but not a guarantee of them. And markets are neither the first nor the last word in human development. Many activities and goods that are critical to human development are provided outside the market — but these are being squeezed by the pressures of globalization. There is a fiscal squeeze on public goods, a time squeeze on care activities, and an incentive squeeze on the environment. When the market goes too far in dominating social and political outcomes, the opportunities and rewards of globalization spread unequally and inequitably — concentrating power and wealth in a select group of people, nations and corporations, marginalizing the others. When the markets get out of hand, the instabilities show up in boom and bust economies, as in the financial crisis in East Asia and its world repercussions, cutting global output by an estimated $2 trillion in 1998–2000. When the profit motives of market players get out of hand, they challenge people's ethics — and sacrifice respect for justice and human rights". (Ibid., p. 2)

Finally, it is ironical that the apostles of unfettered markets, while denouncing government as being an instrument to serve special interests, do not see themselves as a special interest group using the same instrumentality to serve their own ideological and economic interests. The new thesis may well provoke its own antithesis and so the dialectic of social action and social change will continue to unfold. If so, the 21st century will see a continuing evolution of the ideological underpinnings of liberalism and liberal democracy.

Selected Bibliography

Berle, A and G. Means. 1932. *The Modern Corporation and Private Property*. New York: Macmillan Co.

Bird, Richard. 1970. *The Growth of Government Spending in Canada*. Canadian Tax Foundation.

Chamberlin, Edward. 1932. *The Theory of Monopolistic Competition*. Cambridge: Harvard University Press.

Dickerson, Mark and Thomas Flanagan. 1986. *An Introduction to Government and Politics — A Conceptual Approach*, 2d ed. Methuen.

Friedman, Milton. 1962. *Capitalism and Freedom*. University of Chicago Press.

Galbraith, J.K. 1956. *American Capitalism — The Concept of Countervailing Power*, rev. ed. Boston: Houghton Mifflin Company.

Galbraith, J.K. 1982. *Wealth of Nations.*. Penguin Books.

Heilbroner, Robert. 1989. *The Making of Economic Society*, 8th ed. Prentice Hall.

Keynes, John Maynard. 1936. *The General Theory of Employment, Interest and Money*. New York: Harcourt, Brace and World.

Kuttner, Robert. 1997. *Everything for Sale. The Virtues and Limits of Markets*. New York: Alfred A. Knopf.

Marchak, M. Patricia. 1987. *Ideological Perspectives in Canada*, 3d ed. McGraw-Hill Ryerson Limited.

Mishra, Ramesh. 1990. *The Welfare State in Capitalist Society*. Toronto: University of Toronto Press.

Robinson, Joan. 1933. *The Economics of Imperfect Competition*. London: MacMillan.

Roll, Eric. 1953. *History of Economic Thought*, 3d ed. Prentice Hall.

Sabine, George H. 1937. *History of Political Thought*. London: G. Harrap and Co. Ltd.

Tawney, R.H. 1926. *Religion and the Rise of Capitalism*. New York: Harcourt, Brace and World.

Ulmer, Melville. 1969. *The Welfare State — USA*. Boston: Houghton Mifflin Co.

Weber, Max. 1958. "The Protestant Sects and the Spirit of Capitalism" in H.H Gerth and C. Wright Mills, *From Max Weber — Essays in Sociology*. New York: Oxford University Press.

Notes

1. See for instance Eric Roll, *History of Economic Thought*, 3d ed. (Prentice Hall, 1953); and Robert Heilbroner, *The Making of Economic Society*, 8th ed. (Prentice Hall, 1989).

2. Term used by C.B. Macpherson in *The Political Theory of Possessive Individualism — Hobbes to Locke* (Oxford University Press, 1962).

3. For extended discussion see Richard M. Bird, *The Growth of Government Spending in Canada* (Canadian Tax Foundation, 1970).

4. For extended discussion see Dennis Kavanagh and Peter Morris, *Consensus Politics — From Atlee to Thatcher* (Basil Blackwell, 1989).

5. See Michael P. Todaro, *Economic Development*, 7th ed. (Addison-Wesley, 2000).

6. See Robert Kuttner, *Everything for Sale. The Virtues and Limits of Markets* (New York: Alfred A. Knopf, 1997).

7. Stanley Fisher, First Deputy Managing Director, IMF, Forum Funds Lecture at UCLA, March 20, 1998.

8. Robert Kuttner, supra, p. 86.

Introduction to Legal Studies — Law as a Concept and System

Laurence M. Olivo

Introduction[1]

In this chapter, we will first discuss the concept of law in general, and then examine it as a component of a democratic society. While there are certain basic elements that are common to all legal systems, we will see that there are a number of perennial, "open" questions about law to which there is no one "right" answer on which everyone can or does agree. Instead we will see that the answers to questions about law depend in part on the nature of a particular society, and in part on the values and expectations of members of that society. We will see that there are various reasons given for why we obey laws, how we should interpret them, whether they should reflect morality and what the limits of law are. We won't necessarily tell you the "right" answer, because there is not necessarily a "right" answer to all of these questions. There is often simply a range of answers that depend on legitimate, but different, points of view. We hope you will gain an appreciation for the complexity and flexibility of law as a concept and as a system, and feel that you are equipped to intelligently weigh and judge competing points of view. This is not simply an abstract, academic exercise — in a democratic society it is a necessary one. As a

---

1   From *Introduction to Law in Canada*, edited by Laurence M. Olivo (Concord, ON: Captus Press Inc., 1995–2003). Reproduced with permission of author. Note omitted.

responsible citizen, you have to consider points of view, examine your own values and assumptions, analyze and decide. We hope that this chapter will help you to do that, and to appreciate the social context that lies behind the specific areas of law that are discussed in subsequent chapters of this text.

The Concept of Law

What Is Law?

Consider the various definitions of law set out in Exhibit 1.

The definitions of law in the Exhibit are not all the same; some leave out aspects that seem to be important in others. The first definition focuses on law as having a function of regulating behaviour, and instilling tolerance and forbearance. It says nothing about where law comes from, or about what happens if you do not obey. The second definition also refers to ordering behaviour but introduces the further idea of legal rules as being imposed externally, applying within a state, and being enforced if disobeyed. The third definition merely says that in some situations, you will be compelled by state force to obey, but it does not identify the situations in which obedience will be compelled. The fourth definition also focuses on regulating and ordering behaviour, and again

---

Exhibit 1: Definitions of Law

"a set of rules, that enable people to live together and respect each other's right's"[1]

"a body of rules for the guidance of human conduct which are imposed upon and enforced among the members of a given state"[2]

"a statement of circumstances in which the public force will be brought to bear through the courts"[3]

"a body of rules for the guidance of human conduct which are imposed upon and enforced among the members of a given state"[4]

Notes

1. Statement by Irwin Dorfman, President, Canadian Bar Association, 1975, cited in John A. Willes, Contemporary Canadian Business Law, 4th ed. (Toronto: McGraw-Hill Ryerson, 1994), p. 3.
2. William Blackstone, Commentaries on the Laws of England, cited in Willis, op. cit. p. 3.
3. Oliver Wendell Holmes, cited in Willis, op. cit., p. 3.
4. P.S. James, Introduction to English Law (London: Butterworths, 1985), p. 5.

---

talks about imposing rules externally and enforcing them against those who disobey.

Several themes emerge:

- Laws are rules imposed on us by an external body.
- Laws enable us to live together by controlling conflict.
- Laws teach us to tolerate and respect others [and perhaps the rules themselves — telling us what is "right" or "moral"].
- Laws compel us to behave in certain ways because sanctions are applied if we behave improperly.
- Laws indicate when the force of the state will be used to compel you to behave in certain ways.

While these definitions help us to define what law is as a social structure, it leaves us with a variety of questions about law and how it functions. The answers to these questions, as we will see, depend in part on the political, philosophical, religious and social views of the individuals asking the questions.

What Is a Legal Rule?

It should be clear from the definitions at the head of this section that not all rules are legal rules. So, how do we distinguish legal and non-legal rules? Consider the following rules of conduct:

- If someone opens a door for you, you say, "thank you."
- You may not kill another person.

If someone opens a door for you and you walk through and say nothing, you have broken a rule by being rude, but all would recognize that the rule you have violated is a social norm, based on a social value (courteousness). People may avoid you or shun you, or say unpleasant things about you, because your behaviour is unpleasant to them. But no-one will arrest you, find you guilty of an offence, or bring down state supported sanctions on you. If you kill another person, however, you may also be violating a norm based on the high value placed on human life, but all would recognize that the negative reactions would include detention, a formal determination that a legal rule had been broken, followed by legal punishment.

What makes some societal rules "legal" rules and others not? The short answer is that we can identify legal rules because they have certain features other rules do not have: they are backed or enforced by the authority and power of the state. But why are some rules singled out for this kind of treatment and not others? Legal rules are those that are deemed to be very important in preventing a society from becoming dysfunctional and breaking down into anarchy and chaos. In most societies legal rules help to create order and certainty and control the use by individuals of force and fraud to get what they want. For example, most societies will have rules about ownership of property, exchange of property rights, and methods to resolve conflicts and disputes. These rules are so central that all in a society must agree to be bound by them and accept the consequences of not obeying.

How Do Individuals Recognize Some Rules as "Legal" Rules?

In every society, there are clues or indicators to tell members of the society that some rules are legal and must be obeyed. One commentator refers to a list of clues or indicators as the "rule of recognition".[2] They will vary from society to society. In traditional societies the rule of recognition will often involve magic, either alone or mixed with religion, to identify certain basic rules. Supernatural origins for rules go a long way towards getting people's attention.

Consider the Ten Commandments. These are 10 basic rules to govern a simple, tribal society. To get everyone's attention, they are revealed by Moses, a recognized leader, in a dramatic way, as a revelation, directly from God. It must have been quite clear to all but the most dense that these rules were a serious business; this was not just risking others' displeasure for not holding a door open. Look at the nature of the rules: they are not trivial — honouring parents and the deity, no murdering, no stealing, no lying, and so on.

In our society appeals to magic or the supernatural are not entirely absent. Consider the formal court procedures, the judges' robes, and the ritual recitation for the opening of courts calling upon the deity to protect the sovereign, and the use of oaths to ensure that witnesses tell the truth.

In Canada, we have a variety of rules of recognition, based on our political and social values. We recognize sanctions for rule breaking backed by the force of the state as identifying legal rules, and we recognize certain acts — the passage of rules by a legislature, or the pronouncements of judges — as ways of creating legal rules. We also have some rules about rule making and enforcement — constitutional law — that define valid law and valid legal procedure, and tell us whether a rule is a valid legal rule, or something else.

Why Do We Obey Legal Rules?

The first reaction of many would be to say that we obey because we fear we will be punished if we do not. While this is probably true in part, it is not a wholly satisfactory explanation. If fear of punishment were the only reason for obedience, we would need to have, as one English Court of Appeal Judge says, "a policeman at everyone's elbow". But clearly, most of us obey most legal rules most of the time, even when the threat of enforcement is not immediate. Most people do not use force and fraud to get their way. Why is this?

There are a number of reasons: one legal commentator, H.L.A. Hart, has that we obey in part because we have "a habit of obedience".[3] What Hart means here is that through a socialization process we learn and internalize norms and values that help us to recognize legal institutions, laws and the requirement of obeying them. Think of how children are socialized in our

---

2   H.L.A. Hart, The Concept of Law (Oxford: Clarendon Press, 1961) chs. 1 and 2.
3   *Ibid.*

society. From birth, children are taught to follow rules; schools and other institutions further enforce this. Often, we discover there are negative and unpleasant consequences for not following rules. A desire to be accepted, "to fit in", may also contribute to following rules. So may the fact that there are positive benefits for those who obey.

While Hart's approach explains how people learn to obey, it does not explain their motivation for doing so. Explaining motivation requires an examination of human nature. There are two generally competing views on the relationship between human nature and obedience to law. They are associated with two English political writers. The more pessimistic view of human nature is that of the 16th century clergyman and academic, Thomas Hobbes. The more optimistic view is that of the 17th century writer, John Locke.

The Hobbesian View of Human Nature

Hobbes sees human beings as selfish, violent, and predisposed to use force and fraud to get what they want.[4] The society in which they lived was anarchic, where life was, as Hobbes described it, "nasty, brutish and short". It was only when individuals realized that they could improve their lives by entering into civil society that they were prepared to give up their freedom to resort to force and fraud that they had while in the state of nature. Hobbes described individuals as entering into a covenant with a sovereign, in which they gave up their individual rights to act as they wished, by permitting the sovereign to have a monopoly on law making and enforcement and the use of force. A covenant without the sovereign having the power to compel obedience would be worthless: as Hobbes put it, "a covenant without the sword is but words." A just and fair sovereign would insure that individuals lived according to the rule of law, and would punish those who did not. But there was no assumption that individuals would behave cooperatively just because it was to their material advantage. Nor was there any notion that they had any input into the law, or that their consent to its continued operation was required. The threat of state violence beyond their control was still needed to keep them in line and to give them a sense of security. In the end, for Hobbes, we obey the sovereign's rules because we fear the disorder that will arise if we do not, and because we will certainly be punished if we do not.

The Lockean View

Locke, writing in the late 17th century, took quite a different view of human nature and of individuals in the state of nature. His view was that in the state of nature individuals were given to living peacefully with each other and cooperating to assist one another. They were not automatically disposed to engaging in force and fraud. And their lives were not seen as being "nasty, brutish and short." To make their lives easier yet, Locke argued that individuals consented

---

4   The work in which this viewpoint was first set out by Hobbes was in his principal work, The Leviathan. For a summary of his work see G. Sabine, A History of Political Thought, 3d ed. (New York: Holt Rinehart and Winston, 1965), pp. 455–76.

to enter into a civil society by way of a compact, where a ruler ruled and made laws only with the consent of the governed, and where the ruler respected certain basic individual rights: chief among them, the right to own property. For Locke, the purpose of law was not to suppress a violent human nature, but to regulate human activity in the interest of preserving and enhancing property and individual rights. For Locke, individuals obeyed law only so long as they consented to rule by the sovereign, and only so long as the sovereign kept his part of the deal by respecting their political and legal rights, and their right to property. They did not obey out of fear of either the sovereign or each other. Rather, they obeyed because they saw the law as serving their interests, and because they had consented to its creation — it was "their" law: they had some control over what the rules were and how they were enforced.

Locke's approach underlies the view of law we have in a democratic state: we obey, only so long as a majority of us consent to the law making process and to the laws made under that process. Mere fear of disorder and of punishment for breaking the law is no longer the only reason for obedience.

What Are the Limits of Law?

The legal system can bring order and certainty to the law, and control force and fraud, but only so long as the whole of the society is prepared to be governed by the rule of law. We cannot have a situation in a democratic society where the law applies only to some but not others. Another way of putting this is to say that no-one is above the law. If we are all subject to the law equally, we are more likely to accept our obligations under law, knowing that we have lots of company.

Living under the rule of law has another important consequence. Those elected to govern us must obey the same law that we do, and not use their power to ignore laws they don't like. It also means that they must follow the rules for governing and running the state. For example, in Canada political power is exercised by elected representatives. If an army general, unhappy with the civil government, decides to call out his troops and seize power by a coup d'etat, there is no question that he is putting himself above the law. Here, we have rule by physical force rather than by law. At this point, the most elegant and inspiring national constitution is no more than wastepaper.

If the law fails to deal with or contemplate situations of serious evil, we may have to recognize that the law will not assist us in dealing with evil. We cannot expect law to solve every problem, and some matters may have to be left to non-legal means. For example, after World War II, leading Nazis were tried for war crimes that did not exist when the offences were committed. War crimes were not part of international law until after the war, and they were not acts contrary to the valid law of the German state. In this situation, there may be solutions, but they may not come from the law. To deal with these issues in the legal system, we would have to do a number of things that would violate fundamental principles about how the rule of law should operate: for example we would punish people for offences that were not known legal offences at the time they were committed.

The law is also limited in its reach when it simply is not respected or accepted by a majority or large minority of the population. The laws about the consumption of alcohol and drugs furnish very clear examples. The attempt to outlaw the sale of alcohol in the United States in the early 20th century was largely judged to be a failure. It simply did not have any support in urban areas, or among those parts of the population who did not see alcohol as the devil's mousetrap, but instead saw it as part of the expression of their culture. No matter what the law said, and no matter how much effort the government made to enforce the law, it was simply ineffective because large numbers of people were prepared to disobey. In the end, the law was repealed.

The same can be said for the various attempts to prevent the use of controlled drugs, especially cannabis. Some police departments, and even the Canadian Senate, have suggested that the time and effort in trying to control cannabis use is largely time and money wasted. In the United States, a "war on drugs" has been raging since the 1980s with little to indicate that the "war" is being won. Again, many people simply do not accept the idea that using some types of drugs does any significant social harm that requires the law's intervention.

When an individual decides that the law is wrong, or evil, or even silly, they may engage in civil disobedience, either as an individual act or together with others in a group. The early challenges by Blacks in the 1950s and 1960s to state laws requiring segregation on the basis of race were active forms of civil disobedience. They differed from the type of disobedience seen with respect to drug and alcohol consumption laws. The civil rights protesters were not just breaking laws they did not like; they were also making a political statement when they disobeyed segregation laws.

Should Law Reflect Morality?
Whose Morality?

The decision to disobey the law taken by civil rights protesters was because they believed the law to be wrong and immoral. The perception that law reflects morality, or that it should reflect morality, has deep roots in our minds and in our history, going back to Roman law. Today, this view is expressed in a theory of law called natural law, which has its origins in Roman law and the religious law of the Middle Ages. Those who favour this approach argue three things:

Either through a religious or secular perspective, it is possible, through the use of reason, to discover the true morality that the law should reflect. Divine or natural law is superior to human law, and human law should mirror natural or divine law.

- The natural law theorist takes this a step further and states that human law that does not reflect the moral content of natural or divine law is not valid law.
- Last, they argue, law that is not valid need not be obeyed.

Thus, civil rights protesters could argue that segregation laws were immoral because they were contrary to natural law principles and need not be obeyed.

This works as long as we all agree on what is morally right. The problem arises when we ask the question, "By whose morality do we decide what we should or should not obey?" This problem is illustrated by the polarized positions on the right of a woman to obtain an abortion. On the one hand, those who believe that life begins at the moment of conception regard abortion as unlawful killing. On the other hand, those who believe that a pregnant woman has a paramount right to control her own body regard abortion as a right that should be available to every woman without having strangers dictate what happens to her. At present, the Supreme Court of Canada has ruled that the last attempt by Parliament to regulate abortion as part of the criminal law violated the Charter of Rights and Freedoms and was, therefore, unlawful. This left Canada with no law at all regulating abortion, a condition that has prevailed for about a decade, as Parliament has been disinclined to tackle this difficult and divisive issue again, in part, because there are polarized views as to which moral principles apply.

The abortion debate illustrates the problems with respect to the relationship between law and morals. It is simply not possible to "prove" that one side or the other is morally correct in the way that scientific truths are proved. When you ask a scientist how she knows she is correct, she can point to her experiment and observations, which others can repeat. If others obtain the same result, we then know a scientific finding is valid or true. If you ask a natural law theorist how he knows he is right, in the end his answer depends on "right reason" or "divine revelation". But his assumptions cannot be tested or proven to be true. For those who require empirical evidence, the natural law theorist can provide none.

An answer to this problem of morality and law has been proposed in another legal theory called legal positivism. The positivists say that natural law is "nonsense on stilts",[5] and argue that it is ridiculous to suppose that morality is anything more than the assumptions, beliefs and prejudices of those that hold them. This is not to say that moral views are not important or that the law should not reflect them. But it is nonsense to say that we can know for certain which of several competing moral views might be correct and, on that basis, decide what law is valid and what law is not. The positivist answer is to say that:

The law is no more than the language that expresses it.

- The positivist should be concerned with law accurately expressing the intent of the law makers, and that we accurately interpret the language of the law without distorting the meaning of the language used.
- The positivist should not be concerned with the moral content of the law as a test for validity.

For the positivist, the law simply is: it may be morally obnoxious, but the answer is not to deny it is law, but to recognize it as law that needs to be altered. In the meantime, the duty of the positivist is to apply the law as he or she finds it.

The positivist is also concerned with procedure. Once you have determined what the proper procedure is for making, interpreting, administering and en-

---

5   The English 19th century legal positivist, Jeremy Bentham, first used the phrase.

forcing the law, the positivist is content if the law meets those procedural requirements. Behind this lies the positivist concern that the law is made according to the rules for rule making in a given society, and operates with order, certainty and regularity — if it does. then the law is valid. If it does not, then it is not valid. But its validity will not turn on whether its content is morally correct.

Judicial Realism

Positivism and natural law identify two opposed philosophical positions on the role of law as a social institution, and how legal rules should be interpreted. But they do not explain how individuals in the legal system actually engage in judicial decision making. The school of judicial realism that developed in the 1920s and 1930s claims to provide this explanation. This is a behavioural theory that holds he psycho-social makeup of judges as the most important factor in understanding how they interpret and apply law. It provides a way of predicting and explaining judicial behaviour that realists claim more accurately describes the interpretative process than simply trying to determine if a judge is a positivist or natural law adherent. Realism goes further by trying to explain why a particular judge might take a positivist or natural law position, and why a particular judge might be a positivist on some issues and a naturalist on others. From this view came the idea that judicial theories or legal reasons given in case decisions aren't the "real" reasons for judicial decisions, but merely a smokescreen for the real reasons, which are a judge's political, social or moral values, or personality type.

For example, realists argued in the 1930s that the U.S. Supreme Court, in opposing the Roosevelt New Deal legislation, wasn't just applying the common law to strike down these statutes, but was using it as a cover for its conservative social and economic values. Similarly, a realist might argue today that the Supreme Court of Canada, in striking down Parliament's attempts to legislate on abortion, was not just applying the rules in The Charter of Rights and Freedoms, but was using its own values to decide the outcome. Realism does have its detractors, some of whom refer to it as the "what the judge had for breakfast" school of jurisprudence. By this they mean that to focus on a judge's personality and values as the source of a judicial decision overstates the case, and ignores the extent to which judicial values of objectivity, rationality and fairness may minimize the role of a judge's personal views.

What Is Justice?

We can sum up the argument about law and morality by asking the question, "What is justice?" A natural law advocate would argue that justice is providing a morally acceptable outcome. A positivist would argue that justice is applying legal rules literally, without injecting morality or values, so that like cases are treated alike. A realist might argue that asking what justice is is the wrong question. Instead, justice is a legal outcome dependent on the psycho-social makeup of those who decide and interpret the law.

Does Law Lead or Follow Social Change?

The rule maker, be it a king, dictator, legislature or judge, may make rules that may change societal institutions and forms of conduct or behaviour. For example, when Parliament passed the first Canada wide Divorce Act in 1968, it made no-fault divorce possible for the first time, and a divorce, in general, became easier and less expensive to obtain. While attitudes toward divorce were changing anyway, the law brought about an increase in the number of divorces in the country, with various cultural and social changes following the change in the law. There were suddenly more single parent families, divorce was not seen as a social stigma or disgrace, and a new phenomenon, the "combined family", made its appearance, composed of two remarried spouses, and the children of both their previous marriages.

On the other hand, when the rule maker makes or changes law to accommodate changes already occurring in society, then the law is responding to social change that has already occurred in society. When for example, the first legislation giving trade unions the right to bargain collectively was passed in Canada in the late 19th century, the law was merely regulating economic and social changes in labour relations that were already well underway.

These examples are fairly straightforward, but the reality is a bit more complex. In many cases it is hard to say whether the law is bringing about social change or social change is transforming the law. The process of law making is a dynamic process. Lawmakers may be responding to the perceived views of the electorate on some issues, to inputs and ideas from the civil service, to inputs from interest groups and lobbyists. These inputs may represent views and values that are already held by individuals and groups. To the extent that these views become reflected in the law, they, in turn, may bring about further social change.

Consider this example of the complex relationship between legal and social change. In 1990, the Ontario government attempted to change the laws governing employment benefits by extending the definition of who qualified for these benefits. The definition had included married or unmarried spouses of heterosexual employees. It was now proposed to extend these benefits to "same-sex" spouses. The initial impetus was a lawsuit by a government employee who argued that denial of benefits to his same-sex spouse amounted to discrimination on the basis of sex and sexual orientation. But there were also inputs — pros and cons — from various lobby groups, and a lengthy public consultation process, indicating same-sex family benefits had some support in society but also opposition. At that time, the law was not changed by the legislature. The legislation was introduced but failed to pass. However, the law did change as the result of a series of court decisions, taken over a 10-year period, where judges held that denial of benefits to same-sex spouses was a violation of the equality rights under section 15 of The Charter of Rights and Freedoms. The change in the law then attracted little attention as it came incrementally. In the same period, the government had quietly extended such benefits to its employees as had a number of private employers.

How one views the relationship between law and social change depends on what it is one expects of the law. If law is seen as a means of regulating and

---

Exhibit 2: Interpreting Legal Rules: A Discussion

A three-year-old child is walking with his parents into a park, along the path. The child is pulling a toy car behind him on a string. At the entrance to the park there is a sign that says, "Vehicles are not allowed in the park". A police officer sees the family, and issues a ticket to the parents for permitting their child, under their control, to bring a vehicle, albeit a toy, into the park where this is prohibited by law. The parents argue that this is ridiculous. The officer's reply is that it is her job to enforce the law, not question its wisdom.

The example is developed from one used by H.L.A. Hart in The Concept of Law (Oxford: Clarendon Press, 1961). See chs. 1–2.

---

controlling individual behaviour, creating order and certainty, and resolving conflicts, then law's purpose may be to conserve the status quo, not introduce social change. On the other hand, law may be seen as a way of bringing about significant social change. Laws eliminating the consumption of alcohol were designed to make the world a kinder, gentler place. Increasing penalties for drunk driving have brought about a huge change in public attitude and behaviour concerning the use of alcohol and motor vehicles. In these cases, law is seen as an agent for a transformation of society, not just for regulating existing patterns of behaviour.

"Vehicles Are Not Allowed in the Park": How Should We Interpret Legal Rules?

As you can now appreciate how one approaches law can determine how one will interpret it; by way of a summary of our discussion of concepts of law, consider how the natural law adherents, positivists, and realists might approach the problem in Exhibit 2.

How might different approaches to the purpose of law determine the outcome? A realist might say that interpretation means finding and applying the meaning of ordinary English, and interpreting the law according to the meaning of the language used, without going beyond that to draw on external sources as aids to interpretation. This might result in an interpretation that finds the word "vehicle" modified by the word "toy", so as to take the object out of the reach of the law. It might equally well find that a vehicle is a vehicle, and the law has been broken. In either case, the answer is a technical analysis of language rather than content. It may result in an absurdity, but it is for judges to interpret and apply the law, not question the purpose or intent of the law makers. If the law is absurd, then it is up to the democratically elected legislature to make necessary changes, not for judges. Here, the law is seen as limited to what it says — the interpretation is limited to the actual language, is narrow, and somewhat mechanical. But following this approach, we get the same answer every time — the "right" answer, in the sense that we maintain order, certainty and predictability in the law, so we can all easily know the consequences. Like cases are treated alike.

A Natural lawyer might see this differently. She would note the absurdity of arresting a child with a toy truck, and note that it would be immoral to give the law such effect and purpose. She would draw on principals and values, perhaps on a moral code that supports a child's imaginative play to give the words a context, rather than interpret them abstractly and without regard for the results. Here, the law would be interpreted according to a morally proper result.

A realist might look at a case like this in terms of his or her own social and political values, and interpret the law to advance particular political principles. What values and principles the judge chose would come not from an external moral code, but would be influenced by the judge's personality, political or moral views, life experiences, and psychological makeup.

This discussion of approaches to interpreting legal rules can seem to be very academic, based on competing legal philosophies. And for this reason one might be tempted to dismiss the importance of these approaches. But in modern legal systems on some issues, judges can be described in practical terms as being on a continuum running from judicial activist to strict constructionist.

Interestingly, some judges may be strict constructionists on some issues and activists on others. A judicial activist is one who sees interpretation as a quasi legislative function where law is interpreted in a way that is consistent with identifiable principles, values and views of society. A strict constructionist takes a narrower view, looking to the plain or literal meaning found in the language of the law, and ignoring social policy or values. These approaches are particularly true of, and particularly important in, constitutional law. Political values and principles come to the fore in constitutional law, where courts deal with fundamental issues about rights and the uses of political power. Further, the Constitution now requires the courts to decide how fundamental legal principles in the Constitution and in the Charter of Rights and Freedoms are to be interpreted and applied. Judges spend much time trying to fathom the extent of rights identified in the Constitution. For example, section 15 of the Charter sets out certain equality rights by prohibiting discrimination based on a list of grounds, such as race, religion, colour, ethnicity. A strict constructionist would restrict equality rights to the categories listed, arguing that if the framers of the Constitution wanted to be more expansive, they would have been. Activists have said that you must look to the spirit, nature and purpose of section 15, and be ready to expand the list to include, for example, not just discrimination on the basis of sex, but discrimination based on things that are related to items on the list, but not specifically mentioned, such as sexual orientation. A strict constructionist, on the other hand, would say that if sexual orientation is not an already protected category explicitly set out in the charter, it is not the job of judges to put it there. To permit that is to usurp the job of the legislature as supreme law maker.

Judicial activists are often seen as social engineers trying to implement their own view of the world despite the clear intention of parliament. Strict constructionists are often portrayed as narrow and conservative, using narrow interpretation of law to advance a conservative, if not reactionary, agenda. But to say this is probably to overstate the case. In reality, most judges bring some activist and some self-restraint approaches to bear on legal interpretation, but a judge's approach may vary depending on the legal issues or questions before him or her.

Conclusion: The Hallmarks of a Functional and Effective Legal System

So far we have been discussing different concepts of law in terms of its function in society. The concern here has been a political one: what is the role of law in a democratic society? What rules are valid legal rules, and what rules are something else? Most commentators agree that in a democratic society the rule of law should prevail — that is, no-one should be above the law. But beyond that, are there minimal requirements of a legal system that will be generally accepted in a democratic society? What is necessary to get the members of a society to prefer legal solutions to non-legal ones? Lon Fuller, a legal theorist, argues that the reliance on law, rather than on brute force, is a reliance on a rational, consensual approach to problem solving where people defer to norms associated with peaceful conflict resolution.[6] To put it another way, people must have an expectation that the system will work rationally, that like cases will be treated alike and that outcome of conflict resolution, and action in general, will be predictable and certain.

Although Fuller does not say so, the expectation of rationality requires a certain type of society: at a minimum, most members of the society must have access to social and economic resources; they must be free of fear for their own survival and safety. The state apparatus of this society must be seen to be rational and reasonably transparent in its operation, and to have a monopoly over the use of force, which is used with restraint and in accordance with established rules. Examples of political societies that would meet these criteria include Canada, the United States, the European Union countries, and many Asian countries. Examples of states that would not meet these criteria would include countries like Afghanistan, and some of the states of sub-Saharan Africa. These latter are sometimes referred to as "failed states": politically unstable, where many societal institutions are in disarray, where the rule of law is not present, and where life is chaotic, or, to use Hobbes' phrase, "nasty, brutish and short".

The Characteristics of a Functional Legal System in a Democratic State Where the rule of law operates, legal systems usually have the following characteristics:

I.   Laws Are General in Their Application

Legal rules should exist for most of the requirements and prohibitions in a given society. These rules should also be general in nature, and directed at ev-

---

6   See Lon Fuller, The Morality of Law (New Haven: Yale University Press, 1969).

eryone in a specific situation. For example, the rule prohibiting drivers from exceeding a speed limit applies to all persons driving on a particular section of highway governed by that speed limit. An example of a law that fails to meet this requirement is one actually passed in the English Parliament in the reign of Henry VII: "Richard Rose shall be detained, and boiled in oil". Whoever Rose was, he certainly had powerful enemies: powerful enough to get a law proclaimed just to "get" him. This would be regarded as a perversion of the law.

2. Laws Must Be Promulgated

In a rational system of law, we would expect that if we are to obey laws, they must be proclaimed in such a way that we know what they are. In a society like ours there are specific rules about rule making and rule proclaiming that must be followed, or the rules are deemed to be invalid and of no effect. If the rules for making and proclaiming law are followed, it is presumed that we can all find the law and know what obedience is required. In a society like ours, you are presumed to know the law because it is publicly available. The reality is that the mechanisms for finding the law are so technical that most people will need the help of a lawyer to locate the law and determine how it applies to them. There are some who argue that the legal profession and the judiciary contribute to obscuring the process of finding the law by perpetuating the mystery and complexity that surrounds the law.

It follows from this discussion that "secret" law is no law at all. An example arose some years ago when prison reform activists discovered that the prison authorities had, and applied, some internal regulations that they refused to promulgate. Prison reformers succeeded in striking down these "secret" regulations on the grounds that no-one could obey or know that they were disobeying a law that was kept a secret. Nor could anyone know if the rules were being applied properly, if only those who made them knew what they were.

Because law making is complicated in Canada, the courts also require laws to be proclaimed according to the proper procedures. For example, a regulation that is drafted, but inadvertently not posted to the official provincial or federal gazette, is no law at all. In order for the regulation to be valid and in effect, it must be properly proclaimed, or "gazetted".

3. Law Should Be Prospective Rather Than Retroactive

If a law is passed and proclaimed today, then the expectation is that it takes effect as of today, and governs behaviour from today. Past behaviour should not be made illegal today if, at the time the behaviour occurred, it was legal. Also, no penalty should attach for behaviour that was legal when it occurred. For example, if we passed a law today that says, "All persons who let their cell phone go off in class shall be shot", you would all reach for the button that turns off the ringer on your cell phone. You would know what is expected of you, and would be able to take the necessary steps to avoid punishment. However, if we passed a law today that said, "As of last Thursday, anyone who let their cell phone ring in class, shall be shot", it would be seen as very unfair because persons who let their cell phones ring in class before it was outlawed would be punished for doing something that was perfectly lawful when they did it.

There are some situations where the law may permit retroactive application or impact. Under the doctrine of foreshadowing, where a proposed law has had much publicity, and been much discussed, it may apply before it is proclaimed. As its content is well known, it is presumed that people would have already taken steps to obey. Similarly, when a budget is passed, it often is deemed to take effect at some time before its passage. For example, a budget passed in March may be given effect as of January 1, as that is the beginning of the taxation year for many taxpayers, although the budget is usually not ready for a month or two later.

There is one other situation where there is retroactive impact. Where a statute is proclaimed in force, we often will not know how the statute is to be interpreted until someone brings a court case challenging the interpretation of language in the statute. It may take the courts months or years to determine the outcome, and the decision will apply back in time to when the dispute first arose for the parties that were involved in the dispute. For others, the decision should take effect only from the time it is made.

4.   Laws Should Be Clear

This means that the law should not be so obscure or confusing or contradictory that no rational sense can be made of it. It does not mean that the law cannot be complex, or that it cannot be subject to interpretation. The courts have developed various interpretative techniques by which we should be able to clarify and interpret law, so that we know what is required.

5.   Laws Should Not Be Contradictory

A given behaviour or course of conduct should not be legal under one law and illegal under another. In a federal state like Canada, it is possible to have the two levels of government passing contradictory laws. However, the Constitution contains a mechanism that permits the courts to determine which law is valid and should be obeyed, and which is invalid and can be ignored. It does this using constitutional rules to determine which level of government has jurisdiction to enact a particular rule, which in turn resolves the conflict over which law to obey. The problem of contradictory law also looms large in international trade, where in a contract dispute two sets of national laws may apply. Usually these disputes can be resolved by conflict of law rules to determine which of two conflicting rules applies. Similarly, free trade agreements, such as the North American Free Trade Agreement (NAFTA), contain rules for resolving conflicts between domestic rules and rules agreed to by the parties under the trade agreement.

6.   Laws Should Not Make Impossible Demands

The law should not make rules that are impossible to apply on any rational or logical basis.

7.   Law Should Be Reasonably Constant and Durable

While the law needs to change to adapt to changing circumstances, it should not be constantly amended and changed so that there is confusion over what law actually is in operation. In order for people to plan complex, long term undertakings, there has must be some assurance that the laws relevant to that undertaking remain certain and predictable.

There are some laws that are amended frequently, however. Tax law is often amended, sometimes annually, in accordance with the requirements of the government's budget.

8.   Law Should Be Capable of Enforcement

It should be expected in society that when behavioural requirements have been set out in the law, those requirements are enforced, and that there is an expectation that they will be enforced. Where the rules are breached, sanctions or negative consequences should follow reasonably quickly. This is true for criminal law, with its prescribed penalties, but also true for civil disputes where breach of one person's right by another gives rise to negative consequences for the transgressor in the form of a requirement to pay for the harm done to another.

Without penalties or sanctions, the law would be no more than a statement of principle about what we ought to do. It would not be a statement of what we have to do. For the most part, the expectation that sanctions will be applied is enough to ensure compliance without having a policeman at everyone's elbow. But as we noted earlier, there may be circumstances where the failure of government to effectively enforce the law may result in increased disregard of the law. For example, if we know the highway speed limits are not going to be enforced because the government decided not to hire more police, we may disregard them because we know we run little risk of being caught and penalized.

But there are other circumstances where vigorous enforcement does not seem to compel obedience. The American "War on Drugs" has gone on for years, with serious penalties for transgressors. But there seems to be little indication that the non-medical use of drugs is subsiding. Similarly, attempts to enforce prohibition and suppress the liquor trade were largely unsuccessful. These examples indicate that where the law is not accepted as legitimate or valid, harsh penalties will not bring about compliance or deter people from breaking an unpopular law.

Suggested Readings

Finch, J.D. Introduction to Legal Theory 3d ed. (London: Sweet and Maxwell, 1979).

Gall, G.R. The Canadian Legal System 4th ed. (Toronto: Carswell, 1995).

Hart, H.L.A. The Concept of Law (Oxford: Clarendon Press, 1961).

James, P.S. Introduction to English Law (London: Butterworths, 1985).

Lloyd, D. The Idea of Law, Reprinted with revisions (Baltimore: Penguin, 1976).

Laurence M. Olivo

Lloyd, D. & M.D.A. Freeman, Introduction to Jurisprudence 5th ed. (London: Stevens, 1985).

Sabine, G. A History of Political Theory 3d ed. (New York: Holt, Rinehart and Winston, 1961).

Videos

Kramer, Stanley, prod. & dir. Judgment at Nuremberg. With Spencer Tracy, Maximilian Schell. 1961. [Video release, 1989; b and w; approximately 190 minutes.]

Brook, Peter, dir. Lord of the Flies 1963. [Video release, 1993; colour; approximately 90 minutes.]

Websites

Access to Justice: www.acjnet.org

Systems of Law in Canada

Laurence M. Olivo

Systems of Law in Canada*

National Legal Systems

Nation states usually have one legal system. A legal system consists of legal rules, principles, institutions, and procedures that operate in a distinctive way. Modern nation states like Canada that are **federal states** may subdivide their legal system into local and national sy~~~ ~~ e two systems usually operate in the same way, according to the ~~~~ ~~les. Such systems have simply divided **jurisdictions** on a territoria~ ~~ en local and national political units.

Origins of Canada's Legal Systems

The development of legal systems in Canada ~~~~~ ferent from that of most nation states. As a federal state, Canada ~~~~~ s legal system into national and local components on a territorial ~~~~ re provincial and federal laws and courts. But there is another div ~~~~ there is the common law system used at the federal level, includii ~~~~ northern territo-

*   From *Introduction to Law in Canada,* edited by Lauren~~ ~~ cord, ON: Captus Press Inc., 1995–2003). Reproduced with permission of

ries, and in nine of the provinces, and the civil law system used in the Province of Quebec.

This peculiar arrangement is a result of Canada's colonial experience. When France was defeated in the Seven Years' War, sovereignty over Quebec (then called New France) passed from the French to the British in 1760. The British found themselves ruling a colony composed primarily of French-speaking Roman Catholics. The British colonial administrators had to decide how to rule this new colony with its non-British, non-Protestant majority population. British North American colonies up to that time had simply adopted British political institutions and laws when a colony was established. At first, the British followed this policy in Quebec by imposing British political rules and laws on the inhabitants. The latter were unhappy with this arrangement, as social and political institutions were well established, and the intrusion of alien British institutions was disruptive. By the 1770s, as the 13 British colonies on the Atlantic coast inched closer to rebellion, it occurred to subtler minds among British colonial administrators that it might make sense to try to win over the Francophone inhabitants of Quebec by tolerating their religion and accepting their institutions.

By passage of the Quebec Act in 1774, and by some adroit politicking with local elites who were won over and publicly endorsed British rule, Quebec was given the freedom to practise the Roman Catholic religion and exercise other freedoms. Among these was the right to keep its **private law**, the law governing legal relations, rights, and liabilities between individual persons. This law was based on the laws of France in the late 18th century, as well as on local laws and customs. Law governing relations between the subject and the state (often referred to as **public law**) was based on British common law.

Subsequently, the Maritime colonies and Upper Canada were established with legal systems based on the British common law, as were all of the later western additions to the Canadian state. In this way, Canada developed with two quite different legal systems: the civil law system in Quebec, governing private law matters, and the common law system everywhere else.

The Common Law System

Legal Rules Based on Previously Decided Cases

In the common law system, decisions in previously decided cases provide the basis for legal rules. Consequently, much of the law in this system is referred to as **caselaw.** Lawyers also refer to caselaw as **common law** to distinguish it from **statutory law**, which is law passed by parliament or a legislature. There are, in fact, different meanings for the term "common law," depending on the context in which the term is used. This is discussed at the end of this chapter.

How Common Law Developed

The Norman Kings Centralize Law Making

The common law legal system had its origins in feudal England. When the Duke of Normandy invaded England and seized the Crown in the 11th century, his successors faced the political task of consolidating their rule over local populations and over the local feudal lords. The Norman kings sought to do this by establishing a strong, effective, central government as a counter to the power of local feudal lords.

Judges Develop a Law Common to All England

As part of this strategy, the king travelled about the country dispensing justice personally by resolving disputes that were brought to him. In time, responsibility for dispensing the king's justice fell to the king's advisors, from whose ranks there eventually emerged full-time judges. These judges would travel out from London to major towns in the realm to hear cases. The judges, when travelling, were said to be **on circuit.** To this day, in many common law jurisdictions, judges of some courts still go on circuit to hear cases.

Judges, in the course of solving disputes before them, gradually departed from local custom and developed rules that were common to the realm. These rules, derived from cases, and applied as precedents to later disputes, formed the basis for the common law of England. This did not happen quickly or by design. Certain other things had to happen first. Persons who appeared as advocates for disputants, began to write down the decisions of judges and, more important, the judges' reasons for these decisions. Once this was done, it was possible to circulate these reasons among judges and advocates (from whose ranks the legal profession later developed). Advocates would then argue that a judge in a previous case had decided the issue in a particular way, and that the decision, being sensible and wise, should then be followed. Of course the advocate for the other party would argue that the facts of the case currently before the court, or the issue before the court, was different from that in the previous case, so that the previous case was not really a precedent for deciding the present case. Lawyers refer to this latter type of argument as distinguishing a precedent case from the case **at bar** (the case currently before the judge).

Distinguishing cases, and otherwise avoiding the application of an alleged precedent case, are discussed later in this chapter.

Significantly, there was no concerted attempt to attack the common law system of precedent as the basis for developing a system of legal rules. The approach used was practical. Judges saw their role as resolving disputes in a national arena that had little in the way of national law. They developed this law — not consciously or intentionally, but over time — on a case-by-case basis, in reaction to whatever disputes litigants brought before them. It was not elegant; no-one sat down and decided to create a body of national law as a conscious, coherent, related whole, as was the case with Roman law and, later, civil law. Instead, the common law evolved, in bits and pieces over time, slowly growing into a body of law covering most of the problems of life in society.

Precedent and Stare Decisis

Precedent

As noted in the previous section, the common law system is characterized by a particular process of making rules from the decisions of judges in ordinary lawsuits. This form of rule making is based on the use of **precedent cases.** After a judge has given reasons for judgment in a particular case, if a similar case comes before another judge, the judge hearing the later case may be persuaded to decide that case by applying the reasons for judgment in the earlier and similar case to the case before him. When this happens, the judge in the second case is said to be using the reasons for the decision in the first case as a **precedent** for his decision in the second case. The first case is then called a precedent case, and other judges are expected to apply its reasons, and to **follow the precedent** before them, when the precedent case decides legal issues that are raised in the case before the judge. In time a series of cases are decided following the original precedent case. Often the later cases refine and expand the rule (reason for decision) in the original precedent case. In time, the series of cases will develop a number of related legal rules.

It is useful to note, in discussing precedent, that the precedent value of a case does not lie in the actual decision (who won, who lost), but in the legal reasons for the decision. The reason for decision, formally referred to as the **ratio decidendi** or more simply, the **ratio** of the case, is where the precedent value of a case lies.

Stare Decisis

A second important feature of the law-making process in the common law system is the doctrine of **stare decisis.** This term is an abbreviation of a longer Latin phrase that means to "stand by decided matters." It reinforces the operation of the doctrine of precedent by compelling judges to follow precedents, in certain circumstances, even where a judge might otherwise not want to.

This idea of a judge being compelled to follow a precedent case is closely tied to the idea of a **hierarchy of courts.** The idea of a hierarchy of courts involves classifying or ranking courts in terms of their power and authority. Courts can be classified as:

- **courts of first instance**, or trial courts, where legal disputes are first heard and decided
- **appellate courts**, which review the decisions of courts of first instance, and correct errors made by the "lower" courts

Courts can also be classified in terms of the subject matter of cases they can hear and remedies they can grant. The area of activity open to a court to exercise is sometimes referred to as its **jurisdiction.** "Higher" courts have jurisdiction over a broader range of subjects and remedies than "lower" courts do. For example, a "higher" court, the Superior Court of Justice, can hear cases with claims for any amount of money, involving any subject matter. Small Claims Court, which is a "lower court," is limited in the types of claims it can hear, and the monetary value of those claims.

The operation of stare decisis depends on the hierarchy of courts. Generally, courts higher up in the hierarchy of courts can bind judges in the lower courts in the same geographical jurisdiction, so that the latter are bound to follow precedent cases from higher courts. Decisions by courts on a particular level are not binding on courts at the same level, but are considered to be **per-**

Exhibit 1: Which Decision Is Binding?

- A decision of the Supreme Court of Canada binds all courts in the provincial court systems.

- A decision of the provincial court of appeal binds all other courts in the provincial court system, and may be considered persuasive by judges in other provinces.

- A decision of the superior trial court binds lower trial courts in the province and should be considered persuasive by other judges at the same level in the jurisdiction.

- A decision of the lower trial court is not binding on any other court, but may be considered persuasive by other courts at the same level.

---

suasive. For example, a decision of a Superior Court of Justice judge is not binding on another Superior Court of Justice judge, but should be treated as persuasive by being accorded respect and by being followed, if possible. Decisions by judges in courts from other jurisdictions are also not binding, but may be considered as persuasive if the decisions come from a higher court in the other jurisdiction, or if the decisions come from judges in another jurisdiction who are highly respected for their legal knowledge and expertise.

The Role of Precedent and Stare Decisis in a Common Law System

To summarize, if the doctrine of precedent sets out the idea that a precedent case *ought* to be followed, *stare decisis* sets out the idea that a precedent case *must* be followed in certain circumstances. While there have been some recent developments that lessen the force of stare decisis in Canada, making its application less rigid and mechanical, it is considered to be an important feature of a common law legal system.

The common law system differs dramatically from most other kinds of legal systems. Legal rules in this system are not consciously assembled from a series of carefully developed principles laid out and connected in a logical way as is the case in many other legal systems. Instead, judges "made up" the rules as they went along, deciding practical problems that were presented in cases by people with disputes and disagreements. Once a judge made a rule to solve the problem before him, his "solution" would be adopted by other judges with a similar case.

In a sense, legal rules in this system result as a reaction to problems. In other systems, notably the civil law system used in Quebec and in many other parts of the world, rules are often derived from abstract principles, which are organized and codified in a systematic way, ready to be applied to resolve disputes. The latter approach seems simpler, more efficient, less haphazard, and more rational. If this is so, why did the common law not follow this pattern? If we consider the ad hoc way in which the common law developed as an extension of the king's personal power to do individual justice, it is clear that the focus was primarily on the need to make decisions and solve problems, not on developing a systematic and integrated body of law.

A Gloss on the Common Law:
The Law of Equity
Origins of the Law of Equity

While common law developed slowly without anyone consciously managing the process, its growth was checked, after a couple of centuries, by the power of the nobility. The local nobles had watched as the king used the development of a centralized legal system, operating out of London, as one of many ways of consolidating royal power. Eventually, the nobles extracted some concessions from the king to check the expansion of royal power and, in particular, the power of the Royal Courts of Justice, to interfere with the nobles' management of local affairs. They did this by getting the king to "freeze" the expansion of the common law by prohibiting the creation of any further legal rights to sue, or **causes of action**. The common law was thus left for several hundred years with what came to be called the **ancient forms of action**. This step contributed to the common law becoming unable to use precedent to expand or develop the law further. Instead, the law became frozen.

Meanwhile, as society and social institutions changed and developed, the law did not. As well, because the law was frozen and rigid, the application of its rules could and did cause obvious injustice and unfairness. When the legal result was obviously unfair, a **suitor** would occasionally complain about this to the king who, unlike his judges, was free, as the source of justice in the realm, to fashion personal justice as he saw fit. If the king was persuaded by a suitor, he would issue a decree overruling the judgment of the courts. As more subjects brought these complaints to the king, he referred these matters to his chief administrative officer, the **Chancellor.** The Chancellor would then issue a Chancellor's decree to overrule the court, and correct an obvious injustice. Good news travels quickly; in time, the flow of complaints grew so great that the Chancellor had to designate some of his staff to hear these complaints. Gradually the process became institutionalized: the Chancellor's staff became **Chancery judges**, operating out of the **Court of Chancery**. The decrees of the Chancellor, through the use of the precedent process, evolved into a separate body of law called the **law of equity**. Thus a second parallel system of courts was established. As the Chancery system became institutionalized, however, the justice delivered became less personal and less flexible. In particular, Chancery judges resorted to judicial reasoning using precedent. This tended to inhibit the expansion of equity law. The result was that the law of equity also became rigid and unresponsive.

Exhibit 2: Avoiding Precedent

Whether a previous case is actually a precedent is not always clear. Lawyers have a variety of techniques they use to find a way around a precedent case, particularly when they wish to avoid, or get around, a precedent that stands in their client's way.

- **Distinguishing a case on its facts:** When faced with an apparent precedent, a lawyer may argue that it is not really a precedent because it is different in its material facts from the **case at bar** (the case that is being argued by the lawyer before the court).

- **Obiter dicta:** There is no simple, objective test for identifying the ratio of a case. Because finding the "true" ratio is a subjective exercise, it is open to argument that the judicial opinion in a case is not the ratio, but mere **obiter dicta,** or more simply, **obiter.** Obiter dicta is a judicial opinion set out in a case but it is not the opinion on which the decision in the case rests. Judicial opinions that are obiter are thought to have no precedent value in a case, although they may provide insights for deciding other cases, where the judicial observations may be more relevant. However, note that in recent Canadian caselaw there is a suggestion that obiter in cases from the Supreme Court of Canada may be binding on lower courts, if relevant to cases before them.[1] Previously, obiter was thought to be persuasive, but not binding.

- **Per incuriam:** A lawyer may argue that a case should not be followed because the judge based her decision and her reasoning on an error of fact or law. For example, the lawyers arguing a case may have inadvertently failed to cite an important precedent case to the judge, or left out important facts by mistake. In either of these situations, the precedent value of the case is arguably weakened, if its true legal or factual base is other than what the judge hearing the case thought it was.

  The per incuriam problem illustrates the extent to which a judge in the common law system is dependent on the lawyers presenting a case to define the issues, facts and law to be relied on. When a lawyer makes a mistake and fails to find a relevant case when doing his research, and the other lawyer does not catch the mistake, there is no assurance that a judge, busy with a heavy case load, will either. While judges often "check" the cases cited to them, they do not always do this. Further, in the common law system, judges are relatively passive participants in the trial process, reasoning their way to a decision on the basis of legal and evidential information supplied by the lawyers presenting the case.

- **Concurring opinions:** In some proceedings, appeals for example, the case is heard by a panel of several judges, rather than by one judge sitting alone. When this happens, different judges may come to the same conclusion for different reasons. When two or more judges agree on the result, but give different reasons for their decision, their judgments are concurring opinions, but there cannot be said to be a single ratio for the case on which a precedent could be founded. In such a case, the reasons of a particularly eminent judge might carry more weight than the reasons of her colleagues sitting on the same panel, but this does not provide a clear-cut solution to the problem of deciding what the true ratio is.

- **Precedent wrongly decided:** In some cases, it is possible for a lawyer to argue that an earlier case may technically and logically be a precedent, but that the reasoning should not be followed because it is wrong. A case may be seen as wrong when, for example, the social situations that gave rise to the reasons no longer exist, so that the application of the precedent would give rise to ridiculous results. This approach is not used often, as it constitutes a direct attack on the doctrine of stare decisis which lies at the core of the common law system. Lawyers, being masters of legal subtlety, usually can find a more indirect way of avoiding precedent.

  [1] Sellars v. R., [1980] 1 S.C.R. 527.

Features of the Law of Equity

The common law courts continued to administer the common law while the Court of Chancery administered the law of equity. Initially, the law of equity developed a body of legal rules with two main features:

- rules that would "correct" common law results by granting **equitable remedies**
- preconditions that a suitor had to comply with first in order to invoke the law of equity

As a corrective for the common law, equity was sometimes referred to as "a gloss on the common law." For example, at common law, if one party broke a contractual arrangement, the only remedy the common law recognized was money damages. If the breaking of a contract would cause some injury that could not be compensated for in damages, there was nothing the common law could do. The law of equity, however, could be invoked, and an **injunction** obtained to order a stop to the wrongful behaviour.

Before a suitor could resort to the Court of Chancery and the law of equity, she had to satisfy certain preconditions. Originally, before a suitor could get the Chancellor to interfere with a court decision, the suitor had to show

Exhibit 3: An Illustration of the Use of Precedent

A owns a house with a flat roof. B is planning to build a house on the next lot, and right next to A's house. B's house is going to be 10 feet higher than A's. A discovers that B's house, if built, will create conditions that will increase the snowload on A's house, and cause damage to A's roof. A tells this to B and asks him to redesign his proposed house. B refuses.

A wants to stop *B* from building. *A* sues *B* for a tort called nuisance. The tort of nuisance allows one landowner to sue another for damage done to his land as a result of activity by the other on his own land. However, the definition of nuisance, as stated here, is fairly broad, and *A* has to find some cases that show that the definition of nuisance applies to his circumstances.

A finds a case where the court awarded damages to a person whose basement was flooded, when the defendant built a house that diverted rain run off towards the plaintiff's house and into his basement. At the time the defendant built the house, neither party knew that flooding would result.

A can argue that this case is a precedent:

- Its facts on the relevant issue are similar to the case at bar; damage is caused to the plaintiff's property by an act of the defendant on his own property.
- Damage was caused by a natural element being channelled by the defendant where otherwise no damage would have resulted. Whether the element was snow or water, and whether the damage was to the roof or basement is irrelevant, given that the issue is physical damage caused by the defendant.

B can argue that this case can be distinguished on its facts:

- In this case, the defendant had built his house, and the damage to the plaintiff's house had already occurred. Arguably, this case means that you can't sue until damage has occurred. In the case at bar, B hadn't built his house, and no damage had occurred to A's house yet.
- This case creates liability for water damage. But the case at bar involves snowload. Snow and water behave differently. Therefore, this case cannot, on its facts, support a claim for liability for snowload, where other causal factors may be involved, or the risk may be too remote to impose liability.
- This case concerns damage to basements from water. The case at bar is different on its facts, as it concerns snow damage to a roof where other causal factors may be involved, or the risk may be too remote to impose liability.

Exhibit: 4 Avoiding Confusion: Different Uses of "Common Law" and "Civil Law"

By now it should be apparent that both "common law" and "civil law" can have different meanings depending on the situations where they are used.

Common Law

The body of common custom, or law common to all England, which was an early product of the justice system created by the Norman kings. This usage is now only of historical interest and does not have a contemporary meaning.
- The body of caselaw, from which legal precedents are drawn, is called common law to distinguish it from law from other sources, such as statutory law.
- The legal system that developed in England, and that features the use of precedent cases as a major source of law, is called a common law legal system.

Civil Law
- Civil law describes a system of law derived from Roman law and natural law which is usually codified.
- Civil law in the common law system describes private law, consisting primarily of the law of torts and contract.

---

that she had been wronged, that a common law remedy was inadequate or non-existent and that she had behaved properly in her dealings with her opponent. In time, this meant that a suitor in Chancery had to show the court that she had behaved properly in the lawsuit, had not acted underhandedly or oppressively against the other side. If the suitor could not **come into court with clean hands**, Chancery would refuse to hear her or grant the equitable remedies requested.

For example, if a suitor had tried to hide evidence in a case, then it is unlikely that the suitor would meet the preconditions required to invoke the law of equity.

Merger of the Common Law and Equity Jurisdiction
In time, the two parallel court systems and systems of legal rules became cumbersome and rigid. For example:

- It was often difficult for even a highly experienced lawyer to decide whether to start a lawsuit in Chancery or in a common law court. If an error was made, a case would be thrown out and have to start from the beginning in the other court.

• Decrees from the Chancery Court might conflict with, or be inconsistent with, the orders of the common law courts.

These kinds of problems caused uncertainty in the law, delayed proceedings, and made them more expensive. In the late 19th century, a major court reform movement in the common law world, including Canada, resulted in the merger of the two court systems into one superior court with the power to administer the common law and the law of equity together.

While the separate courts administering the law of equity have passed into history, the law of equity is still relevant today. It continues to be administered by superior-court judges who have the power to administer the common law and the law of equity together. Courts today still have available and, where relevant, use powerful equitable remedies, such as injunctions, and orders for specific performance of contracts. These remedies achieve results that cannot otherwise be achieved by traditional common law remedies, which are generally limited to the payment of money for damages sustained.

The Modern Common Law System: Caselaw, Equity, and Statutes

The Modern Common Law System as a "Mixed" System of Law

While the common law originated out of a process where the law developed on a case-by-case basis, modern common law systems are more complex and have more sources of legal rules than previously decided, precedent cases.

The sources of law in the common law system are discussed in more detail in the chapter, Sources of Law; in this chapter, the relationship and development of the main written sources of law are explored.

Modern common law systems are mixed systems in terms of the sources of law. In Canada, the principal sources of written law are caselaw, including both common law rules and equitable rules, and statutory law, which also includes regulations made under the authority of statutes. The development of the law of equity alongside common law has been examined; we now turn to the development of statutory law in the common law system.

How Common Law Developed into a Mixed System of Law

When the common law began to develop, it was the principal source of legal rules. Statutes, which are laws passed by Parliament or a legislature, were not yet a significant factor in legal rule making. In the 11th and 12th centuries, when the common law began to take form, Parliament as we know it did not exist. Over the next several centuries, however, Parliament began to take both a form and function we would recognize today. At first, composed of the Lords (clergy and nobility) and the Commons (representatives of wealthy towns), it was summoned by the king when he needed to raise large sums of money by taxation, usually to finance a war. In time, in exchange for consenting to taxation, Parliament extracted concessions from the king, which resulted in Parliament increasing its participation in government by passing laws or statutes dealing with matters other than taxation.

Parliamentary Supremacy

As this expansion of parliamentary power represented an erosion of royal power, the king sometimes resisted, and from the 17th century on, there was considerable tension between king and parliament over the exercise of power by the latter.

All this came to a head, literally, in 1649, when Charles I lost his, when he tried to dismiss parliament and rule alone. The result was a civil war between the king's adherents and parliament's, in which the king was beheaded and parliament ruled alone. What emerged from the English Civil War was a new legal doctrine, **the Doctrine of Parliamentary Supremacy** (also called Parliamentary Sovereignty), under which Parliament was declared to be the supreme law-maker. This meant that when Parliament passed a law, it negated any other law or rule made outside of Parliament that conflicted with an act of Parliament. Further, not only did ordinary citizens have to obey the law, but so did royal officials, so that those who governed had to do so according to the law passed by Parliament. Another way of looking at this is to say that no-one is above the law. With respect to judge-made law, a statute would cancel out any law developed from decided cases dealing with subjects now legislated on by parliament.

Advantages of Statutory Law over Caselaw

Once parliament had a relatively free hand to legislate, it increased its output of statutes and, from the 17th century onward, it gradually became the source of a growing proportion of legal rules in the common law system. The reason for this growth of statutory law was not simply that parliament now had the power to act. For example, parliament could use statutes to respond to particular problems relatively quickly and in a comprehensive way. As society became more complex, statutes provided a more effective way to make rules than the slow and cumbersome common law process of developing judge-made law on a case-by-case basis.

Sorting Out Conflicts between Sources of Law

It is apparent from this chapter that both statutory law and equity developed, at least in part, because of perceived shortcomings of the common law caselaw precedent system, which was seen as too rigid, too slow, and too unresponsive to the needs of a complex society. However, these later additions to the common law system, when added on to that system, created potential for conflict. If, for example, a rule developed from caselaw conflicted with a statute, which would prevail? Gradually, over time, the answers to these questions were worked out. Briefly, they are:

- if there is a conflict between a caselaw rule and an equitable rule, the equitable rule shall prevail
- if there is a conflict between a statutory rule, and an equitable or common law rule, the statutory rule shall prevail

While statutory law prevails over caselaw, note that there is a continuing relationship between statute law and caselaw. Disputes about the meaning of all or part of a statute are resolved by court cases. Where a case has interpreted part of a statute and expanded or refined previous understandings of what the statute meant, then that case becomes an important determinant of a statute's meaning.

The Civil Law System

In a civil law system, principles and rules of law are found in a set of clearly articulated and connected principles set out in a coherent system of law, in contrast to the common law system, where they are found, if at all, in caselaw. The system of law usually has a base in a legal theory that has an integrated world-view, and which determines the content, focus, and direction of legal rules and principles. For example, modern European (and Quebec) civil law systems owe a great deal to theories of law found in Roman law and in natural law. In addition, the rules and principles are organized in a systematic and logical way. This organizing process, usually called **codification**, results in the codes that are a feature of modern civil law systems.

Key features of a civil law system are:

• a coherent, theoretically interrelated system of law
• the system of law is codified

In Quebec, private law is based on modern European civil law, organized and codified in the Quebec Civil Code.

The Origins of the Quebec Civil Code
The Law of New France at the Time of the Conquest

When the British took over the governance of New France, now to be called Quebec, they found a French-speaking society that had been established on the shores of the St. Lawrence for over a century. While the colony was governed by French officials, its institutions had evolved in response to local conditions. The legal system in use fit this pattern. It was based originally on the customary law of the Paris region. In its origins, it was a mixture of local custom, some of which was rooted in the feudal system of the Middle Ages, and civil law derived from Roman law. It had been codified before being introduced to New France, and was overhauled afterwards. Thus, the French customary law base, by the time the British arrived, had been further customized to suit local conditions, and had been systematized and codified.

The Impact of British Rule on Quebec's Legal Institutions

As noted, the British experimented with several models of government, as they tried to decide how to treat the French-speaking population of their recently acquired colony. With the Quebec Act of 1774, the British opted for leaving the Quebec legal system intact, with respect to the private law. This was not popular with the recently arrived British merchant class, and the Quebec legal institutions did not really become secure until the British, in 1791, separated their colony into Upper Canada (now Ontario) which was primarily English speaking, and Lower Canada (now Quebec), which was primarily French speaking.

In the early British period, the civil law system in Quebec fell into a decline. Based as it was on a civil law base, affecting only private law, in an English colony undergoing rapid change, it was not particularly well suited to solving private law problems. It was also not clear how it could work alongside the rest of the Quebec system of public law, which ran on common law principles. It also did not help that there was no system for legal education in the civil law in Quebec. The civil law system recovered from this decline, however, in part because of a renewal and modernization of civil law in Europe.

The Impact of the Modernization of European Civil Law on Quebec's Legal Institutions

The European systems, while different in substance from each other, shared a systematic codification of legal rules. This was part of a well-established tradition of codification that extended back to codified Roman law. While the influence of Roman law had waned after the collapse of the Roman Empire, it continued to have an impact on European law. The tradition had new life breathed into it during the Renaissance and the **Enlightenment**, with a development of rationally based theories of natural law. Interestingly, none of the intellectual ferment in the civil law reached Britain in any significant way. It had been largely unaffected by Roman law, and the results of changes in the civil law in the early modern period had no effect, either.

In the early 19th century, following political changes brought about by the French Revolution and the reforms to the legal system by Napoleon, law reformers in France and elsewhere in Europe sought to modernize the civil law and recodify it.

Codification was, and is, more than merely collecting all existing law between the covers of a code book. The process also involves a close review of legal rules and principles, to insure that they form a consistent, coherent, interrelated system, based on clearly identified principles. In some respects this is a philosophical exercise in which legal scholars attempt to develop a theory of law that underlies and illuminates the rules and principles in a code.

In Quebec, the reformers, influenced by law reforms in France in the 19th century, recodified private law, abandoning the earlier French customary law base, and replacing it with a system of principles adapted from the Napoleonic Code, or French Civil Code. This code covered both substantive private law (similar to the common law of torts and contracts) and civil procedure. Since the mid-19th century when the Quebec Civil Code was formally adopted, Quebec has periodically reviewed and overhauled the code. The latest extensive revisions were completed in 1993. So extensive were these revisions that members of the Quebec bar were expected to take continuing education courses in the new code if they expected to continue to practise law in Quebec.

Features of a Civil Law Code System in Comparison to a Common Law System

Codified Principles vs. Case Ratios as the Basis for Legal Rules

Codification is a process whereby legal rules and principles are developed and organized into a coherent, interrelated system. The rules or principles, compared to common law rules, are much more general in nature, and are not developed as a narrow answer to a specific case. Instead, the civil law principles are developed as general abstract statements. The general statement of principle or law in the code can then be applied to make a legal decision, with the same principle being applied to many different fact situations.

This is quite different from the common law, where general principles of law are developed as a result of problem solving in specific cases; in other words, judges in the common law system develop legal rules as a result of a search for remedies to practical problems. They reason, inductively, from the particular to the general. In the civil law system, judges start with a general principle, clearly identified and defined, and apply it to particular facts in an attempt to define competing rights. They reason, deductively, from the general to the particular.

The Function of Precedent in a Civil Code System

In reasoning their way to legal decisions, judges using code systems do not rely on precedent cases. The primary source of law is the code itself, which the judge is expected to interpret and apply without resort to secondary sources, such as cases. Judges are not seen as law makers in a code system; they do not make binding rules from cases that can be applied to later cases, or used as alternatives to the code itself. It is not necessary for a judge in this system to find a case that supports his position: finding a principle in the code to solve a legal problem is sufficient. More particularly, in contrast to the common law system, in the code system, the doctrine of stare decisis is non-existent: a previously decided case can never be binding authority for deciding the case at bar.

At the same time, precedent has some function in the Quebec system. One of the weaknesses of a code system is that the principles and rules in the code are based on philosophical and other assumptions about the way society works or should work. Occasionally, a situation arises that is not specifically covered by an **article** in the code. In such a case, it is generally permissible for a judge in coming to a decision to reason by analogy with a previously decided case that is in some way similar to the case at bar.

Precedent cases may also be used in other, more common situations. First, civil code jurisdictions, like common law jurisdictions, have a hierarchy or ranking of courts where, for example, trial courts are seen as subordinate to appeal courts. In this context, the decision in an appeal court, on a case similar to the case at bar in a trial court, may be persuasive for the lower court because of the added authority carried by a decision of a higher court. Note, however, that in the civil code system, a higher court does not automatically bind a lower court as it is presumed to do in the common law system. In a code system, the lower court can ignore a similar decision of a higher court. This is not without a potential cost: a judge in a lower court who ignores a decision of a higher court may find her decision reversed by an appeal court. To put it succinctly, precedent may operate, but the doctrine of stare decisis does not.

Sources of Law in a Civil Law System

The primary source of law is the Civil Code itself, which contains relatively general rules and principles that are grouped together by subject matter. Another primary source is other statutes. A secondary source is **doctrine**, which is a term that describes commentary by legal scholars on the meaning of various provisions of the code. Note that caselaw is not a formal source of law in civil code systems. As well, there is no concept of a separate law of equity, as there is in the common law system. The principles in the code are general rather than narrow or rigid, so that the circumstances that gave rise to the law of equity in the common law system never arose in the civil code systems. However, illustrating Quebec's ability to borrow from the common law, some equitable remedies, such as injunctions, have found their way into Quebec law.

The System of Law in Quebec:
A Mixed Common Law and Civil Law System

We can see that the private law in Quebec is based on the civil law system, using the Quebec Civil Code. To go on from there, to state that Quebec is a civil law and civil code jurisdiction would be to overstate the situation. In fact, the civil law system and the common law system have cohabited in Quebec for over 200 years. As a result of this contact, each has affected the other in a variety of ways. Further, as the result of Quebec's legal system operating in a federal system, large areas of law affecting life in Quebec are based on federal common law. The effects in Quebec of the mingling of the two systems are as follows:

- The private law, affecting the relations between private citizens in their dealings with each other, is primarily codified civil law.
- Commercial law is based on common law, or on statutes.

Exhibit 5: Avoiding Confusion: Different Uses of "Common Law" and "Civil Law"

	Common Law	Civil Law
Use of precedent	yes	rarely
Codified Rules	sometimes (statutes)	yes
Defers to Higher Court	yes	sometimes

- Public law, which governs the relations between the individual and the state (including criminal law), is common law, based on statutes and caselaw.

There is a general acknowledgement that Quebec judges tend to resort to precedents more than judges in other civil code jurisdictions. In particular, attention is paid and deference given to the decisions of the Supreme Court of Canada on issues involving the Quebec Civil Code. As well, ignoring decisions of higher courts within the Quebec legal system is unusual, though more frequent than in other provinces. Much of this judicial behaviour can be attributed to the influence of common law and of common law judges in the rest of Canada.

Suggested Readings

Baker, J., An Introduction to English Legal History, 3d ed. (London: Butterworths, 1990).

David, R., Major Legal Systems in the World Today: An Introduction to the Comparative Study of Law, 3rd ed., translated and adapted by J.E.C. Brierley (London: Sweet & Maxwell, 1985).

Gall, Gerald L., The Canadian Legal System, 4th ed. (Toronto, Ont.: Carswell, 1995).

Keir, D.L., The Constitutional History of Modern Britain Since 1485, 9th ed. (Princeton, N.J.: Van Nostrand, 1966).

Kiralfy, A.K.R., The English Legal System, 8th ed. (London: Sweet & Maxwell, 1990).

Plucknett, T.F.T., A Concise History of the Common Law, 5th ed. (London: Butterworths, 1956).

———, Studies in English Legal History. (London: Hambleton, 1983).

Waddams, S.M., Introduction to the Study of Law, 5th ed. (Toronto, Ont.: Carswell, 1997).

Sources of Law

Laurence M. Olivo

Introduction: Determining What Information Constitutes a Source of Law[1]

The Concept of a Valid Source of Law

In any legal system, the process of solving a legal dispute involves the reasoned application of "law" to the facts of a dispute. However, how do we know what "law" is? To put it another way, what rules or principles that might solve a dispute are acceptable as legal rules or principles? In answering this question we are really deciding, by choosing from among the possibilities, what rules or principles are legally relevant and can be accepted by the users of a legal system as a valid source of law.

For example, if you are supposed to clear your sidewalk of snow and ice, and you forget to do it and someone slips and falls, what is legally relevant to determining whether you are responsible?

- a statute?
- a by-law?
- caselaw?

---

1   From *Introduction to Law in Canada*, edited by Laurence M. Olivo (Concord, ON: Captus Press Inc., 1995–2003). Reproduced with permission of author.

- moral duty not to cause injury to others?
- your standing in the community?
- a revelation from God telling you what to do?

In this example we have to decide which of the above sources of a rule might be legally relevant as the source of a rule in our legal system. Once we have done this, we may describe a source of information that is relevant for inclusion in a legal system as a valid source of law. Then, from among the valid sources of legal rules and principles, we have to choose the rule or principle that is relevant to the problem at hand. In this chapter, we are primarily concerned with the first problem: deciding what are valid sources of law, so that we know where to find rules that are legitimate for use in the legal system.

Determining a Valid Source of Law

There is no automatic, objective formula that can be applied to determine what will be considered a valid source of law in a legal system. In each legal system, what is considered a valid source of law depends on many factors, including historical development, customs, and traditions.

For example, because the common law system developed as a means of enhancing royal power, it was important that the king's judges quickly develop some rules that were distinct from local ones and common to the country as a whole. From that need developed the caselaw system with which we are now familiar and that we accept as a major source of law. In other systems, historical forces led to the government's convening a conference to set up a code of law, as happened in Napoleon's France and in Quebec.

Major Sources of Law in Canada

In Canada, in the common law system, the major sources of law, in the order of their importance to the system, are statute law and caselaw or common law. There are also some other miscellaneous sources of law that are discussed at the end of this chapter.

Another feature discussed here is how the major sources of law are organized, so that legal rules can be found, retrieved from their organizational system, and used. This topic will be explored in more detail in the chapter, Legal Research, which deals with basic legal research skills.

Major Sources: Statute Law

Statutes, or acts of legislatures ("legislature" as used here includes both provincial legislatures and the federal parliament), are perhaps the most important sources of law because of the vast quantity of statutory rules, and because they overrule the common law where they conflict with it.

Exhibit 1: The Statutory Enactment Process

The process of enacting a statute is fairly cumbersome and time consuming. While on the surface it looks inefficient, it does provide time and opportunity for members of a legislature to scrutinize and criticize proposed legislation.

Most bills that are introduced are **public bills** brought in to implement government policy. There are also **private bills,** in which the legislature is asked to implement legislation for some private or purely local purpose. For example, municipalities often request legislation to amend their powers to allow them to exercise some minor power they feel they need. Lastly, there are **private member's bills**, introduced by individual legislators, which deal with subjects that are not taken up by the government as part of its programs. Because most of the time of a legislature is taken up with the government's business, private member's bills are rarely enacted. The enactment process set out below is based on the process in Ontario. Other provinces have very similar procedures. For the federal government, note that after passage in the House of Commons, the bill must go through the same process in the Senate before it can receive Royal Assent.

The Enactment Process

1. **Idea for legislative proposal**. This may come from a minister's initiative, advocacy or lobby group proposal, or other source.
2. **Ministry review of proposal.** Staff advise on proposal, and make recommendations to the minister.
3. **Minister's approval.** A policy submission is prepared by staff and approved by the minister.
4. **Cabinet submission by minister**. A detailed cabinet submission on the legislative proposal is prepared, reviewed, and commented on by other ministries.
5. **Cabinet submission reviewed by Management Board of Cabinet.** Cabinet reviews amended cabinet submission and approves, amends, or rejects submission.
6. **Approved cabinet submission sent to Legislative Drafting Office.** Ministry staff and drafting office staff develop the first draft of the bill. The drafting office will continue to make changes resulting from amendments during the legislative process.
7. **First reading of the bill.** The bill is introduced by the minister, and background information is given to the legislature. The bill is put on the legislative agenda, printed, and distributed to legislators and the public.
8. **Second reading.** The bill is debated in general terms. The minister makes opening and closing speeches. All members may speak once on the bill. There are no amendments at this stage. The

Speaker calls a vote. If there is unanimous consent, the bill goes directly to third reading; if not, it goes to a standing or select committee of the house, as determined by the minister.

9. **Select or standing committee.** Members of the committee can comment on the bill, hold public hearings, allow public input, and call and question witnesses. The committee then does a clause-by-clause examination, and may amend the bill. The bill is then reported back to the whole house, and,, if amended, is reprinted in a second reading version. If there is unanimous consent in the house, the bill may go directly to third reading; otherwise, it is referred to the Committee of the whole house.

10. **Committee of the whole house**. Members debate the bill with less formality than is usual in the house; there is no public participation. Members may pass amendments. If so, the bill is reprinted in a third reading version.

11. **Third reading**. The bill is formally debated in general terms; no further amendments are permitted. Any member may move that the final vote be held on the bill.

12. **Royal assent**. If the bill passes, it is presented to the lieutenant-governor for his signature or assent to the bill's passage. When the bill receives Royal Assent, it becomes an act of the legislature, is given a statute number and reprinted.

13. **Proclamation of act in force**. A section of the act itself will determine whether it is proclaimed in force upon receiving royal assent or on a day fixed by the lieutenant-governor or on a specified date.

Statutes in a Federal System

In a federal system, the constitution divides the power to govern between the national and provincial governments. The subject matter of a statute determines whether it should be passed by Parliament or a provincial legislature. To be a valid law, the subject matter of legislation must come within the heads of power granted by section 92 to the provinces or by section 91 to the federal government, under the Constitution Act, 1867. If a level of government passes legislation on a subject for which that level has no legislative authority in the Constitution Act, 1867, then that legislation is **ultra vires**, or beyond the power of the legislature to enact. In such a situation, the legislation is invalid and need not be obeyed.

Relationship between Statutes and Caselaw

As noted earlier in this chapter, when a statute is inconsistent with previous caselaw, the statute overrules the caselaw. However, it is also important to re-

---

Exhibit 2: The Outline of a Statute

The way a statute is organized will vary with its subject matter. Knowing how a statute is organized, generally, will make it easier for someone reading a particular statute for the first time to find information in a statute easily. The basic organizational scheme for modern statutes is as follows:

1. Long title and chapter number.
2. Preamble. (Usually begins with "whereas" and sets out the main principles and purposes of the act; the preamble is a useful and legitimate aid to interpreting the statute. Not all statutes have preambles.)
3. Introductory sections containing definitions used in the act, the scope or application of the act, powers of officials administering the act, and other administrative matters.
4. Body of the act.
5. Housekeeping sections — proclamation date, regulation making powers, short title of the act.

---

member that a large body of caselaw is caselaw that interprets statutes, giving depth and meaning to statutory provisions. In some circumstances, caselaw develops new directions, giving additional meaning to statutory provisions that they may not have had when the statute was originally passed.

Finding Statute Law

On each of the three readings of a bill, a printed version is available through either the clerk of the legislative body, or from the government's publication centre or bookstore, or on a private or governmental Internet site. Use of anything other than the third reading version is not advisable, as the bill is usually amended to some extent between first and third reading.

Bills are numbered sequentially in the order in which they are introduced during a session, and are referenced and accessed by their bill number. Federal bills have the alphabetical prefix "C" before the sequential number, but are otherwise referenced in the same way as provincial bills.[2]

When a bill is passed and becomes a statute, it is referenced by chapter number in the volume of annual statutes for the year it is passed. Numbers are given sequentially to each bill that becomes a statute. The reference to the annual volume of statutes is "S.O.", for Statutes of Ontario, followed by the year and the chapter.

Example: The Courts of Justice Amendment Act, S.O. 1991, c. 46

---

2   See "Suggested Readings" at the end of the chapter for sources of law databases websites.

Exhibit 3: **Finding a Statute: The Courts of Justice Act, R.S.O. 1990 c. C.43**

The legislature passes The Courts of Justice Act, S.O. 1984, c. 46

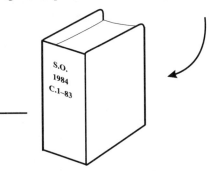

The legislature amends the act in 1989 by passing The Courts of Justice Amendment Act, S.O. 1989, c. 103

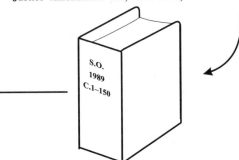

The Courts of Justice Act, S.O. 1984, and all subsequent amendments are consolidated in the 1990 statutory revision process as The Courts of Justice Act, R.S.O. 1990, c. C.43

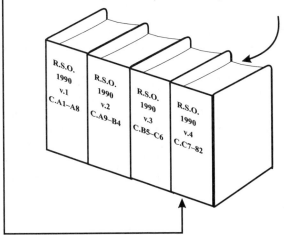

Exhibit 4: Finding a Regulation Made under The Courts of Justice Act

The Courts of Justice Act, pursuant to a regulation, provides for a rules committee that can amend rules of court by regulation. The rules committee in 1985 amended the rules of civil procedure.

The regulation containing the amended rule is gazetted to the Ontario Gazette as O. Reg. 803/85.

O. Reg. 803/85, and all other regulations made under the authority of The Courts of Justice Act, were consolidated and collected under the act during the regulation-revision process in 1990. These regulations were given new sequential numbers based on the alphabetical sequence of the act they are associated with. O. Reg. 803/85 is now Reg. 194, R.R.O. 1990

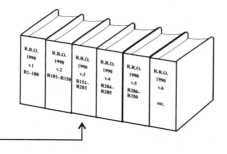

About every decade, at both the provincial and federal level, legislative bodies consolidate all of the statutes and their amendments for the preceding period in a series of volumes called **revised statutes**. These volumes will include all of the public statutes of the legislature in the form they were in at the revision date. The statutes will be set out in alphabetical order and numbered sequentially in the revision volumes, using both the letter of the first word of the act and a number. The volume in which it appears, the Revised Statutes of Ontario, is also cited by its initials, R.S.O., followed by the year of revision and an alphanumeric chapter number.

Example: The Courts of Justice Act, R.S.O. 1990, c. C.43

An example of the history of a particular Ontario statute prior to revision illustrates the revision process: The legislature first passed the Courts of Justice Act in 1984, between the 1980 and 1990 revisions. It was amended on several occasions after 1984, with major amendments in 1989. Amendments are actually in the form of separate acts. Thus the Courts of Justice Amendment Act appeared as a separate statute in the annual statute volume in the year in which the amendment was passed. In 1990, when all statutes were revised, the revised version of the Courts of Justice Act incorporated all of the previous amendments and deleted from the revision anything that had been repealed by an amending act. (See Exhibit 3.)

In some respects a statutory revision resembles a reassembly of a statute using scissors and paste, cutting out parts that have been repealed, and pasting in parts that have been added.

Primary and Subordinate Legislation

The legislatures of the 10 provinces, territorial legislatures, and the federal Parliament all enact legislation by the process described above (with some minor variations). However, the statutes, or **primary legislation**, passed by the legislature may be only the tip of the legislative iceberg on the particular subject covered by the legislation. Many statutes contain provisions, usually found at the end of the statute, in a part dealing with "housekeeping," where either the Cabinet (formally called the lieutenant-governor-in-council for a province and the governor-general-in-council for the federal government) or a minister has the power to make regulations under the act with respect to subject matter that is set out in the section authorizing the making of regulations. Regulations made by this process are called **subordinate legislation**. In practice, the actual creation and drafting of regulations is left to civil servants in the ministry responsible. The subject matter of regulations usually deals with administrative details and procedures for carrying out the statute's general purposes.

For example, procedural rules used in the courts of Ontario could have been included in the Courts of Justice Act. However, if that had been done, the act would have been many times longer than it is now, and the legislature could not have adequately addressed all the technical issues involved in keeping the rules up to date. Moreover, as the rules are amended frequently, the legislature would have to be in constant session to deal with the amendments and would have little time for other government business. Instead, the much more responsive and faster regulation-making process is used. In the case of the rules of civil procedure, the regulations establish a rules committee, composed of persons with specialized knowledge who have the power to make the necessary rule amendments by regulation.

Finding Regulations

A torrent of regulations are passed every year. Initially, before they take effect, they must appear in the government's official publication for public notices, called a **gazette** (the Canada Gazette is at the federal level, and there are gazettes at the provincial level). When a regulation is gazetted, it is assigned a number in sequence for the year in which it is made. The regulation can then be referenced as, for example, Ontario Regulation 803/88. This means it was the 803rd regulation to be gazetted for 1988. The abbreviation of the citation is: O. Reg. 803/88.

As is the case with statutes, regulations go through a revision process about once a decade in most Canadian jurisdictions. In Ontario, for example, the consolidated regulations then appear in bound volumes called the Revised Regulations of Ontario (abbreviated for citation purposes as R.R.O., followed by the year of revision).[3] The plan of the revised regulations is to group the regulations with their authorizing statutes and set the regulations out in the R.R.O. in numerical sequence, with the regulation number being determined by the alphabetical order in which statutes appear in the R.S.O. For example, the rules of civil procedure, made by regulation under the Courts of Justice Act, have a relatively low number because their governing statute, beginning with a "C," comes early in the alphabetical listing. The regulation for the rules of civil procedure is cited as: R.R.O. 1990, Reg. 194.

"The Plain Intention of the Legislature" — Interpreting Statutes

Judges often use the phrase above (or one like it) when interpreting statutes. When they use it, they are saying that the meaning of a section of a statute is clear to them. Yet there are few statutes that have not been the subject of litigation, where one lawyer or another has argued that a section of a statute is ambiguous or unclear. This is why caselaw is sometimes said to give further depth and meaning to statutory rules.

Modern statutes are often very clearly drafted, although the same cannot be said for statutes drafted before 1900. But no statute drafter can foresee every possible situation or contingency that the statute may deal with. Nor does the drafter wish, in every case, to be overly precise, as by so doing, the scope of the statute may become too narrow and inflexible.

The Basic Rule: Determine the Intent of the Legislature

If parliamentary supremacy is to mean anything, it must mean that legislation takes on the meaning that was intended by the members of the legislative body that created the statute. Judges are not free to recreate their own idea of what the statute means.

However, the intention of the legislature is really a fiction. Not all the members of the legislature would necessarily agree on the meaning of the statute; even legislators who are members of the governing party might not agree on the meaning or, even, be aware of what the act is about. But the approach to interpreting an Act begins and ends with finding the legislative intent.

---

3   In addition to bound volumes of statutes and regulations, there are also CD-ROM versions, which have the advantage of being inexpensively updated.

Rules of Construction

A judge begins the search for legislative intent by applying logical and grammatical rules to the language of the statute. Here a judge relies on one or more of the rules of statutory construction. Five of the more common rules of construction are set out below:

1. **The plain meaning rule:** If the words of the statute are clear and precise in their meaning, then that is the meaning the words are to be given, even if the judge thinks the outcome leads to absurdity or unfairness. If Parliament is supreme, then it may be unfair or absurd if it chooses to be, subject to limits on legislative action imposed by The Charter of Rights and Freedoms. (The relationship between the supremacy of the legislature and the Charter is explored in the discussion of the role of the judges and the courts in the chapter on the courts, and in the chapter on constitutional law and the Charter.)

2. **The golden rule**: The words of the statute are to be given their clear meaning, unless this would result in an absurdity, in which case it is permissible to examine the ambiguous part of the statute to see if it is inconsistent with the meaning and purpose of the rest of the statute. This rule expands the first rule by inviting a judge to give meaning to ambiguous language in part of the statute by reading it in the context of the whole statute.

3. **The mischief rule:** This rule is restricted in use to statutes that change the common law, rather than codify the common law. With such statutes, the ambiguity might be resolved by asking three questions:
   (i) What was the common law before the act changed it?
   (ii) What was the mischief or problem that the common law did not adequately address?
   (iii) What remedy did the legislature create to prevent the mischief?

   With the answers to these questions in hand, judges are then supposed to have true insight into the nature and purpose of the act, so that they can interpret the ambiguous language to give effect to the remedy sought and prevent the mischief from occurring.

4. **Ejusdem generis:** This Latin term means that the meaning of a general word or phrase comes from the more specific words that precede it in a sentence or clause. For example, in the clause "no cats, dogs, or other animals shall be permitted in residences," the word "animals" arguably includes domestic pets, but not barnyard animals or wild animals.

5. **Expressio unius, exclusio alterius:** Under this rule, the specific use of one word or phrase, by logic, implies the exclusion of another word or phrase. Often this means that an ordinary dictionary-defined antonym (a word with an opposite meaning) is excluded. At other times, an appreciation of a particular context is required to use this rule. Where the context itself is ambiguous, the rule may provide more problems than solutions.

External Aids to Statutory Interpretation

In addition to the linguistic interpretive rules noted above, there are other sources a judge can use to interpret statutes:

1. **Scholarly and academic writing:** There are a number of articles and texts that deal with major legislation, which judges may cite when interpreting a statute, often as a way of confirming their approach to an issue of interpretation. As well, there are texts, such as Maxwell on Interpretation of Statutes or E.A. Driedger's The Construction of Statutes, that are virtual encyclopedias for statutory interpretation in Canada.

2. **Interpretation statutes:** These statutes exist at both the federal and provincial levels, and attempt to systematically set out some basic rules of interpretation and construction governing all other statutes in their jurisdiction. Such statutes often contain definition sections that give a meaning for words to be used in all other statutes. An interpretation statute will also set out general canons, or rules of interpretation to be used in all statutes. An example is the rule that all statutes are remedial and should be given a broad and expansive interpretation.

3. **Legislative history:** In the search for legislative intent, it has long been traditional in Canada and Britain to ignore Hansard (the official record of debates in a legislature), committee reports, royal commission reports, ministers' speeches, press releases, and other such documents. The assumption in Canada has always been that the intent of the legislature is summed up in the words of the statute itself, and one need go no further than the words of the statute to find the meaning.

   The American experience is somewhat different, and much of what one might call historical documentation from the legislative process may be used as an aid to interpretation, particularly in constitutional cases.

   However, in Charter of Rights cases, there is some indication that legislative history may have a legitimate interpretive role. There is a growing use of the technique in constitutional cases as a way of gaining insight to the meaning of legislation under the constitutional challenge.

4. **Statutory presumptions**: Over time, as a result of custom, convention, historical events, and interpretative caselaw, a number of presumptions have attached like barnacles to statutes dealing with specific subject matter. For example, there is a presumption in criminal law statutes that all crimes shall be interpreted strictly and narrowly rather than broadly. Another is a presumption that no statute is to be read **retroactively**. This means that the statute does not apply to situations that existed prior to the statute's enactment, and only applies to situations arising after its passage.

Exhibit 5: What Judgments, Reasons for Judgment, and Reported Reasons for Judgment Look Like

1. **A judgment or order** is a command from the court; it tells parties what they must do, but not why the judge decided the way he did. Page 1 of a judgment is produced below:

Court file no. 2987/90

Superior Court of Justice

THE HONOURABLE MR. JUSTICE SNORK

TUESDAY, THE 16 DAY OF APRIL 1992

BETWEEN:

HENRY SNOOT

and   Plaintiff

MICHAEL SNIT

Defendant

Judgment

THIS ACTION was heard on the 2nd, 3rd, and 16th day of April, 1992, without a jury at Brampton, in the presence of counsel for both parties,

ON READING THE PLEADINGS AND HEARING THE EVIDENCE and submissions of counsel for the parties,

1. THIS COURT ORDERS AND ADJUDGES that the plaintiff recover from the defendant the sum of $102,000.00.

2. THIS COURT ORDERS AND ADJUDGES that the defendant do pay to the plaintiff his costs of this action, forthwith after assessment.

THIS judgment BEARS INTEREST at the rate of 3 per cent per year, commencing on April 16, 1992.

J.R. Snerg,
Local Registrar

2. A judge's written **reasons for decision** is like an essay, explaining in writing the basis for his decision. Page 1 of a sample reasons for decision is set out below:

Superior Court of Justice		
B E T W E E N:	]	J.W. Tough, Esq.
ANNA ADAMANT	]	for the Plaintiff
Plaintiff	]	
	]	
and	]	
	]	
EDWARD ADAMANT	]	
	]	Sandra Sharp,
Defendant	]	for the Defendant
	]	Heard: July 2,3, 1994

Exhibit 5. Cont.

TRAINOR, J.

The single issue in this proceeding, is the custody of the child, Adam Adamant. born February 1, 1991.

The resolution of that issue is often one of the most difficult problems that judges encounter. It is particularly so where both parents have demonstrated concern over the welfare of their child. The fact that both parents are well educated, sophisticated, professional people having considered and firm opinions about the proper way in which a child ought to....

3. In a **reported reasons for decision** the typed essay in the preceding example is set out in printed form in a law report, and contains additional information. A sample law report version of Reasons for Decision is set out below.

RE GILL AND REGISTRAR OF MOTOR VEHICLES et al.
RE HEFFREN AND REGISTRAR OF MOTOR VEHICLES

Sentence — Driving offences — Provincial suspension of driver's licence — Legislation providing for increased periods of suspension depending on number of convictions for Criminal Code driving offences — Motorist liable for increased period of suspension only where offence for which increased penalty sought occurred after prior conviction — Highway Traffic Act, R.S.O. 1980, c. 198, s. 26.

Section 26(1) of the Highway Traffic Act, R.S.O. 1980, c. 198, which provides that the driver's licence of a motorist who is convicted of a Criminal Code driving offence is thereupon suspended for a period of "(a) upon the first conviction, three months; (b) upon the first subsequent conviction, six months; and (c) upon an additional subsequent conviction, three years" imposes a penalty and should be construed in the same way as criminal legislation which imposes an increased penalty by reason of previous convictions. Accordingly, the rule of statutory interpretation applies that where a statute imposes an increased penalty for a subsequent conviction, the offence for which the increased penalty is sought must have occurred after the prior conviction, before the increased penalty can be imposed. The fact that section 26(1) refers to a "conviction" rather than "offence" is not a significant distinction. An occurrence does not become an offence until there is a conviction but once there is a conviction, the terms "conviction" and "offence" are used interchangeably for the purpose of applying the rule of interpretation.

Benn v. Registrar of Motor Vehicles et al. (1981), 59 C.C.C. (2d) 421, 10 M.V.R. 214, **overd**

R. v. Cheetham (1980), 53 C.C.C. (2d) 109, 17 C.R. (3d) 1; R. v. Skolnick, [1982] 2 S.C.R. 47, 68 C.C.C. (2d) 385, 138 D.L.R. (3d) 193, 29 C.R. (3d) 143, 16 M.V.R. 35, 42 N.R. 460, **apld**

R. v. Joslin (1981), 59 C.C.C. (2d) 512, 10 M.V.R. 29; R. v. Negridge (1980), 54 C.C.C. (2d) 304, 17 C.R. (3d) 14, 6 M.V.R. 14, **consd**

Other Cases referred to:
Christie v. Britnell (1895), 21 V.L.R. 71; Farrington v. Thomson and Bridgeland, [1959] V.R. 286; R. v. O'Brien, Ex. p. Chamberlain (1908), 38 N.B.R. 381; O'Hara v. Harrington, [1962] Tas. S.R. 165

Statutes referred to:
Criminal Code, ss. 234, 234.1, 235, 236

Exhibit 5. Cont.

Highway Traffic Act, R.S.O. 1980, c. 198, s. 26(1) (am. 1983, c. 63, s. 11), (2) (rep. & sub.1984, c. 61, s. 1)

Rules and regulations referred to

(Ont.) Rules of Civil Procedure (Ont.), rule 21.01
(Ont.) Rules of Practice (Ont.), Rule 124
(Ont.)

APPEALS by the registrar from a judgment of Smith J., 12 C.C.C. (3d) 23, and of McKinley J. on applications pursuant to Rule 124 (Ont.) to determine points of law.

Leslie M. McIntosh, for appellants.
Alan D. Gold, for respondent, Sukhpal-Singh Gill.
Robert J. Upsdell, for respondent, Louis Arnold Heffren.

The judgment of the court was delivered by

FINLAYSON J.A.:—Both these appeals are by the Registrar of Motor Vehicles (hereinafter Registrar) with respect to licence suspensions under s. 26(1) of the Highway Traffic Act, R.S.O. 1980, c. 198, as amended, by reason of convictions by the two respondents for certain automobile related offences under the Criminal Code....

Source: "Re Gill and Registrar of Motor Vehicles et al., Ontario Court of Appeal, Houlden, Goodman and Finlayson JJ. A., September 3, 1985" 21 C.C.C. (3d) 1986, pp. 234–35. Reprinted with permission from Canadian Criminal Cases published by Canada Law Book Inc., 240 Edward Street, Aurora, Ontario, L4G 3S9.

Major Sources: Common Law

Common Law or Caselaw

In the chapter on systems of law, it was seen that the use of decided cases as a source of law was a distinctive feature of the common law system of law. The importance of cases as a source of law was due in part to the doctrine of precedent, which requires that cases decided in the past that are similar to the case at bar be followed. The doctrine of stare decisis took the doctrine of precedent a step further by making precedent cases of higher courts binding on lower courts within the same jurisdiction.

Caselaw is not followed if a statute contradicts the ratio of the case, or if the case can be distinguished. It is noted that when a court considers a precedent to be binding, it needs to first determine whether the court that decided the precedent is a "higher court."

Also to be considered is whether a precedent, though not binding, should be seen as **persuasive**. This is determined by a number of possible subjective factors — the reputation of the judge and the reputation of the court. If the case comes from a high-level court in another jurisdiction that is respected by

---

Exhibit 6: How Reasons for Decision Are Set Out in Published Law Reports

Case reports usually follow a generic format, which is set out below:

1. case name

2. court and judge(s)

3. date of decision

4. catch lines — phrases in bold print that can be scanned quickly to identify key facts and issues in the case, and which are also used as index headings and subheadings in the index to the law report series.

5. headnote: a summary of the facts, the decision, and the reasons for the decision, including a list of cases, statutes, and other authorities referred to

6. a brief description of the form or purpose of proceeding (Appeal from ... Motion for....)

7. names of lawyers for the parties

8. full text of the judgment

9. final disposition

---

judges in Canada, deference may be given to its decisions. For example, cases from British superior courts are often deferred to, while cases from American superior courts often are not. Also, on rare occasions, a judge will reject a precedent altogether, and take the law from a line of cases in a new direction entirely. These observations are a reminder that common law can be more flexible than it at first appears to be.

Finding Caselaw

Caselaw developed as an integral part of the common law system at an early stage because it was written down so that it was accessible. No-one had to try and remember all of the rules. Its continued importance owes much to the fact that it continues to be written down and made accessible through **law reports**, which are published reports of decided cases.

There is no particular system to law report publishing, and much of it is in private hands. There are "official reports" published by some courts, such as the Supreme Court Reports, which report the decisions of the Supreme Court of Canada; there are provincial reporting series reporting a medley of cases from a particular province; there are Canada-wide reporting services reporting decisions of note from across the country. There are also reports which focus on specialized areas of law, such as the Canadian Practice Cases, that report cases dealing with procedural law. Some cases are reported in only one reporting series, while others may be reported in several. Some, however, are not reported at all. The decision to report is a subjective one, made by the editorial boards of the various law reports.

An unreported case, though not easily accessed, still has precedent value. In recent years, particularly with the establishment of computer case databases, it has become possible to list and summarize easily many of these unreported cases. As well, there are computerized indices of legal issues, that allow relatively quick and thorough searches to be done that will identify reported and unreported cases. Because the case reporting process is uncoordinated and unsystematic, the process of finding an appropriate precedent case can still be a time-consuming exercise, particularly compared to the search for a principle in the civil law system, where an article in the code that provides the answer can be quickly located. But as more lawyers use indexed databases of unreported cases, such as Quicklaw and LexisNexis, the distinction between reported and unreported cases may diminish. The subject of finding law is explored in the chapter dealing with basic legal research techniques.

Miscellaneous Sources of Law

While statute and caselaw are the most common and most important sources of law in the common law system, there are other sources of law that crop up occasionally.

Practice and Usage

These two terms loosely describe ways in which things may be done that may achieve legal recognition. These forms of behaviour, which have no formal authorization or sanction, will generally be accepted as a source of law if they go unchallenged, and other conduct or consequences that rest upon them will also be seen as legitimate. However, if a practice is challenged, the fact that it occurs is not sufficient to justify it as a source of law.

Custom and Convention

A practice or usage that has been in existence, and in use for long enough (whatever "long enough" may mean), at some point can become enshrined in law as a custom or convention, at which time it is a source of law. Determining when the threshold is reached is a subjective process, with different results in different jurisdictions. The key factors are:

• the activity has gone on for a long time
• there has been no interruption or interference with the activity

In Canada, custom and convention has been a very important source of constitutional law. In 1981, the Supreme Court of Canada decided that the Trudeau government could **repatriate** the Canadian Constitution by taking over control of constitutional change from the Parliament of the United Kingdom.

103

The court's decision turned on a lengthy and detailed analysis of custom and convention with respect to the amount of provincial support required before the federal government could seek an amendment to the Constitution.[4]

Scholarly Legal Writing

On rare occasions, the musings of legal scholars may be a source of legal rules, where no other authority speaks to an issue. More often, however, such works are commentaries on existing law, useful in interpreting the law, rather than being a source of it.

Morality

Ever the delight of natural law theorists, morality has had a rough ride in modern common law. In the 19th and 20th centuries, where the issue was raised, the court would often deflect it by stating that, "the court is not a court of morals." While morality might underlie a particular legal rule or principle, it rarely is the source of law, and operates only when no other source of law provides a solution to a particular legal problem.

The Crown or Royal Prerogative

This describes the power of the sovereign or, in Canada, the sovereign's representative (the governor general, federally, and the lieutenant governor, provincially) to act in certain ways. Historically, the power is derived from the predemocratic era when the King had power to rule personally and use his personal power as a royal right. As the relationship between the King and Parliament evolved, so did the prerogative. Parliaments have steadily taken away parts of the prerogative power by legislating it away; once a prerogative power is lost, by custom and convention, it cannot be revived. Further, the sovereign or his or her representatives rarely exercise a prerogative power without advice from the government.

Some examples of the use of the prerogative are the dissolution of a legislature prior to calling an election and the pardoning of criminals. To the extent that the prerogative can be exercised without having to take or follow advice of elected representatives, to that extent the prerogative can be viewed as a source of law.

Suggested Readings

Attorney General of Canada v. Attorney General of Manitoba et al., [1981] 1 S.C.R. 72; originally called A Reference re the Amendment of the Constitution of Canada, this case contains a discussion of the nature of convention as a source of law.

---

4   Reference re Amendment of the Constitution of Canada, [1981] 1 S.C.R. 753.

Driedger, E., The Interpretation of Statutes, 4th ed. (Toronto, Ont.: Butterworths, 1983).

Fitzgerald, M.F., Legal Problem Solving: Reasoning, Research and Writing (Toronto, Ont.: Butterworths, 1996).

Kiralfy, A.K.R., The English Legal System, 8th ed. (London: Sweet & Maxwell, 1990).

Sullivan, R., Driedger on the Construction of Statutes, 4th ed. (Toronto, Ont.: Butterworths, 2003).

Thornton, G.C., Legislative Drafting, 4th ed. (London: Butterworths, 1996).

SOURCES OF LAW WEBSITES

e-laws: http://www.e-laws.gov.on.ca
(Ontario statutes, regulations and current bills — free access)

Quicklaw: http://ql.quicklaw.com
(all provincial and federal statutes and Canadian caselaw — private subscription service)

LexisNexis Canada: http://www.butterworths.ca for information
(all U.S., provincial and federal cases and statutes — private subscription service)

Types of Law

Laurence M. Olivo

Introduction: A Law Bestiary*

In the Middle Ages, a bestiary was a book that described the animal kingdom.
It was full of fabulous beasts, some of which had not ever been seen by the
authors, and some of which, like the unicorn, did not actually exist.

A formal categorization of different types of law could take the form of a
"law bestiary," full of distinctions that, while interesting, are not particularly
helpful in giving students an idea of the breadth and reach of the law. Instead
this typology will define its organizing principles in terms of the way practising
lawyers look at the law, and then define types of law in the light of the principles identified.

Principles to Consider in Organizing a Typology of Law:
Artificial and Real Distinctions

It is quite possible to build a largely theoretical typology of law that is both
logical and elegant. But to be useful, a typology of law must define law in
terms of concepts and areas of law that will help a student to understand the

---

* From *Introduction to Law in Canada,* edited by Laurence M. Olivo (Concord, ON: Captus
Press Inc., 1995–2003). Reproduced with permission of author.

operation of the Canadian legal system. For example, to simply define law by subject matter alone is to really do no more than give dictionary definitions. Instead we need to identify important elements of law, and see how they relate to each other.

Organizing Concepts

In developing a typology, the following concepts are of some importance:

1. **Positive law:** We need to focus on positive law, that is, the law of the state system. One of the features of a positive law system is that legal rules are in the command mode: *A* shall pay *B*, which means that there was implied an element of compulsion with penalties if *A* did not pay *B*. These are essential parts of any state legal system or positive law system. Contrasted to this are other conceptions of law: norms, values, morality, and religious beliefs, in which there is no physical compulsion involved. Some very interesting typologies of law can be built from norms values, etc., but non-positive law's impact on legal systems in operation in the world is, at best, indirect. Consequently, non-positive law is omitted from our typology.

2. **Domestic and international law:** To some extent, international law has some impact that requires our attention. However, when it has impact, it is usually because it has been incorporated within the domestic system of law of the Canadian state, or influenced the content of that law. For example, the Hague Convention governing international child abduction is a piece of international law. But its rules might as well be yelled out in a desert for all the importance that it has. What makes the Hague Convention important is that it has been incorporated into the Ontario Children's Law Reform Act, and become part of Ontario's domestic law and part of the domestic law of other provinces as well. As a result, the distinctive feature it has is that the law is now enforceable. It can command more than lip service, which significantly distinguishes it from much of public international law. Because public international law usually lacks independent enforcement mechanisms, and because states often ignore it when it suits a state's interests to do so, public international law will be excluded from our typology.

   There is a sphere of international law, however, that is of great practical importance, and that is private international law. Private international law concerns private disputes between individuals that involve more than one national jurisdiction. There are two principal questions that usually have to be considered in the private international law arena:

   • In which jurisdiction shall the issues be determined? This involves deciding which court system of which nation has the right to try the matter.
   • Under the law, of which jurisdiction shall the issues be determined? This involves deciding which national legal system shall be used as a source of legal rules. Even where one national system is determined to have jurisdiction, the law that is applied to the problem may be the

national law of a country other than the one that has jurisdiction to try the matter.

For example, a manufacturer of communication systems in Canada may contract to supply products to a German company making components for a shipbuilding company in Korea. If there are problems with the components that lead to a lawsuit, where would one sue? Canada? Germany? Korea? Which nation's law would apply? The international aspects of these transactions make this an international private law problem, but what actually happens is that private international law, in sorting this out, really converts the problem into a domestic legal matter.

This area of law is of growing importance with globalization and the increase in various kinds of transnational commercial and other transactions.

3. **Private and public law:** Within a system of positive domestic law, there are usually significant differences between private law, which regulates the conduct of individuals as between themselves over private matters, and public law. In private law, the focus is on facilitating and regulating interaction rather than punishing it. Public law regulates the operation of the state and the interaction between the citizen and the state. Here the law is more likely to take the form of commands, spelling out rights and obligations, and visiting sanctions on those who disobey.

4. **Procedural and substantive law:** Procedural law concerns itself with the process of the law, the route one takes to justice. Substantive law concerns rights, obligations and rules of conduct that regulate activity. If substantive law is about the content of rules, procedural law is about how those rules are to be used.

To summarize, our concern is to explore the divisions and elements of the domestic or national state system of law in Canada in terms of the way that law is organized.

Substantive Law of the Canadian Legal System

Public Law

Generally, public law is law that concerns public matters rather than purely private ones. There are four principal substantive areas of public law:

Criminal Law

While crime often has a private dimension in terms of injuries done to victims, it almost always is seen in terms of its public dimension. The theory is that crime tatters the social fabric and threatens social stability. Originally, in common law, criminal acts were those that were socially disruptive and were seen as a personal affront to the sovereign who had primary responsibility for maintaining social peace. At the same time, crime was also seen in terms of the harm to individual victims, so that criminal law had some private law aspects. For example, until this century, it was possible and, in some common law jurisdictions, common for crimes to be privately prosecuted by the victim rather than by the state. Today, however, criminal law rules, and procedures are quite distinct, and the investigation, prosecution, and punishment of crime is a virtual state monopoly.

Constitutional Law

This area of law is concerned about rules by which the state operates. If the functions of the state were a sort of game, constitutional law would describe the rules by which the game is played. It usually takes the form of a statutory document but may also consist of custom, convention and practices. For example, in Canada, it defines what powers each level of government has, determines how the state apparatus is to be operated, and sets out certain areas of individual freedom upon which the state may not trespass. Constitutional law is sometimes described as fundamental law, without which the political and legal system cannot operate. One characteristic it has is that it is more difficult to repeal or amend than ordinary law. Another is that when there is a conflict between ordinary law and constitutional law, ordinary law is subordinate to constitutional law.

Administrative Law

This is a very broad and pervasive area of law, generally concerned with the regulation of activity, often private activity, where there is a perceived public interest. For example, if you own land in a residential neighbourhood, you cannot build whatever you wish on that land, as the land may be zoned for certain types of buildings. If you seek permission to exceed what the zoning allows, you will have to get permission from an administrative board that balances your private right against the public interest.

Taxation Law

This was one of the earliest areas of public law to develop as the sovereign took a personal interest in collecting public revenue, which, in many respects, was personally the King's money. Over time, the state's interest in revenue raising has not diminished, and neither has the citizen's desire to avoid paying taxes. Part of the public law of taxation is concerned with adjudicating disputes between taxpayers and the state. However, where a taxpayer's conduct amounts to fraud, the matter is dealt with as a criminal law matter.

Private Law

Private law is the law concerned with regulating the interactions between individuals as private persons.

Key Private Law Principles

While private law can be characterized in a variety of ways, there is a collection of principles and rules that provides most of the substantive law for almost all private law. These groups of principles are as follows:

- **Tort law:** This area of law can be described as civil wrongs by one individual against another. It includes intentional harm, harm resulting from carelessness (negligence), and some harmful acts where intention is entirely absent. Many torts — assault, for example — are also crimes. This is not surprising, as criminal law developed from tort law. Where a tort has been committed, the remedy granted is usually money damages to compensate the person harmed for the injury sustained.

- **Contract law:** This area developed from the tort of breaking one's word, to become an independent cause of action based on the idea that promises could not be given and broken at will, but were enforceable. Contract law, then, concerns the enforcement of promises, under various conditions. The remedy for breach of contract is usually monetary compensation. Sometimes, however, the courts will order performance of the contract.

- **Property law:** This area of law is concerned with rules for establishing what is capable of ownership, how things are to be owned, how we are to determine who owns something, and the definition of types of property: real property (land), personal property both tangible (chattels or things) and intangible (rights).

Subject Matter of Private Law

The subject matter of private law is capable of almost endless division that would result in an indigestible law bestiary. The areas that are set out below are principal areas of law in the Canadian system. For each of the areas listed, bear in mind that all of them will rely on tort, contract, and property law to some extent, as the source of their rules.

- **Family law:** This area of law was once part of the now vanished ecclesiastical or church law. It was originally seen as involving moral and religious matters. The religious and moral aspects are now largely absent from the law. Today, the law in this area borrows heavily from the contractual concept of partnership, so that the law concerns itself largely with the dissolution of marriage partnerships, and things incidental to that dissolution: property, support, custody, and divorce. There are other areas that are included in family law: adoption, child welfare (dealing with children whose basic family needs are not being met), including, in some instances, law dealing with the crimes of children.

- **Estates, wills, and trusts:** This area of law is closely related to family law and property law as it concerns itself with the distribution of property, often within a family, on the death of an individual. The law of trusts is closely connected to estate law, as it facilitates a person (called a trustee) holding and controlling property for the benefit of someone else (called a beneficiary). However, the law of trusts is also a major part of commercial law.

- **Real estate law:** This area of law is concerned with the highly technical area of transferring and otherwise dealing with interests in land. An important subset also concerns itself with the process of land-use planning, although this may properly be considered part of administrative law.

- **Corporate and commercial law:** Sometimes this area is simply called business law. Closely involved with contract law, it is concerned with the various forms of business organization, banking, insurance, and financial law and, generally, the law governing commercial operations.

- **Patents and intellectual property:** This growing area of law, similar in its basics to business law, is concerned with the law surrounding the protection and marketing of ideas in various forms, whether the substance is patents on things or processes, or copyrights on ideas.

- **Agency:** This area of law concerns itself with the relations of principals and agents, among themselves, and between themselves and others. The focus is on legal rights and obligations that arise when someone acts on your behalf as an agent. This can also be seen as a proper part of corporate and commercial law, or contract law.

Procedural Law

Procedural law is concerned with the legal process by which rights and liabilities are **adjudicated**. Its focus is on the **adversarial** aspect of the law in the context of legal dispute resolution.

Procedural Norms

While we can describe a system of procedural rules as steps to be taken to settle a dispute, procedural law is about more than what steps to take. It is also about attitudes and values concerning how those steps should be taken.

Generally, procedural rules are structured to deal with the three perennial problems of legal systems: fairness, cost and delay. Procedural rules are designed to deliver justice as inexpensively and quickly as possible without sacrificing a just result.

Second, there is also a concern that, whatever procedural rules are, they be uniformly and evenly applied so that similar cases are treated in the same way. Another way of putting this is to say that the rules of the system should be applied objectively and without bias: justice should not only be done, but be seen to be done.

Closely related to consistency in applying procedural rules is the concern that the rules themselves be fair. Procedures that are inherently one-sided or arbitrary, or which cause delay or raise costs, might be seen to be inherently unfair.

Law of Procedure

Incorporating the norms discussed in the preceding paragraph, this area of law concerns the process of settling disputes. It is characterized by detailed, complex, and technical rules of civil procedure to govern private law disputes, and rules of criminal procedure that are tailored to the criminal law process.

It is also looked to to provide fair and transparent rules for regulating activities and resolving disputes in administrative law.

Law of Evidence

This area of law is often considered in the context of procedural rules, both civil and criminal. It concerns the legal rules that determine what kind of information can be used to prove facts that are in issue. It is concerned with reliability, **probative value**, and relevance of information to be considered by the court in deciding a dispute.

Conclusion

The purpose of this chapter is to provide a panoramic view of the Canadian legal system in terms of some of its major components. By talking about divisions of law, it is easy to assume that the law operates in clear and distinct divisions, and that the divisions here are the only important ones. It is important to remember that the borders between the divisions are not all that distinct and sharp, and that there can be considerable overlap among them.

Suggested Readings

David, R., Major Legal Systems in the World Today: An Introduction to the Comparative Study of Law, 3rd ed., translated and adapted by J.E.C. Brierley (London: Sweet & Maxwell, 1985).

Derrett, J.D.M., An Introduction to Legal Systems (New York: Praeger, 1968).

Gall, Gerald L., The Canadian Legal System, 4th ed. (Toronto: Carswell, 1995).

Summary of Constitutional Events*

Janice E. Nicholson
and Diane Jurkowski

During the past decade, the exclusion of Quebec from the final agreement on the Constitution Act of 1982 led to an attempt to remedy a situation in which Quebec regarded itself as excluded from the most important constitutional event in the history of Canadian federalism. In particular, Quebec was concerned about establishing five minimum conditions for its participation in the 1982 Constitution Act. These were

1. recognition of Quebec's distinctive political and cultural nature;
2. limitation of the federal government's spending power;
3. an adoption of the unanimity rule for all constitutional amendments (Section 41 of the 1982 Constitution Act);
4. greater powers for Quebec on immigration; and
5. participation in the appointment of judges to the Supreme Court of Canada.

The 11 first ministers accepted these conditions at Meech Lake on April 30, 1987. They were ratified in their legal form in June 1987. However, Section 41 of the Constitution Act, 1982 specified that the Accord had to be ratified by the Parliament of Canada and all the provincial legislatures within three years.

---

* From *Business and Government: Canadian Materials,* edited by Diane Jurkowski et al., pp. 147–157 (Concord, ON: Captus Press Inc., 2000). Reproduced with permission of author.

113

By the end of June 1990, two provinces, Manitoba and Newfoundland, had failed to ratify the Accord, and the process to amend the Constitution Act of 1982 to make it acceptable to Quebec had failed.

On September 4, 1990, a Commission on the Political and Constitutional Future of Quebec was created under legislation adopted unanimously by all political parties in the Quebec National Assembly. It was given a mandate to study and analyze the political and constitutional status of Quebec and to make recommendations. Its membership included Quebec premier, Robert Bourassa, and the leader of the official opposition, Jacques Parizeau. This commission (the Bélanger-Campeau Commission) submitted its report on March 27, 1991.

Prior to this, in March 1990, the Quebec Liberal Party formed a Constitutional Committee chaired by Mr. Jean Allaire. The committee began its first working sessions in April 1990, but after the failure of the Meech Lake Accord in June 1990, the committee increased its activities and tabled a report with the Executive Committee of the Quebec Liberal Party by the end of January 1991. The report of the Constitutional Committee (Allaire Report) was adopted by the Quebec Liberal Party at its convention on March 9, 1991.

Essentially both reports recommended major constitutional changes and a complete restructuring of the relationship of Quebec and Canada. The Allaire Report, adopted by the Quebec government, proposed three major areas of reform:

1. political autonomy of Quebec, which will be achieved by Quebec assuming a far wider range of powers, including taxation and revenue, immigration, foreign policy and native affairs. Quebec would share these powers with the federal government. The only exclusive powers the federal government would have are in the areas of defence, customs and tariffs, management of the common debt, currency and equalization payments.

2. formation of a Quebec-Canadian economic union that would guarantee free movement of persons, goods and capital; reduction in the size of the federal government; and restrictions on the taxation powers of the federal government.

3. establishment of a new Quebec-Canada structure, including a new constitution, the maintenance of a common Parliament, the abolition of the Senate and reform of the Bank of Canada.

The Quebec government passed legislation to ensure that a referendum would be held by the autumn of 1992. The purpose of this referendum was either to ratify the agreement with Canada on the proposed reforms, or to ratify Quebec's assumption of sovereign statehood along with an offer to form an economic union with Canada.

The reaction of the federal government and the various provincial legislatures was to establish their own commissions and committees, the most publicized being the Citizens' Forum chaired by Mr. Keith Spicer. This commission had the mandate to hear from citizens and groups across the country on constitutional issues. It gave its report by the end of June 1991. Essentially, it reflected the deep disillusionment of the citizens on the current state of affairs: lack of confidence with political parties and politicians, concern for the economic problems and bewilderment regarding the restructuring of the Quebec-

Canada relationship. The report recommended that special constitutional arrangements should be made for Quebec to allow it the freedom and the means to be itself. The report also recommended native self-government for the aboriginal peoples, shorter parliamentary sessions, more free votes and a fundamental reform of the Senate.

Among the many commissions, committees and hearings was the House of Commons/Senate committee known as the Committee for a Renewed Canada or the Beaudoin-Dobbie Committee. It issued its report in the first week of March 1992. Among its recommendations was a Canada clause that states the nation's principles and values. In addition, it recommended the "promotion of Quebec as a distinct society." Other recommendations included:

1. the inherent right of Aboriginal peoples to self-government;
2. property rights should be included in the Charter of Rights and Freedoms;
3. election of senators on the basis of proportional representation;
4. the power of the Senate to be similar to the House of Commons, except on supply (money) bills;
5. an expansion of provincial powers;
6. an economic union that could disallow provincial restrictions on the movement of goods, services, people and capital; and
7. a social covenant that would commit governments to fostering comprehensive and universal social and health services, education, unionization and preserving the environment.

This report formed the basis for the discussions between the federal minister responsible for constitutional affairs, Joe Clarke, the provincial premiers, including Quebec, territorial leaders, and the native leaders. Throughout the summer of 1992 these discussions continued with many trials, tribulations, and doubts. It frequently looked as if no agreement would be reached.

At last, on August 28, 1992, an agreement was reached at Charlottetown, Prince Edward Island. The agreement had a considerable resemblance to the Beaudoin-Dobbie Committee recommendations.

It was recommended that Quebec be recognized as a distinct society, and that there would be:

1. a Canada clause;
2. a social and economic union;
3. recognition of the inherent right of self-government for Aboriginal peoples:
4. a reformed Senate; and
5. greater degree of federal-provincial power sharing.

However, there were differences, and it was some of these differences that became the focus of controversy in the debate leading up to the referendum.

It was proposed that:

1. The Senate should have six elected senators from each province and one senator for each territory, Aboriginal representation in the Senate to be guaranteed by the Constitution.

115

But the Senate would not be allowed to block money bills and it could not defeat a government with a majority in the House of Commons on any legislation. Therefore, this was not a Triple E Senate, as the Senate was not as powerful as the House of Commons. Thus, this part of the agreement was unpopular in the West.

Additionally, Quebec was guaranteed 25 percent of the seats in the House of Commons regardless of its population size. This was also greatly resented in the West.

2. A greater sharing of power between the federal government and the provinces was indicated, but some people in Quebec considered this insufficient.

3. The inherent right to self-government for Aboriginal people was recognized, and it was recommended that the Constitution Act, 1982 should be changed to recognize this right. However, this was opposed by some Aboriginal leaders, especially women, who were opposed to traditional forms of Native government, since they considered that women were put in a subordinate role in such a traditional society.

4. Finally, the amending formula was to be altered so that in some areas a unanimity rule would apply; that is, the unanimous agreement of Parliament and the provinces. These areas would be:
   (a) amendments relating to any changes in the Senate (once it was reformed);
   (b) amendments affecting the House of Commons, including Quebec's guarantee of 25 percent of the seats; and
   (c) matters affecting the creation of new provinces. Critics argued that the introduction of a unanimity rule into the amending formula made it virtually impossible to change the Constitution once it was amended along the lines of the Charlottetown Accord.

Before the federal referendum, the Quebec government withdrew the legislation requiring that a referendum be held in Quebec by the autumn of 1992, since the federal government had agreed to a federal referendum on the Charlottetown Accord.

Despite strenuous campaigning on the part of the federal government and some provincial premiers, the Charlottetown Accord was defeated in the October 26, 1992 referendum. In order to pass, the accord required a majority of affirmative votes in all the provinces. In fact, a number of provinces voted against the accord, including Quebec, British Columbia, and Alberta. In several provinces, including Ontario, the vote was very close.

As a result of this defeat, it is thought that the federal government will not pursue any further constitutional initiatives before the next federal election.

Separatists had received a boost from the election of the Parti Québécois to form the provincial government in Quebec in September 1994. The Parti Québécois was committed to Quebec sovereignty. This was the second occasion on which the issue would be placed before the electorate as a referendum. In the 1980 referendum, Quebecers had rejected independence by a 60 to 40 percent margin. But the Parti Québécois was resolved to try again. If they were successful in the 1995 referendum, the government would then enter into negotiations with the rest of Canada to work out a new political and economic partnership.

On October 30, 1995, a referendum was held in Quebec. The question asked Quebecers was:

"Do you agree that Quebec should become sovereign, after having made a formal offer to Canada for a new economic and political partnership, with the scope of the bill respecting the future of Quebec and of the agreement signed on June 12, 1995?"

The recorded vote was

No:	50.6%	(2,631,526)
Yes:	49.4%	(2,308,028)

The referendum results were perceived as a narrow win of 50,000 for the federal government. The sovereignist forces vowed that they would not stop until they had a nation. A third referendum is planned by the Parti Québécois in two years. However, Quebec law states that two referenda cannot be held within the same mandate of a government. A provincial election is scheduled in 1998.

In response to the Quebec referendum, the justice minister sought a ruling from the Supreme Court to clarify the rules of separation in September 1996. The federal government asked the court three questions:

- Can the government of Quebec take the province of Quebec out of Canada unilaterally?
- Is there a right of self-determination under international law?
- If there is a conflict between domestic and international law on the question, which one takes precedence in Canada?

On February 3, 1996, Bill C-110 passed Parliament and received royal assent granting veto power to Quebec, Ontario, and British Columbia. In addition, any two Prairie provinces with 50 percent of the regional population or any two Atlantic provinces with 50 percent of the regional population, can now veto any constitutional amendment. The law effectively creates four classes of provinces. The new formula for gaining the federal government's approval is an addition to the existing constitutional amending formula, which requires seven provinces with 50 percent of the population to approve most amendments. However, the constitutional validity is in question when a simple act of Parliament can amend the Constitution Act without applying the existing constitutional amending formula.

In February 1997, the federal government filed a brief in the Supreme Court stating that Quebec had no right under domestic or international law to secede unilaterally from the Confederation. However, the brief further stated that Quebec could secede through a constitutional amendment only after holding discussions with the federal and provincial governments. The case was expected to be heard in fall 1997.

Quebec refused to participate in the court hearings, maintaining that Quebec independence would only be settled by the people through a democratic vote in a referendum. Thus, the federal government asked the Supreme Court to appoint legal representation on Quebec's behalf.

In February 1998, sixteen parties — including the federal government, Aboriginal groups, minority rights advocates and the *amicus curiae* representing the government of Quebec's separatist position — presented their cases before the Supreme Court of Canada. The *amicus curiae* made three arguments. First, the Supreme Court's jurisdiction to answer reference questions presented by the Governor in Council (the Governor General) was unconstitutional. Second, even if the Court's reference was constitutionally valid, the questions submitted were outside the scope of the constitution. Finally, these questions were not justiciable.

In August 1998, the Supreme Court of Canada answered the three questions asked by the Governor General on behalf of the Government of Canada. But first, it responded to the concerns expressed by the *amicus curiae*. According to Section 101 of the Constitution Act, 1867, Parliament gives authority to the Supreme Court on reference matters. Therefore, the Supreme Court can direct and interpret the Constitution Act referred to it. Furthermore, the Supreme Court is a "general court of appeal" according to Section 53 within the national court structure.

> Question 1: "Under the Constitution of Canada, can the National Assembly, legislature or government of Quebec effect the secession of Quebec from Canada unilaterally?"

In the 131 years of Confederation, shared values of federalism, democracy, constitutionalism and the rule of law have created interdependence of social, economic, political and cultural ties bonded by the constitution. "A democratic decision of Quebecois in favour of secession would put those relationships at risk". Furthermore, "Quebec could not, despite a clear referendum result, purport to invoke a right of self-determination to dictate the terms of a proposed secession to other parties to the federation".

The Supreme Court stated that there must also be a clear majority vote in Quebec on a clear question in favour of secession. The other provinces and federal government would have no basis to deny the right of Quebec to secede. The negotiations that will follow such a referendum vote would address all the interests of the other provinces, federal government and Quebec both within and outside Quebec and, especially, the rights of minorities.

> Question 2: "Does international law give the National Assembly, legislature or government of Quebec the right to effect the secession of Quebec from Canada unilaterally? In this regard, is there a right to self-determination under international law that would give the National Assembly, legislature or government of Quebec the right to effect the secession of Quebec from Canada unilaterally?"

"Self-determination" under international law usually refers to: people who are governed as part of a colonial empire; where people are subject to alien subjugation, domination or exploitation; and, possibly where people are denied any meaningful exercise of their right to self-determination within the state. "Quebec does not meet the threshold of a colonial people or an oppressed people, nor can it be suggested that Quebecers have been denied meaningful access to government to pursue their political, economic, cultural and social development".

> Question 3: "In the event of a conflict between domestic and international law on the right of the National Assembly, legislature or government of Quebec to effect the secession of Quebec from Canada unilaterally, which would take precedence in Canada?"

"In view of the answers to Questions 1 and 2, there is no conflict between domestic and international law to be addressed in the context of this Reference".

In February 1999, after twenty years of federal government reductions in transfer payments and downloading services to the provincial government, the federal government and nine English-speaking provinces signed "A Framework to Improve the Social Union for Canadian". Absent from the agreement was Quebec. The principles of this social union were to ensure that all Canadians have access to essential social programs and services for health care and education regardless of where they live in Canada; respect for the Medicare principles of universality, accessibility and government-operated; and ensure that funding for social programs is stable, sustainable and affordable. This was seen as ushering a new era of cooperative federalism and a surplus federal government budget. The provinces were given $5 billion over three years for health care, post-secondary education and welfare. There is no agreement for binding dispute settlement that the provinces sought or for preventing the federal government from cutting transfer payments. There can be no opting out, either. If the provinces want federal funding, they have agreed to it under federal terms. The federal and nine provincial governments accepted the conditions of asymmetrical federalism and the strengthening of the influence of the federal government's spending power.

On April 1, 1999, in response to Aboriginal self-government, the Northwest Territories was divided into two distinct governments since joining Confederation in 1949. The eastern Arctic is to be known as Nunavut, meaning "Our Land" in Inuktitut and the western Arctic remains as the Northwest Territories.

Year 2000 — The Clarity Act

In December 1999, the federal Intergovernmental Affairs Minister, Stephane Dion, tabled legislation that would for the first time set out in law the conditions for the next Quebec referendum on secession. The Clarity Act is largely based on the 1998 Supreme Court opinion on the legality of unilateral declaration of independence of Quebec. Under the Clarity Act, the House of Commons will be the sole voice in determining what constitutes a "clear majority" in a referendum on secession. Furthermore, it empowers the House of Commons to determine whether the question posed in the referendum would result in a clear expression of the will of the province with respect to its secession from Canada. The proposed legislation asserts that the referendum question posed to a province must not make reference to any type of political or economic arrangement with Canada following its secession, such as in the 1980 referendum on sovereignty association.

An analysis of the Clarity Act reveals discrepancies with the 1998 Supreme Court opinion. The Act legitimizes through statute law that Canada is divisible. It ignores the rights of the rest of Canada. It does not state how differing opinions on the question and notions of "majority" are to be reconciled by the House of Commons. Furthermore, the Act does not set out what roles Members of Parliament and Senators from the secessionist province are to play both before and after the vote. Although the Supreme Court opinion details the role for the other provinces in Canada in negotiation after the referendum, the Clarity Act ignores this. This Act does not state what a "clear majority" is although the 1982 Constitution Act states a constitutional amending formula. The federal government's role in relation to the Aboriginal peoples is spelled out in the British North America Act, 1867 and the Constitution Act, 1982. The fiduciary duty owed by the federal Crown to Canada's Aboriginal people cannot be obviated. The Clarity Act does not state who is to negotiate on behalf of the federal government.

A number of issues arise. What happens if the Prime Minister represents the secessionist province? Who is to give instruction to the negotiating parties? To whom are they answerable? Does the resultant agreement need to be put to a referendum? Moreover, the Act does not deal with the situation where the parties are unable to reach a mutually agreeable result, or where other provinces do not agree with the arrangement reached between the federal government and the secessionist province.

In the Quebec National Assembly, Parti Québécois complained that the Clarity Act prevents Quebec from freely choosing its own destiny. The law accepts the premise that secession must be negotiated. But Quebec's position is that no negotiations are required and Quebec has only to proclaim itself sovereign to do so. Furthermore, contradictions between the Parti Quebecois and the federal Bloc Québécois appeared when Bernard Landry, the deputy premier of Quebec, stated that the Parti Quebecois government will ignore the referendum rules of the Clarity Act and will conduct the next referendum by the same rules it followed in the past. Daniel Turp, the Bloc Québécois' intergovernmental affairs critic stated that Parliament had the right to evaluate the clarity of the question and the majority after the referendum is held.

In March 2000, the Clarity Act was enacted by the federal Parliament only to raise more questions.

The Constitutional Timeline of Canada*

Diane Jurkowski and
Janice E. Nicholson

1759 — The Battle of the Plains of Abraham

British sieges of French fortresses in Louisbourg in 1745 and 1758 and the War of the Austrian Succession in 1744 had brought armed conflict to the North American colonies. The Battle of the Plains of Abraham, which lasted only twenty minutes, sealed the fate of Nouvelle France. The French commander, General Montcalm, was mortally wounded during the battle. Montcalm's British counterpart, General Wolfe, was killed instantly in battle. A year later, in 1760, British reinforcements marched to Montreal and defeated the remaining French forces.

1775 — Quebec Act

To deal with the mounting problems of unrest in Quebec, the British Parliament enacted the Quebec Act, whereby England restored the old boundaries of Quebec, extending it to the Mississippi River and including what is now Ontario and, also, the American states of Ohio, Indiana, Illinois, and Wisconsin. (This latter territory would change drastically with the American Revolution.) However, the constitutional significance of the Quebec Act was its declaration of religious and cultural recognition: the free exercise of the Catholic religion

* From *Business and Government: Canadian Materials,* edited by Diane Jurkowski et al., pp. 286–298 (Concord, ON: Captus Press Inc., 2000). Reproduced with permission of author.

was guaranteed and the French civil law was recognized as law. Only the language question was unsettled. (French settlers outnumbered the English by thirty to one and all English proclamations were published in both French and English. This set a precedent that would be difficult to change.)

1791 — Constitution Act

The aftermath of the American Revolution brought an exodus of United Empire Loyalists to the maritime colonies, the western regions of Quebec and the surrounding regions of northern Lakes Ontario and Erie in Upper Canada by 1784. They had experienced an atmosphere of political freedom of self-government in the United States. Their intention of immigrating to the British North American colonies was to retain the political association with England. In order to deal with their political agitation, the British Parliament enacted the Constitution Act, which established the representative institutions. Although the Governor was appointed by the Crown, he was to be advised by a council whom he would appoint. The council members comprised a small, elite group of inhabitants representing wealth, education, government, church and society. In Lower Canada, they were known as the Chateau Clique, and in Upper Canada as the Family Compact. In their official capacity, they were known to frequently use their offices to advance their own interests in advising the Governor.

1837 — Rebellions of Upper and Lower Canadas

Reform movements to gain control of the executive powers of the governors and their councils were led by Joseph Papineau in Lower Canada and William Lyon McKenzie in Upper Canada. Among their assertions was for the Governor to appoint to his Council those who had the confidence of a popularly elected assembly.

1839 — Durham's Report

Lord Durham was dispatched from London to restore order in the British North American colonies. His mandate was to inquire into the case of the rebellions and to suggest measures to solve the dilemma. His report was regarded as a constitutional document because it served as the blueprint for self-government of British colonies. Lord Durham's Report made four principal recommendations of significance to a representative, responsible government. First, to resolve the struggle between French- and English-speaking inhabitants, it recommended that Upper and Lower Canadas be reunited. This would result in the absorption and assimilation of the French-speaking people of Lower Canada by the combined forces of the British Crown and the English-speaking people of Upper and Lower Canadas. Furthermore, two recommendations were intended to grant responsible government to the colonial governments. These would not require any radical legislative innovations, but were simply consistent applications of British common law. All Crown revenues were to be placed at the disposal of the colonial governments. Second, all financial issues would originate in the Legislative Assembly and would receive consent from the Crown before being introduced in the assembly. Finally, the report recommended the independence of the judiciary. Members of the court were given a salary and tenure in office based on the British common law system.

1840 — Union Act

The Union Act implemented Lord Durham's recommendations. Upper and Lower Canadas were again united. Members of the council were to be appointed for life by the Crown; however, this was changed in 1856 by making council members submit to an election every eight years. An elected Legislative Assembly of 85 members was also established. English was made the official language of record. However, with the restriction of French, this was unworkable; thus, eight years later, it was amended when both English and French languages were given equal status.

1864

A meeting of delegates from Nova Scotia, New Brunswick and Prince Edward Island was held in Charlottetown to discuss a union of the Maritime provinces. Sir John A. Macdonald and others from the provinces of Canada attended to propose a federal union of the British North American colonies.

1865 — Colonial Laws of Validity Act

A law passed by the British Parliament stating that any law of a British colony that differed from a British law specifically aimed at that colony was null and void to the extent of the difference. This was important because it set aside the older rule that colonial laws that were inconsistent with English common law *could* be set aside.

1866

Delegates from the provinces of Canada, New Brunswick and Nova Scotia met in London to draft the British North America Act.

1867 — British North America Act

The British Parliament enacted the Constitution for Canada. Often referred to as the B.N.A. Act, it created the new Dominion of Canada by uniting the colonies of British North America — Upper Canada (Ontario), Lower Canada (Quebec), New Brunswick and Nova Scotia. It marked no significant break with the past, principally because the colonists desired to maintain many of the colonial relationships and to legislate authority with England. It allocated legislative powers to the federal Parliament and the provincial Legislative Assemblies, thereby establishing federalism. As a British statute, the B.N.A. Act could only be amended by the British Parliament, except in very limited areas in which the Canadian Parliament was given authority. The provincial legislatures were authorized to amend their own provincial constitutions, except in regards to the Office of the Lieutenant-Governor.

1870

The Province of Manitoba was created by the Parliament of Canada.

1871

British Columbia joined Canada by virtue of the United Kingdom Order in Council.

1873

Prince Edward Island joined the federation by virtue of the United Kingdom Order in Council.

1875

The Supreme Court of Canada was established. However, the Judicial Committee of the Privy Council of the Parliament of Westminster remained the highest court of appeal.

1875 — The Northwest Territory Act

The Canadian Parliament made provision for a separate administration of the Northwest Territories. The Territories were administered from Ottawa until 1967, when Yellowknife was designated territorial capital.

1878

Substantial modifications were made in the instructions issued to the Governor General, which had the effect of reducing some of his prerogative powers.

1898

The Yukon was created as a separate territory with Dawson City as its capital.

1905

The Canadian Parliament established the provinces of Saskatchewan and Alberta.

1909

The Canadian Parliament created the Department of External Affairs to protect and advance Canadian interests abroad.

1917

All Dominion prime ministers accepted an invitation to join with the British War Cabinet in an Imperial War Cabinet.

1919

Canadian representatives took part in the Paris Peace Conference and signed the Treaty of Versailles, which brought an end to the First World War. Canada also became a member of the newly created League of Nations and International Labour Organization.

1926 — Balfour Report

Adopted at an Imperial Conference, the Balfour Report defined the Dominions as "autonomous communities" that are "equal in status" and in no way subordinate to Great Britain.

As well, at the Imperial Conference, Prime Minister Mackenzie King issued a formal statement clarifying that the Governor General should cease to represent the British government and become the representative of the Sovereign.

1937 — Statute of Westminster

The British Parliament repealed the Colonial Laws Validity Act (1865), whereby autonomy of the Dominions was given full legal recognition. Because no agreement had been reached on an amending formula, Canada requested that the B.N.A. Act be excepted from the terms of the statute, and that Britain retain the authority to amend the B.N.A. Act.

1939

Canada declared war on Germany one week after Britain had done so.

1945

Canada was one of the founding members of the United Nations.

1947 — The Canadian Citizenship Act

The first such act in the Commonwealth was introduced. For the first time, "Canadian" was defined as "Canadian citizens" rather than primarily as British subjects born or naturalized in Canada.

1949

Canada was one of the founding members of the North Atlantic Treaty Organization.

The British North America Act, 1949

Newfoundland joined Canada through the enactment by the British Parliament of the British North America Act, 1949.

The Supreme Court became the final court of appeal in Canada, ending the role of the Judicial Committee of the Privy Council of the Parliament of Westminster in the interpretation of Canadian constitutional issues.

The Canadian Parliament was empowered to amend the Constitution of Canada with respect to "housekeeping matters" at the federal level. The basic areas of the Constitution still remained within the sole control of the British Parliament.

1965

Canada adopted its own flag.

1980

The Canadian Parliament adopted *"O Canada"* as the national anthem.

The Minister of Justice introduced a resolution in Parliament for a Joint Address to Her Majesty the Queen, requesting that the United Kingdom Parliament enact provisions for the patriation of the Canadian Constitution, the coming into effect of an amending formula and entrenchment of a Charter of Rights and the entrenchment of the principle of equalization.

In 1976, the province of Quebec elected the Parti Québécois with a mandate to hold a referendum on the separation of Quebec. Thus, in the spring of 1980, Quebec held its first referendum on sovereignty-association. The referendum question was defeated by a margin of 40 to 60 percent.

1981

The legality of the justice minister's resolution to unilaterally patriate the Constitution was challenged before the Supreme Court of Canada by Manitoba and several other provinces. The Supreme Court ruled on September 28, 1981 that while the Canadian Parliament could legally act alone, there was a "convention" requiring substantial consent of the provinces. After further discussions in early November, the Prime Minister and nine provincial premiers signed an accord on November 5 that broke the impasse. In early December, the House of Commons and Senate approved the revised resolution which formed the basis of Joint Addresses to be sent to London for action.

1982 — Constitution Act

The Constitution Act, containing *inter alia* the Canadian Charter of Rights and Freedoms and a wholly Canadian procedure for further constitutional amendments, was enacted by the British Parliament. On April 17, in a ceremony on the lawn of Parliament Hill, the Queen signed the Constitution Act.

The Constitution Act of 1982 is an act of the British Parliament which enacted a new Canadian Constitution, ending the British Parliament's function by transferring to the Canadian Parliament the power over future constitutional amendments with the British Parliament never again to legislate in respect of Canada.

The government of Quebec did not sign the Constitution Act. However, it became nonetheless a part of the Constitution because, when the Constitution Act came before the House of Commons for final approval, Quebec members of Parliament voted almost unanimously in its favour (only three opposed it). To date, the government of Quebec has not signed the Constitution Act of 1982.

1987 — Meech Lake Accord

The goal of the Meech Lake Accord was to obtain Quebec's endorsement of the Constitution Act of 1982. It was intended as another constitutional amendment. It recognized five of Quebec's demands, including distinct society, increased powers for Quebec over immigration, a role for Quebec in the appointment of Supreme Court judges, the right of Quebec to a veto over all future constitutional changes, and the right of the provincial government to nominate senators and convene annual constitutional conferences of the Prime Minister and provincial premiers. The Meech Lake Accord was readily ratified by Parliament and, initially, eight of the ten provinces. However, it died in the Manitoba Legislature because a Native member of the provincial Legislative Assembly, Elijah Harper, Jr., refused to give the unanimous approval necessary under Manitoba law for dispensing with public hearings before having the vote on the accord. With that, the premier of Newfoundland concluded that there was no purpose in having the Newfoundland provincial Legislature vote on the accord since its rejection in Manitoba had ended the possibility of the accord achieving the necessary unanimity.

1992 — Charlottetown Accord

Another round of constitutional conferences was held. When the Meech Lake Accord failed two years before, both federal and provincial governments were criticized for much of the deal-making that went on behind closed doors. This same criticism was levied after the enactment of the Constitution Act of 1982. At question were the legitimacy and practice of the federal-provincial bargaining process and federal unilateralism of renewing a constitution. Not only was there a series of federal-provincial meetings of the First Ministers, but committees of Parliament and the provincial Legislatures, as well as Citizen Forums, endeavoured to deal with the arduous issues of constitutional amendments. Furthermore, a national referendum would be held to achieve a consensus on constitutional amendments.

An accord was reached by the First Ministers in August in Charlottetown. The Charlottetown Accord included: a Canadian clause; social and economic union; recognition of Quebec as a distinct society; the inherent right to self-government for the First People; reform of Senate; and a great degree of federal and provincial power-sharing.

The Charlottetown Accord was defeated in a national referendum held on October 26, 1992. In order to gain the consensus that the federal and provincial governments sought to achieve in a referendum, it required endorsement from all the provinces. But, in fact, a number of provinces, such as Quebec,

British Columbia, and Alberta rejected the accord, while in other provinces, the margin was too narrow for either acceptance or rejection.

1995

A second referendum was held in the Province of Quebec. The Parti Québécois was once again elected in 1994 with a mandate committed to Quebec sovereignty. On October 30, 1995, Quebecers were asked once again to decide on the sovereignty of Quebec. This time, the margin against sovereignty had narrowed down to 51 percent from 49 percent.

1996

The federal justice minister petitioned the Supreme Court to clarify the rules of separation. In 1997, the federal Crown attorneys requested the Supreme Court to appoint legal representation on Quebec's behalf since Quebec had refused to participate in court proceedings.

Bill C-110

A federal statute was enacted on February 3, 1996, granting veto power to Quebec, Ontario and British Columbia. In addition, any two Prairie provinces with 50 percent of the regional population and any two Atlantic provinces having 50 percent of the regional population can veto any constitutional amendment. The new formula for gaining the federal government's approval is an addition to the existing constitutional amending formula, which required seven provinces with 50 percent of the population to approve most constitutional amendments.

1997 — The Calgary Framework

The Calgary Framework resulted from a weekend meeting where nine English-speaking provincial premiers and Aboriginal leaders from the territories established the conditions. The premier of Quebec did not attend. The Framework was to provide a balance of a number of principles considered important to all Canadians. Some of the values common to all Canadians are based on traditions and legal rights and freedoms, including tolerance, compassion, economic and political freedoms, diversity, equality and fairness. Though recognizing the unique character of Quebec's language, culture and civil law tradition, the Calgary Framework was a strong statement of equality among provinces. It recommended that if any future constitutional amendments give powers to one province, these powers must be available to all the provinces. The Calgary Framework asserted that federal, provincial and territorial governments work should together to serve the people more efficiently and effectively. It was believed that the Calgary Framework would serve as a draft for discussions on constitutional amendments.

1998

The Supreme Court of Canada answered the three questions asked by the Governor in Council on behalf of the government of Canada on Quebec sovereignty.

The Court first answered the concerns of the *amicus curiae* regarding the Court's constitutionality to answer any issues regarding Quebec. The Supreme Court stated that, under the Constitution Act, 1867, Parliament has empowered it to direct and interpret the Constitution Act and, as a "general court of appeal", within the national court structure, it can answer questions about Quebec.

In response to the first question, "Under the Constitution of Canada, can the National Assembly, legislature or government of Quebec effect the secession of Quebec from Canada unilaterally?", the Court stated that a clearly stated question with a clear majority vote in Quebec in favour of secession would begin the process of sovereignty for Quebec from Canada. The federal government and the provinces have no right to deny Quebec's secession. However, negotiations would follow a referendum vote to address all the interests of the other provinces, the federal government and Quebec and, especially, the question of minority rights.

For the second question, "Does international law give the National Assembly, legislature or government of Quebec the right to effect the secession of Quebec from Canada unilaterally? In this regard, is there a right to self-determination under international law that would give the National Assembly, legislature or government of Quebec the right to effect the secession of Quebec from Canada unilaterally?", the Supreme Court stated that Quebecers were not governed as part of a colonial empire and its people were not denied access to any meaningful exercise of their rights to self-government within the state. Therefore, self-determination in Quebec was not applicable under international law.

In response to the third question — "In the event of a conflict between domestic and international law on the right of the National Assembly, legislature or government of Quebec to effect the secession of Quebec from Canada unilaterally, which would take precedence in Canada?" — the Supreme Court answered that there was no conflict between domestic and international law, based on previous answers to Questions 1 and 2.

1999 — A Framework to Improve the Social Union for Canadians

After twenty years of federal government reductions in transfer payments and downloading of health care, welfare and post-secondary school programs and services, the federal and nine English-speaking provinces agreed to a "social union". Also included was the transfer of $5 billion over three years. If the provinces want federal funding, they will agree to it under federal terms. The federal government and the provincial governments involved accepted the conditions of asymmetrical federalism by strengthening the influence of the federal government's spending power in a new era of cooperative federalism and federal budgetary surpluses.

Establishing the Nunavut and Northwest Territories

On April 1, 1999, in response to demands for Aboriginal self-government, the Northwest Territories was divided into two distinct governments. The eastern

Arctic is to be known as Nunavut, while the western Arctic is to remain the Northwest Territories.

2000 — The Clarity Act

In December 1999, the federal government tabled legislation that would for the first time set out in law the conditions for the next Quebec referendum on secession. The Clarity Act is largely based on the 1998 Supreme Court's decision on the legality of any unilateral declaration of independence of Quebec. Under the Clarity Act, the House of Commons will be the sole voice in determining what constitutes a "clear majority" in a referendum on secession. Furthermore, it empowers the House of Commons to determine whether the question posed in the referendum would result in a clear expression of the will of the province with respect to its secession from Canada. The proposed legislation asserts that the referendum question posed to a province must not make reference to any type of political or economic arrangement with Canada following its secession, such as in the 1980 referendum on sovereignty association.

In the Quebec National Assembly, Parti Quebecois complains that the Act prevents Quebec from freely choosing its own destiny. The law accepts the premise that secession must be negotiated. Quebec's position is that no negotiations are required and that Quebec has only to proclaim itself sovereign to do so.

In March 2000, the Clarity Act was enacted by the federal Parliament only to raise more questions.

Understanding the Canadian Parliamentary Government

George E. Eaton

This paper is intended to be of assistance to students being introduced to the study of public administration. There are two usages of the term public administration. In the broadest sense it encompasses the entire machinery of government, including:

(a) the legislative decision-making bodies (Parliament) through which national or provincial goals and priorities are articulated, debated and translated into specific public policies, programs, or measures;

(b) Executive Organs — including the Crown and Cabinet and the public services especially the civil service, through which the policies are not just interpreted and implemented but are often initiated, and given practical effect to the population at large; and

(c) the Judicial and Legal Services, through which disputes over constitutional questions and rights, as well as other forms of civil litigation and redress are adjudicated, and justice meted out to those accused of violations of laws governing social conduct and order in society.

In its other and more restricted usage, the term public administration is often used to refer to the executive organs of government, mainly the Cabinet and civil or public service.

131

The focus in this paper will be on the term in its broadest usage, looking then, at how society deals with the ordering and running of its affairs: in short, with public affairs.

The public administration, or the machinery of government, involves a complex of institutions and activities, and its purposes are correspondingly varied. They range all the way from establishing and maintaining representative decision-making bodies or institutions to the allocation of the tasks of government so that they can be performed in a manner considered acceptable by the citizenry (which usually involves considerations of efficiency and economy), to defining areas of authority and responsibility of administrative units, so that they can be made properly subject to constitutional and political controls.

In Canada, the machinery or structure of government has been greatly shaped and influenced by the British (UK) Constitution or arrangements of government. Let it be noted right away that there are differing views and perceptions of what a constitution is, depending on one's professional or academic orientation. Thus, we can discern at least five concepts of constitution — philosophical, structural, legal, documentation, and procedural.

From the purely structural point of view, the constitution defines and provides for the establishment of the main organs of government. If, however, the constitution is viewed as a political process embodying certain ideals of government, then the focus will be on the methods or techniques used to establish and maintain effective restraints upon political and governmental action.

The British model of parliamentary government is widely referred to as the Westminster model and/or the Whitehall model and we should be clear as to what these terms connote. The Westminster model derives its name from the physical location of the Houses of Parliament at Westminster, London, England, and is used to identify the classic (British) model of parliamentary government, as well as the countries, typically former British colonies, that have inherited or retained the same functional organization or system of government. There is, however, only one authentic Westminster model and that is to be found at Westminster itself, and there is a lot to be said for reserving the label for the original. To illustrate: a fundamental tenet of British constitutionalism is the doctrine of the Supremacy of Parliament. This doctrine asserts that in the making of laws, Parliament's control over conduct is direct and absolute and not subject to the regularized restraints of fundamental law.

Accordingly, there is no single document or British Constitution that sets out overriding principles of constitutional government or basic rights of citizens that can be enforced against Parliament through and by the courts. The result is that some of the most fundamental aspects of the political and government system are regulated not by law but by "conventions of the constitution". Conventions, it may be noted, are variously customs, usages, rules, or principles that are adhered to, although they may not be legally enforceable. A breach of a convention may be unconstitutional but not unlawful or illegal. It is often this gap between formal theory and practice, between the stated and the unstated, that leaves students confused, and makes the workings of the system of government so difficult to comprehend.

If the Westminster model more appropriately identifies the unique experience and system of government of the United Kingdom, the term Whitehall model is used to denote the colonial or overseas adaptation of the Westminster model. The adjective "Whitehall" gives recognition to the fact that civil servants in Whitehall (the Colonial Office) have been intimately involved in the process of drafting "independence" constitutions, certainly for the newly emergent nations such as all found for example, in the Commonwealth Caribbean.

Some of the features or basic tenets of the Whitehall model that serve to distinguish it from the Westminster model are: a Bill of Rights or Charter of Rights and Freedoms (a Charter was incorporated into Canada's Constitution in 1982) that diminishes the legislative supremacy of Parliament; the entrenchment of certain constitutional articles or provisions that require special and more difficult amending procedures, which likewise diminish the legislative supremacy of Parliament; and the incorporation of previously unwritten conventions into the Constitution. For example, where the dissolution of Parliament remains a convention in the Westminster model, the Constitutions of Trinidad and Tobago and St. Lucia in the Commonwealth Caribbean deal explicitly and differently with the power of dissolution of Parliament.

Let us now turn to the workings of, and interactions between the three main organs or functional branches of the public administration (or government): Legislature, Executive and Judiciary.

The Legislature or Parliament

One of the suppositions of liberal democracy is that the power to set up not only forms and institutions of government — i.e., constituent power — but also sovereignty — the notion of an ultimate source of authority and power that may be exercised within a country and brought to bear against citizens — are both deemed to be vested or inhere in the people. Of course, for many subject (colonial) peoples, constituent power or the right to self-determination was or is a qualified right, as more often than not they have had, sometimes on the basis of armed struggle, to negotiate the terms and constitutional instruments of political independence with an imperial power and to submit draft constitutions for approval. The distinction made earlier between the Westminster and Whitehall models of parliamentary government underscores this point. That sovereignty inheres in the people is all well and good, but how do the people give expression to, and implement their wishes and will, when societies and nations number in millions of people? Even in mini-states, such as in the Commonwealth Caribbean, where populations number over 100,000, it is considered either impractical or inconvenient for citizens to come together in the arena or marketplace as they did in the ancient Greek city states, to discuss and vote directly on matters of public concern. Nor should we forget that this ancient Greek ideal of direct participation in government rested on a foundation of slavery which gave citizens of the city state the time and leisure to congregate in the marketplace.

The only practical alternative where vast numbers are involved is indirect representation, where representatives are chosen through the electoral process to give expression to the desires and will of citizens individually and collectively.

In democratic theory, the Legislature (in our case the elected House of Commons, or Lower House, as distinct from the Senate, or Upper House, whose members are appointed) represents the people or community. Parliament (the House of Commons) is supposed to exercise general surveillance over the Executive to ensure that governmental power is exercised for the benefit of the people and not against them.

Two hundred and ninety-five members of Parliament (MPs) currently sit in the House of Commons, each having been chosen in electoral districts or ridings or geographical constituencies to represent that constituency and, collectively, the nation of over 25 million persons. Because Canada also operates a federal system of government — about which more will be said later — the principle of representation according to population in the Constitution applies only to provinces as such.

How have we been able to decide who can best represent our interests and communal welfare in Parliament? The major instrument or mechanism that evolved as a worldwide phenomenon between 1850 and 1950 to facilitate the process of representation and to enforce electoral accountability has been the political party, or party system of politics.

Party Politics and Electoral Representation

It is not our purpose to trace the development of the national parties or the Canadian party system. Generally speaking, at the national (and provincial) level, Canada has followed the tradition of the Westminster model of a two-party system of government of "ins" and "outs" despite having three major parties — Liberals, Progressive Conservatives, and New Democrats.

As with the concept of constitution — so too the functions of political parties are variously categorized, depending on the predilections of the scholars/practitioners involved. A list of functions is likely to include some, if not all of the following:

(a) Articulation and aggregation of interests: this they do through the brokerage of ideas and interests and presentation of an election "platform or manifesto" designed to attract the widest possible community or regional electoral support. Parties bridge the gap geographically between voters who, at the furthest ends of the country, north or south, east or west, can be united behind a particular party. On an ongoing basis also, parties help to organize public opinion and to communicate demands to the centre of governmental power and decision making.

(b) Political recruitment: that is to say, the selection of political office holders and political leadership.

(c) Articulation of the concept and meaning of the broader community (national consensus), even if the aim of the party is to modify or destroy the community and replace it with something else.

If we accept the essentiality of the functions and role attributed above to political parties, then quite apart from any consideration of how well they perform their functions, we must conclude that political parties lie at the heart of the democratic process. In spite of this, political parties are not mentioned in the Canadian Constitution.[1] Following the Westminster model, they are private and voluntary bodies that control their own internal processes and are formally outside the Constitution. In effect, the most dynamic element of the political process and system of government remains part of the convention of the Constitution. Since the general election of 1993, there has been an interesting turn in the configuration of the three well established and enduring national parties.

The Progressive Conservative (PC) or "Tory" Party, which had won a landslide victory in 1984, taking 211 of 282 seats, and a historic follow-up victory in 1988 was devastated in 1993, and reduced from 169 to 2 seats, one in Quebec, the other in New Brunswick. The New Democratic Party (NDP) fell from 43 seats in 1988 to 9 seats in 1993, with representation being confined to the western provinces of British Columbia (BC), Manitoba and Saskatchewan. Both the PCs and the NDP forfeited official party status in the House of Commons, which requires a minimum of 12 seats.

Also making their first appearances as official parties in 1993 were the Bloc Quebecois (BQ) and the Reform Party. The BQ emerged as a single-issue party, its purpose being to work for the separation of the Province of Quebec from Canada. By winning 54 of the 75 federal seats and 49 percent of the popular vote in Quebec, BQ created a situation, the ultimate in irony, of becoming "Her Majesty's Loyal Opposition", while being dedicated to achieving the break-up of Canada as a nation state.

The Reform Party, a right-wing populist coalition and anti-Eastern Canada protest movement growing out of, and reflecting, western Canada alienation, also won 52 seats, concentrated in the provinces of Alberta (22 seats) and British Columbia (24 seats).

Finally, the Liberal Party, the predominant ruling party since Confederation, survived and took 177 seats to form a majority government.

In the June 1997 general election, the Liberal Party again won another majority term in office with 155 seats but, while it gained modest or respectable representation in the Atlantic provinces, Quebec and the western provinces, its ability to form a majority was made possible by winning 100 of the 103 seats in the Province of Ontario.

The PC party regained official party status by winning 20 seats, but realized support primarily in the Atlantic provinces (13 seats) and in Quebec (5 seats).

The NDP won 21 seats, likewise regaining official party status, but with support concentrated in the Atlantic provinces (8 seats) and in the western provinces (12 seats).

In turn the Reform Party won 60 seats, all in western Canada, thereby displacing the BQ as the official Opposition in Parliament.

In effect, therefore, the traditional two-party system of government of "ins" and "outs" at the national level has been replaced by a collection of region dependent political parties. Whether this is a transitory phenomenon or the harbinger of the new Canadian political reality remains to be seen.

The fragmentation of parliamentary representation does, however, compound the unresolved dilemma of representative and responsible liberal democratic government, namely, meaningful (as distinct from formal) electoral accountability. One of the suppositions of the Westminster model is that "the political party forms the government but does not govern". The rationale underlying this rather subtle distinction appears to be the desire to differentiate between liberal democratic government constrained by checks and balances and totalitarian forms of government in which the political party stands above the government and dictates to it. Be that as it may, the fact remains that in Canada, political parties solicit the support of the electors to give them a mandate to implement their respective electoral platforms or manifestoes. Quite often, however, when party leaders in their capacities as leaders of government or the public administration are quizzed by followers or the electorate at large about failure to adhere to, or implement, their mandated manifestos, the usual rejoinder is that the political administration represents and acts on behalf of all the citizenry and in the national or country's interests and not just on behalf of the factions who voted on behalf of the party candidates. Of course, the converse situation may apply where a ruling party commits itself single-mindedly to carrying through its campaign manifesto even when the electorate may become alarmed and disenchanted with the social consequences. In both situations, whatever may be the avenues available to influence a government during its term in office, in the final analysis, the electorate may be obliged to await the next general election for a reckoning. However, this periodic exercise in electoral accountability may be dominated by the desire to vote against the incumbent party in office rather than to vote positively for an acceptable alternative regime. In other words, the ruling party is punished while its successor wins by default.

An often touted solution that was ardently espoused by the Reform Party as part of its electoral platform and campaign in 1997 is the device of recall. It allows constituents by way of petition to express a vote of non-confidence in a sitting member. If the petition succeeds, a by-election must be held in consistency. The recall mechanism is intended to achieve two objectives concurrently — to encourage the parliamentarian to keep in touch with constituents and to give citizens the assurance that they are, indeed, the ultimate sovereign; that the elected representative is a servant and not master of, the people. In Canada, the Province of Alberta flirted with the recall mechanism as early as the 1920s, but the enabling legislation was repealed when the premier became the subject of a recall petition. The courts also were of the view that recalls violated the principle of the supremacy of the legislature.

It may be noted, by way of comparison, that in the United States about nine states have recall provisions in their constitutions. However, while recall is permitted at the state and local levels, it is not at the federal level of government. Local recall is allowed in at least 37 states with various signature percentage requirements ranging from 5 percent to 50 percent.

The Legislature — The Gap
between Formal Theory and Practice

As was the case when specifying the functions of political parties, so too, the functions of Parliament have been variously enumerated to include: law-making, surveillance or control of the Executive, representation and electoral conversion, recruitment, socialization and training (of political leadership) and conflict management or integration, and legitimization.

This writer's preference is to see Parliament as having three functional roles: (1) As Legislature; (2) As Representative Assembly, and (3) As Deliberative Assembly.

In formal theory, the primary function of Parliament as Legislature is to enact legislation. The primacy of the law-making function is consistent with the notion of the supremacy and sovereignty of Parliament. It grew out of the long struggle in Great Britain between monarch or Sovereign and Parliament over control of the purse string. Buttressing the principle of no taxation without representation was the conviction that freedom and liberty of citizens might best be assured by a separation and balance of powers and function — between legislation (the Legislature), execution (the Executive) and the enforcement of laws and administration of justice (the Judiciary). To the extent also that Parliament came increasingly to embody the principle of representation, and of public deliberation, it seemed best placed and suited to serve as the counterpoise to the powerful Executive — the Sovereign.

The notion of supremacy of Parliament rests on a number of propositions:

i.   that there is no higher legislative authority than Parliament
ii. that there is no limit to Parliament's sphere of legislation
iii. that no Parliament can legally bind its successor or be bound by its predecessor, and
iv. that no court can declare Acts of Parliament to be invalid.

Parliamentary supremacy is also reinforced by the principle of Parliamentary Privilege, that is, a series of rights given uniquely to the legislature to ensure that Parliament as an institution and its members are collectively and individually protected against outside control. Thus, while the House of Commons is sitting and its members are within its chambers, they are exempt from the laws of libel and need not respond to subpoenas requiring attendance at court trials. Parliamentary Privilege also allows the legislature to determine remuneration of members, to set its own rules of procedure and conduct and to discipline members. Indeed, it may determine its own membership and expel members temporarily or even permanently as was done at the provincial level by the Saskatchewan legislature in relation to a member who was convicted for the murder of his wife.

The Westminster notion of supremacy of Parliament has, however, been qualified in Canada, first by the operation of a federal system, under which exclusive areas of jurisdiction have been allocated to two levels of government — central or federal and regional or provincial. Second, and more recent, the Charter of Rights and Freedoms incorporated into the Constitution in 1982, gives formal recognition to, and enshrines the rights of individuals. These rights are now protected by the Constitution and their enforcement falls within the jurisdiction of the courts. Parliament therefore performs its functions subject to these additional constitutional restraints.

The one area over which Parliament historically has been most concerned to assert its supremacy as Legislature has been in the area of public finance, to which we have already alluded. The formal supremacy of Parliament — and I stress *formal* — has been reflected in the application of special rules to so-called money bills. Bills for the appropriation of public funds or for the raising of any tax or duty must originate in the House of Commons. *But*, special rules applied to money bills also *confine initiation of financial measures to responsible Ministers*, which in effect means the Cabinet. Furthermore, the House of Commons may not adopt any financial measure unless recommended to the Commons by the Governor General (the Formal Executive), which as we shall see, also means the Cabinet or political executive. Thus, while Parliament has formal primacy in the sense that it gives effect to policy by legislating, *it is the Cabinet* — the political executive — decides what Parliament may legislate.

The fact is that Parliament is no longer the prime initiator of legislation, having been superseded by Cabinet dominance of the machinery of government. Realistically, therefore, it is the two other functions of Parliament, as Representative and Deliberative Assembly, that have become the main function of Parliament today. As a representative Assembly, Parliament gives legitimacy and authority to government, and facilitates stable government by reassertion of confidence in political administrations. As a Deliberative Assembly, Parliament engages in public/popular education by bringing public policy issues into focus, examining the pros and cons, and engages in propagandizing, i.e., the selling by the government and belittling by the Opposition of government programs with a view to influencing the electorate. In the process of parliamentary give-and-take, a measure of integration of conflicting interests and views is achieved.

Freedom of speech (and immunity against laws of slander and libel within Parliament) is considered essential to the representative and deliberative functions of Parliament. But freedom of speech cannot be absolute, as democratic expression has to be tempered by considerations of efficient performance — getting things done. Hence, the need for rules of procedure and rules of debate and, in particular, rules of closure of debate — and in this, the office and role of the Speaker, as presiding officer, is crucial. One of the reforms recently carried out to enhance the independent and impartial status of the Speaker, is that the holder is now chosen in secret ballot by MPs rather than by the Prime Minister as a sinecure to be bestowed.

The Senate or Upper House

The Senate has a normal complement of 104 members (Ontario 24, Quebec 24, Maritime provinces, six each totalling 24, western provinces six, each totalling 24, Newfoundland six, the Northwest Territories, and the Yukon one each). However in 1988, the Conservative Prime Minister Brian Mulroney invoked, for the very first time, a provision — thought by conventional wisdom to be inoperative by virtue of disuse — to increase the membership to the maximum allowable at any time: namely, 112. Sections 26–28 of the Constitution Act of 1867 provide for the addition of from four to eight senators, representing equally the Four Divisions (Regions) of Canada. The procedure was invoked to prevent the Liberal-dominated Senate from blocking passage of the very unpopular Goods and Services Tax legislation. The appointment of the additional 8 senators withstood legal challenges and raises speculation as to whether other provisions of the Constitution deemed to have been made inoperative by the convention of disuse could, likewise, successfully be invoked in appropriate circumstances. Of particular interest are the powers of the federal government, unrestricted at law, to disallow provincial legislation and to direct the withholding of assent to provincial bills by the Lieutenant Governor, the representative at the provincial level of the Queen (Head of State) of Canada. The Lieutenant Governor also has the constitutional power to reserve a bill for the signification of the Governor General, the representative at the federal lever of the Head of State in Canada.

Canadian senators used to be appointed for life, but since 1965 must retire at age 75.

The Senate of Canada, at the time of Confederation, was intended to play an important role and to be a social balancing mechanism between Upper (English) Canada and Lower (French) Canada; hence the equal representation and appointment rather than election to office. It was also designed to serve as a restraint on "hasty or ill-conceived legislation" (which might compromise the interests of private property) emanating from the popularly elected House of Commons.

Criticism of the Senate has been the favourite pastime of students and practitioners of Canadian politics and public administration and, more recently, of the premiers of the western provinces. Now, virtually trapped in a posture of western alienation — based on alleged bias of the Canadian government towards the dominant concerns of Quebec as a distinct society and of Ontario as the industrial heartland of Canada — western political leaders have been arguing for a Triple E Senate (Elected, Equal, Effective).[2] In 1989, the Government of Alberta, under the leadership of Premier Don Getty of the ruling Progressive Conservative Party, instituted a province-wide election to choose a senator-designate to fill a Senate vacancy. A political complication arose when a maverick candidate put forward by a fringe (separatist) party gained the majority vote — and thus became the Senator designate. Premier Getty has, however, forwarded his name to the Prime Minister of Canada for appointment, raising a number of interesting constitutional and political issues that cannot be pursued here.

Both friends and foes of the Senate have conceded that the Senate has made a useful and often significant contribution in discharging its functions as a revising chamber for general legislation originating in the House of Commons. The Senate retains a critical role in the process of constitutional amendment, as its approval is needed for any amendments to the "safeguarded" or "entrenched" clauses (this would include any changes that were made to the status of the Senate itself). Actually, the Senate can delay certain motions (constitutional amendments) passed by the House of Commons for a maximum of 180 days, after which it can be approved by the Commons unilaterally. What this means is that senators cannot indefinitely block amendments that would reform or abolish the Senate itself.

Parliamentary Government as Cabinet and/or Prime Ministerial Government

The Formal Executive — Queen and Crown

The Queen of the UK is also the Queen of Canada and the government of Canada is conducted in her name. However, she herself does not — by constitutional convention — govern, either in the UK or in Canada. The monarchy is institutionalized in the Crown, the legal entity or institution that embodies all the powers of executive government, whether exercised by ministers or public officials. Put another way, the Crown, as a legal abstraction, represents the government, but is not accountable for the actions of the government. The Queen of Canada can do no wrong, and cannot be sued, but the Crown (by virtue of the Crown Liability Act of 1952) can be.

The powers of the Crown derive from two sources — statute and common law.[3] The statutory powers both to administer laws (executive power) and to make laws (legislative power) are conferred upon the Crown by Parliament and is, thus, a delegated power subject to the discretion of Parliament. (e.g., to summon senators, to summon or call the House of Commons, appoint the Speaker of the Senate, assent to or refuse to assent to bills that have been passed by both houses of Parliament, and so on).

The fact is, however, that the exercise of these statutory powers is subject to *convention*, or long established constitutional doctrine, that the Governor General, the Queen's personal representative, acts on the advice of the Privy Council (the Cabinet).

The common law or residual powers may be considered part of the prerogative powers. The Sovereign (Queen) also possesses certain "personal prerogative powers" are still important constitutional reserve powers: for example, the right to act independently of ministerial advice in certain circumstances.

The most important prerogative power of the Crown exercised in Canada by the Governor General is the finding of the Prime Minister, in the choice of which the Governor General acts on his own authority (prerogative). The Governor General likewise has a prerogative right to be consulted in the appointment of ministers of the Crown, and the much more controversial right to refuse the Prime Minister's request for the dissolution of Parliament.

The exercise of prerogative power again shows how formal theory and requirements may, and have been, circumscribed by *convention*. In normal circumstances, convention requires that in the choosing of the Prime Minister, the Governor General call upon the leader of the political party that has gained a majority of seats in the House of Commons to accept the Prime Ministership and form the government. The Governor General may, however, enjoy much greater scope for discretionary prerogative where no party has a clear majority, or where a Prime Minister becomes incapacitated or dies in office, and his party has not yet chosen a successor.

Dominance of the Cabinet
or Political Executive

The Cabinet has become, and is, the unchallenged centre of political power in the Government of Canada. Technically, the Cabinet comprises of Crown's confidential advisers and is a Committee of the Privy Council.[4]

The Cabinet, however, is not mentioned in the Canadian Constitution. While there are other statutory references to the position of Prime Minister, there is no legal definition of the Office of Prime Minister. The earlier title — First Minister — implies that the Prime Minister was supposed to be the first among equals (primus inter pares), but has achieved such a degree of pre-eminence that it is now plausible to speak of Prime Ministerial government rather than Cabinet government. Indeed, it is fair to say that the life of the Cabinet is linked to the will and life of the Prime Minister.

The power of the Prime Minister stems in part from the exclusivity of certain functions that he performs and in part from the nature of electoral politics and the role of the media in mass society.

The Prime Minister advises the Sovereign (Queen) on the appointment of the Governor General, her personal representative in Canada. He alone recommends to the Governor General the appointment, dismissal or acceptance of resignations of ministers. He has the right to determine what ministerial offices are entitled to Cabinet rank and who may attend Cabinet. His own resignation may bring not only his own ministry, but his government to an end. The Prime Minister has the right to advise on the dissolution of Parliament, a threat that he can hold over the heads of fractious or rebellious colleagues.

The Prime Minister presides over the Cabinet and Cabinet Secretariat, so that he, in effect, controls the agenda and recording of decisions. He can easily dominate Cabinet proceedings, more so when he is a highly popular or charismatic leader on whose coattail many party candidates may have been carried into political office.

In this writer's experience, based on three and a half years of participation in Cabinet and Cabinet Sub-Committee meetings in a comparable Whitehall model situation, that genuine free for all discussion takes place in Cabinet only when the Prime Minister does not have a very direct personal interest in a matter and plays the role of elder statesman. If there is a strong opposing consensus, the Prime Minister is likely to remind that it is he who will have to pull the political chestnuts out of the fire and repair the electoral damage. When there is dissatisfaction with the Prime Minister's performance, it is the other ministers who bear the brunt of Cabinet shuffles designed to give the administration a new look or a new lease on political life.

Again, and most surprisingly, the mystique of the Cabinet appears to be at its strongest in the privacy of closed meetings, where ministerial colleagues and close political associates who would otherwise address the Prime Minister by first name (and this applies to close relatives also) feel constrained to use the formal addresses of Prime Minister or Sir.

The Prime Minister has the right to issue orders in any department or ministry with or without consulting the incumbent minister and may, indeed, place any ministry under his direct control or trusteeship, so to speak.

141

George E. Eaton

It is also the Prime Minister who exercises the prerogative of advising the Governor General whether Cabinet secrecy may be relaxed, so that a disaffected, dismissed, or resigning minister may find himself effectively gagged from publicly telling his side of the story because of the constraint of the Official Secrets Act and the Privy Council oath of secrecy.

The nature of electoral politics in mass society and the influence of the media, especially television, also serve to enhance the dominant role of the Prime Minister. The ruling political regime is identified by the name of the Prime Minister. He can, at short notice, pre-empt prime time of the electronic media, commandeer the print media to press conferences, photo opportunities, and so on.

Paradoxically also, high levels of popular education in the modern administrative or bureaucratic state, with its emphasis on rational/legal procedures and administration, have not diminished the tendency towards veneration of political leadership. As social existence and interaction and the world of work become more complex, and the rapid rate of socio-economic change becomes more bewildering, it appears that even an educationally more sophisticated electorate seems inclined to suspend its critical faculties and to seek a leader or saviour who will provide the solutions or lead into the promised land.

The challenge to enhance citizenship participation in the democratic processes and the politics of participation, or to make Parliament a more effective instrument of representation, may lie not in making political parties or Parliament more effective instruments of democratic will, but in curbing the power of the Prime Minister, and making the holder of the office a first among equals and nothing more.

The dominance of the Executive over the Legislature — from which ministers are overwhelmingly drawn (Senators may be appointed to ministerial portfolios, but cannot sit in and report to the House of Commons) — has also been made possible by the invoking of party discipline and voting on strict party lines in the House of Commons. Full and frank exchange of views on the part of MPs, especially back-benchers who do not hold ministerial or junior ministerial appointments, tends to take place within the confines of private party meetings (caucus) held before the sitting of Parliament. Once the caucus has agreed on a government or opposition position MPs are expected to toe the line in the Commons, and vote along strict party lines. Only on issues of conscience (e.g., death penalty or abortion) are MPs especially on the government side, free to vote in accordance with personal and/or constituency inclinations.

A device often used to allow MPs to avoid embarrassing voting dilemmas is pairing where an MP of one party may join an opposite colleague so that both can absent themselves from the Commons, and thus not jeopardize the outcome of a vote.

Failure to observe party line and party discipline in the House of Commons is likely to impact unfavourably on the career prospects of a recalcitrant or rebellious back-bencher or even parliamentary secretary (minister in training). A powerful Prime Minister, can also, as party leader, but obstacles in the way of re-election of the troublesome MP as a candidate for the general election the next time around.

142

Other factors which have served to promote the dominance of the political executive are the sheer volume of governmental activity arising from the expanded role of government in the modern welfare state — even parliamentary committees tend to be overburdened — and the complexity of the issues in the modern state, which require expertise that is found concentrated in the civil service: the permanent arm and mainstay of the Executive.

The Civil Service

The basic unit of organization in the Civil or Public Service is the ministry or department. A ministry is a grouping of governmental functions or departments headed by a minister. A measure of confusion has been created by the fact that in the British tradition the term ministry is used interchangeably with department: thus, the Ministry of Finance is referred to as the Department of Finance.

Strictly speaking, a department is an agency or major unit of government, usually discharging a single substantive function (e.g., Department of Labour or of Public Works). In some countries the department is known as Bureau, Service, Office, or Administration.

A department may be headed by a political officer or a technical officer or a career official. A department usually is structured into Divisions, Branches, or Sections.

The underlying principle of organization is functional homogeneity: that is to say, there is usually an attempt to group functions into units as nearly related or as homogeneous as possible.

However, the grouping of ministries or departments to constitute the portfolio of a minister is, in the final analysis, a political function. The Prime Minister may realign ministries/departments because of the particular skills (or lack of skills) of a MP earmarked for Cabinet appointment or for other purely political considerations.

The Functions and Role of
the Civil Service or Bureaucracy

The main thrust of this paper has been to try and make the Canadian parliamentary system (Westminster/Whitehall model) more comprehensible by distinguishing between formal theory and actual practice, between legally enforceable constitutional provisions and informal provisions or conventions that are accepted as part of the political culture.

It is in examining the functions and role of the civil service that we can best get an overview of the conventions that link the machinery of government and appreciate the extent to which certain of these conventions have persisted as rationalizations or folklore of "responsible" government, long after they have ceased to describe or correspond to political and administrative realities.

In the Westminster/Whitehall tradition, the constitutional convention that defines the responsibilities and role of the public service especially in relation to the Legislature and political executive is known as the doctrine or model of neutrality. Strict adherence to this conventional doctrine requires that the following conditions be met.[5]

1. The separation of politics and policy-making from administration, with politicians making the policy decisions and public servants executing them.

2. Public servants are independently appointed and promoted on the basis of qualifications and merit rather than on the basis of political patronage (party affiliation or contributions).

3. Public servants do not engage in partisan political activities.

4. Public servants do not express publicly personal views (in praise or criticism) of government policies or administration.

5. Public servants provide the best and most honest advice they can to political executives who, in turn, accord them "anonymity" (no-name-calling) by accepting ministerial responsibility for departmental decisions and actions.

6. Public servants, regardless of their personal opinions or social philosophy, zealously carry out the decisions of the party in power, irrespective of the latter's ideological commitment and program emphases.

Politics and Administration

According to the doctrine and model of political neutrality, politics is concerned, in all spheres of government, with the whole business of deciding what to do and getting it done. Deciding what to do properly belongs in the realm of policy formation, which is equated with politics and is, thus, the prerogative and responsibility of legislators and political executives. Getting things done, on the other hand, falls in the realm of administration and is, thus, the concern of administrators or public servants. Given this dichotomy, policy decisions are political, administrative decisions are non-political.

However, this distinction between policy formulation or politics and policy execution or administration cannot be sustained in today's administrative state. The fact of the matter is that while the legislators may give legal effect and governmental force to certain directions in policy or priorities in terms of programs and activities, it is in the process of implementation by way of delegated powers and authority that policies become meaningful and make their impact on particular groups or the society as a whole. It is no secret that much of the legislation enacted by Parliament or the legislative authority (as much as 80–90 percent) originates within the civil service and, certainly, the regulations made to give practical effect to enabling legislation are almost always subject to the decisive influence of civil servants.

Public servants also have been forced increasingly by the logic of the development of the administrative or Welfare State to assume the role of social change agents. Not only do ministers of government expect and seek advice from senior civil servants on policy, but they encourage them to promote new and innovative solutions to social problems. These expectations are derived from the status and role of senior civil servants. If their academic and professional training, as well as long experience in public affairs guaranteed by security of tenure of employment mean anything, they should mean the ability to anticipate social and economic problems and to help find solutions to them. Hence, the job of a senior civic servant or public servant must involve, to a greater or lesser extent, ongoing evaluation and scrutiny of the ideas and proposals that emerge from the political process. It is difficult to see how it could be otherwise. The administrative and advisory role of the senior civil servant places him or her in a special relationship to the minister, the limits of which are set by mutual confidence and respect rather than formal constitutional theory or supportive rationalizations.

Another of the realities faced by the senior civil servant in the parliamentary system of government is that of growing exposure to pressure groups or interest groups seeking to influence policy formation and policy execution. Given the dominance of the Cabinet as the principal instrument of policy formation and execution, and the strict adherence to party discipline that requires voting along party lines in the Legislature, the individual member of Parliament usually has relatively limited sway or ability to influence policy measures and/or subsidiary regulations. Interest groups have recognized this by shifting their representations and lobbying to the ministries of government and to the senior public servants who advise and influence ministers.

In the Westminster/Whitehall tradition, the permanent civil service head of a ministry is typically known as the "Permanent Secretary". The designation carries a number of connotations. For one thing, it suggests that the civil servant is the permanent and immovable expert while the political executive is essentially a transient amateur or "bird of passage" to be tolerated until another comes home to roost temporarily. For another, it could reinforce the impression that the Permanent Secretary is the sole repository of executive authority and the only person constitutionally responsible for the proper administration of a ministry or department, whereas it would be far more helpful to view the office as that of Chief Executive or General Manager, coordinating the efforts and activities of the senior management team.

In some Caribbean (though not Commonwealth Caribbean) jurisdictions, the designation used is Vice-Minister, while in many Western European and Afro-Asian jurisdictions with much the same British civil service traditions, the title used is Director General. Whatever the title used, the fact remains that the permanent chief administrator is a co-policy maker and joint executive with the political administrator (minister).

The Canadian public administration has given recognition to the unique role played by the chief administrator by an innovative adaptation of the Westminster model. The Permanent Secretary has been redesignated "Deputy Minister" and is an appointment that is the prerogative of the Prime Minister who is supported in the selection process by other senior officials. Deputy Ministers are legally appointed by, and serve at the pleasure of, the Governor General, acting on the recommendation of the Prime Minister. The performance of Deputy Ministers is appraised annually by a Committee of Senior Officials (COSO) or Executive Personnel with inputs from the appropriate Ministers and central agencies. The committee reports its findings to the Cabinet, and it is on the basis of these recommendations that the Cabinet makes its determination of performance and compensation awards. Appointments below the grade of Deputy Minister are made by the Public Service Commission after consultation with the Deputy Minister.

The convention has developed that, provided the Deputy Minister does not become too publicly identified with the political regime in office, or become too overtly partisan in his support of the policies and programmes of the government in office, he or she enjoys much the same security of tenure enjoyed by other officials below the grade of Deputy Minister. This arrangement thus leaves open the possibility of a new government being able to appoint a Deputy Minister from outside the ranks of the civil service, although here again the convention is that the outsider should have professional qualifications or experience and attainments at least equal to, if not more impressive than, candidates with the public service who may be considered logical contenders.

Political Patronage

The appointment of persons to the government service on the grounds of contributions to the governing party or political or ideological affiliation is regarded as a blatant violation of the traditional doctrine of political neutrality. The main objection is that such a course of action is at odds with the merit principle, the premise of which is that public servants are appointed on the basis of merit or fitness for the job rather than on the basis of political affiliation or contribution.

It may be noted that this problem usually becomes particularly acute when a political party comes to office espousing significant shifts in programs or governmental policies, or alternatively a more radical ideology that envisages profound reconstruction of the socio-economic and political systems. The argument most often heard is that the natural tendency of the bureaucracy to administrative inertia will be compounded by resistance to, and sabotage of, change. It is further contended that the resistance to change may be expected because career officials will most likely have been recruited from the dominant social (and wealthier) groups within the state, and will be loyal only to the political leadership that evidences the same political attitudes as those held by the permanent officials.

To prevent political patronage and other considerations from impinging on the establishment of a career responsibility for recruitment, appointment, transfers, discipline, promotions — in sum — career advancement and development is vested in a relatively autonomous Public Service Commission. There appears to be a great deal of misunderstanding, however, about what political neutrality means. If it means non-direct involvement in partisan political activities, it is a reasonable proposition. If it means a lack of political awareness and acumen, it is not.

Politically, the administrator must not only be responsive to external direction and control, but have a "political sense" which leads to an appreciation of major political shifts of opinion and the pressures to that members of the political directorate are subject. They must have faith then in popular values and popular institutions.

Satisfactory public service is best guaranteed by public service employees with professional competence. If not, inability to perform new tasks or meet new challenges is likely to be mistaken for disloyalty and sabotage.

Political Activity

The tradition of political neutrality requires that public servants do not engage in partisan political activities. Historically there has been a close link between the patronage and spoils system and political activity on the part of public service officials. Political sterilization of public servants was deemed to be a reasonable quid pro quo for the elimination of spoils and patronage in the public services.

It still appears to be a reasonable expectation and a practical consideration that public servants do not become actively engaged in partisan political activity in the course of performing their duties and responsibilities. It may be noted that the Public Service Employment Act of 1967 provided that public servants, with the exception of Deputy Heads, may, with the approval of the Public Service Commission, take leave of absence to stand for election to public office, but must resign if they are elected. There is a continuing embargo, however, against public servants actively campaigning for or against a candidate or political party.

Public Comment

The prohibition against publicly expressing personal views on government policies or administration is another integral component of the doctrine and model of political neutrality. Increasingly, it is a prohibition largely observed in the breach, because public servants unavoidably become involved in public comment in the regular performance of their duties.

The prohibition is also at odds with the growing demand for, and trend towards, openness in government and greater participatory democracy. Citizen participation in the political and governmental processes can have no meaning unless politicians and officials are prepared to, and are capable of, discussing basic policy issues in the public arena.

Anonymity and Ministerial Responsibility

The concept of anonymity on the part of public servants depends upon, and reinforces, the doctrine of ministerial responsibility, which however, has been suffering erosion for some time. Ministers of government are no longer expected to resign in response to revelations or disclosures of maladministration in ministries and departments.

Government and the public administration have become so large and complex that ministers can hardly be expected to have knowledge and control of all the activities and actions of officials. As the Head of the British Cabinet Office observed to the Expenditure Committee of the British House of Commons, which undertook an extensive review of the structure and role of the civil service between 1974–1977, "The concept that because somebody whom the

Minister has never heard of, has made a mistake, means that the Minister should resign, is out of date, and rightly so. I think equally, that a Minister has got a responsibility which he cannot devolve to his Permanent Secretary, for the efficiency and drive of his Department".

Tenure and Permanency in Office

The changing role of public servants and the increasingly high profile of so-called "mandarins" have led to the questioning of the principle of security of tenure or permanency in office on the part of public servants.

Increasingly, also the right to security of tenure (not just for public servants but for university academics, for whom it is an equally hallowed tenet), has been made subject to budgetary considerations. The fact of the matter is that security of tenure is no longer the unique or characteristic feature of public service employment that it once was. The quest for job security is no less a preoccupation of the private sector, and grievance procedures in collective agreements and employment contracts for managers and professionals are being used to offer a measure of job security. What may really be at issue is not the principle of security of tenure, but revision of extremely cumbersome and time-consuming procedures by which public servants can be separated for valid causes.

The Status of the Doctrine of Neutrality

The doctrine of neutrality, based as it is on a presumed dichotomy between politics and administration is difficult to sustain. It is also based on a definition of politics that is narrow, misleading, and dangerous. Politics is concerned with the exercise of power and not just with the manoeuvrings of politicians, political parties, and interest groups.

The distinction between policy or politics and administration undoubtedly has served some purpose, otherwise it would not have so long survived as one of the canons of parliamentary government. Analytically, the dichotomy makes it possible to distinguish between the constitutional and legal functions of political executives and permanent administrators. Practically, it has served the interest of both civil servants and politicians. Civil servants have been shielded from attacks by politicians and the public, while politicians have invoked it to maintain appearances before the public, giving the impression that they may be acting more objectively than is in fact the case.

The greatest limitation and danger of the doctrine of neutrality is that it exposes the society at large to fraud and the civil service to moral corruption. To fraud, because political and administrative decisions can be taken without fear of awkward enquiry or demands for public scrutiny either by Parliament or other legislative body, the press, and the citizenry at large. To moral corruption, because if *all* governments are to be served with equal impartiality and legality, there can be little grounds for criticizing the officials who serve regimes that commit heinous crimes and infamy against a society or even humanity.

A recurrent theme appearing in the now fashionable genre of political biographies of former or retired political leaders is the feeling of frustration and inadequacy engendered by the inertia and/or resistance to change, especially ideologically inspired change, on the part of the administrative bureaucracy. But apart from recourse to special advisers, who are political appointees and may play a facilitative but not executive role, no attempt has been made to provide a more appropriate constitutional framework or set of principles to reconcile the concept of responsible and responsive bureaucracy with the more positive role of public servants as agents of social change. The starting point would have to be explicit recognition that the public administration is managed jointly by a political and administrative directorate rather than by presumed political masters and self-effacing and neutral public servants. The traditional concept of neutrality can only serve to make even less meaningful the already difficult task of enforcing governmental and administrative accountability.

The Judiciary

The Judiciary and courts in Canada have drawn their decisive legal and judicial traditions from Great Britain. In the Westminster model, because of the assertion and acceptance of the supremacy of Parliament, the Judiciary cannot declare legislation unconstitutional, and are limited to interpreting the meaning of legislation when disputes turning on its meaning and application arise.

Unlike Britain, which is a unitary state, the British North America Act of 1867 created a federal union, with legislative power and functions being assigned, explicit and otherwise, to the federal Parliament and provincial legislatures. The Canadian courts since then have emerged as the arbiters of the balance of the Constitution, with the authority to declare laws ultra vires or null and void when a litigant, whether individual or corporate citizen, or one level of government or the other, alleges that there has been an encroachment upon or usurpation of jurisdiction. Since 1949, final interpretation of the Canadian Constitution has fallen mainly to the Supreme Court of Canada. Before that, the Judicial Committee of the Privy Council of the UK had constituted the ultimate court of constitutional appeal.

Outside of its role as arbiter of the constitutional balance of powers, however, there was little scope for judicial activism, as the Judiciary felt constrained by the notion of the supremacy of Parliament.

The inclusion and proclamation of the Charter of Rights and Freedoms has enlarged the role of the Canadian courts, giving them a more central role in deciding public policy and social values. A case in point was the decision of the Supreme Court of Canada in 1989 that the provisions of the Criminal Code governing accessibility to abortion infringed upon certain rights of women under the Charter of Rights and were, therefore, null and void. To the extent, therefore, that the courts may now entertain litigation contending that a contested law is not only beyond the jurisdiction of the enacting legislature, but may also be in contravention of the Charter, the Canadian courts will now be closer to the American system of courts, where the Supreme Court has served as the "living voice" of the Constitution. In the US Constitution, the application of the doctrine of separation of powers between Legislature, Executive, and Judiciary has resulted in a system of constitutional checks and balances designed to achieve limited government.

In Canada, the independence of the Judiciary has become a matter of fundamental constitutional principle, rather than of fundamental law. It is reflected in the guarantee of security of tenure, both general and specific to judges and autonomy in the operation of the courts. The general right of tenure ensures that judges of all but the lowest level of courts, once appointed, may serve without fear of being removed from the bench until age 75. The specific right of tenure is reflected in the requirement of specific procedures for the removal from the office of the judges in question.

It may be noted that while the judicial branch is treated as distinct and independent, there is, in fact, a near fusion of the Legislature and Executive. Legislature and Executive are inextricably intertwined in that the political executive is drawn from the Legislature and the government will not survive a vote of no-confidence unless it can command a majority vote in the House of Commons. We also saw that while Parliament gives effect to policy by legislating, it is the Cabinet or Executive that decides what Parliament is to legislate. At the same time, under the concept of ministerial responsibility, the political directorate are accountable to Parliament for the direction of their respective ministries or portfolios.

Concluding Observations

While Canada has a written constitution based on the British North America Act of 1867, and other related legislation, the functioning of the system and the machinery of government depend a great deal on conventions or unwritten rules. As we saw, while the Cabinet (as distinct from the (Queen's) Privy Council of Canada) is not mentioned in the Constitution — there are the Cabinet conventions — of Cabinet Solidarity (ministers collectively accepting responsibility for Cabinet decisions), of ministerial responsibility to Parliament, which also entails according anonymity to civil servants.

Likewise, the Governor General in his choice of a Prime Minister is bound by the convention that he should first call upon the leader of the majority party to form the government. In the exercise of statutory and prerogative powers, the Governor General is likewise bound by convention to accept the advice of the ministers of the Crown — or the Cabinet. The very appointment of the Governor General is done by the Queen, as Queen of Canada, on the advice of the Prime Minister of Canada. There is the firm, unwritten rule that the government must hold the support of a majority of the House of Commons or resign.

Political parties are not mentioned in the Constitution, but constitute the lynch-pin of responsible representative government and political debate and voting in the House of Commons takes place normally on the basis of party affiliation and party discipline. The convention of the doctrine of neutrality governs the role and its relationship with the Public Service to the Political Executive and Legislature (although certain of its tenets no longer appear to be congruent with objective reality, constitutional change may also be brought about by the disuse of a convention). For instance, under the BNA Act the federal government has the power, unrestricted in law, to disallow provincial legislation. The power has not, however, been used since 1943, and its use is now highly improbable, given the coming of age of the provinces.

The federal government also has the power, again unrestricted in law, to instruct the Lieutenant Governor, the Queen's representative at the provincial level, to withhold assent to provincial legislation, but this power must now be considered incongruous and a constitutional anomaly, as its use would put the provinces in a position of inferior (colonial) status.

It is by recognizing the gaps between formal theory and practice and action, and by linking constitutional and legal requirements with constitutional conventions, that we can make sense of the Canadian parliamentary system of government.

Notes

1. The British North America Act of 1867, which created the Federal Union of Canada and its subsequent amendments, stood as the basic Constitution of Canada until the passage of the Constitution Act of 1982, which modernized the Canadian Constitution. It did so by patriation of the Constitution, which had been domiciled in the UK because of the lack of an amending procedure. The Constitution Act of 1982 not only remedied this defect but incorporated the Canadian Charter of Rights and Freedoms.

2. It is a development arising out of the Meech Lake Constitutional Accord, which is dealt with in the next article.

    The idea behind the Triple E Senate, is that with each province having equal representation — the Senate could more effectively balance provincial interests.

3. See J.R. Mallory, *The Structure of Canada on Government*, Rev. Edition (Gage, 1984), for extended discussion.

4. In the 12th century, the King of England was advised by a Great Council of the principal men of the Kingdom. The King developed his own Inner Circle of that Council. It in turn evolved into sections based on functional separation and the general purposes section became the permanent council or privy council.

5. For extended discussion see K. Kernahan and D. Siegel, *Public Administration in Canada: A Text* (Toronto: Methuen, 1987), Chapter II.

Public Administration and Business Administration

Inter-relationships and Tensions

George E. Eaton

Scope of Paper

This paper begins by examining the nature of administration, its relationship to politics and administration and management as generic concepts. Next, it traces the conditions that historically distinguished public sector from private sector employment, that gave rise to traditional models of public and private sector administration; models characterized by sharply differing expectations of values of service, loyalty and commitment, as well as systems of governance and accountability. It then discusses changes, most notably the rise of large scale organizations and bureaucratic administration which, it is argued, served to mitigate the traditional differences and made them differences of degrees rather than of kind. Next, it traces the growing importance of the role and influence of public administration occasioned by the emergence of the Modern Welfare State, and the growing involvement of the state and public administration in the economy and society; the combination of regulatory, promotional, developmental, and entrepreneurial roles; and the shifts in political and economic ideology that accompanied these changes. Finally, the paper examines the factors leading to disenchantment with, and hostility towards the Welfare State; the attempts to dismantle it, and apply the private sector or business model to the public sector, and replace the traditional model of public administration by developing a new corporatist model and theory of administration, referred to as "The New Public Administration".

Introduction

Definition and Nature of Administration

Administration, simply put, is the art of getting things done. It is prompted by the desire or necessity on the part of human beings to circumvent individual limitations that stand in the way of achieving personal goals or objectives. To illustrate, let us suppose that an individual encounters a large boulder blocking access to a desired path or entrance. In this situation, he faces two limitations: relative to the size of the obstacle, he is too small, and thus *physically* incapable of moving the stone; and second, he has no *environmental* or exogenous control over the size of the boulder. By himself, therefore, he does not have the resources to remove the obstacle that prevents him from achieving his goal — continuing along the (blocked) path. However, let us also suppose that others have arrived on the scene, and are faced with the same dilemma. By pooling their resources, and focussing on the common goal of removing the obstacle from their path, the boulder can be moved and the path cleared. In effect, the group constitutes the formation of a social unit that, collectively, has created a rudimentary organization.

The growth of administration, as our illustration suggests, has been prompted by two fundamental reasons — the first is material, the other social. In the first instance, cooperative or determined action in pursuit of a common goal serves to enlarge individual abilities, and shorten the time needed to achieve objectives. With the latter, human beings are gregarious and like to associate with each other. In other words, it is hard to contain the human spirit.

Organizations are formed, then, to achieve objectives or goals that can best be met by joint, or collective action. Thus, organizations are constructed and reconstructed to meet the various needs of human beings, or members of society. For instance, emotional or gregarious needs may be met by service clubs, spiritual needs by churches, intellectual needs by schools and universities, economic needs by enterprises, the conduct of public affairs by government, and so on.

Organizations and the pursuit of organizational goals also involve the mobilization of resources and, more important, the effective utilization and replenishment of such resources. This is particularly relevant because it appears to be universally the case that the human capacity for "wants" is virtually unlimited, whereas available resources to meet these wants are limited. Indeed, the pervasiveness of markets and allocative price mechanisms for determining what is to be produced (theory of demand), how it is to be produced (theory of production), and who gets what (theory of distribution) lends support to the presumption of ever escalating and competing demands, and relative scarcity of resources.

It is the existence, then, of organizations that provide the raison d'etre for administration. It is a process that entails the organizing, planning, structuring, directing or coordinating, and funding of the efforts of individuals and groups to accomplish specific goals, whether they be in the public or private, or non-profit sector. So defined, Administration is a generic concept.

Administration and Politics

To the extent that an organization also brings together employees or members who seek to influence the administration of policy and the allocation of resources through structured interaction, and in a variety of functional roles, it constitutes a political system. Organizational stability may be disturbed by internal as well as external changes in the environment, which threaten the status quo and induce affected individuals or groups to seek to realign the authority structure (distribution of decision-making opportunities) and the power structure (the importance or essentiality of functions). Politics is all about the exercise of power; it is the ability to determine ends or preferences through institutional mechanisms, and this holds true to a greater or lesser extent, whether one is dealing with the family (nuclear or extended), the church, school, a social club, community based organization, a corporation, or the government, albeit at a different level.

The politics of Government, however, differs from institutional politics in that it entails "authoritative allocation of resources"[1] or, in somewhat broader terms, "activity by which people define themselves and their world and publicly seek their goals".[2]

Administration and Management as Related Concepts

Prior to the 1930s, the leading writers and thinkers, including what came to be known as *The Scientific (or Classical) Management School* (F.W. Taylor, 1856–1915), used management as a generic term interchangeable with administration. Accordingly, business management was considered to be a subset, or specialized area of general management. By the 1950s, however, a sharp differentiation had emerged between public administration and business administration or business management, leading to the identification of "management" with business management. In the USA, according to Peter Drucker,[3] what led to the identification and preemption of the term "management" by the private sector was the Great Depression, the animosity it engendered towards business, and the contempt for business executives it inspired. To avoid attracting the same opprobrium, management in the public sector was re-christened "Public Administration", proclaimed a separate (i.e., sectoral) discipline, and given its own departmental status within the university system.

By the 1960s, however, business management (or business administration) had regained respectability as a field of study, largely as a result of the performance of business management during World War II; and it led to a burgeoning of "business schools". Drucker further adds that, in recent times, this mistake of identifying management with business is being undone, and business schools are being converted into "schools of management", offering courses/

programs of study on non-profit management, as well as "executive management" programs for both business and non-business executives.[4]

Differences between Public and Business Administration

Significance of Differences in Employment Conditions

By the end of the nineteenth century and continuing well into the 20th century, inspired by the Prussian (later German) model of the civil service, state or public service employment had typically acquired distinctive, unique characteristics that sharply differentiated it from private sector employment. These characteristics included the concept of a public service career: lifelong employment, or rights in jobs guaranteed by the security of tenure; entitlement to salary on a regularized basis and generous compensatory, non-wage fringe benefits and entitlement to a pension.

Concept of a Public Service Career

Consistent with the concept of a career, the civil servant or Public Servant (the terms will be used interchangeably) was expected to make a commitment of lifelong service to the state. By definition, a career provides a vista, or set of expectations of progression from the point of entry, through the stages of professional development and achievement, to retirement. Over time, the concept of a career in the Public Service was transformed into a career merit service; employees would be recruited on the basis of qualifications rather than political patronage or nepotism, with promotion and advancement on the basis of length of service (progressive experience), and merit (ability) as measured by performance. Hence, the necessity of placing these personnel functions under the jurisdiction of autonomous, quasi-independent bodies (commissions) to prevent or minimize political interference, or the "spoils system".

Employees of the state, certainly in the UK, Europe, and other colonial administrations before and after independence, typically enjoyed high social status and considerable prestige. This was, in part, a reflection of stratified social class and caste systems, and class oriented recruitment. At the same time, civil servants, as agents of the state, were required to observe values and conventions demanding the highest standards of personal conduct and probity.

Security of Tenure and Rights in Jobs

The commitment on the part of the civil servant to lifelong service to the state was reciprocated by the government by way of a guarantee of lifelong employment, through security of tenure. This meant that once past the initial probationary period, the employee could expect continued employment until retirement, unless found guilty of gross misconduct or dereliction of duty. Job security, or permanence in office, was also justified by special, elaborate disciplinary procedures, making it extremely time consuming, albeit no less difficult, to dismiss an employee, regardless of the cause.

George E. Eaton

Entitlement to Pay on a Rational and Regularized Basis

Whereas legislation was required to prohibit private sector employers from making unauthorized deductions and offsetting payments in kind from the wages of workers, civil servants received salaries based on classification and ranking of posts, and regular incremental increase as reward for professional employment experience and career advancement. Generous leave benefits were also provided to compensate for salaries that were proportionally lower (discounted) than those within the private sector.

Entitlement to Pension

In comparison to the private sector, the right to a pension or retirement income constituted, for a long time, one of the most distinctive features — and advantages — of public service employment. Usually, on a non-contributing basis, upon completion of the prescribed years of service, civil servants could expect a retirement income based on retiring salary multiplied by eligible years of service. Residual benefits could also devolve upon widows and orphans.

Transference of Distinctive Public Service Employment Entitlements (Rights) to the Private Sector

While governments were prepared to confer on civil servants the entitlements mentioned above, there was almost universal resistance, certainly until the post World War II era, against conceding two rights — the right of unionization, and the right to collective bargaining, including the right to strike. These were rights that had been won by private sector workers through political agitation, in tandem with industrial and legislative action.

The argument put forward against conceding unionization and collective bargaining to civil servants was two-fold. First, civil servants were instrumental in providing a range of essential services to the society at large, some exclusively so by the state; accordingly, the state should not be held to ransom by its employees. Second, government, as the agent of a sovereign state, could not be coerced to accede to the demands of its employees, or be bound by the constraints of a collective agreement. Moreover, the cost of any settlements had to be paid for out of taxation exacted by Parliament or the Legislature, and control over budgetary finances was an essential component of Parliamentary supremacy. Hence, Parliament could not subordinate its fiscal responsibilities to a joint bargaining process. This did not, however, prevent civil servants from forming associations for consultative purposes (the Associational Model).

On the other hand, unionized private sector workers effectively used collective bargaining and the right to strike to establish retirement income schemes, as well as fringe benefits that closely approximated those traditionally enjoyed by civil servants. The emergence of Personnel Administration (later, Human Resources Management) as specialized areas of general management also facilitated the introduction of rationalized compensation systems, not unlike those of the public service, particularly in large bureaucratic firms. Unionized workers also achieved some measure of job protection through grievance procedures established in collective agreements procedures designed to curb the arbitrary exercise of authority by the employer. The process required the employer to provide just cause for disciplinary action (including dismissal) deemed in violation of the collective agreement. In Canada and several other jurisdictions, grievances that are not resolved by the grievance process must be referred to third party arbitration, without recourse to strike or industrial action. Under this system of industrial jurisprudence, the arbitrator who finds evidence of unjust dismissal may award compensation to the grieving employee, or order job reinstatement without loss of income or employment rights. Admittedly, the measure of job protection afforded by the grievance procedure and industrial jurisprudence falls far short of the security of tenure accorded to public servants. Parenthetically, it is worth noting that while civil servants in Canada enjoy a general right of security, some officials, most notably judges, the Auditor General, and the Governor of the (Central) Bank of Canada, have the benefit of a specific right to security of tenure; removal from office requires special investigative and disciplinary procedures and, ultimately, endorsement by the Parliament of Canada.

Finally, the concept of career has also become rooted in the private sector. The rise of modern corporations embodying the bureaucratic (hierarchical) form of organization, and characterized by separation of ownership from management and control, has fostered the notion of management as a profession, and the value of education and training to prepare employees at all levels to effectively perform job-related tasks and responsibilities.

Changing Perceptions and Appreciation of the Status and Role of Civil Servants

It was noted above that a number of employment entitlements, formerly considered unique to the civil service, provided justification for levels of compensation proportionately lower than for comparable categories in the private sector. These entitlements were transferred to the private sector through the medium of collective bargaining and political action. Civil servants, therefore, were left to contemplate the disparities in pay between the two sectors.

Conferment of Collective Bargaining and its Impact

The parastatal sector provided another point of reference for civil servants. In Canada, for instance, state owned enterprises engaging in commercial activities and operating under the rubric of Crown corporations (analogous to private sector companies), not only paid salaries comparable to those in private industry, but they had to live with unionization and collective bargaining. Federal civil servants began to press for the right of unionization and collective bargaining, and were granted it by the Public Service Staff Relations Act (PSSRA) of 1967. The sovereignty argument was laid to rest by pointing out the obvious: that a sovereign Parliament had delegated policy- and rule-making processes to the Executive (Cabinet), administrative agencies and tribunals. An official representative or agency to conduct negotiations with public service unions could accomplish the same. Coinciding with the changeover from the rather ineffective system of representation of civil servants by associations and non-legally binding consultation with government representatives was the redesignation of civil servants to "public servants" under the Public Service Act, 1967. Until then, the term civil servant referred to a full-time employee working in departments and agencies that came under direct ministerial jurisdiction, and who were eligible for pensions under the Superannuation Act. It is worth noting that while all civil servants (establishment positions) are government employees, not all government employees (that is, paid by the government) are civil servants. The change from civil to public servant was in recognition of the fact that public employees now had the right to bargain collectively, with the government as employer.

The Concept of Controlled Strikes

The PSSRA also introduced the novel arrangement of the controlled strike. It required unions to declare, at the onset of negotiations, whether they would opt for binding arbitration without the right to strike or, alternatively, choose the freedom to strike. In the case of the latter, negotiations would extend to designating a certain number of employees who would be obliged to remain on the job, to maintain critical levels of service or maintenance of facilities. In terms of public perceptions, however, it appeared that public servants were trying to get the best of both worlds, public and private sector; the lofty ideal of dedicated "servants of the public" was no longer sustainable.

Adverse Economic Conditions since the 1970s

Another contributing factor[5] to the changing and negative perceptions of the role of state was the seeming inability of government bureaucracies to deal with unexpected crises that erupted during the 1970s; for instance, the phenomenon of "stagflation", or concurrently high levels of unemployment and price inflation occasioned by the OPEC oil crisis. In light of the inadequacy of the prevailing Keynesian approach to management of the economy, government seemed unable to find more appropriate levers of control. Fiscal crises that persisted during the 1970s and 1980s also provided fertile ground for increasingly vocal conservatives and free market protagonists to launch a sustained assault on the Welfare State and its alleged incompatibility with the capitalist free enterprise system. Furthermore, increased competitiveness in domestic and international trade put additional pressure on employers to lower costs, resulting in "restructuring" (reorganizing) of businesses, accompanied by "downsizing" (retrenchment) of full-time employees, and, increasingly, recourse to part-time employees. In these circumstances, unemployed (and precariously employed) private sector workers could not but adopt an increasingly jaundiced view of the security of tenure in the employ of the public sector.

Proponents of globalization, the new mercantilism being spearheaded by mega-transnational corporations, hastened to portray it as an irresistible force against which national governments were powerless. The sensible approach, they maintained, was for government to adjust, as best as it could, to the new realities.

The Comparison Between Public and Business Administration of Five Functional Tasks of Management

Having looked at the relative significance of differences in employment conditions as a basis for differentiating between public and business administration, and at changing perceptions of each, it is now timely to look at the relative significance of the political framework and environment for both public and business administration, and then to compare differences between them in five functional areas of management; namely, authority, impartiality, legal and financial accountability, measuring performance and efficiency, and personnel administration and control.

Whereas business administration, or business management, focuses primarily on the operation of the company, public administration embraces the entire machinery of government. There are: the legislative decision-making bodies through which national goals and priorities are articulated, detailed, and transformed into specific policies and measures by elected politicians; the Executive organs, including the Prime Minister, or Chief Executive and Cabinet; the Public Service or Bureaucracy, through which policies are initiated, interpreted, implemented, and given practical effect; and the judicial or legal services, through which disputes over constitutional issues and other forms of litigation are adjudicated, and justice dispensed to those accused of violating laws governing social conduct and societal order.

This framework provides a degree of complexity not experienced by the private sector in three ways. First, it combines policy formulation, or the setting of objectives driven by the imperatives of democratic, "representative and responsible" government, the end result of which may be mutually exclusive goals or mandates that conflict with each other. Second, a regime of public management, under which public managers/administrators are subjected to ministerial and political oversight, and the advice given may be overruled if political considerations are deemed more important. Ultimately, the overriding goal of the political administration in a system of competitive politics is to get re-elected and, thus, retain power. Herein, perhaps, lies the most fundamental difference between private sector and public servant employees: namely, the proximity of the latter to politics and to daily interaction with politicians. It requires a tremendous bureaucratic balancing act to reconcile traditional perspectives of the passive role of administrators with the power and influence derived from the essentiality of their functions. On the one hand, they are under the oversight of political heads and ministers of government but, at the same time, as advisers they exercise considerable influence with the same ministers because of their permanence, authority of knowledge, and expertise.[6] Third, there is the judicial and legal services system, through which public servants may be held accountable for their exercise of public authority, to a greater degree than their private counterparts.

Authority — Size and Scope

In public administration, law, or more precisely, public law is the chief source of authority; that is, the ability to make and enforce decisions that guide or influence the behaviour of others. Law is the primary source of authority in the sense that every ministry and agency is established by law, whether as an act of the legislature or by delegated legislation. The law that creates the ministry or agency will usually set out its objectives and policies, defining the scope of, or setting limits on the exercise of authority. It may even provide guidelines relating to conduct and behaviour.

The legitimacy of authority is of critical importance because, in the tradition of liberal democracy, public administration is not an end of government, but a means of serving public interests. Hence, the manner in which the instrument or modality is used is of key importance. Moreover, citizens tend to feel that they have specific rights in relation to the public administration, including the right to be treated with due observance of the rule of law and the dispensation of justice; and, as a corollary, the right to appeal administrative decisions as a protection against capricious or arbitrary treatment. Thus, when an official or public servant is perceived to have exceeded his/her authority, the aggrieved citizen has recourse, through the courts, to seek redress. No such claim exists against the private firm. Once it has met the legal requirements for incorporation, and has registered its memorandum (or article of association), the private company, within this framework, is relatively free to pursue its corporate objectives and interpret subsequent actions as it sees fit, subject only to any legal interdiction or sanctions that might apply in the event of fraud, misrepresentation, or other malfeasance. Generally, however, relations between individuals and corporations fall within the purview of private law.

Impartiality

It is a fundamental axiom of the rule of law, and one of the most valued tenets of liberal democracy, that citizens should enjoy equality under the law, without discrimination. Paradoxically, this implies universal application of established precedent, thus leading to impartiality or detachment, a characteristic of large bureaucracies that is anathema to most citizens. Moreover, the best guarantee of impartiality is to minimize the need to exercise discretion by substituting for it written rules, guidelines, and manuals. In other words, the greater the degree of personal discretionary decision-making, the greater the probability of capricious judgement. To illustrate, the discretionary authority of customs officers to decide whose baggage may be searched or waved through untouched has been a source of aggravation to many international travellers, including returning residents of a country. Likewise, before the advent of radar enforcement of speed limits on public thoroughfares, the subjectivity apparent in the selection of drivers charged with speeding infractions created a constant source of friction between the police and the driving public. This was further compounded by other factors such as ethnicity, sex, or age of the driver. The move to sophisticated radar devices, the primary focus of which is the vehicle's speed and not the identity of the driver, represents the ultimate in impersonality and efficiency.

While equality of treatment may be assured by impartiality and observing the letter of the law, it may do so at the expense of the special case that is better served by equitable, not equal, treatment because equitability allows for greater personal discretion. It seems to be the predisposition of large-scale organizations to require staff at the lower levels of authority to adhere strictly to the letter of the law, leaving the application of the spirit of the law to those occupying higher supervisory or managerial positions, who are more closely involved with formulation of policy.

In comparison with public administration, where impartiality is imposed as a matter of duty, business administration is free to discriminate in favour of, and give preferential treatment to its clients. Indeed, the purpose of "product differentiation", advertising, and consumer motivation is to attract and retain clientele by making them feel that they are as "special" as the products and services they receive.

Legal and Financial Accountability

Legal Accountability

While legislators may pass laws outlining directions for public policy, it is in the process of implementation by the public service that policies become meaningful, and make their impact on individual groups, or society in general. The bulk of the regulations that give practical effect to enabling legislation is almost always subject to the decisive influences of bureaucrats by way of delegated power and authority. Moreover, these regulations are usually tabled in Parliament without debate or public scrutiny. Since the law comprises the chief source of authority at the operational level, there is always the question of legal obligations imposed both on the administrators of the law, and the general citizenship.

Let us examine, for instance, the matter of obtaining a driver's license. There are legal obligations to be discharged by the applicant: written, physical, and road tests; fee payments. Once these requirements have been properly met, the issuing authority has a legal obligation to issue the appropriate license; failure to do so would entitle the applicant to have recourse to legal action to compel issuance of the license. Therefore, the courts, to either require performance on the part of the administration, or to determine whether such decisions are within the jurisdiction granted by law, may review administrative decisions.

In the private sector, where the corporation is governed mainly by private law, there can hardly be any question of legal recourse by the client/customer, to determine whether an employee (or manager) of the company has gone beyond the prescribed limits of his/her authority. Typically, the legal obligation of the organization to the customer is restricted to the conditions attached to the product warranty; the issue of exceeding legal authority does not arise.

Financial Accountability

Control of the purse strings is a central tenet of the notion of Parliamentary supremacy in the tradition of the Westminster or British model of Parliamentary government. Accordingly, the Executive (Cabinet) and supporting bureaucracy may not have any money that has not been granted, or otherwise approved by, Parliament. Likewise, the Executive should make no expenditures beyond those specified and approved by Parliament.

In effect, therefore, since the public administration is financed by taxation, the most rigid accounting and accountability procedures are imposed. For example, when Parliament approves the annual budget, it approves allocation of funds to each ministry, department, or agency on the basis of line items or sub-heads and, in the event of changed circumstances, those funds cannot be transferred from one line item to another without first seeking the approval of the Ministry of Finance. The Ministry of Finance acts on behalf of the government through powers delegated to the Executive by Parliament. In Canada, the Financial Administration Act governs the expenditure process, and delegates to the Treasury Board, a statutory committee of the Cabinet, responsibility for overseeing the pre-budget estimates. The office of the Comptroller General is responsible for developing and instituting control procedures, and for ensuring that they are adopted in all government programs.

Finally, the Auditor General, an officer of Parliament who enjoys both general and specific tenure, is responsible for checking up on the financial expenditures in the public service; to access the government's financial records, make public any breaches or indiscretions, and confirm that money has been spent in accordance with the law. Since the 1970s, the audit role has been expanded to include "value for money" audit. However, it is fair to say that public administration may be differentiated from business administration by the extent to which the element of control is emphasized. Over two decades ago, in an effort to reform and restructure the civil service of a particular Commonwealth Caribbean nation, to encourage operational cost effectiveness and savings in expenditure, this writer recommended that, at the fiscal year-end, unused funds be carried forward and not allowed to lapse in accordance with existing financial regulations.[7] However, this ran counter to the notion of the supremacy of Parliament, wherein the Executive should have no money that is not provided or granted by Parliament. The result was the unseemly practice of ministries and departments rushing with great abandon to find ways of spending surplus funds, in order to support demands for the same level of funding in the succeeding financial year.

In the area of financial control and accountability, therefore, public administration can be sharply differentiated from business administration by the pre-eminence attached to the control and accountability functions. In business administration, on the other hand, management enjoys a much greater degree of flexibility in the allocation, deployment, and redeployment of financial resources and expenditure budgets. Reviews of budgeting, programs, and activities can be used as tools for planning, and to facilitate other line management functions.

Measuring Performance or Efficiency

In the private sector, profitability provides a convenient yardstick for measurement of performance and efficiency, however defined. It is an organizing principle for all activities. The company that successfully generates profit is presumptively deemed to be well managed and operating efficiently, since profit is a residual over and beyond costs. Conversely, failure to make a profit, or the threat of bankruptcy, constitutes poor and inefficient management. In both situations, the enforcers of accountability are primarily the owners or shareholders. Institutionally speaking, public administration does not exist to generate profit, but to provide a range of services, including those considered essential to societal well-being. Accordingly, levels of customer satisfaction within the general population become the performance yardstick of effective service delivery. For instance, when confronted with an epidemic outbreak of a potentially life-threatening disease, cost effectiveness becomes a secondary consideration in the face of a public health crisis. The same principle applies to national — and natural — disasters. Decisions based on cost effectiveness, or economic efficiency criteria, must also consider socio-political factors. A clear illustration of this dichotomy is seen in the proposed closing of a school because pupil enrolment has fallen below economically viable levels. Officials may be constrained by social considerations of the impact of school closure on individual families and the neighbourhood; the implications of relocating students, and the disruption of social fabric of the community, and so on. Furthermore, the goals of government, as determined through the representative process, may be in conflict, if not mutually exclusive; consider the trade-off between economic growth and full employment and price stability, or containment of inflation; or a balanced budget in a time of economic recession.

Personnel Administration and Control

In the private sector, the personnel function, or personnel administration (the authority to hire or fire, discipline, transfer, and promote) is derived from property rights, or ownership of the means of production. It is also an integrated process in the sense that the supervisory and management hierarchy has control over virtually all facets of the process. The only constraints on the process may be statutory provisions against various forms of discrimination deemed contrary to public policy, and grievance procedures contained in collective agreements that attempt to circumscribe the unilateral exercise of authority by the employer.

Public sector personnel administration and control are derived from the constitutional and legal authority of the state, and are based on the commitment to career merit service, alluded to earlier. This authority is also considerably more diffused than in the private sector. The personnel process and functions are fragmented, and shared between senior managers/administrators and central agencies. In Canada, at the federal level, the Treasury Board has responsibility for the system of industrial relations (including collective bargaining instituted under the PSSRA of 1967), as well as for classification of positions and pay, and developing standards of discipline, training, and development. The Public Service Commission, in turn, is responsible under the Public Service Employment Act of 1967 for staffing, promotion, and discipline, and for maintaining the integrity of the merit system. There is also cross delegation of functions between the two agencies.

Differences of Degree Rather than Kind — Size and Bureaucracy

Undoubtedly, the differences highlighted above in the areas of authority, impartiality, legal and financial accountability, measurement of performance, and personnel have been significant in shaping perceptions of public and business administration, as well as influencing operational norms and practices. However, one could argue that the differences are of degree rather than of kind, since the element of size coupled with the necessity of bureaucratic organization and hierarchical management, have tended to mitigate the differences.

It is instructive that in Great Britain, during the immediate post-World War II era when the British Labour Party's socialist led government nationalized a number of key privately owned industries, the most significant change was in the financial structure where the state became the shareholder. The functional tasks of management or administration remained the same. Planning, communication, supervision, public relations, and so forth, and the range of skills remained the same. Indeed, in most of the industrially advanced countries, both during and after World War II, there was a great deal of interchange of administrative and professional personnel between the private and public sectors, a practice that continues to the present day. The same observation applies to the United Nations' family of international development institutions, such as the World Bank and IMF. Size, therefore, rather than sector appears to be the decisive factor in determining organizational structure and method or style of operation. It seems appropriate, then, to explore briefly the concept of bureaucracy, especially since it will impinge on discussion of the concerted movement, beginning in the 1980s, to transform the character of traditional public administration by "reinventing government": applying the private sector "business model" to public enterprise, thereby laying the foundation for the "New Public Administration".

Bureaucracy

In popular imagery, "bureaucracy" has long been used as a derogatory term, associated with "red tape" or paper shuffling, impersonality and inefficiency. Bureaucrats have also been stereotyped as clock-watchers, inept, lazy, and insensitive to the needs of those who indirectly pay their salaries through taxation, and whom they are supposed to serve. These all represent expressive or behavioural traits. To organizational theorists, on the other hand, bureaucracy constitutes a form of organization that embodies certain objective, structural characteristics; as such, therefore, it constitutes a neutral or descriptive term. The underlying causal factor here is large size and resulting complexity, reflecting the need for division of labour, task differentiation, a chain of command, and a communication network. It becomes apparent, therefore, that bureaucracy means different things to different people, as evidenced by the radically differing perceptions outlined above. The possibility of reconciling them lies in recognizing that they represent two basic approaches to, and understanding of, the dynamics of bureaucracy.

Structural Approach to Bureaucracy

The "structural" approach was given its classical foundation by Max Weber (1864-1920), the founder of modern sociology. Drawing on personal experience, observation, and empirical research, Weber articulated an "ideal construct", or type of organization that is also referred to as a legal-rational social organization. His ideal abstraction of reality is similar to the economists' idealized model of the perfectly competitive market structure, or ideal model of market efficiency.

According to Weber, there are five organizational features of large-scale (bureaucratic) organizations: *Division of labour*, or clear out, and *official distribution of tasks* and duties that facilitate specialization. Since these first two features tend to pull organizations apart, there is the need for co-ordination, or the *principle of hierarchy* (Scalar principle), by virtue of which subordinates are under the control of superior ranks. Likewise, a consistent system of *impersonal legal rules* is conducive to the routinization of administrative tasks and the establishment of precedents, as well as the dispassionate performance of duties. To ensure professionalism, *staff* must be recruited on the basis of *qualifications and competence for office*.

The presence of all five features constituted, for Weber, a model of superior administrative efficiency. Weber also argued that market capitalism provided the impetus for the expansion of bureaucratic organization because of the emphasis placed, in economic theory and capitalism, on the rational allocation and utilization of resources, and self-interested maximization of profits. Thus defined, bureaucracy represented the highest form of organizational efficiency, and any departure there from would impair that efficiency in much the same way that economic theorists juxtaposed perfect and imperfect competition.

The Behavioural Approach to Bureaucracy

As political scientists and other behaviouralists began to explore the general applicability (and validity) of Weber's structural model, it became evident that while the structural features were indeed important, they were not, by themselves, sufficient for achieving maximum efficiency. Equally important were the ways in which the formal structure and rules of behaviour were complemented by informal structures of behaviour (for instance, the "grapevine"). Furthermore, it was unreasonable to expect employees to always behave rationally. In fact, it was often the exercise of human ingenuity and inventiveness that explored practical alternatives ("short cuts") or novel applications ("bending") of the rules, which contributed to the more effective attainment of organizational goals. Paradoxically, strict adherence to formal rules can be inimical to efficiency, as it produces "go slow", or "work to rule", a form of industrial action that can be highly disruptive and bring operations to a near halt; employers usually counter these measures with "lock-out", an appropriate response to what is, in effect, a partial withholding of labour.

Behavioural research identified certain traits as typical characteristics of bureaucrats, including objectivity, precision, consistency, and discretion (secrecy).[8] Similarly, psychologists began to focus on what appeared to be dysfunctional aspects of behaviour, more consistent with the popular negative stereotype of the bureaucrat: the inclination to "sanctify" rules, and treat them as ends in themselves rather than as means of achieving a desired end; administrative inertia and resistance to change, playing it safe by relying on precedent; "goal displacement", or moving away from original goals or purposes; "goal succession", or strategic expansion of activities ("empire building"); and obsession with job status, a function of hierarchical authority and communication structures.

The Process Approach to Bureaucracy

As is usually the case, where there are highly differentiated, polarized concepts, there will be attempts to blend them. In this case, synthesis was provided by the Process Approach associated with the work of Peter Blau,[9] who argued that, a priori, there is no ideal structure or pattern of behaviour that must be adhered to by all organizations. Rather, bureaucracy should be viewed as a form of organization, manifest in all sectors of the economy, that maximizes efficiency in administration: "an institutional method of social conduct in the interests of administrative efficiency". Both structural and behavioural characteristics are thus made variable, since the test for determining whether or not an organization is a bureaucracy is the extent to which it is achieving its purpose. The elements of structure and behaviour required to achieve objectives efficiently may shift from time to time and place to place.

This eclectic approach implied a refutation of the assumption first put forward by the Scientific Management School (or Classical School of Management) and its disciples, that there is one right organization, and one right way of motivating and managing people. Interestingly, there is now a plethora of different approaches to the study of management and administration: political scientists focus on the exercise of power, psychologists on interpersonal relations. Sociologists centre on group behaviour and human relations, cooperative social systems and organization theory, industrial engineers on socio-technical systems, and mathematicians on decision theory and management science; Neo Classical management theorists stress operational/functional tools and roles and, finally, there is the multi-disciplinary systems approach.[10]

It is of more than passing interest, therefore, that since the 1980s, there has been an ideologically inspired movement — the New Public Administration — to apply a single business or economic market model, and its theory of human motivation, to public administration. This is based on the premise that all areas of human endeavour, and spheres of activity, may be treated as markets and, hence, everything is for sale.

The New Public Administration
Contributing Factors

The rise of the so-called New Public Administration has to be appreciated as a reaction to developments beginning in the 1970s, and gathering momentum during the 1980s and 1990s. In addition to factors previously mentioned, they included: economic crises and scarcity of resources; the breakdown of societal consensus of the 1950s and 1960s; disenchantment with the role and ability of the state or government to deal effectively with socio-economic changes and social problems; revival and resurgence of laissez-faire and anti-state ideologies; and the emergence of a new economic and trading environment (globalization) characterized by global integration of production, and increased mobility and internationalization of financial capitalism.

The Rise and Fall of Keynesianism
— Keynesian Dominance 1950s to 1960s

The Great Depression challenged fundamental assumptions of Classical and Neo-Classical Economic Theory that had assumed the status of a secular dogma. It postulated the existence of a natural economic order adroitly driven by the "invisible hand", the laws and forces of the market — demand for, and supply of — goods and services that mirrored the pursuit of self-interest by consumers and producers. Market transactions were coordinated by the price mechanism that impersonally (efficiently) allocated resources, provided there was freedom of competition and no intrusive government intervention. In this scheme of things, national income represented a circular flow of income, where production generated the income used to purchase production, so that what was produced overall was purchased. The result was neither over production nor under consumption and, given the capacity of the economy to regulate itself, mass or involuntary unemployment was not a possibility. Then the unthinkable happened, the Great Depression of the 1930s, and with it the worldwide collapse of the capitalist or market economy, leading to millions of people being visibly and involuntarily unemployed. The conventional economic wisdom having been rendered ineffectual, it was replaced by the so-called Keynesian Revolution, or the "New Economics", which shifted focus to the general level of economic activity, and the importance of maintaining aggregate demand or purchasing power while sustaining total expenditures (the other side of the coin) at desired levels of employment.

The New Economics clearly encouraged a greatly expanded role for the state and its agent, government, in the economy; and, as anti-depression economics, Keynesianism rapidly gained universal acceptance. Compensatory fiscal and monetary politics provided the tools for government to fine tune the economy. The level of economic activity could be stimulated or restrained by public budgetary expenditures and incentives, affecting both public and private sectors; and by monetary policy to stimulate (or restrain) consumption and investment by manipulating the money supply and interest rates.

During the 1950s and 1960s, Keynesianism became the conventional wisdom and, very important, elevated the national annual budget to a position of central importance as the key to economic prosperity. Budget deficits, typically, were comparatively small, and manageable as a percentage of GNP. In western countries, conflict over budgets was muted by the Cold War, which provided an external focus for conflict. The politics of the budget was not central to the politics of governing, and budgeting tended to be regarded as a dull and technical exercise, the preoccupation of legislative committees and academics concerned about the necessity for, or implications of, "trade-offs". These two decades, then, represented the Golden Era of the positive state, witnessing a period of growth in size and influence of the public administration, abetted by the availability of fiscal resources. War battered and shattered economies of victors and vanquished alike were being constructed, certainly in western Europe and Japan, by the generosity of the American government under the Marshall Plan, named after the US Secretary of State, Dean Marshall.

Thus, the era of fiscal activism reflected a consensus among major economic stakeholders in the society, built around: the commitment to a mixed economy, full employment, unionization and collective bargaining; tripartite consultative mechanisms involving capital, labour, and government; and the core services of the rapidly ascending welfare state.[11]

The Era of Fiscal Crises and Resource Scarcity in the 1970s and 1980s

Inflationary pressures occasioned by the upward trend of prices appeared to be the most worrisome trend confronting public policy makers and business leaders during the golden era of Keynesianism. However, its persistence during the 1960s enabled believers in the free enterprise, free market system to sow the seeds of disenchantment with the interventionist role of the government and with the welfare state generally. The major centre providing intellectual and ideological support was the Chicago School of Economics, inspired by Professor Milton Friedman, and identified as the Monetarist School. Its central theme was that changes in the money supply caused changes in the level of business activity, and that inflation was always a monetary phenomenon. Fiscal policy that allowed the government to play an activist role in the economy was likely to impair the efficiency of the market or price mechanisms and, thus, result in inferior outcomes. Monetary policy, on the other hand, fell under the purview of autonomous central banks (or their equivalents), and their operations were more in accord with market forces.

The politicization of oil by OPEC in the early 1970s spurred dramatic price increases in oil and petroleum products in a short period of time. This produced worldwide external (or "supply") price shocks, leading to severe cost-induced inflation. The result was a phenomenon not anticipated by Keynesian economics, "stagflation", the co-existence of high rates of inflation with high rates of unemployment, which defied the Keynesian post-depression policy of compensating fiscal and market policy. Therefore, the 1970s bid farewell to the post-war commitment to full employment.[12]

By the 1980s, monetarism dominated and, with it, preoccupation with control of inflation; all levels of government budgeting became subject to the discipline of Central Bank management of monetary policy. Faced with a situation of mounting deficits and expanding long-term commitments for the core "safety net" programs of the welfare state (education, health care, income support, and so forth), governments were left with little budget flexibility. Thus, once shrouded from public scrutiny, and concern moved to the centre of representational and competitive politics, budget politics became a major battleground for partisan and ideological struggles over the appropriate role of government, and the scope of its intervention.

168

The Ideological Triumph of Neo-Conservatism
and Neo-Liberalism

Neo-Conservatism offered an alternative vision of economy, society, and government, based on a number of suppositions or shared views:

i. The welfare state had achieved its original purposes, but its programs were no longer affordable. Furthermore, its very existence was incompatible with economic progress in a capitalist, free market economy.

ii. The public sector had become too large, and too demanding of resources. It was crowding out the private sector, and needed to be reduced both in terms of sheer size and the scope of programs that pre-empted resources (e.g. core social services).

iii. The private sector was over-regulated, imposing unnecessary costs and impairing competitiveness; hence the need for "de-regulation".

iv. Removing state-owned enterprises from being competitors with the private sector, and limiting government primarily to a regulatory and facilitative role through privatization.

v. Espousing economic policies that stress the need for balancing budgets and effecting tax cuts.

Neo-liberalism goes beyond neo-conservatism in its new-found reverence for, and exaggerated belief in, the efficacy of the free market. Thus, virtually everything is for sale. All areas of human endeavour may be treated as markets, including political democracy. Consequently, the business model of the private sector can be applied to the civil bureaucracy, and services provided accordingly (reinventing government). Executive agencies or autonomous units can be deemed to enter into implied social contracts, to deliver services to "clients", not citizens (reinventing the personnel function).

One consequence of the neo-conservative and liberal focus on redefining and delimiting the role of the state has been an intensification of "bureaucratic bashing", an element of which may be attributed to political opportunism. Administrative reform in large-scale organizations tends to be very complex and time consuming, especially in the public sector. Some of the reasons have already been touched on in earlier comparisons of employment (career expectations) and operational differences between public and business administration. Candidates for political office often find it expedient, therefore, to portray themselves as agents of reform, promising to bring the bureaucracy to heel, and making it more responsive to the needs of citizens (namely, the electorate). Ironically, regulations crafted by bureaucrats are invariably to implement policies made by elected politicians.

The New Public Administration Paradigm
and its Compatibility with Popular Democracy

The theoretical and ideological rationale for applying the "business sector model" to the public sector is provided by Public Choice Theory, or the New Political Economy Approach. It draws on a number of assumptions borrowed from economic theory, namely that human conduct is motivated by the pursuit of self interest and the maximizing of that self interest; that the public interest is nothing more than the aggregation of private or individual interests; and that the public sector is merely another market. Thus, the rational self interest generally attributed to business leaders, executives, and consumers may also be extended to politicians, bureaucrats, and citizens. Similarly, the operational norm of profit maximization in the private sector has its counterpart in the politicians' goal of re-election, and, for the bureaucrats, budget minimization to foster growth and/or empire building.

It stands to reason, then, that the notion of public interest clouds the issue and must be rejected. The public service bureaucracy has traditionally been envisaged as an instrument for social betterment; but in reality, the public sector is nothing more than an alternative market that ends up distorting private economic behaviour, reducing individual freedom, and impeding economic efficiency. This occurs because government runs contrary to the dominant human motivation of self-interest, resulting in a three-way tug-of-war between the demands of special interest groups (privileged political and bureaucratic elite), business interests (including unionized workers), and the general public; all of whom are seeking to use the instrumentality of the state to further the purposes of self-interest. Once government becomes larger and more powerful, individuals and groups use it to gain advantage over others. The economic efficiency of government is thus reinforced by rent seeking, monopolistic behaviour.

The aim of the New Public Administration is, therefore, to make the public service into an efficient instrument for implementation. This requires reverting to the traditional doctrine of neutrality, the first premise of which is the separation or dichotomy between policy formation and policy execution. Policy, or deciding what has to be done, falls within the realm of politics, and is thus the prerogative of the legislators and the political executive, while getting things done falls within the realm of administration and is, thus, the responsibility of administrators or public servants. It is worth reiterating that, in reality, political executives and senior public service administrators serve jointly as co-policy makers and co-administrators, and that the presumed dichotomy has long ceased to be tenable.[13]

The reasoning behind the belated attempt to revive the doctrine of separation of politics and administration is that public administrations are unelected, and need to be held more directly responsible for providing efficient government. Again, there is an analogy to the private sector, where business executives are forced by competitive market forces, as well as the pressure of shareholders and customers, to adopt sound business practices. The argument that public service administrators face differing expectations from citizens is dismissed as an excuse of incompetent bureaucrats. Citizens, as consumers, are entitled to expect the same efficient provision of services as their counterparts in the private sector.

The New Public Administration as a Worldwide Phenomenon

With its rallying clichés, "Reinventing Government" and "Reinventing the Personnel Function", the New Public Administration has assumed the proportions of an international movement. One reason is that the Commonwealth of Nations, the family/club made up of the UK, as the former imperial power, the older dominions, Australia, Canada, and New Zealand, as well as former colonies in Africa, Asia, and the Caribbean (which achieved political independence in the post-World War II era), has served as a vehicle for diffusion of the new paradigm. Not only is there the legacy of shared Parliamentary and Administrative systems, but the wealthier members of the commonwealth, led by the UK, have been willing to provide financial and technical assistance in support of administrative reform.

The pioneer, or front runner, of the privatized model was New Zealand which, under a conservative political administration, responded to the challenge of fiscal limitations and the new international economic movement by carrying through radical and extensive reforms to produce the most advanced, and apparently successful, prototype. However, it should be noted that more recently, the return to office of a more social welfare minded political administration has led to some reversal of the process of reform.

The preferred structure is the Executive Agency (EA), a form of corporatism that is deemed to have two advantages. First, it serves to clarify and provide an organizational solution to a major shortcoming of the Doctrine of Neutrality: namely, the blurring of the differentiation between policy formation, primarily the responsibility of politicians, and policy execution, the primary responsibility of public servants.

Second, it also allows for differentiation and separation of government's role of funder, purchaser and provider of services to "clients", and for new structures and modalities for delivery of public goods and services, including: new arm's length contractual arrangements; competition between service providers, both within the public sector and between public and private sectors; full cost pricing systems that reflect efficient allocation and utilization of resources; and "bench marking", or the addition of "best practices" developed within the public sector, or drawn from the private sector.

This privatized or business model of the New Public Administration has been problematic in that it has raised, and left unanswered, as many questions and issues as it has sought to resolve. For instance, is there an interchangeability of the private sector and public sector ethos? In the UK, the so-called "New Labour Party" government led by Prime Minister Tony Blair has tried to address this issue by linking the privatized model to broader "democratic renewal", the aim of which is to "create a distinctive public service management philosophy which adopts management techniques from the private sector, while enforcing long standing public service values". But who will decide what the best management techniques are in the private sector, and by what criteria, and whose standards; and what is the basis of the expectations that the adoption of private sector values and operating norms will enhance long standing public service values? Both these issues, among others, will be addressed in

171

the ensuing discussion of whether, and to what extent, the entrepreneurial or business model is compatible, or reconcilable, with the tenets of democratic government.

The Privatized or Entrepreneurial Model of Public Administration and Issues of Democratic Accountability

Managerial Authority

The main objective of the restructuring, or decentralization of the personnel function is to provide greater management autonomy or discretion. This typically involves transferring the personnel functions traditionally vested in the Public Service Commissions (PSC) to administrative heads, variously designated Deputy Minister in Canada, and Permanent Secretary and/or Director General in the British Westminster tradition. Where the PSC is constitutionally entrenched, as is typically the case in the post World War II Independence Constitution of former British colonies, the delegation of the personnel functions usually requires the issuing of Public Service Regulations in the name of the formal Head of State, the Governor General. It also may involve, as is the case in Jamaica, the largest of the island states in the Commonwealth Caribbean, the signing of an Accountability Agreement between the Administrative Head and the PSC to enhance managerial flexibility. It does so by conferring the power: to recruit and dismiss staff, select staff for training and development, assign, transfer and promote staff on the basis of performance evaluation and incentives; to handle grievances and disciplinary procedures; and to impose appropriate penalties for infractions. The traditional security of tenure of employment is also subordinated to contractually fixed, but renewable terms of employment.

Entrepreneurial Vision of the Future

In the Jamaican example cited above, the PSC also indicated that the signing of the agreement was in keeping with the wider public sector reform agenda, which is geared primarily towards improving public service delivery to clients/customers. Moreover, by virtue of being empowered as entrepreneurial managers, administrative heads or Chief Executive Officers, consistent with their mandate (statement of objectives) are expected to generate extra revenues by user and other fees that the market can bear, so as to generate surpluses. In other words, the adoption of the entrepreneurial role carries with it the added responsibility of trying to generate new sources of revenue for financing existing services, or providing new services to pay for themselves. In effect, therefore, the Public Service Executive Manager more closely approximates an independent contractor, separated from the public and concerned more about money and freedom to exercise maximum discretion in the determination of priorities of expenditures. The notion that citizens can be regarded and treated as clients or customers is at odds with the democratic theory of government. The customers in the private sector tend to respond to a business agenda determined by others, and their preferences are likely to be ascertained by market surveys prepared at the discretion, and for internal purposes, of management. In this scenario, the values of citizenship are secondary, whereas it is a fundamental premise of political democracy that citizens should have a say, on the basis of majority determination, as to what services should be provided and in what manner. Put another way, the focus of the entrepreneurial approach, or managerialism, is aimed at creating a happy or satisfied customer, not an informed and involved citizen. The reality is that the customer is not a building block or foundation of democratic government. On the other hand, citizenship derives from mandatory membership in a nation, or its subsets — communities, towns, cities, and states or provinces — and carries with it certain inescapable obligations, most notably the right of participation if one is so inclined. As has been observed, "Governments that buy too easily into the idea that customers are a higher form of life than citizens risk losing the participation of taxpayers as partners".[14]

The differentiation of the quality of service offered on the basis of differential fees is even more problematic. A case in point, again based on the Jamaican experience, is a two-tiered fee structure for the issuing of passports, where the usual time delivery may be reduced from weeks to a few days, by the payment of a substantially higher fee. This practice leads inevitably to differentiation of citizens and fragmentation of society on the basis of ability to pay. In this case, it is manifest in a country where there is general recognition and admission at all levels of leadership in the economy and society; that there are great disparities in income; of the importance the provision of basic living necessities; and in the importance of the availability and delivery of services to various segments of the society, including the critical area of the administration of justice.

Equality of treatment, as noted earlier, is a fundamental value of liberal democracy, and this precludes the citizen from being treated as a customer, and made subject to the exercise of managerial discretion. It cannot be left, for instance, to entrepreneurial initiative or direction to decide that one prisoner may be granted parole and another is denied. Such determination should be made on the basis of "due process" and "objective evidence". If taken to its logical conclusion, the adoption of the private sector orientation would make government agencies more responsive to their clients/customers, but denude them of their legitimacy as public institutions. The public sector values of integrity, transparency, and equality of access and treatment have external or social costs in that they require a public administration based on due process, rules and regulations, which slow things down, especially since the public sectors are the cornerstone of social life.

The British experience is instructive. Between 1984 and 1994, nearly eighty percent of civil servants moved from central departments to semi-autonomous agencies. Concern, previously unknown, about the preservation of traditional public service values of probity and dedication to the public led to the establishment in 1994 of a UK Committee on Standards in Public Life under the chairmanship of Lord Nolan. To ensure just and honest government, the Committee recommended seven principles of public service, including selflessness, integrity, objectivity, accountability, openness, honesty, and leadership. One may question, however, the presumption that public office holders should take decisions solely in terms of devotion to public service and the public interest, when the premise is that a collective public interest does not exist, but rather atomized individuals seeking each one opportunistically, to maximize individual self interest or satisfaction.

Deregulation — The "Common Sense Revolution"

Along with entrepreneurship, decentralization and customer orientation, deregulation (the removal of government controls on market activities) is one of the core ideas of re-inventing government. Indeed, the neo-conservative agenda successfully pursued in the province of Ontario since the mid 1990s purported to be the "Common Sense Revolution", a terminology apparently borrowed from the United States. Proponents of the Common Sense approach to deregulation in the USA[15] have argued that legal regulation in the country has achieved the worst of both worlds, in that it goes so far to achieve so little. The greater the attempt to make rules more precise, the greater the loopholes created. The shortcomings of over-regulation can be overcome by the application of common sense, by reinventing the personnel function and the adoption of managerialism, or business ideology and practices.

There is no denying that the multiplicity of regulations in the public sector has contributed to the popular perception that public service systems are inefficient and insensitive. The question, however, is whether Common Sense by itself provides sufficient reason to regulate or deregulate. The point made by leading American scholars[16] is that government structures and processes were not intended to be efficient but, rather, to protect the rights of citizens, and to guarantee equality of treatment. Moreover, the value of accountability on the part of the public services to elected leaders ranks higher than that placed on efficient low-cost provision or delivery of services. Regulations are themselves the product of contradictions inherent in the democratic process, in that they are usually arrived at by negotiation and compromise. For instance, procurement rules that require all contractors be given equal opportunity to bid on every project are probably not the most efficient way of getting the job done. But efficiency is merely one of many public values and imperatives that have to be balanced. The call for deregulation in the final analysis must, therefore, be seen as part of a political and economic strategy that includes other items on the anti-government, pro-free market movement. "Cost-benefit analysis attempts to bring into the price-auction system, things that most people think should not be for sale".[17]

One final observation: as long as the "New Public Administration", or the privatized public sector model, remains part of the prevailing or conventional wisdom, it will have the effect (which can sometimes be a positive one) of forcing greater attention to be paid to performance motivated administration and the integration of more workable economic concepts into the traditional body of public administration and administrative theory.

Notes

1. David Easton, *The Political System*, 1960. p. 129
2. Kenneth Dolbeare & Murray Edelman, *American Politics*, 1985
3. Peter Drucker, *Management Challenges for the 21st Century*, 1999
4. *Ibid.*
5. For fuller discussion of this and other related factors, see Chapter 1, pp. 4–53, *Liberal Democracy and Its Underpinnings*
6. For extended discussion of the functions and roles of the legislature, political executive, public service, and their inter-relations, see Chapter 8, pp. 131–151 *Understanding Canadian Parliamentary Government*
7. The author, Dr. George E. Eaton, as Administrative Head of the Central Personnel Ministry and Head of the civil service undertook this initiative while on extended leave of absence.
8. Carl Friedrich, *Constitutional Government and Democracy 2nd ed. N.Y, Boston Ginn, 1952*
9. Peter Blau, and Meyer, M., *Bureaucracy in Modern Society 2nd ed. Random House 1971*
10. H. Koontz, C. O'Donnell, H. Walrick, *Essentials of Management*, 3rd edition, McGraw-Hill Book Co., p.14-36
11. For more background information see Chapter 1, pp. 4–53, *Liberal Democracy and Its Underpinnings*
12. For a more technical discussion see Chapter 1, pp. 4–53, *Liberal Democracy and Its Underpinnings*
13. *Ibid.*
14. For discussion of the conditions of the doctrines of neutrality, see Chapter 8, pp. 131–151, *Understanding Canadian Parliamentary Government*
15. Cited and attributed to K. Barrett, and R. Greene, *Consumer Disorientation* Governing 11 in Peter Kobrak, *The Political Environment of Public Management*, 2nd edition, Longmans, 2002
16. P.K. Howard, *The Health of Common Sense: How Law is Suffocating America*. Reviewed by Joseph A. Repato in Peter Kobrak, *The Political Environment of Public Management* , 2nd edition, Longmans, 2002 pp. 10–20
17. *Ibid.*
18. R. Kuttner, *Everything Is For Sale*, N.Y., Knopf, 1997 p. 300

The Case for a "Triple E" Senate

Howard McConnell

Canada is demographically, sociologically, and in the unevenness of distribution of its natural resources, one of the most disparate federations on the globe. It is a country riven at times with regional conflicts. No matter what political party is in power federally, there are regional issues on which a strong central Canadian majority in the lower house can dictate policy to the peripheries. The regions, whether they be in the east, west, or north, can be overridden with relative impunity because their comparatively sparse population gives them scant weight in a House of Commons dominated by Ontario and Quebec. This has engendered much frustration, and could lead to disunity, since the outlying provinces and territories lack a countervailing voice, such as exists in the American and Australian senates, in our central parliamentary institution. It will be argued here that the present moribund Senate should be replaced by an elected Senate, with effective powers, in which, as in the US and Australia, the constituent units would possess equal representation. While such a revised body would have a special responsibility to articulate provincial and regional concerns there are constitutional safeguards which would still maintain much of the House of Commons' present dominance in Parliament.

---

1 From *Queen's Quarterly 95(3), (Autumn 1988)*: pp. 683–698. Reproduced with permission.

176

A "Triple E" senate refers to a reformed upper house which is "equal, elected, and effective," having the same number of senators from each province, elected by the provincial electorates, and possessing effective legislative powers to offset, at least temporarily, initiatives by the House of Commons deemed harmful to the provinces or regions. It seeks to provide a countervailing regional voice in a lower house having 282 members, 180 of which (or just under 2/3 of the total) represent the two large central provinces.

If the upper houses in the federal systems bearing the closest resemblance to Canada are examined, it will be seen that they play a far more vigorous role in representing local interests than does the Canadian Senate.

In the US there was extensive debate between the large and the smaller states at the Philadelphia convention in 1787 on the rival principles for apportioning seats in the Senate.[1] It was agreed there that seats should be allocated proportionally on the basis of population in the House of Representatives, and there were some who favoured the same method of distribution of seats in the upper house. An unsuccessful motion by Charles Pinckney of South Carolina and James Wilson of Pennsylvania would have provided for a variable number of senators for the states, the number depending on approximate population density, with Rhode Island having one, New York three, and Virginia five, and the other states being ranged in population groupings with from one to five senators. Population having been used as the distributive principle in the lower house, however, the smaller states were adamant that equality should be the rule in the Senate. "The smaller states can never give up their equality," said Jonathan Dayton of New Jersey. "For myself, I would in no event yield that security for our rights"; a colleague, Roger Sherman of Connecticut, stressed that it was not solely the interest of the small states that was at stake; all states should be represented on an equal basis in the upper chamber. That chamber should reflect the interests of all state governments. (Peters 126)

James Madison, one of the erudite expositors of the ideas underlying the American Constitution, describes the outcome in *Federalist* No. 39:

> The House of Representatives will derive its powers from the people of America; and the people will be represented in the same proportion and on the same principle as they are in the legislature of a particular state, so far the government is *national* not *Federal*. The Senate, on the other hand, will derive its powers from the states as political and co-equal societies; and these will be represented on the principle of equality in the Senate.... So far the government is *Federal* not national. (244)

The resulting legislative system, accordingly, united the national and the federal governmental principles. The lower house represented the people and the upper house the states. Either principle without the other would result in a perversion of federalism, since in a legislative body organized according to population alone there would be no assurance that imperilled regional or state interests — which might not much preoccupy that lower house since it represents the "people" — would be adequately taken into account. The loose coalition or "league" of states represented by the Articles of Confederation (1781–89), on the other hand, with its excessive dependence by Congress on the states both for funds and the execution of its decrees, had little real contact with the citizenry. It erred too much in the other direction. For true federalism, on the Madisonian model, the people should be represented according to population in the lower house and the states, or local units, on the basis of equality in the Senate. Although the two chambers would respond to the same issues, they would take different constituencies into account in making laws and policies, and the interests that they respectively represent, as will be argued later, must both find effective expression if the central legislative organ of the federation is to respond both to popular and to regional concerns.

The same contention between states' rights and centralized authority helped to shape the Australian Senate, with Sir John Cockburn of South Australia declaiming at the 1891 Convention:

> We know that the tendency is always to the centre, that the central authority constitutes a vortex which draws power to itself. Therefore, all the buttresses and all the ties should be the other way, to enable the States to withstand the destruction of their powers by such absorption.... Government at a central and distant point can never be government by the people, and may be just as crushing a tyranny under republican or commonwealth forms as under the most absolute monarchy. (Cockburn 155, 157)

The balancing of central and regional concerns, again, was an influential factor in the design of the Australian upper house. As L.F. Crisp states in his work, *The Parliamentary Government of the Commonwealth of Australia*, "Central to the position of the 'States' Rights' spokesmen was their idea of the constitution of the Senate. It must, they urged, be founded alike in equal representation of the States and in equality of status with the Lower House in respect of powers over all classes of legislation"(26). Although the Australian Senate has sometimes been criticized for not being sufficiently energetic, when required to do so it has played a significant role as a guardian of local interests. To give just two examples, in 1939 Western Australian senators helped to defeat a gold-tax bill which in their judgement would have retarded the expansion of the gold-mining industry in their state. A later, more acceptable bill, at a reduced tax rate, was subsequently passed. In 1958 Southern Australian senators ensured over strong opposition that their state would get an equitable share of River Murray water for a hydroelectric project which drew largely from their local resources (*Australian Senate* 5).

A common problem mentioned by Crisp is that an over-zealous and encroaching executive power will sometimes virtually pre-empt policy formulation or effective debate by taking initiatives that present Parliament with a *fait accompli*. For example, the Australian Commonwealth government made decisions at the 1931 Ottawa Economic Conference intimately affecting the economic interests and industries of Australian states without consulting them. Neither was there effective debate by the Senate at Canberra of the issues raised at the Conference (Crisp 189). While the Senate cannot really be a substitute for inter-governmental consultation, in areas of central-regional conflict it could perform a more effective role in putting forward provincial or regional points of view.

From its inception in 1867, the Canadian Senate possessed only very modest powers; it did not, as did its American and Australian parallels, represent the constituent federal units equally, nor was it effective, having no popular constituency to appeal to; in any confrontation with the elected lower house it could do little more than delay unwanted initiatives for a limited time. Its weakness arose not through inadvertence but by design. A noted Canadian historian has summed up well the purpose of the Senate as envisaged by the Fathers of Confederation:

> Though the designers at Quebec turned naturally to the United States to study federalism in North America, they did so largely to see what to modify or avoid. The Canadian Senate, for example, had only the same name as the powerful American chamber. As an upper house on the British parliamentary model it was not meant to be more than a revising body, or a brake on the House of Commons. Therefore it was deliberately made an appointed house, since an elected Senate might prove too popular and too powerful, and be able to block the will of the House of Commons. The Canadian Senate was really the old British colonial legislative council under a new name. Besides, it did not represent separate provinces or states, as in the American system, but sections; Ontario and Quebec each had twenty-four members, and Nova Scotia and New Brunswick twenty-four together. This 'section' principle was continued as new provinces were added to the Dominion. (Careless 256–57)

The present complement of 104 senators was made up by adding a new "western section" of 24 senators to the other three in 1915, composed by six senators from each of the four western provinces (Constitution Act, 1915), six more for Newfoundland on its admission to Canada in 1949 (Constitution Act, 1949), and one each for the Northwest Territories and the Yukon in 1975 (Constitution Act, 1975)

As with the case of the colonial legislative councils to which Careless rightly compares the Canadian Senate, appointments to the upper house are the virtually unfettered gift of the incumbent prime minister. Those to whom political debts are owed have a greater claim on the appointing authority's beneficence than those who have achieved distinction in various areas of national life. In Canada where, historically, there have been long periods of one-party dominance, of the Conservatives in the nineteenth century and the Liberals in the twentieth, this can lead at times to disconcerting political imbalances. One of the most glaring examples of this trend occurred in 1955 when, after 20 uninterrupted years of Liberal federal power, a minuscule Conservative opposition of seven senators faced 75 Liberals in the then 102-seat Senate. Even so, Prime Minister Louis St Laurent refused either to relinquish such an important source of patronage or to make new appointments as vacancies arose, leaving a large number of seats to be filled in 1957 when the Conservatives, after 22 years in the wilderness, unexpectedly achieved power under John Diefenbaker (McConnell 68).

It was episodes like the above, along with the moribund nature of the institution, which led to various reform proposals for what most observers saw as a very imperfectly constituted legislative chamber with little real power.

One of the most recent reform proposals emerged in the twilight days of the second Trudeau administration in 1984, when a joint Senate and House of Commons committee recommended the future election of senators, representing major "regions" of the country as well as minority groups (Canada Special Joint Committee). The present chamber would be expanded to 144 seats to provide additional representation for the smaller Atlantic and western provinces. One-third of the reconstituted House would be elected at two-year intervals. Under the proposal, Ontario and Quebec would each retain its present complement of 24 senators, while the four western provinces would be enlarged from six to 12 each, with Newfoundland, Nova Scotia, and New Brunswick also being increased to 12 and Prince Edward Island advancing from four to six. Instead of their single senator, as at present, the Yukon would receive two and the Northwest Territories four.

Any such uneven allocation of seats to the various provinces and territories raises important issues. If relative population density is the criterion, why should British Columbia, with three times, or Alberta with twice Saskatchewan and Manitoba's population, receive the same number of seats? Or why should British Columbia, with more than 20 times Prince Edward Island's population, receive only twice the number of the island province's contingent? Some areas of the country are growing relatively more rapidly than the others, and there are indications that others are stagnant or could even be in decline. Substantial population shifts are bound to take place in future. If we assign such uneven numbers, it is inevitable that further reallocations will be needed at indefinite intervals in the future. If, a hundred years hence, the four western provinces acquired a greater population than central Canada, would the latter region agree to giving a preponderance of senators to the West? Would not the better course be to assign all the provinces an equal quotient of seats, since population density is *already* taken into account in the lower house, and the upper house should give the provinces equal representation so that valid provincial concerns will not simply be overwhelmed by numbers. By definition, the Territories have a subordinate constitutional status, and some numerical discrimination against them is justified until they become provinces.

Relative population disparities among the varied constituent units have not been an impediment to equal representation in the American or Australian senates. In fact, as mentioned above, the reason for equal representation is to forestall undue domination of the lesser-populated peripheries by the centre. If the examples of Wyoming or Alaska are taken in the US, for example, the populous state of California has more than 50 times the population of either, yet each of these three states has the same entitlement to two members in the US Senate. While population disparities in Australia are not so great, the small state of Tasmania, with about one-tenth the population of New South Wales, has the identical representation, ten senators, as the other five states of the Australian Commonwealth.

Another contentious feature of the 1984 reform proposal is the limitation of senators to a single nine-year term, with incumbents not being eligible for a second term. The purpose of creating a single relatively longer term was evidently to make the elected Senate a genuinely independent body by relieving its members of some of the political pressures and anxieties contingent on the necessity of presenting themselves for periodic re-election, pressures that would be felt particularly towards the end of their terms. The undesirable concomitant of such a proposal, however, would be that the valuable fund of accumulated experience of long-serving members in other upper houses (one thinks of Senators Fulbright or Goldwater in the US or Lords Beaverbrook or Shinwell in Britain) would be lost in the Canadian upper house. Independence could be better achieved by reconstituting the upper house on different lines, with a distinct mandate, which would create a dynamic interaction between the two chambers: former Prime Minister Pierre Trudeau's concept of the "counterweight" comes to mind here. There would arise a creative interplay between two legislative bodies each considering the same laws and policies, but with the needs of different constituencies in view. Because of party discipline, lack of political legitimacy and effective power, the present Senate cannot perform such a role. It is as moribund and stagnant as a "federal" chamber as it is in other respects.

Another reform plan with some of the same undesirable features was Trudeau's proposal, in Bill C–60 (Constitutional Amendment Bill), advanced in the spring of 1978, to establish a new upper house along lines radically different from the present Senate. Rather than the existing 104-member Senate appointed by the governor-general on the recommendation of the prime minister, a 118-member House of Federation was to be elected indirectly, with half of its membership being contingent, respectively, on the relative proportion of votes received by the various parties in the last preceding elections for the provincial legislatures and the House of Commons. With each successive such election, consequently, the composition of the new upper house would undergo a shift. While there would be some increase in seats for the Atlantic Provinces and the West in the new body, with Ontario and Quebec retaining their present numbers, representation would still be unequal. The new chamber would accede to such novel functions as confirming federally-appointed judges and senior federal executive appointees. It would also act as a watch-dog of French-English linguistic rights, with a double majority of English- and French-speaking senators (federators?), constituted for this purpose as separate "colleges," so to speak, being required to approve basic changes in language laws.

Some critics, and notably William Lederman of Queen's University law school, strongly contested Trudeau's contention that Parliament acting by itself possessed constitutional jurisdiction to reform the upper chamber. The prime minister's assumption appeared to be that Parliament as a whole was a *national* legislature: if the provinces could unilaterally reform provincial legislatures (e.g., Premier Jean-Jacques Bertrand's abolition of the Quebec legislative council on 31 December 1968), then Parliament, by a simple bill, could reconstitute the Senate into a House of the Federation. There was no need, indeed, for prior provincial consent to a constitutional amendment for that purpose. The doubts of experts like Lederman, however, prompted Trudeau to initiate a constitutional reference to the Supreme Court to determine whether Parliament possessed the challenged jurisdiction. The tribunal held unanimously against the prime minister's proposal (Authority of Parliament). One of the main factors persuading the Court against the initiative was the compelling argument that the Senate, as originally conceived, was designed expressly to protect sectional or provincial interests[2] and Bill C–60 was attempting fundamentally to alter the character of the upper house without seeking provincial consent.

The federal government did not dispute that the historical intention was to create an upper chamber representing local interests, but it contended that the present Senate no longer performed such a task. It had been superseded long ago as a guardian of provincial or regional interests by a "federalized" cabinet, the members of which were drawn from every province in the country. The fact, nevertheless, that the Supreme Court had so emphatically rejected the logic underlying the government's argument (which, it might be added, was still valid in an empirical if not in a strictly constitutional sense) dramatically emphasized the need for genuine reform of the upper house so that the reconstituted body could more effectively discharge its original constitutional mandate.

But what are the types of controversies which so imperatively demand such an alteration of the upper house? There are significant provincial and regional issues with respect to which the lack of an appropriate forum places the smaller provinces, particularly, but all provinces potentially, at a decided disadvantage. For example, take the controversy in October 1986 between Manitoba and the federal government about the awarding of the CF–18 maintenance contract to Canadair of Montreal rather than to Bristol Aerospace of Winnipeg. According to documentation later obtained by the *Globe and Mail* under the Access to Information Act ("Taken for a Ride"; York)[3] the awarding of the contract to the Quebec firm, as determined by the federal government's own experts, "would cost 13 percent more in the first four years of the contract and 1.8 percent more each year after that. While the Canadair bid was technically acceptable, the advisers preferred the Bristol bid 'based on a significantly higher technical assessment'" ("Taken for a Ride"). Although not everything was revealed about the award of the contract to Canadair, enough was known at the time for the matter to be debated vigorously in a chamber more aptly designed to ventilate regional grievances. In the lower house, with its substantial central Canadian majority, the issue did not provoke the intense debate it should have. In all frankness, the leaders of opposition parties were just as much aware as was the prime minister that Quebec had 75 seats in the House of Commons as compared to Manitoba's 14, and did not want considerations of equity to interfere inordinately with partisan electoral prospects in the coming general election. From a realistic standpoint, as practical politicians, they could hardly be censured for such an assessment, especially when Quebec voters were in a volatile mood in the wake of the September 1984 federal election.

Had there been an independent, elected senate, where each province had equal representation, and minority viewpoints would not have been inundated by sheer force of numbers, such regional issues could have been more rationally dissected and debated. Senators who owed their seats not to one or another prime minister, but to the electorate in their respective provinces, could have debated such matters with greater vigour and independence, and without the inhibitions imposed in the lower house by party discipline. Such a body could act as a real brake on possible excesses by the dominant lower chamber, balancing provincial and regional requirements against the unconstrained "popular will" to which the more *jacobin* House of Commons is designed to give expression. In such a reconstituted Parliament, whenever the regions or provinces lost out, as they not infrequently would, they would at least be cognizant that their viewpoints had been articulated and duly weighed before being rejected.

It is not merely the smaller provinces, however, which would benefit from such a reconstituted senate. Sometimes, a province such as Ontario finds itself in disagreement with the other provinces on matters of high provincial interest. In 1980–81 during the acerbic national debate over the patriation of the Constitution and the adoption of the Charter, Ontario and New Brunswick found themselves isolated from the rest of the provinces in their support of Trudeau's unilateral constitutional initiative. Much of the rancour and bitterness that surrounded that incendiary debate might have been avoided were it not for the strong perception, at least until the Supreme Court's cautionary decision in September 1981 (Reference re Amendment), that the ultimate fate of patriation would be determined by a centralist-dominated House of Commons in which there was no authentic provincial presence. Everybody expected, under current constitutional arrangements, that the Senate would more or less uncritically follow the lead of the lower chamber, as indeed it did. This would not have happened, of course, in a truly "federal" senate with eight provinces opposing, and only two supporting, Trudeau's original project. Some might say that in such a new institutional framework we still might not have patriation or the Charter. More likely, we would probably have achieved both, but perhaps in an altered form, and arguably with greater political legitimacy. It is also likely that Quebec, the shunned partner, would not have been subject to a midnight deal consummated in a kitchen behind her back. It would have been, rather, a continuing party to the negotiations and the outcome, and we would, mercifully, never have heard of the Meech Lake Accord. Instead of this, the perception that parliament was a monolithic entity with a single corporate will produced a mood of exasperation in those who questioned either the process or the substance of what our prime minister was doing.

More recently, Premier David Peterson of Ontario has diverged from a large number of his fellow premiers in opposing the US-Canada free trade pact. As Canada's richest and most industrialized province, Ontario assuredly has a high stake in the economic consequences of the deal, and could be severely hurt by a bad result. But where is the parliamentary forum where the distinctive Ontario point of view, rather than that of national party leaders, can be put forward? There is, of course, no such forum. What is needed is a new upper house where issues dividing the regions and the centre can be resolved. When it comes to matters of detail, for example, Peterson challenges the mandate of Ottawa, under the free trade agreement, to dictate the prices of imported wines on the shelves of his province's liquor stores. Citing the Privy Council's 1881 ruling on trade and commerce (Citizens Insurance), and its 1937 decision in the International Labour Organization (ILO) case on the treaty-implementing power (Labour Conventions), Donald S. Macdonald, a strong proponent of free trade, puts the federal argument in its most uncompromising form: "A federal statute, therefore, assuring the nationals of a foreign state freedom from discriminatory trade barriers would take precedence over provincial trade restrictions, and so it should" (Letter). Would Ontario's present discretionary legal competence to set prices for wine in its liquor stores constitute a "discriminatory trade barrier?" How far would the trade pact go, without a further constitutional amendment, to empower Ottawa to regulate matters formerly considered as falling under provincial jurisdiction? Surely, local jurisdiction over wine pricing, local marketing, and consumer protection, falling as they do under the provincial head of "property and civil rights in the province" (Constitution Act, 1867), would not be transferred to federal jurisdiction by the trade pact alone? Does the 1937 ILO case (Labour Conventions) *really* support Macdonald's (or the federal government's) position? Should not such issues profitably be debated in a reformed upper house? It is of some interest that a closely related issue was raised in the US Senate by Senate Bricker in 1954, when he proposed a constitutional amendment which would have allowed treaties to become effective only through legislation valid in the absence of the treaty (Corwin 133) (which is, *pace* Macdonald, the present Canadian position). The fact that Bricker's proposal ultimately failed to attain the required two-thirds majority by only one vote is not the point; the point is that it was possible to debate fully in the American Senate this issue of primary importance to the federal system and to bring it to a resolution after canvassing both the national and the local implications of the contested constitutional jurisdictions. With members of the Canadian Senate (disregarding some untypical recent exceptions) (Lynch) deferring excessively to their national leaders in the lower chamber, either through political impotence or the strong tradition of party discipline, the Senate too often is simply a weak echo of what happens in the other place. What is needed, again, is a reconstituted second chamber reflecting provincial concerns with greater authenticity, with a mandate from provincial electors which would give its members greater independence.

Other specific contemporary issues which have occasioned sharp federal-provincial discord have been numerous and often protracted. Among such disputes was the recent disagreement between Alberta and Ottawa over the taxation and regulation of energy; the controversies between British Columbia and Ottawa, and between Newfoundland (and some other Atlantic provinces) and Ottawa, over the ownership and control of mineral rights in the sub-soil under territorial waters and in the adjacent continental shelf; the dispute between Saskatchewan and the federal government over the rescinding of the "Crow rate" for hauling grain, a dispute, indeed, with large ramifications for all of western Canada; the disputes between provinces on both coasts and Ottawa over the fisheries; the disputes between New Brunswick and, incipiently, Manitoba, with the federal government and other provinces over the ratification of the Meech Lake Accord; and the ongoing dispute between Quebec and Ottawa over educational language rights (as well as related disputes on the rights of linguistic minorities both inside and outside Quebec); and other contentious political conflicts, all of which might more effectively be debated in a revised upper house.

In addition to such specific disagreements, there are more general, overarching issues which impinge on both orders of federal government, which could be canvassed in a reformed senate. Among such issues would be the respective federal-provincial responsibilities for the establishment of Aboriginal self-government, and for environmental controls, and oversight of the constitutional division-of-powers generally. It has been suggested at times that the upper house could also oversee Canadian compliance with treaties, especially in the human rights area, and that a subcommittee of the reconstituted senate could confirm prospective federally-appointed judges and senior government officials.

Another general issue that could be debated more effectively in the upper house of a federation constitutionally committed to reducing regional disparities (Constitution Act, 1982) would be the overall equity with which Ottawa treats the different provinces and regions. This is a matter best not left to prime ministers with huge majorities in the lower house, or to opposition leaders who must soon confront the regional electorates they might otherwise accuse of enriching themselves extravagantly from federal coffers. Party leaders may be more frank on the hustings than within parliament, of course. At a nomination meeting in western Canada, for example, NDP leader Ed Broadbent (who was very muted in his criticism in Parliament of the CF–18 deal) charged that "Pierre Trudeau's Liberals spent 13.9 percent of the federal procurement budget in the west where 29 percent of Canada's population live, while in the past four years the Mulroney government has used just 11.5 percent of the budget beyond the Manitoba-Ontario border..." (qtd. in *Star-Phoenix*). Even if Broadbent's numbers are right the federal government may have a good explanation for them: the problem is that the bald statistics are troubling, and are not likely to be effectively discussed in a legislative chamber with a weighty majority from central Canada. In a senate with equal representation from all provinces there would be a more propitious climate for dealing with such figures adequately. But how could such a "Triple E" senate be set up, and what might some of its powers be?

As a senate of about the present size seems practical, an elected upper chamber with 10 senators for each of the provinces, with perhaps two for the Yukon, and four for the somewhat large and more diverse Northwest Territories, would be workable. When the Territories became provinces they too would be entitled to equal provincial representation. This would establish an upper house with 106 members as compared to the present 104. A smaller senate would probably not have enough numbers adequately to perform committee work and other legislative responsibilities.

There is a certain arbitrariness about any internal boundaries, but the continuance of the practice of maintaining "sectional" rather than provincial equality in the Canadian Senate is simply not justifiable. It is "provinces" not "sections" whose constitutional and political rights may be jeopardized by action in the House of Commons. It is typically provinces which are in confrontation with Ottawa, rather than sections, although there may be moments where there is a considerable degree of "sectional" agreement on certain issues. There can also be, and often are, disagreements between provinces in a section of the country on important issues. The possible continuation of "sectional" representation raises the question of just how many shared interests there are between adjacent provinces. How much sectional or regional homogeneity is there? Alberta and Saskatchewan disagreed on the Crow rate, for example, and Saskatchewan and Manitoba for many months had major differences on constitutional patriation. Nova Scotia and Newfoundland had distinctly different perspectives on the ownership of offshore resources, and if central Canada is considered as a region, Quebec and Ontario have strong differences on free trade. The differences in industrial development between Prince Edward Island and Nova Scotia, or between Saskatchewan and Alberta make it difficult to classify either pair, on rational criteria, as members of a common section with uniform interests. In most ways, with some exceptions, our typical perspective is provincial rather than regional or sectional. It would seem to underlie the postulate of equal sectional representation that there is a community of economic or other interests binding together members of a section, but there isn't. Even if Ontario is taken as a "section" (which apparently it was) the northern Ontario hinterland has more affinities with the adjacent prairies than it does with the industrialized south of the province, and "sectionalism" might be questioned even here.

Taking the 10 provinces, then, as the more typical federal units, for representative purposes, the units in which constitutional rights, duties, and interests inhere, *these* are the entities which must be accorded representation in the upper house, and that representation must be equal. The provinces must have equal status in the upper house because the more populous areas of the country already have greater weight in the lower chamber. In a properly balanced federal system the weight of population should not be felt in *both* houses, since that would tend towards an overcentralized *national* rather than a balanced federal polity.

As in other federations, continuity in the upper house could be ensured by providing for a six-year term for senators, with one-third of the body being elected at two-year intervals.

Like the other provinces, Quebec would be represented by 10 senators. If the criticism were made that the proposed new upper house did not adequately take Quebec's specific interests into account, it could be met by providing that no legislative action could be taken derogating from the province's linguistic, cultural, or other rights without the assent of a majority of Quebec senators, present and voting, which would be considered as a unit for that purpose. This would not, in any event, seem to be a major obstacle, since some of Quebec's most important existing rights are already entrenched and beyond alteration by a simple parliamentary bill: a constitutional amendment would be needed for that purpose. The protection envisaged here, however, contemplates that cultural or linguistic rights in ordinary legislation specifically protecting Quebec's interests would not be abrogated without the "collegial" consent of the province's senators.

As argued above, the primary aim of the reconstituted Senate would be more effectively to advance provincial points of view, so that there would be an authentic central legislative organ in Ottawa to articulate local interests there that are not now adequately put forward. Far from exacerbating regional tensions, such a revitalized body would inject needed harmony into federal-provincial relations. Much of the fractiousness between Ottawa and the provinces in recent years has arisen because there was no "presence" in the national capital to effectively represent the provinces. The new Senate would in no manner replace the intermittent meetings of federal and provincial First Ministers, or so-called "executive-federalism," which is an extra-parliamentary, extra-constitutional forum without specific legislative powers. The First Ministers do valuable work, but their task is essentially that of inter-governmental consultation and compromise, and is more specific in character, being largely confined to constitutional and economic matters. These areas are, assuredly, of great importance, but the work of the Senate would be more continuous and of even greater breadth, embracing virtually all jurisdictions, and it would have its appropriate legislative dimension which the First Ministers, as an executive body, lacks.

And to be truly effective, the new Senate should have not merely a delaying power, or "suspensive veto," but a real veto on virtually all laws emanating from the lower house, except for constitutional amendments,[4] and for the not always clear restrictions circumscribing the action of the upper house where the "spending power" is concerned. If a mere delaying power were involved, in any federal controversy the lower house would need only to wait through the moratorium period and then unilaterally do whatever it pleased. Disagreements, even so, would not be very frequent; they are not endemic in other federations. Where such disagreements did arise, a "conference committee" of both houses could decide on joint action. A possible device to break any unusually intractable disagreement could be similar to that contained in section 57 of the Australian Constitution. That provision provides that in such a contingency the governor-general can convoke a joint sitting of both federal houses, with an absolute vote of both senators and members of the lower house, sitting together, being necessary to break the log-jam.

But in collaborating in the establishment of such a potentially powerful new legislative body, would the House of Commons be creating a powerful rival? In some respects, unquestionably, it would be, but its position of dominance in the overall legislative framework, which Canadians have come to accept, could still be maintained. There are at least three reasons why, in any reconstitution of the upper house, the House of Commons would continue to play its present dominant role. First, by the unwritten convention of responsible government, it would continue to be only a want-of-confidence motion in the lower house which would entail the defeat of the government. Second, the primary function of the new senators would be to represent their home provinces; their purpose is principally to voice the needs of their local constituencies while bearing broader national interests in mind. That being the case, it is envisaged that the prime minister and virtually all of the federal cabinet, and certainly the holders of major portfolios, would continue to be drawn from the House of Commons. This would certainly ensure that the formulation of policy would continue to be the main prerogative of that House. The Senate, however, would be a more powerful watch-dog of regional interests than the present upper house, perhaps forestalling by its mere presence the initiation of ill-advised measures in the Commons. And third, money bills, as at present, would continue to originate only in the lower chamber.

The continuance, therefore, of the present convention of responsible government, and the presence of a powerful cabinet in the House of Commons would ensure that the new parliament would not merely be a pale replica of the American Congress with its more stark separation of powers. While maintaining the traditional dominance and legislative leadership of the House of

Commons, the reconstituted Senate would infuse a needed, and now absent, federal balance in the halls of Parliament.

Notes

1. The three rival plans put forward at the Philadelphia constitutional convention of 1787 are known, respectively, as the Virginia Plan, the New Jersey Plan, and the Connecticut Compromise. The Virginia Plan provided for a bicameral legislature with proportional representation in both houses, with the executive and judicial branches to be chosen by the legislature. The New Jersey Plan provided for a single legislative house with equal representation for each state. The Connecticut Compromise, which was ultimately adopted, provided for equal state representation in the Senate and proportional representation in the House of Representatives. See Madison, *Debates, passim.*

2. Liberal leader George Brown, an influential Father of Confederation, was quite explicit about the role of the Senate as a guardian of local interests, and was quoted by the Supreme Court to that effect, in Authority of Parliament, 67, 102 DLR (3rd) 10: "But the very essence of our compact is that the union shall be federal and not legislative. Our Lower Canadian friends have agreed to give us representation by population in the Lower House, on the express condition that they should have equality in the Upper House. On no other condition could we have advanced a step...."

3. Statistics Canada, and see York A3, and "Taken for a Ride on the CF–18."

4. Pursuant to s. 47(1) of the Constitutional Act, 1982, the Senate cannot veto, but may only delay constitutional amendments for a 180-day period; on re-adoption by the House of Commons after such delay, parliamentary assent thereto is effective.

Public Sector Restructuring
Eight Minor Details*

D. Wayne Taylor

Pride is unCanadian. At least it was when I was growing up in the shadow of Canada's Protestant, Tory past. This began to change ever so slowly as Canadians basked in the Centennial celebrations of 1967. This change in attitude towards pride accelerated with the rapidly increasing Americanization of our institutions, communications and pop culture, and with the swelling, non-European immigrations of the 1980s and 1990s.

Ironically, when it was unCanadian to exhibit pride, I was proud to be a public servant. I believed Herschel Hardin when he said Canada's was a public sector culture.[1] This was a good thing; I was part of it; and I was proud.

Today, pride is less of an interdiction. But, ironically, I am again no longer proud of our public service. It is with a sigh, mixed with relief and remorse, that I am often introduced as a former public servant. And it seems that I am not alone.[2]

The Case Against the Public Service

In 1996, Environics, a commercial market research firm, reported that only three percent of Canadians had a lot of confidence in their government(s).[3] A year

---

*   From David Barrows and H. Ian Macdonald, eds., *The New Public Management: International Developments*, (Concord, ON: Captus Press Inc., 2000), pp. 106–123. Reproduced with permission.

later, the National Quality Institute (NQI) reported that government ranked last among 21 sectors of the economy in consumer satisfaction. In fact, the public sector was a low-end outlier with only a 40 percent approval rating.[4] In satisfaction survey methodology, market-driven entities consider 80 percent as the generally acceptable cut off; 90 percent plus as the desirable result. Government occupied the basement along with the banks, department stores, Canada Post and cable television. The one commonality across the five was bigness.

Although we cannot in any way suggest that the public sector is a homogenous monolith,[5] it is nonetheless an unsympathetic leviathan[6] to those it supposedly serves. Banks, cable television, Canada Post, government and department stores (the latter of which is paying the price as they exit the marketplace one by one) all exhibit the same bureaupathology — an indifference to the client, arrogance, long cycle times, a lack of courtesy, a lack of promptness, poor public information, and inattention paid to complaints.[7]

As expected, of course, not all public services are viewed equally by their clients. In 1998, the Canadian Centre for Management Development (CCMD) discovered that 15 distinct public services, some from each of the federal, provincial and municipal levels of government, ranked significantly different, one from the other, in terms of perceived service quality.[8] Fire departments received an 86 percent level of satisfaction — the only one to surpass the market researcher's 80 percent cut off. Road maintenance occupied the basement, with a 45 percent approval rating. Libraries, garbage disposal, provincial parks, Canada Pension/Old Age Security, the RCMP, the passport office, motor vehicle licensing, electric utilities, health cards, customs, Canada Post, Revenue Canada, and hospitals completed the continuum in descending order of approval.

The CCMD study also revealed that 95 percent of Canadians expect equal to or better service from the public sector than from the private sector.[9] And so they should.

The bureaupathetic behaviour identified in the NQI study was compounded in the CCMD study by the explosive use of voicemail — a supposed technological answer to the "wrong door" phenomenon encountered by Canadians trying to negotiate the public labyrinth that, in fact, has complicated things for many. Incompetence and a lack of fairness were also added to the list of dissatisfiers.[10]

Satisfaction with "Movement"

Most interesting, however, was the CCMD's finding that the number one priority for improvement, as identified by the citizens surveyed, was the reduction of "red tape"[11] after a decade of government at all levels across Canada attempting to do just that! With respect to most aspects of social organization and social responsibility, for most people, perception is reality.[12] In this case, public sector management in Canada has a lot to improve and a long ways to go to regain the public's respect.

Canadians are no longer proud of their public sector management because of poor public sector service access and delivery; and yet, for ten years or more, that has been the major content of Canada's journal-of-record for all things public, *Canadian Public Administration*, published by the Institute of Public Administration of Canada (IPAC). In 1989, *Canadian Public Administration* identified the middle manager (all but eradicated in the private sector by then) as the "crucial link" in public service delivery.[13]

As we entered the 1990s we were treated to "Public Service 2000: the renewal of the public service," touted by a then-Clerk of the Privy Council who has since found both fame and fortune in the private sector by resurrecting in phoenix-fashion a moribund, privatized Crown corporation.[14] In the very next issue, readers were propelled "beyond 2000" with a series of reports from the Education, Training and Development Committee of IPAC focussing on the development of leaders for the public sector.[15] Then, in 1991, this reader/ author gagged, for want of a better descriptor, when an article appeared entitled, "Service to the public: A major strategic change".[16] It was almost like an epiphany; the public service finally discovered the meanings of the words "public" and "service". (Forget management for the time being.) In fact, it was such an important and novel idea that the article was published in both official languages.

Then we heard about administrative reform in the federal bureaucracy and Career Public Service 2000.[17] Before the mid-1990s, decentralization, power-sharing and "downloading" had come into vogue[18] — downloading from Ottawa to the provinces, from the provinces to the municipalities, and from government to the non-profit sector.[19] We then began to mystify the entire process of public sector reform by invoking values, ethics and culture.[20]

Then, as if much had been accomplished in the first half of the decade, the literature shifted to topics of evaluation, introspection, comparative reforms, codes of conduct, barriers to change, and "managerialism" — the latter representing a perceived shift in the recruitment of senior public executives to those with managerial expertise from those with technical expertise.[21] Ignoring front-line reality even further, the 50th Anniversary Issue of *Canadian Public Administration* (CPA) chronicled the "intellectual odyssey of Canadian public administration".[22]

Worthy of note and absent from discussion in the 1990s' issues of *CPA* are Special Operating Agencies (SOAs) — probably one of the most creative and promising, yet dishonest, reforms in government. Jumping onto the reform bandwagons of customer service and user-pay, a number of federal government bureaus within departments (as well as some similar provincial and municipal agencies) were carved out of their mother-departments as independent "businesses" charged with developing excellence in customer service and fiscal self-sufficiency.[23] The most pathetic example was the Passport Office. Although the user fee paid to acquire a passport almost tripled overnight, offices still staffed themselves at about one-third complement at lunch hours, when the lion's share of passport clients attempt to acquire their passports. Prices soared, and client satisfaction went from poor to worse. But the Passport Office's Estimates were now off the Government's books.

Reviewing the *CPA* literature reminded me of a former Assistant Deputy Minister I know who, when we were both in the employ of the Crown, used to be quite satisfied with events so long as there had been "movement". Well, there has certainly been a lot of movement (as Peters says, "change in the public sector is the rule rather than the exception"[24]), but there has been very little tangible, measurable, substantive improvement; just a lot of smoke and mirrors, political symbolism,[25] and subterfuge.

Of course, all of this writing in Canada's journal-of-record has occurred at the same time as other researchers and practitioners were writing about the need to not just download but downsize governments at all levels. The University of Toronto/Donner Canadian Foundation's Monograph Series on Public Policy and Public Administration, as an example, concentrates on the diminishing role of government in Canada. Not only do these monographs identify how governments have failed at most economic and social policy forays they have entered, but also how most government initiatives are not sustainable for the future. Some even go so far as to claim that not only is government not the solution, but it has become the problem. Government programs, prone to "unintended consequences, perverse incentives and slippery-slope excesses," in many cases actually exacerbate the social and/or economic "ills" they are intended to heal, and/or create ills anew.[26]

In one such monograph, economist Fred Lazar documents 25 years of federal government failures in policies addressing research and development, regional development, small business, labour markets, industry and agriculture.[27] Totalling hundreds of billions of dollars, these programs have failed to meet their objectives and, in many cases, actually undermined their objectives. But did Ottawa learn any lessons? No, in fact they continue to do more of the same.

In this country — the living laboratory of Keynesian and Galbraithian economic theories — we did not even get the basics right. Most of Canada's public sector debt was incurred as a result of deficit spending during an era of prosperity — when we were supposed to be saving![28]

Coincidental, but prophetic, was the lack of fiscal prudence exhibited by one of Ottawa's founders, Colonel By, and its correlation with the fiscal habits of Ottawa during these past 25 years. Charged with building the Rideau Canal in the late 1820s and early 1830s from Kingston to Ottawa as part of Upper Canada's defence against an expanding, militaristic United States, Colonel By was given a budget of £169,000. The final price tag for the Rideau Canal came in at £1,134,000.[29]

Downsizing of government in Canada in the next millennium makes sense for a number of reasons, many of which are reviewed in the Monograph Series. But if for no other reason, public sector downsizing makes sense because only 25 percent of Canadians today are engaged in wealth creation — the rest do nothing more than shuffle it around.[30] Within this 75 percent of Canadians who are employed in "services," the private sector's share will probably decline in both relative and absolute numbers as the microchip globalizes the key players: telecommunications, finance, transportation and information technology. A huge public sector employment base creating not a loonie's worth of wealth is not sustainable without serious rending of the Canadian economic and social fabric.[31]

(I know someone will argue that Crown corporations and all the other forms of state enterprise that produce goods are wealth-creating, public sector entities, but their impact on Canada's Gross Domestic Product and labour market have already been accounted for in the 25 percent figure. Believe me, I am giving government all the benefit of the doubt I honestly can.)

One Not-So-Quiet Revolution

All of this Canadian research, experimentation, and the chronicling of same has transpired against a backdrop of governmental "reforms" in almost every other country in the world at the same time. There has been some mimetic isomorphism[32] (me-too-ism) across governments, as well as novel initiatives created in isolation from any others. But generally, the outcomes have been the same — movement. New Zealand stands alone as the only industrialized nation to have truly revolutionized its public sector.[33] (Sweden may be, but it is too early to really tell.)

Challenging the traditions of its Westminister model of government, New Zealand replaced many of those traditions with ideas straight out of public-choice economics and best practices from private sector management. New Zealanders faced up to the truth: that public servants of the 1990s were only human, self-interested, rational, utility maximizers and not the super-human, values-free, public administrators of myth sacrificing self for country in disinterested and rational fashion.[34] In New Zealand today, public sector management is governed by objectives. Results are measured and managers held accountable for their achievement, or lack thereof. Responsibility, accountability and authority are balanced. Departmental objectives are aligned with the collective goals of the government. Senior executives are placed upon term-specific, performance-based employment contracts.[35]

So What? ... Eight Minor Details

Economic power is rapidly shifting to the global stage and local backlots. This "glocalization" is transforming the nation-state, making market-driving metropolises and sub-regions the *bona fide* players in a global economic game, relegating arbitrarily defined national governments — and even more so, the arbitrarily defined provincial governments in a confederation like Canada — to the sidelines.[36] Such change, at one level, makes the content of this whole symposium moot — especially for federal states.

A simple, logical response to glocalization could call for unitary states with the elimination of provincial governments, and the devolution to and empowerment of regional/local entities. But this is a political decision, not a management decision — and such a sea-change decision no one at this symposium today will likely live to witness.

So, given no substantive change in the constitutional division of powers, how can our public service improve its crafting and delivery of public services, and regain the confidence, trust and respect of Canadians? All the paddling in shallow water will not put the public juggernaut back on course. The public service needs to return to first principles, specifically eight not-so-minor first principles.

I. Visualizing for Success

Although "reform" has been talked about in, and for, public sector management — and much "movement" has taken place — there is no consensus on what reform means and where it should take us.

Restructuring needs focus and direction. Take a look at the difference between winners and losers in sports and business (another unCanadian thing to do). The very elite amongst high performance athletes seldom have to change their mechanics before a big meet or game, or scrap their routine or game plan minutes before competing. They prepare for their future by visualizing their success: visualizing nailing that dismount, scoring that overtime goal, crossing the finish line first, with time to spare.

The highest performing companies in the world do likewise. Collins and Porras[37] have empirically demonstrated that mission/vision/values are the reasons "visionary" industry leaders leave competitors in their wake: why General Electric has surpassed Westinghouse; why Disney outpaces Columbia; why Sony outdistances Kenwood; why Ford is overtaking General Motors. And I am not referring to the generic "vision statements" that many have adopted in the 1990s that amount to little more than fluff, puff and pixie dust.

If public sector management reform or restructuring is to be meaningfully successful, then the public sector needs to have defined for it a core ideology or a set of core values that are non-negotiable and circumscribe expected behaviour, goals and performance; and an envisioned future — a "big, hairy, audacious goal" (as Collins and Porras would say) with vivid descriptions of success and measurement.[38]

The difference between athletic champions visualizing their success and organizations with benign vision statements is that athletic accomplishment is measurable, time-specific and the responsibility of the athlete. Similarly, the difference between visionary companies and organizations with benign vision statements is that visionary companies have measurable goals that really stretch them, with deadlines and managers held accountable for their achievement.

In short, public sector restructuring needs to achieve a specific, defined, envisioned future with measurable end-points for which senior managers will be held accountable. It needs ideological focus. New Zealand is doing this. So can we. But beware the trap of mimetic isomorphism. Let us not just copy New Zealand. There are significant cultural and institutional barriers to the transfer of other countries' experiments to Canada.[39] We need to be bold, innovative, unwilling to subscribe to the past, and follow the principles outlined in a process we call MVP (Qtr)™ — Managing with Vision for Performance (Quantified, time-specific, responsibility)™.

This is not another flavour of the month. The public service is no different from Alice in Wonderland when she meets the Cheshire Puss and asks which path she ought to take without knowing where she wants to go. All of this movement in public sector restructuring is tantamount to choosing pathways to follow without knowing the destination desired. The Cheshire Puss is grinning at us all.

But where to start?

2. Essential Services

Brady once said "the role of the state in the economic life of Canada is really the modern history of Canada".[40] As an historical observer Brady was correct. However, given the reality of glocalization, Brady as a futurist would be wrong. Governments have failed in many of their economic and social policy forays, and the general public is fed up with this mediocrity in governance.

The public sector needs to focus on essential services only — that is, those that demonstrate empirical correlation with successfully fulfilling a public need that is essential to the nation's, province's or municipality's well-being and is not available by any other means. I am not sure whether I would subscribe to the libertarian's definition of government as purveyors of only justice, defence and the protection of life and property. But I also know that much of what governments do today is not essential to our well-being.

If it is essential, then do it; if it is not, then get out of it. Why? If current levels of government programming are not sustainable — and all indicators point that way[41] — then better to do the essential ones well, than continue to nickel-and-dime ourselves across-the-board into a perpetual state of mediocrity. And that is where the NQI and CCMD surveys place us.

Zero-based budgeting (ZBB) — introduced in municipalities across the continent 20 years ago — did just this. It rank-ordered all services. The trouble was that the politicians of the day could not see the wisdom of strategic, surgical program cuts. But the fiscally tight late 1970s and early 1980s were replaced with the boom of the late 1980s and ZBB was soon forgotten. Most municipalities are paying for this today as roads deteriorate, utility infrastructures rot, parks become overgrown, social services fall short of expressed needs and user fees are initiated.

An "essential" service could easily be described as being one that we have no choice but to require. If you are acutely ill, you need a hospital; if your house is on fire, you need a fire brigade; if you drink, you need clean water. There are no choices to be made here. You do not choose to be ill, to have a disaster fall upon you, or to be born. But where we do make choices, we should bear the consequences — not the state.

An immutable definition of "essential service" could go a long way to providing the public service with some badly needed focus.

3. Unions

Hand-in-hand with the concept of an essential service goes the argument that any service deemed truly to be essential — and, therefore, will continue to be provided by government — should not be withheld from the general public by anyone else's right-in-law to do so through work action. Essential public services should be protected from all the arbitrariness of unions and so-called professional associations. The right to strike should be denied all public service employees.[42] If they argue that the right to strike is legitimate because the public will not be hurt by such action, then the service they provide is not essential — and should be delisted from the public agenda.

The fundamental issue of essentiality aside, unions: inflate the cost of labour beyond its market value in a monopsonistic fashion; inflate the costs of operations due to the obligations incurred in administering collective bargaining agreements; oppose meritocracy (one of those old British North American tenets of public administration); and promote mediocrity through their opposition to performance-based pay. None of this is managing the public trust in the public interest — this has been self-interest through and through.[43]

Providing only essential services, with those providing these services not having a right to strike — this could be a "big, hairy, audacious goal" for Canada's public service.

4. User-Pay Financing

The concept of user pay financing goes beyond the band-aid fiscal tactic of imposing user fees on heretofore "free" government services. User fees were predictable as the cost to the consumer for services like health care and elementary/secondary education reached zero. As price approaches zero, demand explodes exponentially. This is basic price theory.

User pay financing calls for "corridors" or "streams" of revenue earmarked for, and spent on, specific programs and services. No more black hole of "general revenue". When Tommy Douglas envisioned medicare, he envisioned insurance premiums and user fees to fund a system that inherently would not place a financial barrier between any one person's medical need and care. Today, the lion's share of medicare is financed out of personal and corporate income tax. Of the billions raised through gasoline taxes for road construction and improvement, only a very small fraction is spent on transportation — it subsidizes health care, education and welfare.

How do you begin to measure value-for-money or any other such customer satisfaction criterion if there is no direct link between payer, what is paid, the service provided, and the provider? The answer is, you cannot, so you do not. Let taxation be directly correlated with services provided. Raise and spend what we need for roads — no more, no less. Likewise for health, education, environmental protection, and so on.

5. Real Balanced Scorecards

If items one to four are implemented successfully, then — and only then — can the public service become truly accountable, through their political masters, to the general public. A "dashboard" of success measures, or indicators, could be created to gauge the efficiency and effectiveness of the public service — indicators grounded in a definable vision of the future, measuring goal accomplishment, client satisfaction, and financial performance. Such a scorecard closes the MVP (Qtr)™ loop.

The value of such a management tool lies in the public service's need to align targets, behaviours, resources, initiatives, activities, incentives and accountabilities with set goals, to celebrate successes, and to deal appropriately with failure — or worse still, mediocrity. Real balanced scorecards are about management, not measurement, and vision achievement.

6. Redefine and Develop Leadership

Leadership is not simply charisma or popularity. Leadership is being able to pull an organization as well as to push it; to inspire as well as to direct; to understand what motivates someone and to use it; to set an example. Leadership is about responsibility and accountability. Leadership is about courage.

Effective leadership is about producing useful change. Not every manager needs to be a leader. But public sector management definitely needs a good dose of leadership as we enter the new millennium. And those chosen to lead must understand what leadership is all about. Effective leaders: (1) *select* the right people for the right job at the right time and right place for the client, (2) build and enhance relationships to *connect* them to the right cause, (3) *solve* problems that arise and produce results, (4) enhance individual performance by *evaluating* progress towards objectives, (5) serve the client by achieving consensus and/or *negotiating* resolutions to conflict, (6) tend to the fabric of organizational life by *healing* wounds inflicted by change, (7) *protect* their cultures/values from crises and threats; and (8) *synergize* all stakeholders, enabling them to achieve together more than by themselves.[44] Few of the above eight points surfaced in any of the *CPA* issues mentioned earlier.

The first and foremost predictive criterion for a high leadership IQ is being an achiever.[45] The key ingredient for being an achiever is competence.[46] The public service needs to define, promote, recruit for, and reward the competence-achievement-leadership chain if it is to truly restructure itself as a purposeful, meaningful management cadre for the 21st century. Effective leadership will promote the realization of first principles one to five listed above.

7. Tough Love Human Resource Management

How do we assist in the leadership development identified above? There are five essential human resource management components that together can take any organization a long ways along the competence-achievement-leadership chain. Since there are five elements involved — recruitment, just-in-time training (JITT™), appraisal, reward and firing — corresponding to the five major points of a maple leaf, we have called this Maple Leaf HRM™.

1. To paraphrase W.E. Deming, the father of total quality management, you can burn the toast and scrape it, or make it right the first time. Therefore, *recruitment* is key! You can always train for skill, but hire for attitude. How many public servants are hired today for their attitude?

2. In total quality companies, at least two percent of payroll is spent on *training*. The first thing to get chopped in government downsizing is the training budget. Little wonder the public does not see much quality in the public service today. Training should be targeted at closing skill gaps, whether in terms of mass training across-the-board (computer skills), strategic training for selected personnel (emergency response teams), or competency upgrading. Training should also be delivered just-in-time to optimize value-for-money and desired outcome (JITT™).

3. Performance *appraisal* or measurement should be quantifiable within a specific time frame. Public servants should be retained, promoted, demoted, compensated and fired based upon such appraisals. Performance targets need to be mutually agreed upon and part of the organization's mission, which, in turn, should be part of the public service's big, hairy, audacious goal.

4. Reward needs to be tied to performance. If a public servant achieves beyond what is expected, that public servant needs to be rewarded above what was promised; otherwise, this "achievement-oriented" behaviour will soon disappear. This also begs the whole union issue above.

5. Finally, the best time to plan for a public servant's departure is at the beginning of employment. *Firing* should be based upon performance expectations, performance appraisal and fiscal realities. The public service can no longer afford to be a high-class, make-work program for millions. And let us be honest: we owe it to the public servants who do what is asked of them day in and day out to fire the two percent or so who do not.

This is Maple Leaf HRM™ — a Canadian's version of tough love human resource management. We owe this to ourselves, as managers, to the public who foot the bill, and to our number one resource — those who go home at the end of their work day.

8. Choice

Finally, the public service in Canada needs to realize that socialism is dead. With the crashing of the Berlin Wall in 1989 came the rapid demise of socialism worldwide. The Marxist cookie-cutter has grown dull. China is adopting market economics; Sweden is de-socializing itself. Only Cuba holds out against this sea-change in ideology. And a lot of public servants in this country.

In particular, for the sustainability of any significant form of public service in the future, Canadians need choice once again in our lives. We have no choice of family doctors (most have closed their doors to new patients and specialists are only engaged upon referral). We have no choice of hospitals (most denominational hospitals are being closed in many provinces). We do not have the best medical technology (we are in the bottom one-third of the OECD, even though we are the fifth highest spender on health per capita in the world).

And choice does not mean unaffordable. In fact, the exact opposite is true. We have private schools for which parents pay out of their own pockets, with no tax relief, while at the same time paying their full share of the public education bill. Why not do the same in health care? Is health any higher a privilege than education? Australia has a parallel private health care system, paid for in the same way we pay for private schools in Canada, yet Australia's per capita health bill is lower than ours, and its medical technology ranking is higher! Choice saves the public purse, stimulates innovation, and makes for a much more satisfied population footing the bills. Choice preserves democracy.

Conclusion

As you probably can tell by now, I, and most Canadians, it would seem, have lost patience with public service reform and public service reformers.

It is clear that public service reform has not worked in this country. During ten years or more of formal restructuring and reform, public confidence in, and satisfaction with, government has waned. Public service reform has been misdirected and ineffective. Public sector management needs to return to first principles — specifically, the principles of visualizing for success, essentiality, freedom from labour arbitrariness, channelled user pay financing, balanced scoring, real leadership, tough love human resource management, and choice.

A lot of my time these days is spent teaching, researching and consulting in the healthcare sector, so please indulge me as I adopt a healthcare way of expressing myself in summing up this paper. Focus on the eight determinants of good health for the public service identified in this paper. Cosmetic surgery, the likes of which *Canadian Public Administration* has been reporting for a decade, is not enough. The patient needs to be prepared with an enema and then undergo radical surgery. No more band-aid reforms.

Notes

1. H. Hardin, *A Nation Unaware: The Canadian Economic Culture* (Vancouver: J.J. Douglas, 1974).
2. A.A. Warrack, "The Private Sector and Intergovernmental Relations," *Proceedings of the Forum of Federalism in an Era of Globalization* (Mont-Tremblant, QC., 1999), p. 5.
3. D. Zussman, "Do citizens trust their governments?" *Canadian Public Administration* (1997), vol. 40, no. 2: 234–54.
4. R. Ferguson, "Being big a liability, consumer survey says" *The Toronto Star* (October 8, 1997): D3.
5. D.W. Taylor, A.A. Warrack and M.C. Baetz. *Business and Government in Canada: Partners for the Future* (Toronto: Prentice-Hall, 1999), Chapter 7.
6. W.T. Stanbury, *Business-Government Relations In Canada: Grappling with Leviathan* (Toronto: Butterworths, 1985).
7. R. Ferguson, "Being big a liability, consumer survey says" *The Toronto Star* (October 8, 1997): D3.
8. B. Marson, "Citizen Centred Service: Canadian's Service Expectations, Satisfaction, and their Priorities for Improvement," *Management* (1999), vol. 9, no. 3: 10–12.
9. Ibid.
10. Ibid.
11. Ibid.
12. W.I. Thomas, *On Social Organization and Social Responsibility* (Chicago: University of Chicago Press, 1966).
13. P. Aucoin, "Middle managers — the crucial link: summary of discussions"; W.D. Mitchell (1989), "The 'new' middle manager: unleashing

entrepreneurial potential"; and R. Paton, "Middle managers: upscale supervisors or emerging executives" all in *Canadian Public Administration* (1989), vol. 32, no. 2: 187–209, 244–60.

14. P.M. Tellier, "Public Service 2000: the renewal of the public service," *Canadian Public Administration* (1990), vol. 33, no. 2: 123–32.

15. *Canadian Public Administration* (1990), vol. 33, no. 3.

16. F. Séguin, "Service to the public: A major strategic change," *Canadian Public Administration* (1991), vol. 34, no. 3: 455–73.

17. K. Kernaghan, "Career Public Service 2000: Road to renewal or impractical vision?" *Canadian Public Administration* (1991), vol. 34, no. 4: 551–72.

18. *Canadian Public Administration* (1994), vol. 37, no. 3.

19. M.H. Hall and P.B. Reed, "Shifting the burden: how much can government download to the non-profit sector?" *Canadian Public Administration* (1998), vol. 41, no. 1: 1–20.

20. K. Kernaghan, "The emerging public service culture: values, ethics and reforms," *Canadian Public Administration* (1994), vol. 37, no. 4: 614–30.

21. *Canadian Public Administration* (1996), vol. 39, no. 4 and *Canadian Public Administration* (1997), vol. 40, no. 1.

22. *Canadian Public Administration* (1997), vol 40, no. 2.

23. See Note 5.

24. B.G. Peters, *The Future of Governing* (Lawrence, Kansas: University Press of Kansas, 1996).

25. M. Edelman, *The Symbolic Uses of Politics* (Chicago: University of Illinois Press, 1980).

26. F. Lazar, *How Ottawa Rewards Mediocrity* (Toronto: University of Toronto Centre for Public Management, 1996).

27. Ibid.

28. D.W. Taylor, A.A. Warrack and M.C. Baetz (1999): 49.

29. D. Morton, *A Military History of Canada* (Edmonton: Hurtig Publishers, 1985), p. 72.

30. D.W. Taylor, A.A. Warrack and M.C. Baetz (1999): 70.

31. Conference Board of Canada, *Performance and Potential 1999* (Ottawa: Conference Board of Canada, 1999).

32. P.J. DiMaggio and W.W. Powell, "The iron cage revisited: Institutional isomorphism and collective rationality in organizational fields" *American Sociological Review* (1983), vol. 48: 147–60.

33. See Note 24.

34. J. Boston, J. Martin, J. Pallot and P. Walsh, *Public Management: The New Zealand Model* (Auckland, New Zealand: Oxford University Press, 1997).

35. Ibid.

36. T.J. Courchene, "Glocalization: The Regional/International Interface" *Canadian Journal of Regional Science* (1995), vol. 18, no. 1.

37. J.C. Collins and J.I. Porras, *Built to Last: Successful Habits of Visionary Companies* (New York: Harper Business, 1997).

38. Ibid., 91–114, 236–39.

39. D.W. Taylor, "TriPartism in Canada and the Socio-Historical Determinants of Industrial Relations Systems" *Business in the Contemporary World* (1990), vol. 2, no. 2: 55–62.
40. A. Brady, "The State and Economic Life in Canada" in K.J. Rea and J.T. McLeod (eds.) *Business and Government in Canada: Selected Readings*, 2nd ed. (Toronto: Methuen, 1976).
41. See Note 5.
42. D.W. Taylor, "Taylor's Ten: Suggestions for Managing the Crisis in Health Care" *Canadian Health Care Management* (1993), DP87: 28–34.
43. Ibid., 31.
44. E.C. Murphy, *Leadership IQ* (New York: John Wiley & Sons, 1996).
45. Ibid., 14.
46. Ibid., 15.

A Comparison of Public and Private Sector Restructuring

Their Impact on Job Satisfaction

Tom Wesson and
David Barrows

Introduction[1]

Due to unprecedented competitive pressures, firms everywhere are cutting costs by restructuring and downsizing.[2] In the United States during the 1990s, several million workers lost their jobs through restructuring. Even in transition economies such as those in Eastern Europe, the transition from a state-dominated system to a market system has resulted in widespread job losses as privatized firms have adjusted to their new environment. Meanwhile, firms have restructured in developed countries like Norway and Japan that have historically maintained nearly full employment. These restructurings have contributed to increased unemployment in these nations.

The practices of downsizing and restructuring, which began in the private sector of the North American economies, have not only spread geographically, but have also spread from the private sector to the public sector in many diverse nations. However, this spread of restructuring practices to the public sector is based on a major assumption which has, to a large extent, gone unchallenged. It is assumed that the adoption by the public sector of these pri-

---

1   From David Barrows and H. Ian Macdonald, *The New Public Management: International Developments*, (Concord, ON: Captus Press Inc., 2000) pp. 152–172. Reproduced with permission.

2   We will use the terms downsizing and restructuring more or less interchangeably. Although in theory all restructurings do not result in downsizings, in practice they most often do.

vate sector managerial practices is appropriate. A major goal of our ongoing research program, of which this chapter represents a summary to date, is to explore the validity of this assumption.

We see two major aspects of this assumption that are worthy of further exploration. First, it is now clear in private sector management literature that downsizing and restructuring is not a panacea that is always effective in different private sector situations. It is all too clear that the cost savings forecasted often do not materialize as a result of restructuring. In fact, because restructuring is essentially certain to have a negative effect on organizational morale, it can be the case that the cure is worse than the illness, and that the net effect of restructuring on the organization is negative. Thus, we fear that by taking a medicine that has only limited proven effectiveness in one situation and applying it in what is in many ways a very different environment, it is likely that a compounding of errors will occur. If restructuring has a high variability in its effectiveness across the private sector, that variability is bound to be even greater across the public and private sectors combined.

Our second, albeit related, concern with the assumption that downsizing and restructuring is a valid managerial tool for public sector managers to employ is that the short-term goals achieved by downsizing and restructuring may not be consistent with the long-term goals of public sector organizations. Downsizing and restructuring can, at least in theory, be related directly to the private sector goal of profit maximization. However, it is much more difficult to relate downsizing and restructuring to the more diverse and more complex goals of public sector organizations.

A frequently observed lesson from failed private sector restructures is that often the problem was not that the firm had too many employees, but rather the problem was at a higher strategic or policy level. In other words, downsizing and restructuring initiatives are essentially tactical actions and cannot solve strategic problems — even when there is a direct link between the cost reduction goals of the restructuring and the long term profit maximization goal of the private sector organization. Again, this problem can only be compounded when looking at public sector organizations.

A second major goal of our ongoing research is to examine the extent to which, in borrowing the managerial tools of downsizing and restructuring from their private sector counterparts, public sector managers have been able to learn from the successes and failures of the private sector. There is a developing literature exploring best practices for downsizing and restructuring. We hope to understand to what extent this literature has influenced the design of public sector downsizing and restructuring initiatives.

This chapter will proceed as follows. First, we discuss briefly the precedence and pattern of private sector downsizing. That will lead into a discussion of best practices in downsizing. We will then compare those best practices to the results of a survey we conducted of senior mangers in several ministries of the Government of Ontario, asking them about their experiences with downsizing and restructuring initiatives. Next, we will use the results of this survey and some apparent contradictions in its findings as a lens with which to look at the results of a relatively small and narrowly focussed survey we performed comparing job satisfaction between public and private sector workers. We will conclude by outlining a view that emerges from this analysis, admittedly with very narrow empirical support, of the effectiveness with which downsizing and restructuring practices have been transferred to the Ontario public service.

Private Sector Downsizing and Restructuring

It is believed that the wave of downsizing that has caught the world by storm originated in the United States during the merger bloom of the 1980s and a subsequent recession in the early 1990s. Downsizing has occurred at an unprecedented rate in an attempt to cut costs and increase productivity, customer service and competitiveness.

McKinley, Sanchez and Schick (1985), drawing on institutional theory, suggest that three types of social forces help to explain the prevalence of downsizing in recent years. The authors label these forces constraining forces, cloning forces, and learning forces. These forces represent, respectively, the pressure on the decision makers to do what appears to be the "right thing"; pressure on the decision makers to imitate the steps taken by other organizations; and pressure exerted on decision makers by the network of professional organizations, academic institutions and consultants with which they interact.

Whatever the factors that led to the spread of downsizing and restructuring, there is no denying that it has been widely adopted, particularly by American firms. But, to what effect?

As stated above, restructuring is not a quick-fix solution to a firm's existing problems. In fact, downsizing and restructuring polices are often indicative of underlying problems at the core of the organization. The assertion is supported by a study commissioned by the US Department of Labour (Cacio, Morris and Young, 1999). The study showed that companies that had more successful downsizing and restructuring experiences were those that carried out downsizing and restructuring of their human assets at the same time that they underwent a restructuring of their physical assets. It may be assumed that these companies took stock of their core competencies and shed entire business units that were unproductive and/or did not utilize the companies' strengths. Similarly, in successful firms, acquisitions were made in order to strengthen existing core competencies.

In general, however, it seems that the downsizing programs of many companies do not produce their expected profit improvement. In a Wyatt Company survey conducted in 1991 of 1,005 firms that had downsized, only 21 percent indicated that there had been improvements in return to shareholders as a result of the downsizing (Cacio, 1993). Fewer than one in three indicated that profits increased as expected and only 46 percent of companies stated that their downsizing efforts actually reduced costs, while four out of five firms admitted to having to replace some of the employees that were dismissed. Yet, despite these results, 65 percent of firms that downsized in any particular year did so again the next (Mroczkowski and Hanaoka, 1997).

Looking in more detail at how these firms handled their downsizing and restructuring efforts, we see little evidence that firms attempted to reduce job losses through techniques such as reducing pay or job sharing. In fact, on average, work days lengthened for "survivors". Furthermore, it seems that most companies would prefer to shed employees rather than reapply them — 40 to 45 percent of employers were offered extended severance pay or health benefits, but only 10 to 18 percent were offered retraining (Mroczkowski and Hanaoka, 1997). Similarly, in a poll of 1,204 companies that engaged in downsizing, Right Associates discovered that only 14 percent had created job sharing plans, nine percent used vacation without pay, another nine percent shortened work weeks, and six percent attempted to cut pay (*Wall Street Journal*, 1992). Meanwhile, a Time/CNN poll of workers indicated that 80 percent of respondents would prefer a 10 percent cut in pay as opposed to a workforce reduction (Greenberg, 1990).

A question inevitably raised by this discussion is the extent to which morale been affected by downsizing and restructuring. A 1995 American Management Association Report (cited in Mroczkowski and Hanaoka, 1997) indicated that, in the private sector, decreased morale is one of the most probable effects of downsizing. Decreased morale occurred in 86 percent of the companies studied by the Association. Another study by Bennett (1991) found that two thirds of private sector firms reported that morale was seriously affected by downsizing.

Allen et al. (1994) found that while individuals do adjust, at least in part, to organizational restructuring, this adjustment process was influenced by the career stage of the employee. Specifically, it was found that managers early on in their careers were more negatively impacted than mid-career managers. The authors offered three possible explanations for this trend. The first is that early career managers have higher expectations and, therefore, experience higher levels of disappointment when these expectations are not met. Second, mid-career managers may have more experience with the restructuring process and may, therefore, feel more comfortable with organizational changes. Finally, as mid-career managers are generally in higher positions in an organization, they may have greater access to information, giving them a better understanding of the change process.

There is also evidence to suggest that the impact of restructuring is also mitigated by other factors, such as union and organizational support. Greenglass and Burke, in three research papers (1998a, b, c) examining downsizing and restructuring in Ontario hospitals and its psychological impacts on nurses, note several factors that can reduce the perception of negative outcomes. Nurses at affected hospitals reported fewer negative feelings related to downsizing and restructuring when they had a high degree of support from their union throughout the downsizing and restructuring process. This was most evident in situations where restructuring was most significant and the threat to personal employment was high.

Similarly, organizational support appears to lessen the perception of negative outcomes for those experiencing restructuring and downsizing. Greenglass and Burke argue that companionship and open, honest communication are key to forming positive global beliefs amongst employees about an organization. The converse of this is also true, they state, in that employees are more likely to perceive threats to themselves where there is little support for what they do

205

or what they need in order to provide good service. In summary, Greenglass and Burke state the following factors as key to ensuring good morale during restructuring and downsizing initiatives:

- A vision of what the organization will look like post-restructuring;
- Complete, timely and repetitive communication with employees;
- Recognition of the organization's past accomplishments;
- Celebrating the organization's current accomplishments;
- Using staff reductions only as a last resort;
- Investing in training and development of staff; and
- Career transition assistance to facilitate employment elsewhere.

Greenglass and Burke appear to confirm other researchers' findings that the highest anger and hostility reactions against restructuring and downsizing are found amongst middle managers, particularly where the level of service provided to clients appears to be declining. Furthermore, anger levels seem to be related to tenure and hierarchical level in these circumstances. Contributory factors include the clarity of the vision for the organization, whether the organizational leadership is demonstrably committed to the stated goals, and whether the new direction is respectful of the organization's past accomplishments.

Public Sector Downsizing

While almost all of the existing research on downsizing has focussed on private sector firms, as was discussed above, downsizing is also very prevalent in the public sector. The effects of public sector downsizing are of particular interest for several reasons. First, the public sector is highly labour intensive and relies upon professionals from all fields. Furthermore, the public sector relies on the expertise of such professionals to effectively design and implement government policies. The recruitment and retention of qualified employees, then, is an integral part of the operations of any civil service. It has often been posited that the low pay, limited flexibility and limited opportunities for promotion are characteristics of the public sector that prevent the most qualified workers from remaining in government agencies and rising to the top. The result can be a loss in productivity and initiative in the public sector. These hindering characteristics also discourage young people from engaging in civil service careers. A recent Executive Institute Alumni Association Survey in the United States indicated that public careers are not recommended for young people (Emmert and Walied, 1992).

The downsizing of the public sector also carries with it potential economic costs. As more and more government employees are displaced and turnover rates increase, the costs of retraining and repositioning employees grows steadily. There is also concern that the effects of the reduced morale that often accompany downsizing and restructuring could have grave consequences in the public sector. The popular caricature of the bloated and bureaucratic civil service greatly belittles the essential role civil servants play in both policy design and implementation in modern democracies. If our civil service is left disgruntled and discouraged by poorly conceived and executed downsizing and restructuring initiatives, the effectiveness of our government will be greatly reduced.

We will continue our exploration of public sector downsizing by examining what are considered to be among the more successful public sector downsizing initiatives in three countries — the United Kingdom, New Zealand and Australia.

Public Sector Reform in the United Kingdom, New Zealand and Austria

The United Kingdom, New Zealand and Australia engaged in major reforms during the 1980s and 1990s, resulting in considerable reductions in the size of the public sectors. The United Kingdom reduced the size of its public service by 28 percent, New Zealand by 60 percent and Australia by 17 percent. For all three countries, the objectives of the reforms were to reduce costs and improve productivity.

In the United Kingdom, a large section of the civil service was privatized, while other programs operated on the "Next Step Agencies" principle, which focussed on cost effectiveness. Still other programs imported private sector practices in order to modernize the civil service. These served to improve both the efficiency and quality of services to the public.

In 1991, a Treasury document entitled, "Redundancy: Principles and Procedures" was made available to British ministries in order to assist them in negotiating arrangements for redundant employees. The criteria for determining redundant positions included level, speciality, geographic area and functional area of the work. The selection criteria for active employees included abilities, personal suitability, performance assessments, attendance and disciplinary record, with seniority as the tie breaking factor.

The British government experienced difficulties with the reforms in that they were implemented over a long period of time, undermining employee commitment and energy applied to change. Also, because the process was undertaken with little legislative guidance, there was a lack of clear role definition that resulted in employee distrust and a lack of control and accountability in many budgetary problems. Initially, the problems that were generated in the short term overshadowed the key objectives of improving quality of service. However, in the long run, the British service achieved its objectives of improving efficiency, accountability and quality of service.

The New Zealand government enacted reforms aimed more at improving the country's international competitiveness than merely the efficiency of its civil service. The public sector particularly sought improvements in financial management and leadership. It reorganized by transferring activities to both the private sector and the semi-public sector. Similar to British ministries, the ministries of New Zealand were able to autonomously administer the downsizing of their personnel after 1988, although the state services commissioned remained available to provide consulting in training services for those involved in the downsizing process. Also similar to the British reforms, the New Zealand government realized difficulties after an assessment in 1990 revealed a lack of role and output definition, and a need to improve recruitment and training of senior executives.

Another inherent difficulty with the massive public sector reform in New Zealand was the loss of institutional memory that occurred as a result of the huge job losses. Despite improved performance in the public sector, the impact on human resources was immense, as many people were required to retrain or end their careers. Nonetheless, the country was successful in implementing its strategy to reform its public service.

In Australia's case the impetus for reform was the country's poor economic condition. The government strove to create an efficient and cost-effective public service. The reforms were successful in that the public service became less unwieldy and more agile in its decision making. Downsizing occurred through both privatization and commercialization and was administered by the ministries, with mandatory disclosure of methods and costs to the public service commission. A series of legislative reforms assisted the government in adopting strategies on how to manage downsizing situations. For example, the 1986 legislation set out the heuristic for attrition, voluntary departures, redeployment and training, and included guidelines on negotiations, as well as on job search and financial support services. The legislation provided for voluntary retrenchment by providing an incentive program, including significant monetary incentives.

Similar to the British case, the Australian government experienced difficulties in acculturation. The workforce was accustomed to stability, and had difficulty adjusting to the reforms, particularly since improvements in training and information systems were required. Initial lack of communication and employee involvement in the reforms led to an unmotivated civil service. Nonetheless, the reforms were a success in the long run as the Australian government, like the British and New Zealand governments, achieved its quantitative objectives.

As these three examples clearly show, even in the most successful downsizings there can be problems along the way — problems that can have far-reaching consequences. The potential economic and social costs of public sector downsizing are clearly sufficient to warrant a closer examination of the current trend towards creating a leaner public service. Despite the importance of this topic and the role of the civil service in the formulation of public policy, there is relatively little information about public sector downsizing and restructuring and how restructuring affects the attitudes of public sector employees toward their work, their managers and their employers. Furthermore, the literature that exists is varied and inconclusive. One issue on which there is apparent agreement is the lack of data available on this topic. Our major goal in the work described here is to close some of the gaps that exist in this literature. As a first step towards that goal we will present the preliminary results of a survey that we carried out in the summer of 1999.

Top Management Experiences with Downsizing in the Ontario Public Service

During July and August of 1999, we surveyed 100 senior managers (directors, assistant deputy ministers and deputy ministers) in the Ontario public service concerning their experiences with downsizing and restructuring. The rate of response to the survey, which was conducted by fax, was approximately 30 percent. Almost all of the respondents had been involved in some kind of downsizing or restructuring exercise in the past five years. Of the 78 percent of the respondents who had been involved in workforce reductions, most describe their organizations' downsizing efforts as an ongoing process in which they were still involved, not as a single "one-off" event.

In the section of the survey dealing specifically with the goals of the restructuring in question, 73 percent of the respondents reported their organization had set specific goals before embarking on the downsizing or restructuring initiative. Almost all (92 percent) of those who set specific goals set quantitative ones. Goals that focussed on measures of cost and/or efficiency were more common than those that focussed on service quality and/or organizational effectiveness.

Most respondents also reported the goal setting process in their organization was a top-down one. Fifty-three percent of the respondents reported that the government was involved in the goal setting process, 68 percent reported that the organization's executives were involved, while only 16 and 26 percent reported involvement by either line managers alone or both line managers and employees, respectively.

Another important set of questions in the survey dealt with communication during the restructuring process. Most of the respondents reported that their organization had put considerable effort into communicating with employees during the restructuring process. Eighty-nine percent of the respondents reported that they held regular meetings with employees during the restructuring. This finding can be regarded as evidence that the public sector managers who responded to a survey had learned from the private sector experiences in literature regarding downsizing. This is a point to which we will return later.

The responses to a series of questions concerning the methods used to reduce staffing levels revealed that the organizations represented by the respondents to our survey relied predominantly on traditional methods of workforce reductions. Fifty percent of the respondents reported that their organization used attrition as one of their methods of workforce reduction; 55 percent reported that they used severance packages and 47 percent reported that they used early retirement programs. However, only 11 percent of respondents reported that they dealt with excess staff by reducing the length of the work week, and only 24 percent reported that they dealt with excess staffing levels by retraining redundant staff to assume new jobs in the organization.

The emphasis on traditional, monetary methods of dealing with departing employees shown in the response pattern regarding methods of staff reductions is echoed in the responses to a question dealing with the compensation and services that the organizations offered departing employees. Sixty-five percent of the respondents reported that they offered departing employees monetary incentives or compensation; 42 percent reported that they provided departing employees with counselling; while only 30 percent reported that they provided placement assistance; and 29 percent reported that they provided training opportunities for departing employees.

Although the responses described in the preceding paragraph suggest that, in general, the organizations represented in our survey did a poor job in assisting departing employees, the situation is, in some ways, worse for employees retained by the respondents' organizations. Only 16 percent of the respondents reported that they provided any counselling to retained employees, while only 11 percent reported that they provided mentoring opportunities for surviving employees. Although a somewhat larger number — 34 percent of respondents — reported that, as part of their downsizing and restructuring program, they empowered retained employees to a greater degree, it can be argued that "empowerment" is often used as a euphemism for reducing the support provided to employees.

In general, most of the respondents to the survey felt that their organization had achieved its goals for its restructuring initiative. Respondents typically viewed the organization as being both more efficient and more effective as a result of the downsizing and restructuring undertaken. They were, however, more likely to feel that their organization had achieved its short-term goals than its longer-term goals.

The respondents were more likely to attribute their organization's success in its downsizing and restructuring efforts to good implementation than good planning. Most respondents felt that management in their organization did a good job at communication and maintaining openness by making themselves available to staff during the restructuring process. Neither employee trust in management nor having the goals of the restructuring process well understood throughout the organization were seen as significant contributors to the success of the downsizing and restructuring initiative.

This last finding highlights an important issue for further study. Much research has shown that shared goals through the organization and employee trust in management are both important contributors to the success of downsizing and restructuring initiatives. There are several possible explanations for this apparent inconsistency between our results and what is generally accepted to be best practices. It is possible that the managers responding to our survey either underestimated the contribution of these factors to their success in the downsizing and restructuring initiatives or overestimated the success of the initiatives. Finally, of course, it is possible that, for some as yet undetermined reason, our results are truly different from the norm.

An additional section of the survey sheds further light on this issue. Despite their general confidence that they had done a good job communicating with their employees throughout the restructuring, when asked what they would do differently were they to undertake the process of restructuring again, just over half of the respondents stated that they would improve their communications with employees. Nearly half of the respondents said that they would focus more on their organization's strategic goals in planning and undertaking major organizational change. Finally, about a third of the respondents stated that they would have involved employees directly in the process to a greater extent.

The fact that the respondents would focus more on strategic issues and goals is very interesting in light of the point made earlier: that the key concern regarding the transferability of private sector management tools to the public sector is the fact that public sector organizations have different and more complex goals than private sector organizations, which, at some level, are driven by the profit motive. The finding that the respondents would direct more effort towards communications and fostering involvement in the restructuring process is not surprising given the work of Greenglass and Burke and other authors who have shown these things to be important elements of a successful restructuring initiative.

The final section of the survey asked respondents how the restructuring in which they were involved had affected them directly. Seventy-one percent of the respondents felt that they themselves worked harder as a result of the restructuring. However, 68 percent also felt that they worked smarter. Perhaps somewhat alarming was the finding that 60 percent of the respondents felt more stress after the restructuring, while only 37 percent felt more motivated in their work.

The Effect of Downsizing on Surviving Employees in the Ontario Public Service

In addition to our survey of upper level managers in the OPS, we performed a survey aimed at comparing job satisfaction and attitudes toward work among mid-level managers and professionals in the private and public sectors in Ontario.[3] In order to ensure comparability and to facilitate the administration of the survey, we targeted lawyers in each of the two sectors for this study. While this choice of sample group may raise questions about the ability to generalize our findings, it provided a good environment for this early stage of research, since it ensured that many of the respondents' personal attributes, job requirements and work environments were consistent across the private and public sector samples.

Measuring Job Satisfaction

While numerous measures of job satisfaction exist, we elected to develop a survey based upon the Job Satisfaction Survey (JSS, Spector, 1997). The JSS was chosen in part because it yields not only an overall measure of job satisfaction, but measures of satisfaction on nine sub-scales as well.[4]

In addition to the questions from the JSS, we included additional questions on our survey relating to burn-out. The literature on burn-out has identified three major elements of burn-out: a feeling that one's life is dominated by one's work; a feeling of emotional exhaustion; and a feeling of detachment from those around oneself. We included one question relating to each of these elements of burn-out in our survey. We also asked two questions concerning an aspect of job satisfaction closely related to burn-out — the ability of respon-

---

3   This survey is discussed in much more detail in Wesson and Barrows (2000, forthcoming).
4   Nine sub-scales measure satisfaction with pay, opportunities for promotion, supervision, general operating conditions in the organization, benefits, contingent rewards, the respondent's co-workers, the nature of the respondent's work (job contentment) and communications within the organization.

dents to strike the right balance between the demands of their work and personal lives.

We also included two simple questions to explore the respondents' assessment of both their employers' current level of effectiveness and how that effectiveness has changed over the past three years. We took a similarly straightforward and simple approach in addressing a single question regarding the respondents' perceptions of their employers' effectiveness in meeting their needs for training.

In another series of additional questions, we asked respondents for their assessments of the leadership provided by senior management in their organizations. This is an important element of job satisfaction — especially during times of restructuring — that is not directly captured by the JSS. One can easily argue that many of the keys to successful downsizing reported by Burke and Greenglass and others relate directly to the effectiveness of the top leadership of the downsizing organization.

Results

We received 60 responses (40 percent response rate) from the private sector lawyers, and 38 responses (25.33 percent response rate) from the public sector lawyers. An unfortunate drawback to the mail survey approach is the typically low response rates associated with this method. These response rates are in the range to be expected from this type of survey. Perhaps what is somewhat surprising is that the response rate from the private sector was higher than that of the public sector.

Sectoral Differences in Responses

The results of our survey indicate significant differences between public and private sector lawyers in Ontario with respect to both intrinsic and extrinsic satisfaction with their job. Furthermore, our findings indicate that differences in the actions and attitudes of top management between the two sectors are directly responsible for a large part of these differences in the attitudes of their employees.

In general, the results of our survey indicate that the public sector respondents were significantly less satisfied with most aspects of their job than the private sector respondents. However, there was one striking exception to this general trend: respondents from the two sectors showed nearly identical levels of satisfaction on the JSS sub-scale that measures respondents' satisfaction with the nature of the work they do. We argue that because the employees in the two sectors are equally satisfied with this most fundamental aspect of their job, they should be able to achieve similar levels of overall job satisfaction.

There are two other aspects of their work in which the two groups did not have significantly different responses: their feelings of burn-out and their feelings about their abilities to balance their work and personal lives. Given the responses we received to the open-ended questions on the survey, it is clear that these results would surprise some of the private sector lawyers, who clearly feel that their public sector counterparts do not work as hard as they do themselves. Members of both groups felt, on average, what could be described as a moderate degree of burn-out (the average score of 3.38 across both groups of respondents on a six-point scale on the three burn-out related questions). The private sector respondents did report slightly higher feelings of burn-out. Both groups reported higher and nearly identical levels of agreement with statements that indicated a lack of ability to find time for themselves and their families (an average score of 4.59 across both groups).

While there are these three areas of similarity between the public and private sector responses to our survey, there are vast differences between the responses of the two sectors in the rest of the survey. The public sector respondents were significantly less satisfied with their pay and benefits, their opportunity for promotion and the performance-contingent rewards they receive (such as recognition for a job well done and a feeling that the organization appreciates one's efforts). The public sector respondents also felt, to a greater extent, that they were bogged down by paperwork and red tape.

The public sector respondents were also less satisfied with the performance of those around them. They were significantly less satisfied with their co-workers, their immediate supervisor and their organization's leadership. Given these results, it is not surprising that the public sector respondents were also significantly less satisfied with the quality of communication in their organization.

Another major area of difference between the two groups of respondents is in terms of their feelings about the training they are receiving. For the public sector respondents, the questions in which they were asked to indicate their level of agreement with the statement that they were receiving adequate training received the lowest average response of any on the survey, indicating that there are vast differences between the training these lawyers think they need and that provided by the Ontario Government. In contrast, the private sector attorneys were relatively well satisfied with the training they were receiving.

A final pair of questions relate to the respondents' perceptions of their organizations' overall effectiveness. Here we see not only that the public sector respondents agree much less than the private sector respondents with the statement that their organization is effective in achieving its goals, but that they are also less likely to agree with the statement that the organization is performing better today than it did three years ago. In fact, this statement is one with which the public sector respondents on average disagree, indicating that the Crown Attorneys responding to our survey see their organizations' performances worsening of late.

Our overall findings are indicative of systemic unhappiness with their work environment on the part of the public sector respondents to our survey, particularly in comparison to the private sector respondents. However, respondents from the two sectors are equally satisfied with the actual work that they perform. That is, the differences we see are not differences in satisfaction with job content, but rather differences in satisfaction with the environment in which the respondents' work is performed.

We also performed an analysis of the correlations among the sub-scales for each sector and between the various sub-scales and some of our demographic variables. The findings of this analysis were consistent with the view that leadership and leadership-related activities are key factors in determining overall levels of employee satisfaction.

The findings of this survey shed important light on differences in the downsizing and restructuring process in the public and private sectors in two important ways. First, much of the downsizing and restructuring literature discussed earlier points to the importance of such factors as strong leadership, effective communications across levels of the organization and fostering a sense of purpose and belonging in survivors as key factors in determining the ultimate success of any downsizing and restructuring initiative. These are all aspects of the work environment in which the public sector organizations represented in our survey seemed to be performing worse than the private sector respondents. Second, the public sector respondents were less positive about their employers' current performance and, perhaps more important, did not feel that this performance was improving.

Conclusions

While we are still at an early point in our research program, there seems to be a consistent story emerging from our work that indicates, based on the first survey described in this paper, that a gap exists between what the literature would have recommended in terms of an optimal downsizing and restructuring strategy to be employed in the Ontario Public Service, and what has actually been done. The results of the second survey provide some evidence of the effects of this gap on the outcomes of downsizing and restructuring exercises in the Ontario Public Service.

If our ongoing work corroborates the effects of these two preliminary studies, then we could apply the following description to downsizing and restructuring in the Ontario Public Service:

> "Instead of using an open, participatory, institution-building approach to downsizing and restructuring, the Ontario Public Service seems to have adopted a top down approach in which leadership was seen to perform poorly by the employees. As a result, the workforce is dissatisfied, unhappy with the performance of their superiors all the way up the organizational hierarchy and left feeling that their organization is, at best, failing to improve."

A further concern with our preliminary findings is that they indicate a marked difference between the perceptions of upper level managers in the Ontario Public Service and those of their subordinates. Again, if our ongoing research continues the pattern seen to date, we will have a situation in which upper management perceives that their restructuring efforts were successful, while further down the organization the view is very different.

Perhaps one reason for this difference in perceptions about the effectiveness of public sector restructuring is that those carrying out the restructuring are looking at it through the lens of cost cutting and efficiency enhancements (hence the emphasis on quantitative goals we found in our survey), while those on the receiving end of the restructuring, as it were, are measuring its effectiveness against different yardsticks. We might also expect that other stakeholders in the process, such as the organizations' specific clientele, would evaluate the effectiveness of downsizing and restructuring against goals that extend beyond the purely monetary (although perhaps this would not be the case for the tax-paying general public). If this difference in evaluation criteria is indeed a contributor to the apparent difference between senior management and their subordinates in their evaluations of the effectiveness of downsizing and restructuring, then it could be argued that this difference is symptomatic of the fact that the use of downsizing and restructuring in the public sector represents the transfer of a private sector model to the public sector, where organizational goals are more complex than in the private sector.

A final conclusion of our research is that there is little evidence of what could be called a "Second Mover Advantage" — that is, there is little evidence that public sector managers, as late adopters of downsizing and restructuring, were able to learn from the experiences of their private sector counterparts. Although the respondents to the first survey reported here claim that they focussed on communications and other inclusionary practices in their downsizing and restructuring plans, their statements about what they would do differently in the future and the results of our second survey cast serious doubts on this assertion.

As a final note, we should emphasize again that all of the findings presented in this paper can only be thought of as tentative. The size and scope of the surveys upon which our study is based do not allow us to make firm conclusions, only to speculate about potential firm conclusions that could be made based on a larger study. Clearly then, it is our goal to continue our work with much larger and broader studies based on large sample surveys and in-depth field interviews with managers and professionals at various levels in both the Ontario Public Service and comparable private sector organizations.

References

Allen, T.D., D.M. Freeman, R.C. Reizenstein and J.O. Reatz, *Just Another Transition? Examining Survivor's Attitudes Over Time*. The University of Tennessee, Department of Management, 1994.

Bennett, A., "Downscoping Doesn't Necessarily Bring an Upswing in Corporate Profitability" *The Wall Street Journal*, June 4, 1991, pp. B-1 and B-4.

Burke, Ronald J. & Esther R. Greenglass, "Organization Support during Health Care Downsizing and Restructuring" York University, mimeo, 1998.

———, "Union support during organizational restructuring," York University, mimeo, 1998.

———, "The Relationship Between Hospital Restructuring, Anger and Hostility in Nurses" York University, mimeo, 1998.

Cacio, W.T., "Downsizing: What do we know? What have we Learned?" *The Academy of Management Executive* (1993), Volume VII, number 1.

Cacio, W.T., J.R. Morris and C.E. Young, "Downsizing after all these years: Questions and answers about who did it, how many did it, and who benefited from it," *Organizational Dynamics* (Winter 1999).

Tom Wesson and David Barrows

Greenberg, E.R., "The latest AMA Survey on Downsizing," *Compensation and Benefits Review* (1990), Volume 22.

McKinley, W., C.M. Sanchez and A.G. Schick, "Organizational Downsizing: Constraining, Cloning and Learning," *Academy of Management Executive* (1995), 9: 32–42.

Mroczkowski, T., and M. Hanaoka, "Effective rightsizing strategies in Japan and America: Is there a convergence of employment practices?" *The Academy of Management Executive* (1997), Volume XI, Number 2, pp. 57–67.

Spector, Paul E., *Job Satisfaction: Application, Assessment, Cause and Consequences*, Thousand Oaks, California: Sage Publications, 1997.

Wall Street Journal "Lack of Communication Burdens Restructuring," November 2, 1992.

Role of Interest Groups in Influencing Public Policy in Canada

W.T. Stanbury and
Sean Moore

Introduction[1]

The purpose of this paper is to describe and discuss some of the important aspects of the role interest groups[2] play in seeking to influence public policy in Canada. The issues on which they focus are highly varied: civil rights, contraception, the prevention of nuclear war, tax policy, gender, sexual orientation, international trade policy and the preservation of everything from particular languages or cultures to wilderness areas, heritage buildings, dairy farms and endangered species.

The interests represented by one or more groups may be material, or symbolic, or both. Indeed, any one of the enormous range and variety of factors that motivate human behaviour may be represented by an interest group. Salis-

---

1   This paper draws heavily upon Stanbury (1994) with the kind permission of Captus Press, but all that material has been revised where necessary or desirable. Far more comprehensive analyses can be found in Stanbury (1993a), (1992). See also Pross (1992), Phillips et al. (1990); Thorburn (2001); Pross (1982), (1986), (1992); and Phillips (1994), (2002). This paper is to be included in a textbook being prepared by Professor Diane Jurkowski of the School of Administrative Studies, York University for a course entitled *Business in the Canadian Context*.

2   We use the term interest group broadly to refer to any effort by any group or organization (formal or informal) to influence any public policy. Thus, when Ford of Canada is seeking a subsidy to build a new plant, it is acting as an interest group.

bury (1991, p. 376) argues that "no firm or permanent line of demarcation differentiates political interest groups from those that are not political. Interests change, emerge or are discovered; the actualization of interests is a dynamic process". He suggests that "much of the task of interest group representatives lies in discovering what their groups' interests are so as to protect and perhaps advance them" (Salisbury, 1991, p. 373). At the same time, not all interests — even some very important ones — get organized and participate in policy-making processes due to what might be called the "logic of collective inaction" (see Olson, 1965).

Would-be managers and ordinary citizens need to understand how interest groups operate in the political arena and policy-making processes for a variety of reasons. First, many interest groups make such an effort to influence public policy that different groups become rivals both in trying to place their issues on the policy-making agenda (see Kingdon, 1995) and in trying to influence policy makers. Second, many groups obtain direct financial assistance from government, and individual business firms obtain indirect assistance because their expenditures on government relations, including membership fees in industry associations, which lobby on their behalf, are tax deductible.[3] Third, a number of interest groups seek to influence the behaviour of business firms as well as government. For example, a number of environmental groups tried to stop the cutting of old-growth timber by BC forest companies by blockading logging roads and by persuading their customers to stop buying from them (see Stanbury, 2000). This was part of a larger effort to get the Province to change its forest policies. Fourth, interest groups perform important functions in a democratic society, through both lobbying and involvement in consultations, improving the making and implementation of public policy.

Interest groups attempt to influence governments to take certain actions, but government actions may also have the effect of creating interests, directly or indirectly. For example, when it established the old age pension, the federal government created a flow of income that each pensioner has a direct interest in having continue. People quickly become accustomed to any benefit. Expectations soon form about the continuation and, perhaps, increase in size of a benefit, and so any threatened reduction in the flow of benefits is likely to provoke a hostile reaction, and this may result in the formation of an interest group.[4]

The motivation behind many actions by interest groups is negative — to stop a proposed action by government (or reverse a recent one). The fear of the loss of an accustomed position is stronger than the anxiety over opportunity losses.

The body of this paper is organized as follows: Section 2 describes the focus of interest group activities, namely government actions that embody public policies (and also those of the courts). Section 3 briefly identifies the actors and institutions involved in policy-making processes and explains the nature of the exchanges that occur in them. In Section 4 we discuss the various types of

---

3   See the discussion of government of the voluntary sector in LeRoy (2002a).
4   For example, the Canadian Federation of Independent Business was established in the early 1970s in direct response to proposed changes in tax policy that would have reduced important tax breaks then enjoyed by small businesses (see McQuaig, 1988).

interest groups and review their functions in a democracy. Section 5 notes important characteristics of business firms as interest groups. Section 6 describes the increasing number of government relations consultants and the kinds of things they do for their clients. Section 7 examines several of the most important techniques interest groups use to influence public policies (lobbying, stimulating the grass roots, direct action tactics, advocacy advertising, and litigation). Section 8 sketches how new information and communications technologies are influencing the creation and operation of interest groups. Section 9 outlines the regulation of interest groups by the federal government. Finally, we offer some brief conclusions in section 10.

This paper focuses primarily on a positive analysis of the activities of interest groups in their efforts to influence public policies; i.e., it is descriptive, outlining in an analytical framework what groups do. We provide little normative analysis, i.e., what groups *ought* to do in order to increase the odds they will obtain the kinds of changes in public policy they seek. That would require a separate volume.

Actions that Embody Public Policy: The Focus of Interest Group Activities

In general terms, public policy can be thought of as various actions of a government designed to modify the behaviour of citizens. These actions are ultimately backed up by the legitimate (constitutional) coercive powers granted to a government by a democratically-elected legislature.[5] Interest groups seek to influence public policy in all of its many forms. Government actions that embody public policy include the following:

- New statutes enacted by the legislature;[6]
- Amendments to existing statutes;
- Subordinate legislation, such as regulations or orders-in-council, that need be approved only by the cabinet or a single minister (not the legislature);[7]

---

5   Note that the ultimate source of such power in a democracy lies with citizens — they delegate it to their representatives.

6   Under Canada's version of the Westminster model of government, the cabinet (appointed by the prime minister) controls the executive and effectively controls the legislature so long as the party in power has a majority of the seats in the House of Commons. Thus cabinet ministers have an effective monopoly over the supply of new legislation (statutes and amendments) to the legislature. Party discipline is used to ensure that what the cabinet proposes is, in fact, enacted. For this reason, interest groups seeking to influence legislation must focus on the minister (and, particularly, his/her departmental officials and ministerial advisers) who sponsors new legislation, and on the central agencies that provide advice (notably the Privy Council Office) and generally control the Government's agenda (the Prime Minister's Office). There is no doubt, however, that the prime minister, by far, exercises the most power in the federal government (Savoie, 1999).

7   Subordinate legislation (called the sinews of government) has the same force of law as does legislation, but it is usually created by (or approved by) a committee of the cabinet (the

- Formal decisions of regulatory agencies to grant licenses to enter an industry, alter the terms of such licenses, set tariffs or otherwise constrain private-sector decisions;[8]
- Cabinet decisions on appeals from the decisions of regulatory agencies;[9]
- The exercise of discretion by line departments and regulatory agencies in day-to-day dealings with private-sector actors.[10] These take the form of the application of regulations and the interpretation of policy guidelines, internal policy manuals or interpretation bulletins available to the public;
- Ministerial policy statements (in the legislature, or in the form of press releases or internal guidelines to bureaucrats);[11]

Special Committee of Council). Since 1985, the federal government has required that departments putting forward new regulations (or amendments to regulations) engage in consultation with affected interests, pre-publish a draft of the proposed regulations in the *Canada Gazette*, allow time for the public comment on the draft, and include with the draft regulations a regulatory Impact Analyses Statement that is to contain a cost-benefit analysis. Then, after the sponsoring department responds to comments, the Special Committee of Council enacts the regulations they are published in the Canada Gazette. For interest groups to be able to exercise influence, they must get into the process as early as possible — no later than the consultation process.

8 Regulatory agencies are important elements in the policy-making processes. While they operate under various statutes and (sets of) regulations, they exercise considerable discretion in interpreting legislation and policy statements when they apply both to specific cases. Their important decisions follow public hearings at which both the parties directly involved present their positions (sometimes aided by experts), and interveners offer advice on the matters before the agency/tribunal. While there has been some liberalization and even some outright deregulation in Canada (see Ostry & Stanbury, 1999), government regulation shapes a great deal of economic activity in Canada. In the cultural industries, such as broadcasting, government regulation (and other forms of intervention) has increased over the past two decades or so (see Stanbury, 1998). Despite trade liberalization agreements, supply managed agricultural products (chicken, turkeys, eggs, milk) remain a bastion of government-mandated monopoly (see Stanbury, 2002c).

9 Regulatory agencies in Canada are subject to far more political control by the Cabinet than most of their counterparts in the US One key tool is that of political appeals from agency decisions to the cabinet, which has very wide discretion in modifying a decision (even reversing it) or sending it back to the agency for reconsideration in light of issues emphasized by the cabinet. Since there are no public hearings by the cabinet, parties with the largest stakes often lobby ministers. In this way, they can raise issues addressed in their formal submissions that are likely to be in the public domain. Note, however, that appeals to cabinet do not occur frequently and most are not successful. At the same time, it appears that their frequency has increased (see Fraser, 2002).

10 The exercise of discretion by ministers and public servants (middle and senior levels) is endemic in governments. Discretion means that individuals are able to exercise their judgement within the criteria set out in a statute or regulations. The scope of discretion may be narrow (usually at lower levels) or wide (usually at higher levels). Discretion is a double-edged sword — it can be used to help or to harm the person/group seeking a decision from government. Much lobbying focuses on persuading the government decision-maker (individual or group of individuals) to exercise their legitimate discretion in favour of the group (or individual). For example, when the very wealthy Reichmann family proposed to acquire Gulf Oil, their lawyers were able to persuade the Department of Finance and the cabinet to interpret the tax laws in such a way as to save the family some $500 million in tax payments. The Reichmanns lawyers argued that without this exercise of discretion this Canadianization of a US-owned oil company would not proceed (see McQuaig, 1988).

11 Since the language of key statutes may be very broad, it is often made operational by means of ministerial policy statements. A very good example is that of federal aviation policy since

- The annual Estimates — expenditure allocations among departments and agencies;[12]
- The Revenue budget[13] (changes in tax policy, including tax expenditures);
- Central agency directives to line departments that affect that department's "clients" (these agencies include Treasury Board, Privy Council Office, Department of Finance);
- Direct financial benefits (e.g., grants, loans, loan guarantees);[14]
- Procurement contracts to sell goods and services to government[15] (the federal government is the largest single buyer in the economy);
- Intergovernmental (i.e., federal-provincial-territorial) or international agreements; and
- Appointments of individuals to government positions (the federal government has about 3,500 order-in-council appointees, and the choice is made largely by the prime minister).

the 1990s. That policy has been driven largely by various official statements of the Minister of Transport (see Ross & Stanbury, 2001). Therefore, airlines, potential entrants and consumer groups interested in changing aviation policy have had to focus most of their efforts on convincing the Minister (often through his senior officials) that certain changes should be made.

12 In general, expenditures still constitute the largest tool governments use to effect public policies. The total outlays by the federal government in 2001/2002 amounted to $164.4 billion (Department of Finance, 2002), or about $5,346 per capita. Program spending amounted to $126.7 billion, while public debt charges were $37.7 billion. Budgetary revenues in 2001/2002 were $173.3 billion. And note that provincial plus local government expenditures far exceed federal outlays. The annual Estimates process that leads up to Parliament's approval of each year's expenditures is very well defined. Lobbyists seeking to modify the level and direction of expenditure flows must begin putting pressure on various targets in government at least a year prior to the start of the fiscal year (April 1 through March 31) in which they expect the change to occur (see Hartle, 1988). There is, however, some opportunity to get ministers to move smaller amounts around within their total envelope during the course of a year. And in the odd case, new money can be obtained during the fiscal year through the Supplementary Estimates process (although it is used largely to increase the budget of programs whose expenditures are running ahead of the level approved in the Estimates).

13 The timing of the Revenue budget (often called *the Budget*) is largely up to the Minister of Finance, in consultation with the Prime Minister, although in recent years the Budget has usually been introduced in February or March. While it now is the practice to engage in consultations in the weeks or months leading up to the Budget, the import of such consultations varies greatly depending upon the inclination of the Minister of Finance. Both the Department of Finance and the Commons Finance Committee hold consultations of various sorts prior to the Revenue budget. Lobbyists seeking changes in the tax system and, particularly, specific rulings may involve several years of sustained effort by various groups posing much the same point (see McQuaig, 1988). Note that the creation of the Revenue budget is shrouded in secrecy — unlike the Estimates process.

14 Some companies, e.g., Bombardier, have a reputation of being able to obtain a great deal of direct financial help from Ottawa. Recently, Ford, General Motors and Daimler Chrysler obtained a subsidy of $625 million over five years from the Ontario government after intense lobbying (Corcoran, 2003). Ford Canada and Daimler Chrysler were also seeking $250 million and $400 million respectively from the federal government to help build new plants.

15 Huge amounts of money move from the federal to provincial governments and from the have to have-not provinces, via complex federal-provincial fiscal arrangements. These involve shared cost programs and revenue sharing. Naturally, the provinces lobby hard to get more money from Ottawa.

We emphasize that each of these actions that embody government policies are the result of a distinct process with its own policy community, venue and mechanics. In short, federal government policies are the result of at least a dozen different policy-making processes.

Public policy is also made by the courts, which are part of the state, but independent of government, although judges are appointed by a province or by the prime minister. The courts make public policy in two main ways: (I) decisions flowing from judicial review of administrative actions (including those of regulatory agencies). These involve providing authoritative interpretations of statutes and appeals based on alleged failure to abide by the rules of natural justice, and (ii) decisions that interpret the Constitution, including the Charter of Rights and Freedoms. The most authoritative decisions are those of the Supreme Court of Canada.

Public policy is most obviously embodied in new legislation or amendments to existing legislation — statutes enacted by Parliament or a provincial legislature (municipal by-laws would also be included here). A widely debated new statute is certainly the most dramatic and obvious instrument of public policy (e.g., Bill C-68 in December 1995, which greatly extended the federal regulation of firearms). But it is only one of many; it would be a major mistake for interest groups to concentrate all or even much of their efforts in seeking to influence new legislation (including amendments). The fact is that a great deal of law (let alone policy) is not enacted by the legislature. The consequences of many statutes are only understandable by reference to the regulations passed by a committee of the cabinet pursuant to the statute. As important in many cases are the operational interpretations of statutes and regulations, as well as the less frequent but important formal interpretations made by the courts. Because the enactment of new statutes (or amendments) is so visible, uninformed students of government tend to spend too much time on this one expression of public policy and too little on the other less visible, more arcane, but nevertheless important instruments of public policy.[16]

While it is common to speak of the policy-making process, this is misleading because there are multiple policy-making processes. They do have one key thing in common — each process operates within a legal framework authorized in a statute or in subordinate legislation (which has the same force of law). Thus, one of the earliest things a would-be lobbyist must determine is which policy-making process is relevant to the *issue(s)* his/her group wants addressed, and the type of *action* the group wants the government (or possibly a court) to take. There may be several actions that could achieve the same purpose. and so

---

16   Further, Doern and Phidd (1983, p. 103) explain that there can be policies without resources (money, personnel, time and political will) to support them. Many governments find it necessary to enunciate policy to express their concern about, and support for, a particular constituency or group, since this is usually preferable to expressing no public concern whatsoever. This takes us into the world of symbolic politics, where the object is to show concern, to temporize, to husband scarce resources whose expenditure may produce little or no substantive result, but above all, to be seen to be doing something in response to interest-group pressures or a politician's identification of a latent concern of important groups of voters.

the lobbyist must consider both the likelihood of success of each and also the different costs of each alternative.

Actors, Institutions and Exchanges

The major actors and institutions in the various policy-making processes include the government (notably its departments, agencies and Crown corporations), the cabinet, public servants, voters, political parties, news media, interest groups (including corporations, trade associations and unions) and the courts (judiciary). The role of each is outlined in **Figure 1**.

The public-choice approach offers a way of understanding what goes on in political markets. A key idea is that policies are exchanged by political parties for financial and other resources. For example, in Albert Breton's view, "the trading process can be caricatured as follows: 'if you will donate some money to our party, we will provide you in exchange with a tariff which will allow you to reap monopoly rents of such and such magnitude, or we will allow you to form a professional or trade association that will have the power to set standards, to define the terms of licenses, to set the rates that can be charged for services rendered, and so on'" (Breton, 1976, p. 16). In other words, political parties obtain campaign contributions from firms and other interest groups in exchange for promises of favourable policies when they gain or retain power.[17]

However, the political exchange process is rather more complicated in reality. First of all, in Canada, even the implicit exchange of policy favours for campaign contributions is widely condemned as undesirable or even immoral behaviour. Second, an MP (or public servant) who accepts money for actions by the government beneficial to the person paying the money may be violating the Criminal Code (see Federal Government Regulation of Lobbyists and Interest Group Activities, below). Third, contributions to political parties and candidates seldom exceed $50,000. Moreover, there are legal limits in the *Canada Elections Act* on the "election expenses" of parties or candidates during the official campaign period, and both are required to disclose the names of all donors (individuals or organizations) contributing more than $200 p.a. in cash or kind.[18]

---

17   Hartle (1988, p. 52) suggests that donations by rent-seeking interest groups to political parties and to the election campaigns of particular candidates can be looked upon as a siphoning off of some of the rents by those who make it their business to put together coalitions of rent seekers and who garner rents on behalf of the members of the coalition through the introduction of appropriate policies.

18   For the November 2000 federal general election, the average limit on election expenses for candidates was $68,000 (the amount varies in part based on the number of electors in the constituency) and less than 10 percent of candidates came within 5percent of their limit. A party running a full slate of 301 candidates had a limit of $12.7 million. Only the Liberal Party came close to the limit set for each party. (Note that there are no limits on what parties can spend outside the official campaign period, now usually 36 days.) On January 29, 2003, Bill C-24, amendments to the *Canada Elections Act* dealing with political finances, was given First Reading. It proposes to set a limit of $1000 per year on contributions to candidates and nomination contestants by corporations, unions and unincorporated organizations. Individuals are to have three limits of $10,000 p.a. depending on to whom

All of this indicates that policies are not simply "sold" for campaign contributions. A richer explanation is required. In practice, what is the medium of exchange between interest groups and political parties? First, interest groups may spend their own money (in lieu of a party's money) directly on campaigns to support candidates, parties and policies following an agreement by the party to take the actions requested by the interest group.[19] However, if Bill C-24 becomes law, interest groups could only contribute $1000 p.a. to candidates and/ or nomination contestants — and nothing to a party per se. Second, and more important, the interest group can co-operate with the party in power — it agrees to go along with the party on policy A (which it would otherwise oppose) in exchange for the party implementing policy B (which the group favours).[20] Where trust is well developed, the exchange may not be contemporaneous. Government (and the party in power) seeks public "buy-in" from interest groups, including public endorsement of the initiative (i.e., providing laudatory comment and giving the government credit) and, possibly, some form of participation in its implementation. In dealing with business interests, governments want more than anything else, tangible responses from business interests, such as announcements of new investment or job creation, as evidence that their policies are working.

Third, possibly the most valuable resource the interest group has to offer a politician or party is information, the exchange of which is subject neither to campaign-financing legislation nor to moral strictures. The information most valuable to politicians consists of (a) knowledge of the preference of voters, particularly uncommitted voters (those who may be persuaded to vote for the party); (b) knowledge of the likely political reactions of voters to both existing policies and potential policies that the party might propose; and (c) knowledge of the most efficient and effective ways to influence uncommitted (or "marginal") voters,[21] by means of both substantive policy actions and intentionally persuasive communications. Politicians and public servants appreciate the fact that the information provided by interest groups is not so much likely to be wrong or untruthful but rather selective in terms of the facts presented and in terms of the interpretation placed upon those facts. These groups are acting as advocates in their own cause. However, an interest group (or professional lobbying firm) that lied or engaged in misrepresentation would soon lose its credi-

---

their donations are directed: a) $10,000 for each registered party, including its electoral district associations, nomination contestants and/or candidates for MP, b) $10,000 for the leadership contestants of each party holding a leadership race, and c) $10,000 for each independent or non-affiliated candidate for MP. The loss of contributions from corporations and unions is to be offset by a new annual public subsidy for registered parties equal to $1.50 per vote obtained in the last general election. See Stanbury (2003d).

19   Note, however, that there are tight limits on so-called third parties who wish to spend money during official election campaigns. See section 9a) below.

20   It should be obvious that there is a potential for deception, bluffing and other forms of strategic behaviour. For example, a group could launch a vigorous campaign against an existing policy, toward which it really was indifferent, to create a bargaining chip to be exchanged for an action on a policy it really cared about.

21   Duffy (2002, p. 36) points out that during the nineteenth century [in Canada] the largest single vote swing from one election to the next was 8 percent [sic, 8 percentage points]; most of the time it was more like 2.5 [percentage points]. Today, swings of 9 [percentage points] are the norm, and up to 20 percent of voters can switch sides in the middle of a campaign.

Figure 1: **Major Actors and Institutions and their Roles in Politics and Policy-Making Processes**

Governments
- Exercise legitimate power of coercion through governing a variety of instruments (taxes, expenditures, regulation, "tax expenditures," loans/guarantees, suasion)
- Are subject to the Constitution as interpreted by the courts (but able to amend it
- ·Exercise social control over behaviour of business and other groups
- Effect income/wealth transfers to alter the distribution of income
- Arrange for provision of many collective goods

Cabinet
- Is collectively responsible for the executive to the legislature
- Through its committees, "filters" major policy initiatives of individual ministers All members are appointed and removed by the Prime Minister
- Amounts to a periodically elected collective kingship where their party has a majority in the legislature
- Has virtual monopoly over the supply of legislation
- Is able to create law by approving regulations (subordinate legislation)without reference to the legislature (provided the statue authorizes it to do so)

Public Servants
- Provide the Government with technical knowledge/policy advice
- Administer public policies/programs
- Are a "permanent," professional cadre (not partisan)
- Implement policies chosen by politicians who make the values choices and are responsible for these policies to the legislature, and ultimately to voters

Voters
- Collectively select the Government of the day by electing local MPs
- Create public opinion, which constrains/encourages government
- Join interest groups which seek to influence government between elections
- Rely heavily on the news media (particularly TV) for information on policy making and knowledge of the world generally

Political Parties
- Are organizations of individuals that compete for office
- Act as a mediating institution between individual and the state
- Select a leader whose words and actions come to symbolize the party
- Seek a majority of seats in general elections to become the government of the day
- Organize election campaigns, solicit funds and develop policy promises
- Offer policy promises in exchange for political support

Figure 1 Cont.

News Media
- Provide a major communications channel among all actors
- Define, select, amplify, distort the "news"
- Are business enterprises (selling audiences to advertisers)
- Sometimes act as the unelected opposition
- Help to shape public opinion (primary source of political news)
- Are relied upon by voters for information about politics and policy-making (TV more so than newspapers)

Interest Groups (including corporations and unions)
- Aggregate interests (reduce cacophony); provide information to policy makers
- Seek to advance the interests of members by a variety of techniques to influence governments and the courts
- Represent "values" as well as economic (pecuniary) interests
- Mediate between citizens and government
- Often use the news media strategically to influence governments
- May employ government relations consultants to assist them
- All interests do not get organized due to the "free rider" problem

Courts/ Judiciary
- Independent of the executive, the legislature, interest groups and voters
- Judges of superior courts are appointed by the Prime Minister
- Adjudicate private and public disputes
- Interpret the laws (including the Constitution) and regulations; review the actions of administrative bodies upon appeal
- Have played a greater role in shaping public policy since the Charter of Rights and Freedoms was enacted in 1982 (as part of the new Constitution). Interest groups have played an important role in bringing/financing cases and as interveners.

bility with those it was seeking to influence.[22] Virtually all writers on the politics of interest groups emphasize the importance of the credibility of interest group representatives.

The fourth possible medium of exchange between interest groups and political parties relates to the capacity of the former to shape public opinion and to

---

22 The public seems to make an exception in the case of at least some environmental groups (see Stanbury, 2000).

help define the limited number of issues that make up the public policy agenda (see Stanbury, 1993a, Chapter 10).

Interest Groups: Definition, Functions and Types

Definition

Jeffrey Berry (1989, p. 4) states that an interest group "is an organized body of individuals who share some goals and who try to influence public policy". Wilson (1990, p. 8) states that interest groups are formal organizations (social movements are excluded) that try to influence public policy (although this may not be their primary activity), and have some autonomy from government and political parties.[23] Wilson (1990, chapter 2) argues that four features set interest groups apart from other forms of social organization. First, they are multi-member organizations, although the members may be individuals, firms or other organizations. Second, membership is voluntary. While interest groups may have fairly restrictive criteria for membership, members cannot be formally prohibited from leaving. Third, interest groups are highly dependent upon the active involvement of members in joining and conducting their activities. ("Staff groups" are an exception — they are discussed below.) Fourth, interest groups have a narrow focus of concern — it may be a single issue or a variety of related ones in a wider domain, but is far narrower than that of a political party, for example. In addition to these characteristics, the central or defining characteristic of interest groups is that they seek to influence public policy, directly or indirectly, by trying to influence public opinion.

Schlozman and Tierney (1986, pp. 9–10) use the term "organized interests", rather than "interest groups", so as to include not only membership associations, such as trade unions and environmental groups, but also politically active organizations that have no members in the ordinary sense (such as universities, corporations and hospitals). In their view, "organized interests" refers to "the wide variety of organizations that seek joint ends through political action".

Functions

Interest groups perform a variety of functions in a democratic society, including the following:

  i. Acting as Signalling Mechanisms: General elections occur only every three to five years at the federal or provincial level in Canada and they are relatively crude mechanisms for transforming the policy preferences of individuals into government action (see Stanbury, 2002d). Interest

---

23   Wilson (1990, p. 6) notes that most organizations that participate in interest group politics do recruit individuals with the promise to represent their views or interests politically, referring to business firms, unions and professional organizations. In each case, the primary activities of the organization do not relate to influencing public policy.

groups can play a valuable role in "signalling" the preferences of citizens between elections — particularly in a world that is continually changing and, thereby, creating new information and new issues of concern to citizens. Interest groups are not the only mechanism available for signalling preferences, of course, nor are all important interests represented by such groups. That is one of the reasons why all modern democratic governments make considerable use of scientific public opinion polls. It is also why the federal government is planning to make more extensive use of public consultation and "citizen engagement" exercises.

ii. Aggregating Interests: Groups are able to aggregate individual interests into more manageable units. It is very difficult for governments to listen to millions of voices speaking independently. Further, participation in groups may inculcate respect for democratic values, such as debate, tolerance, negotiation and compromise. Because they may well represent and defend minority interests, interest groups can temper the possibility of the "tyranny of the majority".

iii. Providing Information: Interest groups provide information to government through their specialized technical knowledge and information about political support for proposed and existing policies. A former senior official in the Ontario government suggests that the "client groups" of government departments "can be of considerable assistance to the Government because of the particular knowledge and insight which they possess, and their reaction to contemplated policies and programs can be invaluable in assessing their appropriateness" (Stewart, 1989, p. 81).

iv. Contributing to Policy Development: Interest groups propose policy options and changes in public policy. Interest groups — even those seeking to advance private, pecuniary interests in the political arena[24] — may increase society's welfare, depending upon the nature of society's "welfare function," the degree of competition in the policy process, and other factors.

v. Providing Resources: Interest groups can help to finance the electoral activities of parties and candidates. They do so, of course, in the expectation of influencing public policy. In Canada, however, the data indicate that financial contributions from interest groups other than business firms and trade unions are very small (Stanbury, 2001). (This is not the case in the United States, however.)

vi. Acting as Agents of Government: Interest groups may, in some cases, act as agents of government to regulate members and administer government programs, such as occupational groups. Charitable groups have established hospitals that now depend on government funding. There are many voluntary agencies, some of which receive funds to provide services

---

24 For example, if there is a widely held preference for a more egalitarian distribution of income, and a group succeeds in obtaining policies that redistribute income from the rich to the poor, then it may have improved society's welfare.

to citizens.[25] Such groups may help implement public policies at less cost than would public servants in a government department.

Types of Groups

There are a number of ways of classifying interest groups and other entities that seek to influence public policy. This section outlines several classifications.

Institutional Groups versus Issue-Oriented Groups

Professor Paul Pross (1986, chapter 5) explains that institutional groups are characterized as having organizational continuity and cohesion, extensive knowledge of areas of government relevant to members, easy communication, stable membership, concrete and immediate operational objectives, and organizational imperatives that are more important than any particular objective. Institutional groups are more likely to be successful because they recognize that "[O]rganization is the key to the exploitation of power in the modern community" (Pross, 1986, p. 114). The attributes of organization are as follows: a formal structure incorporating at least several people (or several thousand people) — a hierarchy; a clear definition of roles (specialization and division of labour); and the ability to generate and allocate resources. In addition, an organization has a collective memory, rules governing the behaviour of members and leaders, and procedures for reaching and implementing decisions.

In contrast, issue-oriented groups have the following characteristics, according to Pross (1986, chapter 5). They have limited organizational continuity and cohesion; most are badly organized. They have limited knowledge of how government functions; they are often naïve. Their membership is fluid, often depending on the visibility and immediate salience of particular issues. These groups have considerable difficulty in formulating and adhering to longer-range objectives. In general, they have a low regard for organizational mechanisms to achieve their goals. Perhaps because of their lack of organization, issue-oriented groups can act in ways quite different from institutional groups. Being flexible, they may be able to generate immediate public reactions to government action. Since members usually have little or no pecuniary stake in the issue, they can indulge in tactics not acceptable if used by institutionalized groups. They are able to command media attention, possibly embarrass the government and force a change in policy or in its short-run behaviour. Finally, issue-oriented groups may serve as more radical proxies for established interests that cannot afford to be seen to be using certain tactics.

While issue-oriented groups lack all of the characteristics of institutional groups, some do become institutionalized in time — the Canadian Federation of Agriculture and Canadian Federation of Independent Business are two well known examples. In between these two poles are what Pross (1986, pp. 120–121) calls the "fledgling" and "mature" interest groups.

---

25 Indeed, some interest groups (e.g., those supporting immigrants from various countries) help to finance their efforts to influence government policy by making a margin on the activities they perform which are funded by government. Generally, see LeRoy (2002a).

Staff versus Membership Groups

Hayes (1981) draws a careful distinction between staff and membership groups. The latter are characterized by a large number of contributors from the general public and a governing board that is not controlled by the full-time staff people who manage the daily operations of the group. The key distinction is whether the group seeks a membership base or not. Staff groups do not seek an active membership base; rather, they seek contributors to causes that are defined by the staff, which forms the leadership cadre which governs the organization. Note, however, that donors to staff groups may well be called members even though they play no role in governance (see Stanbury, 2000; and Jordan & Maloney, 1997).

Most US authors emphasize that the majority of more recent public interest or citizen's groups are not traditional, membership-based organizations. They have overcome the "free-rider" problem by limiting effective participation in the development of the organization's strategy to their small professional staffs (see Berry, 1977; McFarland, 1976, 1983). The staff has effective control; it identifies the issues to be addressed and determines the targets and tactics of the group. Staff often have a high degree of commitment to the organization and are willing to pursue distant and intangible goals. Further, the staff develop a strong interest in sustaining the group as such because it is the vehicle by which they can earn income as well as try to achieve their non-pecuniary collective goals, such as environmental protection legislation (see Stanbury, 2000).

Single-Issue Groups and Protest Groups

By definition, single-issue groups are those organized around a single policy issue. The classic example consists of anti-abortion groups, but the category also includes animal rights groups and those environmental groups with a very narrow focus (such as saving the whales or preserving old growth forests). Single-issue groups are often hard to accommodate in the political/policy-making process. For members, the issue on which they focus their efforts is a matter of primary importance; it holds trumps over all other matters. There is little or no room for compromise. Moreover, negotiation is seen as moral betrayal by the most righteous supporters. Such groups are inevitably conflict-ridden, as the "true believers" seek to overcome those who would compromise with policy makers (see Stanbury, 2000).

Single-issue groups appear to be growing in importance, for a number of reasons. First, they are a reaction to the growing complexity of political processes and institutions. While social and economic problems are complex, people yearn for "simple solutions". Second, there has been a decline in the influence of political parties and other mediating institutions, such as the family and the church. Third, new information and communication technologies make it easier to mobilize a constituency (see New Information and Communications Technologies and Interest Groups, below).

So-Called "Public Interest" Groups

Jeffrey Berry (1989, p. 7) defines a public-interest group as "one that seeks a collective good, the achievement of which will not selectively and materially benefit the membership or activists of the organization".[26] In his earlier book, Berry (1977, p. 137) defined collective goods as those policies for which the benefits may be shared equally by all people, independent of membership or support for any given group. He excluded groups that receive their funding from governmental sources[27] from his definition of public interest groups because they operate under much different constraints (Berry, 1977, p. 143).

Phillips, Pal, Hawkes and Savas (1990, p. 1) describe a public interest group as one whose members act together to influence public policy in order to promote their common interest, and whose objective is to benefit people beyond their own membership.[28] Their intentions are not centred upon providing direct economic benefits to their members. Membership is voluntary and relatively open; restrictions are likely to be based only on the interest and identity base of the group. Phillips et al. (1990) describe the following types of groups as being public-interest groups: ethnic or multiculturalism groups, minority language associations, Aboriginal groups, women's groups and disabled persons' groups. The breadth of the definition has been strongly challenged (see Stanbury, 1993b).[29]

The amount of resources available greatly shapes the specific objectives and activities of public interest groups. It is common for much of the staff's time to be spent on fund-raising (and for one quarter to one half the amount of funds raised to be absorbed by fund-raising costs). Hence, the leadership may have to be responsive to different entities outside the group's membership. For quite a number of groups, the ability to issue tax receipts for contributions is very important. Some groups, such as the National Citizens' Coalition, are not able to issue receipts to make contributions eligible for the tax credit available for contributions to registered charities (see Federal Government Regulation of Lobbyists and Interest Group Activities, below). In some cases, "advocacy groups" take actions in order to create visibility for the group, which can use it to attract members and funding (see Stanbury, 2000).

---

26 The scope and scale of the collective good pursued by public interest groups varies greatly. Some organizations (such as feminist, peace and environmentalist groups) seek to transform the most basic as well as the most embracing of human relationships: those of the sexes, nations, and of humanity to nature. Others are less expressive: for example, the student and consumer movements (Phillips et al., 1990, p. 16).

27 Note that in the early 1990s, the federal government made grants to only 1000 interest groups (see Phillips, 1991). During efforts to cut the deficit, the number and size of such grants declined a great deal. Unfortunately, even the most detailed parts of the Public Accounts make it impossible to provide current data on such grants/contributions. For a broad picture of government support for voluntary organizations, see LeRoy (2002a).

28 In some cases, these groups may advocate politics that produce selective benefits that go largely to their membership, but the core of their activities must be focused on the broader collective.

29 Over two centuries ago, Adam Smith wisely counselled his fellow citizens to be sceptical of persons advocating various types of government action for the public good. He said "I have never known much good done by those who affected to trade for the public good". This advice seems as appropriate today as it was then.

Business Firms as Interest Groups
Business' Common and Conflicting Interests

In everyday speech, in the newspapers and, frequently, in the political arena, reference is made to "the business community," to "business interests" or to the power or weakness of "business". Such terms imply that business in Canada is a homogeneous or even monolithic entity. This is not true, of course, but it is often convenient to speak in terms of large aggregations such as business, labour,[30] and government (or governments). When we look more closely we often find that intra-group differences in interests (not to mention other matters) are as great as inter-group differences. There are often disagreements or even overt conflicts among different segments of the business community on public policy issues. These disagreements mean that business does not speak with one voice and that a government often receives conflicting advice on specific policy issues. Indeed, it may even receive conflicting advice from different firms in the same industry on an industry-specific issue.

Common Interests

While these differences can be important, it is useful to identify and consider interests that all or nearly all business firms share. They have a common interest in having a political environment in which they have a great deal of freedom to make and sell goods and services with the objective of earning a profit. The key characteristics of such an environment appear to be the following:

- Political stability — in the sense that governments change in response to democratic elections, that the decision-making "framework" and important public policies are not changed capriciously;
- Legal and, preferably, constitutional protections for the rights of private property (while governments must pay compensation when they formally expropriate ["condemn"] private property under various federal and provincial statutes, property rights are not expressly protected in the 1982 constitution);
- Macro-economic stability — monetary and fiscal policies that act in a contra-cyclical fashion to reduce the amplitude of economic cycles;
- Well-defined and practicable "framework" legislation in areas such as corporation, bankruptcy, intellectual property, labour,[31] competition and contract legislation;
- The process for making public policy should be quite well-defined, accessible and reasonably predictable or, at least, the changes should be subject to reasonable notice; further, the policy actions produced by the process should be based on rational argument and subject to appeal to the courts;

---

30   A standard mis-generalization is to illustrate the interests of labour by quoting the statements of the senior officials of the Canadian Labour Congress. While the CLC represents 2.5 million workers, less than 30 percent of the labour force in Canada is unionized and, in Quebec, there are other peak labour organizations.

31   Business is usually concerned that labour legislation strike a careful balance between the interests of employees and employers.

- An efficient, effective and non-partisan public service;
- Reasonable tax burden — governments should be concerned that the total net burden of its interventions on business (taxes, regulations, subsidies, etc.) is comparable to that of Canada's trading partners and competitors;
- An independent judiciary to settle both private interest disputes (over contracts or torts) and challenges to the constitutionality of the actions of the executive and the legislature (see Litigation, below); and
- Easy access to foreign markets: Because Canada is so dependent on foreign trade (almost 46 percent of GDP), many firms have a strong interest in having the federal government negotiate and maintain trade as free of discriminatory regulatory constraints as possible.

Bases of Conflicting Interests

A president of the Toronto Board of Trade observed that "...business in our society is a kaleidoscope, as diverse in its problems and aspirations as the country itself" (Board of Trade *Journal*, Christmas 1976, p. 9).

The bases of these conflicting interests begin with the fact that all firms face direct or indirect competition from domestic or foreign rivals: intra-industry rivalry. However, the typical industrial structure in Canada is that of a moderately to highly concentrated oligopoly — see Green (1990).[32] In other words, firms recognize their interdependence and perceive themselves more as head-to-head rivals than do firms in an atomistic industry unaffected by the actions of any single firm. In dealing with government, firms often seek to reinforce their competitive advantage over rivals (or obtain one) by gaining discriminatory benefits — benefits that improve their position relative to their rivals.[33]

Different industries tend to be concentrated in certain provinces or regions in Canada. Ontario accounts for half of Canadian manufacturing activity, while a large fraction of Canada's exports of forest products come from BC Governments within a province or region tend to support its major industries. The effects of this tendency are exaggerated by the important role of the provinces in Canadian federalism. This inter-regional rivalry is a major source of conflict within the business community in Canada. Polices that favour one industry or region (such as protectionism for central Canada's manufacturing — despite the liberalizing effect of the FTA and then NAFTA) impose costs on others (e.g., the resource-based industries in western Canada).

Closely connected with conflicts brought about by inter-regional rivalry are conflicts that originate between those industries favouring free trade and those favouring protectionism. Canadian firms that sell a substantial fraction of their

---

32   Of course, when foreign trade is important in an industry, even high domestic concentration ratios may not permit domestic firms to exercise much market power.

33   For example, a pulp and paper company whose mills are new (and less polluting) may urge stringent enforcement of across-the-board pollution controls in order to force its rivals with older mills that produce more effluent to incur higher costs in the form of expenditures on abatement or new, less polluting production equipment.

output abroad[34] are naturally concerned about terms of access to foreign markets and the exchange rate. Firms that focus on the domestic market are likely to be more concerned about competition from imports and macroeconomic policies that stimulate demand. Further, there are attitudinal differences between Canadian-owned and foreign-controlled firms operating in Canada.

Comparing Business Firms as Interest Groups to Other Interest Groups

A business firm or a trade association is one of many interest groups seeking to influence public policy. It is useful to consider the characteristics of a business firm as an interest group. In general, a business firm (particularly a large one) has certain advantages as an interest group relative to other interest groups. First, the firm is already organized for other purposes so that the "free rider" (collective action) problem has already been solved (see Olson, 1965). Second, the firm's "agency problem" is tiny compared to those of interest groups with a broadly based membership. Third, business executives are familiar with strategic thinking, which is very useful in the political arena. Fourth, business firms have a well-defined, functional role in society, which provides them with legitimacy. They are seen to play an important role in maintaining a high standard of living in society. Fifth, large firms have extensive economic resources, which can be used in their efforts to influence public policy. They can hire expertise in business-government relations and pay the cost of major efforts to influence public policy. Sixth, expenditures on lobbying and other efforts to influence public policy are tax-deductible expenses (but they are not for trade unions or other not-for-profit organizations).

At the same time, business firms face a number of *disadvantages* in their efforts to influence public policy relative to other interest groups. First, pecuniary private interests are widely perceived to be morally inferior; business firms are deemed to be exclusively focussed on increasing profits (see Stanbury, 1993a, Chapter 5). Second, in Canada many people believe that business interests are antithetical to "the public interest," a highly evocative but ill-defined concept (see Stanbury, 1993a, Chapter 13). Third, as noted above, there are plenty of internal cleavages within the "business community". Fourth, market or institutional failures (such as pollution) are often blamed on firms — they are seen to be attributable to the greed of managers rather than the absence of individuated property rights in the atmosphere, rivers, lakes and oceans. Fifth, periodically capitalism exhibits an "unacceptable face"; its periodic excesses[35] often lead to more general government intervention. Sixth, the public appears to be highly tolerant of the direct action tactics of environmental groups when they

---

34   Canada's exports as a percentage of GDP increased from 25.6 percent in 1989 to 45.3 percent in 2000. Exports to the U.S. rose from 15 percent of GDP in 1989 to 28 percent in 1998 to 32 percent in 2001. In 2001, 85 percent of Canada's merchandise exports went to the U.S. (Statistics Canada data).

35   See Macklem (2002). *The Economist* (May 3, 2003, pp. 67–68) reports that 10 Wall Street firms paid US $1.38 billion to settle the cases against them.

are focussed on business firms and the claims of such groups are far more credible in the public eyes (see Stanbury, 2000; Solomon, 2003).

Government-Relations Consultants

Business and other interest groups may employ government-relations consultants and consulting lobbyists to assist them in influencing government. These firms can provide a variety of services to their clients.

Number, Size and Activities

Government-relations consulting firms (GRCs) have been growing in number and size in Canada in the last decade. As of March 31, 1991 there were 658 Tier-I ("professional") and 2182 Tier-II ("employee") lobbyists registered under the federal Lobbyists Registration Act (which came into effect on September 30, 1989). There were 2878 Tier-I and 2249 Tier-II registrations[36] active on the same date (Consumer and Corporate Affairs Canada, 1991, p. 7).

The Lobbyists Registration Act was amended effective January 31, 1996 to require three types of lobbyists to register: a) Consultant lobbyists — individuals who, for pay, lobby for clients, b) In-house lobbyists (corporate) — employees who, as a significant part of the duties, lobby for an employer that carries out commercial activities for financial gain, and c) In-house lobbyists (organizations) — these are not-for-profit organizations in which one or more employees lobby, and the collective time devoted to lobbying amounts to the equivalent of at least a significant part of one employee's duties. It is the senior officer of such organizations who must register, and he/she may not be the person(s) who actually do the lobbying (Industry Canada, 1996, p. 3).

As of March 31, 2002 there were 858 consultant lobbyists, 233 In-house lobbyists for corporations and the head of 351 not-for-profit organizations were registered under the Lobbyists Registration Act.[37] These data indicate that the number of consultant lobbyists increased by 30.4 percent over 12 years. On the other hand, the number employee lobbyists — whether for for-profit corporations or not-for-profit organizations — declined from 2,182 to 584, or by 73 percent. Some of this decrease, however, may be attributable to the fact that since 1996 only one employee had to register for each not-for-profit organization — even if a handful devoted a significant part of their time to lobbying.[38]

---

36 This term refers to the name of the organization for which the registered lobbyist is working as a consultant or as an employee. It appears that there was a huge growth in the number of fee-for-service lobbyists from 1985 to 1990, although there are no official statistics we can cite.

37 Annual Report on the Lobbyists Registration Act for the year ended March 31, 2002 (Ottawa: Industry Canada, 2002).

38 For there to have been no decrease in the number of in-house employee lobbyists between 1991 and 2002, each not-for-profit organization would (on average) have to have had 5.46

What Do GRCs Do?

Gary Ouellet, former chairman of the now defunct GCI — Government Consultants International once stated that "[C]ompanies come to us when they want results. They don't want policy papers, just resolution of the issue" (*Globe and Mail*, June 5, 1989, p. B28). The objectives of firms hiring a GRC include: to get a contract (the Department of Public Works and Government Services alone spends over $10 billion annually on procurement); to get a favourable regulatory decision from an "independent" agency, from a line department, or from the cabinet; to obtain or block new legislation or subordinate legislation, e.g., regulations.

In the world of lobbying and government relations, clients of GRCs talk of two types of consultants: Contact and Content. The Contact Consultants are those perceived to be wired to politicians, principally to ministers. They can be counted on for some broad strategic advice quite apart from performing whatever "dating service" function someone thinks needs to be filled. But they're also often seen as being light on policy which, conversely, is the perceived strength of the Content Consultants (Moore, 2002).[39]

Government-relations firms offer a range of services. They may a) provide intelligence on what is going on in Ottawa and predictions about future developments; b) develop the interest group's strategy for trying to influence government, either on an ongoing basis or for a specific issue or problem. This may include the following aspects: identifying and defining problems; identifying key people who are likely to influence the decision itself (or the process by which it is made); generating and describing alternative influence strategies, such as traditional lobbying, public relations, advocacy ads, media campaigns, and political contributions; and identifying and evaluating strategic alliances or coalitions; c) develop a detailed program to co-ordinate efforts to influence government; d) provide advice on the group's proposed strategic approach; and e) prepare the persuasive materials to be used to lobby government, such as briefs, speeches, advocacy ads, press releases and internal communications programs. In some cases, a GRC may carry out some or all of the set of persuasive activities for the client ("get into the trenches").

The larger public affairs/government-relations consulting firms[40] monitor social, economic and political issues relevant to their clients or potential clients. They try to identify as early as possible, the issues that are likely to be subject to some form of policy action by government. While consultants will develop strategy and prepare briefs for clients, few make presentations directly to public officials. Many strongly believe that senior executives of their client organizations are likely to be more effective. By maintaining close contact with public

---

persons devoting a significant part of their time to lobbying. This seems far too high, given the nature of many of these organizations.

39   In the same vein, Curtis (2003) suggests that there are, roughly speaking, two types of consultant lobbyists — policy experts and political operatives. The former tend to be experts in the bureaucracy and sectoral areas, and the latter have pipelines to cabinet ministers, their aides and political parties, and know how the political winds are blowing. Most lobbyists are a little of both. The best are a lot of both.

40   Note that many GRCs are one-person operations, and many of these are former public servants.

servants, politicians and regulators, consultants are able to indicate whom their clients should contact and what arguments are likely to be more effective. Both formal and informal contacts are used. Such contacts are based very heavily upon the exchange of information that is valuable to all participants.

One of the important steps in influencing government is gaining access to decision makers. First, the GRC may be able (for a fee) to obtain a meeting with a government official (elected or appointed) that the interest group could not have obtained solely through its own initiative. Second, the business firm or interest group could have eventually obtained a meeting, but the GRC greatly speeded up the process (and for some problems, time is of the essence). Third, the GRC may be able to provide the client with valuable insight on how the issue in question is being viewed in government and the alternatives that public officials may be willing to consider, the particular concerns they may have which need to be addressed and the themes that are likely to have the greatest resonance among policy-makers. This is the greatest significance of "access" by government relations consultants — that is, by dint of their contacts in government and their familiarity with the personalities, process and substance of public policy decision making; they are able to provide the client with valuable information, insight and advice that is generally not available to those without such contacts and experience. In some cases, certain government relations consultants hold out the prospect that, because of their personal contacts and relationships among key advisers and decision makers, they are able to more directly influence government decision-making to the client's advantage due to their past associations (not simply because it is able to make the client's argument more persuasive). When this occurs, GRCs are really selling influence, not merely obtaining or facilitating access.

How Interest Groups Try to Influence Public Policy

Section 5
question 3b

The techniques used by interest groups to influence public policy take a wide variety of forms, as Figure 2 makes clear. These techniques can be grouped into two broad categories: direct and indirect. **Direct** approaches consist of bringing organizational representatives into direct contact with public officials. Consulting with legislators or their staff, presenting committee testimony, presenting research and interacting with regulatory agency personnel are all forms of direct approaches. **Indirect** approaches consist of more circuitous methods of influencing policy makers. For example, lobbyists can try to put pressure on public officials by generating support or opposition at the local riding level. They can also launch mass media campaigns or establish opposition groups. Direct lobbying, the main focus of this paper, consists of efforts to communicate with decision makers and their advisors directly to persuade them to adopt the firm's position. This may be done in a number of ways: meetings with the "target" (i.e., the person(s) to be influenced); testimony before a parliamentary committee; the submission of a brief to a committee, a government department and/or a minister; telephone calls; contacts at social events; and participation on

Figure 2: Techniques Used by Interest Groups to Influence Public Policies

1.   Direct Influence Techniques

Direct Lobbying:
- Hold formal and informal meetings with policy makers and their advisors (public servants and politicians); may be part of an ad hoc or ongoing consultative process;
- Submit briefs to departments or ad hoc policy processes (for example, advisory committees);
- Testify before Parliamentary committees or other entities (such as regulatory agencies) formally addressing policy/legislative issues;
- Use various means of communication (telephone, email, fax, letters) to advocate one's (the group's) position (these may also be used to acquire information about the process and other players).

Stimulation of the "Grass Roots"
Get "ordinary citizens" to signal their views to politicians through tactics like mass mail/fax/email/telephone campaigns from members of the interest group and/or other supporters.

Direct Action Activities
Include demonstrations, rallies, protest marches; boycotts of the product/services of the target; planned violence (the strongest form of direct action); civil disobedience, such as blockades of streets, bridges, building entrances; the appurtenances of these activities may include placards, signs, burning in effigy, grotesque masks, speeches, spontaneous behaviour (a "happening") and use strong colourful language.

Litigation
May be used to try to block some policy action, or also compel government action, such as a full-scale environmental review of a project; constitutionality of a law may be challenged under the 1982 Charter of Rights and Freedoms and, as a result, the courts may create new law.

Coalition
Create an alliance among several groups and utilize one or more of the techniques.

2.   Indirect Techniques

Media and Public Relations
Getting favourable media coverage for positions, speeches and publications through interviews, press releases, video tapes, press agents, websites.

Advocacy Advertising:
Selling ideas (rather than products) designed to influence public policy. May use paid media, but can also use own website.

Figure 2 Cont.

Think-Tanks
Try to change the composition of the set of **ideas** in good currency (ideas can have practical consequences) by funding research and dissemination of ideas through publications (print and electronic), speeches, and news stories using the research.

Election-Related Activities:
political contributions to parties and/or candidates; running ads on specific policy issues; volunteer work for a party and/or candidate(s); creating a "third party" to oppose or support candidates/party.

Doing Favours:
Trying to build up "credits" by helping ministers, MPs and public servants, then relying on reciprocity to achieve greater influence for the group when it asks these decision makers for help on the group's concerns/issues.

---

advisory committees. In most cases the person(s) doing the lobbying are employees of the interest group but, in some cases, they may be accompanied by a GRC who has been hired to assist the group in making its case.

Indirect lobbying focuses on mass marketing and the "packaging of issues". It is wholesale lobbying, in contrast to the one-on-one approach of retail lobbying (Smith, 1988, p. 235). The indirect techniques for influencing public policy include efforts to influence the news media with the objective of influencing public policy by gaining visibility for the firm's (other interest group's) views and, thereby, influencing public opinion. Advocacy advertising is designed to sell ideas primarily to the public, but may also be targeted at policy makers. The state of public opinion can make it either easier or harder for a government to implement particular policies. Even less direct techniques include political contributions and the funding of think-tanks (e.g., the Fraser Institute, Canadian Policy Research Network, the Institute for Research on Public Policy). The latter involves trying to alter the volume and types of ideas in the policy-making political arena. Obviously, it is a longer-term approach to shaping the policy agenda. It is impossible in the space available to discuss each of these techniques even briefly. Therefore, a handful have been chosen to give readers a feel for the ways interest groups go about their work.

Lobbying

Defining Lobbying

Who is a Lobbyist? In colloquial terms, "lobbying" often refers to any and all of the activities of representatives of organized interest groups that are designed to influence public policy. This is the broad, loose use of the term. But lobbying also refers to a narrower set of activities centred on direct communications between an interest group's representative and the persons they are seeking to influence. See Figure 2. In the most general terms[41], a lobbyist is any person who seeks to influence public policy (whether for remuneration or not). Hence, the term could be applied equally to the senior citizen who writes a letter urging her MP to fight the proposal to de-index the old-age pension and to a partner in a government-relations consulting firm retained by a large trade association to advise it on how to persuade the cabinet to increase subsidies for the firms in that industry. Lobbyists also include the head of the Canadian Federation of Agriculture, who regularly meets with politicians (and public servants) urging them to resist the efforts to dismantle supply management marketing boards (see Stanbury, 2002c). Fred Moonen, then vice-president of government relations for MacMillan Bloedel, Canada's largest forest products company, described his role as a lobbyist as "creative loitering". By this he meant that he haunted the corridors of the legislative building in Victoria waiting to catch cabinet ministers and backbenchers (including those in opposition) for a few minutes' discussion about MB's views on certain legislation or administrative policy (Comparelli, 1983). Therefore, lobbyists may be paid professionals representing a firm or other interest group, or they may be "amateurs" representing only themselves or a volunteer group.

Focussing on Public Servants

The key to success in many advocacy campaigns is often the degree and quality of engagement with government officials well below the ministerial level. While the popular view is that successful lobbying is principally a function of getting at, and working on, ministers, real effectiveness is more often a function of the degree to which lobbying organizations are able to take into account the many factors that public servants and ministers must consider as part of the decision-making process. (This often requires a substantial commitment of human and financial resources that is beyond the means of many interest groups.) It is all the more important these days, as governments' own, in-house policy units are leaner than ever despite ever-increasing demands on their resources. There is both a challenge and an opportunity for advocates. They must be prepared to engage in some "Do It Yourself Public Policy," by working on their issues in much the same way as public servants are required to do: considering a variety of factors critical to the political and public-policy process of modern governments in Canada.

These factors include a consideration of such things as the definition of the problem, purpose or principle at issue. A common question posed by government officials, particularly at the political level, whenever they are being pitched on an idea by an advocate is: "What problem are we trying to address here? Is it really a problem?" Also vitally important is the matter of precedent, one of the most ubiquitous considerations in government decision-making. It includes not only the matter of legal precedent (about which government lawyers are always vigilant) but, also, administrative and political precedents. Regardless

---

41   The federal *Lobbyist Registration Act* contains the legal definition of a lobbyist, which focuses on persons who get paid to engage in efforts to influence public policy.

of the issue in question, both bureaucrats and politicians will always be concerned about the precedents their decisions are making or changing. They will always be thinking about how they justify providing a benefit to one organization, when others will likely line up asking for the same. Advocacy groups must be prepared to help think through justifications for what they seek. They can't just leave it for government officials to do so.

Careful consideration must also be given to how the government is "positioning" the issue. In determining this, an advocacy group should examine both the stated and unstated objectives and considerations held by the government. Stated objectives are relatively easy to decipher. Government news releases, background papers, speeches and web sites contain most of what is needed to get a handle on the administration's stated or official objectives. What is often at least as important — and more difficult to discern — are the government's unstated objectives. They are usually not publicly cited because they are likely to be more difficult to explain (i.e., moving federal offices or installations from one part of the country to another in the interests of spreading federal largesse more equitably). They may even be impossible to justify (i.e., doing something to help a candidate in a critical by-election or confronting a problem that is viewed as politically incorrect or hazardous to publicly acknowledge.)

The politics of an issue is also vital for interest groups to understand, but it's also important for there to be a sophisticated and detailed appreciation of political factors, far beyond the facile, cartoonish politics of what Canadians see in the daily Question Period in the House of Commons.

An Exchange Process

At first glance, lobbying appears to be a unilateral activity: the group seeks to have government do what it wants. Wise lobbyists, however, recognize and seek to benefit from the pervasiveness and power of the norm of reciprocity.

Lobbyists are more likely to be successful if they start out with the view that lobbying is a process of exchange. Since lobbyists want something from government (a decision by a minister, a senior public servant, etc.), they should begin by thinking of what the interest group has that it can offer to the targets of its lobbying efforts in exchange for what it wants from them. What sort of information might be useful to the target? What kind of political support might the group offer the minister? On the negative side, what actions might the group take that the target would *not* like to occur?

A Negotiating Process

Lobbying is often a negotiating process, but interest groups must recognize that a lobbyist negotiating with government is not the same as a firm negotiating a contract with a supplier, or negotiating a collective bargaining agreement with the union. Indeed, most public-policy processes are not construed by government officials or the public as negotiating situations at all (or even implicit invitations to negotiate).

Negotiating with a government is different from negotiating with private parties in a number of ways. First, lobbyists have to appreciate that, ultimately, government can exercise legitimate powers of coercion to force people to do what it wants (subject to the Constitution). Second, governments are probably more sensitive to public opinion than are most private parties (except, perhaps, some businesses selling directly to the public). This fact may be used to advantage, but the lobbyist has to be careful that information openly given or leaked to the press that is perceived as going beyond the normal range of tactics to increase pressure on a minister or the cabinet may result in a loss of access or credibility in the future. Third, government probably has a "taller" hierarchy (more steps) than most business firms and has to consult more players than private negotiators because policy-making is more pluralistic.[42] Fourth, wise lobbyists appreciate that a government's goal structure is usually more complex than that of business firms (or interest groups): it has more goals; many are less tangible; some goals conflict with each other; and the set of goals and their priority ranking is subject to change. Thus, agreements or understandings with government are often harder to reach, are more complex, and have more elements that are implicit than those reached between private parties. Fifth, a government has no economic "bottom line" analogous to that of a firm.[43] In some ways, this makes it easier to "cut a deal", but in others it makes it more complicated because governments are more willing to use economic resources to achieve the political goals of the party in power (all in the name of the "public interest" of course). Sixth, lobbyists have to realize that a government probably has to be more careful about setting a precedent (which may have unattractive consequences in the future) when it negotiates. Demands for equity, in the sense of treating people in similar circumstances in the same fashion are ubiquitous in Canada. Finally, governments are subject to a larger number of statutory constraints than are most businesses.

A Rivalrous Process

Lobbying (like all efforts to influence public policy) is often a rivalrous or competitive process in which different interests are in conflict over what each is urging government to do or not do. These conflicts stem largely from the differential impact of alternative policy actions on the income/wealth or utility of members of various organized interest groups, including firms. Conflicting claims may be couched in the rhetoric of the public interest or in ideological terms. However, the best way to predict a group's position on an economic issue (as opposed to a non-pecuniary or "values" issue) is to determine whether its members believe they are likely to be economically better- or worse-off because of a particular proposal. Even on a values issue, such as environmental protection, self-interest often lurks just beneath the surface. In the case of Canadian nationalism, it is hard to avoid the conclusion that the strongest proponents of policies in the name of such nationalism also stand to gain in

---

42   Thus, negotiating with government over a policy issue is very seldom a strictly bilateral process. Explicitly or implicitly, other interests are involved; government has to find a solution that a number of contending interests (stakeholders in the relevant policy community) can live with.

43   In order to eliminate the large annual deficits, for the past few years the federal government has had to stick to its fiscal framework. The Minister of Finance has emphasized that spending can be reallocated, but that the total must be tightly controlled.

economic terms from such policies. While wrapping themselves in the flag, they are also advancing their economic interests (see Stanbury, 1998).

Coalitions

An old maxim of warfare and politics is that there is strength in numbers. There is evidence that ad hoc lobbying coalitions are becoming more important in policy making in Canada. Some are only very loose arrangements among groups that are moving in the same direction and keep each other informed so that each can improve its effectiveness while acting independently. Other alliances take the form of a more formal — albeit ad hoc — coalition in which lobbying and other persuasive activities are closely co-ordinated.

Coalitions can have several advantages. First, a coalition, particularly one that is well organized, may represent a sizeable number of votes directly or be able to make a credible claim to be able to influence a large number of votes. Second, coalitions can reduce the costs of advocacy for each participant. Third, ad hoc coalitions of groups that are perceived as "strange bedfellows" (those normally in conflict with each other) are likely to have a greater impact on both public opinion and on politicians precisely because the alliance appears to be so unnatural — so they may signal the seriousness of the problem. Fourth, lobbying coalitions or alliances, by incorporating groups with widely differing interests, can give the appearance of "representing everybody". Therefore, it is easier for them to argue that what they want from government is "in the public interest".

Coalitions may have disadvantages. The cost of putting a coalition together and keeping it together may be prohibitive. Second, decision-making may be too slow to deal with fast-changing events. Third, participants have an incentive to try to "free-ride" on the efforts and financial contributions of other members.

Stimulating the Grass Roots

The Funk and Wagnall's *Standard College Dictionary* states that "grass roots" is an informal term, of American origin, referring to "those people often living in rural areas, thought of as having fundamental, practical, and highly independent views or interests". The term has come to be used to refer to people whom the government does not usually hear from directly on public-policy issues (except on election day) because they are "ordinary folks" who are normally too busy with the practical business of making a living, tending their gardens and supervising their children. There is a clear implication that such people represent the true "voice of the people". They are closely related to what Richard Nixon called "the silent majority".A firm or other interest group tries to produce signals from a large number of people at the grass roots level that **appear** to be spontaneous and unorganized, but support its position. The word "spontaneous" is the key.[44] Opinions of people at the grass-roots level can be triggered by a

---

44   When politicians know that the grass roots signals they receive are the result of interest group efforts, they refer to them as astroturf.

number of new technologies. Individuals can be "aroused" (made aware of an issue that is likely to have specific consequences for them) by mail, fax, email, or even automatic telephone dialling machines with a pre-recorded message linked to a computer data bank of telephone numbers. It is usually easier to mobilize opinion at the grass-roots level if people perceive that their health, safety, primary values or income are threatened by a proposed policy action.

A firm can begin by making an effort to stimulate communications from its stakeholders, such as employees, stockholders, suppliers and even customers. In addition to communicating with politicians, signals from the grass roots may be focussed on the news media. Outpourings from the grass roots can be focussed on regulatory agencies to back up a group's brief.[45] In general, the objective of generating signals from the grass roots is to show politicians that voters are interested and willing to act on a particular issue. The telephone calls, letters, postcards, fax messages and emails are also a means of demonstrating the organizational strength of a group and its leadership on a particular issue. A large number of messages from the grass roots is a way of showing that ordinary citizens, not just activists or paid staffers, care about the issue.

Canadians have to appreciate that differences in the design of our political institutions (notably cabinet government and the emphasis on party discipline) limit greatly the utility of grass roots pressure on individual Members of Parliament. For efforts to stimulate the grass roots to be effective in Canada, it is essential that they focus on the party in power[46] rather than the opposition. But even then, the key target must be the cabinet, since ministers are the key policy-makers. And efforts to change policies need to occur early in the process of developing a policy. Once a government has publicly committed itself to a specific course of action (for example, introduced new legislation or amendments to existing acts), it is very difficult to obtain other than minor changes.

Direct Action

Direct action or "expressive activity" as a technique of influencing public policy embodies a variety of specific tactics, including the following: (I) Verbal assault on a minister (or possibly a public servant) in a context designed to obtain coverage in the news media; (ii) Occupying a government's (or a firm's) office with the objective of shutting it down (or disrupting its work) and obtaining extensive coverage in the news media; (iii) "Eco-tage" — a wide range of tactics designed to inflict damage on the firms or people seeking to utilize areas environmentalists want left in their original state;[47] (iv) Blockades of transportation "bottleneck" points (such as bridges, or tunnels), so thousands of ordinary peo-

---

45   An alternative is a scientific opinion poll, which may focus on the total population, a region or a particular segment of the population.

46   Signals from the grass roots to a large number of Government MPs are likely to be carried into Caucus meetings and so examined by ministers. But if the PM is not convinced they are worthy of attention, such efforts will not be effective. Party discipline will ensure that Government MPs will toe the line laid down by the PM. Those MPs are then expected to try to sell the Government's position to the grass roots.

47   This may include tree spiking or pouring sand in the gas tanks of vehicles, earth-moving equipment, logging equipment, etc.

ple become aware of the group's issue (see Stanbury, 2000, chapter 3); (v) "Bodies-on-the-line" — direct efforts to stop activities the group opposes, such as shutting down an abortion clinic, disrupting whale hunting or killing baby seals (white coats), "tree-sitting" to prevent logging of old-growth forests, etc.; (vi) Civil disobedience — actions designed to provoke the police into arresting the protesters, preferably while the television cameras roll,[48] such as blockading an abortion clinic or violating a court order limiting the number of information pickets outside a particular business or government office; and (vii) Boycotts of a firm's products either by urging consumers not to buy at the retail level or by putting pressure on wholesalers or retailers not to stock the goods produced by the firm(s) whose behaviour the group is seeking to change.[49]

Illustrations of legitimate direct-action techniques are not hard to find, for example, demonstrations and rallies by pro-choice groups; a rally by students protesting budget cuts; a hunger strike organized by environmentalists; a series of protests, rallies and other means by which farmers signalled their fear and a sharp decline in their income. Legitimate tactics are usually the choice even of groups that are "outsiders" or are marginal in society, although some groups choose such tactics because, for them, they appear to be useful in both influencing public policy and in building the organization by attracting more members, by providing a means for members to vent their feelings and to create solidarity within the group — see Phillips et al. (1990).

Illegitimate activities — those that violate widely held social norms about how interest groups and their members ought to behave — generate a variety of consequences. First, there is the possibility of extensive coverage in the news media, so the group's message is carried to a larger audience. Television coverage is the oxygen of radical interest group tactics. Second, such activities may provide reinforcement of the most activist members' motivation; the expressive actions may assist the organization in recruiting new members who seek an outlet for their frustrations and desire to give voice to their values. Third, illegitimate activities may stiffen the resolve of less radical or mainstream groups to ask for more and/or refuse to settle for less in their efforts to obtain changes in public policy. Fourth, among more radical interest groups, illegitimate activities may boost the group into a leadership position, so that other groups will acknowledge it as the one most willing to make real sacrifices for the cause. Fifth, these activities may enhance the reputation and increase the legitimacy of the group among those relatively narrow segments of society that believe such actions are justified. Sixth, publicity associated with illegitimate activities, if properly managed, can indirectly enhance the group's legitimacy with broad segments of society that support its goals, if not its tactics (Elsbach and Sutton, 1991, p. 5). Seventh, illegitimate activities may reduce the legitimacy of the group and its demands in the eyes of the public or segments of public opinion (see Stanbury, 2000, Chapter 11). Eighth, one of the objectives of illegitimate activities may be to provoke opponents of the group or the police into extreme

---

48   See Blatchford (2003).
49   This tactic brought the most pressure on BC forest products companies regarding the cutting of old-growth forests. The key targets were major big box retailers of lumber in the US See Stanbury (2000).

reactions in front of the news media, preferably television. Then the issue becomes the "pornography of violence" rather than the illegitimate actions of the group. This creates a new (diversionary) issue that invests the initial action with more moral force. It also displays the "corruption" and lack of legitimacy of those who oppose the radical tactics.

Advocacy Advertising

Advocacy advertising consists of paid commercial messages that seek to sell ideas rather than goods and services. It is based largely on the assumption that an organization can influence public-policy decision makers both directly and indirectly by shaping public opinion through such advertising. Advocacy or "issue" or "controversy" advertising is often used in conjunction with other actions designed to influence policy, notably lobbying (see Stanbury, 1993a, Chapter 11). Organizations other than business and labour appear to be making increased use of such ads (e.g., environmental groups; see Stanbury, 2000).

Advocacy advertising has been defined as "any kind of paid public communication or message, from an identified source and in a conventional medium of public advertising, which presents information or a point of view bearing on a publicly recognized controversial issue" (Stridsberg, 1977, p. 18). The advertiser's intention is to have an influence on a matter of recognized public controversy. The results sought range from the correction of factual information to a change in the opinions of members of a target audience, to the mobilization of supporters, to the solicitation of financial contributions and the passage or defeat of a specific piece of legislation. The main characteristics of advocacy ads are the following: (i) they are paid communications in electronic and/or print media; (ii) they are designed to "sell" ideas, not products or services; (iii) they may be aimed directly at policy makers or at some segment(s) of public opinion; and (iv) their ultimate objective is to influence public policy on an issue (or issues) that is important to the firm or organization paying for the ads.[50] In most cases, advocacy advertising is only one of several techniques being used to influence public policy at the same time.

The Ottawa weekly, *The Hill Times*, has become a popular outlet for advocacy ads relating to the federal government. In the May 26, 2003 edition, there was a full-page ad by the Canadian Generic Pharmaceutical Association attacking what it calls the "unjust regulations within the Patent Act" which, it argues, "enable patent drug makers to stall or halt release of less costly generic alternatives". In the same edition, there are full-page ads by patent medicine manufacturer Astra Zeneca responding to the sort of arguments posited by the generic drug makers represented by the CGPA: "They don't want to spend time and money developing their own delivery formula, and they don't want to wait for our hard-earned patent rights to expire". The May 26 edition also featured: large ads by the International Association of Machinists and Aerospace

---

50   Our brief survey of advocacy ads in the past few years suggests that an increasing number focus on gaining support — including donations — for particular interest groups. See, for example, the two-page, full colour ads by World Wildlife Fund Canada in *Maclean's*, January 27, 2003 and March 10, 2003.

Workers presenting its case that it's being reasonable in its negotiations with financially troubled Air Canada; a joint Boeing and CAE ad extolling their partnership in responding to a major Defence Department procurement; and an ad by the Lubicon Legal Defence Fund pressing Prime Minister Chrétien to honour what it says is his long-standing commitment to settle the First Nation's 64-year-old land dispute with the Government of Canada.

As a technique of influencing public policy, advocacy advertising is not without some risks. Those using such ads need to be aware of them. First, the ads themselves could cause controversy instead of helping to influence public policy in the way the sponsor intended.[51] They may be counterproductive for several reasons: the target audience may resent them, perhaps by thinking about their cost if an extensive campaign is mounted; politicians and senior public servants may perceive the ads as "going public" on an issue that should remain in the policy community, or as an effort to generate pressure from the public. Second, there is the possibility that the ads will be ineffective — thus wasting the sponsor's money. Since a major campaign could cost $500,000 to over $2 million, this is a serious matter. Third, the ads may be somewhat effective in moving public opinion, but not as effective as other, less costly, techniques of influencing public policy. The head of the sponsoring organization can become enamoured with seeing its position "up in lights," e.g., in full-page newspaper ads or even in 30- or 60-second ads on television.

A variety of concerns have been raised about advocacy advertising as a technique for influencing public policy. First, it is argued that advocacy advertising favours the political interests of those with "deep pockets". It is a form of interest-group representation open only to those with larger financial resources; hence larger corporations or trade associations have an advantage in the process of influencing government policy. Moreover, some argue it adds insult to injury because the costs of advocacy ads by corporations are tax deductible. Second, critics ask, whose interests are being advanced in corporate advocacy ads? Where there is a separation of ownership and control, professional managers may be using shareholders' money in ways they would not approve. Third, potential advertisers ask, should the media have the right to reject advocacy ads? For example, in October 1990, the CBC rejected a commercial prepared (at a cost of $400,000) by the Dairy Farmers of Canada because it expressed "a point of view or course of action on a matter of public interest". Both the CTV and Global television networks ran the ads, however.

Litigation

In the past two decades, interest groups have increased their use of litigation as a technique to influence public policy. Litigation can be seen as nothing more

---

51 For example, the BC Government Employees Union was criticized by the president of British Columbians for Mentally Handicapped People for using an "offensive, awful and unreal" advocacy ad in an effort to portray the effects of de-institutionalization of the mentally handicapped and mentally ill. A *Vancouver Sun* editorial called the ad "irresponsible almost to the point of being scurrilous." Two cabinet ministers called the ad "factually misleading and irresponsible." See *Vancouver Sun*, January 27, 1986, p. A1; January 29, 1986, p. A4; January 31, 1986, p. A20.

than the continuation of lobbying by other means. Organizations that fail to achieve their objectives in the political area seek decisions from the courts that help to achieve their goals.[52]

Litigation can be used to stop actions by others, such as an injunction to stop the construction of a dam, power plant or logging roads; force positive action, such as make an agency establish regulations according to a schedule established in a statute; test the interpretations of a regulatory agency by appealing them to the courts;[53] and test the constitutionality of legislation that goes against the group's interests.[54]

In Canada, since the Charter of Rights and Freedoms was entrenched in the revised Constitution of 1982, the number of cases in which individuals, firms and interest groups of all types have sought to use the courts to achieve their political and policy objectives has expanded greatly. Morton (2000) states: "Under the 1960 Bill of Rights, the Supreme Court of Canada declared only one law invalid over a 22-year period. In just 16 years under the Charter, the court has struck down 68 statutes — 31 federal and 27 provincial".

An analysis of the first 100 Charter cases decided by the Supreme Court of Canada by political scientists Peter Russell and Ted Morton indicated that the success rate for litigants relying on the Charter after the first two years began to fall precipitously (*Toronto Star,* May 28, 1990, p. A20). During the first two years the Court awarded victories to nine of 14 Charter claimants (64 percent). Over the next four years the success rate fell, averaging 27 percent to 37 percent. Overall, the success rate of charter claimants was 36 percent resulting in the Court striking down 12 provincial and eight federal laws. As for the subject matter of the first 100 Charter cases, 74 dealt with questions of Charter rights in the criminal justice system (Knopff and Morton, 1992, p. 22).

Gregory Hein of McMaster University reviewed 2588 Federal Court and Supreme Court of Canada (SCC) decisions from 1988 to 1998. He found that what he called the social activists of the "New Left" launched 104 cases challenging elected officials to extend and clarify rights, compared to 92 launched by corporate interests to push back the constraints on their commercial activities. "However, the propensity of activist groups to litigate under the Charter was much higher. One in eight activist groups launched a suit, compared to one

---

52 Generally, see Morton & Knopff (2000), Knopff & Morton (1992), Mandel (1994), Brodie (2001), (2002a), Manfredi (2000), Stanbury (1993a, Chapter 12).

53 A firm, as a party to a decision of a federal regulatory agency, may seek review of the decision: by the Federal Court, based on an error in law or violation of the rules of natural justice, or by the regulatory agency itself (separate appeal panel), or by the federal cabinet (a political appeal).

54 Constitutional challenges tend to be the highest profile form of litigation used by firms and other interest groups. A firm could challenge the constitutionality of a statue or part of a statute. This may come about in several ways. A firm may seek a reference to a provincial court of appeal or to the Supreme Court of Canada. A firm may launch an ordinary action starting in the provincial supreme court and, possibly, working up to the provincial court of appeal and the Supreme Court of Canada. A firm may challenge the constitutionality of legislation under which the firm is the subject of a criminal charge by the Crown. The charge may be "provoked" by the firm in the sense that it deliberately violates the law in order to test the law, or it may be the result of an inadvertent action resulting in a charge by the Crown The constitutionality of certain legislation may be raised by a firm in the context of a private action.

out of every 399 corporations". "Politicians and scholars of the right are essentially correct when they say that social activists are urging judges to make political choices" (quoted in Chwialkowska, 1999; see Hein, 2000 for the full paper).

Hogg and Bushell (1997) found that since the Charter of Rights and Freedoms had come into effect between 1982 and 1996 there were 66 cases in which the Supreme Court of Canada struck down a provincial or federal law. In two-thirds of these cases, law makers went back and rewrote the law to make it conform to the Court's requirements re constitutionality. In 98 constitutional rulings between 1996 and 1998, the Supreme Court of Canada ruled parts of 12 different statutes to be unconstitutional, according to a study by Patrick Monaghan of Osgoode Hall Law School (*Vancouver Sun,* April 15, 1999, p. A22); and Janice Tibbets, *National Post,* April 9, 1999, p. A4).

Brodie (2002a) shows that for the period 1976 to 1986, there were few applications for intervener status and the SCC granted few of them. However, between 1987 and 1999, the number of applications increased greatly (to a high of 125 in 1996) and the Court granted about 90 percent of them. Brodie (2002a, p. 41) found that "unions, native groups and individual Canadians have had the most trouble getting into the Court's hearings." On the other hand, the Women's Legal Education and Action Fund (LEAF) and the Canadian Civil Liberties Association (the two most frequent non-government interveners) were granted access in *every* case they sought it from 1987 to 1999. The explosion of Charter-related litigation was aided by federal funding, notably the Court Challenges Program (CPP)[55] (see Brodie, 2001; 2002b). One of the most prominent recipients was LEAF. It was established in April 1985, the month in which the equality rights provision (section 15) of the Charter of Rights and Freedoms came into effect. The LEAF sought to advance women's interests by using the Charter as a sword to attack existing statutes. By mid-1990, LEAF had been involved in about 80 cases, 12 of which went to the Supreme Court of Canada. It became the most frequent non-government intervenor in charter cases before the Supreme Court. The LEAF's activism continues to the present day.

In Figure 3 we provided brief summaries of recent notable cases in which five interest groups played an important role and resulted in a court, usually

---

55 In 1985, the Mulroney Government extended the CCP (created in 1978 to help language groups pressure the provinces for more bilingual services) to fund "equality seeking groups" such as feminists, gays, lesbians and multiculturalists. At that time, the government contracted out the administration of the program to the Canadian Council on Social Development. The CCSD, in turn, asked the applicant organizations to help run CCP. Thus, in 1994, ShelaghDay, co-founder of LEAF, helped re-design CCP and then became co-chair of one of its decision-making/grants-making panels. The Court Challenges Program was funded in 1985 at $200,000 p.a. By 1995, the federal grant was $2.75 million and it increased to $5.9 million in 2000 (LeRoy, 2002b, p. 12). Brodie (2002b) states that the federal funding was $2.75 million in 2002. In 2000, it became impossible to determine who actually gets how much money from CCPs. The latter claimed it has a confidential lawyer-client relationship with those it funded. This approach was supported by a decision of the Federal Court. So CCP does not publish the names of those it funds and its files are no longer available under the *Access to Information Act* (Brodie, 2002b). Brodie (2002a, p. 118) found that 22 percent of the interventions by public interest groups between 1984 and 1995 were paid for by the federal Court Challenges Program, which does not fund groups that oppose the "disadvantaged" agenda.

the Supreme Court of Canada, making new law.[56] Note that in only one of the five (#1) did an interest group actually take the lead in launching the litigation (although in #5, three groups acted as co-plaintiffs with an individual). In most cases, interest groups play one of two roles: they finance the litigation conducted in the name of an individual, or they act as an intervener. Note that in case #5 (Vriend) three government bodies and 14 interest groups acted as interveners.

Litigation as a technique to influence public policy has both advantages and disadvantages. The advantages include the following. Litigation can produce a sweeping change in operative public policy with a stroke of the highest court's pen. For example, a law may be declared unconstitutional and the government may not wish or be able to produce new legislation that has the same effect but is constitutionally valid — for example, the Province of Ontario moved to change its policy with respect to prayers in public schools after a Court of Appeal decision (*Globe and Mail,* October 15, 1989, p. A4). As noted in case #5 in Figure 3, the SCC read into the Alberta human rights law sexual orientation as a prohibited ground for discrimination.

Litigation is subject to an elaborate set of procedural rules (and customs) that limit and channel hostility into a socially accepted method of conflict resolution. One of the primary functions of the court is to resolve a variety of conflicts, including those concerning the constitutionality of legislation and the interpretation of the key terms and phrases in legislation.

On some policy issues, the political process culminating in the legislature has simply not been able to resolve sharp conflicts in basic values. Thus, statutes are often vague (the Charter is conspicuously so in many places) or, even, contradictory. In effect, the legislature has delegated to the courts the difficult task of translating broad concepts/principles into action. Where they are not clear or are conflicting, judges are effectively forced to apply their own value judgements.[57] Some people find this preferable to continued conflict in the political arena. Others do not because it seriously threatens their view of the proper roles of the legislature and the courts in a democracy.[58]

It has been argued that the courts represent a better forum for the "underdogs" — if they can get there (that is, obtain standing and have the money to pay the lawyers' bills).[59] In litigation, the grounds for battle are narrowed. There is equality of argument, where facts and logic really do count. In litigation, the focus is often on **individual** rights. In some cases, activist judges with

---

56 A much longer list of earlier cases can be found in Stanbury (1993, Chapter 12) and Knopff and Morton (1992). A longer and more detailed description of cases in the last decade can be found in Brodie (2002a).

57 The judges of the higher courts are appointed by the prime minister, and are not subject to public hearings (unlike those in the U.S.). During his tenure as PM, Jean Chrétien has made five appointments to the SCC and elevated another to become Chief Justice. Before he retires, he may make at least one other appointment to the SCC (Spector, 2002).

58 See Bork (1990), Knopff & Morton (1992), Morton & Knopff (2000).

59 As noted above, financial assistance from the federal government through the Court Challenges Program has made this easier.

a streak of noblesse oblige are prepared to make decisions in terms of their views on what is desirable social policy.[60]

The courts may provide an avenue of appeal from decisions rendered by governments, which have great powers of coercion. They are the protectors of the rights of private individuals (firms, organizations) in the sense of deciding fairly the operational scope of constitutional rights.

The disadvantages of litigation include the following: Litigation can be extraordinarily costly, and hence is beyond the means of many individuals or organizations (including firms). Further, litigation involves several types of risks. First, there is the risk of losing and, hence, becoming liable for the costs of the other side — and now, in light of the Lavigne case, the costs of interveners as well.[61] Second, there is the risk that, even if the firm or group wins the case, that its own legal bills (including experts and the time of its executives) will be much more than it forecast. Such costs are hard to control short of discontinuing the action — and then the firm could be hit with the other side's costs. Third, there is the risk that the substantive outcome will be not only negative, but worse than living with the law as it was prior to the case; the courts may close and bar a door that was partially open but that the litigant wanted to open wider. Alternatively, the litigant may win in the courts, but find that the government responds by changing the law in ways adverse to the litigant and succeeds in making the new legislation (apparently) immune to constitutional challenge.

The critical point is that a new law (embodying a particular policy disliked by a potential litigant) may remain in force for several years even if it is challenged immediately and is eventually overturned. In that time, irreversible changes may have occurred that limit the utility of winning in the courts.

Litigation may force issues into the courts that would be better determined in the political arena (through elections, intra-party debates, the legislature and the legitimate exercise of discretion by public administrators). The courts may be called upon to make value choices in interpreting a statute or the constitution. Through strategic use of the judicial system, an elite that is unable to win election or command the majority of the legislature may well be able to influence judges and gain the force of law. (This point is emphasized by Knopff and Morton, 1992 and by Morton and Knopff, 2000.)

---

60 Supreme Court of Canada Justice Claire L'Heureux-Dube (who retired July 2002), at a gay rights symposium in England, said in part: "There is a general failure in the political process."... "Radical ideas such as gay marriage need the pressure of the court to become law. "I will do anything I can," she told delegates. "We [judges] have lots of discretion ... I am not afraid to strike down laws". (quoted in a *National Post* editorial, August 23, 2000, p. A17).

61 Merv Lavigne, funded by the National Citizens Coalition, brought a case against his union, arguing that compulsory union dues should not be used to support the NDP, the peace movement and efforts to make abortions more easily available (causes with which he disagreed). Such use of union dues violated his freedom of association rights under the Charter. He won at the trial level, but that decision was reversed by the court of appeal, and at the Supreme Court of Canada and Lavigne lost in 1991. Most unusually, the SCC ordered Lavigne to pay the costs of the three labour organizations that intervened in the case — some several hundred thousand dollars. Yet it gave no reasons for doing so. See Stanbury (1993a, pp. 414–415).

Figure 3: **Notes on Selected Recent Legal Action in Which Interest Groups Were Heavily Involved**

1. In September 2000, Stephen Harper, then head of the National Citizens' Coalition[62] launched a constitutional challenge to parts of Bill C-2, amendments to the Canada Elections Act (effective on September 1, 2000) dealing with the rules governing expenditures by so-called "third parties," during election campaigns. It was the fifth time in the previous 17 years that NCC had mounted a challenge to legislation relating to "third parties".[63]

On June 21, 2001 the trial court held that the spending limits and anti-bundling provisions were unconstitutional as infringing Harper's right to freedom of expression and to freedom of association guaranteed in S.2(b) and S.2(d) of the Charter of Rights and Freedoms. In December 2002, the Alberta Court of Appeal (2 to 1) upheld the trial court's decision which ruled that parts of the new legislation were unconstitutional. In January 2003, the federal government stated that it would appeal to the Supreme Court of Canada (SCC)[64] (Globeandmail.com, January 24, 2003).

2. In December 2002, the Supreme Court of Canada decided a class action case brought by Quebec welfare recipients (Louise Gosselin v. The Attorney General of Quebec). The amount claimed was $388.6 million based on a change in policy in the late 1980s that greatly reduced payments to able-bodied adults. The SCC dismissed the action but didn't award costs against the plaintiff. It left open the possibility that similar claims might succeed if politicians impose welfare rules that appear to be "stereotypical or arbitrary". The Court had been asked to rule whether the reduction in welfare rates violated S.7 of the Charter re "life, liberty and security of person". The case had been dismissed by the Quebec Court of Appeal (see Seeman, January 2003, p. 3).

At the SCC level, there were nine interveners: four provinces (Ontario, New Brunswick, British Columbia, and Alberta) and five other organizations: the International Centre for Human Rights and Democratic Development (based in Montreal and funded largely by the fed-

---

62   In March 2002, Mr. Harper was elected Leader of the Canadian Alliance party and is now Leader of the Opposition in the House of Commons.

63   In 1984, and twice in 1993, NCC convinced the courts to overturn legislation governing electoral spending by "third parties".

64   In October 1997, in the Libman case, a unanimous SCC held that Quebec's Referendum Act's (passed in 1978 by the PQ) almost total ban on spending by individuals or groups not under the umbrella of either the official Yes or No sides violated the freedom of expression and of association provisions under the federal Charter and under Quebec's Charter of Human Rights and Freedoms. Robert Libman was the leaders of a small political party when he began the litigation in 1992 and his legal action was financed by Howard Galganov's Quebec Political Action Committee.

eral government), Commission des droits de la personne et des droits de la jeunesse, National Association of Women and the Law (NAWL), the Charter Committee on Poverty Issues, and the Canadian Association of Statutory Human Rights Agencies (which is effectively funded by the federal and provincial governments). It is not clear from the decision who funded Ms. Gosselin's challenge, but she certainly did not have the resources to do so herself. It is likely to have been an interest group.

3. On October 31, 2003, the Supreme Court of Canada, in a 5 to 4 vote, ruled that inmates in penitentiaries serving a term of over two years were entitled to vote in federal and provincial elections. The decision was based on an uncharacteristic literal reading of S.3 of the Charter: "Every citizen of Canada has the right to vote". The case had been brought by Richard Sauvé who had been serving a life sentence for first degree murder. The Court Challenges Program financed the litigation conducted in Sauvé's name and that of several Native inmates. The interveners at the SCC level were the British Columbia Civil Liberties Association, Aboriginal Legal Services of Toronto Inc., Canadian Bar Association, the John Howard Society of Canada, the Canadian Association of Elizabeth Fry Societies, and two provinces (Alberta and Manitoba).

Jeffrey Simpson (2002) pointed out that previously the SCC struck down a section of the Canada Elections Act of 1985 that deprived all prisoners of the right to vote. In 1993, Parliament amended the Act to limit the ban on voting to prisoners serving terms of two years or more.

4. On December 20, 2002, by a vote of 7 to 2, the Supreme Court of Canada ruled that the British Columbia School Act does not allow a school board to proscribe certain books for classroom use where the decision is inconsistent with "the broad principles of tolerance and non-sectarianism underlying the School Act". The case was launched in 1997 by James Chamberlain, a teacher in Surrey, BC after he was ordered by the Surrey School Board not to use three books dealing with same sex parents in his kindergarten and Grade 1 classes that were on the resource list of the Gay and Lesbian Educators (GALE) of BC, of which he was a member.

Some 65 affidavits were filed in that court in support of the Board's decision. One came from 32 evangelical churches. A poll conducted for the School Board's legal counsel in February 1998 found that 61% of adults in Surrey opposed the use of same-sex books in kindergarten and Grade 1 classrooms.

The following groups were interveners at the SCC level: EGALE Canada Inc., Elementary Teachers Federation of Ontario, BC Civil Liberties Association, the Board of Trustees of School District No. 34 (Abbotsford), Canadian Civil Liberties Association, Families in Partnership, the Evangelical Fellowship of Canada, the Archdiocese of Vancouver, the Catholic Civil Rights League, and the Canadian Alliance for Social Justice and Family Values Association.

Mr. Chamberlain said the case cost him and four other litigants $400,000 (but it seems likely that much of this was borne by GALE BC). The Surrey School Board is on record as having spent $880,000 to defend its position (Makin, 2002c).

5. On April 2, 1998, the SCC released its 6 to 1 decision in the Vriend case, the substance of which was to read sexual orientation into Alberta's Individual's Rights Protection Act because failure to include it violated S.15(1) of the Charter. In 1991 the appellant Delwin Vriend, an employee of King's College in Edmonton was fired apparently because, in response to an inquiry by the president of the College, he disclosed that he was homosexual. The Alberta Human Rights Commission advised Vriend that he could not make a complaint under IRPA because the legislation did not include sexual orientation as a protected ground against discrimination. Vriend and three gay/lesbian interest groups went to court and the case worked its way up to the SCC.

The SCC granted intervener status to 14 interest groups as well to the Attorney General of Canada, Attorney General for Ontario, and the Canadian Human Rights Commission. The interest groups included EGALE, LEAF, Canadian Bar Association, Canadian Jewish Congress, Focus on the Family (Canada) Association, Canadian AIDS Society, the Foundation for Equal Families, and the Canadian Labour Congress. A total of 22 lawyers represented the interest groups.

The resolution of the matter took 70 months from the time Vriend attempted to file a complaint with the Alberta Human Rights Commission (June 11, 1991) to the release of the decision of the SCC (April 2, 1998).

Changes in public policy brought about by litigation may be an unintended consequence of defending either a private action or a criminal charge rather than the result of a conscious effort to reshape public policy by means of a legal decision. In the latter situation, the accused care only for their own skins and use the constitutionality sword because it is just another weapon that may work. The key point is that, in many instances, the defendant has not set out to use the Charter as a tool to change public policy. The defendant would be entirely happy to "get off" without any change in public policy at all. Finally, the decision rendered by courts (even after all appeals have been exhausted) may turn out to be very narrow, with only a very limited range of applicability to other people.

New Information and Communications Technologies and Interest Groups[65]

In this section we discuss briefly the effects of new information and communications technologies on interest groups and their activities.

New Information and Communication Technologies

What do we mean by NICTs? One approach to defining NICTs is to focus on the *hardware* that symbolize and embody the NICTs. These include the following: wireless telephony (e.g., cellular phones; desk-top and lap-top computers with increasingly powerful and cheaper, microprocessors); the Internet (the network of networks) and World Wide Web (the Web); handheld video cameras; digital cameras; satellite transmission of telecom and broadcasting signals; fibre optic "wires" to transmit telecom and other signals with broad band capacity; and digital switching for telecom operations. Note that almost none of these advanced innovations could deliver the new/better services they do without advances in *software,* i.e., the instructions that are loaded into a computer or hardwired onto a chip.

One of the most important NICTs for interest groups is the World Wide Web. It is a means of storing digitized content in a server that can be retrieved remotely. This digitized content includes print (text), graphics, sound, videotape, and numerical data. The Web is based on hypertext — a way of embedding codes in text that permit near instant electronic links to other digitized content at the same site, or at another website anywhere else on the Net. Browser software is essential to search the Web to find content for which a person does *not* have the exact electronic address.

Many of the pieces of hardware were not invented or even marketed last year. They have existed in a somewhat similar form (i.e., substitute) for some years, even over two decades.[66] What makes them new is the *non-incremental change* in one or more of the following characteristics:

- Price: e.g., long-distance calls at five cents a minute are quite different than the same calls at 60 cents[67]; a fax machine (of a given quality) at $199 is different than the same one at $1000.
- "Power": this term refers to the range of functions a piece of hardware can perform/handle and/or the speed/ease/convenience with which it functions.

---

65   More extensive discussions can be found in Stanbury & Vertinsky (1995a) 1995b); Hill & Hughes (1998), Davis (1999).

66   The core technologies are the telephone (invented in the late 19th century), the desktop or personal computer, which first came to the market in 1974, and the Internet, established as a link among four main frame computers in 1970. The first cell phone was introduced by Motorola in March 1983. It weighed 28 ounces and was 13 inches long. The Web was created in 1991, but its use was limited until the early versions of what became the Netscape browser became available in 1993.

67   Recall that the first trans-Atlantic telephone calls cost over US $10 per minute in 2003 dollars.

- Mobility: this includes all types of wireless transmission but also size: e.g., the 20 pound portable video camera became the 18 ounce, handheld minicam with a 20 to 1 zoom lens with playback capability through the flip-out viewfinder.
- Speed: this not only refers to computer processing speed, but also bandwidth (capacity) of various types of telecom transmission.

When several or all of these attributes improve quickly at the *same time*, the change can be (and has been) extraordinary.

NICTs and the Creation of Interest Groups

The Net provides the ability to "aggregate" into a group a minute percentage of the population no matter where located on the globe (if they have access to the Net).[68] Using the Net, it is possible to create virtual communities based on very specialized, shared interests. The Net provide "broadcast" capability to groups and even to individuals who create a website. This capability can be used to try to *create* a group by recruiting others on the Net.

A growing number of people have access to the Net.[69] This makes the Net more powerful in both the creation of interest groups and their ability to communicate with the public, news media and government. At present, a high percentage of users are male, better educated, with a higher income — but users are becoming a closer reflection of the population. The Net subverts geography — location is irrelevant for online communication, but legal actions, protests and sit-ins are location-bound, of course. The Net is a social space — people use it to seek out like-minded people no matter where they are located. It allows people to build emotional/intellectual ties across space. The Net has been described as the practical embodiment of the "global village" (of McLuhan).

NICTs and the Operation of Interest Groups

The Net has near zero marginal cost of transmission.[70] (But the "front end" costs, i.e., a personal computer with a modem, and an ISP connection, are still beyond the reach of many in poorer countries.) It also provides near instant communications worldwide. The Net can transmit anything that can be digitized — thus allowing multi media messages (which are presumably more powerful,

---

68   The Net tends to be particularly valuable to minorities of any kind. It can be used to help identify each other, and to help dispersed minorities communicate (e.g., the Welsh). The Net permits a group to create a presence far greater than any geographic concentration of the minority.

69   Canada is one of the leaders among industrialized countries. Over 70 percent of adults have access to the Internet a home, school, work or public libraries. Some 60 percent of households have access at home (and almost half have broadband access). Source: www.ipsos-reid.com.

70   There do not appear to be economies of scale in the creation of content; i.e., the costs are essentially fixed. At the same time, once the content is created it has many of the characteristics of a "public good", as economists use the term.

i.e., persuasive). The Net is now being used for even lower cost long distance telephony.[71]

The Net can make it easier/cheaper for a group to raise funds across a nation and across nations/continents (with the advent of secure, inexpensive, easy to use payment mechanisms). It also permits the mobilization of individuals across borders.[72]

A website provides a convenient way to "publish" materials an interest group wants to diffuse: Any digitized media can be made available. The site is open 24 hours per day. Material can be added or updated every few minutes if desired. Material can be put into PDF format so that the words, graphics, etc. are "fixed" on each page and are not addressable by the recipient. The cost of creating and maintaining a site is modest, and the number of times a site is contracted ("hits") can be counted.

Using the Net, people can interact either in real time, or asynchronously. It is easy for information consumers to be information *providers*. At the least, the Net can permit rapid feedback to leaders of interest groups. A group can use the Net for confidential communications accessible only by those given the code/descrambler.

It is easy to utilize decentralized intelligence by means of the Net. This intelligence can be embodied in people or, data/information deposits. The Net facilitates collaboration by small to large numbers — it is easily scaleable.

The Net is a means to get around (bypass) traditional gatekeepers in communication channels, e.g., the print and broadcasting news media. For example, the Net has been used to subvert official authority's control over traditional media. Protests and other efforts to influence the government in Belgrade, Serbia in November-December 1996 were organized using the Net (see Friedman 1997, Ch. 4).[73]

We are just beginning to see how the Net and text messages on cellular telephones can be used to mobilize from hundreds to many thousands of people for political protests — either in person or for a "virtual demonstration". For example, on March 5, 2003, "more than 400,000 antiwar protesters...jammed switch boards in the White House and Congress with a flood of phone calls, faxes and emails in what was billed as the first nationwide virtual demonstration" (Taylor, 2003). According to the same source, the international coordinator of Moveon.org (which has only four paid staff members) can "ask any army of 750,000 protesters to take to the streets whenever he chooses..."

---

71   See, for example, www.net2phone.com.
72   See Stanbury (2000), Vertinsky & Stanbury (1995a), Keck & Kikkink (1998).
73   Pal (1998) argues that there are two views about the impact of NICTs on politics. View #1 suggests that the new technologies empower individuals; reduce the need for intermediaries, e.g., news media; subvert the power of governments and other intermediaries; facilitate the creation and operation of interest groups (including mobilization of people for political activity); and makes international mobilization of interests easier/cheaper. View #2 suggests that NICTs are most likely to be used by those who already have power/position; that they are likely to increase power at the centre — incumbent's ability to influence voters via much greater personal information; and that the Net facilitates disaggregation (fragmentation) of the polity into many, specialized interests — there is less feeling of being part of a larger whole (community).

Indeed, he helped create the antiwar protests in the US on February 15, 2003 (and which occurred in other major cities around the world).

Federal Government Regulation of Lobbyists and Interest Group Activities

As the number of interest groups and professional lobbyists has expanded, so has the regulation of their activities. In this paper, we can only sketch some of the more notable provisions created by the federal government.

Lobbyists Registration Act (LRA)

The LRA was enacted in 1988, coming into effect September 30, 1989. It was extensively amended effective January 31, 1996.[74] Amendments to the LRA were introduced on October 23, 2002, but they have not become law (as of May 2003).

Under the LRA effective January 31, 1996, three types of lobbyists must register and provide information about themselves, the persons/organizations they represent, and the government department/agency being lobbied.

- Consultant lobbyists — individuals, such as lawyers, accountants and government relations consultants, who are paid to lobby for clients;
- In-house lobbyists for corporations — employees who, as a significant part of their duties, lobby for an employer who carries out commercial activities for financial gain; and
- In-house lobbyists for organizations — not-for-profit organizations in which one or more employees lobby, and the collective time devoted to lobbying amounts to a significant part of one employee's duties[75] (Industry Canada, 1996, p. 3).

Certain public officials when acting in their official capacity are *exempted* from the registration requirements: e.g., MLAs, employees of provincial, territorial and local governments, members of local municipal governments and their staff, members of Indian band councils, official representatives of foreign governments, officials of U.N. organizations. Note, however, that if any of the organizations to which these public officials are attached employs a consultant lobbyist, the latter must register.

The following activities do *not* require registration: oral or written submissions to parliamentary committees or government agencies (e.g., CRTC, NEB) where there is a public record; oral or written submissions to a public official engaged in the enforcement/application of a federal statute or regulation; and

---

74   The is R.S.C. 1984, c.44 (4th supp.) including the 1996 amendments [www.laws.justice.gc.ca/en/L-12.4/text.html]. The Lobbyists Registration Regulations can be Found in *Canada Gazette* Part II, December 27, 1995]

75   When the accumulated lobbying duties by all paid employees would constitute 20% or more of the duties of one employee, the senior officer must complete the registration form in which those employees would be listed.

oral or written submissions made in response to a written request by a public office holder (MPs, Senators, Ministers, employees of federal departments) for advice or comment with respect to any matter referred to in the Act.

The definitions of persons who must register exclude the following persons engaged in lobbying: individuals seeking to influence government on their own behalf (e.g., obtaining a pension), members of interest groups making representations on behalf of the group, and academics submitting briefs or testifying before parliamentary committees or inquiries (provided that they are not being employed by any of the persons who have to register). Further, the LRA does not cover communications between federal public office holders and employees of commercial organizations whose job it is to sell their company's products or services (to the federal government).

Among the things consultant lobbyists must disclose on the registration form (within 10 days of beginning to lobby) is the subject matters of their lobbying, the source and amount of government funding provided to the client, whether payment is contingent upon the success of their efforts, and the communications techniques used (including grass roots lobbying).

The "Guide to Registration" for the LRA defines grass roots lobbying as "a communications technique that encourages individual members of the public or organizations to communicate directly with public office holders in an attempt to influence the decisions of government. Such efforts primarily rely on use of the media or advertising, and result in mass letter writing and facsimile campaigns, telephone calls to public office holders, and public demonstrations" (Industry Canada, 1996, p. 10). It also states that if a person is not engaged in any registerable lobbying activity, it is not necessary to register for a grass roots campaign.

The *Lobbyists Registration Act* does not, per se, "regulate" the activities of lobbyists. It is primarily a disclosure tool. The only thing in the federal domain that deals with specific behaviour of lobbyists is the Lobbyists Code of Conduct[76], but it does not have the same force of law as, say, the Criminal Code of Canada (see below).

The purpose of the Lobbyists' Code of Conduct is "to assure the Canadian public that lobbying is done ethically and with the highest standards with a view to conserving and enhancing public confidence and trust in the integrity, objectivity and impartiality of government decision-making". It includes a range of principles (i.e., "Lobbyists should conduct with integrity and honesty all relations with public office holders, clients, employers, the public and other lobbyists", and, "Lobbyists should at all times be open and frank about their lobbying activities, while respecting confidentiality"). These, according to the Office of the Ethics Counsellor, "set out in , in positive terms, the goals and objectives to be attained without establishing precise standards." The rules then provide more detailed requirements for behaviour in certain situations: (i) requiring transparency (e.g., "Lobbyists shall, when making a representation to a public office holder, disclose the identity of the person or organization on whose behalf the representation is made;" "Lobbyists shall provide information

---

76   The text of the Lobbyists Code of Conduct can be found at www.strategis.gc.ca/SSF/lr01044e.html.

that is accurate and factual to public office holders..."); (ii) conflict of interest ("Lobbyists shall not represent conflicting or competing interests without the informed consent of those whose interests are involved"); and (iii) "improper influence" ("Lobbyists shall not place public office holders in a conflict of interest by proposing or undertaking any action that could constitute an improper influence on a public office holder").

The Ethics Counsellor has the power to investigate breaches of the Code and report to Parliament. But beyond the potential embarrassment of the person or organization under investigation, there are no other sanctions for violations of the Code. Moreover, the powers of investigation that are provided to the Ethics Counsellor are only to be triggered where an alleged breach of a rule is reported to him. There is no proactive compliance-monitoring and enforcement of the Code.

Canada Elections Act

Although the finances of parties and candidates have been regulated since 1974, there have been no limits on the size of political contributions that could be made to parties, candidates, nomination contestants or electoral district associations (constituencies) by individuals, corporations, trade unions, or other organizations. Bill C-24, given first reading on January 19, 2003, proposes to limit contributions by individuals, corporations, unions and not-for-profit organizations as indicated in note 18 above. Most interest groups will be limited to $1,000 per year in donations to candidates and nomination contestants.

Non-resident foreigners are prohibited from giving money to federal parties, to candidates and to electoral district associations. Nor can US TV and radio stations just across the border be used to broadcast election campaign ads as a way to try to get around the limits on party and candidate "election expenses"[77] during official campaign periods (now 36 days).

Effective September 1, 2000, so-called "third parties" (defined as individuals or organizations *other* than a registered party, a candidate or an electoral district association of a registered party) have been limited to spending no more than $150,000 nationally during a general election, *and* not more than $3,000 in any one electoral district (Stanbury, 2002b). These limits are indexed to the CPI, so the actual limits for the November 27, 2000 election were $152,550 and $3,051, respectively.[78]

Interest groups (through staff and members) and consultant lobbyists can exploit the provisions concerning volunteer services to parties and candidates. So long as the volunteer is not being paid by their employer and is not making a donation in kind (e.g., by doing work that they normally do as an employee or professional), then the value of their efforts does not count as an "election expense" (which are tightly limited for candidates, but less so for parties), nor

---

77   The key limit is that for candidates. For the November 2000 general election, the average limit was $68,000. The limit for a party running a complete slate of 301 candidates was $12.7 million.

78   In that election, 40 third parties spent a total of $570,688, or an average of $14,267. Only two organizations spent $150,000 or more; only six organizations spent more than $10,000. (Data from Stanbury, 2002b, updated by the late filing by CUPE, see Waldie, 2002.)

would they be counted as in kind contributions that are to be limited under Bill C-24 (see Stanbury, 2003b).

Prior to June 12, 2002, when the PM announced his "Guidelines to Govern Ministerial Activities for Personal Political Purposes" (Prime Minister's Office, 2002) the only rules governing leadership races were those established by the parties themselves. In some cases these became fairly elaborate and, in most cases, included limits on leadership campaign expenditures (although the Canadian Alliance did not impose such a limit in the race won by Stephen Harper in March 2002 (see Stanbury, 2002a). The PM's "Guidelines" (which require more extensive disclosure) apply only to cabinet ministers, but if Bill C-24 is enacted, there will be a limit of $10,000 that can be given in aggregate to rival candidates for leadership of the *same* party. Further, corporations, unions and not-for-profit organizations are to be *banned* from making any contributions to any leadership candidate under Bill C-24 (see Stanbury, 2003b).

Also under Bill C-24, money from a political trust fund created by an interest group (or by an MP) will not be payable to a party, EDA, candidate or nomination contestant.[79] But such trust funds could spend money on political activities between elections benefiting a party, sitting MPs or persons expecting to run in the next election (see Stanbury 2003b).

If an interest group wants to form a political party (e.g., to avoid the tight constraints on "third parties) that is eligible for various financial benefits under the CEA,[80] it must become registered with the Chief Electoral Officer, and the key condition (since 1993) is that it field 50 or more candidates in the upcoming federal general election, each of whom must meet certain conditions (a deposit of $1000 and the signatures of 100 electors in the district in which the candidate will run). These conditions, however, have been the subject of a constitutional challenge in the Figueroa case, which has gone to the SCC.[81]

Income Tax Act

The maximum tax credit for contributions by individuals, participants, and corporations to political parties and candidates is currently $500, based on contributions totalling $1,075. If Bill C-24 is enacted as introduced, the limit will rise to $650 p.a., based on contributions totalling $1,275 (and the credit of 75 percent will apply to the first $400).

---

79   Note that money paid into such a trust fund is not accountable (i.e., need not be publicly reported), nor are the expenditures from such a fund.

80   These include the right to issue receipts for the income tax credit for contributions (now 75 percent of the first $200), access to free time on the electronic media, and a 22.5 percent rebate on its "election expenses". The provisions will become more generous if Bill C-24 is enacted as introduced: the 22.5 percent rebate will go to 50 percent and each registered party will get an annual subsidy of $1.50 per vote in the previous general election (Stanbury, 2003b).

81   Figueroa, then leader of the Communist Party of Canada, brought an action against the federal government and won at trial level in Ontario (March 10, 1000), but the Ontario Court of Appeal upheld only part of the trial court's decision. The case was heard by the Supreme Court of Canada in November 2002 (see Makin, 2002b).

Registered charities — those permitted to issue receipts for the income tax credit on contributions[82] — may engage in only very limited efforts to influence public policy: only 10 percent of their annual expenditures may be devoted to such efforts. But such entities may spend as much as they want on efforts to "educate" the public.[83] It is under this provision that some thinktanks are able to issue tax receipts for the donations made to it (or to its endorsement) by corporations and individuals. Yet it seems clear that thinktanks sponsor and publish research that makes specific proposals for changing public policy, or it is easy to infer from the author's discussion that certain changes should be made. The crucial fact is that the law in relation to what charities can and cannot do with respect to efforts to influence public policy, while retaining their authority to issue tax receipts, to put it politely, is imprecise.[84] Greenpeace Canada, for example, has had its status as a registered charity taken away twice. Some organizations, all of whom seem to be on the right, have never succeeded in gaining this status.[85] However, a variety of highly activist organizations continue to enjoy the benefits of charitable status even though much of their expenditures are on efforts to influence public policy.

Business corporations (and other tax-paying entities) are able to deduct as expenses in the computation of taxable income their fees and other outlays to belong to trade/professional associations that lobby on their behalf, and their own expenditures on all efforts to try to influence government policies/actions. Thus, when the tobacco companies challenged the constitutionality of Bill C-57 (enacted in June 1988), and took the case to the Supreme Court of Canada (where they won), the millions of dollars in legal and experts' fees were tax deductible. On the other hand, trade unions, environmental groups, and many other interest groups are non-taxable organizations.

Criminal Code and Other Statutes

Interest groups sponsoring a demonstration or protest need to be aware of S.63 of the Criminal Code. It deals with an unlawful assembly, which is defined as:

> An assembly of three or more persons who, with intent to carry out any common purpose, assemble in such a manner or so conduct themselves when they are assembled as to cause persons in the neighbourhood of the assembly to fear, on reasonable grounds, that they

---

82 Under the *Income Tax Act*, an organization must be registered by the Canada Customs and Revenue Agency before being granted charitable status. Non-profit agencies denied charitable status, while tax exempt, are not able either to issue tax receipts or to receive foundation grants the way registered charities can (LeRoy, 2002b).

83 The leading legal definition (the Pemsel case, 1891) sets out four broad categories of charitable activity: religion, relief of the poor, education, and other purposes beneficial to the community (LeRoy, 2002b; Webb, 2000).

84 This point was recognized by the SCC in the *Vancouver Society of Immigrant Women* case ([1999] S.C.R.1), but the Court urged Parliament to act to clarify the legislation. (Generally, see Webb, 2000).

85 Such organizations can appeal to the Federal Court of Appeal, but this is a costly and slow process.

(a)   will disturb the peace tumultuously; or

(b)   will by that assembly needlessly and without reasonable cause pro-
       voke other persons to disturb the peace tumultuously.

Those guilty of participation in an unlawful assembly are punishable upon summary conviction. Section 64 defines a *riot* as "an unlawful assembly that has begun to disturb the peace tumultuously". Participation in a riot can result in
imprisonment for up to two years.

The Criminal Code of Canada has numerous provisions covering "Offences
Against the Administration of Law and Justice," proscribing various types of activity associated with illegal dealings involving government officials. They include
S.119 (bribery of public officials, including elected officials or public servants);
S.121 ("frauds on the government" and influence peddling); S.122 ("breach of
trust" by public officials); S.123 (corruption of municipal officials); S.124 ("selling or purchasing office"); and S. 125 ("influencing or negotiating appointments
or dealing in offices").

Bribery and influence peddling are also covered in the offence of "prohibited compensation" in the *Parliament of Canada Act*. Section 41(1) makes it an
offence for MPs to "receive or agree to receive any compensation, directly or
indirectly, for services rendered or to be rendered by any person...(a) in relation to any bill, proceeding, contract, claim, controversy...or other matter before
[Parliament], or (b) for the purpose of influencing or attempting to influence
any member of either House". The penalty is a fine of $500 to $2,000 and dis-
qualification from being an MP and from holding any office in the public service of Canada. A similar provision applies to Senators.

Section 41(3) makes it an offence to "give, offer or promise" to any MP
"any compensation for services described in subsection (1)..." The punishment
is a fine of $500 to $2,000 and imprisonment for up to one year. A similar
provision applies to Senators.

Finally, we note that there is a provision in the General Conditions of federal procurement regulations[86] that prohibits contractors from paying, directly or
indirectly, a contingency or "success" fee for "the solicitation, negotiation or
obtaining of contracts to any person other than an employee "acting in the normal course of the employee's duties". Bidders on federal contracts must certify
as part of their bid that they have not and will not pay a contingency fee to
anyone other than an employee. Specifically included in this prohibition is any
individual who is required to file a return under the terms of the *Lobbyists
Registration Act*.

Conclusions

The design of Canada's form of government (the Westminster model) greatly
influences how interest groups must operate if they are to increase the likelihood that they will be effective.

---

86   Standard Acquisitions Clause and Conditions SACC - Manual - General Conditions DSS-
      MAS 1011A-21.

Interest groups seeking to influence the federal government are more numerous and, apparently, better funded than they were two or three decades ago (although there are no authoritative statistics on their expenditures). The number of fee-for-service lobbyists registered in Ottawa grew from 658 in 1991 to 858 in 2002.

Important and widely-shared interests — because of the "logic of collective inaction" — are not represented by one or more interest groups. However, individual MPs and political parties do seek to advance those interests, either because they believe it is the right thing to do or, more likely, they are seeking votes (also a perfectly legitimate reason). At the same time, to a surprising degree, interest groups have been able to overcome the free rider problem. One of the main ways they do so is to supply (excludable) goods and use part of the price of membership to fund lobbying activities.

Frustration with the limited role of MPs in Canada's version of the Westminster model, and with the shrinking of the role of political parties (to that of near election-fighting vehicles), appears to have made interest groups the primary signalling device for citizens between general elections. At the same time, the federal government spends heavily in public opinion polling to find out what voters want, and also how to "sell" the policies the party in power wants to implement.

It appears that many interest groups have become more sophisticated about influencing government. This may be attributable to the greater use of professional lobbyists or hiring persons with substantial experience in policy-making. But many employees of interest groups have learned the game on the job. Some of these persons have shown remarkable imagination in finding new ways to try to influence governments.[87]

Since the enactment of the Charter of Rights and Freedoms in the new Canadian Constitution in 1982, there has been a huge growth in the use of litigation by interest groups to achieve changes in public policy. It is clear that judges — particularly those on the Supreme Court of Canada — have become law makers. There is considerable debate over the desirability of this change.

New information and communications technologies (NICTs) are changing the ways interest groups operate. In general, their effect has been to lower the cost of entry into the market for voices, and to provide means to bypass the "filters" of traditional communications channels. At the same time, both MPs and government departments are making greater use of the NICTs. It is far too early to say what the full range of consequences of NICTs for policy-making will be.

It is very likely that the amount of cross-border lobbying will increase for two main reasons. First, the key decision-makers that interest groups want to influence may be located in a foreign country (due to globalization). Second, the NICTs make it far easier to do this either alone or, more likely, in cooperation with other groups in the nation where the "target" operates.

---

87   Many of these work for environmental groups. For a list of almost 30 tactics and techniques used by various environmental groups in the conflict over B.C.'s forests, see Stanbury (2000, Table 11–1).

The regulation of interest group activities by the federal government has increased notably since the late 1980s, when the *Lobbyists Registration Act* was enacted. Parliament has made repeated attempts to curb spending by "third parties" during election campaigns, and the current and most restrictive legislation is now before the Supreme Court of Canada in a case brought by an interest group, the National Citizens' Coalition.

The effectiveness of the efforts of interest groups to influence public policies is extremely difficult to determine — and far beyond the scope of this paper.[88] The fact that the number of groups engaged in the process has increased as have the expenditures by existing ones, strongly suggests that the groups believe that the game is worth the candle. Hence, we believe that more academics and others should pay more attention to the role of interest groups in helping to set the federal government's agenda, and in influencing public policies.[89] At present, Canadian political scientists devote far more ink to political parties, for example, even while they acknowledge that their role has declined a great deal (although they continue to provide the organizational shell and legal basis for election campaigns and leadership races).

---

88   For studies that try to do this, at least in part, see Stanbury (1977), (2000); Egri & Stanbury (1989); McQuaig (1988).

89   They have devoted even less effort to understanding the role of thinktanks (public research organizations) in the market for political ideas and the extent to which they help to shape public policies.

Introduction to Part II

Cases and Articles of Government Intervention

The second part of the book presents cases and articles of what is often referred to as the Canadian mixed economy.

The first two articles, respectively entitled, "Representative Government and the Provision of Public Goods" and "Pension Fund" relate to the first article in the first part of the book on ideological considerations of government's roles.

The third article, entitled, "A General Model of Government Intervention" presents a model whereby interactions between business and government can be described and explained. The author defines intervention as the application of any governing instrument to give an effect to its policy decisions through modifying the behaviour and/or economic and social circumstances of individuals or groups within the private sector.

The fourth and fifth articles examine challenges in the Canadian health care system. "Myths and the Canadian Health Care System" challenges four propagated myths about health care in Canada. "The Medical Centre: Strategic Alternatives for A Private Health Care Provider" is based on a private hospital seeking to make decisions about its role in the challenges of health care delivery.

The next three articles examine the protectionist policies towards Canadian indigenous industries. "The Book Publishing Industry Development Program: An Evaluation" is a report prepared in December 1998 for the Department of Heritage Canada to evaluate various Departmental programs to assist the Canadian book publishing industry. "Federal Government's Industrial Strategy to Regional Economic Disparities" examines the various federal government policies and programs to readdress regional economic disparities. The focus has always been on loss of employment and industry. "Cultivating Cash: How to Grow a Farming Business in Canada" examines the changing nature of the agriculture sector. Although the family farm is still barely thriving, agricorporations have breathed new life into the agriculture sector.

The next series of case articles deal with privatization. There has been the assumption that government enterprises are often dumped at a loss after consuming great amounts of public money. Privatization has not always been properly used to reduce government deficits, except by the difference between the sale price and the value at which the assets are carried on government's books. The reasons frequently given for the privatization of government activities include:

- To improve efficiency
- To reduce the public sector borrowing requirements
- To reduce government involvement in enterprise decision making
- To ease problems of public sector pay determination
- To widen share ownership
- To gain political advantage

In "Privatization of Pearson International Airport", there are two examples of privatization. The first decision was to reduce the public sector borrowing by selling Pearson International Airport which would then permit businesses to develop, expand and manage the Airport. The second decision was to see the establishing of the Greater Toronto Airport Authority to work in partnership with the Department of Transport, thereby reducing government involvement in enterprise decision making. In "Privatization of Highway 407", there are again two examples of privatization. The first decision was to establish a working partnership with the Ontario Ministry of Transport to finance, develop and construct Highway 407. The second decision was the sale of Highway 407 to a private sector consortium. In "Commercialization of the Liquor Control Board of Ontario", the Ontario government sought to re-invent the once lucrative revenue producer by changing the image and business activities of a Crown Corporation. In "Solid Waste Management in Toronto", the city of Toronto sought to establish policies and programs that would change how the city viewed garbage as a resource. Attention is paid to establishing partnerships with businesses in the removal, disposal and management of solid waste.

The thirteenth article entitled "The Stakes in the Canadian Airline Industry" traces the growth and tribulations of a former Canadian Crown Corporation and a national icon, Air Canada. Air Canada assumed a monopoly position. With its own growth and incurring debts and global situations, Air Canada, much like its global competitors would file for protective bankruptcy in April 2003. The story is not completed.

The fourteenth and fifteenth articles address the issues of Canada's position in globalization. Under the North American Free Trade Agreement, Canada and the United States have created the world's largest trading co-operative. ""The Canada — US Softwood Lumber Dispute" discusses and explains the dispute between Canada and the United States over softwood lumber in 2000 represents the challenge of protectionist policies in a global economy. "Canadian Provinces, US States and North American Integration: Bench Warmers or Key Players?" discusses a number of past disputes involving US States and Canadian or foreign jurisdictions and argues that such frictions should inform strategy toward integration.

Representative Government and the Provision of Public Goods*

Janice E. Nicholson

> [The governments of all parties] have managed to create a tax
> and social security system of such complex detail that they could
> not possibly understand it. The only explanation for their
> achievement is that it happened piecemeal, each change being
> made in pursuit of the latest fashion, social purpose or whim.
> (*Economist*, October 1983)

In the continuing debate surrounding the imperfections of the social security
systems in developed countries, two themes emerge: the application of the
market concept to the provision of public goods, and the role of the state in
providing a rational, planned approach in both the provision of public goods
and the establishment of priorities concerning them.

Both themes trace their roots to the Classical Economists of the eighteenth
and nineteenth centuries, and the fundamental issues raised by these political
theorists have remained unresolved.

The emphasis of the Classical Economists upon free enterprise and the
market was a result of their rejection of the Mercantilist State. They were sus-
picious of state intervention, which had served the interests of special groups by
providing protection for their various economic interests. They wished to see
the social and economic system cleared of abuses. They argued that the people

---

* From *Business and Government: Canadian Materials,* edited by Diane Jurkowski et al., pp.
190–207 (Concord, ON: Captus Press Inc., 2000). Reproduced with permission of author.

are more ardent and skilful in the defence of their own interests than the state would be. Thus, the state should remove itself as far as possible from the economic sphere, so that the individual, in pursuing his own interests will, in the end, pursue the interests of society.

However, Robbins argues that their attachment to the laissez-faire principle has been exaggerated. While they did have a general presumption of free economic activity, they were not opposed to state activity per se. Their principle was utility and they did not think that wide state activity led to utility. On the other hand, they were not so naive as to believe that the establishment of complete economic freedom would lead to harmony among different economic interests.

> The most that can be said of the Classical Economists in this respect is that they believed that in a world of free enterprise, certain relationships would arise which were of a mutually advantageous kind to the individuals concerned and superior to those resulting from alternative systems.[1]

Within this framework the state was given a limited role. Adam Smith saw the state performing three main functions: external defence, protection of the individual from injustice at the hand of any other member of society, and some public works.[2] Smith perceived education and justice as the chief public functions. But Jeremy Bentham and John Stuart Mill extended the role of the state. They believed that public goods should be financed as 'collateral aids', which private enterprise would not provide, but that would create improved economic and social conditions so that the individual could pursue his enlightened self-interest.

At this point, the line becomes blurred. It is no longer possible to distinguish between those social goods that the individual is responsible for providing for himself via the marketplace, and those that the state should provide as "collateral aids".

This ambiguity is reflected in the work of Jeremy Bentham. In some of his work, Bentham does have a general presumption against government activity. In his "Institute of Political Economy", he outlines a general rule:

> Nothing ought to be done or attempted by government for the purpose of causing an augmentation to take place in the national mass of wealth, with a view to increase of the means of either subsistence or enjoyment without some special reason.[3]

But he was also capable of arguing that a group of individuals acting in their own best interests could not alone bring about the end of maximizing happiness:

> that the uncoerced and unenlightened propensities and powers of individuals are not adequate to the end without the control and guidance of the legislator is a matter of fact of which the evidence of history, the nature of man, and the existence of political society are so many proofs.[4]

271

He appeared to pursue this point further when he went on to outline several ends of economic activity. He refers to these ends of subsistence, security, opulence and equality as subordinate ends, but it is implied in his analysis that they are, in fact, components of the ultimate end of the greatest happiness of the greatest number. Once Bentham outlined a multiplicity of ends for society, he implied a broadening of state intervention. Although he asserts that government activity may not be necessary in the spheres of 'subsistence' and 'equality', the possibility arises that with a multiplicity of ends, government intervention may be necessary to deal with conflicts in the pursuit of different ends.

The work of Bentham highlights the problems that arise once a move is made away from individual freedom to choose in an open marketplace. Once the assumption is made that the state has an obligation to provide some social goods, the question arises as to which social goods should be provided, at what cost and to what end.

The Utilitarians tended to answer that question by reference back to the principle of utility. This principle can be defined in terms of either individual self-interest or social stability, or by the Benthamite terms of the greatest happiness of the greatest number. However, whichever way it is defined, it does not provide a guide as to the means society should use either individually or collectively to pursue such a goal. As long as the individual is perceived as being best able to determine his own needs, then social goals remain an aggregate of individual choices. Once this view is abandoned and the state is seen as having an obligation to pursue certain ends for the benefit of society, then choices must be made between both different means and ends. But the question recurs: on the basis of what criteria and what values shall these choices be made?

> The welfare and happiness of millions cannot be measured on a single scale of less or more.... It cannot be adequately expressed as a single end, but only as a hierarchy of ends, a comprehensive scale of value in which every need of every person is given its place.[5]

But how is the state to construct this hierarchy of ends? On what basis can it assess the every need of every person?

One answer to this question is to see societal values in a constant state of evolution. Gradually, the norms and values of the society emerge and can be translated into state action. Thus, Edward Burke saw government conducted by the leadership of a public spirited minority that the country would be willing to follow since it understood and expressed the prevailing communal values.[6]

Such a view was unacceptable to the Utilitarians, even those who saw a very limited role for state intervention, since "a policy based on natural evolution is a paralysis of inaction".[7] In this situation the state cannot act until society's norms have evolved to the point where clear messages can be sent to the government.

A compromise was suggested by both John Stuart Mill and Alexis de Tocqueville. Both saw the polity as a product of man, but subject to a series of constraints. Within these constraints policies and institutions can be a matter of choice. The constraints define the scope of ideological or technical possibilities for development.[8]

Within the limits of the present evolved values of society, some choices can be made with regard to ends in the provision of public goods. This allows for both evolutionary and planned change. These choices may be influenced by the examples set by other societies when faced with the same challenges. Thus, both the constraints and the choices may be partly determined by decisions made outside the society.

But this does not tell us the process by which the society selects certain values and constraints as a basis for action. This process is best described in the discussion of representative and responsible government. Theories of representation attempt to answer the questions of:

- Who has the authority to speak for the whole?
- How is this authority attained?
- Do any particular groups or interests have the right to be heard and to take part in the establishment of that authority?

Much of the work of John Stuart Mill is devoted to the subject of representative government. His views reflect the influence of Utilitarianism, although he diverges from his father's theory of representation in several important respects.

Basically, the Utilitarians viewed citizens as politically rational human beings who would exercise their political rights by choosing freely among rival candidates and conflicting policies. They assumed that although men's opinions and personal interests may vary, there were no fundamental conflicts of interest in the society. As the state was assumed to be neutral, minorities would be willing to accept the decision of the majority, since they had the opportunity to convince the majority of the error of their views.

James Mill did not concern himself with the problems arising from the power of the numerical majority, as he assumed that the "middle rank" formed the largest proportion of society, and that the virtue and wisdom of the "middle rank" would prevail in a representative government. He stressed that the benefits of the representative system were lost if there was not an identity of interests between the community and the body that chooses the members of Parliament.

However, John Stuart Mill argued that this was not the only aspect on which good government depended, and in any case such an identity of interest could not depend on the conditions of elections alone. But the main difference between John Stuart Mill and his father was that they differed over the end of representative government. For James Mill the most important end was to secure the greatest happiness of the greatest number; for John Stuart Mill, it was to secure the intellectual and moral advancement of society.

J.S. Mill bases his argument in favour of representative government on the grounds that a person's interests are only secure when he is able to defend them himself, and it is only when the whole community can play a part that the maximum moral and intellectual improvement occurs. As it is no longer possible for all to participate directly in the political life of the community, then the best alternative is one based on representation.

The best form of representative government is one in which the representative body has the duties of control and criticism, while the actual control of affairs is left in the hands of a well trained and intelligent few.

There are two great dangers in representative government. First, there is the danger that the representative body will consist of mainly unintelligent members who are controlled by an equally unintelligent popular opinion. Second, the numerical majority will concern itself only with its own interests which will result in a predominance of legislation in its favour. Minority opinion will not be heard and minorities will, in effect, be disenfranchised.

It is of great importance, then, that the representatives are of a high calibre who will be able to take a wider and more informed view than their constituents. Thus, the representative is not a 'delegate' in the sense that he simply reflects the views of the majority of his constituents, he is a more knowledgeable and informed person than his electorate, and thus better able to make decisions regarding their interests.

As Currin Shields argues, "This claim implies that standards of political value exist external to and independent from the government; by consulting these objective principles, an elite can determine how authority should be exercised to promote the general interest".[9] Shields accuses Mill of advocating an elitist society where, in theory, the people are supreme, but in practice they are without power and are ruled by an elite minority that is chosen on the basis of merit. But Mill does not indicate where this elite group will obtain its superior standards and values, or why its values will have a greater utility for the society than those of the "uninformed" majority.

The Utilitarian/Liberal view essentially saw society in terms of individuals presenting their interests to the state, which in turn governed in a way that aided this aggregation of individual interests. The questions was: how best could these individual interests be represented?

But there is an alternative view of representation that sees society divided into strata, or functional groupings. Each of these groupings has a right to be represented, due to their importance to society. This collectivist view of representation may be expressed by those with varying ideological beliefs. Socialists may see society divided into various socio-economic strata. These socioeconomic interests may be best expressed by a party system in a parliamentary democracy. Pluralists see society as being divided among a wide diversity of interests, some of which will be expressed via the political party process; but others will need to seek access to the political system by other means. Conservatives may see society in a traditional organic form, with part of that society, the governing elite, being more able to express the will of the society as a whole than any other part. Whatever the ideological approach, however, it is difficult to reconcile these collectivist theories of representation with a system of representation that drew its inspiration from the liberal emphasis on the individual as the basis of society and state.

One way in which this can be done is to perceive the political party as a bridge between the individual voter and the state. The political party expresses both the views of its members via intraparty democracy and, at the same time, provides alternative policies to the voters at election time. In Schumpeter's terms, voter participation in the political process is restricted to choosing between political party contestants at regular intervals.[10] In this sense there is no direct expression of the individual voter's interests in the political process. But if the citizen's interests are not expressed via this channel, then he may choose to combine with others of similar interests, and form an interest group.

At this point, the discussion of representation turns from the contrast of individual versus collectivist theories of representation to a consideration of the potentially harmful effects of powerful interest groups on the political decision making process in contemporary society.

Mill's concerns, that majority views would prevail over those of the minority regardless of the merits of their case, have been replaced by the concern that the views of powerful interest groups will prevail over both individual interests and those of other interest groups.

One possible approach to this problem is to suggest that the methods of representation be brought into line with the actualities of the political process. Representation should be based on the collectivity. Interest groups should be represented in Parliament on the basis of their functional utility to society. There are two problems with this approach: one is the question of who is to decide on the comparative functional utility of each group. The second problem is the dynamic and changing nature of the society itself. Interest groups that would have a "right" to representation at a certain time may lose their economic and social utility as time passes and need to be replaced by others.

It is difficult to imagine such groups voluntarily relinquishing their representation on the grounds that they no longer have a useful function in society. If it could be shown that their economic utility had waned, they would most likely stake their claim on the basis of social utility — a far more ambiguous category.

Contemporary Western political systems can be seen as a compromise between the nineteenth century liberal theory of representation, with its emphasis on individual interests, and a collectivist theory of representation expressed through the activities of interest groups in the political process. This means that we have left unresolved the question of whether the common good is best expressed via an aggregate of individual interests, or whether the common good can only be pursued by collectivities. Both the aggregate of individual interests, as measured by the Gallup polls, and the degree of political pressure exerted by interest groups play a role in determining political outcomes. The result appears to be haphazard, piecemeal, incremental changes in the provision of social goods. This is frequently called "disjointed incrementalism". It is regarded as an irrational and often unpredictable process by which decisions are made in the political system. It is the opposite of the planned rational approach that we tend to regard as desirable in the decision making process. It indicates that within the evolved values of society we face both choices and constraints. These may vary according to both issues, time and place, and may explain why societies differ in the choices they make when faced with similar sets of circumstances.

An example of this process is the problems that most developed countries face in the provision of health care services. They are confronting similar problems: the escalation of costs in technologically sophisticated health care systems, the need to integrate services increasingly fragmented by specialization, and to develop new and more economic ways to provide primary services to the population.

David Mechanic relates these problems to the fact that the systems of rationing in health care systems are in a process of transition. He identifies three rationing systems: rationing by fee, implicit rationing and explicit rationing.[11] At each phase in these rationing systems, we move from situations in which choices are made by the individual user — the closest to a free market system — to one where the choice tends to be made by interest groups — a semi market system — until we finally reach the point where most of the important choices are made by the state and rationing is imposed upon both the consumer and the supplier. Under the system of *rationing by fee*, those with the financial means were able to obtain whatever level of health care was available. Those people who did not have sufficient funds were dependent upon whatever services were provided by the government, the philanthropy of the churches and the medical profession. As long as medical technology remained unsophisticated, this system worked reasonably well, since health professionals were only able to offer the public a limited range of health services.

Once medical technology and knowledge began to develop more rapidly after World War I, and far more active medical intervention became possible, the costs of a serious medical episode became much higher. There was a growing demand for a system that would help individuals share the risk. This was expressed through the development of private insurance plans; and, as costs mounted, government intervention in the health insurance field was sought. With the introduction of third party payment, a system of *implicit rationing* was introduced. Implicit rationing depends upon a queue. Limited resources, facilities and manpower are made available. It is assumed that the medical practitioner will make a rational choice in distributing the limited resources giving the highest priority to those whose health care needs are most acute. But he may have his own biases as to the relative importance of various health needs and, at the same time, some groups of consumers may be more demanding than others.

A contemporary example of implicit rationing is the establishment of pre paid medical plans and Health Maintenance Organizations, especially in the US Under these arrangements private insurance companies contract with a group of doctors who agree to provide all outpatient services to a group of patients for a capitation fee. From the monthly premiums it collects the insurance company creates a fund to cover the costs of hospitalization. If the doctors and the affiliated hospitals spend less on hospitalization than the insurance company has earmarked, they may have the opportunity to share the savings. Thus, both doctors and hospitals have an incentive to reduce costs. This implies rationing, with both the medical profession and the hospital administrators the main decision makers. Certain interest groups — the insurance companies, the purchasers of insurance packages (usually large companies), the medical profession and the affiliated hospitals — play a major role in deciding the choices and the constraints in the provision of public goods.

As the provision of health care moves from the private sector to the public sector, the range of interests involved in the decision making process become much broader. It is at this level that the state has the prime responsibility to reflect the interests of the citizens as a whole. Thus, in the face of ever increasing costs, it may need to move to a system of *explicit rationing*. Under this system, limits are set on total expenditures for care, and there is an attempt to develop mechanisms to arrive at more rational decisions regarding investments in different types of facilities and manpower. Mechanic argues that the difficulty in establishing priorities and standards in this way is the overall lack of definitive evidence as to which health care practices really make a difference in illness outcomes.[12] Wagner and Zubkoff support this view when they claim that there is mounting evidence that many health services have made little difference in health outcomes. Nonmedical factors appear to have been more important in reducing mortality and morbidity rates over the past fifty years.[13]

Mechanic is searching for a rational, planned basis on which to justify explicit rationing of health care by the public sector. This would require a statistical analysis of the health outcomes of specific treatments, an analysis of the extent of iatrogenic disease, especially related to the overuse of certain medical treatments such as prescription drugs, and an evaluation of costs and health outcomes of innovative medical technology. Such a thorough analysis of the health care system in any country seems unlikely. If it was undertaken, it seems probable that its results would be challenged by threatened interest groups.

Thus, the question recurs: If decisions cannot be made regarding the provision of public goods on a planned, rational basis, how is the decision to be made? It seems the answer lies in most pluralist societies in a balancing, by the political system, of individual and interest group demands and expectations. As a result, countries with similar political systems may supply different answers to the same social question, depending upon the balance of political groups existing at the time crucial decisions were made.

A case in point is the varying approach of the Canadian and Australian federal governments to the question of national health insurance plans. The two countries have many cultural, economic and political similarities, yet their approach on this issue has been different.

Both countries have a federal parliamentary form of government with a political culture strongly influenced by the British. Their economies are heavily dependent on natural resources, yet their labour forces are employed primarily in the industrial and service sectors. The majority of the population live in urban areas surrounded by a vast, largely uninhabited, hinterland. In terms of development, standard of living, influence of other English speaking cultures, and activity of interest groups in the political process, both countries have very much in common. They differ in respect to the degree of regionalization.

With two official languages and at least two separate cultures, Canada has a much greater degree of regional heterogeneity. This is not the case in Australia. Both linguistically and culturally, there is a high degree of homogeneity in Australia. Each state has a largely urban workforce and its own natural resource base. In view of the cultural and economic homogeneity of the states, it would be assumed that they, and the federal government, would find it easier to reach agreement on social issues than in the more diverse Canadian political system.

In fact, the reverse appears to be true, as far as health insurance is concerned. In Canada this issue has been largely resolved for almost 20 years.[14] In

Australia there has been continuing controversy and debate, with complete policy reversals occurring as late as the 1970s.

After the Second World War there was a growth of voluntary health insurance plans in Canada and Australia. Although there had been discussion of publicly supported health insurance schemes during the Second World War, they had not been made operational. In Australia the Labour Party government adopted a National Health Insurance Plan in 1942. It was incorporated into the necessary legislation, but it was never implemented because of the opposition of the Australian branch of the British Medical Association.[15]

The progress toward a national health insurance program in Canada was less direct, but no more successful. In early 1943 the proponents of such a plan were able to establish a House of Commons Special Committee on Social Security, with the responsibility to report on the practical measures required to implement a comprehensive social security plan. The Committee heard the opinions of a number of groups, including the Canadian Medical Association and the Canadian Hospital Council. Both groups supported a national health, although the Canadian Medical Association made it plain that the schedule of fees should be under the complete control of the organized profession in each province.[16]

Despite the support of major interest groups, the proposals to implement a national health insurance plan became a victim of the federal-provincial disputes over taxation changes at the Dominion Provincial Conference in August 1945.

In the ensuing years the voluntary private health insurance plans grew in both countries. By 1952 almost 5.5 million people were insured for hospital benefits in Canada through voluntary and commercial insurance plans. Almost 4 million were insured for medical and/or surgical benefits.[17] The success of the commercial plans probably provoked a reversal of the previous positions of the main interest groups. The Canadian Medical Association abandoned its 1943 policy of support for a national health insurance scheme, and proposed instead the extension of voluntary plans to cover all Canadians. The task of the government would be to pay the premiums for low income and indigent Canadians. The Canadian Hospital Association and the commercial industry supported these proposals.

According to Taylor, the Liberal government under St. Laurent had become reluctant to commit itself to a federally supported national health insurance program. There were several concerns. In the first place, it was clear that the Canadian Medical Association, the Canadian Hospital Association and the commercial insurance industry were now opposed. There was some concern about the cost of the program, since a publicly supported plan cannot exclude poor risks. Finally, there was the realization that a high degree of cooperation was required between the federal and provincial levels of government.[18]

On the other hand, there were several provincial health insurance plans. Saskatchewan led the way, and Alberta and British Columbia had followed. In Taylor's view, the federal government was gradually pushed toward developing a national health insurance plan by Premier Frost of Ontario.[19] As the Ontario government maintained pressure on this issue for several years, the federal government was pushed first to announce a national proposal in January 1956, and then a compromise proposal in early 1957. In April 1957 the legislation was passed, despite the fact that six of the provinces had not indicated that they would be willing to join. By 1961 all provinces had joined, and almost the total population of Canada was covered.

Despite the resistance of important interest groups, the unwillingness of some of the provinces, and the reluctance of the federal government, Canada had legislated and implemented a national hospital insurance plan. Taylor explains this success in terms of two major factors: the skill of the Premier of Ontario in pursuing this end and the problems of operating a fragmented system.[20] The Premier had gradually persuaded the provincial interest groups to accept his approach. The Ontario Hospital Association had been drawn into the discussions at an early date. The Ontario Medical Association came to accept the plan tentatively, so long as medical services in the diagnostic field were considered separately from hospital care.

Faced with a similar political and economic situation, the Australian government moved in the opposite direction. In 1953 the Liberal/Country Party government introduced a Voluntary Health Insurance Plan. It provided a subsidy to those citizens who voluntarily joined private health insurance funds. This scheme persisted without substantial amendments until the late 1960s. However, the program was regarded as unsatisfactory and this eventually led to the appointment of a Commonwealth Committee of Inquiry under Mr. Justice Nimmo. The Committee found that the program was unnecessarily complex and beyond the comprehension of many. The benefits received were often much less than the cost of the hospital and medical treatment. The premiums had increased substantially so that it was beyond the capability of lower income groups to pay them. Furthermore, the rules of many of the insurance companies limited claims for particular conditions.[21] The Nimmo Committee visited Canada and were impressed by the Canadian system. They noted that, despite the fact that the Canadian system gave universal and comprehensive coverage, it had been more effective in containing overall health costs than the US. This appeared to be due to the lower cost of physician services in Canada and, in particular, to the lower costs of administration.[22]

Australian Health Care System

In the federal election of 1972 the Labour Party was returned to office after a long period as the opposition party. During their period in opposition they had developed a comprehensive health insurance program designed to cover the entire population, funded from a health tax and administered by a federal government authority. Attempts to introduce the legislation for this program were strongly opposed by the federal opposition parties, the Australian Medical Association and the voluntary health insurance funds. The legislation to introduce Medibank, as the health insurance program was called, was twice rejected by the Senate. The legislation was only passed after a new election in which the Labour Party was once more returned to power.

After considerable negotiation the medical insurance aspects of Medibank were introduced on July 1, 1975, and a federal Health Insurance Commission was established. However, after the election of the Liberal-National Party coalition in December 1985, the new government systematically dismantled the main features of Medibank. By 1981 this government had essentially returned to the private voluntary health insurance program. The federal subsidy was payable only to members of voluntary registered health funds.

With another swing of the political pendulum, the Labour Party was returned to power in 1983. The party reintroduced a system of universal tax funded health insurance administered by a federal Health Insurance Commission. Medicare, as the new plan was called, differed from Medibank mainly in that part of the increased cost to the federal government was met by a one percent levy on taxable income.

Opposition to the new health insurance program was more subdued on this occasion. The Australian Medical Association indicated that, despite its philosophical objections to compulsory health insurance, it would not actively oppose the program. However, the Liberal Party, in the 1987 federal election campaign, again indicated its intention to dismantle the principal elements of Medicare. As it has not yet succeeded in defeating the Labour Party, the basic Medicare plan is still in operation as of 1993.

A major point of conflict since the introduction of Medicare has been the method of payment to physicians providing medical services to patients in hospitals. Under the original Medicare arrangements, physicians treating patients in public hospitals were normally paid by the hospital on a part-time salaried (seasonal) basis. Physicians' treatment of private patients in public hospitals was on a fee-for-service basis. Much of the physicians' opposition to Medibank and Medicare was based on the expectation that as the number of private patients declined the physicians' incomes would decrease, since sessional payment arrangements were substantially less than the amounts they would receive from fee-for-service.

This was the basis for the doctors' dispute that occurred mainly in New South Wales where many orthopaedic surgeons and ophthalmologists resigned from the public hospital system. Palmer and Short[23] suggest that one possible solution to the problem would be to move to the Canadian practice of permitting physicians to bill on a fee-for-service basis all patients in public hospitals. In this way, there would be no automatic income advantage attached to privately insured patients. This would require an increase in the health tax levy to offset the higher cost of medical services, but it would also mean the removal of a continuing source of irritation among physicians.

It is unlikely that there will be a fundamental change in the Australian health care system as long as the Labour Party continues to control the federal government. However, if the Liberal/National parties had won the 1993 federal election, they may have been tempted to dismantle the present system and proceed once more with a system based upon voluntary private health insurance.

The decision to do this would depend upon a number of factors:

- the length of time the present system has been in place;
- the degree of opposition by the medical profession to the present system;
- the amount of public support for a comprehensive Medicare program.

Over the past four decades, a publicly funded health insurance program has been a far greater political football in Australia than it has been in Canada. While there have been a number of disputes relating to health care in Canada, especially over such issues as extra billing, the fundamental principles of a publicly funded program have not been seriously questioned. In contrast, in Australia, the debate relating to the costs and efficiency of a publicly funded system continued throughout the 1970s, despite the fact that the original Medibank scheme proved to have one third of the administrative costs of the previous fragmented private system.

It is hard to find any fundamental differences in the political, economic, or social environment of Canada and Australia that would explain the difference in public policy direction in the health field. At most, it is possible to point to a higher degree of regionalization in Canada, and to perhaps a slightly more conservative orientation in the Australian political scene. But these two aspects appear to provide an inadequate explanation. Premier Frost headed a Progressive Conservative government in Ontario, and the greater degree of regionalization in Canada would presumably be more of a hindrance to developing a national plan than an aid. In both countries a national health insurance plan had been discussed in detail and even accepted in principle during the Second World War. In both countries private health insurance plans had become well established after the war. Neither the Australian nor the Canadian federal governments had shown any particular interest in developing a national health insurance plan in the 1950s.

The difference, if there is one at all, seems to lie in the greater degree of heterogeneity among the Canadian provinces. Since the provinces tend to differ economically, socially and sometimes culturally, this may lay the foundation for a greater degree of experimentation. Taylor regards Saskatchewan's contribution to the establishment of a national health insurance program as very important. On both occasions, that is, for both hospital and medical insurance, it led the way and demonstrated to the rest of the country that it could be done.[24]

Taylor tends to attribute Saskatchewan's initiative to a combination of characteristics unique to the province:

> the precarious underpinnings of the one crop economy and the severity of the depression; the geography of the province that yielded a uniformly thin distribution of population in small rural municipalities and urban centres; the high proportion of citizens serving as local government councilors and school trustees together with the extraordinary number of cooperative associations that also contributed to widespread citizen participation in policy making and reinforced an orientation directed to collective action to solve mutual problems....[25]

In other words, the dire economic circumstances and the lack of political power within Confederation tended to force Saskatchewan into collective social action and experimentation to find a solution to some of their problems. They demonstrated that publicly funded hospital and medical insurance programs could work effectively, and a wealthy and powerful province like Ontario could start the move for a national plan and effectively manoeuvre the federal government into supporting it.

Once a program is securely established, and it is perceived as serving the interests of individual citizens, then it becomes difficult to remove. The balance between the aggregate of individual demands and the demands of affected interest groups shifts in favour of the aggregate of individual citizens. Individual voters can become united around issues that affect their own interests directly. The disadvantages that arise from their lack of organizational unity is offset by their direct access to the vote. Governments respond to them at election time and to the polls that indicate their preferences between elections.

Interest groups, on the other hand, only have indirect access to representation. They may seek to influence the political process by lobbying, and they may threaten to use their power to influence blocks of voters at election time. But they cannot usually directly participate in the political process. If they enjoyed some type of functional representation, then presumably they would be able to shift the political decision making process more directly in their favour. While their indirect influence on the decision making process may be useful and very effective on a number of occasions, it is probably ineffective once a substantial proportion of the voting public supports a particular policy or plan of action.

Notes

1. L. Robbins, *The Theory of Economic Policy in English Classical Political Economy*, p. 28.
2. *Ibid.*, p. 37.
3. Werner Stark, *Jeremy Bentham*, Vol. III, p. 333.
4. T.W. Hutchinson, "Bentham as an Economist", *Economic Journal*, June 1956, p. 303.
5. F.A. Hayek, *The Road to Serfdom*, pp. 42–43.
6. G.H. Sabine, *History of Political Theory*, p. 607.
7. R.J. Bennett, *The Geography of Public Finance*, p. 17.
8. *Ibid.*
9. C.V. Shields, Introduction, in John Stuart Mill, *Considerations on Representative Government*, p. xxxiii.
10. Schumpeter, *Capitalism, Socialism and Democracy*, p. 273.
11. D. Mechanic, "Growth of Medical Technology and Bureaucracy: Implications for Health Care" in *Technology and the Future of Health Care*, edited by J.B. McKinlay, p. 3.
12. D. Mechanic, *Ibid.*, p. 7.
13. J.L. Wagner, and M. Zubkoff, "Medical Technology and Hospital Costs", in *Technology and the Future of Health Care*, edited by J.B. McKinlay, p. 106.
14. The National Medical Care Insurance Act 1966–1967 established the current medical insurance plan.
15. For an account of the health insurance programs in Australia from the time of the Second World War, see B.S. Hetzel, *Health and Australian Society*, Ch. 8.

16. M. Taylor, *Health Insurance and Canadian Public Policy*, p. 28.
17. *Ibid.*, p. 171.
18. *Ibid.*, p. 183.
19. *Ibid.*, pp. 135–38.
20. *Ibid.*, pp. 158 & 159.
21. *Op. cit.*, p. 269.
22. *Op. cit.*, pp. 271 & 272.
23. S.R. Palmer, and S.D. Short, *Health Care and Public Policy: An Australian Analysis*, p. 69.
24. M. Taylor, p. 418.
25. *Ibid.*

Pension Fund Capitalism — The Latest Stage in the Evolution of Capitalism

Issues of Governance and Accountability

George E. Eaton

Introduction

Capitalism, defined as an economic system in which the means of production are predominantly privately owned and economic activity is spurred by the expectation and pursuit of profit, had its precursor in commercial capitalism. Several factors contributed to the development of commercial capitalism, some of which will be noted here in passing, namely: the growth of modern nation states, which began to appear after the Protestant Reformation; maritime discoveries, often inspired by the quest for gold and spices, and which provided the impetus for the expansion of trade and, ultimately, for the establishment of colonies and colonial empires; and the devising of joint stock or huge trading companies, which facilitated joint ventures between sovereign rulers and merchant adventurers. The result was a form of state capitalism based on an alliance of convenience between authoritarian rulers and private entrepreneurs, who were mainly traders. The intervention and regulation by the state, including the provision of incentives, were considered essential for the widening of the market and to enhance the competitive advantage of producers and traders.

Commercial capitalism over time evolved into industrial capitalism as a result of the Industrial Revolution. It profoundly altered structures of production and social relations. The application of science and technology and a series of inventions led to the harnessing of energy from natural resources, to significant

284

improvements in the physical movement of people and materials and to mechanization and factory employment. It also led to a much sharper differentiation
between the new class of businessmen, capitalists, who, by virtue of ownership
of the means of production, claimed the prerogative right to hire, fire and direct the activities of workers, skilled and unskilled, constituting a new working
class dependent solely on the sale of services or gainful employment for
income.

The new capitalists were entrepreneurs in the sense that they were inven-
tors, investors and owner-managers who were identified with the engineering
function and were largely responsible for carrying forward the industrial revolution and laying the foundations for heavy goods and mass production
manufacturing industries.

As with commercial capitalism, there was a complex of factors that contributed to the transition to industrial capitalism. The Protestant Reformation engendered changes in religious attitudes towards economic activity, money
making and the accumulation of wealth or material possessions and towards the
worth of the individual; the belief in a natural economic order governed by the
laws of the impersonal market or forces of demand and supply, driven by, and
responding to, the pursuit of self interest on the part of both producers and
consumers; a utilitarian or instrumental view of the necessity for government
based on the primacy of individual self interest over the interest of society, in
short laissez-faire government implying that government is best which governs
least.

During the latter part of the 19th century, both the organization and the
processes of production further evolved to more fully realize the potential of
technology and economies of scale of large-scale production. The increase in
concentration of both size and ownership reached its fullest expression in the
USA where the merger and trust movement resulted in giant corporations
founded by the so-called "robber barons". Unlike the Industrial revolution
which placed a premium on the engineering function, the new entrepreneurs
were industrial and financial strategists. The engineering function became the
responsibility of paid professional staff. This period also saw the fleshing out of
the characteristic features of corporate civilization: the legal personality of the
corporation and presumed equality before the law; the changing concept of
property based on shareholding or fragmentation of property into pieces of paper along with dispersal of ownership; the separation of ownership from management and control — "the managerial revolution"; in effect, a shift from the
property system to a power system.

Notwithstanding these developments, the legal model of the corporation,
that of principal and agent, articulated a system of governance predicated on
the theory that managers are subject to general oversight of the Board of
Directors, fiduciary trustees chosen by the shareholders, to whom, as owners,
both directors and executives alike are accountable.

The separation of ownership from control and management has now been
carried to the extreme by the phenomenon of the institutional ownership of
equity on the part of employees through their pension and mutual funds investments in securities and financial markets

The purpose of this article is to examine the proposition that capitalism has entered another evolutionary stage represented by the advent of full blown pension or employee capitalism, in which employees have become the new long term owners of the largest publicly owned or traded corporations. It will show that the implications have yet to be fully appreciated and be reflected in more appropriate socio-legal and organizational structures.

The Emergence of Pension Capitalism

The closing decades of the 20th century gave added momentum to the evolution of "the Employee Society". In every developed country, at the beginning of the 1980s between 85 and 90 percent of GNP was being paid in the form of wages and salaries and even the self-employed (including medical practitioners, lawyers and engineers), were being compensated for labour services rendered.

The rise of the "Employee Society" also witnessed the phenomenal growth, concomitantly, of funded pension schemes, the virtues of which soon became part of the conventional wisdom of finance theory, both public and private. To governments, the particular merit of funded pension schemes was that they would relieve the public treasury and, inferentially, the taxpayers of the burden of paying retirement pensions. In relation to the private sector, pension fund contributions also could be channelled into the securities markets to provide savings for the financing of capital investment. Certainly in the UK, the US and Canada (prominent members of the so-called Anglo-American Economies), private pension assets now have attained prodigious proportions surpassing all other forms of private savings. To illustrate, in 1950 in the US, households owned 91 percent of all equities but by 1994 that figure had fallen to 48 percent. On the other hand, whereas in 1950 public and private pension funds owned less than 1 percent of all equities by 1994 they owned more than 25 percent. Combining pension funds with other investors and players (mutual funds, banks and near banks, insurance companies and public and private endowments), these institutional investors control about 45 percent of all equities. Even more striking is the fact that pensions funds and institutional investors control the majority of stock (variously 56 to 60 percent) of the largest 1000 US corporations. Similar trends have been noted for Canada and the UK. In Canada in the mid 1990s, the financial assets of institutional investors collectively represented 35 percent of total equity, with mutual and pension funds accounting for 25 percent of that amount.

It is now evident that in the industrially advanced countries, employees and their pension funds are now the only source of the enormous amount of capital needed for investment purposes, not only nationally but also internationally. In the latter case, the largest 25 pension funds in the US (those with assets over one billion dollars), account for 42 percent of foreign equity held by all US investors. To appreciate the importance of workers savings via pension funds to the performance of the economies of the developed countries (and some developing countries), we may note that in the advanced economies, with the exception of Germany, national savings rates declined appreciably over the period 1980 to 1996 (OECD, 1997). The capacity of many of these countries to accumulate public savings was handicapped by the recession of the early 1980s, ensuing slow growth rates as well as the early 1990s recession and its lingering effects.

Of the several factors that have contributed to the rather phenomenal growth of pension assets and their institutional impact on capital and financial services markets, labour market considerations feature prominently. " In the Anglo-American economies the growth of private pension assets reflects, in part, the rapid post 1950 expansion of employment and increased participation in employer or multi-party sponsored private pension plans. The fact that private plans must be fully funded, the fact that pension benefits have come to be an important component in employees' wages, and the fact that those of the baby boom generation have moved into their peak earning years means that the net flow of assets to pension funds has become a tidal wave" (Clark 2000)[1]. Other factors that may be mentioned are governmental fiscal crises and resource limitations obliquely referred to above, and the ideological siege, and retreat of, the modern welfare state, as well as the new economic and trading environment encapsulated by the term "globalization".

Pension Capitalism and Issues of Governance
Impact of Globalization

When the expansion of funded pension schemes was being strongly advocated during the 1970s, exponents, more so in the USA, Canada, and the UK, argued that the build up of contributions would, among other things, provide long-term finance in the capital markets for the growth and development of businesses and reverse the trend to de-industrialization or reduction in employment due to rationalization of operations. This expectation that relatively cheap long-term finance would foster productive investment has proven illusory. "The contribution of funded pension schemes to corporate economy of the UK and the US has been to inflate capital markets in which unproductive take over and corporate restructuring activity flourishes while industrial production and employment activity stagnate". [2]   The huge flow and reservoir of pension contributions that are used to buy securities have provided a cheaper source of financing than the banking system and both governments and companies have replaced short-term borrowing from banks by issuing short term bills or paper. One effect (exploration of which would take us outside the limits of this paper) has been to discourage fixed capital productive investment. "When capital market inflation is depressing fixed capital investment, and by implication real economic activity, most companies would lose less money entrusting it to commodity or derivative traders than they would by issuing securities to finance fixed capital investment. Assets in financial markets are more liquid than fixed capital. Even if the company may not make more money out of financial assets, it certainly sees its money more frequently, which is reassuring in uncertain times. Most likely, if the capital is being systematically inflated, profits can be made from the purchase and sale of financial assets, even if there is no improvement in the productivity of the real assets underlying those instruments"[3]. The reason is that while fixed assets are specific to industrial processes and facilities, funds raised in the securities market can be rolled over more quickly.

The mobility of capital also has been greatly enhanced by electronic information devices that transcend spatial distance, time zones and national borders and the real economy. The materials based economy, now being referred to as the "old economy", and the "symbol" or paper economy of money appear to have been diverging and operating more independently of each other, rather than being tightly bound together, in theory and practice, as they were in the past. The increased mobility of capital also has given impetus to a new international division of labour and shared production, now popularly referred to as "globalization". Capital flows and foreign direct investment, in particular, can now react more rapidly to new profit making opportunities by shifting production to places where wages are low relative to potential productivity. Thus, in effect, national economies have become production stations for trans-national corporations and trans-national confederations

Globalization and Impact on Labour Markets

Employment Trends and their Implications

Perhaps the most striking characteristic of globalization of production or shared production and enhanced mobility of capital is the so-called restructuring of economies and of business and governmental units.

In terms of economies, it has been reflected in trends in employment, unemployment and earnings. The decades of the 1970s through the 1990s saw a slow growth in both output and productivity and the disappearance of jobs, especially in the manufacturing (blue collar workers) and largely unionized sector, a trend generally applicable to both developed and less developed economies. Relatively high levels of unemployment (there were major recessions in the early 1980s and 1990s) also were aggravated by continuing downsizing as a means of increasing profits and enhancing share values, if not to meet the challenge of increasing competition at regional and international levels.

Where employment grew, it was predominantly in the collective service economy — two out of three jobs in the OECD area and, most notably, in the financial services sub-sector. The composition of employment also was affected by a rapid growth in non-standard jobs that is to say of part-timers, self-employed and dependent and independent contractors. To the extent that this is a segment of the labour force that is dominated by women and is not readily susceptible to unionization, it is also the most vulnerable in the economy. Incidentally, in the OECD area in 1991, between 20 and 30 percent of all part-timers declared themselves to be working part-time involuntarily. The increase in part-time employment has also been accompanied by an increased polarization of both working time and income. The rapid growth of part-timers increases the numbers working short hours while, at the same time, permanent employees who survive "downsizing" are expected to put in longer hours to take up the work of those who have left.

Polarization of working hours between full-time and part-time also has contributed to polarization of income to the extent that those with adequate or high incomes are working longer hours to stay where they are, while those with low incomes are trapped in jobs that are not full time or that might not last very long.

The combination of increased competitiveness and increased mobility of investment capital could be expected to exert strong pressures on employers to lower costs, but the cost reductions seem to end up being directed at variable costs, the most important of which is labour. Hence the cry on the part of employers for less costly separation benefits as they focus on core operations or leaner organizational structures and downsizing. The rapid introduction of product technology, equipment technology and process technology also has intensified management demand for "flexibility" to alter either output and/or work processes associated with existing production. Flexibility is often achieved not only by reducing the number of permanent full-time workers to a minimum, but by making the regular hours of work more variable or increasing reliance on people whose work can be changed easily: namely, temporary workers, part-time workers and so-called self-employed contractors including home workers who by definition usually do not participate in private pension and benefit plans. Everywhere, the once standard eight-hour-day, five-day workweek is increasingly being pushed to the margin and there is a constant ratcheting effect as enterprises and individuals operating on non-standard hours demand goods and services from those who have not yet made the shift.

It is not surprising, therefore, to find that income inequities and amelioration of poverty have emerged as central concerns in reports on Labour Market Reforms recently released by international development organizations and national governments.

Employment and Income Insecurity

It is ironic, though not surprising, that while employees, through their pension funds, have become the new owners of capitalist enterprises, they are bearing the brunt of globalization. In 1976 leading management theorist Peter Drucker[4] opined that pension funds presaged the era of pension fund socialism. Yet two decades later American labour leaders were lamenting: "The dilemma facing workers is that their own pension funds, as owners of almost one-third of all US financial capital, are behind the scene fuelling these activities. (Spiral of corporate mergers and downsizing). They finance overseas plants. They agree to outrageous pay packages for corporate management that have shown only mediocre performance. They reward the slash and burn practices of customers that serve up quarterly to shareholders. They finance mergers and acquisitions in the name of retirement security. They ignore investments in job-creating ventures, instead preferring to finance leveraged buyouts that mean further layoffs".[5] Accordingly, the unions had to develop strategies to take back their money in support of long term, quality jobs in local communities. They appear to have made little progress. Indeed, a recent reviewer has suggested that, far from presaging the advent of pension socialism, the phenomenon of employee pension funds ownership of business enterprises represents a further evolution of capitalism, rather than a break with the past. "Pension Funds depend upon the performance of national and international markets for their accumulated wealth. Their assets are the product of the employment relation and agency relationships with the investment management industry. The concentration of financial assets in pension funds, coupled with the facts that trustees and their advisers have considerable autonomy from plan beneficiaries, is analogous to the separation of ownership from control characteristic of modern corporations".[6]

Further, in Anglo-American economies, company sponsored plans are precluded from holding a large portion of stock in their sponsoring company. Similarly, individual pension funds would not normally sponsor such large holdings as to be able to directly control corporate managers' disposition of company resources. It appears then, that a mutually interdependent or symbiotic relationship exists between owners/trustees of pension funds and corporate managers who are utilizing these resources. Indeed, owners now have the compound agency problem of getting fund managers (agents) to act in their best interest by getting corporate managers (agents) to act also in their best interests. In other words, can agents watch agents or who will monitor the monitors?

There is no denying, however, that the "employee society", or pension capitalism, still poses the paradox that employee investment power does not confer commensurate employee responsibility. Mutual funds are controlled by fund managers, and workers/employees as institutional investors have little direct control over the financial resources they invest in pension funds. Indeed, they are more vulnerable than investors in mutual funds (pooled financial resources), in that while these funds are controlled by fund managers, exit from pension schemes is costly, if not impossible, for workers. Even more disconcerting is the fact that they have become exposed to a double jeopardy — on the one hand to loss of retirement savings arising from corporate failures and the vagaries of financial markets and, on the other to loss of jobs and employment income as cutbacks in the workforce becomes the preferred technique for dealing with short term variations in profits and earnings.

In a speech defending the Canadian banking industry's record C$5.2 billion profit during 1995, even while continuing to downsize during a period of economic depression and high unemployment, the CEO of one of the country's five largest chartered banks who earned C3$.1 million as the highest paid banker in the country, reminded the public that members of pension plans were, indirectly, the biggest shareholders, numerically, and thus, the bank's profits were really theirs and, accordingly, protection of profit levels must take precedence over job creation. The irony of this situation is that while the management of pension and mutual funds, on the one hand, are to be found pressuring corporate executives for shorter term improvements in returns on investment, on the other hand, corporate executives, find reduction in variable costs, and labour costs in particular, much easier to achieve than the alternative of longer-run growth and job creation; hence the continuing recourse to retrenchment. Thus workers as the "new owners" are being made poorer in terms of gainful employment and income security from pensions.

One inference that can be drawn from the new ownership structure is that management generally can no longer claim legitimacy on the traditional capitalist grounds of ownership, and that it is because employee-owners have not yet been able to exercise ownership rights — either through boards of directors or other participatory mechanisms — that professional managers have been able to lay claim to compensation levels that have led to a significant widening of the gap between those at the top and those at the beginning of the organizational hierarchy.

Economic theory has long held that increases in real output (productivity) are the source of economic growth and development and of higher standards of living for workers to the extent that wages bear some relationship to productivity. However, a study also undertaken in 1995 by the Conference Board of Canada, an influential independent but business-oriented research body, reported that structural changes in the economy were severing the links between profits, productivity and income growth. This was reflected in the fact that while unionized and non-unionized employees could anticipate wage increases in line with the rate of inflation, managerial compensation was increasing by leaps and bounds. In fact, by 1996, CEO's of the 255 largest companies listed with the Toronto Stock Exchange had received an 11 percent increase in compensation over 1995, whereas the average employee earned a 2.8 percent increase. In the US in 1997, CEO compensation was nine times higher than that of the average white-collar worker and 13 times higher than that of the average blue-collar worker. The average CEO or boss earned 326 times what a factory worker did.

A major contributory factor is that companies may now more readily move production to, or import labour from, low wage countries, thereby putting downward pressure on wages. Another is that, faced with alternate strategies for growth of either taking a bigger share of the market from competitors or cutting costs, management tends to opt for the easier of the two — cutting labour costs.

In spite, therefore, of the evolution of industrial capitalist society into an employee (or people's capitalist) society, institutionalizing the economic interest of employees has not kept pace. One important reason for this may be that the issue of governance of mutual and pension funds has not been properly addressed and until this is done, the issue of voice representation at the corporate level likewise cannot be dealt with more effectively. Nevertheless, three distinctive employee-oriented labour market arrangements have emerged: the Japanese, the Western European and the British/North American.

The Japanese attempt to institutionalize the employee society is represented by life long employment, which rests on the premise that ownership (property) is, in effect, a relationship of mutual obligation rather than right. Ownership and its obligations encompass employees who are assured of rights in jobs or life long employment; banks, which have preferential rights in the event of insolvency; and nominal shareholders, with claims to investment returns.

In western Europe, the employee society has been reflected in comprehensive and strict employee protection legislation, with costly redundancy provisions being used to discourage retrenchment and unemployment. Employee claims

291

also take precedence over creditors, even banks, in the event of bankruptcy. There are also additional forms of social protection accorded workers in the EU Social Charter. All these forms of employment protection have been challenged in the name of "labour market reform" to meet increased competitiveness heralded by globalization.

In the UK and the US. the employee society has been institutionalized only indirectly, through financial intermediaries representing essentially the resources of employees through pension funds and insurance companies that own minority and, often, majority business interests. At the work level, direct stock ownership (ESOPs) has been pushed in both countries. However, in the US, ESOPs have featured more as a form of pension benefit. As such, ESOPs have been criticized on the grounds that they tie employees to a particular company and, thus, might have the effect of impeding labour mobility in periods of rapid social, technological and economic changes. Related criticisms are that since businesses go through periodic ups and downs and may not sustain adequate levels of investment return, workers are likely to feel cheated. Questioned also is the wisdom of employees who already have a stake in the company by virtue of investments of their jobs, exposing savings that should be treated as a provision for the future outside the employing company to the same financial risks associated with their continuing employment.

Corporate Governance and Employee Participation in Decision-making in the 21st Century

The juxtaposition of full-blown Pension plan capitalism and the universally disruptive effects of global integration touched upon in this paper could be counted upon to ensure that corporate governance and employee participation would become not just additional footnotes to age-old debates, but central concerns in the opening decade of the 21st century.

For one thing, there could be no gainsaying that, in the course of making routine decisions, mega corporations, both national and trans-national, exercise as much, if not more, power than most national governments to determine where people live; the character and location of the work they will perform; and job skills preferred as well as consumption patterns and life styles of current and successive generations. Indeed, the on-and–off Multilateral Agreement on Investment, initially pushed very hard by Canada, came close to extending even further the power of multinational/trans-national corporations by conferring upon them the right to exercise the same constitutional democratic rights guaranteed to individuals, notwithstanding that corporations do not operate as democratic institutions. It would be difficult also to shrug off the growing income inequality between social classes and occupational groups both within and between countries being exacerbated by globalization and increased competitiveness and the skewing of compensation in favour of virtually non-accountable corporate/executive management. Indeed, insecurity of employment and acceptance of relatively high unemployment rates, key elements of an anti-inflation strategy, appeared to leave trade unions little option but to negotiate rather than increase wages. Finally, as it appeared that universally the top twenty percent of income earners were increasing their share of income at the expense of the corresponding lower income strata, so rising tide of concern was being voiced that growing income disparities and concomitantly heightened class and social tensions could become a greater threat to the stability of liberal democracy than anti-capitalist ideologies.

The Corporate Governance and Accountability Scandal and Crisis in the USA

That questions about corporate governance and accountability posed by full blown pension capitalism could be expected to become of increasing concern in the opening decade of the 21st century could reasonably be predicted. What was not anticipated, however, was that they would so soon, in such a dramatic way, become the national concern of legislative policy makers and financial market regulators, leading, in the United States, to the introduction in the year 2002 of far reaching legislative and administrative measures for reform of corporate governance and accountability. The catalyst was the spectacular collapse and bankruptcy of several mega national and multinational American Corporations predominant in, but not limited to, the telecommunications industry. In particular, the declarations of bankruptcy of Enron Corporation, an energy trader (December 2, 2001), Global Crossing Telecommunications (January 28, 2001), Adelphia Communications (June 2002) and WorldCom Inc. (July 21, 2002), the last named being the largest bankruptcy in United States history, produced a litany of corporate management abuses and scandals, seemingly with the complicity of leading audit/consulting companies, stock brokerages, and investment and law firms.

Investigations by Congressional and financial regulatory bodies (e.g., the Securities and Exchange Commission, or SEC) led to allegations of deploying sham transactions involving off-the-book partnerships to move billions of dollars off balance sheets, thereby masking worsening financial situations; inflating profits through manipulative accounting, and mind boggling personal aggrandisement by CEO's and senior executives based on insider trading of stock options and other fraudulent practices and outrageous "golden handshakes" or separation packages; even as thousands of workers were losing 401 (K) pension savings and jobs as prices of company held stock collapsed and bankruptcies ensued. Charges for fraud involving false filings, accounting improprieties, insider trading and misuse of corporate funds, have been laid by the appropriate government authorities against selected executives of a number of corporations and further arraignments are expected.

Commenting on this crisis of epidemic proportions, the Chairman of the Federal Reserve System, Alan Greenspan, observed that "rapid enlargement of stock market capitalizations in the latter part of the 1990s engendered an outsized increase in opportunities for avarice. An infectious greed seemed to grasp most of our business community". Further, stock options "perversely created incentives to artificially inflate earnings to keep stock prices high". To stave off the "contagion effect" and a major economic crisis, the United States Congress moved with alacrity to enact legislation (Sarbanes-Oxley Act of 2002), including:

- New criminal penalties and jail terms for company fraud and the shredding of documents.
- Stiff fines and imprisonment for CEO's and Chief Financial Officers (CFO's) convicted of fraudulently certifying company financial reports.
- The creation of an independent private sector board, with subpoena powers, to oversee the accounting service. Auditors must register with the new Board in order to provide audit reports to the SEC.
- Audit Committees: Listing of securities is prohibited where the company does not have an audit committee that satisfies specific criteria, including independence from management.
- External Auditor independence and rotation: Auditors are prohibited from providing certain services (e.g. consulting) to companies they audit. The lead or coordinating partner for a company must be rotated if the partner has performed audit services to the company in each of the past five years.
- Disclosure in Periodic Reports of off-balance-sheet transactions and Pro Forma Figures.
- Most types of personal loans to Directors and Executives prohibited.
- Recapture of bonuses or profits: If a company is required to restate its financial statements due to misconduct, the CEO and CFO must reimburse gains made during the period covered by the financial statements.
- Timely disclosure of material changes in a company financial condition or operations.
- Insider Trading during pension fund blackout periods: directors and executive officers may not trade equity securities during periods when employees who participate in benefit plans are prohibited from trading company securities.
- Whistleblower protection: Employees are protected from retaliatory discharge or other adverse employment for providing to the US Congress, or to regulatory or enforcement agencies, information believed to be in violation of securities or anti-trust laws.
- Disclosure as to whether companies have adopted a code of ethics for senior financial officers and prompt disclosure of any changes in them or waivers thereto.
- Management Assessment of Internal Controls: Annual Reporting and disclosure of the effectiveness of such procedures.
- Extension of statute of limitations for private securities fraud.
- Lawyers as Gatekeepers: Attorneys practising before the SEC are required to report material violations of securities law or breaches of fiduciary duties to the Chief Legal Officer or CEO, and/or to the Audit Committee or full Board of Directors.
- Setting up a new federal account for defrauded investors that would take in all civil fines, payments and assets from corporate wrongdoers.

The SEC has been strengthened to more effectively perform its monitoring and policing functions, including the enforcement of the new legislative provisions, and has imposed on the 1000 largest publicly traded corporations the obligation to provide sworn statements from their CEO's vouching for the accuracy of financial reports. Also being touted is a similar obligation on the part of financial analysts to certify that their recommendations for stock trading are not influenced by their own firms' investment from client companies.

Post-Enron Impact in Canada

The Canadian corporate governance reform initiatives have been much more muted and limited than in the United States. A Canadian Public Accountability Board has been set up to be an independent accounting watchdog. It is administered by an 11 member Board appointed by a Council of Governors comprising the three chairs of the major securities commissions and government financial regulators. The Board is dominated by professionals from outside the accounting business and is charged with conducting yearly inspections and ensuring the expeditious preparation of new accounting standards. Under the threat of cancelling audit contracts, it can require firms to rotate lead auditors on a regular basis and have a second partner review every audit.

More important, however, is the fact that the provisions of the Sarbanes-Oxley Act cover Canadian companies that are either listed in the United States or required to file annual and other periodic reports to the SEC. Thus, for example, executives of Canadian cross-border issuers must now personally certify SEC filings that contain financial statements and face significant fines and terms of imprisonment if they knowingly and wilfully give false certification. Additionally, they are prohibited from making loans to their directors and executives, and may also be affected by the auditor independence rules.

While these measures may be expected to serve as a deterrent to corporate governance malfeasance, they are not, in and of themselves, a sufficient answer to the proposition that, in the same way that the preservation of liberal democracy and government required a system of checks and balances, so too the stability of "employee society" or of "pension" and/or "fiduciary" capitalism will require a system of checks and balances more reflective of the new system of financing and ownership of private enterprise. Employees, through their pension plans, constitute a new class of permanent and universal owners of private (and public) enterprise systems. They are long-term owners whose interests are congruent with those of society. Indeed, numerically, they are the society at large and, as such, may claim to be the only group capable of providing normative direction for corporate enterprise. The long-term perspective derives from the fact that, on average, employees contribute for 30 years before taking out a pension, and by then a new generation of employees will have begun paying in. The governing principle that pension funds should be invested for the exclusive benefit of plan members and their beneficiaries also implies that all conflicts should be resolved in their favour. By the same token, plan fiduciaries (trustees and fund managers) should be guided, in terms of investment decisions and their ramifications, by similar long-term considerations. Logically, therefore, institutional investors, and the pension system in particular, are strategically placed to serve as the foundation for a new system of corporate governance and accountability.

Contradictions/Challenges to be Resolved
Long-term Owners but Short-term Perspectives

Although employees collectively, through their pension plans, now constitute the new and long-term owners of the private enterprise system, the trustees who legally administer scheme assets on their behalf typically have little to do with management or determination of the corporate equity investments.

What is more, in discharging their fiduciary responsibilities — duty of loyalty (sole purpose doctrine) and of care (skill and diligence/prudence) — trustees and/or competing professional managers retained by them have felt constrained to realize the best possible returns for plan participants by focussing on short-term considerations — especially last quarters fund results, and taking advantage of any premium opportunities. This short-term perspective has been reinforced by the growing presence among institutional investors of mutual fund trusts, which have been designed for total liquidity. By being geared to investors who come in and out of the money market on a daily basis, mutual funds have been dubbed "the one night stands of institutional investing". Although aggregate shareholdings are large, they are dispersed over a large number of individual funds and, thus, mutual fund owners and managers act as passive participants rather than longer-term owners of the companies in which they put their money.

Pension Capitalism
and Employee Responsibility
The American Experiment
with Pension Shareholder Activism

In the US, the California Public Employees Retirement System (CalPers) has been acclaimed since the 1980s as the standard bearer of a shareholder activism movement aimed at increasing participation of shareholders to the benefit of both interests. CalPers has interpreted its duty of loyalty and of care to include a duty of active monitoring of corporate performance that it considers inherent in the concept of prudence. With a view to enhancing the long-term value of shareholdings, CalPers has used shareholder proposals as a means of enacting general governance reforms, such as eliminating the poison-pill in the anti-takeover atmosphere of the mid-1980s; more representative and accountable boards of directors, including greater shareholder freedom to elect Directors; increasing the number of independent (non-management nominated/appointed) Directors; determining criteria for director qualifications and for performance evaluation of both directors and executive management of targeted companies. The ouster of a number of CEO's of large corporations has served to dramatize the effectiveness of CalPers' strategy of exercising responsible ownership rights. But to the extent that its first priority is the maximizing of albeit long-term value of shareholdings, CalPers appears to be less concerned with employment generation and employment stability.

Pension Plan Capitalism and Models of the Corporation

Another approach to the issue of corporate governance and accountability in the post-industrial or employee centred society, has been to question the relevance of traditional legal and economic theories of the corporation. For example, in the UK and the Americas (and, indeed, in the Common law world) the corporation tends to be viewed as a private agency defined by a set of relationships between the principals and agent. Though legally the owners, shareholders usually are too numerous and too busy to undertake the responsibilities of ownership and hire salaried executives to run their affairs. The shareholder-agency model conforms more to the entrenched authoritarian type of political system of government, in that the managing elite tend to be self-perpetuating, and are only nominally accountable to the shareholders/electors: be it through Directors who have been chosen by and are compliant to executive management or through Annual General Meetings, which are, again, manipulated by management and are largely ritualistic.

Financial Model

Much of the debate about corporate governance in the US (and Canada) has flowed from acceptance of the financial approach or model associated with "fiduciary" capitalism. Its major premise has been that the only goal of the corporation is to maximize long-term shareholder wealth, a goal shared by institutional investors. From the fiduciary perspective, the challenge of corporate governance has been largely one of finding efficient solutions to the problem of divorce of ownership from control, and to ensure that professional managers do not act contrary to the interests of owners. In the idealized free market scenario, the solution lies in the "market for corporate control" or "hostile take-over". If a corporation was badly enough managed, its share price would decline relatively, making it a target for take-over by more aggressive entrepreneurs and efficient managers who would displace the current managers and proceed to reap economic gains. Thus, the threat of hostile take-overs provided the incentive for managers to run companies in the interest of shareholders. Indeed, it has been argued that there was a direct correlation between legislation enacted during the 1980s to curb hostile take-overs and the escalation of executive compensation (Henry G. Manne, Financial Post, June 28, 2002). The "market for corporate control" approach raised questions on the grounds that the wholesale assault on the firm, that it entailed was an extremely expensive and inefficient way to enhance corporate performance, and a more generalized approach to corporate governance appeared to be needed. This was provided by the "political model" or broadening of the finance model, which has focussed on influencing legislators and regulatory agencies, as well as litigation, to secure reforms and rule changes that would allow owners/ institutional investors to pursue collective action against individual companies. CalPers, already referred to, exemplifies this type of institutionalized shareholder activism.

In the post Enron/World Com era, one may, however, question the wisdom of identifying maximization of shareholder wealth with maximization of share prices, especially when it may entail understatement of costs, inflation of profits, and manipulation of employment levels by continuous downsizing. In other words, longer-term rates of return or profitability geared to long-term survival of the firm may be equally legitimate objectives.

The Social Institution or Trusteeship Model

In contrast to the "Anglo-Saxon" model touched upon above, the Continental European and Japanese model — the "social institution" model — has been touted as more relevant and worthy of adaptation, if not emulation, in the Americas. In this model, the corporation is treated as an "institution", as distinct from an organization, with its own personality and character and its own objectives and aspirations and with obligations to a wide range of stakeholder groups — investors/shareholders, employees, suppliers, customers and the society at large represented by the public administration. Thus, the corporation as a social institution and a social system, in which the whole is greater than any of the parts, has social (public) responsibilities, including recognition of a public interest in governance. The Corporation is not governed or driven by the principal/agency contractual relationship or the goal of maximizing shareholder value as postulated by neo-classical economic theory of firm. Rather, it is obligated, as part of the socio-economic structure, to *sustain the interests of all stakeholder* groups, without necessarily giving priority to any particular one. Executive management function, therefore, as trustees, seeking to serve and to be responsive to this broad range of vested interests of stakeholders.

It may be noted that the notion of corporate management being regarded as trustees was instrumental in altering traditional labour-relations approaches in the United States as a result of New Deal pro-labour legislation that created a charter of trade union rights, including compulsory recognition and collective bargaining. The trusteeship concept of management emerged as the counterpoint to the residual or sovereignty thesis of management, which held that management enjoyed certain "prerogatives" derived from property rights and that management retained a residual or absolute prerogative right of discretion to deal with matters not ceded to unions within the framework of the collective agreement or labour contract. The trusteeship theory of management was increasingly espoused by professional corporate management, who were concerned to achieve stable labour-management relations, and derived its rationale from the fact that the traditional concept of ownership had undergone a number of changes. First, share ownership represented an intangible asset rather than physical property. Second, the separation of ownership from management and the fact that operational control could be achieved with less than full ownership. It is instructive that the courts in Great Britain have determined that legally the corporation is not owned by shareholders. "The Company is at law a different person altogether from its subscribers". Indeed, the British Companies Act of 1985 reversed a 1962 rule that shareholders had exclusive claim to the residual assets in the event of liquidation, by entrenching employees' interests and imposing on Directors a duty to strike a balance between employee interests and shareholder interests.

In this broadening of shareholder interest to encompass stakeholder interests, executive management are seen as trustees rather than mere agents of owners, having a responsibility to temper the wealth maximizing presumption of liberal economic theory, by taking account of obligations to: (a) employees retaining a stable and productive workforce; (b) suppliers, a part of the supportive infrastructure; (c) the consuming public (quality goods and services at competitive prices; (d) investors, entitled to a reasonable rate of return; and (e) public policy makers, concerned with growth and development, price stability, and equity. British Prime Minister Tony Blair, as part of the vision of his (New) Labour Party government for modernizing the economy and political economy of the UK, advocates a "stakeholder society" based on a "relationship of trust not just within a firm but within society". Just as the debate about "corporate" or "corporate citizenship" responsibility has never been conclusively decided one way or the other, so the issue of defining and the weighting of stakeholder values and interests will be on-going ones.

The appeal of the Trusteeship model, which generally prevails in Europe and Japan, is that it is more compatible with Pension Fund (or Employee) Capitalism. It recognizes, to an extent that the principal/agency model does not, that businesses are not just groups of people expediently linked by contractual relationships (which may or may not be renewed on the basis of essentially short-term considerations), but by a nexus of long established trust relationships. Thus, there is recognition that the profit maximization norm may be subject to a set of social constraints, such as, for example, taking account of environmental concerns and ethical investing, and the human and social costs of downsizing and reducing employee protection as well as the consequences of rising income inequality in the winner-take-all ethos of competition in the so-called "new economy". However, some protagonists of the American corporate model argue that in comparison with the "social institution" model, be it Japanese or western European, the principal-agent model not only has produced better results for shareholders, but is superior in its ability to unravel misallocations of capital and to quickly pick up the pieces, so to speak.

It is possible, also, that as the United States clearly establishes its hegemony in the evolving global economy, and its trans-national corporations play an equally pivotal role in the new mercantilism of trans-national confederations, the European model of the corporation as a social institution may, by dint of circumstances, be forced to move towards the Anglo-American model. It is, nonetheless, reasonable to predict that for the immediate future, as pension funds and assets continue to accelerate in growth and become even more powerful players in the equities markets, they will, as the new class of owners, assert the rights and entitlements: to be adequately and continuously provided with information necessary to enforce accountability of performance; to deal directly with management about policy concerns; to determine criteria for the membership of boards of directors; and to nominate and elect new board members.

The new environment may also have confounded expectations as to how the widening of market participation would affect the dynamics of politics. Among the rationales provided by neo-conservative and neo-liberal regimes for including privatization of public enterprises and services in their political agendas during the 1980s and 1990s were that it would serve both to limit the scope and role of government in the economy and to widen share ownership. As more workers came to own shares, they would absorb the predominantly "small government" attitudes of business owners. But in the United States, when that stake in capitalism, extending to about one in two households (as opposed to about one in five in 1980), appeared to have been put in jeopardy by reckless corporate behaviour employees, past and present, as well as householders cum investors, turned to the one institution they deemed capable of protecting their interests and well-being. Put another way, as the stake of householders (Main Street) in the stock market (Wall Street) has increased, so has the political system's sensitivity to issues related to investor and pension protection.

Notes

1. Clark, Gordon L. (2000) *Pension Fund Capitalism, Oxford University Press,* p.17
2. Toporoski, Jan (2000) *The End of Finance, Routledge, London and New York*
3. Toporoski, Jan, supra, pp. 52–53
4. Peter Drucker (1976) *The unseen Revolution — How Pension Fund Socialism Came to America,* (New York, Harper Row)
5. *United Steelworkers of America (1996) Conclusions-Industrial Heartland Labour Investment Forum*
6. Clark, Gordon L Supra, p.43

References

Clark, Gordon L. (2000) *Pension Fund Capitalism*, Oxford University Press
Drucker, Peter (1976) *The Unseen Revolution — How Pension Socialism Came to America*, Harper Rowe, New York
Government of Canada (1994)
Report of the Advisory Group on Working Time and Distribution of Work, Arthur Donner, Chairperson

Kay, John & Silberstone, Aubrey (1996) *"Corporate Governance", The Guardian Stakeholder Debate,* Guardian Media Group plc, 1996 (Extracted from *National Institute Economic Review,* August, 1995)

Monk, Robert A.G. & Minnow, Nell (1996)

(1995) *Watching the Watchers: Corporate Governance in the 21st Century,* Blackwell Publishers

Corporate Governance, Blackwell Publishers

OECD (1994) *The Jobs Study: Facts, Analysis, Strategies,* Paris

Toporoski, Jan (2000) *The End of Finance,* Routledge, London & New York United Steel Workers of America (1996)

Conclusions: Industrial Heartland Investment Forum

A General Model of Government Intervention*

Randy G. Hoffman

The ongoing interactions between government and the governed can be considered as the dynamic aspects of an extremely complex (highly interconnected) system that is in itself conceptually inseparable from the entire national society. Any attempt to predict the broader consequences of an alteration in the behaviour of any group within society must, due to considerations of this complexity, take one of two forms. In one, a particular behavioural change, either transient or sustained, is examined with analytical techniques appropriate to it. The use of this method does not typically involve an understanding of the system that goes beyond what may be learned from such casual observations. Historical evidence from similar phenomena affecting the same group(s) can then be employed to hypothesize the nature of the interactions and dependencies of immediate interest. The weakness of this method for prediction is that the accuracy of predictions will depend upon each new phenomenon being a close replication, in terms of the whole system and the nature of the apprehended changes, of the prior phenomena.

A second method is to study a class of phenomena through the construction of a model that simplifies reality in order that its essential, salient features and cause and effect relationships can be understood. The model will therefore not comprehensively simulate reality; but it should specify logical inter-

*   From Diane Jurkowski et al., eds., *Business and Government: Canadian Materials.* (Concord, ON: Captus Press Inc., 2000), pp. 229–236. Reproduced with permission of author.

relationships among its components, and be complete enough for whatever purpose it is designed.

In this paper, I introduce a model of government intervention to be employed for the purpose of discerning whether a particular application of a governing instrument, regardless of the policy area, is likely to be effective for its stated goals, or at least better or worse than alternative policies for the same purpose. The benefits to be ultimately derived from such a model are the ability to select policy formulations that are of high quality, and to predict the likely performance of intended measures.

Intervention is defined here as the application of any governing instrument: whether moral suasion, resource allocation, or regulation: in short, any way in which a government can give effect to its policy decisions through modifying the behaviour and/or economic and social circumstances of individuals or groups within the private sector. This is a broad working definition of intervention consistent with my aim to model a broad class of phenomena. I shall attempt to show below that the quality and effectiveness of interventions are related to measurements along selected dimensions that may be applied to all interventions. The price of such generality is the lack of an assurance of rigorously accurate determinations of effectiveness in all instances.

The Model

In the literature, two methodologies for studying government intervention commonly emerge. In one, the policy area of intervention is acknowledged, and that area (such as health care or broadcasting) will suggest an appropriate analytical framework, different in many respects from those that might be employed for other interventionist activities. An example is the "General Theory of Regulation" developed over the past two decades by Stigler and Peltzman. Those authors have suggested a transactional analysis specific to regulatory activity in which goods (votes, redistributed wealth, market power etc.) are exchanged between the regulating body and affected groups. The transaction takes place in a way that maintains an equilibrium between the utility values received by the most materially-affected parties. The government, as well as some private sector groups, who will then support the government, perceive a profitable transaction; while those suffering disutilities tend to be affected only marginally, perhaps subliminally, on a per capita basis.[1] This approach, dealing with the exchange of resources, can be employed to explain the motivating factors behind government's choice of regulation and society's acceptance of that choice. More recently, Bryson and Ring[2] have established transaction dimensions that pertain to various policy mechanisms (governing instruments), and generate qualitative measurements of performance stated in terms of governing principles, such as the degrees of efficiency, justice, and liberty. This analysis, as is generally the case with transactional approaches, does not adequately address the questions of whether the regulations effectively satisfy their policy goals.

Also, this phenomenological approach addressing motivating factors is tied to particular policy areas. The analytical framework devised is context specific. In Canada, discussions of diverse areas of government activity treat them as distinct phenomena, and focus upon the goals to be achieved, the methods of achievement, and the perceived desirable and undesirable consequences. Although there are linkages to other concerns, for example, the effect of regional development policy upon national, aggregate economic performance, the quantitative or literary models advanced typically do not exhibit the qualities of generality. Their analytical methods are more or less confined to a select area of policy.[3] In addition, Morah has pointed out that even in context specific analyses there are many barriers between the measurement of an outcome or result of policy and the assessment of what formulation and implementation factors were responsible for the degree of success or failure obtained. He further states that political considerations are more involved in the selection and alteration of policies than are considerations of effectiveness based on historical experience.[4]

There has also been significant attention paid to the formulation of a taxonomy of governing instruments with appropriate categories that could then be used to explain the preferences for each category according to the situational variables surrounding each policy decision. Howlett has described American, British, and Canadian work in these taxonomies, and has observed that the categories selected reflect national "characteristic processes by which they arrive at policy decisions".[5]

Generally, the categories of governing instruments are depicted as following a continuum from the least coercive (moral suasion), through expenditure solutions, to the most coercive (direct regulatory action). Doern and Wilson, commenting in their 1974 collection of Public Policy essays, and Doern, commenting in his 1978 collection of essays on the Regulatory Process, suggest that lack of effectiveness of exhortation (moral suasion) and the limited supply of expenditure instruments, respectively, tend to motivate government to move along the continuum to direct regulation. Conversely, they observe that this motivation is opposed by the requirement for constitutional clarity (and public acquiescence) that enables direct regulation. Therefore the more "mature" issues, in which well-known and stable public opinions exist, are the likely candidates for this latter treatment.[6]

The concept of a continuum in the selection of governing instruments, and the linkages that Doern and Wilson in Canada and others, internationally, have suggested that exist between points on that continuum and the effectiveness (both in terms of economic efficiency and goal accomplishment) of government's actions, seem to be promising areas for further development. However, it is necessary to develop a comprehensive definition of effectiveness that incorporates qualities related not necessarily to political "spin" or ideological preference, but rather to whether the *tangible* goals of the policy were effectively accomplished. In this way an analytical framework for intervention would exist independently of specific policy areas and ideological preferences. By choosing the measurement dimensions of an intervention appropriately, I shall attempt to show that a generic model can be devised that will have some significant predictive value regarding the consequences of the implementation of the policy. The model that follows does not, however, overlap the territory of the transactional theories of regulation. It does not model the motivational forces that generate intervention. It rather seeks to describe, in terms of dimensional measurements, only the type of intervention. The predictive aspects are then derived from linkages between the particular measurements and useful indicators of quality or effectiveness.

As will soon be apparent, the weakness in this model is its generally qualitative rather than rigorously quantitative nature. It was not my intention, however, to create only a literary model. I shall attempt to show that predictions of effectiveness can be considered as reasonably accurate indications without being overly concerned with precise quantitative determinations. Predictive statements will therefore be analogous to: "tall people are heavier than short people." This is a useful observation that is generally true, although it will sometimes be in error. In this case, the model of people that prompts this statement is one of classification by height. The intervention model below is comprised of classifications that enable conclusions of general truth at least with respect to the relative effectiveness of alternate forms of intervention. But in the study of a specifically intended or completed action, the current role of the model shall be mainly to provide an analytical framework to facilitate a more insightful analysis of the nature of the intervention and its linkage with results or performance.

Dimensions of Measurement

The essential nature of the model being proposed is the establishment of three independent dimensions by which an intervention can be measured. They are not the types of intervention suggested by Lowi: distributive, redistributive, regulative, and constituent, or subsequent formulations by others that still follow the traditional political science descriptions of such activities.[7] The critical qualities that the dimensions must possess are that they can be applied to a broad range of actual policies, that they can yield categorical measurements of such policies, and that they can be axiomatically linked to useful and comprehensive quality characteristics. The latter is necessary as, otherwise, empirical evidence would have to be gathered to substantiate the linkages, and such evidence must always be situationally specific. The dimensions are, as it turns out, more related to Lowi's political characteristics that are differentiated by degrees of directness or indirectness in the application of legitimate coercion.[8] Below, the dimensions are described, following which I shall attempt to show a relationship between the model as defined by measurements along these dimensions, and the effectiveness of an intervention.

Strategic/Reactive

This first dimension probably presents the most severe measurement problem. Although these terms have been widely employed, it is difficult to isolate precise meanings. Such is necessary, however, if the dimension is to be useful; and it is further required that the working definitions chosen should be as unambiguously applicable as possible to actual interventions. Therefore, a purely reactive intervention is defined as one that responds only to the superficial aspects of the issue, without visible concern for underlying or root causes. The word "visible" is important, as otherwise it would be necessary to try to examine the thought processes of members of governmental policy-making bodies, not a particularly rewarding line of inquiry. Suppose, for example, a regulatory response to inflation consisted of only a total, permanent ban on price increases. This would be indicative of a complete disregard for the national economic environment and its complex workings, despite what reasoning may have led to this action.

The term reactive is employed because it has been extensively applied by those authors who carry out the analysis of intervention in particular policy areas. Their use of it often denotes a "kneejerk" governmental response to a highly salient and specific issue that gives scant consideration to deeper or broader priorities or consequences. The decision-making process that gives rise to such measures has been termed by Lindblom and others "incrementalism", or steps in the process of successive limited comparisons.[9] The term "satisficing" is also employed in these instances. It suggests that, when an optimizing policy is not discernible or is impossible, only small policy changes are advisable, which are perceived to offer acceptable results, and which may be thought of as experimentation unlikely to lead to disastrous results. The rationale for reactive interventions, that may or may not be defensible depending upon circumstances, is, however, not of interest here. I simply note it as an "ideal type" which locates one extreme in the continuum that defines this dimension of measurement.

At the other end of the continuum, the probably unattainable ideal type is a purely strategic response that would consider and deal with all the underlying, root issues to any issue. The identifiable, environmental ramifications of any intervention in the short and long terms would be perceived, and a policy would be formulated that would attempt to deal with them, along with satisfaction of the primary goal(s).

The literature generally refers to strategic planning rather than strategic intervention itself. The relationship between them is, however, very close, as strategic planning will logically result in the formulation of a strategic intervention. For example, Hartle, writing as a Deputy Secretary of the Treasury Board, defines strategic planning as: (1) forecasts of the changes in the indicators of goal achievement that would occur in the absence of changes in the policy instruments; (2) the assignment by ministers of priorities...to problems...on the basis of this information; (3) identification of...policy instrument changes that might be used...; (4) assessment of their relative effectiveness...; and (5) selection...of the changes in the policy instruments that would most effectively resolve the highest priority problems....[10] This description, which states the necessity of a broad analysis of the impact of alternative interventions is essentially the same process by which I identify strategic intervention as the one that accounts for environmental consequences. The consequences of importance are virtually the same as Hartle's areas of priority.

Real interventions will likely fall along the strategic-reactive continuum according to the analyst's perception of how many of the root causes and potential environmental interactions are being included in a significant way in the formulation of the governmental response. Note that although ex poste analysis will likely, in all cases, expose previously unforeseen areas of both omission and inclusion, I must take care to separate true omissions from attempts at inclusion that simply missed the mark. The accuracy of an attempt to deal with causal factors of an issue must be treated as one measure of the effectiveness of the intervention. It is, in fact, one of the quality characteristics that shall be dealt with later. Much of the difficulty in measuring the position of an intervention along the strategic-reactive continuum disappears if absolute (and therefore quantitative) determinations are less important than a comparison of the position among two or more alternative interventions designed to fulfil the same policy objectives. Since this relative assessment of effectiveness is often what is precisely at issue when a decision must be made concerning how best to intervene, an ordinal measurement of effectiveness between alternatives is valuable. The model is probably best employed for this purpose.

For example, suppose several firms are discharging industrial waste in a small river. Although there is concern for the quality of the environment, there is also a danger that pollution controls may severely affect the economic life of the community, for which these firms are the principal employers. Government could simply: (1) regulate an immediate reduction in effluent levels; or alternatively, (2) such reductions could be phased in over a certain period of years. Government may also agree (3) to provide grants or tax reductions to defray part of the costs. These monies could be calculated as less than the expected discounted value of future unemployment insurance/welfare payments, and loss of creation of economic surplus that would be required should direct regulation cause plant closures. Suppose the adverse environmental developments of interest are, in order of priority, (1) destruction of the local economy (with a potentially broader multiplier effect), (2) the setting of a precedent in assisting private industry to meet pollution requirements, and (3) the increased expenditure of public funds. It would then appear that the second alternative action, which best deals with side effects one and three is the most strategic in nature. With respect to causal factors, this alternative avoids the outlay of public funds. One identifiable causal factor of pollution could be the private sector's perception that it is government's job to remedy pollution and business' job to operate economically. Note, however, that the second alternative may not necessarily be the highest quality intervention in all respects. For that determination, I must apply the other two dimensions of the model and generate a quality prediction based upon a complete measurement, as I shall show below.

Direct/Indirect

Figure 1 schematically depicts the sequence of effects caused by the intervention "A". For the purpose of a measurement along this dimension, "A" is considered to be either a single component of the exercise of a governing instrument (e.g., a regulation from a group of regulations) or multiple components that are very closely related, both in mode and purpose, and that have the same goal(s). As will become clear below, a single measurement of multiple policy components may include some which are direct and others that are indirect. Similarly, if the intervention is aimed at the accomplishment of multiple goals or objectives, then the measurement of whether it is direct or indirect may also depend upon which goal is specified. The same policy may be direct in respect of one goal, but indirect in respect of another. This can be contrasted to the measurement along the strategic-reactive continuum where all components of an intervention must be considered simultaneously.

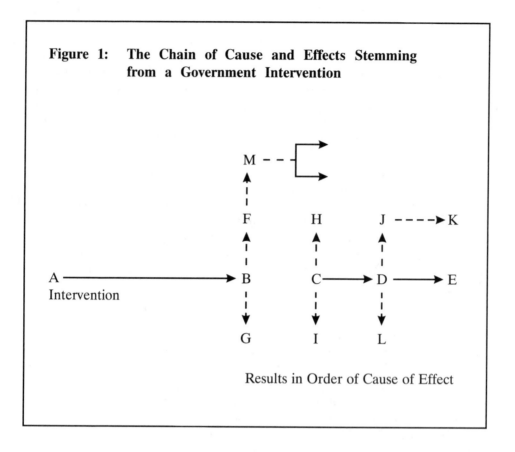

Figure 1: The Chain of Cause and Effects Stemming from a Government Intervention

Results in Order of Cause of Effect

The direct effect of the intervention (component) "A" is "B". (There may also be several direct effects.) All other effects that are in turn caused by "B" are indirect. Some of them may be desirable, indirect goals, while others may be side effects that are undesirable. To specify whether an intervention is direct or whether it has various degrees of indirectness, it is only necessary to ascertain whether the action leads to the specific goal being considered without intermediate stages of cause and effect. For example, government subsidies to farmers may have two goals — directly to assist farmers and indirectly to assist food purchasers. The latter result depends upon the price supports being passed to consumers through the distribution system, and is, therefore, indirect. Below, I will show that the degree of indirectness is also important in making predictions of effectiveness. Other authors have tended to associate direct intervention with the exercise of coercion in the context of regulatory activity. But in this model, it denotes only the closest possible causal link between the application of any governing instrument and the realization of its goal. It is defined in this way because I shall be able to correlate measurements along it with predictions of effectiveness or quality; and because directness is a distinctly separate (independent) aspect of an intervention. In the above example, farmers may be given a choice whether to subscribe to the price support program. (In doing so, they may, for instance, have to adhere to acreage restrictions.) There may be other direct formulations that aspire to the same goal that would be coercive; and the intervention may or may not be strategic, depending upon how well it deals with underlying factors.

As with the Strategic-Reactive Dimension, it is easier to compare one intervention with alternatives to determine the degree of indirectness. Nevertheless, the chain of cause and effect is usually identifiable, so that determinations with a useful degree of objectivity can be performed; for example, a public infrastructure improvement project to benefit indirectly the local economy. Ordinal determinations of indirectness are logically carried out by counting the various stages of cause and effect until the goal in question is reached. (In Figure 1, it is schematically depicted as the number of links separating it from "B".)

Coercive/Voluntary

There is no continuum for this dimension. The group or individual that the intervention directly affects must either adhere mandatorily to its provisions, or its acceptance is voluntary. Many direct regulations are not coercive. For example, government supported health insurance is voluntary in Ontario, although its main goal of subsidizing the cost of health care is certainly direct. It is not coercive even though a person would have no rationale for declining the coverage. Therefore, in the application of this dimension, it should be appreciated that certain "voluntary" measures may be tantamount to coercion.

It should be noted that in the case of indirect interventions that are also coercive, the intervention can only be coercive with respect to its direct effect ("B" as depicted in Figure 1), which is not the intended goal. Therefore, the targeted group of the indirect goal of a coercive intervention may not be the one being coerced. The establishment of an import tariff, for instance, to assist domestic manufacturers to acquire a larger market share is certainly coercive, but only when it is on importers of the foreign, competitive goods. If the goal is defined as encouraging the sales of domestic products, then the consumers who are targeted are not the group being coerced. As was the case when making direct-indirect measurements, it may be necessary to split an intervention into its components in order to measure coerciveness unambiguously.

Measures of Effectiveness

The linkages that will be demonstrated between the measurement of an intervention along each of the three dimensions and its effectiveness can at best suggest likely results or, at worst, provide a frame of reference for a latter, detailed study that would then add the context-specific component as an overlay. It is important here that the existence of these linkages is supported axiomatically, because such requires no proof or empirical support that might be valid only if given a narrowly defined sphere of activity. That is, the predictions must follow logically from the nature of the dimensions and the measurements that can be made. The dimensions were chosen with this requirement uppermost.

The choice of what quality measures constitute effectiveness of an intervention has been made in what I feel is the most obvious manner, although it may well be that other choices appear equally valid, and could perhaps be considered in addition to those below:

Accuracy

The accuracy of an intervention is simply the degree to which the intended or stated goals are satisfied, when all effects and interaction are substantially complete, or have reached a state of equilibrium. That is, the process of change is virtually completed. If there are goals stated in objective terms, then a quantitative measure of accuracy is simply the ratio of actual to intended accomplishment. When the expected time of goal accomplishment forms part of the statement of a goal basic (as it should), then the ratio measurement should take place at that time. Otherwise, if a reasonable time passes and equilibrium is still not obtained, there must be the exercise of judgement as to when to determine the accuracy.

This definition of accuracy does not include any measure of precision. If the government wished to stimulate the house construction industry, it might offer all taxpayers a continuing shelter allowance tax exemption based on some proportion of their housing expenses. The measure, if sufficiently generous, might be quite accurate, as all those who are prospective home purchasers would then perceive mortgage and other housing costs as partially defrayed, and they would have a higher propensity to buy. But the measure would not be precise. Much of the resources thus distributed would accrue to those occupying rental units or home owners with no intention to purchase another unit. Yet, in some cases, the requirement for accuracy might be sufficiently strong that precision considerations are secondary. In other cases, as in the above example, the reverse might be true. Precision must be treated as a separate entity in order that any desired priority between it and accuracy can be reflected in the design and assessment of interventions.

Precision

From the foregoing, precision can be defined as the degree to which the effect of the intervention is limited to only the intended goal(s). The amplitude of all intended effects is compared to those that are unintended (although not necessarily unanticipated) to arrive at this measure. This definition does not presuppose that all unintended results are undesirable, although that is clearly the general case (else they likely would be intended). A plethora of scattered results is at best an indication of uncontrolled intervention which will increase environmental turbulence; and at worst, is counterproductive to the intended measures.

Precision is intrinsically a qualitative measure although still an important one. Undesirable environmental consequences can clearly have visible, deleterious social or economic effects, although quantification of them may be impossible.

Efficiency

This is a difficult measurement to assess in the public sector, even qualitatively. It measures the difference or ratio between the resources or utilities created (benefits) and those expended (costs). However, given that such exchanges of value may take place among any groups in any sector of society, economic measures are nearly always insufficient. Values also expressed in terms of social or economic utility units generally pertain. It is perhaps the search for efficiency and the lack of an objective, common unit of value that renders decision making in the public sector a complex activity. In the United States during the early 1970s, top level executives were exchanged between business and government to promote a better understanding of the people and their respective task environments in each sector. The following comment was typical of those business executives who spent time working at a policy-making level in the public bureaucracy.

"Most decisions there are very complicated in terms of who they affect what groups in the country for instance and the way those people are affected...there is no right decision...so you settle for the best of a series of alternatives, none of which is close to ideal".[11]

These executives were directly addressing the difficulties in ascertaining an optimal balance of costs and benefits in public sector interventions. Their sensitivity to the problem was due to their prior private sector experience where purely economic measures, such as return on investment, generally suffice, or at least predominate over other criteria for judging decisions.

Nevertheless, merely because efficiency is difficult to ascertain (and attain) is not a reason to omit it from my measures of effectiveness. The implication is rather that the use of the linkages between the model's dimensions and that determinant of quality are rendered less distinct than for the other determinants.

Time Delay

The nature of intervention that stems from a political decision is that sufficient public support (whether broadly based or located within influential pressure groups) must be perceived before action is taken. Governments far prefer to act when they have established a defensible rationale. This fact tends to force a "management by crisis" flavour to the use of governing instruments, which certainly degrades the public sector's ability to act in timely fashion. When the government is ready to act, results are often required "yesterday". Any additional time delay caused by the design of the intervention is generally an adverse quality of some importance.

Time delay is not a difficult factor to measure even quantitatively. It is simply the period of time between the implementation of an intervention and the accomplishment of the desired goals. In order that it not be confused with accuracy, the ultimate level of achievement is not at issue. Of importance is only that the degree of achievement is no longer significantly increasing at the time that defines the end of the measurement period.

Private (Productive) Sector Environmental Effect

The definition of this last suggested determinant of quality has to be carefully, and somewhat narrowly, defined to avoid it becoming too vague to be used. Obviously, certain measures (for example, the establishment of a minimum wage, unemployment insurance, laws governing product safety, pollution standards, and even corporate income tax) could have a measurable, deleterious effect on the private sector's environment that may be evidenced by a reduction in economic performance indicators such as the GNP. These effects are derived from the chosen, intrinsic nature of a specific intervention and are, therefore, not to be considered here. They result from an exercise of political preference. My concern is in respect of the choice of the mode of the intervention as described by the dimensions of the model. I wish to establish a linkage by which a mode of accomplishing the same results will be perceived to affect the environment of the private sector more or less deleteriously than other modes, given that government wishes to maintain a viable private sector.

A relatively complex example is the effort to reduce inflation. Allowing and encouraging high and highly variable interest rates is one method in which environmental instabilities are established or increased. Industrial expansion plans are in doubt because of the cost of debt capital and the reception of the stock market to a share offering making the consumer demand for products all the more volatile. Behaviour that will optimize on the part of corporations is less discernible by their managements. Profits will then tend to be adversely affected: unless the nature of the business offers built-in protection, such as for chartered banks. Alternatively, wage and price controls are aimed at the same objective with relatively little short run environmental turbulence. This is not to say that the latter mode is preferable to industry. But it seems to be resisted more for the ideological aspects the removal of management and labour's discretionary power over price and wage decisions, and the long run distortions it would cause if the regulations remained in place. (And which might then have to be resolved by rationing.)

Whether business favours the objective of government action is not at issue here. It is arguable, in any event, whether the private sector was happier in 1981, with high interest rates, than in the earlier 1970s with wage and price controls. It can be shown that, in Canada, for many key industries such as steel, automobile manufacturing, appliances, transportation, food production etc., performance has been more severely disrupted in the more recent attack on inflation. Some of the blame for that must be attached to the environmental instability inherent in the chosen mode of action to combat inflationary pressures.

The assumption upon which the inclusion of the environmental effect is justified is that the maintenance of a favourable business environment is desirable. This is easy to demonstrate. Canadian society, even though existing as a mixed economy, is still almost totally reliant upon the private sector for the production of most of its goods and services. While the government may have interventionist objectives, there is nothing to be lost, and much to be gained or maintained by pursuing these aims in a less disruptive fashion, if it can be so done with similar effectiveness. This is not tantamount to a pro-business orientation for government. Adherence to that value also requires that the goals of interventions themselves will reflect it. In the context of the above examples, those goals may be perceived by business interests as very unfavourable. But even in these instances, the infliction of further damage purely through the choice of the means to achieve those goals, can only be judged as a negative contribution to the intervention's quality.[12]

A useful characterization of business environments depicts them as consisting of both formal and informal groups that interact through resource exchanges. Turbulence, which is the unpredictable component of variability inherent in those interactions,[13] is the parameter of environmental degradation that government intervention (among, of course, other causes not at issue here) can engender, apart from any deleterious effects that result solely from the specific goal of the intervention. Turbulence causes change that is less predictable as its intensity increases. Excessive turbulence will tend to degrade the performance optimizing competence of private sector organizations.

Linkages between the Model and Effectiveness

Figure 2 summarizes the linkages that are discussed below. I have attempted to impute a linkage only where there is a logical justification for it that is not derived from specific examples of intervention. Rather, it must be based upon an easily demonstrated, abstractly justified relationship between the dimension and the determinant of quality. Of course, as observed above, the requirement of generality and measurement difficulties leads to exceptions or examples where contradiction is unavoidably perceived. The relationships between the quality determinants and the position of an intervention along the three dimensions of the model are best considered as likely tendencies. This can yield useful information, as it establishes an analytical frame of reference by which historical, present or future interventions can be considered. It follows that the most reliable predictive use of the model is to compare two or more alternative modes of intervention designed to accomplish the same goal. A search for tighter, more deterministic linkages would, at this stage of the model's development, be fruitless; the result being that no linkage could be established.

Figure 2: Linkages Between Dimensions of the Model and Quality Measures of Effectiveness

Three Dimensions of the Model

Quality Determinants	Strategic/ Reactive	Direct/ Indirect	Coercive/ Voluntary
Accuracy	*/*	greater/less	greater/less
Precision	greater/less	greater/less	*/*
Efficiency	*/*	greater/less	greater/less
Time Delay	*/*	less/greater	less/greater
Environmental Effect of Private Sector	less/more deleterious	less/more deleterious	marginally less/more

* indicates the lack of a generally supportable linkage

With respect, first, to the strategic-reactive dimension, the very nature of the strategic approach, as defined above, almost assures a more precise accomplishment of the government's goal. The highly strategic intervention attempts at the outset to counteract, through its design, the dampening of undesired side effects and unfavourable changes in environmental interactions through a close analysis of cause and effect in the context of the issue at hand. For that reason, an unplanned deleterious environmental effect upon the private sector is very likely minimized. Less turbulence (uncontrolled changes) will, by definition, create less environmental disruption. Other quality determinants, however, do not suggest linkages with the strategic-reactive dimension that can be logically supported.

The dimension that suggests the strongest overall linkage with effectiveness is the direct-indirect. The depiction of the causal chain of intervention consequences in Figure 1 is a useful illustration in this regard. First with respect to accuracy, a direct intervention (the intended result would be "B" in Figure 1) is clearly likely to better reflect this quality. A measure that directly accomplishes the intended result(s), and that does not rely upon an extended chain of cause and effect (as would be increasingly the case if the intended result was C or D, etc.), is much easier to design accurately. The shorter the chain of events between cause and desired effect, the easier it is to perceive the details of the relationship and incorporate them in the design of the appropriate intervention (cause).

The argument to support generally greater precision for direct intervention, as opposed to indirect, rests upon a similar rationale. Unless the environment is in an extreme state of instability (turbulence), any changes in existing interactions, such as those caused by an intervention, will eventually allow the environmental area affected to settle to a new stable state. The analogy of ripples in a pond dying out as their distance from the original splash increases is appropriate. Therefore, it is probable that as the effect being considered moves from B to E, J, K, or M, the amplitude or intensity of the effect lessens. If one of the latter results is a desired indirect goal of the measure, unwanted antecedent effects that are direct, or less indirect, may well be stronger than the desirable one(s).

It can be concluded, therefore, that precision of indirect interventions is generally inferior to the direct or less indirect modes. And if the precision is lower for the reason of an extended chain of cause and effect, the amount of resource expenditure in that instance is likely required to be greater to accomplish a given indirect, desired result. There will be a tendency for the resources expended to be spread out over unwanted effects. Therefore, efficiency of the direct intervention also tends to be superior. This latter linkage can only apply when the direct intervention requires an expenditure of public money; or decreases the utility of some group(s) and increases it for others. Direct actions that do not perceptibly involve value exchanges would avoid an efficiency measure, except perhaps in terms of sociopolitical utility, measuring the latter always being difficult.

Finally, there are two reasons to suspect that environmental degradation will usually be more severe in the case of indirect intervention. First, the higher relative amplitude of unwanted (and perhaps unplanned) antecedent and/or side effects may engender the results. Second, the longer the chain of cause and effect, the more difficult it is to design the intervention for the desired intensity of results. This may lead to some situations where "overkill" occurs. The stronger measure will then adversely affect environmental stability throughout the causal chain (which will be more extensive than the illustration of Figure 1). Conversely, the inherent lack of predictability in lengthy causal chains may lead to interventions that underachieve the results, and force a revamping of the policy and adjustment of initial measures. In that instance, additional environmental changes are generated. Neither of these problems would be as prevalent when the direct mode is used.

The coercive-voluntary dimension separates measures that are mandatory and, therefore, more predictable in effect from those that may be avoided by the exercise of such a preference on the part of the intervenees, and which are, therefore, less predictable in effect. It is precisely the degree of predetermination that provides the linkages with the quality determinants. The two most obvious linkages concern accuracy and time delay. When it is known that the group(s) primarily affected by the intervention must comply, accuracy will generally be greater than for the converse. Similarly, with coercive measures, the variable time required to decide whether to comply is omitted. Time delay for effects is nearly always less.

The argument for a linkage to the quality determinant of efficiency is almost as straightforward. It rests upon the proposition that in order to attract adherence to a voluntary measure, more resources will tend to be required than if a coercive approach was taken.[14] As an example, consider that to raise funds voluntarily, government must offer bonds at competitive interest rates while a mandatory tax suffers no such constraints.

Finally, the environmental effect on the private sector has a weak linkage to this dimension that may still be useful, if less reliable. First, mandatory measures will certainly change the environment in a more predictable way than measures that may be optionally avoided. The accomplishments (and hence environmental consequences) of voluntary interventions can only be well assessed ex poste. However, coercive measures tend to reduce flexibility of response to environmental change. Flexibility of response assists the strategically superior firm to achieve differential advantages over less apt or less efficient competitors. Reduction of such flexibility is, therefore, a deleterious environmental change, in that excellence in strategic and tactical planning may yield less tangible results. These two effects can perhaps be perceived as striking a rough balance. To tip that balance, consider that, additionally, a more complex formulation is often required of the voluntary intervention. It must attract adherence through shifting existing environmental opportunities and constraints as perceived by firms or individuals in order to alter their voluntary behaviour. And if satisfactory, results are not forthcoming, then adjustments must be performed. All in all the linkage in this instance is not very strong; but coercive measures seem to logically cause somewhat less degradation.

Conclusion

It is intended that the model presented above and the established linkages will help to provide an analytical frame of reference for the examination of the use and effects of governing instruments. Overall, it has been demonstrated that a strategic, direct, and coercive intervention is a superior mode to accomplish a given goal, assuming that the quality determinants, as defined, are reasonable indicators of such effectiveness. Government has likely perceived this tendency, since, on a case by case basis, the historical trend seems to be toward these types of measures.

As an illustration, consider the formation of the Foreign Investment Review Agency, which had to approve or disapprove of significant foreign investments in Canadian Business. Since it could assess the broad impact of the investment on Canadian society before reaching a decision, it should be considered quite strategic. Certainly, it is both direct (with respect to the goal of limiting foreign ownership) and coercive. The more reactive, indirect and voluntary measures it generally supplanted were such formulations as tax credits for domestic equity investments by Canadians. Whether or not FIRA appealed ideologically to the private sector, the agency, by setting appropriate standards, was able to fine tune its efforts to exclude or include foreign buyers to whatever extent and for whatever reason was desirable. A contrast with the alternative mode shows relative deficiencies with it in respect of all measures of effectiveness.

The dimensions of the model and their individual linkages to the quality determinants can additionally provide insights into the performance of interventions that cannot be categorized as extreme positions with respect to all of the dimensions. For example, it is likely that a direct and coercive intervention that is reactive would have relatively high qualities with respect to accuracy, efficiency, and time delay, but poorer performance with respect to precision and the environmental effect.

This model may be useful in examining the probable outcome of a measure; or, better still, by using it to select an intervention to implement from alternatives. Inherent in the selection of any mode of intervention (as well, of course, in the selection of the goals of the intervention) are political, social, economic, and ideological choices. These cannot appear in the model as they require the application of values that will change from time to time, and from government to government. Therefore, it may be that the practical use of the model is in its consideration as a "template" that can underlie and, therefore, inform prevailing socio-political preferences.

Notes

1. See George J. Stigler, "The Theory of Economic Regulation", *The Bell Journal of Economics and Management Science*, 1971, 2(1): 3–22; and Sam Peltzman, "Toward a More General Theory of Regulation", *The Journal of Law and Economics*, 1976, 14(2).
2. See John M. Bryson and Peter Smith Ring, "A Transaction-Based Approach to Policy Intervention", *Policy Sciences*, 1990, 23.
3. Publications that study the interventionist concerns of government by methods specific to distinct policy areas include: R.W. Phidd and G.B.

Doern, *The Politics and Management of Canadian Economic Policy* (MacMillan of Canada, 1978); G.L. Reuber (ed.), *Canada's Political Economy* (McGraw-Hill Ryerson, 1980); G.B. Doern and R.W. Phidd, *Canadian Public Policy: Ideas, Structure, Process* (Toronto: Methuen, 1983).

4. Erasmus U. Morah, "A Comprehensive Approach to Public Policy Evaluation: The Implementation-Outcome Connection", *UBC Planning Papers, Discussion Paper #21*, University of British Columbia School of Community and Regional Planning, July 1990.

5. Michael Howlett, "Policy Instruments, Policy Styles, and Policy Implementation: National Approaches to Theories of Instrument Choice," *Policy Studies Journal*, Spring 1991, 19(2): 1-21.

6. G. Bruce Doern, and V. Seymour Wilson (eds.), *Issues in Canadian Public Policy* (MacMillan of Canada, 1974), p. 339; and G. Bruce Doern (ed.), *The Regulatory Process in Canada* (MacMillan of Canada, 1978), pp. 13–18. See also G.B. Doern and R.W. Phidd, *Canadian Public Policy: Ideas, Structure, Process* (Toronto: Methuen, 1983).

7. Theodore Lowi, "Four Systems of Policy, Politics and Choice", *Public Administration Review*, July-August 1972, pp. 298–310.

8. *Ibid.*

9. See C.E. Lindblom, "The Science of Muddling Through", *Public Administration Review*, 1959, XIX(2): 81; A.O. Hirschman and C.E. Lindblom "Economic Development, Research and Development, Policy Making: Some Converging Views", *Behavioral Science*, April 1962, pp. 211 ff.

10. D.G. Hartle, "A Proposed System of Program and Policy Evaluation", *Canadian Public Administration*, 1973, 16(2): 243–66.

11. Herman L. Weiss, "Why Business and Government Exchange Executives", *Harvard Business Review*, July-August 1974, p. 134.

12. To carry the argument further: if it were deemed favourable to damage the business environment through the choice of a mode of intervention, then that would become one of the *goals*; and this determinant of quality would become inoperative — perhaps being replaced by the contrary statement.

13. This is a simplified depiction of a complex phenomenon that will suffice for the present argument. For a more detailed description of the nature and causal relationships of turbulence, see Shirley Terreberry, "The Evolution of Organizational Environments", *Administrative Science Quarterly*, March 1968.

14. From the viewpoint of the private sector's environment, the government typically creates opportunities for altered behaviour when it intervenes voluntarily, and rigid constraints on behaviour when it intervenes coercively. The nature of the voluntary opportunity is that it must compete with other opportunities for adherence; and it is typically more expensive to create than an involuntary constraint. Other societal costs and benefits associated with the goal (rather than the mode) of the intervention are assumed to generally remain constant.

Myths and the Canadian Health Care System

Janice E. Nicholson

There are several myths associated with the Canadian health care system. They describe the system as:

1. the best in the world;
2. underfunded;
3. moving toward a two-tier system in which a substantial proportion of the health care system will be privatized; and
4. moving toward the US health care model and abandoning the comprehensive universal coverage that has characterized the Canadian health care system since the 1960s.

Some of these myths are propagated by the media, partly because they are unaware of the actual facts and their dramatic conclusions make excellent headlines. There is also an assumption that the public's attention is easily captured in matters of health care.

In fact, these myths can be easily exploded by simply using comparative data from other industrialized/urbanized countries of comparative wealth.

Statistics are readily available from the Organization for Economic Cooperation and Development (OECD), which provides comparative data on both the

---

*   From Diane Jurkowski et al., eds., *Business and Government: Canadian Materials.* (Concord, ON: Captus Press Inc., 2000), pp. 229–236. Reproduced with permission of author.

health status of the population in OECD countries and the cost of the health care system, both public and private, for each country.

Myth One: The Canadian health care system is the best in the world.

A useful and standard way to estimate the health of the population is to look at infant mortality rates and life expectancy at birth. When Canada is compared to other countries on these indices it is clear that, while Canada is certainly among the best in the overall health of its population, it is not the best. As Exhibit 1 shows, other countries also have excellent life expectancy and infant mortality statistics: especially countries such as Japan, Sweden, Finland and Ireland.

Myth Two: The Canadian health care system is underfunded.

Comparative data from other OECD countries show this assumption to be completely unfounded. In fact, the Canadian health care system is the second most expensive system in the world. Only the United States is more expensive, and by a wide margin, as Exhibit 2 indicates.

When the two exhibits are compared in terms of health status of the population and the cost of the health care system, it is quite clear that some countries have a similar population health status at a much lower cost than either Canada or the United States. This raises a number of questions:

- Why are some health care systems so much more expensive than others that produce similar population health outcomes?
- Why is there a perception that there is underfunding in a country such as Canada where clearly there is a high per capita spending on health?

The answer to the first question ties in with the way the health care system is organized. If the emphasis is placed on preventive measures, such as immunization, vaccination and maternal and child health, that are delivered by medium- to low-cost health professionals, then considerable improvements can be made in the population's health status at a modest cost. If, on the other hand, emphasis is placed on curative rather than preventive medicine, and that curative medicine is delivered by expensive health professionals, then the cost of the health care delivery system will rise substantially. Thus, one of the factors contributing to the high cost of the American health care system could be due to the fact that primary health care is often delivered by specialists. In comparison to other countries, the United States has a lower proportion of general practitioners and a higher proportion of specialists.

The answer to the second question is possibly more complicated. Even in an expensive system such as that which Canada enjoys, there may be areas that are underfunded. Resources tend to flow to the regions that have the most political influence. Consequently, there has been underfunding for health care in some rural and northern regions of Canada. Some categories of health professionals have been reluctant to provide services in these regions. This problem is not exclusive to Canada. Other countries, especially developing countries, have difficulty in attracting health professionals in remote areas. Generally, health

Exhibit 1: Infant Mortality and Life Expectancy, OECD Countries, 1990 and 1995

Country	Infant Mortality per 1,000 live births		Life Expectancy at birth, Males (years)		Life Expectancy at birth, Females (years)	
	1900	1995	1990	2002	1990	2002
Australia	9.9	5.9	79.9	77.15	80.1	83.00
Austria	7.8	5.4	72.3	74.85	78.9	81.31
Belgium	8.0	6.1	72.4	74.80	79.1	81.62
Canada	6.8	6.0	73.8	76.30	80.4	83.25
Czech Republic	12.5	7.9	67.5	71.46	76.0	78.65
Denmark	7.5	5.1	72.0	74.30	77.7	79.67
Finland	5.6	4.0	70.9	74.10	78.9	81.52
France	7.3	4.9	72.7	75.17	80.9	83.14
Germany	7.0	5.3	72.7	74.64	79.1	81.09
Greece	9.7	8.1	74.6	76.17	79.4	81.48
Hungary	14.8	10.7	65.1	67.55	73.7	76.55
Iceland	5.9	6.1	75.7	77.42	80.3	82.07
Ireland	8.2	6.3	72.9	74.41	77.5	80.12
Italy	8.2	6.2	73.5	76.08	80.0	82.63
Japan	4.6	4.3	75.9	77.73	81.9	84.25
Korea			67.4	71.20	75.4	78.95
Luxembourg	9.0	5.3	72.3	74.20	78.5	80.97
Mexico	36.6	30.5	67.7	68.99	71.0	75.21
Netherlands	8.0	5.6	73.8	75.70	80.1	81.59
New Zealand	10.9	7.2	72.4	75.17	78.3	81.27
Norway	7.0	4.1	73.4	76.01	79.8	82.07
Poland	19.3	13.6	66.5	69.52	75.5	78.05
Portugal	16.3	11.2	70.9	72.65	77.9	79.87
Spain	7.6	5.5	73.4	75.63	80.5	82.76
Sweden	6.0	4.1	74.8	77.19	80.4	82.64
Switzerland	6.9	5.1	74.0	76.98	80.9	82.89
Turkey	57.6	45.6	64.1	69.15	68.4	74.01
United Kingdom	9.4	6.2	72.9	75.29	78.5	80.84
United States	12.6	8.0	72.8	74.50	78.8	80.20

Source: Organization for Economic Cooperation and Development Health Data, 1997.
Health Affairs, 16(6): 170.

Exhibit 2: Spending on Health Care, 1990 and 2000

Country	Percent of GDP spent on health		Per capita spending[n] (in US dollars)	
	1990	2000	1990	2000
Australia	8.2%	8.3%	$1,316	$2,211
Austria	7.1	8.0	1,180	2,162
Belgium	7.6	8.7	1,247	2,269
Canada	9.2	9.1	1,691	2,535
Czech Republic	5.5	7.2	838	1,031
Denmark	6.5	8.3	1,069	2,420
Finland	8.0	6.6	1,292	1,664
France	8.9	9.5	1,539	2,349
Germany	8.2	10.6	1,642	2,748
Greece	4.2	8.3	389	1,399
Hungary	6.6	6.8	c	841
Iceland	8.0	8.9	1,375	2,608
Ireland	6.6	6.7	748	1,953
Italy	8.1	8.1	1,322	2,032
Japan	6.0	7.8	1,082	2,012
Korea	3.9	5.9	310	893
Luxembourg	6.6	6.0b	1,499	2,701a
Mexico	c	5.4	c	490
Netherlands	8.3	8.1	1,325	2,246
New Zealand	7.0	8.0	937	1,623
Norway	7.8	7.8	1,365	2,362
Poland	4.4	6.2b	c	576a
Portugal	6.5	8.2	616	1,441
Spain	6.9	5.9	813	1,556
Sweden	8.8	7.9a	1,491	1,847b
Switzerland	8.4	10.7	1,782	3,222
Turkey	2.5	4.8d	119	320b
United Kingdom	6.0	7.3	957	1,763
United States	12.7	13.0	2,689	4,631

Source: Organization for Economic Cooperation and Development, OECD Health Data 2002 (Paris 2002), 22(3): 91.
a 1999 data.
b 1992–2000.
c 1991–2000.

professionals will have better career opportunities in the urbanized areas, and they will have greater exposure to the newest medical technologies.

Myth Three: The Canadian health care system is moving toward a two-tier system in which a substantial proportion of the health care system will be privatized.

This myth usually arises in conjunction with news reports concerning patients who would rather pay for treatment than wait for the publicly funded treatment to become available. Such "queue jumping" is often portrayed as an increasing trend, but it is rare that such claims are backed by statistics.

In these debates the fact that Canada always has had a substantial private sector is ignored. When the two basic pieces of legislation establishing the present Canadian health care system were passed (Hospital and Diagnostic Services Act 1958 and the Medical Care Act 1968) there was well-established private sector health insurance. This private sector health insurance was normally linked to employment, with employer/employee contributions to voluntary or commercial health insurance companies providing coverage. This type of coverage did not disappear with the introduction of public sector coverage. Instead, it continued to exist, providing additional coverage to that of the public system. Thus, people covered by private insurance can obtain private/semi-private hospital accommodation, dental care and other extra benefits.

Most, if not all, publicly funded health care systems have a private sector, including those of former socialist countries. The real issue concerns the proportion of the health care system that is in the private sector. As long as the major proportion of health care spending is funded by the public sector, then the public sector is able to provide the regulation and direction of the health care system. However, even in the United States, a substantial proportion of the health care system is funded by federal and state governments through the Medicare and Medicaid programmes. Approximately 48 percent of health care spending in the United States comes from public funds. This is not sufficient, however, to allow the public sector to play the dominant role in regulating the health care system. (*Health Affairs* January/February 1998, Exhibit 4)

Myth Four: The Canadian health care system is moving toward the US health care model, and abandoning the comprehensive universal coverage that has characterized the Canadian health care system since the 1960s.

This view tended to be more popular in the 1980s when certain innovations in the American system, such as Health Maintenance Organizations, were perceived as having some direct applicability to Canada. Such views overlooked the fact that the Canadian health care system is organized on a quite different basis from the American system. It is true that some American innovations, such as diagnostic related groups (DRGs), have been introduced in hospitals in Canada as well to have some control over medical and surgical procedures. However, when the Clinton administration attempted to reform the American health care system in the early 1990s, it became obvious that there were severe deficiencies in the system. In particular, it is clearly the most expensive health care system in the world, though approximately 35 million people are not covered by either health insurance, Medicare or Medicaid. Additionally, health care expenditures are higher in the United States than they are anywhere else. As Exhibit 2 indicates, not only does the United States have the highest per capita spending on health care of all the OECD countries, but it also has one of the highest compound annual rates of growth. The American experience suggests that a health care system primarily funded through the private sector does not necessarily lead to a more economical or better health care system.

Comparing the Canadian and American health care systems provides an excellent basis for a general debate on the issues surrounding public versus private sector funding, and government control versus control by market forces.

Public versus Private Funding, Government Control versus Market Forces

The general criticism against publicly funded institutions is that they are usually less efficient and innovative, more wasteful and bureaucratic than privately funded institutions. This generalization may apply in certain sectors of the economy, such as telecommunications or airlines, but there is little or no evidence that this is true in the health care field.

On the contrary, one of the major reasons for transforming the Canadian health care system from a privately funded basis to a publicly funded one was the recognition that the privately funded system was not working well. A considerable proportion of the population was not covered. The infirm, the aged and the disabled were often refused coverage, and hospital deficits remained large.

Many similar criticisms are still levelled at the American health care system. In addition, the administrative costs are thought to be higher in the United States since there are multiple third-party payers, rather than just a single third-party payer as in Canada. The existence of multiple third-party payers means that both hospitals and physicians in the United States have a much greater burden of paperwork when they seek payment for their services.

The other part of the debate, concerning the relative merits of public versus private sector control, is the degree to which either sector can successfully control rising health care costs. Advocates of the public sector point to the successes of other countries, such as Germany, the United Kingdom and Sweden in introducing regulatory measures that have controlled costs and, even, reduced them, in the last decade. In other words, champions of publicly funded health care systems see government regulation and control as the most effective form of health care cost control, since ultimately the government is the final payer and can change the rules.

On the other hand, advocates of the private sector regard the interplay of market forces and competition as the most effective form of cost control. In this scenario, the consumer is free to shop around and find the best health care coverage at the best price. In this context, the private sector purveyors of health insurance will lose business if they do not provide their customers with a satisfactory product. However, in the American system, it is not the potential patient who is the customer but the business corporations that buy health insurance coverage for their employees. It is in their interests to control or lower the cost to the company of health insurance coverage. Therefore, in the last two decades, there has been increased pressure on the insurance companies to stabilize or lower their insurance premiums. In turn, the insurers introduced a number of reforms aimed at controlling the prices of the providers, primarily hospitals and physicians. To this end, they introduced Preferred Provider Organizations, Health Maintenance Organizations, procedures such as preauthorization for admission, concurrent review and required second opinions for surgery.

In a sense, market forces have brought about changes in the American health care system, so long as one regards the corporations as the final customer. If, however, one regards the potential patient as the final customer, then obviously the individual citizen has little or no choice but to accept the decisions of their employer. If they are dissatisfied with the health care they receive, it is difficult to change plans without changing the employer.

However, on the wider question of whether competition and market forces have helped to stabilize and/or reduce costs in the health care system, the result of the American experience so far would appear to indicate a negative answer.

The Medical Centre

Strategic Alternatives for a Private Health Care Provider

Lilian Liao and Laura Ng

The Medical Centre

In the spring of 2003, the Managing Director of The Medical Centre is preparing the strategic plan for the hospital for the next three years. The hospital clinic has experienced steady growth over the years, but the management team believes that it is time to re-evaluate the current organizational strategies and explore other growth alternatives. Although the company has moved from its traditional strategic small 'g' growth plan to embrace a new strategic growth plan, there has been some reluctance from key management personnel.

The alternatives available are:

- Diversification into other simplified medical treatments, for example, hernia repair and cataract surgery
- Expansion of the current facility
- Franchise The Medical Centre
- Expansion into the United States market

A physician founded The Medical Centre in 1965. Initially, The Medical Centre only treated gallbladder disease patients with open incision surgical

*   This article was written by Lilian Liao and Laura Ng under the guidance of Randy G. Hoffman and Diane Jurkowski.

method, but by the end of the 1960s, other treatment methods, such as dietary and medication, were offered. In 1990, the laparoscopic surgical method was introduced. The founding physician was born and educated in the United Kingdom. At the age of 23 years, he completed his studies and worked in an urban hospital and specialized in gallbladder surgeries. He immigrated with his family to Toronto, Ontario and eventually settled in the city of Mississauga, Ontario a suburban community west of Toronto. It was in Mississauga that he opened a clinic that specialized in treating gallbladder diseases. At first, the clinic included only him and two nurses. The demand grew rapidly in a period of less than three years; so, he decided to expand the clinic. He purchased 100 acres of land several blocks west of the original location. No interest had been expressed by anyone for this parcel of land until he came along and purchased it. It had been listed at $250,000. He was able to purchase the land for the very reasonable price of $150,000. In the summer of 1965, he opened The Medical Centre.

Presently, The Medical Centre is situated on 35 acres of land (25 acres stands vacant). The Medical Centre is world-renowned for being the leader in gallbladder treatments, as well as being a highly efficient model of health care service delivery. This reputation has prompted many clinics all over to study The Medical Centre's surgical method as well as the efficient service delivery model developed at The Medical Centre. As a result, there are many imitators internationally. However, this also has its downfalls, as The Medical Centre is unfairly blamed for their ineffective imitations.

The Medical Centre consists of a three-storey building. The lowest level comprises seven fully equipped operating theatres, surgical recovery room, a dining room, laundry facilities, the central supply centre, a patient lounge and mechanical rooms. On the second and third levels, the patient rooms and lounges are located. The five-winged hospital has 108 beds, which is operating at maximum capacity. The patient rooms are designed to have a non-institutional appearance. The Centre is an approximate 30-minute drive from downtown Toronto. This distance enables easy access, but also provides the tranquillity of a rural setting.

The Medical Centre has two divisions that include the not-for-profit hospital and the for-profit examination centre. The not-for-profit centre is approximately 40 percent (with slight variations from year to year) funded by the government. On the other hand, The Medical Centre privately funds the examination centre. As for any not-for-profit entities, profit made by the hospital division has to be returned to the government in the form of a cheque. The founding family has 55 percent ownership in The Medical Centre and the employees have The Medical Centre hold 45 percent ownership. Employee ownership was offered as an Employee Stock Option Plan. The Medical Centre believes the Employee Stock Option Plan is more beneficial to the organization as this increases employee motivation, strengthens corporate culture and eliminates the need for unions.

The five members of the Board of Directors govern the hospital and clinic divisions of the Centre. The son of the founder is a member of the Board and is appointed by the Chair of The Medical Centre. Quarterly Board meetings are held with members of the Board and the management team, usually at the beginning of each quarter. This allows the Board to evaluate the progress of The Medical Centre's operations and provide consultation to prospective operating decisions. Department heads report to the Managing Director who, in turn, reports directly to the Chair of The Medical Centre.

The Managing Director plays a vital role in the organization. She is responsible for all departments of the hospital and clinic. She also acts as a coordinator between departments and deals with strategic decision making matters. Her responsibilities are less directed to the daily operational activities because each department manages tasks very well, thereby allocating more time for strategic planning. The role of Managing Director was established a decade ago after the organization became more stabilized. This permitted her to withdraw from daily operational activities. She is responsible for almost every aspect of the hospital, directly and indirectly.

She integrates the flow of communication in The Medical Centre by using an open-door policy in order to resolve human resources issues that arise. She is known as a warm and friendly person. She believes that this enhances communication between employees and herself. The open-door policy also is an effective means of keeping up with the pulse of the Centre. This is also an important source of gathering information about the professional operations within the hospital and clinic. Many employees welcome her open-door policy and are comfortable in approaching her even when seeking personal advice. She has found that this bonds the employees and management together. With workplace issues, she encourages employees to first communicate with their respective department before coming to her. Only if the department head cannot resolve the problem, will she intervene.

The Managing Director is responsible for all employees. It is her responsibility to ensure their job satisfaction. Her belief is that employee performance affects the overall performance and reputation of The Medical Centre. Management is responsible for the supervision of employees' performance on a daily basis in order to make the necessary adjustments that benefit patient care and The Medical Centre. Yearly assessments are conducted to determine the appropriate stock option payments to employees and other rewards offered by the Centre. Employees are paid comparable wages in most instances. The pay scale is higher than the union scale for comparable jobs in the sector.

The hospital division of The Medical Centre has five departments consisting of physicians and surgeons, nurses, administration, food services and environmental services. Job rotation is practised in the hospital division. The staff in some departments, such as administration, familiarize themselves with tasks within the same department, thereby enabling them to fill in other roles in days when colleagues are absent. Multi-tasking is also practised at The Medical Centre. Multi-tasking is a unique aspect of the administrative department. Each administrative secretary is trained to do another's work. Therefore, when the need arises, secretaries are able to switch from one job without disruption to the flow of work. A distinctive outcome of this teamwork has left The Medical Centre without a very detailed organizational chart. The organizational chart would box the employees into a specified role. With multi-tasking, each employee frequently assumes a broad collection of job activities in the administrative department.

Lilian Liao and Laura Ng

The clinic division consists of three departments, physicians, nurses and administrative staff. They are responsible for diagnosing gallbladder disease patients and determining which methods of treatment should be used. There is some overlapping between some of physicians and surgeons in the two divisions because of the diagnosis and treatment procedures of patients.

The organization chart for The Medical Centre, as represented by Figure 1, does not clearly identify or distinguish roles. This is because there are over-

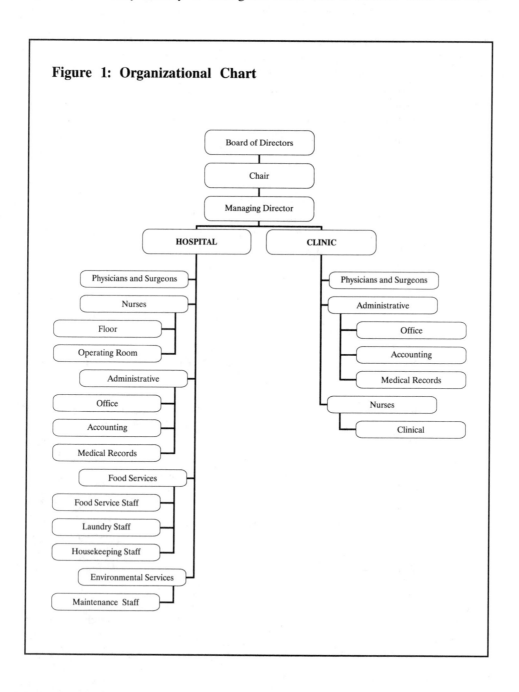

Figure 1: Organizational Chart

lapping tasks between nurses and administrative staff from the two divisions resulting from the role similarities. In addition, administrative staff in the two divisions is knowledgeable about each other's work. This also occurs between the nursing departments of the two divisions. The Medical Centre employs 189 staff members, consisting of:

- 30 physicians and surgeons
- 2 anaesthetists
- 57 nurses
- 36 administrative staff
- 64 maintenance workers

Supervisors are responsible for recruitment in their departments. The turnover rate of employees is low, with employees averaging ten years with the Centre. They express dedication to the Centre and think of it as a second home.

Extrinsic rewards are given to motivate employees. As well as the Employee Stock Option Plan, employees with children who want to pursue post-secondary education can apply for educational bursaries. Educational bursaries of $4,500 are available to employees with five years or part-time or two years of full-time tenure. Funds for all bursaries are derived from donations and money received from filming movies on The Health Centre property. Employees are also recognized and rewarded for their dedication and years of services at The Health Centre with prestigious awards. A part-time employee who works at The Health Centre for five years receives a bronze medal; a full-time employee with the same five years of tenure receives a silver medal. A full-time employee who has worked for ten years receives a gold medal.

Recently, unions have unsuccessfully attempted to persuade nurses to unionize. Nurses have been migrating to the United States because of better incentives to popular destinations, such as Texas and Florida. At The Medical Centre, recruited surgeons undertake a training program of approximately half a year to qualify to practise at the Centre. Non-surgeons, that is, family physicians, can apply for a position and be trained. With the Centre's training, they become qualified to work at the Centre, but this qualification is limited to working only at the Centre and nowhere else. In recent years, many foreign-trained physicians have faced difficulty entering the Canadian medical profession because of the high costs and restrictive Canadian medical licensing legislation. Cutbacks in educational funding and high entry barriers have resulted in decreasing the number of medical school enrolments. Another growing trend is the refusal of physicians to practise in northern and rural areas in Ontario. Reasons for physicians' reluctance to practise in these northern and rural areas are the problems of administering health care to scattered populations, lack of entertainment, harsh weather conditions, isolation and the great distances from major cities where there are teaching hospitals and medical schools and the lack of incentives. Many of these factors have adversely affected the number of physicians and create a problem for the government and industry to provide health care delivery.

The Medical Centre has adopted technology to assist in achieving its world-renowned reputation. There is an intricate network of approximately 40 personal computers that allows employees to have access to a computer with a newly installed database. The adoption of laparoscopic equipment and techniques has established equity built by this technique. The Centre concentrates solely in diagnosing and treating gallbladder diseases. Methods of treatment offered at The Medical Centre include dietary modification, medications and both incision and laproscopic surgeries. Although there are a number of treatment methods available for patients, most often surgery is recommended by physicians. The surgical removal of the gallbladder has proven to be the most effective treatment for the disease. Hence, more than 70 percent of The Medical Centre's patients are treated surgically and 80 percent of these patients undergo the laparoscopic surgical treatment.

The Medical Centre treats approximately 14,000 cases of gallbladder disease annually. Approximately 10 percent of the patients are treated by dietary modification; 20 percent are treated with medication; 14 percent are treated with open incision surgery; and the remaining 56 percent are treated by the laparoscopic procedure. Dietary modification and medicated patients do not need to have hospital stays. However, surgical patients need to stay at least 24 hours at the hospital post-surgically. The number of days of hospital stay varies depending on the individual patient, but the average patient stay is approximately three days. Patients treated with the laparoscopic treatment usually remain at the hospital for a period of at least 24 hours. Patients who have undergone open incision surgery are usually required to remain in hospital from five to eight days. This results in an annual hospital stay of approximately 30,000 days. Due to the need for patients to stay overnight, the hospital offers semi-private and private rooms at a cost of $100 per night and $150 per night, respectively. This cost includes accommodation and meals. For complete financial information regarding the company and each division, refer to Figures 2, 3 and 4. The financial statements are used to illustrate the financial resources the company will have in the future to enable the company to select strategic alternatives.

The Medical Centre believes in treating the patients physically and psychologically. Therefore, there are other aspects that the Centre deems to be more important than just making a profit. For years, the Centre has promoted the importance of patient accessibility, affordability, high quality patient well-being and employee empowerment. With a firm grip on these beliefs, the Centre is world-renowned for offering quality care and has gained the advantage of cost leadership over many other comparable clinics.

Individual Stakeholders at The Medical Centre

The majority of employees have worked at The Medical Centre for at least eight years, with approximately two-thirds working full-time. There is high employee morale. There is a low turnover rate for the staff at the hospital, with approximately an employee turnover rate of five years. Great benefits and high job security have contributed to this low turnover rate.

Figure 2: The Medical Centre Consolidated Balance Sheet

As at March 31

	2003	2002	2001	2000	1999
Assets					
Current					
Receivable from the Ontario MOH	2,273,568	2,190,784	2,130,138	2,497,059	2,638,798
Accounts receivable	349,030	330,657	319,540	356,921	300,832
Inventory of supplies	300,294	267,351	285,390	287,648	291,826
Prepaid expenses	65,294	60,843	63,906	74,257	75,645
Total current assets	2,988,186	2,849,635	2,798,974	3,215,885	3,307,101
Land	4,520,958	4,398,502	4,099,543	3,985,430	3,754,290
Land improvements	178,820	168,998	172,176	175,354	178,532
Buildings	1,200,528	1,313,438	1,476,348	1,529,258	1,582,168
Furniture and equipment	398,456	365,035	288,667	301,723	315,684
Automobiles	13,425	14,321	15,365	16,531	20,653
Total capital assets, net	6,312,187	6,260,294	6,052,099	6,008,296	5,851,327
	$9,300,373	$9,109,929	$8,851,073	$9,224,181	$9,158,428
Liabilities & Shareholders' Equity					
Current					
Accounts payable and accrued liabilities	230,247	150,516	135,650	165,381	200,516
Shareholders' Equity					
employees	1,561,091	1,697,059	1,794,436	1,844,931	1,865,011
owners (Lloyd Family)	3,642,547	4,154,869	4,614,264	4,988,146	5,308,109
Retained Earnings	3,866,488	3,107,485	2,306,723	2,225,723	1,784,792
Total Liabilities and Shareholders' Equity	$9,300,373	$9,109,929	$8,851,073	$9,224,181	$9,158,428

Figure 3: The Medical Centre Hospital Division Statement of Operations and Deficit

Year ended March 31	2003	2002	2001	2000	1999
Expenses					
Gross salaries, wages and benefits	5,905,630	5,792,876	5,720,945	5,829,004	5,730,956
Medical and surgical supplies	512,960	387,309	394,509	501,901	462,856
Drugs and medicines	110,068	89,067	84,200	105,679	104,940
Other supplies and expenses	2,980,765	2,509,854	2,400,695	2,803,451	2,503,546
	9,509,423	8,779,106	8,600,349	9,241,035	8,802,298
Deduct					
Revenue from preferred accommodation	4,503,281	3,664,908	3,565,342	4,200,198	4,004,761
Meal recoveries	70,954	60,984	55,609	68,201	65,612
	4,574,235	3,725,892	3,620,951	4,268,399	4,070,373
Net operating expenses	4,935,188	5,053,214	4,979,398	4,972,636	4,731,925
Deduct					
Revenue from other non-Ontario Ministry of Health sources	903,764	800,318	793,508	899,213	810,208
Net Ontario Ministry of Health liability	4,031,424	4,252,896	4,185,890	4,073,423	3,921,717
Funds provided by the Ontario Ministry of Health	4,008,538	4,218,656	4,093,767	4,101,001	3,850,035
Net income (loss) for the year	(22,886)	(34,240)	(92,123)	27,578	(71,682)
Deficit, beginning of year	(537,089)	(502,849)	(410,726)	(438,304)	(366,622)
Deficit, end of year	(559,975)	(537,089)	(502,849)	(410,726)	(438,304)
Total Revenues	$9,415,583	$8,683,882	$8,452,617	$9,200,412	$8,665,004

Figure 4: The Medical Centre Clinic Division Consolidated Income Statement

As of Mar 31	2003	2002	2001	2000	1999
Revenues					
Diagnosing fees[1]	1,020,382	1,000,329	985,643	1,201,932	1,302,864
Treatment fees, Dietary Modification[2]	502,365	490,302	465,065	535,003	542,831
Treatment fees, Medication[3]	750,821	700,153	679,430	760,124	793,103
Net Billing to MOH	2,273,568	2,190,784	2,130,138	2,497,059	2,638,798
Proceeds from sale of Land Acreages	523,000	623,050	0	0	123,075
Donations	39,800	35,025	34,043	45,035	56,008
Rent — Filming	95,621	93,452	76,500	104,298	113,973
Net Revenue	2,931,989	2,942,311	2,240,681	2,646,392	2,931,854
Expenses					
Gross salaries, wages and benefits	1,340,983	1,300,657	1,356,786	1,403,289	1,450,364
Medical and surgical supplies	301,231	287,009	277,345	320,854	330,674
Drugs and medications	468,025	450,643	432,763	473,026	500,021
Other supplies and expenses					
Net Expenses	2,110,239	2,038,309	2,066,894	2,197,169	2,281,059
Net Profit (Loss)	$ 821,750	$ 904,002	$ 173,787	$ 449,223	$ 650,795

[1,2,3]Billed to Ontario Ministry of Health

The administration and management teams are consistently trying to recruit new physicians, nurses and other staff members because of the shortages predicted for the future. They must begin recruiting and training the employees to sustain the high performance and competitive advantage in the hospital in the long term.

The administrative department is also concerned about the budget and costs to finance the hospital. They need to know how much funding will be received from the Ontario Ministry of Health and other shareholders in order to operate the facility. Rules and regulations must be followed because the health sector is highly regulated by both the federal and provincial governments. The administration and management team must ensure that The Medical Centre operates efficiently and consistently.

The nursing staff consists of 39 full-time and 18 part-time employees. They are distributed among the hospital, operating room, laboratory and central supply. Each organizational unit has its own supervisor. The nurses at The Medical Centre perform services that are not replicated in a general hospital setting. A low nurse-to-patient ratio offers more individualized attention to each patient. The major part of the nurses' work is spent providing counselling to the clients/ patients to ensure that they are comfortable with the prescribed treatment.

The nurses have sought more job autonomy in their work. They do not want to perform repetitive tasks on a daily basis, but seek more variety in their job routine and higher salaries. The nurses are also concerned about the treatment and high quality of health care services that each client/patient receives at the hospital. To ensure that the patients receive a high quality of patient care, nurses receive performance appraisals from their supervisors annually. This helps to benchmark their performance with their competitors.

There are 18 full-time surgeons, 12 part-time surgeons and two anaesthetists at The Medical Centre. These physicians play a vital role at The Medical Centre. They are directly responsible for patient care and treatment. In order to ensure the effective health care delivery service of The Medical Centre, physicians evaluate whether the patient is healthy enough to undergo surgery and if sufficient equipment and technological supplies are available to perform the surgery. The physicians must carefully and systematically follow The Medical Centre protocol. This method has proven to be effective for over 30 years at The Centre demonstrating a 98 percent success rate in the treatment of gallbladder diseases.

As employees of the Centre, physicians are also concerned about their benefits package, salary and job security. Status is another important aspect for the physicians. Their status depends upon the success rate of their surgical skills and the positive reputation of the hospital. In order to continue the positive standing of The Medical Centre, physicians can only perform surgical procedures outlined by The Medical Centre protocol. In other institutions, ingenuity is applauded; however, at The Medical Centre, physicians must refrain from being "creative" and concentrate on the proven method of health care at the Centre.

The government plays a dual role at The Medical Centre. It is an independent governing body, mandated to ensure the five principles of health insurance: universality, portability, accessibility, comprehensiveness and public administration. Whether these principles are achieved through public or private or public-private partnerships, the Ontario Ministry of Health requires that patients receive quality health care in a timely fashion.

The Ontario Ministry of Health is also a source of revenue, providing The Medical Centre with more than 50 percent (clinic and hospital division) of its annual budget. Currently, the Ontario Ministry of Health is under tremendous pressure to clean up backlog of patients waiting for health care and to reduce the time for patients awaiting surgical procedures. Whether the Ministry grants an increased amount of funds to either the private, public or private-public partnership hospitals, the actions of the Ministry of Health will always impact on future decisions at The Medical Centre.

Although the Ontario provincial government assumes a central role in financing the hospital, the federal government decides the allocation of health care funds. The federal government is not constitutionally required to provide money to the provincial government for health services. However, the federal government provides transfer payments to the provinces on a contingency basis. Therefore, if the federal government does not approve provincial government spending, it can refuse the transfer of funds to a province. This is an important aspect to consider. The federal government has gone on record in opposing private and public-private partnerships. The federal government is a supporter of the public health care system and free access for every Canadian citizen to the health care delivery system. This was affirmed in the Romanow Report. The Romanow Report is an example of the federal government's view of the current unacceptable health care system and its plans to change the system to one that supports more public health care facilities.

The provincial governments in Canada are left in a difficult position. They are under pressure to alleviate backlogs and waiting times; however, if the provincial governments engage in an increased number of ventures with private health care companies, they risk not receiving additional financial aid from the federal government. Therefore, additional investment in new public-private partnerships or current private facilities may lead to a shortage of health care funds and services in provinces.

The clients or patients of the hospital have demonstrated a great interest, support and loyalty towards The Medical Centre. The calm and homey atmosphere of the clinic that is unduplicated by any other hospital ensures patient comfort during her or his stay. The uncomplicated admission process is easy to understand and follow. The highly effective, technologically innovative surgical method ensures low risk and, quick recovery time as well, as minimum rates of recurrence of gallbladder diseases and minimum wound infection rates. The Medical Centre's clients are dedicated patients and promoters of the Centre. It is through word-of-mouth advertising by former patients that most potential patients learn about the hospital and its methods.

Clients have multiple interests in The Medical Centre. They want an effective procedure with a minimal recovery time and financial cost. They also do not want to wait for a long time for their surgical procedures. The patients also rely on the longstanding reputation of The Medical Centre. Since their treatments are guaranteed for life, patients want the clinic to be as profitable and as available for them in the future, in the event that they experience problems.

The External Environment
of the Health Care Sector

Recently, major external forces have bombarded the health care sector. In March 2003, the emergence of Severe Acute Respiratory Syndrome (SARS) has driven all Canadian hospitals to take drastic measures to prevent the cross-transference of the disease. In order to minimize the risk of infections, hospitals follow detailed clinical guidelines provided by the federal government's Health Canada to control and recommend actions for public health. The use of masks, the implementation of such procedures as the 24/7 surveillance and monitoring, the no visitation policies and other precautionary measures have resulted in the disruption of health care services. By mid-June, the Ontario government announced that $1 billion had already been spent managing the SARS outbreak. The federal government offered only $250 million to compensate the province. The provincial government rejected the offer, claiming that it was "outrageous" and insulting and would not cover the shortfall in health care costs for Toronto area hospitals.[1] Private facilities have not been affected by SARS to the same extent as general public hospitals. Nevertheless, private hospitals are still obligated to follow Ontario Ministry of Health rules and procedures.

Another significant event in the health care sector occurred in September 2002. Roy Romanow, the current Commissioner of the Royal Commission on "The Future of Health Care" issued the Romanow Report. The main objective of the Report was to "carefully examine the public health care system in this country and to recommend ways it could be made sustainable into the twenty-first century".[2]

The Romanow Report mainly focuses on funding issues between the federal and provincial governments. Other federal health reports that have impacted the health care sector include the Kirby Report and the Mazankowski Report. The report written by Senator Michael Kirby was intended to provide recommendations to improve funding and increase the involvement of the federal government in the restructuring and renewal of the health care system. The Mazankowski Report focused mainly on the province of Alberta's restructuring of the payment of health care services by Alberta's unsustainable health care system.

Another factor to consider in the external environment is the increasing trend of globalization. Globalization presents many opportunities and constraints for the Canadian health care system. The global health care market is estimated at $2 trillion annually. Canada currently supplies 2 percent of that market or approximately $40 billion.[3] Globalization has the potential of providing a company with vast monetary benefits. However, it can lead to the disruption of proper treatment as the interpretation and disputes of health care would come under the umbrella of international trade agreements. This would severely hamper Canada's ability to protect Canadian public health services and set domestic policies. Globalization also threatens the Ministries of Health's ability to recommend and implement reforms to the existing health care system. Therefore, the Ministry of Health would no longer be responsible for determining appropriate health care policies; rather multinational corporations and the World Trade Organization would set global health care policy.

There are currently 27 private hospitals and 968 general public hospitals in Canada. There is only one private hospital that specializes in the repair and treatment of gallbladders: The Medical Centre. A majority of the general hospitals have a specific department allocated to this disease. The Medical Centre is the only private hospital in the gallbladder sector. While general hospitals participate in the same treatment process as The Medical Centre, they do so without the personalized approach.

The threat of new entrants into the gallbladder sector is limited due to the amendment of the 1972 Ontario government Private Hospital Act to prevent any future growth in the private hospital sector. At the time of the amendment to the Act, approximately 100 hospitals were licensed in Ontario. From 1972 to the present, only 10 private hospitals were remaining in the province. The government has claimed that the closure of nearly 100 hospitals was due to a number of building code and fire violations. From the point of view of a new private entrant, the gallbladder sector appears to be a very attractive market. It illustrates high entry barriers, few substitute products and high demand. Despite the amendment to the 1972 Private Hospital Act, the threat of new entrants is not zero. The emergence of the public-private partnerships, as seen by Shouldice Hospital Limited and newly established health care institutions in Alberta, a private clinic can enter into an agreement with a provincial Ministry of Health and start a private-for-profit health care clinic.

The available treatments for gallbladder diseases include: dietary modifications, medications, extracorporeal biliary lithotripsy, open cholecystectomy or laparoscopic cholecystectomy. Diet is the basic factor in the treatment of gallbladder disorders.[4] There are many variations of the diet, each incorporating the use of fruit juices and mono unsaturated oils. With the elimination of fatty foods in diet, gallbladder pain may be minimized. There is even the belief that gallstones can be passed. However, in most instances, gallstones cannot be dissolved by medical treatment; the gallbladder must be removed along with the gallstones.

There are two standardized surgical repair methods: open cholecystectomy and laparoscopic cholecystectomy. The former describes the classic, traditional operation procedure that requires a large incision. The latter describes the current treatment of choice using keyhole size punctures in the abdomen. A recent technique started only 12 years ago is the laparoscopic cholecystectomy, which is a minimally invasive surgical procedure. It is now the treatment of choice in 80 to 95 percent of cases in the United States, most Western countries and most of the developed and developing countries.[5] The distinct advantages of laparoscopic cholecystectomy over the traditional open cholecystectomy include: minimum scarring, lessening the procedural time from 36 to 60 minutes in most cases and negligible post-operative pain. Patients have been known to eat after waking up from the anaesthesia and return to her or his usual work in two to three days without restrictions. Laparoscopic cholecystectomy is usually offered as the first alternative treatment if surgery is required. Open cholecystectomy is the second option.

An emerging technique has been recently developed to aid in the treatment of gallbladders with tools that are increasingly minimally invasive. The micro-laparoscopic repair involves the use of 3-mm instruments instead of the traditional 5-mm or 11-mm tools. Patients incisions are two-thirds smaller, thereby reducing pain and trauma. There is no removal of stitches. Their local physicians can check out-of-town patients. However, not all gallbladder diseases are resolved by the micro-laparoscopic cholecystectomy. Furthermore, because the instruments are so delicate, they are subject to shorter life utility and result in a recurrent expense. Presently, this method is only available in a few centres in the world. It is forecast to be the standard method within the next ten years and be available at all surgical facilities.

Gallstones occur in up to 20 percent of Canadian women and 10 percent of men by the age of 60 years.[6] Women between the ages of 20 and 60 years are three times more likely to develop gallstones than men. The incidence of gallstones is higher in certain racial groups. For example, in Canada 70 to 80 percent of the North American Native People population is affected with this disease.

With rising demands for laparoscopic repairs, the surgical waiting time for treatment has been extended to approximately 1.4 months. The widespread acceptance of the gallbladder procedure has led surgeons to apply the laparoscopic technique to broad range of other surgical procedures, including hernia repair, hysterectomy, appendectomy and lung and bowel surgery.

There is a current shortage of nurses due to the cutbacks on costs in the health care sector. Enrolment in nursing and medical schools has resulted in a "brain drain". Canadian health care workers are leaving Canada in search of better foreign opportunities offering comparable salary incentives. Demands have been made to politicians and health care professionals to invest additional funds in the health care system, not only to maintain the existing conditions, but also to ensure the future of proper health care in Canada.

The Role of 3P Partnership, Private and Public Health Care Systems

The foundation of the Canadian health care system has been based on five principles of health insurance. These are to ensure accessibility, universality, portability, comprehensiveness and public administration in the public health care system. Traditionally, these principles have been achieved through the public means. However, in the face of government's ability to build or remove barriers to entry into the health care sector, private for-profit clinics are able to aid in the achievement of these health care principles. In 1931, the Government of Ontario enacted the Private Hospital Act. This legislation enabled private for-profit clinics to deliver health care services. At the time of its enactment, there were 100 private hospitals. In 1970, The Medical Centre legally became a private hospital. In 1972, the Ontario Private Hospital Act was amended to prevent new private entrants in the Canadian health care system.

There were only 14 private hospitals remaining. At present, there are 27 private hospitals in Canada, with 10 of these facilities located in Ontario.

The private sector plays an important role in the transfer of health care services. It provides quick and effective services in order to alleviate the backlogs and waiting time and provides for a more efficient health system with a lower fixed and variable cost structure. The federal government recognizes the importance of private services and the effective delivery of health care. It has led new areas of growth within the private sector, especially in western Canada. Public-private partnerships, or "3P" Partnerships began in the 1990s with the treatment of over 10,000 people.[7] It is a relatively new practice in Canada, but it is present in other countries. For example, the United Kingdom has approximately 26 hospitals built on the "3P" Model in 2002 and another 40 hospitals are approved to be built on the "3P" Model.

The usual model is that public-private partnership hospitals are built and financed by the public sector and leased back to the private sector for a predetermined fee. The public still maintains control over determining the public needs, priority setting and other public policy elements, even though a project is carried out using a "3P" Model.[8] This unique contractual relationship between the public and private sector allows for a more resourceful and productive delivery and treatment of health care to Canadians across the country. Some of the key benefits of "3P" Partnerships are stated by the Ontario SuperBuild 2001, "A Guide to Public-Private Partnerships for Infrastructure Projects":

- Risk sharing
- Maintaining or improving service levels
- Reducing cost/improving revenue
- Accessing new sources of capital
- Accessing new or better skills
- Realizing the value of under-utilized assets
- Realizing economic development opportunities

The Role of Government Support for the Health Care Sector

In Canada, both federal and provincial governments subsidize health care. The federal government provides provincial governments with financial aid for health care services with the Canada Health and Social Transfer (CHST) payments. Figure 5 represents the state of health care costs as presented by the Minister of Finance Janet Ecker in the 2003 Ontario Budget.[9] The amount expended by the Ontario government on health care is increasing steadily. The federal government was once responsible for most of the health care costs, but an erosion of Canada Health and Social Transfer payments have placed the burden of funding more than 60 percent of health care expenses on the provincial government. She further stated, "While the total CHST funding for 2002–2003 has increased by $2.1 billion, the increase in federal transfers does not begin to make up for the loss of previous federal cutbacks."[10] The province has

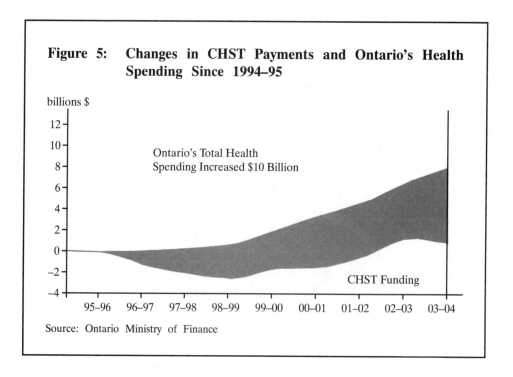

Figure 5: **Changes in CHST Payments and Ontario's Health Spending Since 1994–95**

billions $

Ontario's Total Health
Spending Increased $10 Billion

CHST Funding

95–96   96–97   97–98   98–99   99–00   00–01   01–02   02–03   03–04

Source: Ontario Ministry of Finance

increased the amount spent on health care funding by $1.9 billion, while the federal government increased its funding to Ontario by $143 million. It is obvious that the federal government does not keep up with Canadian and Ontarians' demands of health care services.[11] It is increasingly apparent that the federal government is not committed to the recommendations of the Romanow Report.

As presented by Figures 6, 7 and 8, health care is a significant part of Ontario's budget expenditures. Even though the federal government's Canada Health and Social Transfer payments represent 10 percent of the budget dollar revenue (see Figure 6), the Ontario government expends 39 percent of its revenue on health care (see Figure 7), while 47 percent of the revenue falls into health care program expenditures (see Figure 8).[12] Hospital operating expenditure by the province comprises approximately 15 percent of the total provincial operating expenditure, as seen on Figure 9. Therefore, in order to ensure sustainable health care for future generations, both federal and provincial governments are encouraged to work together.

Health care funding has steadily increased, paralleled by an increase in health care expenditures. Figure 10 illustrates the increase in Health Base Operating Spending. The Ontario Ministry of Health is planning to renew the Ontario health care system and restore public confidence in the system. As stated in the 2003 Ontario Budget, the Ontario government plans to:

• Increase the number of available health care workers
• Decrease wait times
• Increase access to technology

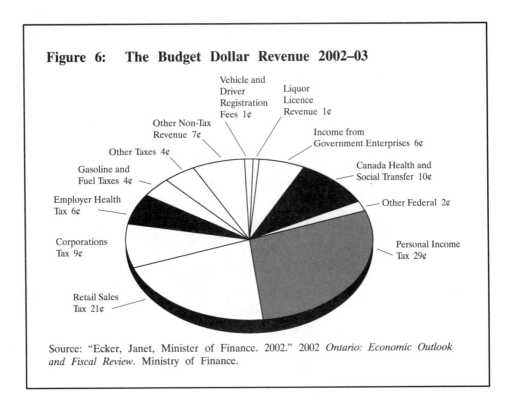

Figure 6:   The Budget Dollar Revenue 2002–03

Vehicle and Driver Registration Fees 1¢

Liquor Licence Revenue 1¢

Other Non-Tax Revenue 7¢

Income from Government Enterprises 6¢

Other Taxes 4¢

Canada Health and Social Transfer 10¢

Gasoline and Fuel Taxes 4¢

Employer Health Tax 6¢

Other Federal 2¢

Corporations Tax 9¢

Personal Income Tax 29¢

Retail Sales Tax 21¢

Source: "Ecker, Janet, Minister of Finance. 2002." 2002 *Ontario: Economic Outlook and Fiscal Review*. Ministry of Finance.

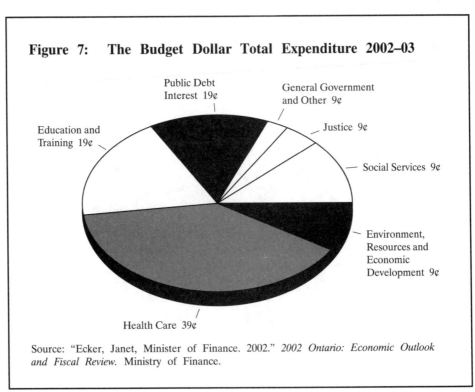

Figure 7:   The Budget Dollar Total Expenditure 2002–03

Public Debt Interest 19¢

General Government and Other 9¢

Education and Training 19¢

Justice 9¢

Social Services 9¢

Environment, Resources and Economic Development 9¢

Health Care 39¢

Source: "Ecker, Janet, Minister of Finance. 2002." *2002 Ontario: Economic Outlook and Fiscal Review*. Ministry of Finance.

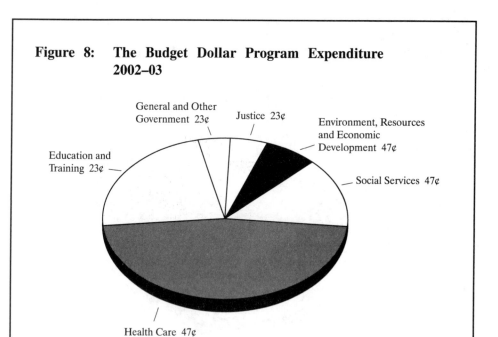

Figure 8: The Budget Dollar Program Expenditure 2002–03

General and Other Government 23¢

Justice 23¢

Environment, Resources and Economic Development 47¢

Education and Training 23¢

Social Services 47¢

Health Care 47¢

Source: "Ecker, Janet, Minister of Finance. 2002." *2002 Ontario: Economic Outlook and Fiscal Review.* Ministry of Finance.

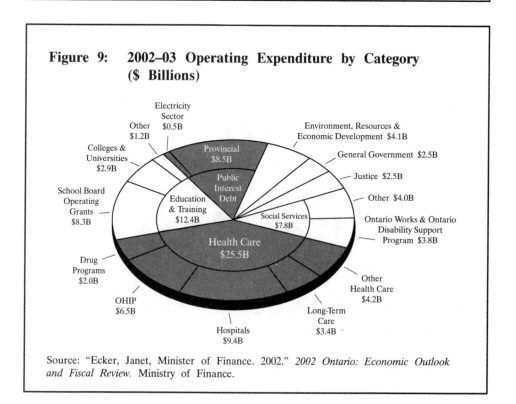

Figure 9: 2002–03 Operating Expenditure by Category ($ Billions)

Electricity Sector $0.5B

Other $1.2B

Colleges & Universities $2.9B

School Board Operating Grants $8.3B

Drug Programs $2.0B

OHIP $6.5B

Hospitals $9.4B

Provincial $8.5B

Public Interest Debt

Education & Training $12.4B

Social Services $7.8B

Health Care $25.5B

Environment, Resources & Economic Development $4.1B

General Government $2.5B

Justice $2.5B

Other $4.0B

Ontario Works & Ontario Disability Support Program $3.8B

Other Health Care $4.2B

Long-Term Care $3.4B

Source: "Ecker, Janet, Minister of Finance. 2002." *2002 Ontario: Economic Outlook and Fiscal Review.* Ministry of Finance.

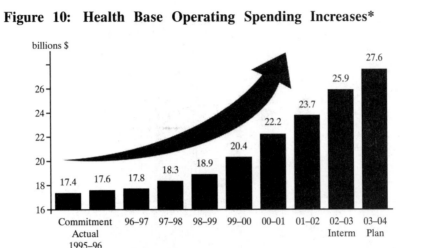

Figure 10: Health Base Operating Spending Increases*

billions $

27.6
25.9
23.7
22.2
20.4
18.9
18.3
17.8
17.6
17.4

Commitment   96–97   97–98   98–99   99–00   00–01   01–02   02–03   03–04
Actual   Interm   Plan
1995–96

*Ministry of Health and Long-Term Care base operating spending excludes capital, restructuring and major one-time costs.

- Provide better mental health services
- Ensure a stronger focus on keeping people healthy[13]

Figures 11 and 12 illustrate Ontario's Operating Expenditures and Program Expenditures for a five-year period, respectively. Health care expenditures represent a significant portion of the total provincial funding. This is increasing each year. The Ontario government plans to expend the money invested by:

- Supporting health care facilities
- Advancing primary reform
- Increasing the supply of health care professionals
- Improving access to health care services[14]

Since 1998–1999, the Ontario government has managed to increase funding to hospitals by 50 percent.[15] Figure 13 demonstrates a five-year historical operating fund gained by Ontario hospitals. Ever since 1995, the Ontario government has managed to increase the amount of funding in the health care sector by $10 billion, from $17.5 billion to a projected $27.6 billion in 2003–2004.[16]

Reports of the Federal Government on Health Care

The federal government's mission is to change the current health care system. Dissatisfied with present results, it has enlisted the services of Royal Commissions and Task Forces to ensure compliance with the five principles of health

Figure 11: Operating Expenditure by Category Per Cent of Total 1998–9 to 2002–03*

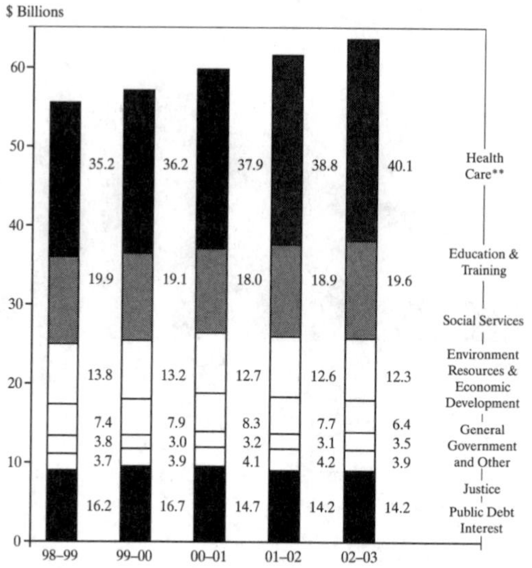

$ Billions

*As at September 30

**Includes Major One-Time Health Care Costs and Health Care Restructuring.

Source: "Ecker, Janet, Minister of Finance. 2002." *2002 Ontario: Economic Outlook and Fiscal Review.* Ministry of Finance.

insurance. Listed below are three current health care reports that have served as guiding documents for the federal government to base its decision on the future of the Canadian health care system.

The Romanow Report

The Romanow Report is the one of the most comprehensive overhauls of the health care system in 40 years. Roy Romanow, a former Premier of Saskatchewan and the current Commissioner of the Royal Commission on the Future of Health Care was appointed by the Prime Minister to examine the future of the public health care system. The primary focus of the Report was to examine the inefficiencies of the current health care system and to suggest measures that would make it efficient and effective for future generations.

It was suggested that Canada is lagging behind in the funding of health care services. However, Charts 1a and 1b below illustrate that Canada is not behind in the funding of health care. In fact, Canada ranks fifth among the 17 other countries studied by the Organization for Economic and Co-operative Development (OECD) for the most money spent on health care expenditures as a percentage of Gross Domestic Product. Canada places sixth for public health care expenditure as a percentage of Gross Domestic Product. Therefore, it can

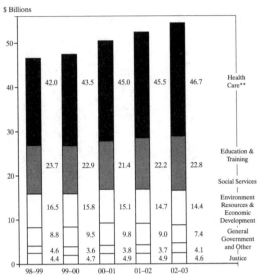

Figure 12: Program Expenditure by Category Per Cent of Total 1998–9 to 2002–03*

*As at September 30
**Includes Major One-Time Health Care Costs and Health Care Restructuring.

Source: "Ecker, Janet, Minister of Finance. 2002." *2002 Ontario: Economic Outlook and Fiscal Review.* Ministry of Finance.

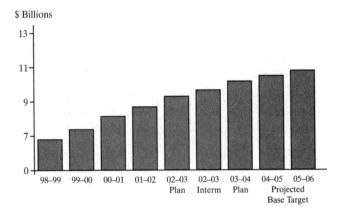

Figure 13: Program Expenditure by Category Per Cent of Total 1998–9 to 2002–03*

Note: Excludes major one-time costs.

Source: "Ecker, Janet, Minister of Finance. 2002." *2002 Ontario: Economic Outlook and Fiscal Review.* Ministry of Finance.

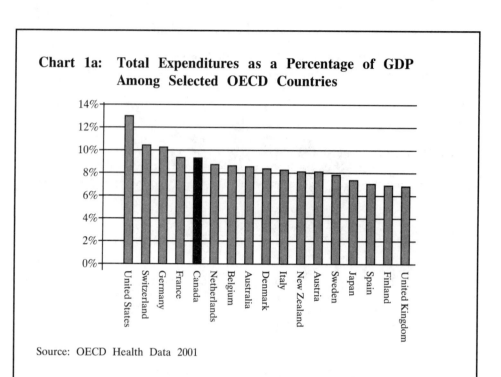

Chart 1a: Total Expenditures as a Percentage of GDP Among Selected OECD Countries

Source: OECD Health Data 2001

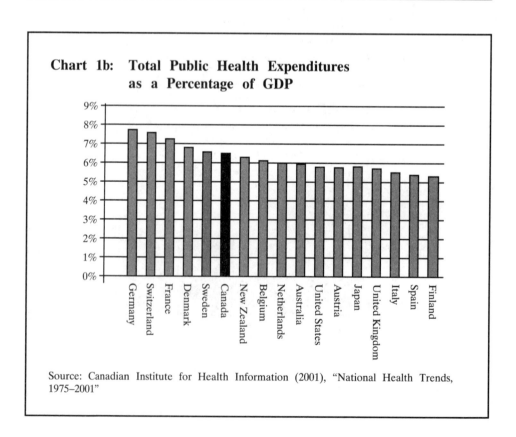

Chart 1b: Total Public Health Expenditures as a Percentage of GDP

Source: Canadian Institute for Health Information (2001), "National Health Trends, 1975–2001"

be seen that Canada is spending the same amount of money, if not more, on health care than most countries in the world.[17]

Charts 2 and 3 that indicate the amount of money spent on health care is increasing, but not at a linear pace. As a result, the amount spent on health care in previous years is not a determinant of future spending habits of government. Chart 4 shows the increased amount in health care spending with Ontario leading the way.

The Romanow Report proposes some major recommendations focused on building a mandate to recommend improvements in the public health care system. The Report further suggests that more money be transferred to the public health care system instead of to the private health care system. The reason is that "no evidence exists to show that the private health care system improves patient treatment; private clinics will erode the principle of equal access in the system."[18] The Romanow Report fails to recognize some of the significant and positive attributes of the private health care sector. These include an increase in the amount of resources, choices and competition, which, in turn, increases the amount of efficiency and effectiveness in the health care system as a result of private or public-private partnerships.

Chart 2: **Per Capita Health Expenditures — Total Health, Provincial-Territorial Health Expenditures, Hospital and Physician Services Expenditures**

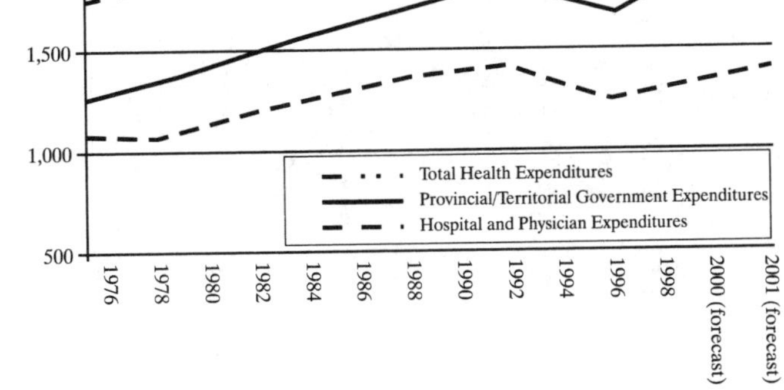

Source: Canadian Institute for Health Information (2001), "National Health Trends, 1975–2001"

Chart 3: Annual Rate of Change — Public Health Expenditures as a Percentage of GDP

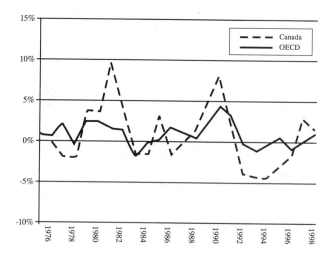

Source: Canadian Institute for Health Information (2001), "National Health Trends, 1975–2001"

Chart 4: Preliminary Provincial Government Health Expenditures as a Proportion of Provincial Government Programs (Current $)

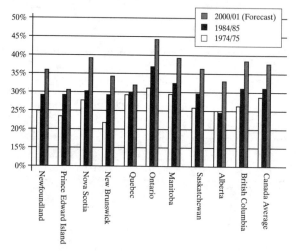

Source: Canadian Institute for Health Information (2001), "National Health Trends, 1975–2001"

An increase in the number of private or public-private partnership agreements, coupled with the increased trend of globalization could lead to damaging effects on the Canadian health care system. In order to combat any negative effects that may arise from globalization, the Romanow Report suggests:

- Prevent potential challenges to Canada's health care system by ensuring that any future reforms that are implemented are protected under the definition of "public services" and be included in international laws and trade agreements
- Reinforce Canada's right to regulate its internal health care policy
- Build an alliance with other countries, especially with members of the World Trade Organization to ensure that future international trade agreements allow for the maintenance and expansion of public health care
- The federal government should play a more prominent role in international efforts to assist developing nations in strengthening the health care system, especially in training health care providers and on public health initiatives
- Federal government and health care providers want to reduce the reliance on recruiting health care professionals from developing countries.[19]

The Report also concentrates on establishing the Health Council of Canada to help focus on the understanding of Canadian values. Other primary goals include:

- Ensuring sustainability and proper funding
- Providing top quality and accessibility to medical services for Canadians
- Ensuring leadership, collaboration and responsibility in the health care system
- Assessing benchmarks on performance
- Collecting information
- Assessing new technology[20]

The First Ministers Conference on February 5, 2003 was the first step of the Romanow Report. It concentrated on the primary health care sector, home care and catastrophic drug coverage for long-term sustainable health care provision.[21] The federal government continues with its intent to focus on building a mandate to recommend improvements in the public health care system by providing an annual report to citizens regarding what it has done during the year.[22] This will provide information on current expenditures and programs by providing a baseline against new investments, service levels and outcomes. It will also provide a benchmark for all other health care services to be measured. This will result in an increased measure of transparency and accountability to achieve public health care outcomes.

The Kirby Report

Senator Michael Kirby tabled the Kirby Report in April 2002 from the Senate Standing Committee on Social Affairs, Science and Technology. This Report was in response to the following three main areas of concern:

- The unsustainability of the current Canadian health care system given its current funding levels
- The desire for a stronger federal government role in facilitating health care restructuring and renewal
- The need to introduce incentives for all participants in the publicly funded hospitals and for the doctor system providers, institutions, government and patients to deliver, manage and use health care more efficiently.[23]

Given the fundamental realities of health care, public policy planning is required to explore additional sources of funding for health care. The Kirby Report also placed a greater emphasis on the funding debate becoming more patient-focused rather than dollar-focused.

The Senate Committee on Social Affairs, Science and Technology believed in splitting the incentives into finance, delivery and evaluation of the health care system to provide for a system that would be more patient-oriented than cost-oriented. By following this method, the patient would be able to receive the most appropriate health care in a timely fashion from a qualified provider. By separating the government-funding provider from the evaluator, the intention was to enhance transparency and accountability in the use of public funds. Based on the trends expressed by the Kirby Report, the stated recommendations are for the increase in funds in health care technology, health infrastructure, health research and human resource planning in health care.

The Mazankowski Report

The Honourable Donald Mazankowski, Chair of the Premier's Advisory Council on Health was responsible for A Framework for Reform for the Alberta health care system. The Council strongly suggested that without fundamental changes in how Albertans pay for health services, the current health care system was not sustainable.[24]

Current problems in the Alberta provincial government health care system include:

(a) Spending on health is crowding out other important areas, such as education, infrastructure, social services and security.
(b) Despite recent funding increases, access to health care continues to be a problem.
(c) Support of many expensive new treatments is difficult to assess.
(d) Limited revenue sources (provincial and federal taxes) have resulted in rationing of services, which further leads to an un-serviced segment of the population.

Overall demands for health care services are increasing, as are aggregate costs. Waiting times continue to grow and so are health provider shortages, as workers are not motivated and are demoralized and pessimistic about the future. If the health spending trends do not change, by 2008 the Alberta provincial government could be spending half of its provincial program budget on health care alone.[25]

The Mazankowski Report recommendations for reform include:

- Promotion of healthy living as opposed to treatment — By being proactive, Albertans can refocus on education and various lifestyle factors that affect their health.
- Adjust the focus of the system to the "customer" — Reduce waiting times by introducing centralized booking, posting waiting times for selected procedures on a website and allowing people to access services from any physician or hospital.
- Redefine "comprehensiveness" — Make some choices about what services are covered by the system and which services the patient should cover. An expert panel would decide which services should be covered and establish criteria by which each treatment would be judged.
- Invest in technology and establish an electronic health record — Lack of good information is a serious impediment in Alberta's health system. It creates difficulty in tracking the results and gathering of evidence about whether a new approach is effective or not.
- Reconfigure the health system and encourage choice, competition and accountability — This should be accomplished by setting clear and distinct responsibilities for government and regional health authorities, setting performance targets, encouraging health authorities to establish service agreements with a wide variety of providers, and to develop centres of specialization, and encouraging an innovative blend of public, private and not-for-profit health organizations to deliver health care services.
- Diversify the revenue stream — If Alberta continues to depend only on provincial and federal government revenues to support health care, options will be severely limited. If Alberta opens itself up to other sources, it will have the opportunity to improve access, expand its health care services and realize the potential of new techniques and treatments.
- Put better incentives in place for attracting and retaining health providers — This could be accomplished by encouraging regional health authorities to develop and implement strategic initiatives to improve workforce morale, to increase work satisfaction and improve the retention of the workforce.
- Make quality the top priority — Set standards, measure results and hold people accountable for achieving better outcomes. Alberta needs to establish a permanent "Outcomes Commission" with a responsibility of measuring outcomes, tracking progress and reporting results to achieve goals and targets on a long-term basis.
- Recognize and promote Alberta's health sector as a dynamic and powerful asset to the provincial economy — Currently, the health sector is viewed as a cost centre, but with new sources of revenue, the health sector has the potential to make significant contributions to Alberta's economy and help expand the province's reputation.

Summary of Reports

All of the reports urge a greater emphasis on staying healthy, with emphasis on preventive health care. They seek to embrace broader determinants of health and reorganization of the primary health care sector. The difference between the reports lies in the role of the state versus the role of the individual in terms of financial responsibility and scope of service available to the average Canadian citizen. The Romanow and Kirby Reports focus on an increased amount of federal government involvement in the health care sector. The Mazankowski Report focuses on opening up the health care sector to the public and private domains. The implications of each Report are yet to be experienced.

Tables 1 and 2 indicate that health care spending is increasing. Real spending per capita is growing faster today than at any other time during the 1980s.[26] This increase in health care spending is necessary in order to provide an appropriate level of care in response to current population needs and to be sustainable in the long term. There is an upward pressure on the Canadian health care system to improve its costs in order to sufficiently accommodate growing public expectations, close gaps in the health care safety net and provide restructuring solutions. Table 3 illustrates the increase in Canadian health care costs.

The federal government has to significantly increase its financial support over the years and gain new forms of funding in order for the current level of health care to continue for future generations. This may require changes that can only be achieved by establishing an appropriate system of incentives:

Table 1:   2002 Ontario Economic Outlook and Fiscal Review — Operating Expenditures

$ millions	Actual 98–99	Actual 99–00	Actual 00–01	Actual 01–02	Outlook 02–03
Health and Long-Term Care	18,867	20,373	22,184	23,713	25,452
Major One-Time Health Care Costs	639	286	487	197	—

Table 2:   2002 Ontario Economic Outlook and Fiscal Review — Gross Capital Expenditures

$ millions	Actual 98–99	Actual 99–00	Actual 00–01	Actual 01–02	Outlook 02–03
Health and Long-Term Care	187	338	182	205	342
Major One-Time Health Care Costs	—	1,004	140	—	—

Table 3:   Pressures to Increase Health Care Spending

• **Drug costs:** $14.7 billion was spent in 2000, up 9 percent from the previous year.

• **New Technology:** $6 billion to $10 billion is required to achieve the full implementation of a Canadian health infrastructure.

• **Ageing Population:** By 2010, seniors will equal 14.6 percent, which will represent approximately $1 billion, increase in health care costs.

• **Human Resources:** According to Mazankowski approximately 75 percent of health care spending is directed towards salary costs of health care workers, which could be attributed to salary increases in the health care system.

• **Health Research:** $40 billion (US) is spent by G-7 countries for health care research in 2002.

• **Growing Public Expectation:** as stated by the Romanow Report.

• **Gaps in the Health Care Safety Net:** Especially home care and drugs require more of an investment to close the gap.

• To introduce constructive competition among health care institutions.
• To encourage more efficient use of all health care providers.
• To encourage more appropriate utilization of health care technology.
• To put in place a structure that will result in better ongoing evaluation of the system as a whole and of health care outcomes in particular.
• To ensure that patients receive timely and quality care.
• To encourage patients to make cost-effective use of publicly funded health care services.

Implementation Results of Past Reports

The concern for health care has resulted in both federal and provincial governments annually using task forces that take on the challenge of diagnosing the problems in the health care system. Annually, the process results in recommending possible remedies that would enable the system to fulfil the expectations of its citizens and to be sustainable in the long term for future citizens. The ramifications of each report and each restructuring recommendation are yet to be seen.

The Mazankowski and Kirby Reports have not resulted in any significant changes in the health care sector. Both reports stress general themes for additional funding to be invested in the health care sector for a sustainable health care system. Also, there is the emphasis on refocusing on the patient to provide timely and effective treatment and increased use of technology and utilizing it to its full advantage as well as transparency and accountability in the health care sector. The Romanow Report also echoes these theses in its recommendations for improvements and restructuring. However, unlike the Mazankowski and Kirby Reports, the Romanow Report has received the most publication and media attention. It is the most current and the most extensive study of the health care system. Its effects have resulted in the First Ministers Conference, a demonstration of the federal government's intent to pursue reform and restoration of the Canadian health care system. The federal government may be keen on seeing the health care sector revamped, as illustrated by the numerous commissions and reports that it has produced; however, its lack of action in restructuring of the health care system is also evident. "Past governments knew for years that health care needed to be reorganized, but no one did anything about it; investments in long-term care were neglected, waiting lists were too long and essential diagnostic equipment were virtually inaccessible to millions of Ontarians."[27] The implications of these reports have yet to be acted upon.

Strategic Alternatives

The Managing Director of The Medical Centre has studied and reviewed the external forces and internal stakeholders of the Centre. At the next Board of Directors meeting, she will propose the following strategic alternatives:

Contract Surgery

There is increasing demand for cataract surgeries due to the aging baby boomers. Hospitals are unable to support the backlog of all cataract surgeries. These outstanding cases will be distributed to The Medical Centre. In launching this alternative, The Medical Centre will form a partnership with the Toronto Western Hospital.

Toronto Western Hospital is located in the heart of Toronto on Bathurst and Dundas Streets. It has over 100 years of history and is known for the technological advancement used in the care of its patients. Toronto Western Hospital is also a teaching hospital affiliated with the Faculty of Medicine, University of Toronto, and a partner in the University Health Network with Toronto General Hospital and Princess Margaret Hospital, which are also teaching hospitals affiliated with the Faculty of Medicine, University of Toronto. Toronto Western Hospital has approximately 320,000 patient visits annually. Over the last year, the hospital performed 13,156 surgeries. The hospital is only equipped with 272 beds and with the various types of surgeries associated with a general hospital, patients experience long waiting times for surgeries, with the wait for cataract surgery being one of the longest.

Because of the insufficient surgical time and resource allocation to cataract surgeries, a long waiting list and a big demand have been created. Currently, the median wait time for cataract surgeries is approximately 12 weeks and about 20,000 patients in Ontario are currently waiting this surgical procedure. Cataract surgery takes approximately 45 minutes and is performed as outpatient elective surgery. Cataract surgery must be performed by ophthalmologists. The cost of this surgical procedure is approximately $450, but the reimbursement from the government is usually a little more than $1,000. Therefore, this is a very attractive market because of the high profit margin.

If The Medical Centre decides to select this alternative, it will need to modify its current facilities in order to equip itself. Changes need to be made to the current accommodation facilities because patients will not be advised to stay overnight. Moreover, The Medical Centre will need to recruit an ophthalmologist and acquire new equipment for cataract surgeries. The costs associated with such modifications and purchase of new equipment would be a one-time investment of approximately $2 million. Furthermore, ophthalmologists are leaving public hospitals and entering the private sector due to insufficient operating time allocations in public hospitals.

Laparoscopic Hernia Surgeries

As of this date, the backlog of hernia patients is unmanageable in public hospitals. The government has put much effort into private hospitals and provide funding for those hospitals in a lump sum amount to reimburse them for their services. The situation is similar at The Medical Centre, as similar relationships have been established with government.

The approximate wait time for hernia surgeries is one month and over 35,000 patients are currently waiting. The cost associated with laparoscopic hernia repair is approximately $650 and government reimbursement is approximately $1,250.

In North America, more than ten private hospitals treat hernia diseases. Thus, competition is quite fierce and many of these hospitals have been established for a long time.

Shouldice Hospital Limited is in Thornhill, Ontario, located 30 kilometres north of Toronto. Shouldice Hospital is a not-for-profit hospital that specializes solely in hernia repairs. Dr. Edward Earle Shouldice first established Shouldice Hospital in 1945. For almost 60 years, it has built up a world reputation for quality and cost efficient health care. This was achieved by adapting the *Shouldice Method* of performing hernia operations. This proven effective and cost efficient method attracted many people from all over the world. Consequently, patients have strong brand loyalty when it comes to hernia repair. Although, the hospital solely performs open-incision hernia repairs, patients still find it to be their number one choice (including over methods such as laparoscopic).

With this alternative, hernia surgeries will be performed solely with the laparoscopic methods, rather than open incision. However, the recruitment of physicians is effortless as regular physicians can be trained in a period of no longer than half a year to be qualified as specialized hernia surgeons.

The current facility at The Medical Centre would not need any alterations, as the only requirement would be to recruit new physicians or train the current surgeons to be specialized hernia surgeons. The same equipment used for gallbladder surgeries can be used for hernia surgeries. The initial investment in this new sector would be less than $500,000.

Expansion of the Current Facility

The current facility at The Medical Centre can support up to approximately 15,000 cases of gallbladder treatments annually. It is believed that a total demand of 500,000 cases of gallbladder treatment exists annually in the North American market. Among those, The Medical Centre would absorb 5 percent of the cases.

Expansion of the current facility requires that the Centre build an additional wing(s) to accommodate the excess demand. Aside from the physical building, the Centre also has to recruit more employees and acquire more equipment. Undertaking this alternative will require the Centre to concisely plan the amount of space needed to accommodate the expected demand and the appropriate number of employees and new equipment. The cost of adding another wing to the hospital is approximately $500,000 and an additional two wings would be an additional 50 percent of the initial $500,000. This cost includes the additional costs for recruitment and equipment.

Franchise

The success of the Centre has brought about the consideration of franchising the current name, The Medical Centre. The current demand of gallbladder treatments opened an opportunity for more repair centres in North America. Like many successful franchisers — McDonald's, Second Cup, etc. The Medical Centre is confident that it can be one in the future.

Franchising requires more management involvement and, therefore, it is necessary that The Medical Centre build a stronger management team. Recruitment of more executive members or internal promotions of current executive members can achieve this.

An annual franchising commission from one franchisee would generate approximately $2 million from a hospital the same size as The Medical Centre. However, the Centre would be responsible for marketing and brand management. One significant challenge to franchising would be the difficulty of quality control among franchisees. Any negative outcomes originating from the franchisees would have adverse effects on The Medical Centre.

In the initial stage, The Medical Centre would only consider franchising in North America with the intention of obtaining better quality monitoring due to the proximity of location. International franchising is a possibility for the future.

Expansion to the United States

The United States has a population of more than 300 million; this is ten times the Canadian population. Hence, The Medical Centre believes that the United

States is a country with high demand potentials. Although more competition exists in the United States, the larger demand for gallbladder treatments due to the larger population compensates this negative factor. To expand to the United States requires that the company establish a facility in the United States.

A private hospital in the United States, similar in size to The Medical Centre, treats approximately 15,000 cases of gallbladder diseases annually. Furthermore, demand statistics indicate that the sector can still support another 20 to 30 hospitals, similar in size to The Medical Centre.

The positive statistics indicate a possibility for The Medical Centre, but the cost of building the facility and all associated costs in order to begin servicing are worrisome. A rough estimate of the start-up cost is approximately $5 million. Obtaining a loan from a financial institution can raise the capital.

The health care system in the United States is quite different from the Canadian system. In Canada, legitimate citizens and residents benefit from "free" health care. Any employed or unemployed person who holds an Ontario Health Insurance Protection (OHIP) card is eligible to utilize the health care facilities and services at no cost. This is due to the heavier income taxes levied on Canadian citizens and, as a result, health care is funded by the public. However, this is not true in the United States, as a lower percentage of income tax is levied. In the United States, only those employed are covered by public health insurance. Health care expenditures are held liable to those patients that are unemployed. In Figure 14, the percentages represent the population distribution of health insurance coverage insurance status. Medicaid and Medicare are health insurance programs that assist to the elderly and poor.

The average cost per case of operation is approximately $750 US. The government usually compensates for the surgery and medications, but the patients pay for semi-private and private accommodation. The hospital can probably

Figure 14: Population Distribution by Insurance Status

United States	Percent
Employer	58%
Individual	5%
Medicaid	11%
Medicare	12%
Uninsured	15%

Source: Population Distribution by Insurance Status, State Data 2000–2001, U.S. 2001. The Henry J. Kaiser Family Foundation: State Health Facts Online "Personal Health Care Expenditures, 1998". Retrieved from the World Wide Web on July 7, 2003 at: http://www.statehealthfacts.kff.org/cgi-bin/healthfacts.cgi?action=compare&category= Health+Coverage+%26+Uninsured&subcategory=Insurance+Status&topic=Distribution+ by+Insurance+Status

collect an average of $1,100 per case. This amount is receivable from the government and the patient.

Figure 15 indicates the number of hospitals in the United States. As we can see, private hospitals represent 15% of the total number of hospitals in the United States. Of the 754 private hospitals, approximately 24 of them specialize in gallbladder surgeries. Furthermore, Figures 16 and 17 display the hospital-adjusted expenses per inpatient day and personal health care expenditures respectively. Based on the statistics provided by these two figures, The Medical Centre can further deduce the optimal location to situate the facility.

Figure 15: United States Hospital Ownership

	US (# of Hospitals)	US (%)
Non-Profit Hospitals	2,998	64%
For-Profit Hospitals	754	15%
State/Local Government Hospitals	1,156	24%
Total	4,908	100%

Source: "Hospital Ownership". The Henry J. Kaiser Family Foundation: State Health Facts Online. Retrieved from the World Wide Web on July 7, 2003 at http://www.statehealthfacts.kff.org/cgi-binhealthfacts.cgi?action=compare&category=Providers+%26+Service+Use&subcatecorgy=Hospitals&topic=Ownership

Figure 16: Hospital Adjusted Expenses per Inpatient Day

Rank		Adjusted Expenses per Inpatient Day
	United States	NA
1	Alaska	$1,756
2	District of Columbia	$1,745
3	Washington	$1,595
4	Oregon	$1,548
5	California	$1,527
6	Massachusetts	$1,493
7	Utah	$1,473
8	Maryland	$1,422
9	Nevada	$1,410
10	New Jersey	$1,409

Source: "Hospital Adjusted Expenses per Inpatient Day, FY2001". The Henry J. Kaiser Family Foundation: State Health Facts Online. Retrieved from the World Wide Web on July 7, 2003 at: http://www.statehealthfacts.kff.org/cgi-bin/healthfacts.cgi?action=compare&category=Health+Costs+%26+Budgets&subcategory=Hospital+Expenses&topic=Adjusted+Expenses+per+Inpatient+Day

Figure 17: Personal Health Care Expenditures

Rank		Total Expenditures
	United States	$1,015,988,000,000
1	California	$ 112,008,000,000
2	New York	$ 85,531,000,000
3	Texas	$ 67,117,000,000
4	Florida	$ 60,344,000,000
5	Pennsylvania	$ 50,027,000,000
6	Illinois	$ 45,780,000,000
7	Ohio	$ 42,001,000,000
8	Michigan	$ 36,090,000,000
9	New Jersey	$ 34,057,000,000
10	Massachusetts	$ 29,566,000,000

Source: The Henry J. Kaiser Family Foundation: State Health Facts Online "Personal Health Care Expenditures, 1998". Retrieved from the World Wide Web on July 7, 2003 at: http://www.statehealthfacts.kff.org/cgi-bin/healthfacts.cgi?action=compare&category=Health+Costs+%26+Budgets&subcategory=Personal+Health+Care+Expenditures&topic=Total+Expenditures&link_category=&link_subcategory=&link_topic=&datatype=&printerfriendly=0&viewas=&showregions=0&sortby=area#sorttop

Notes

1. (www.toronto.cbc.ca/regional/servlet/View?filename=to_sars20030620)
2. (www.healthcarecommission/ca/Suite247/Common/GetMedia WO.asp?MediaID=401&Filename=Commission_Interim_Report.pdf)
3. (www.healthcarecommission/ca/Suite247/Common/GetMedia WO.asp?MediaID=401&Filename=Commission_Interim_Report.pdf)
4. (www.healthlibrary.com/reading/ncure/chap49.html)
5. (www.geocities.com/mydoc01/medinfo-gallbladder.html)
6. (www.cag-acg.org/patinfo/gall_bladder.htm)
7. (www.canada.com/national/features/healthcare/story.html?id={455713BA-4726-8E79-2942326C9606})
8. (www.globeandmail.com/serlet/ArticleNews/PEstory/TGAM/20030106/COWILSON/Health/health/health_temp/1/1/3)
9. "Ecker, Janet, Minister of Finance. 2002." 2002 Ontario: Economic Outlook and Fiscal Review." *Ministry of Finance*. Queen's Printer for Ontario 2002: Toronto.
10. (www.gov.on.ca/FIN/english/budeng.htm)
11. (www.gov.on.ca/FIN/english/budeng.htm)
12. (www.gov.on.ca/FIN/english/budeng.htm)
13. (www.gov.on.ca/FIN/english/budeng.htm)
14. (www.gov.on.ca/FIN/english/budeng.htm)
15. (www.gov.on.ca/FIN/english/budeng.htm)
16. (www.gov.on.ca/FIN/english/budeng.htm)
17. (www.hc-sc.gc.ca/english/pdf/care/romanow_e.pdf)

18. (www.healthcarecommission.ca/Suite247/Common/GetMedia_
     WO.asp?MediaID=401&Filename=Commission_Interim_Report.pdf)
19. (www.healthcarecommission.ca/Suite247/Common/GetMedia_
     WO.asp?MediaID=401&Filename=Commission_Interim_Report.pdf)
20. (www.healthcarecommission.ca/Suite247/Common/GetMedia_
     WO.asp?MediaID=401&Filename=Commission_Interim_Report.pdf
21. (www.healthservices.gov.bc.ca/bchealthcare/publications/health_accord.pdf)
22. (www.healthservices.gov.bc.ca/bchealthcare/publications/health_accord.pdf)
23. (www.oma.org/pcomm/kirby.htm)
24. (www.gov.ab.ca/home/health_first/documents_maz_report.cfm)
25. (www.gov.ab.ca/home/health_first/documents_maz_report.cfm)
26. (www.gov.on.ca/FIN/english/budeng.htm)
27. (www.gov.on.ca/FIN/english/budeng.htm)

The Book Publishing Industry Development Program

An Evaluation

Department of Canadian Heritage

*This report was prepared by the Universalia in December 1998 for the Department of Heritage Canada and has been implemented as policy to assist Canadian book publishers.**

2. The Canadian-Owned Book Publishing Industry

2.1 Introduction

The Canadian-owned book publishing industry reflects both a cultural dimension and an industrial dimension. This chapter has been organized to reflect these two interrelated aspects. It provides a brief historical overview of the two aspects and reviews the involvement of government in the industry. The chapter then describes the industry today, its quality, economic status and its

* From Department of Canadian Heritage, Corporate Review Branch, *Evaluation of the Book Publishing Industry Development Program December 1998.* pp. 9–20. Source of Information: Canadian Heritage — Corporate Review Branch. Reproduced with the permission of the Minister of Public Works and Government Services Canada, 2003.

problems. These topics provide the context required to examine and evaluate the BPIDP in Chapter 3...

2.2 Historical Development of Book Publishing in Canada

2.2.1 Overview of the Cultural Dimension of Development

Finding 1: Since the 1950s the Canadian Book Publishing Industry has moved from a cultural wasteland lacking in authors and literature to a diverse, culturally rich fertile area of growth that defines Canada to its citizens and the rest of the world.

Cultural diversity is as important as biodiversity.
Sheila Copps, Quill and Quire, Aug. 1998.

In Northrop Frye's words, "In an immature society culture is an import; for a mature one it is a native manufacture which eventually becomes an export." In less than four decades, Canada has moved from an immature to a mature society, with a homegrown culture that is in demand beyond our borders. Nowhere is this more evident than in the writing and publishing produced within the country. In the words of Rowland Lorimer (1996), director of the Canadian Centre for Studies in Publishing at Simon Fraser University, "The cultural achievement of the industry has been spectacular. Canadian creative genius and sensibility and Canadian commentary and analysis are recognized worldwide — just the opposite of thirty year ago" (p. 3).

Perhaps the most notable change in Canadian writing in the past decade has been the development of regional and multicultural voices, writers telling their own specific stories, but telling them in a way that communicates universally.

Among the first who were successful at reaching a world-wide audience for stories about Canadian life, in such regions as Francophone Manitoba or small town Ontario, were Gabrielle Roy and Alice Munro. Now there exists a whole chorus of voices from throughout the country. Kevin Major evokes the outports in his books for young readers. Antonine Maillet and David Adams Richards give us their unique pictures of life in New Brunswick. Poets Anne Szumigalski and Lorna Crozier, and playwrights Ken Mitchell and Sharon Pollock, speak to us from the prairies, and George Woodcock has dissected all of Canadian literature from British Columbia. From the more densely populated Quebec and Ontario, the voices are too numerous to begin to classify, but among the strongest have been Michel Tremblay, Anne Hebert, Mordecai Richler, Marie-Claire Blais, Timothy Findley, Farley Mowat, and Janet Lunn and Tim Wynne-Jones with their stories for young readers.

Perhaps the most exciting development in recent years has been the new voices of multicultural Canada. These writers would probably not have found publishers two decades ago — especially when writing about their homelands. Now Canadian readers and Canadian publishers have adopted them as our own and enabled these authors to reach audiences around the world. Wayson Choy and Joy Kogawa allow us to experience something of Chinese and Japanese life in Canada, while Olive Senior and Dany Laferrier write from a Caribbean background. Neil Bissoondath, Shyam Selvadurai and Rohinton Mistry make their stories of India our stories. Michael Ondaatje discovers a new mythic Canada, while Nino Ricci introduces us to the Italian experience.

Federal and provincial programs, such as Writers-in-Residence and Writers in the Schools, have introduced students to many of these Canadian voices, and have made the idea of life as a writer a possibility for budding talent. More recently, the Wired Writers Program allows students to find a writer mentor through the Internet, and get advice and encouragement from a professional.

> Short story writer Merna Summers on first reading *Who has Seen the Wind* by W.O. Mitchell in grade 11: "I had not known it was allowed to write books about places like Saskatchewan and Alberta. I already knew...that I wanted to be a writer when I grew up, but I had always supposed that I would have to find a way of moving to some place like Connecticut or California to do it."
>
> Globe and Mail, Feb. 26, 1998.

The Public Lending Right Commission, through funding from the Department of Canadian Heritage, pays writers, translators and illustrators for the use of their books in public libraries. The program was launched in 1986 and in the first year, $2.75 million was distributed to 4,553 authors for 16,584 titles. Eleven years later, in 1997, a 267% increase in the number of eligible books resulted in $8 million being dispersed to 11,151 authors for 44,360 titles. This signals the success of Canadian writing. When taken together with the acknowledged quality of Canadian books in recent years it is something to be proud of.

> European and USA readers...like the diversity of multicultural Canadian writing, be it the setting or influences of the book or even the writer's background.... It's ironic to see that just as years of cultural subsidy for writers are paying off with all this success, this infrastructure is being dismantled.
>
> Dennis Duffy, Professor of Literature at the University of Toronto, *Globe and Mail*, Aug. 18, 1997.

2.2.2 Overview of the Industrial Dimension of Development

Finding 2: Since the 1950s, in industrial terms, Canadian Book Publishing has moved from a cottage industry to an important aspect of the Canadian economy resulting from the continual growth in the number and size of Canadian-owned publishers, industry revenues, and export sales.

The publishing industry was virtually non-existent prior to 1950 (see section 2.2.3). The growth in Canadian publishing in the past decade is shown in Exhibit 2.1. Both the number of firms and their size has increased over this pe-

Department of Canadian Heritage

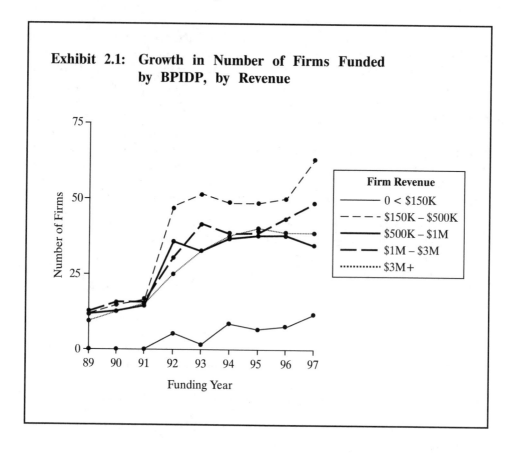

Exhibit 2.1: Growth in Number of Firms Funded by BPIDP, by Revenue

Number of Firms

Funding Year

Firm Revenue
— 0 < $150K
--- $150K – $500K
— $500K – $1M
– – $1M – $3M
···· $3M+

riod. In some cases, firms have clearly moved from one size category to the next.

Finding 3: Preservation of the diversity of Canadian publishers contrasts with experience in the United States and at the same time opens a window of comparative advantage for Canadian publishers in increasingly global markets.

So far Canada has escaped the unfortunate experience of the United States. There, independently owned publishers, at one time, showed a diversity similar to that in Canada. Over the past decade or two, most of these previously editorially driven houses have been bought by large international conglomerates such as Bert[el]smann, Pearson, or the Murdoch empire. The objective of these internationally owned companies was to concentrate on popular best-sellers (cookbooks, diet books, light fiction) and drop what is referred to as mid-list books — influential titles containing challenging ideas, or books of cultural interest.

The real problem with Globalization is that it is actually Americanization.

A Focus Group Comment.

364

The consolidation of American publishing houses as the giants (many of them German companies such as Bertelsmann) buy up the competition has not been healthy for their industry. Over the past few years, Canadian book exports to the USA have seen exceptional growth. Some publishers note that, with few American publishers remaining in the mid-range, serious titles with sales that are considered by the giant companies to be too low to be profitable are no longer being published. For Canadian publishers these sales — of five to ten thousand — are a tremendous addition to the home market, and Canadian titles in niche areas, such as Native studies and children's books, have been doing very well.

> In the global market, Canada is a micro market. Now that Bertelsmann has bought Random House, there is a theory that Germany will control book publishing world wide, and the USA will control book selling. But the jury is out on whether the superstores, over time, will expand the market. In the meantime, they destroy the good independent infrastructure.
>
> A Publisher Interview.

A number of factors, some planned and some based on luck, have seen Canadian publishing maintain a balanced approach concerning what gets published, with books both serious and popular finding their niche.

Finding 4: About a third of firms receiving BPIDP funding have moved upward in PCH's revenue classification since they entered the program.

Currently the BPIDP programs categorizes firms into five financial brackets for reporting purposes. These categories are: $0–149,000, $150,000–500,000, $500,000–1 million, $1 million–3 million and $3 million+. Firms are placed into these categories based on the net profit they report on their annual application. While these five categories do not represent equal units of measurement (a restriction in this type of analysis), it is possible to examine the "churn" in the recipient pool by identifying the amount of movement between these five categories. Exhibit 2.2 illustrates that 56% of the firms have remained in the same financial category from the time they entered the program until present. (Obviously, for firms in the $3 million+ category, positive movement cannot be represented). An additional 34% of the firms moved into a higher revenue category, 28% moving up one level, 6% moving up two levels. For the two firms, for example, that went from the $500,000–1 million to the $3 million+ category, this represents substantial growth in firm revenues. Ten percent of the recipient pool moved into a lower financial category.

2.2.3 Overview of Government Involvement in the Industry

Finding 5: Development of the Canadian Book Publishing Industry over the past 30 years has been a cooperative venture between Canadian-owned publishers and the Government of Canada.

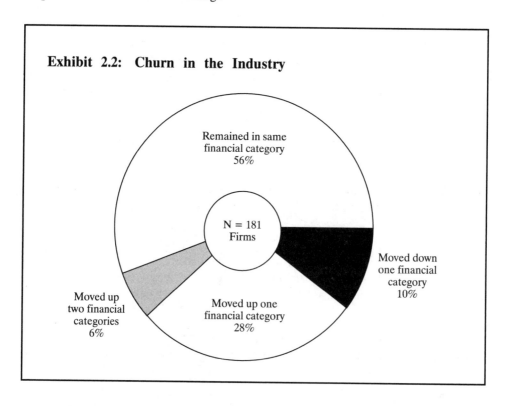

Exhibit 2.2: Churn in the Industry

Remained in same
financial category
56%

N = 181
Firms

Moved down
one financial
category
10%

Moved up
two financial
categories
6%

Moved up one
financial category
28%

The industry rests on the creative talents of the many writers working in communities from coast to coast, while the development of the industry which has allowed them to flourish during this period is the result of a unique collaboration between the book publishers and government. This is particularly true at the federal level where, in a carefully woven network of programs developed over the years in collaboration with the industry, the government has helped the industry survive and grow. The following is a brief historical synopsis of how this came to be:

1951: The Royal Commission on National Development in the Arts, Letters and Sciences. The Commission (commonly referred to as the Massey-Levesque Commission) was surprised to hear the statistics on the number of Canadian books published each year at the time of their meetings; in 1948–1950, only 70–80 were reported in all. Their report portrayed the country as "hostile or at least indifferent to the writer". "Is it true then," they asked, "that we are a people without a literature?" The key recommendation of the report was to establish a council for the arts to support cultural activity at all levels.

1957: The Canada Council for the Arts. It took six years, but the founding of an arts council to "foster and promote the study and enjoyment of, and the production of works in the arts, humanities and social sciences" was to have an enormous effect on the future of the country and its artists. The Council began at once, in a small way, to include grants to book publishers based on an assessment of individual literary titles.

1960s: A Literary Flowering. A new generation of fiction writers began to make their mark during this decade: in English Canada, Mordecai Richler, Margaret Laurence, Hugh Hood, and Margaret Atwood. In Quebec, where only 27 novels had been published in 1961, there were 100 by 1974, including major works by Gérard Bissette, Marie-Claire Blais, Hubert Aquin, Jacques Godbout, and Gabrielle Roy. In both languages this burst of creativity was stimulated by the emergence of the small, literary publishing houses that began operating in the late sixties.

1970s: A Critical Decade. Canadian publishing in the seventies was in the throes of severe difficulties. Old established Canadian firms were in danger of going under or being sold to foreign interests. Although a number of exciting new houses had been created, they too were struggling to survive. English publishing was then still highly centralized in Ontario, and the province reacted quickly with a Royal Commission which led to the establishment of a loan program just in time to rescue McClelland and Stewart and a number of smaller houses.

1972–79: Major Programs of Support for Publishers. The federal government responded to the publishing crisis in a number of ways. First, it introduced a major program for publishers to be administered by the Canada Council and the Social Sciences and Humanities Research Councils. Then, towards the end of the decade, the federal government undertook a direct, comprehensive policy review through the Department of the Secretary of State, (later, the Department of Communications in 1980 and finally the Department of Canadian Heritage in 1993) which included providing significant support for the sale and marketing of Canadian books, and for structural and professional improvements within the industry.

1982: Report of the Federal Cultural Policy Review Committee. Federal concern during this period resulted in the first comprehensive review of cultural policy and institutions since the Massey-Lévesque Commission. In what is commonly referred to as the Applebaum/Hébert Report, the committee took note of the "marked flowering of artistic achievement" that had occurred between 1952 and 1982. Among its recommendations it advocated increased funding for book publishing and for the development of the structure of the book industry, as well as programs to ensure writers would receive payment for the use of their books in libraries and for the photocopying of their work.

1980s: A Time of Consolidation and Development. Throughout the seventies and eighties, with the realization that Canadian book publishers lacked the kind of network needed to support a mature industry, there begin to spring up a number of organizations: l'Association des [é]diteurs [c]anadiens; Association of Canadian Publishers; Conseil Supérieur du Livre in Quebec; the Literary Press Group; l'Union des Écriv[ai]ns; Canadian Writers' Union; Canadian Book Information Book Centre; Book and Periodical Development Council, Children's Book Centre; Communication-jeunesse; and many others. In addition a number of programs such as Cataloguing-in-Publication and the Public Lending Right Commission were initiated.

For writers and publishers it was a time of rapid artistic development with which the market did not keep pace. The period was one of consolidation in which a number of major publishing houses underwent significant changes: Peter Martin Associates, House of Anansi, and Clarke Irwin all folded into Stoddart Books, Hurtig Publishers and Lester & Orpen Dennys went out of business. By the middle of the nineties, Boston Mills Press, Macfarlane Walter and Ross, and Cormorant Books had also become owned or partly owned by Stoddart, and Tundra Books had been bought by McClelland & Stewart.

At the same time, the government and the publishers worked together to adjust the industrial support programs so that they responded more directly to the needs of the industry itself.

1990s: Roller Coaster Funding. The sudden and sweeping cuts to programs both federal and provincial in the mid-nineties were devastating to book publishers, threatening fewer new Canadian books and increased difficulties for beginning writers. Book publishers were innovative in coping with these unanticipated cuts. They responded by reducing staff, narrowing lists, increasing cooperation and amalgamation, targeting foreign sales, and diversifying their activities. Major projects were put aside until better times. With renewal of programs underway towards the end of the decade, publishers are beginning to feel that they can now attend to the new challenges of a new century.

> Canadian publishers say they will publish fewer new writers, fewer reference books, and a lot less drama and poetry this year in an effort to keep up with the deep reductions in federal and provincial grant money. Many have already laid off staff, some have decided to forego the spring season altogether, and others are teetering near bankruptcy and are seeking new investors or mergers with larger houses.
>
> *Quill & Quire*, January, 1996.

In describing the economic side of Canadian publishing one of the most frequently used adjectives is "fragile", because, in spite of its evident success over the past decades, the industry continues to operate on a shoestring. Although most companies, with government assistance as part of the mix, are now showing small profits, any significant change on the business side of the enterprise can spell catastrophe.

2.3   Current Status of Book Publishing in Canada
2.3.1   Cultural Significance

Finding 6: Canadian books are acknowledged as a major cultural success around the world.

The written word illustrates perfectly the Canadian situation ... it is an area of astonishing success. Some 20 writers — Anglophone and

Francophone — have won large publics outside Canada. This involves translations into a dozen or so languages and healthy sales.... Many foreigners, when they think of Canada, think first of these writers and books.

John Ralston Saul, *Position Paper on Culture and Foreign Policy*, 1994.

One indication of the success of books by Canadians abroad lies in reports of some of the most successful titles that have found audiences throughout the world. The following are taken from articles recently published:

- As the *Globe and Mail* of March 21, 1997 revealed, in Britain, "Can Lit is hot." It is now rare to see the famed Booker shortlist without a Canadian writer's name on it (both Margaret Atwood's Alias Grace and Rohinton M[i]stry's A Fine Balance made it in 1996.). The reputations of writers such as Margaret Atwood, Rohinton Mistry, and Michael Ondaatje have opened the doors to newer novelists including Gail Anderson-Dargatz and Ann-Marie MacDonald. During the second week of February of this year, novels by Anne Michaels, Margaret Atwood, and Kathy Reichs appeared as 12th, 20th, and 23rd on The Times of London's bestseller list.

- In recent years France has awarded its highest civil honor, the Chevalier des Arts et Lettres, to Jane Urquhart, Margaret Atwood, Michael Ondaatje, and John Ralston Saul. The books of novelists Timothy Findley and David Homel are now just as popular there as in Canada.

- In Italy, Canadian writers such as Marie-Claire Blais, Sandra Birdsell, and Monique Proulx are the subject of special newspaper and magazine stories, and are widely studied at universities. John Ralston Saul's Voltaire's Bastards was recently on the Italian bestseller list.

- In Germany, where Farley Mowat's books have found their biggest market anywhere, the interest in Canadian writers is intense. Writing about the Frankfurt Book Fair in the book industry's Quill & Quire last December, the reporter referred to "the apparently insatiable appetite among German publishers for Canadian fiction."

- Rights to Anne Michael[s'] Fugitive Pieces have been sold in at least 25 countries. It was awarded Britain's Orange Prize for fiction last year, but its biggest success has been in Germany where more than 40,000 copies were sold within a few months of publication. "In almost no time, apparently," wrote critic Robert Fulford, "*Fugitive Pieces* will be at home all over the world."

- The highly successful Franklin series of books for children (by Paulette Bourgeois and Brenda Clark, published by Kids Can Press) has sold worldwide, is the subject of a CD-ROM, has a series of toys created from its characters and has been made into a TV series for the Family Channel and CBS by the Canadian company Nelvana.

Carol Shield's *The Stone Diary* was winner of the Pulitzer Prize and the National Book Critic's Circle Award in the USA Her latest novel *Larry's Party* just won the British Orange prize — the second year a Canadian has been so honored.

Maclean's, 1 June 98.

> At least five universities [In China] offer Canadian literature courses, and books by everyone from Susanna Moodie to Michael Ondaatje are available in Chinese translation.
>
> *Globe and Mail*, February 28, 1998.

The list could go on. Without Canadian publishers, most of these writers would never have been published — many of them were first published by one of the smaller literary presses found across the country. In the *Globe and Mail* of August 18, 1997, Toronto literary agent Beverley Slopen notes, "Good books are not written in a vacuum. They don't get written if there is no publishing infrastructure." She attributes this international success to the cultivation of an enthusiastic audience in Canada. "And it's the publishers who create this audience," she says, praising the federal support that has helped to make this happen.

In the case of many of these highly successful titles, the sales figures do not show up on Canadian publishers' balance sheets, since the rights are handled by the writer's agent. In spite of this, publisher[s'] direct export sales have continued to grow significantly. For the total industry, Statistics Canada reported a 172% overall increase in book exports from Canada from $93 million in 1990 to $254 million in 1996.

Finding 7: The industry is active in all major genres; however, the economic viability varies greatly among genres.

The BPIDP and the Canada Council both give publishing assistance to book publishers but they do so on a different basis and thus to a somewhat different group of publishers. Those in the Council's programs but not in the BPIDP tend to be smaller, more literary publishers, or presses in their first few years before they have reached the required sales level for the BPIDP. Since the Council's programs (which cover essentially all Canadian publishers with the exception of educational publishers) are based on title grants, they have been able to collect a broad range of information specific to costs and sales by genre. Exhibits 2.3 and 2.4 give a picture of the change in the number of new, Canadian-authored titles, by genre, published by companies in the Canada Council's Block Grant program between 1985 and 1997.

Non-Fiction

By far the most titles published by Canadian publishers fall into the category of non-fiction. So successful have books of history, biography, and current affairs been in recent years that it is difficult to remember that, only a few decades ago, Canadians had a tendency to believe that we were a country without interesting heroes and heroines, and with little history worth recounting. Now fascinating books about explorers, settlers, and political figures are readily available; as are local, regional and national histories. This fall alone, biographies with subjects ranging from Nicole Brossard to Craig K[ie]lburger, and from Bill Reid to Maude Barlow will appear; along with current affairs titles commemorating such subjects as the devastating Quebec ice storm, the death of hockey and a season of opera.

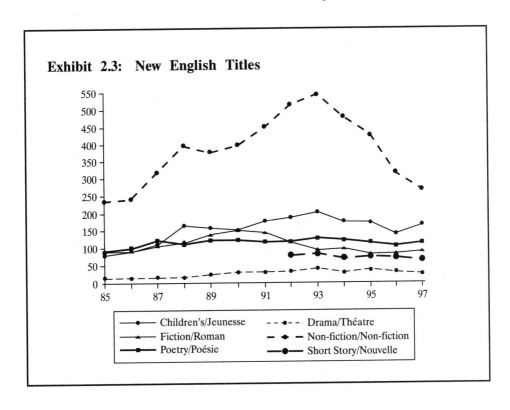

Exhibit 2.3: New English Titles

Children's/Jeunesse — Drama/Théatre
Fiction/Roman — Non-fiction/Non-fiction
Poetry/Poésie — Short Story/Nouvelle

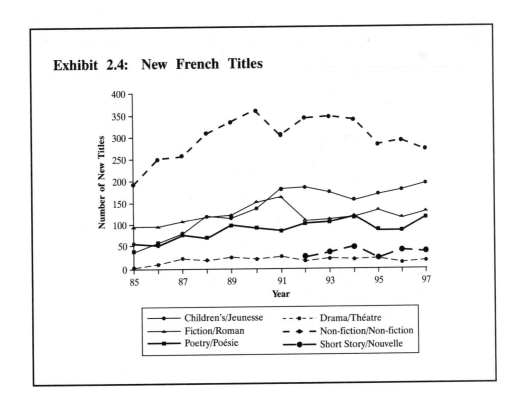

Exhibit 2.4: New French Titles

Children's/Jeunesse — Drama/Théatre
Fiction/Roman — Non-fiction/Non-fiction
Poetry/Poésie — Short Story/Nouvelle

Our contemporary Canadian literature, both English and French, reflects many of the tensions of our often embattled present-day Canada...the public's encounter with those words, painful, exciting, transforming, is an essential experience for bringing change, for instilling reflection, for creating perspective. That is reason enough for Canadians to take pains that the words will continue to be our own, that our books will reflect what we are both in reality and in our most trenchant dreams.

> Tom Henighan. *Ideas of North: A Guide to Canadian Arts and Culture*. Vancouver: Raincoast, 1997.

The number of titles published increased dramatically between 1985 and 1992, with a subsequent drop between then and 1997 which can be attributed to cuts in funding at that time. (All genres experienced a drop between 1993 and 1997 with the exception of poetry which costs the least to produce. Non-fiction, as the most costly, dropped most severely.) And while all English language genres dropped in numbers, French language titles actually increased for fiction and children's books. The increase in titles during this period did not hurt sales of each. On the contrary, sales per title increased as well, with average titles selling 2,037 copies — an increase of 28% over the seven year period.

Unfortunately, in spite of the fact that list prices increased by 44% for both French and English books in this category, average deficits after two years of sales also increased by 33%.

Fiction

As noted previously, this is a period of intense interest in Canadian fiction abroad — an interest that would have been impossible without the excitement our fiction writers have engendered at home. Canadians are reading more Canadian novels: average sales increased by 25% during the period under consideration and this was the only category in which sales did not drop when the GST came into force. These figures fail to tell the whole story, however. What has really changed has been the significant number of Canadian books of fiction that have become best sellers, remaining on the lists for months, and making their authors household names — recent writers such as Ann-Marie Macdonald and Andre Alexis, and writers at the height of their careers such as Marie-Claire Blais and Guy Vanderhaeghe. Their success depends not only on the creative strength of the writers, but on the financial ability of the publishers to take advantage of this interest by increasing advertising and making more copies available.

Successful though it has been, Canadian fiction requires investment. Almost all of the Canadian stars started ou[t] with small print runs of books of poetry or short stories that sold only in the hundreds. On average, all books of fiction published in 1992 required an investment over income of $8,236 ($10,232 for English titles and $6,694 for French).

Poetry

In Canada the average sale of a book of poems in 1991 was 514 copies.... In the USA, with an English-speaking population 10 times the size of Canada's, a book of poetry sells only an average 1,200 copies.... In Britain, with a population triple ours, average sales are also 1,200.

Judy Stoffman, *Toronto Star*, Jan. 1995.

Canadians are among the most enthusiastic poetry-readers in the world. Unfortunately this does not convert into very large sales. Considered the most literary of creative writing, poetry is also, in many ways, the most difficult to sell. Long the subject internationally of articles such as "the death of poetry", it continues to find a small but dependable audience. Many of its sales are made at public readings given by the authors. The distilled language of the very best of our poets becomes an integral part of the way we understand ourselves and our country. Canadian sales of poetry stand up with the best in the world on a per capita basis.

Most books of poetry are published by small literary presses (82% of the titles come from publishers with sales of less than $250,000). And many of our most famous novelists (Margaret Atwood, Michael Ondaatje) started their writing careers as poets.

Interestingly, the highest deficits on books of poetry are experienced by the largest publishers, illustrating the effect of the free labour well known to be a significant factor for small literary presses.

Drama

Books of plays are the smallest category of titles reported on statistically by the Council. They have fairly low sales as well — about 700 copies a year — but their importance is greater than such a figure would indicate. It is the availability of Canadian plays in published form that often leads to their production in the theater, as well as their study in schools. The number of plays published in French has increased from only 6 in 1985 to 20 in 1992, an interest mirrored in the relatively large number of these that have been translated and published in English — notably the work of Michel Tremblay.

Children's Books

The brightest light in Canadian publishing has, for some years now, been books for children. Canada Council statistics show average sales for children's books of 7,990 for 1992, up 67% from 1985, and considerably higher than average sales of adult fiction and non-fiction during the same period.

In quality too, books for children excel. They are respected worldwide and are an important presence at the Bologna Book Fair, the most important international venue for children's books; so much so that Canada was asked to mount a special exhibition of Canadian children's book illustration over the previous decade in 1990.

Authors Sheila Egoff and Judith Saltsman in *The New Republic of Childhood* (Toronto: Oxford, 1990) credit government support with being the prime influence in bringing about the rapid growth of Canadian children's book publishing in the eighties, which fostered so many admirable works of literature and art. "It took such government intervention," they wrote, "to prove that this relatively small and individualistic society ... does not need to accept a situation in which foreign imports determine the cultural development of its children."

2.3.2 Present Characteristics of Book Publishing as an Industry

Finding 8: Canadian-owned publishing houses range from one person micro-enterprises to multi-million dollar conglomerates resulting in a diverse industry representative of Canada and Canadian values.

The Canadian aim, of both publishers and government, has been to encourage diversity in writing. The result has been a wide range of publishing companies — small and large — operating in all regions of the country, with individual houses specializing in every aspect of writing, aiming at differing tastes and interests, and representing the multicultural nature of the country.

The BPIDP Aid to Publishers component includes publishers from every province in the country, from one in P.E.I. (Ragweed Press) to 81 French and English houses in Quebec. It includes educational presses from small (Fernwood Publishing) to large (Canadian Publishing); university presses from Les Presses de l'Université Laval to University of British Columbia Press; literary presses such as Turnstone Press in Manitoba, Nuit Blanche Éditeur in Quebec and Talon Books in B.C.; publishers of books for children such as Annick Press and Éditions de la courte échelle; publishers who concentrate on books about their own regions such as Harbour Publishing in B.C. and Boston Mills in Ontario; publishers of plays (Blizzard in Manitoba); and publishers of native materials such as Pemmican in Manitoba.

In addition to this range of publishers and interests, two specific areas deserve additional attention: 1) the recent development of presses specializing in Aboriginal interests, and 2) the difficulties faced by Canadian-owned educational presses, particularly in English-language publishing.

One of the positive developments in recent years has been the increase in Aboriginal publishing. The arts and history of Native peoples in Canada has long been an important element in Canadian books, from such standbys as *The Canadian Indian* by Fraser Symington, and *Natives and Newcomers* by Bruce Trigger to more recent titles such as *Women of the North* or *The Architecture of Douglas Cardinal*. There are now a number of companies organized and run by Native entrepreneurs with programs devoted to the work of Aboriginal writers, books such as *Stories of the Round Allowance People* published by Theytus Books and *No End of Grief: Indian Residential Schools in Canada* published by Pemmican Publications. Although small in size, these two publishers have received BPIDP support since 1993–1994 and 1992–1993 respectively, and they bring a new perspective to the stories of the First Nations. Smaller similar presses too are in the development stage, including Nortext Multimedia (although not a Native-owned press) publishing school books in Native languages of the Arctic. In Quebec no Aboriginal presses as such exist, but publishers there are taking an increasing interest in the writing of their Native authors.

Many of these presses are members of the newly formed Organization of Aboriginal-controlled Publishers.

The picture for Canadian textbook publishing is much less encouraging. In this category, huge capital investment is required; for instance, it is not unusual for American publishers to spend $35 million to develop a new textbook series. The results can be significantly profitable, but few Canadian companies have the assets that would enable them to enter the field, and no government programs approach this level of funding. In English Canada the field is dominated by American companies, with a few small Canadian companies, such as Between the Lines and Fernwood Books, carving out niches in the university market, and Gage Educational Publishing providing a strong presence at the elementary and high school level. In Quebec, Canadian-owned companies are much more active, but here too, foreign-owned firms have budgets that enable them to control about half the market. No positive changes in this situation are on the immediate horizon, and the recent decision by the Ontario government to no longer insist that authors of their textbooks be Canadian is discouraging.

Finding 9: Publishing is active in both French and English and is carried out in every region of the country.

The bulk of the publishing industry has always been centered in Ontario and Quebec. However, the 1960s and 1970s saw an increase in the number and type of presses in every region, and publishing now relates more closely to the population across the country. This regional growth of publishers has had a number of important benefits. Some are economic. Publishing companies in provinces such as Alberta and B.C. stimulate a whole range of activities around them, including work for freelancers, designers, typesetters and printers, in addition to their own staff. In a cultural sense they seek out material that would be overlooked by larger companies in the densely populated centre of the country. They are aware of what readers in, and visitors to, their regions want to know, and are therefore in a position to encourage the creation of a whole range of material on history, geography, or social problems that may otherwise go untapped. These works in turn lead to other material, specialized and general, that becomes a part of the country's special story. It would be no exaggeration to say that specialized regional titles have an [e]ffect on tourism, creating a new interest in the province or region.

The influence of regional publishers on writers is just as significant. As Merna Summers makes clear in the quote in Finding 1, when no writers, publishers or books relate closely to one's own world, young writers see no possibility of a future in writing or they assume, as she first did, that to be a writer meant leaving home and creating stories about the 'real' world. This was the situation for most writers throughout Canada in the forties and fifties. Morley Callaghan, Mavis Gallant, Mordecai Richler, and many others felt forced to leave the country to do their work. Their early writing reflects this, and some never did tell their own stories about their own home.

During the period under consideration in this evaluation, the number of firms eligible for BPIDP, by language and region, has remained constant. French-language publishing, considering the significantly smaller size of the population, is remarkably similar in size and range of publishers, to that of English. The following exhibits give a picture of where the publishers are, across the country, as well as give a comparison of the range of publishers working in French and English.

Publishers in the BPIDP program, when compared linguistically, are comparable in size (Exhibit 2.5). It is interesting to note that a higher percentage of French-language firms fall into the largest category of companies — those with sales of over $3 million. When examining the number of firms by region, according to size of revenue (Exhibit 2.6), the most striking observation is that the majority of the firms (French and English) fall within the $500,000 to $1 million revenue bracket. BPIDP recipients, of varying size, are located in each region, with the exception of the Maritimes which lacks publishers in the smallest and largest categories.

Publishers in the BPIDP program are asked to record their sales according to three categories: trade, educational or scholarly. The BPIDP then categorizes the publishers by their largest sales market. Publishers with significant sales in two or three of the markets are included in 'Hybrid'. For this reason, scholarly presses may seem under represented in this exhibit for they are absorbed in the hybrid section (Exhibit 2.7).

Finding 10: The purchase of Canadian books is fueled by Canadians who average 4.4 hours of book reading per week and international audiences with their increasing appetite for our award winning authors and children's books.

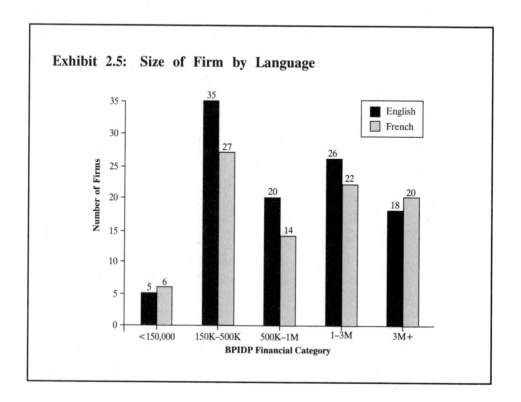

Exhibit 2.5: Size of Firm by Language

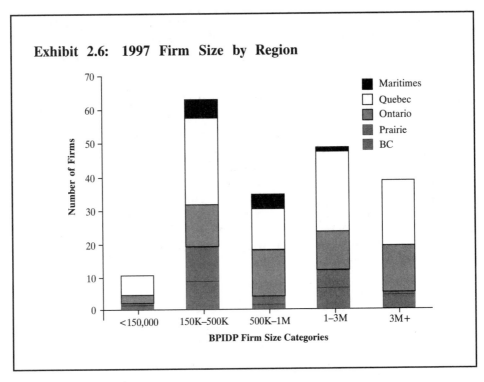

Exhibit 2.6: 1997 Firm Size by Region

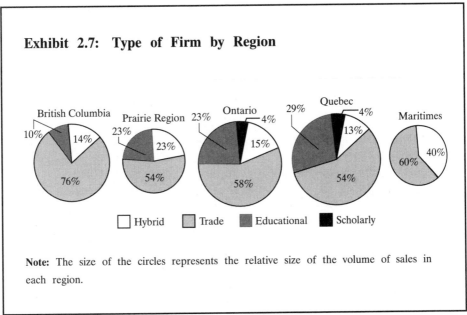

Exhibit 2.7: Type of Firm by Region

Note: The size of the circles represents the relative size of the volume of sales in each region.

Canadians have become a reading public and book reading is now a major leisure-time activity. According to Statistics Canada, 44% of the Canadian population had read at least one book in the week prior to the survey (General

Social Survey, 1992). In the Reading in Canada Study (Statistics Canada, 1991), Canadians reported spending 4.4 hours a week reading books and said they had purchased six books over the previous three months, at an average cost of $12.00.

Canadian writers and publishers have been highly successful at reaching this reading audience with significant cultural titles. For instance, sales of books of poetry and fiction by Canadians, when compared with that of other countries, show a higher penetration of the market. Average sales of Canadian poetry in English in 1992, the last date for which figures are available, were 436 (514 in 1991). In Holland, a country with about the same population has average sales of about 350 for their poetry. In the United States, a country with well over ten times our English population, poetry sales average only 1,000 to 2,000 copies — far from ten times the sale of Canadian poetry. Average sales for poetry in French at 314 copies in 1992 and 462 in 1991 are even more admirable. Similar comparisons can be made for other literary genres.

Federal Government's Industrial Strategy to Regional Economic Disparities

An Historical Overview

Diane Jurkowski

379-396

Canadian federal and provincial governments have been preoccupied with developing a regional industrial strategy. Industrial strategy can be said to refer to any attempt by government to apply a coherent and consistent set of policies that are designed to improve the performance of the economy. The idea is of particular concern in those regions of Canada suffering from regional economic disparities: in particular, high unemployment, slow or no growth and loss of industry. These policies are frequently directed at the manufacturing sector. But an industrial strategy can also focus on the performance of a number of other sectors in the economy, ranging from resource production to manufacturing to services sectors. Industrial strategies have been oriented towards correcting imbalance in the economy's performance and involve the assumption by government of a prominent role in facilitating or effecting economic change. Sometimes, the means deployed are either direct or indirect government interventions in the marketplace.

Although the debate about industrial strategy is recent, the use of government powers to shape the economy is not new. The National Policy of Sir John A. Macdonald in the late nineteenth century can be credited as a major effort to build an integrated national economy through tariff protection, the construction of the transcontinental railways and the encouragement of immigration to settle western Canada. Each of these initiatives complemented the others to develop a national framework for development. The intention was to encourage

379

manufacturing in central Canada through the use of tariffs. Creating a wheat-based agricultural economy in western Canada through settlement policies expanded markets for the manufactured goods. The western wheat economy, in turn, provided the agricultural exports needed to support the new western population and to pay for eastern manufactured goods. A transcontinental railway tied all this economic activity together. The politicians of the time were concerned that if political means were not used to promote the emergence of a national transcontinental economy, Canada's future as an independent country would be seriously compromised.

In more recent times, external forces have also prompted the interest in industrial policy, most importantly by international trade. At the end of World War II, Canada emerged as a middle power both militarily and politically. Canada's economic strengths lay in low-value added resource exports, principally with the United States and in the expansion of manufacturing, primarily through foreign-owned subsidiaries oriented towards domestic, as opposed to export, markets. By the early 1960s, the manufacturing sector was under pressure. Europe had fully recovered from war and was expanding its industrial base. The United States dominated the international trading system. While international demand for traditional resource products, such as pulp and paper and minerals was still strong among Canada's industrialized trading partners, international trade in manufactured goods became more competitive and the manufacturing sector began to experience increasing difficulties. This resulted in a national debate about the future prospects of the Canadian economy, including the issue of whether Canada would revert to its former status as a resource producer or whether it would succeed in expanding its manufacturing base.

The federal government's approach to the question of industrial policy has externalized the major elements of liberalization of trade. Canada was a strong supporter of the principles of the General Agreement on Tariffs and Trade (GATT). In the mid-1960s, the Canada-United States Automotive Products Agreement legitimized a modified bilateral sectoral free trade agreement in the North American automobile manufacturing industry. This allowed the major North American car manufacturers to import and export cars free of duty provided that certain minimum production levels were maintained in both countries. In the late 1980s and early 1990s, successive federal governments aimed to establish first, Canada-United States Free Trade Agreement and then the North American Free Trade Agreement (NAFTA). The Free Trade Agreements are based on a desire to ensure access for Canadian industry to an increasingly protectionist United States market. This was seen by some of as providing, through increased trade and competition, a powerful instrument for restructuring the Canadian economy and making it more efficient and competitive.

Continentalization and globalization have a major effect on the Canadian economy. It is difficult to precisely measure benefits and threats to regional aspirations and national sovereignty. Supporters of the Free Trade Agreements argue that these are simply economic agreements with no impact on politics and culture. They are simply tools to enhance the economic well-being and strength of the nation. Nor is it possible to measure the extent to which Canadians have voluntarily and willingly absorbed American values. But certainly economic ties, proximity, population distribution and the fact that a majority of Canadians share a language with Americans means that the United States' values are easily transmitted and willingly accepted by Canadians.

The challenge of successive governments is to prevent the balkanization of the Canadian economy on regional lines and, at the same time, develop a national industrial strategy that is sensitive to regional aspirations. A dichotomy appears between government's attempt to develop a national industrial strategy and the challenge of ameliorating regional and/or provincial aspirations. Attention becomes focussed on a number of salient characteristics in Canadian society that are part of its regional diversity. The characteristics include geographic, economic, cultural and historic elements.

These characteristics can be examined as a reflection of federalism. The study of federalism has been dominated by a recurring theme in Canada, that is, the divisions of economic, constitutional and political power of the central and regional governments. In a federal system, the division of political powers questions the extent to which federal and regional governments can intervene effectively in economic and social issues as both authorities are constrained. Federalism operates to preserve the *status quo*, and militates against the formulation of appropriate policy responses to changes. Thus, federalism acts as a barrier to change. For example, in Canada, federalism first slowed the expansion of the welfare state, and then, in the 1980s, it operated to protect social programs from those who would dismantle them.

Geographic differences stemming from long distances and scattered population persist even after modern technology and transportation has reduced the barriers of distance itself. This simple geographic distance appears to be one factor accounting for the great sense of remoteness and isolation from Ottawa found in British Columbia, Alberta, Newfoundland and even Toronto.

There are more important regional influences. Great differences among regions in Canada persist in wealth, income and the nature of regional economies. These differences have led to great variations in outlook with, for example, regional economic interests battling for freer trade and protectionism. These regional differences remain a prime source of conflict.

Coupled with economic influences are differences in historical tradition between the various regions. Ontario, Quebec, the Maritimes and British Columbia had an independent existence as British colonies long before Confederation. Many of the distinctive characteristics engendered by the pre-Confederation experience have persisted, especially in Quebec and the Maritimes. As a result, it appears reasonable to conceive of Canada as a collection of regional cultures rather than one "national" culture.

The most salient and historically most important basis of social diversity in Canada, of course, is the existence of what is commonly referred to as the two cultures of, respectively, the French and English Canadas. The French-Canadian minority is highly distinctive in its language, history, religion and culture. It is heavily concentrated in Quebec, with its significant French-speaking origin. However, there are French-speaking Canadians in northern Ontario, Manitoba and the Maritimes. There is a tendency to ignore the political implications of differences in the regional subculture of English-speaking Canada. With Canadian politicians attentive to the bilingual and bicultural nature of Canada, there has been ignorance of the Celtic and Acadian cultures of Atlantic Canada and the Aboriginal culture of Canada's First People.

Quebec is the home of a distinct culture. It has an autonomous educational system, a code of Civil Law and a distinctive pattern of institutional and associational life. In addition, it has its own political voice, the provincial government. Moreover, French-Canadians have been imperfectly integrated into national life. English-Canadian and United States industries have dominated the province of Quebec's economy. French-English relations have been a central problem facing the Canadian system since before Confederation. A major reason for federation itself was the political deadlock, that developed when what are now Ontario and Quebec were combined in the united province of Canada. Since 1867 there have been recurrent conflicts between French and English Canadians over language and religious rights, education and conscription during both World Wars. The "crisis" of federalism has often focussed on Quebec's relationship with Confederation. This was the case in the 1960s and 1970s as well as for the two Quebec sovereignty referenda held in the 1980s and 1990s.

These widespread regional differences in Canada result in regional and ethnic cleavages. Regionalism is partly a function of patterns of immigration and settlement. Different groups of people have settled in different parts of the country at various times in Canadian history. This reinforces the regional nature of the Canadian culture. Immigration and settlement are also functions of economics. Regional differences in economic activity have contributed to the development of regional Canadian cultures. Harold Innis was among the earliest proponents of this view. In the industrialized heartland of Quebec and Ontario, the occupational mix of working populations is quite different from that found in the Prairies, the Atlantic provinces and British Columbia, all of these latter regions relying heavily on resource-based economic activities or staples. Economies that over rely on staples are subject to the fluctuations of world demand for their products, a factor over which there is no control. Regional economies fluctuate in terms of prosperity at different rates and times depending upon the particular economic base of the region. While some regions enjoy prosperity, other falter, aggravating regional differences.

Regional dynamics has an impact on Canadian business and government. First, there is the raw fact of electoral arithmetic. About 60 percent of Canada's population live in two provinces, which means that the votes in the region carry enormous electoral weight. They can make or break a national elected government. This is also the heartland of Canada's manufacturing, commercial and financial centres. It is often stated that elections are over before voters in western Canada have even had a chance to cast their ballots. This can only contribute to feelings of alienation and powerlessness among Canadians in regions outside Quebec and Ontario, who have few reasons to believe that their influence will be felt nationally, that their influence can be exercised effectively or that their interests will ever occupy a place of importance on the national agenda, except in a regional political party sitting in Opposition in the House of Commons.

Another argument that aggravates rather than moderates regional divisions is based on Canada's style of federal Parliamentary institution. It is particularly seen in Canada's Senate, which is an appointed legislative body and appears largely ineffectual in the main task for which it was created: that is, representing regional interests. The Senate's representative role has decreased, creating the feeling among regional populations that they are without an effective champion in Ottawa's halls of power.

To some extent regional economic disparities have narrowed over the decades. Some regions, such as Newfoundland and Alberta, appear to have gained relative to the national average as a result of the oil and natural gas resource sectors. Other regions such as British Columbia and parts of Atlantic Canada have fallen below the national average because of soft wood lumber and fishing sectors experiencing problems. In the absence of opportunities for economic growth, regions experience high unemployment rates and few opportunities for development.

A region's capacity to grow and develop depends on a number of factors that vary from region to region and, even, province to province. Such growth and development are necessary in many cases to produce equal standards and quality of life throughout the country. These variables have particular significance in those regions and even provinces suffering economic disparities.

The first variables are market size and market access for products. In regions with small populations, companies serving the regional market may fail to reach a size sufficient to exhaust economies of large-scale production. These companies will be subjected to competition from companies in more heavily populated regions, where economies of large-scale production can be achieved in the context of larger markets for products. If companies in the small market are to survive, wages must be low enough to offset cost advantages in other regions adjusted for transportation costs. Companies that do reach efficient size by serving the markets of other regions must absorb transportation costs in order to have access to these expanded markets and must pay lower wages to remain competitive. However, in regions where there is a large population, this provides for a local market for goods and services. Also, where there is an opportunity to access larger markets, possibly within an international trading system, this allows for much greater economic growth and development. Consider sourthern Ontario and Quebec, the industrial and commercial heartland of Canada. Approximately 60 percent of Canada's population reside in the corridor between Quebec City and Windsor. Companies are presented with an ease of access to much larger global markets from the St. Lawrence River to the United States.

A second variable is the quality of natural resources, including agricultural land. Natural resource extraction and processing can offer a viable alternative to a secondary manufacturing sector for a region. Low quality resources will also reduce the tax base available to provincial governments for maintaining and improving regional public services. High quality and plentiful natural resources would increase tax revenues accruing to the regional government while, at the same time, attracting capital into the resource sector. Resulting increases in the demand for the regional labour force would increase wages and enable lightly populated regions to import manufactured goods from metropolitan regions. Canada has had a long tradition of building its economy on the low-value added resources sector and been criticized that this has not served Canada's industrial and trade relations when they have to operate in a volatile price-sensitive market.

The third variable is occupational mobility and skills. This refers to the mobility of the region's labour force, both from one occupation to another and from one place to another. An absence of adequate training for industrial labour force and an absence of skilled organizational and entrepreneurial factors of production can prevent a region from achieving its full production potential. Both sources of inefficiency will reduce personal income in regions. A skill mix that is appropriate and rigid can reduce regional income disparities. This is particularly evident in regions dependent on a single industry, such as fishing or mining. When the fish supply is depleted as in the case of cod in Atlantic Canada, or a mining company has stripped the ore and left town, people do not possess the skill variety to seek occupations where jobs exist.

The fourth variable is spatial immobility. This refers to the skills of the region's labour, including its ability to take advantage of new technologies and apply old techniques efficiently. The inability or unwillingness of individuals to change their geographic locations is the root of regional differences in per income capita. When wages are low in one region compared to another, individuals do migrate away from low wage regions and towards high wage regions. They do not move fast enough and in large enough numbers, however, to eliminate the wage disparity as population growth replaces out-migrants from low-income regions. This variable constitutes a very special problem. People are attached to home, family and community. When employment is lost in a region, it is very difficult to leave home and community to seek an unfamiliar future elsewhere. Also, it is often very difficult to attract people who have been accustomed to a quality of life and standard of living associated with a metropolitan area to move to a regional depressed area, even when there is promise of employment.

Finally, claims on capital refer to the extent to which residents of the region posses income claims on capital employed within or outside the region. If those receiving incomes as interest or dividends reside predominantly in metropolitan regions, outlying regions will posses lower per capita incomes than metropolitan regions. To some extent, this source of regional inequality is related to disparities in wage and farm incomes. Banks and other financial institutions are not that eager to loan prospective entrepreneurs capital where there is high bankruptcy. Of course, large multinational corporations have their sources of raising capital and negotiate with head offices of large financial institutions.

The regional cleavages have dominated federal government interests. The political machinery of political parties and Cabinet are expected to accommodate these interests. There is a history of federal government intervention in regional issues. This also bridges the relationship between business and government, as each government policy and program is related to an industry sector.

Early federal regional programs to address disparities demonstrated *ad hoc* approaches to cope with demands in specific locations or from particular groups with different problems. For example, the Prairie Farm Rehabilitation Programme and the Maritime Marshland Rehabilitation Scheme dealt with problems associated with drought and flood, respectively. These programs were directed at a given geographic region. The Agricultural and Rural Development Act of 1961 was broadened to include fisheries and tourism problems. On the whole, an attempt was made to extend earlier programs in at least three respects. The first was to expand the original rural base of the earlier programs to include urban and metropolitan regions. Second, there was an emphasis on both economic and social aspects to include job creation programs as well as job re-training and subsidization of employment incomes. Third, there was the extension of programs throughout the country rather than restricting them to given regions.

The federal government assumed responsibility for co-ordinating federal and provincial government programs and, as such, also recognized the facilitation of planning for interdepartmental co-ordination, federal-provincial co-operation and effective policy implementation. The recognition of the need to improve consultation and co-ordination between the various federal departments was achieved through decentralization with their provincial counterparts. Inherently to policies and programs of regional development is Co-operative Federalism whereby, the federal and provincial governments attempt to resolve problems of concern to them. This mechanism of problem solving is established in institutions and in the Constitution Act of 1980 in the distribution of transfer payments or conditional grants and equalization payments or unconditional grants. The impetus of resolving economic and social disparities in Canadian regions was initiated by the federal government as it is in the position of financing policies and programs. The implementation and administration of programmes and funds are undertaken in a co-operative endeavour by federal and provincial governments as well as by municipal governments.

There are three broad policy areas that the federal government has sought to manage economic and social issues related to regional economic disparities. The first is industrial incentive programs. They have the objective to create continuing productive employment by making investment in viable industries more attractive in relatively slow-growth regions of the country. The federal government offers low interest loans, grants, tax credits, seed money and consulting services to companies with the condition that they must locate or re-locate in one of the designated economically depressed regions. Their programs are based on the understanding that companies create jobs in depressed regions where there is high unemployment and an available labour pool.

The second area is infrastructure assistance programs. They assist in providing additional capital for water and sewage systems, road construction and improvement, housing and transportation construction and hospital and educational construction and expansion. These are necessary prerequisites for economic and social adjustment in depressed regions of the nation as it is yet another way in which governments create jobs.

The third area is social adjustment and rural development programs. They facilitate the access of people in rural areas to productive employment opportunities as well as to improve individuals' incomes. This is achieved through more efficient utlilization of rural resources, especially land. Unequivocally, Canada has a large land mass with scenic lakes, rivers, forests and mountains. Canada is also grossly underpopulated, given this vast land mass. What can governments do in those regions where there are little or no opportunities for economic employment? What can governments be expected to do where the one-industry town has become a ghost town with the departure of the that industry? What can be done when there is a high rate of available labour force lacking transportable skills and a labour force that does not want to seek its fortunes in a large metropolitan region? With these programs, governments encourage entrepreneurialism in providing financial and consulting services for skills retraining and seed money to establish small businesses such as artisan and craft shops, bed and breakfast accommodations and dude ranches. On a much grander scale, governments negotiate with corporations to attract corporate development in the resort, casino and recreational industries. These ventures are intended to create an economy in the region and provide employment opportunities not only for the residents of the region but, also, for those seeking to move to where the jobs are.

Underlying all of these programs is a basic theme: job creation. Ultimately, what most people want is a job. A job defines who a person is; a job provides dignity and self-esteem; a job sustains a family. Governments are empowered to make effective use of their resources, including power to make laws and administer and implement programs that their electorate deem representative, responsible and accountable. This creates the environment for both individuals and companies to work together.

Criticism of the Canadian government's regional policies has centred on the use of cash grants to companies locating or modernizing in designated regions. It has been questioned whether or not the companies receiving these cash grants really require grants as part of their decisions to locate in these regions. The industrial incentive programs have further been criticized on the grounds that the grants favour the adoption of relatively capital-intensive techniques in areas where one of the major problems is excessive labour supply. Grants that increase the profitability of particular enterprises in a designated region may cause difficulties for other companies not receiving subsidies. This results in the reduction in product price and/or increases in input price thereby reducing the profit of unsubsidized companies below normal levels leading them to close operations in the long-run. There are problems in providing such incentives. First, it discriminates in favour of those enterprises locating, expanding or modernizing their plants or equipment. It also results in creating an artificial marketplace condition when examining such variables as market size and access, quality and availability of natural resources, occupational immobility and skills, spatial immobility and, finally, claims on capital. The incentive programmes have also been criticized for producing windfall profits for large corporations, some of which will accrue to foreign owners in foreign countries.

There is a real dilemma in mixed economies in determining how much of public funds should be spent to encourage new employment opportunities. While the utilization of cost-benefit analysis can improve the ratio between jobs created and cost incurred, the decision to expend public funds is highly political and discretionary. There is also the issue of federal-provincial relations which presents political and administrative problems. The fact is, the federal government has the financial resources and the administrative machinery to initiate economic policies, the provincial governments that are directly affected by economic and social dysfunctions often lack the financial resources, especially in many of these depressed regions of the country to address particular regional problems on their own. There is also the complex relationship with business. Businesses do establish relations with government based on government satisfying their needs. There is yet one other factor that should be considered in the relationship between business and government in dealing with regional industrial strategy. This is the growth of government intervention. There is no single accepted explanation for the growth of government in Canada. There are many explanations, some competing and others complementary. Each contains some element of truth. The list includes growing industrialization, the rising level of incomes, and the effects of inflation, increased urbanization, ideological shifts, emerging technologies, federal-provincial relations and the nature of the political and bureaucratic structures of government.

Especially since the early 1960s, governments have put in place a variety of incentive programs for business. In certain regions of Canada, there is government subsidy available for virtually every type of commercial activity. Government intervention in the economy is particularly pervasive in Canada because both the provincial and federal governments have become involved in decisions about the location of new or expanded economic activities by the private sector. Market forces alone no longer dictate a company's response to emerging opportunities or its decision with regard to location. With their shareholders' best interests in mind, companies will search out government programs to see if public funds are available to assist in promoting their development of business plans.

The federal government supports business in numerous ways. It gives cash grants, loan guarantees, funds federal-provincial agreements designed solely to assist the private sector and makes tax incentives available. Other federal policies include special grants to support firms facing economic difficulties and to organizations or groups established to promote the views of business.

Early Keynesian economists believed that government could fine tune the economy through incentives to the business community. Some federal government assistance programs, including the Maritime Freight Rate Acts, date back to the Depression years of the 1930s. But it was only in the late 1950s and 1960s that government grants to the private sector became fashionable. Before that time, the federal government had considered that the best means of adjusting fiscal policy lay in offering generous subsidies to provincial governments for public works projects. The federal government felt that this alone would allow a concerted attack on unemployment. Later, it introduced equalization payments to poorer provinces to even out the fiscal capacities of all provincial governments. This policy was intended to reduce disparities between regions, to achieve a national standard in public services and at the same time, to equalize provincial government revenues. It was only during World War II that the federal government sought to act as a high profile economic manager and to intervene in private sector decisions. The government intervened in numerous ways. For example, when the private sector proved reluctant to produce synthetic rubber for the Allied war effort, the federal government established Polymer, a Crown Corporation that created a rubber industry in Canada.

When World War II came to an end, the federal government withdrew and let the private sector set the pace of economic development. C.D. Howe, the "Minister of Everything" during the war years, had a business view of the limits of government programming and of Canadian economic development. Howe did not believe that government could or should force the pace of development faster than the private sector could support. He was content to see relations between business and government fall into a much more American-like mould, with business being more the engine and architect of development. He had a bias in favour of private enterprise and was happy to wield public power vigorously to help private enterprises achieve what seemed like national goals.

When the Conservative government of John Diefenbaker came to power in 1957, there was no single cabinet minister with the stature of C.D. Howe to shape government-business relations. The government also inherited a recession. The previous Liberal government had appointed a Royal Commission on Canada's Economic Prospects, known as the Gordon Commission. In its 1957 Report, it urged that a bold, comprehensive and co-ordinated approach to development was needed to resolve the underlying economic problems of Atlantic Canada. The Report advised that a federally sponsored commission be established to provide infrastructure facilities to encourage economic growth. The Report also called for measures to increase the rate of capital investment in the region. In many ways, the proposal to involve the private sector in promoting development in slow-growth regions was breaking new ground. However, the Commission remained cautious in its recommendations, stating that special assistance put into effect to assist these regions might adversely affect the welfare of industries already functioning in most established areas of Canada.

The government did not immediately embrace the proposals. With the recession worsening, the persistence of regional imbalances was critical. All regions felt the effects of the recession, but it was more severe in the four Atlantic provinces. This helped convince the federal government that undirected financial transfers in the form of equalization payments were simply not sufficient to bring about structural changes in the slow-growth regions. Certain Ministers were also pointing to what they viewed as unacceptable levels of poverty in numerous rural communities and arguing for special corrective measures.

The 1960 Budget Speech unveiled the first of many measures the federal government has since developed to assist the private sector. The Budget permitted companies to obtain double the normal rate of capital cost allowances on most of the assets they acquired to produce new products if they located in designated regions with high unemployment and slow economic growth.

Other measures quickly followed. The Agriculture Rehabilitation and Development Act was passed in an attempt to improve the depressed rural economy. This began as a federal-provincial effort to stimulate agricultural development in order to increase income in rural areas. It aimed to increase small farmers' output and productivity by providing assistance for alternative use of marginal land, creating work opportunities in rural areas, developing water and soil resources and setting up projects designed to benefit people engaged in natural resource industries other than agriculture, such as fisheries. However, the Agriculture Rehabilitation and Development Act was widely criticized because, among other things, it lacked an appropriate geographical framework.

The Fund for Rural Economic Development (FRED) programme broke new ground in northeast New Brunswick. It provided special inducements to private enterprises. Assistance was given to projects that were considered capable of creating long-term employment in the natural resources and tourism sectors, but that could not be carried out without some form of public assistance. An interest-free forgivable loan of 50 percent of approved capital costs of up to $60,000 for new manufacturing or processing industries and up to 30 percent of modernization or expansion was available. It was explicitly designed to encourage new entrepreneurs and expansion of small existing businesses.

The federal government introduced in 1962 another development initiative, the Atlantic Development Board (ADB). Largely inspired by the Gordon Commission, the Board was given a special Atlantic development fund to administer. By and large, the fund was employed to assist in the provision or improvement of the region's basic economic infrastructure. It did not provide direct assistance of any kind to private industry as the Gordon Commission had recommended and, on this point, the Atlantic Development Board was heavily criticized.

The federal government dealt with this criticism by providing "limited" and "direct" assistance to the private sector. It introduced the Area Development Incentives Act (ADIA) and, in 1963, the Area Development Agency (ADA) within the Department Industry. The central purpose behind these initiatives was to turn to the private sector to stimulate growth in economically depressed regions. Regions of high unemployment and slow growth were the targets. Only regions reporting unemployment rates above a specified level would be eligible. Manufacturing and processing companies were then invited to locate or expand operations in these regions. Three types of incentives were applied sequentially: accelerated capital cost allowances, a three-year income tax exemption and higher capital cost allowances. In 1965, a program of cash grants was introduced over and above the capital cost allowances.

Assistance was provided automatically on a formula basis. It was applied in a non-discretionary manner to areas chosen solely on the basis of unemployment levels. The federal government was told that it had limited potential as a development tool. Virtually no opportunity existed to relate assistance to development planning. In addition, because of the program's regional formula, the areas eligible for assistance did not include main population or industrial centres within slow-growth regions where new manufacturing initiatives could be expected to have a better chance of success.

In 1968, there was a change in government with the election of Prime Minister Pierre Trudeau's Liberal government. For Pierre Trudeau, national unity extended well beyond English-French relations. Regional employment was given increased priority. Trudeau appointed Jean Marchand, a close friend and trusted Quebec lieutenant, to his newly established Department of Regional Economic Expansion (DREE).

Marchand immediately set out to modernize the government's incentive program. He decided to build the new incentives package from the existing Area Development Agency program by taking from the Area Development Agency most of its positive attributes and discarding its less desirable features. The new program would be discretionary. Grants would now be available for selected industry sectors. However, the program would also be available over a much wider area by providing incentives in growth centres and in selected urban areas. The new programme would confine itself to development grants and would set maximums, if circumstances warranted. It would establish a two-part grant structure, one for capital costs and the other according to the number of jobs created. Maximum levels for both were also more generous for the Atlantic provinces.

Not surprisingly, the most contentious issue confronting the new program was its geographical applicability. Marchand was adamant on two points. First, the regions designated had to be sufficiently limited so as not to dilute the effectiveness of the program. Second, unlike the Area Development Agency program, it should apply in growth centres such as Halifax, Moncton, Saint John's and others.

Regions designated for the program included all the Atlantic provinces, eastern and northern Quebec, parts of northern Ontario and the northernmost regions of the four western provinces. Thus, regions were designated in all ten provinces for a three-year period ending in 1972. The regions designated accounted for approximately 30 percent of the Canadian labour force and the average per capita income within them was approximately 70 percent of the national average. On the face of it, this coverage may appear excessive in terms of the program's regional applicability. However, initially at least, Marchand was successful in getting what he wanted. He was successful in limiting the program's coverage to the areas he had first envisaged. Parts of Ontario, Alberta and British Columbia were also designated, but more as a gesture to ensure that they would not feel completely left out. As well, Marchand feared that these provinces, given their relatively strong fiscal positions, might establish their own incentives programs, thereby greatly inhibiting the new federal initiatives.

It was not long before strong political pressure was exerted on Marchand to extend the program's regional designations further. Cabinet ministers and Members of Parliament from the Montreal area frequently made the point that Montreal was Quebec's growth pole and that, if the Department of Regional Economic Expansion were serious about regional development, it ought to designate Montreal under its industrial incentives program. Montreal's growth performance rate was not keeping pace with expectations, particularly those of the large number of Liberal Members of Parliament from the area. The city's unemployment rate stood at 7 percent in 1972, compared with 4.6 percent for Toronto. Furthermore, Quebec's economic strength was directly linked to Montreal and, unless new employment opportunities were created there, little hope was held for the province's peripheral areas. Montreal required special measures to return to a reasonable rate of growth.

In the end, Marchand chose to include Montreal in a special region, known as 'Region C'. In this newly designated area, which consisted of southwestern Quebec, including Hull and Montreal and three counties of eastern Ontario, the maximum incentive grant was lower than elsewhere. The grant could not exceed 10 percent of approved capital cost, plus $2,000 for each new direct job created. Elsewhere in the designated regions of Quebec and Ontario, the maximum incentive grant was fixed at 25 percent of approved capital costs and $5,000 for each new job created. Finally, the changes stipulated that "Region C's" special designation was to be for two years only. This would be sufficient to help Montreal return to a reasonable rate of growth. The changes, however, extended the designated regions to cover about 40 percent of the population. Marchand assured his colleagues that the special Montreal designation was temporary and committed his Department to de-designating the city after two years.

By 1976, Montreal area Members of Parliament were pressing the new Minister of the Department of Regional Economic Expansion, Marcel Lessard to re-designate their city under the Department's incentive programme. Unemployment in Quebec had risen to 300,000, half of it in the Montreal region. The election of the Parti Quebecois in November 1976 resulted in a sudden downturn in private investment in the province and the widespread fear that head offices of major companies would leave Montreal because of proposed language legislation.

When Lessard first went to the Cabinet with the proposal to designate Montreal, he met with stiff opposition. If the Department of Regional Economic Expansion could justify a presence in Montreal, why could it not also justify one for Vancouver and Toronto? Fundamental questions were asked about the Department's mandate and its role in alleviating regional disparities. Cabinet ministers from the Atlantic provinces remembered well Marchand's comment about the necessity of spending 80 percent of the Department's budget east of Trois-Rivieres. How would a Montreal designation affect other regions? Would it still be possible, for example, to attract firms into depressed regions if they could obtain a cash grant for starting new productions in Montreal?

Lessard, with considerable help from seven Ministers from the Montreal region, was able to convince Cabinet to designate Montreal under the Regional Development Incentive Area (RDIA) program. In 1977, the Department of Regional Economic Expansion introduced a discretionary incentives program for selected high-growth manufacturing or processing facilities. Only certain industries could qualify, including food and beverages, metal products, machinery, transportation equipment and electrical and chemical products. Projects would be limited by a lower maximum grant than elsewhere, that is, 25 percent of total capital cost.

In obtaining Cabinet approval for the Montreal designation, Lessard promised his colleagues to look at the possibility of designating other regions, including northern areas of British Columbia and the Northwest Territories. He also committed the Department to undertake special development efforts in eastern Ontario, notably the Cornwall area.

By the early 1980s, the regional incentive program in the private sector had been pulled and pushed to cover fully 93 percent of Canada's landmass and over a significant percent of the population. Candidates for Parliament from all parties pledged, if elected, to make every effort to see their Riding designated for regional incentives. Local chambers of commerce and other business groups continually applied pressure on their Members of Parliament and the Department of Regional Economic Expansion Minister to have their communities designated. From the time the program was introduced in the late 1960s until the early 1980s, the federal government spent well over $1 billion in cash grants to the private sector.

The constant pull to extend the government's regional incentives program to the private sector, among other things, led the federal government to revamp its regional and industrial programs and its delivery mechanism. The Department of Regional Economic Expansion was disbanded and replaced by the Department of Regional Industrial Expansion, which was designed to combine both industrial and regional perspectives. The newly appointed Liberal Minister, Ed Lumley, reported that he had finally solved the designation problem for regional incentives to the private sector. He unveiled a new programmed labelled the Industrial and Regional Development Programme (IRDP) that would apply *everywhere* in the country. All constituencies were eligible for assistance. The program accommodated a variety of needs. It could be used for investment in infrastructure, industrial diversification, establishing new plants and the launching of new product lines.

An important distinguishing characteristic of the Industrial and Regional Development Programme was the "development index" that was designed to establish the needs of individual regions, as far down as a single census tract. All are arranged in four tiers of need. The first, for the most developed 50 percent of the population covers districts with a need for industrial restructuring. In this tier, financial assistance is available for up to 25 percent of the cost of modernization and expansion. At the other end of the spectrum is the fourth tier, which includes the 5 percent of the population living in areas of greatest need based on level of employment, personal income and provincial fiscal capacity. In this tier, financial assistance is available for up to 60 percent of the cost of establishing new plants.

The program can provide financial assistance to both business and non-profit organizations through cash grants, contributions, repayable contributions, participation loans and loan guarantees. This assistance is available for the various elements of "product or company cycle", for example, economic analysis studies, innovation including product development, plant establishment, modernization or expansion; and marketing, including exact development measures and restructuring. Lumley believed that through this program the government could be involved in every stage of the development of a business — from start up, to expansion, modernization and restructuring.

The year 1984 witnessed a change in government with the election of the Progressive Conservative government of Brian Mulroney. Only some relatively minor modifications were made to the Industrial and Regional Development Programme (IRDP). Restrictions were imposed on Tier 1 regions, or the most developed regions of the country so that modernization and expansion projects would no longer qualify for assistance. It was clear by then that the private sector was taking full advantage of the government programs, even firms in the most developed regions of the country. For the first full year of operation, for example, the program was more successful in the Windsor-Quebec City corridor than elsewhere and the estimated number of jobs created or maintained under Tier 1 was well over twice the number estimated for tiers 3 and 4 combined. In terms of financial resources, the Department of Regional Industrial Expansion funds earmarked for Tier 1 projects alone amounted to over $229 million, compared with $23 million for Tier 4, $46 million for Tier 3 and $74 million for Tier 2.

In time, the program favoured Tier 1 regions, or the more developed regions of the country even more. By 1985–6, over 70 percent of the Department of Regional Industrial Expansion funds to the Industrial and Regional Development Programme (IRDP.) went to Ontario and Quebec. This led to a series of charges from both the Atlantic and western regions that private sector firms in central . Canada were being given preferential treatment. The Department of Regional Industrial Expansion was disbanded in 1988 after separate Atlantic and western agencies had been established. The focus of both agencies, with their billion dollar budgets of new money over five years and the inclusion of ongoing programs, begun under the department of Regional Industrial Expansion was on the private sector. Both had programs in place, that could fund virtually any conceivable private sector plan or initiative. In addition, a new department called the Department of Industry, Science and Technology was also established in 1988. This Department was present in all regions of the country and also made cash grants available to the private sector.

Cash grants to the private sector have not by any means been limited to regional incentives programs. The federal government has, since the 1960s, made cash grants available to businesses in the shipbuilding industry, energy exploration and the defence industry, to name just a few. It also provides cash grants to the private sector for human resources training and development, for example research and development and for transportation. Under various federal-provincial programs, cash grants are also available to the private sector for almost any kind of business activity. Tourism, agriculture, fisheries and mining have all benefited. In addition, whenever a sector is experiencing difficulties, the federal government often moves in with its own program or enters into a federal-provincial agreement to assist firms in "adjusting to new or emerging circumstances". There are numerous examples. Agreements were signed in the late 1970s and early 1980s with the provinces of Ontario ($180 million), Quebec ($282 million), New Brunswick ($42.5 million), Nova Scotia ($21.7 million) and Newfoundland ($33 million) to fund pulp and paper firms to modernize their operations. Another example is the major appliance industry. By the early 1980s, it was obvious that this industry, located in southern Ontario and Quebec, was in difficulty and was the least likely to survive tariff cuts of the Canada-United States Free Trade Agreement. In 1987, the federal government announced a $15 million assistance package to help restructure the industry.

In the 1980 Budget Speech, the Minister of Finance announced a major initiative to promote industrial restructuring and manpower retraining and mobility in areas of particular need. Communities were designated on the basis of need as measured by the number of layoffs from an industry, whether the adjustment was recent or chronic and whether the layoffs were structural or cyclical. One such example was the Industrial Labour Adjustment Programme, which was applied to various sectors, including the auto parts industries.

Another regionally oriented initiative was the Adjustment Assistance Benefit Programme, which granted some $250 million over a five-year period. The federal government sought to update its textile and clothing policy. In 1978, it negotiated nine bilateral arrangements stating a preference for freer trade and for the removal of special protection measures over the long terms.

The Nielsen Task Force reported that there were some 218 distinct federal or federal-provincial programs costing in aggregate $16.4 billion in 1984–85 and requiring the services of more than 68,000 federal public servants. The Task Force concluded that programs to business were overly rich, overlapping and required rationalizing. It argued that there were compelling reasons to change incentives programs to make them more efficient and that there were many existing programs that would probably not be invented today. However, the Task Force held little hope that the problem would be correct. It was believed that the problem at the political and senior bureaucratic levels lacked rewards for doing more with less. In fact, governmental bureaucratic middle managers were all too aware that their pay and classification levels depended in part on the number of people they supervised and the dollars they spent. Such incentives have predictable results.

There is yet another instance of government intervention resulting from businesses' demand for government action. This is the case of bailing out firms. Textbook economics suggest that bankruptcies are normal in a private enterprise economy. By weeding out the unsuccessful firms, bankruptcy provides additional room for growth by the more productive, job-creating businesses. When a company fails, its shareholders lose their investment, and unsecured creditors obtain less than full compensation for their loans, with company's assets being sold to other firms at depressed prices. But those assets, in turn, if placed in the hands of energetic managers, lower the cost of production. Productivity and international competitiveness thus are both increased, with the result that sales grow and new employment is created. Accordingly, government intervention to save a failing firm is considered to be counterproductive.

However, the federal government has tossed aside textbook economics on many occasions, opting instead for intervention. Others include the cases of Chrysler Canada, Massey Ferguson, Cooperative Implements, Maislin Industries, Lake Groups Inc., CCM Inc., White Farm Equipment, Consolidated Computer Inc., Electrohome Ltd., Pelromont Inc., National Sea Products, H.B. Nickerson and Sons Ltd., fisheries Product International and General Motors of Canada. Without government aid, these companies would not exist or, in some cases, they would have gone bankrupt earlier.

The federal government responded on several occasions to requests for financial assistance from failing businesses in the early 1980s in the midst of world recession. Interest rates were both high and unpredictable. In Canada, something like two-thirds of corporate earning went to pay interest. With weak markets, several major corporations had inadequate earnings to meet their interest payments. Faced with bankruptcy, the firms turned to the federal government for help. Often the appeals came at the eleventh hour, which put enormous pressure on the government. Financial deadlines, especially loan repayment dates, could not easily be postponed without causing damaging stock market reactions. Ministers, particularly those representing the affected regions, either had to push the Cabinet for a quick decision to support the firm, despite the limited information available, or risk seeing thousands of workers in their ridings or regions being laid off. Inevitably, they chose the former course. But once the government bailed out high-profile corporations in central Canada, such as Chrysler and Maislin, other regions insisted on equal or better treatment for their corporate citizens. It was extremely difficult for the Ministry of Industry, Herb Gray and the Minister of Finance, Marc Lalonde in the Liberal Trudeau government to oppose similar assistance for Cooperative Implements in western Canada and National Sea in eastern Canada. Similarly, after bailing out corporate giants in central Canada, it became difficult to turn down pleas for aid from smaller companies also facing bankruptcy. Numerous small firms, including some in the retail industry, did receive special assistance through various federal and federal-provincial programs. Government bailouts of firms has not been limited to recession years. The practice continued, though with less frequency, in the late 1980s and 1990s with western Canada bank bailouts and General Motors closing in Sainte-Therese plant in Quebec.

Federal and federal-provincial intervention in private industries can be explained in terms of economic nationalism in the protectionist policies governments have practised. The writings of Harold Innis asserted that the origins and purposes of the federal government are to be understood in terms of an economic territory dependent upon the export of certain staples. To make it commercially feasible production entailed heavy public expenditures on such capital facilities as railways and canals. The significance of Harold Innis's thesis is the concept that the state fills an important vacuum by being the substitute for private enterprise in the building and developing of Canada. Thomas Hockin argues that the Canadian government was given an active role in national development and the fostering and protecting of certain cultural and economic characteristics.

When Canada entered nationhood in 1867, the federal government was allocated legislative power for "Peace, Order and Good Government". By allocating residual legislative powers to the federal government, the intent of the Fathers of Confederation was to establish a strong central government that could unite, expand, develop and settle a newly established nation. This is especially evident in allocating to the federal government legislative power "to regulate trade and commerce". When the western provinces joined Confederation, the federal government made special efforts to build a united Canada. The very small population was scattered across a large geographic land mass. One way to unite and connect the country was to construct a railway. This would have an impact on trading patterns. Trading patterns were in a north and south configuration because, like today, people lived near the United States border.

The United States was developing faster, with a larger population and a bigger economy providing products not available in the Canadian provinces, either because they were not produced in Canada or there was no transportation to distribute them in Canada. This resulted in the Canadian government, starting with Canada's first Prime Minister, Sir John A. Macdonald developing the National Policy. The National Policy placed high tariffs on imports from the United States to protect Canadian manufacturing, which then had higher costs. In addition, the federal government began to wrestle with the difficult question of building a costly rail line to the west coast. These two issues initiated the continuing involvement of Canadian governments developing and maintaining Canadian society.

Economic nationalism has played an important role in the development of relations between business and government. In Canada, economic nationalism is a movement aimed at achieving greater control by Canadians of their economy. There are two types of economic nationalism. The first, protectionism in trade, is represented in the establishing of a system of tariffs to favour domestic production of goods and to discourage foreign imports. This policy dates to Sir John A. Macdonald's National Policy of 1879. It was partly intended to encourage the creation of an industrial base in Canada by protecting "infant industries" against the competition of larger and more established firms abroad.

The second type of economic nationalism is concerned with the ownership of Canadian businesses by foreign investors. This is largely a post-World War II phenomenon. The rapid rise of foreign ownership in Canadian business after World War II was linked to the rise of multinational corporations. Various multinationals realized they could bypass tariff restrictions by building and operating their own branch plants or subsidiaries in Canada. This accorded them access to markets, resources and capital, and favour with Canadian governments. However, as these multinational corporations expanded, economic nationalism was concerned with the special problems created by this type of investment, particularly the stunted and distorted pattern of economic development. Such investment also tended to shift control over economic decision making outside Canada to the head office of these foreign-owned corporations. Economic nationalists began to demand legislation to monitor the activities and restrain the growth of foreign ownership in the Canadian economy.

Over the next several decades, the federal government responded with a series of four government sponsored reports. They included the Gordon Commission on Canada's Economic Prospects (1955–57), the Watkins Task Force on Foreign Ownership and the Structure of Canadian Industry (1968), the Wahn Report on the Eleventh Report of the Standing Committee on External Affairs and National Defence Respecting Canada-US Relations (1970) and the Gray Report on Foreign Direct Investment in Canada (1972). As a result of these reports, the Foreign Investment Review Agency (FIRA) was established in 1974. FIRA reviewed all proposals for foreign take-overs of existing business and the creation of new foreign-owned businesses in Canada for the purpose of ensuring maximum benefits to Canadians. However, in the mid-1980s, the Foreign Investment Review Agency was disbanded.

Government intervention in the guise of protectionism, as expressed in terms of federal and federal-provincial assistance programs or economic nationalism has provided assistance to domestic and foreign-owned businesses in all regions of Canada. It had a precedent in the early periods of Confederation, and This continued throughout the twentieth century. By the 1980s, liberal democratic governments began to reject Keynesian principles and accept Monetarism of Milton Friedman. Monetarism seemed to revert to the nineteenth century classical philosophy of Adam Smith. The federal government began negotiating the Free Trade Agreement with the United States: with this came the dismantling of economic protectionist policies. Furthermore, under the Free Trade Agreements, companies receiving subsidies would be subject to countervailing and anti-dumping tariffs equal to the subsidies received. The days of protectionism were ebbing.

Cultivating Cash
How to Grow a Farming Business in Canada

Andrew Sutherland

Introduction

Canadian farmers are essential not only to the well being of our food supply, but to the sustenance of many other industries. Equipment dealers, fertilizer and pesticide companies, railways, processors, restaurants, and retailers all depend on the annual harvest to turn a profit. Despite the crucial nature of agriculture for our economy, farmers are being forced off the land at an alarming rate. Statistics Canada has found that the price of fuel, chemicals, seeds and other necessities has increased almost five-fold since 1974, while food prices have not seen a similar jump. An Ontario Federation of Agriculture study shows that, of the $1.99 retail price of Great Harvest Bread and $4.69 for Oatmeal Crunch Cereal, farmers receive only eleven and six cents, respectively. Needless to say, there is a great opportunity for producers to add value to the products sold to distributors in order to increase these figures.

Before any conclusion can be drawn on the state of agriculture in Canada, a distinction must be made between the different types of farmers. Banks distinguish between the types of farmers in evaluating loan applications. Traditional or "lifestyle farmers" continue to play an integral role in Canadian heritage, but are increasingly folding their businesses due to rising costs and competition from larger farms. Meanwhile small business farms, often operated by entrepreneurs and university graduates, are managing to profit in spite of re-

397

cent droughts. Many successful small business farmers are advancing and growing their operations into agricultural corporations, that are experiencing incredible profits and benefiting from government support. Part-time farmers represent one-fifth of all producers in Canada. They fall into two categories. The first group is often traditional farmers who were forced to scale back the production. The second group is small business farmers gaining entry into the market.

Government subsidy programs heavily influence the economics of farming in Canada. While organizations such as Farm Credit Canada and the Net Income Stabilization Account act as safeguards to farmers, it is ultimately the level of business education obtained and technology used that determines the fate of a farm. The Canadian government plays an active role in regulating and protecting the agricultural sector, and receives input on the issues that concern farmers from several large interest groups. The Ontario Federation of Agriculture has been in the forefront in lobbying on tax, income support and regulatory issues. Foreign agricultural sectors are heavily subsidized, forcing the Canadian government to decide between losing its farmers and protecting them. Ultimately, the agriculture industry *must* be supported and regulated to maintain employment, global trade, high food quality and environmental sustainability.

Profiles

Note that the following distinctions are based on the banking industry's criteria for evaluating farm type.

Lifestyle Farmer

Lifestyle farming perhaps exemplifies Canadian history and heritage better than any other profession. While farming has been a mainstay in the economy for centuries, many are concerned that with the loss of small farms also goes the rural culture that they define. In the early twentieth century, rural towns revolved around the farm. The farmers' market, town fair and 4H club (Head, Hands, Heart, and Health) dominated the rural culture in a way that makes modern corporations jealous because they were part of the culture of farming and the lifestyle of farming.

The values engendered in farming life have been eroding. The 4H club began in Manitoba in 1913 as a community program geared toward the development of rural youth. Local farms were the sites of national agricultural competitions, which took the spirit of rural Canada to new heights. Today, the rural agricultural spirit has been replaced with the sombre knowledge that, one by one, families are fleeing the farm because they simply cannot afford to survive. The stress brought on solely by the harsh economics of the industry has led to many immeasurable human effects that Statistics Canada could never account for. Marital problems, substance abuse, spousal and child abuse, crime, depression and suicide plague rural areas at a significantly higher rate than urban cities. The shame and despair of not making enough money to feed children and maintain the family farm has led the government to set up exit programs and toll-free numbers to deal with the emotional aspects of being forced off the farm. The Farm Health and Safety Council was formed by the Saskatchewan provincial government to combat the displacement of financial burden to social problems. With the increase in petty thefts, crime and vandalism, it became clear that economic conditions were taking their toll on farming communities. The Farm Stress Line was created in 1992 to offer counselling for farm-related stress. Since 1999, the toll-free number has experienced a significant increase in the number of calls, and the nature of these calls is becoming more serious: "More than 600 callers identified financial concerns as their primary reason for calling, while 'stress burnout' prompted another 233 people to phone. There is at least one call a week from someone considering suicide". (Boyens, 54)

Traditional farmers often tend to their crops with poor or outdated equipment and little knowledge of how to run a business. Despite efforts by banks, government and private organizations to train and empower farmers, educational resources are being utilized at far less than maximum capacity. Farmers are often unaware, unwilling or financially incapable of new methods of production and cultivation that, if adopted, would significantly increase yields. Financial institutions are more than willing to lend to large agribusinesses, which employ hundreds nationwide and supply the majority of the food exports, but leave small farmers without a viable plan to fend for themselves. Drought, flood, spills and parasites have a greater effect on smaller farms, since any disaster could wipe out the entire acreage.

Small farmers may be behind in terms of competitiveness, but their conservation efforts do not go unnoticed. They protect their land because they know some day they must pass the farm down to their children, in the same spirit as it was passed on to them. Demographic statistics show that the average farmer in Saskatchewan is 58 years old and many of these operators have lived on the farm their entire life. Farming in rural Canada has become a hereditary way of life, with families having deeps roots in the history of their community. Whether it is the value placed on this heritage or the stubbornness of lifestyle farmers, many parents are sacrificing their children's education in lieu of the farm. Rather than gain an education or seek better employment in the city, many farmers are willing to do absolutely anything necessary to stay. In many Prairie farms, the wives and children are forced to take on part-time jobs, in addition to farm work, to provide enough income to sustain the farm.

Demographics presents an interesting understanding of farming in Canada. While the average farm *size* is rapidly growing, it's only a sign that small farmers are being pushed away from the land to the city.

Farm population has also significantly declined as a percentage of rural population. In 1931, farmers represented 68% of the rural population; the latest census results only count farmers as 13% of the same group. Perhaps more disturbing is the breakdown of *who* exactly is leaving the rural and small towns. University graduates represent the greatest number of those to migrate out of the province, while those with less than grade nine are leaving at only one-quarter the rate.

Table 1: **Number and Percentage of Canadian Farms by Gross Receipts**

Canada	1995	2000	1995 to 2000
		Farms Reporting Number	% Change
All farms in Canada	**276,548**	**246,923**	**−10.7**
Gross receipts class:[3]			
Less than $10,000	71,175	54,166	−23.9
$10,000 to $49,999	85,608	76,284	−10.9
$50,000 to $99,000	42,587	35,255	−17.2
$100,000 to $249,000	51,221	47,079	−8.1
$250,000 to $499,000	17,579	21,396	21.7
$500,000 and over	8,738	12,743	52.1

1. Data are reported on Census Day for the preceding calendar or fiscal year
2. As in previous censuses, response errors have resulted in an under-reporting of total gross farm receipts. However, the data are comparable with previous censuses.
3. At 2000 prices.

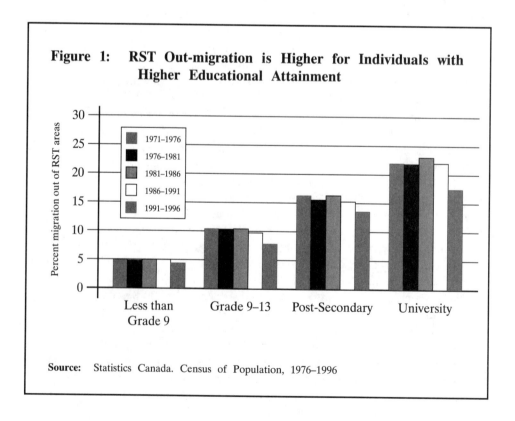

Figure 1: **RST Out-migration is Higher for Individuals with Higher Educational Attainment**

Source: Statistics Canada. Census of Population, 1976–1996

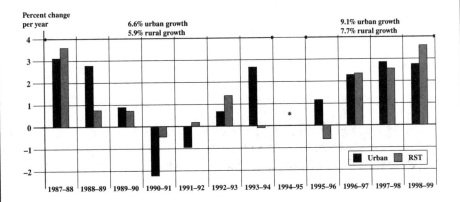

Figure 2: **Rural and Small Town Employment Almost Keeps Up to Urban**

Note: In 1995 the LFS changed its urban geographic boundaries from the 1981 designations.

Source: Statistics Canada. Census of Population, 1976–1996

The average person who leaves a rural or small town will have a higher education than one who moves into one. And while Canada has experienced a positive net rural migration since 1991, many of those entering are unemployed. Interestingly, rural and urban labour forces are beginning to resemble one another.

Clearly, rural Canadian cities are not far behind in terms of services available and quality of work. No longer is farming the only way to make a living away from the city. No longer does the rural town revolve around the farm as it used to, as factories and service providers are turning into a dominant force in the economy. The development of rural areas improves the overall standard of living in many ways. Farmers no longer have to drive for hours to buy groceries, visit a doctor or buy equipment. Rural youth are encouraged to finish school and contribute to the community because they do not have to go to another town to find a job or get an education. Developing rural areas also attracts railways and equipment dealers essential to the farming industry. However, this growth has not led to an increase in employment in traditional sectors. Primary industries such as agriculture, mining, and fishing are experiencing a serious decline in employment levels.

Agricorps

Agricorps are farming corporations with annual gross receipts of over $5 million. Large agribusinesses are boosting profits through developing close relationships with suppliers, economies of scale in the industry and collecting government payouts. Agricorps often qualify for government subsidies intended for smaller farmers and take full advantage of them. Loans offered by Farm Credit Canada and the Net Income Stabilization Account contain no criterion of farm size; so, large operations, while already able to garner plenty of support from banks and investors, would rather receive the loans at special rates and conditions. All levels of government enjoy working with agricultural corporations because they employ many people, invest in crop diversification and supply lots of food. Once established, agricorps enjoy greater efficiency, productivity, competitiveness and profit from grand scale production and expensive technology. Thousand acre farms utilize the latest Global Positioning Systems that monitor their crops and tell them where to apply and not to apply chemical fertilizers and pesticides. The agribusiness operators seek to make a profit and will never be forced to consume their own harvest or keep their children out of school because they cannot afford to hire another hand.

McCain Foods, based in Florenceville, New Brunswick, has become Canada's largest and best-known food company in the world. They produce hundreds of products including french fries, pizzas, frozen vegetables, desserts, oven dinners, specialty meat products and juices. In fact, of all the french fries consumed in the world, McCain produces an astounding one-third! McCain also maintains diversification through its customers: restaurants, grocery and retail chains, and catering services order McCain products on a regular basis. Due to customer concerns, McCain refuses to use genetically modified potatoes; however, it is interested in the potential benefits the new science may produce. In Canada, McCain employs over 3,300 workers in 11 processing plants, and many more worldwide. The company's success (over $6 billion in worldwide annual sales) can be credited to aggressive marketing, new product development and investment in agronomy. Agronomy is defined as the application of soil and plant sciences to land management and crop production. McCain's researchers identified the Ranger Russet as the ideal potato for growing, based on its size and shape. However, with Canada's cold climate and short growing season, harvesting this particular crop was extremely difficult. So McCain, while working with Agriculture Canada, developed methods for farmers to produce top quality crops of a long season variety in colder climates. Additionally, they discovered the Shepody, a potato that requires a much shorter growing season, allowing farmers to rationalize equipment costs over longer growing cycles and reduce the astronomical costs of labour and storage. As a result of the investment in agronomy, McCain has never failed in a new factory location.

Maple Leaf Foods, based in Toronto, is Canada's largest food processing company, with annual sales reaching $3 billion globally. Maple Leaf brand offers hotdogs, sliced meats, canned meats, bacon, ham and deli meats to grocery chains. Additionally, Maple Leaf owns several other processing companies, including Dempster's bakery products, Tenderflake, Olivieri, and Prime Turkey and Chicken. Clearly, the diversification tactic has succeeded in capturing the processing market: all three separate segments of the company achieved growth in earnings from operations in 2001, with $38.1 million for Meat, $37.9 million for Bakery, and an outstanding $81.5 million for Agribusiness. Maple Leaf builds tight relationships with suppliers, dealers, breeders, farmers and retailers

Table 2: Maple Leaf — Financial Highlights

For years ended December 31	2001	2000	1999	1998	1997	1996
Consolidated Results						
Sales	$4,775	$3,943	$3,530	$3,281	$3,678	$3,210
Earnings from Operations (I)	158	90	147	103	117	112
Net Earnings (Loss)	57	37	77	(23)	47	42
Return on Net Assets (RONA)	7.6%	5.4%	9.5%	6.2%	7.7%	7.7%
Financial Position						
Net Assets Employed	$1,405	$1,298	$1,148	$ 998	$1,073	$1,012
Shareholders' Equity	660	451	465	395	338	298
Total Net Borrowings	599	722	566	480	594	583
Per Share						
Net Earnings (Loss)						
As reported	$ 0.55	$ 0.34	$ 0.77	$(0.25)	$ 0.51	$ 0.46
Before Unusual items (ii)	$ 0.55	$ 0.22	$ 0.68	$ 0.34	$ 0.51	$ 0.46
Dividends	0.16	0.16	0.16	0.16	0.16	0.16
Book Value	5.05	3.77	3.93	3.28	3.64	3.22
Number of Shares (millions)						
Weighted Average	95.9	95.1	94.4	93.6	92.8	92.2
Outstanding at December 31	112.0	9.51	95.0	94.1	93.0	92.3

(In millions of Canadian dollars, except per share and percentage information)
(i) Before Usual Items
(ii) In 2000, gain on sale of short investments have been excluded.

in order to maximize its market potential. By using a Vertical Coordination Strategy to link and coordinate operations within the value chain, the company's sales have soared 21 percent over the past year. Two key strategic business acquisitions have also enabled them to grow: the purchase of Schneider foods in Winnipeg and Multi-Marques in Quebec, the province's leading fresh bread business.

McCain's and Maple Leaf are model cases of agricultural corporations operating in the farming sector like businesses. While smaller farms may be unable to compete with the amount of capital and level of technology possessed by these billion dollar companies, they can learn from their level of diversification. By offering a wide array of products to multiple buyers, the corporations minimize risk associated with varying commodity prices and droughts. If there is a period without rain, revenues can still be collected in the harvests of other products with different growing seasons. By maintaining close relationships with all entities in the value chain, McCain and Maple Leaf are able to better control their environment.

Small Business Farmer

The increased competitiveness of the agricultural sector has led to the emergence of the small-business farmer. A farm with gross annual receipts of

$100,000 to $5 million is classified as part of this category. While it may not operate on the same scale as the agricorp, the small business farmers develop relationships with suppliers. They are constantly updating their training with the latest business management, market and farming method information. Successful small business farmers are characterized by the way they treat their land as a resource in the exact same way a factory treats the raw materials as the life-blood of its business. Many of them actively participate in interest groups to voice concerns about public policy and communicate and learn from other's ex-periences. A small business farmer distinguishes himself/herself from the tradi-tional farmer in the level of technology s/he employs and the education s/he has attained. Statistics Canada has established a link between computer use and level of education, as the most educated are the highest users of computers, while those who have not completed high school are the lowest users. Higher income earners not only are more likely to own computers, but have completed some level of training in their use.

If farming is to be treated like a business, record keeping and sufficient communications technology must be a priority. While it is difficult to directly link computer and internet use to profit margins, the most successful farms are visibly benefiting from technology use.

It is common for the small business farmer to have an off-farm income to act as a safety net in the event of drought, flooding, or infestation; it is a prac-tice borrowed from the part-time farmer.

Part-Time Farmer

Finally, there is the "weekend farmer", one who operates the farm part time or as a hobby. While many hobby farmers have no intention of making money from the farm, some turn a profit. The Census of Agriculture defines hobby farmers as those whose main operator reported more than 190 days of off-farm work and whose farm did not employ any year round labour. Part time farming allows people to engage in agricultural sectors while spreading the risk and maintaining off-farm income. The devastation of a drought or a poor harvest can be offset by income from off-farm work. Many get involved in hobby farm-ing based on interest in the sector, desire for a tax break or as an alternative to exiting full-time farming. Census figures indicate that between 15 and 20 percent of farmers in Canada are part time farmers, and this population has been steadily growing since 1971.

Statistics Canada finds the average part-time farmer to be 45.2 years old and to have 1.3 years more education than the average full time farmer does. Of all part time farmers, 57 percent report losses from operations, 32 percent report profits under $10,000 and 11 percent profit over $10,000. Hobby farmers balance the risk and cost of operating by supplementing their income through off-farm employment. Tackling off-farm employment is a characteristic not unique to part-time farmers. The number of unpaid family farmers has steadily decreased over the past 50 years, as wives and children often get jobs off the farm in order to provide a safety net in the event of a catastrophe. Even farm operators are working away from the farm: almost half of all farmers reported another professional activity, be it paid off-farm work or non-agricultural busi-

ness activity. In spite of the disappearance of farms across the nation, agricul-
tural-related employment has remained relatively steady over the past 10 years.

Economics of Farming

Entry Barriers

Loans, government subsidies, and relatively flexible licensing standards aid entry
into agriculture. While numerous charities and benefits, such as the Agricultural
Income Disaster Assistance program (AIDA), have raised money and awareness
for struggling Canadian farmers, their ability to survive is not improving. The
reality is that the profit for small farmers is rapidly shrinking, while the cost to
harvest grows every year. Revenues are not keeping pace with rising equipment,
transportation, fertilizer and pesticide costs. The prices of food are largely un-
related to the costs incurred in cultivating, transporting, processing and selling
the food.

Even well established farmers who have borrowed to invest in equipment
and land would find themselves in debt if they sold everything they had. Recent
droughts and floods have not made yields very promising either. No private insurance companies offer coverage for weather-related catastrophes and government funds are often delayed and insufficient. The hardest hit by these factors
have been the small farmers. Of all farms reporting a loss of income of over
$10,000, small farmers make up the majority.

While much of the vulnerability of small farms to natural disaster is attributed to widespread effects, farmers can plan to minimize the damage incurred.
Farmers susceptible to variable conditions must save and invest during profitable years so they do not end up bankrupt during downswings. The most successful farmers plan and anticipate fluctuations so they do not have to rely on
government support in the case of drought or flooding. This is another case
where farmers, like any other business owners, can ensure stability and long
term growth through planning in cyclical markets.

Banks

Due to the enormous risk and expense of starting or expanding a farm, banks
like to work closely with clients to ensure they are on the right path to success.
Visiting the farm once a year is a bare minimum; most clients are assessed
three or four times a year to continually monitor progress of their investment.
Banks are more than willing to lend funds to farmers with a *formal, viable business plan* to guide operations. Lifestyle farmers are known for repeatedly applying and being repeatedly rejected for loans. Banks are only interested in
producers who are ready to prepare to run a business; any other client puts
them at a great risk of never being paid back. Applicants are screened based
on the cash flow of their operations, similar to the way any other business
owner would be evaluated. A farmer may be able to put up a great deal of
valuable land as collateral, but if his farm is not making money, why should the
bank lend to them?

The Royal Bank breaks farmers into three distinct categories for lending purposes:

1. Lifestyle farmers, whose annual receipts total under $100,000
2. Business farmers, whose annual receipts total between $100,000 and $5 million
3. Commercial farmers, whose annual receipts total over $5 million

Some top clients report over $175 million in annual revenue. "Lifestyle farming is no longer a viable industry," says Vaughn Stuart, Sales and Marketing Manager for Royal Bank Agriculture in an interview in October 2002. He explains that if a family of four requires $50,000 to sustain and revenue from operations is under $100,000, there is little chance of surviving solely from the farm. In fact, most banks encourage families to get involved in off-farm employment during the off-season to maintain a steady income and minimize risk. Mr. Stuart has noticed a steady decrease in the number of business farmers, as the successful ones are being helped by the banks to grow into commercial farms, while the less fortunate are quickly vanishing from rural Canada. While there exists a surplus of available credit in Canada, there are not enough qualified farmers demanding it. Banks are making a clear statement to operators: either run the farm like a business or we won't help you.

Land Management

If a farm is to be operated as a business, land becomes the most precious resource. Farmers can significantly increase yields through efficient equipment, new technologies, and application of chemicals. Use of pesticides, fertilizers, and herbicides may improve annual harvests, but long term effects on the environment must be considered. Like any primary industry, the balance between preservation and production is often difficult to achieve. If Canadian farmers neglect and abuse their land, future generations of rural families will be out of work. Furthermore, the nation will have to rely on imports for food, and the 14 percent of Canadians employed in the food industry will become unemployed. An encouraging study from Environment Canada suggests that it is actually more profitable to consider environmental implications of production: farmers who practise conservation improve their income by an average of $32.78/hectare. While investing in environmental research and new production methods may not deliver immediate visible benefits, the long term advantages are immeasurable. The cost of food poisoning and water contamination on the health care system is enormous; therefore, ensuring inspection and grading of all products is a necessity. Canadian food products are highly regarded on the world market for their high safety standards and quality, giving Canada significant revenues from the industry. If our agricultural exports are to continue to be a major part of Canada's economy, the very means of production, the soil, must be aggressively protected.

Fertile soil is an irreplaceable resource that is already eroding because of ploughing techniques in addition to overexposure to harmful chemicals. Healthy soil provides for plant growth, holds air, nutrients and water, recycles organic waste and breaks down contaminants. Yet few farmers seem to care that the overfertilization of nitrogen leads to erosion, pollution of ground water and the release of greenhouse gases. Research in timing of fertilization and improved manure storage methods is being conducted to make the most of precious soil. Environment Canada's extensive research on the effects of pesticides has led them to promote their findings to farmers. Pesticides are proven to be harmful to all forms of life: humans, the pest to be controlled, the land, birds, fish and insects. Residues from pesticides can accumulate in the crops, causing birth defects in the species inhabiting the farm. Not only have pesticides never been able to completely eliminate an entire species, but they've led to the creation of resistant species that are much more difficult to control. The effects on the water supply of a farm using chemicals can be devastating in the case of a spill or improper use. The Environment Canada website suggests many alternatives to pesticide use, including the increasingly popular genetic engineering. This process allows you to kill insects without harming the environment. The use of insecticides has declined over the past several years.

The federal government recently implemented the Pest Control Products Act, which outlaws the import of pesticide products in Canada, or in between provinces, unless the manufacturing establishment is licensed and complies with the respective region's conditions. It is also illegal to wash pesticides down drains, submerge exposed equipment in water or dispose of pesticides unsafely. Farmers are required to maintain a minimum distance of separation for manure and fertilizer application near wells and waterways.

Much has been made about the introduction of organic products to the food market. While statistics are just beginning to be gathered on organic farming, nearly 1 percent of farms in Canada are producing organic products.

Government Influence

Interest Groups

The Ontario Federation of Agriculture (OFA) is a corporation dedicated to "improve the economic and social well being of farmers in co-operation with county, commodity, and rural groups". (Ontario Federation of Agriculture: About) Made up of 49 county and district federations, the OFA has 43,000 operators paying $150 annually for membership fees. Government policy states that farming groups such as the OFA *must* charge $150 per year for membership; therefore, money cannot be raised by increasing fees. Membership with the OFA also carries many fringe benefits, such as discounts on telephone rates, car rentals with Budget, insurance with Cooperators, as well as health and dental packages for employees at group rates. The OFA has 31 organizational members and affiliates in most commodity groups in Ontario, such as wheat, poultry, and dairy. They partner with these affiliates in lobby efforts of mutual interest, strengthening the farm voice by unifying it. Government representatives in the past have balked at negotiating with farm groups because of the lack of agreement on significant issues. In many cases the OFA will compromise on issues of concern to be certain that their voice is heard.

The Ontario Federation of Agriculture (OFA) is a grass roots organization, meaning it is democratically organized. If a farmer has a concern or recommendation, they contact their local representative on the board of directors. Then the issue is debated and, if deemed relevant, brought to the attention of the Ontario Federation of Agriculture. The OFA then may adopt the policy into its program and bring it to the attention to the Canadian Federation of Agriculture (CFA), a body that sits over lobby groups in many provinces. If the issue is relevant on an international scale, the CFA might bring it to the attention of the IFA, the International Federation of Agriculture. In fact, Ontario farmer Jack Wilson was recently nominated president of the International Federation of Agricultural Producers. Over the Board of Directors in the OFA sits an elected Executive Committee that consists of seven members. The Board of Directors holds meetings nine times per year that are open to the press, members and the general public. The OFA also keeps in touch with members through regular emails: their list contains over 5,000 members. Monthly and quarterly farming magazines and newsletters also advertise OFA announcements. While it's up to the farming community to voice concerns, the OFA's role is to mobilize members and develop lobbying tactics through a strategically organized association.

The government has been active in contacting the OFA for help in developing public policy. In light of the Walkerton disaster, government has launched a joint research program to guarantee quality water for citizens of Ontario. Canada's first Agriculture Policy Framework (APF) has also benefited from OFA contributions and collaboration.

Another key topic is the decrease of farm income over the past decade. Last year, farmers from all over the province were outraged over the lack of government support in wake of rising operating costs and poor yields. The Ontario Federation of Agriculture organized a rally in Queen's Park and a mass phone, email and fax campaign to government representatives. Volunteers posted advertisements in farm supply stores and popular rural coffee shops to notify farmers of the efforts. Letters, emails and faxes were sent out to members with instructions about how to contact officials and attend the downtown rally. The results were overwhelmingly successful. Government phone lines were kept busy through repeated calls by members and volunteers. Queen's Park and many of the province's highways were shut down by the thousands of tractors and ploughs of angry farmers demanding attention. Government immediately gave in to the farmer's requests and worked with the Ontario Federation of Agriculture in creating necessary support programs and a feasible Agricultural Policy Framework.

Participation in the creation and administration of legislation is crucial to the well being of farmers. In many cases, simple environmental policy changes will be of great relevance to producers. For example, Nutrient Management Regulation Bill 81 contains very specific conditions for the use and storage of manure. It is no longer permitted to be stored on clay because of the effects on soil and water run-off, forcing some farmers to build concrete storage, costing tens of thousands of dollars. In many cases, such capital improvements are more beneficial to society than to the farmer, but the farmer is forced to pick up the bill. Similarly, measures to guarantee food safety are provided by the farmer, despite the fact it is the consumer who is benefiting. Many problems in the industry can be attributed to Canadian consumers' refusal to recognize and pay for value-added to the products produced. Since farmers are not able to re-coup their expenses through sales, government subsidies are required to support them. The OFA is also involved in hydro-deregulation procedures, as farmers are affected by the smallest of price increases of electricity. Tax policy, global trade, and rural child care are also issues of concern for the organization.

Successful lobby efforts of the OFA include:

- Reducing the Retail Sales Tax farmers pay by $10 million per year.
- Working with county federations to reduce or eliminate municipal development charges on agricultural outbuildings.
- Lobbying to have electricity development rates reduced, saving about $30 per farm.
- Receiving an equity based formula for federal safety net funding distribution, resulting in an increase in Ontario core safety net funding.

A more recent project of the Ontario Federation of Agriculture has been the campaign for the dire need for high speed internet connections presently not available in many rural areas. The future of the industry is "e-farming", says OFA General Manager Neil Currie. With many farmers already operating satellites and computers on their tractors, those without a decent internet connection have difficulty keeping in touch. The OFA aims to bring technology to those who wouldn't otherwise have it. Moreover, improving internet access in rural Canada will keep rural youth from migrating to the cities. The OFA website contains online tutorials to educate farmers on issues such as gas rebates and hydro billings. With declining membership revenues, the OFA sees an opportunity to recoup money through administering required pesticide management courses over the internet. Presently, farmers must take a Pesticides Management course every five years at a cost of $100. The OFA hopes to be able to provide the program over the internet, charge less, and save farmers time travelling across the province. In addition, the website could generate revenue by selling advertising space.

The Odyssey Report, published in 2001 by the Ontario Federation of Agriculture, contains a series of recommendations based on a study conducted on Ontario farmers and market conditions. Among sections on food safety, marketing, and rural development, the Odyssey Report provides an in depth analysis of measures that need to be taken to stabilize and protect farm income. "Perhaps above all, farmers themselves must realize that the so-called independent farming 'lifestyle' under which previous generations of farmers have operated is no longer economically feasible". (Odyssey Report) More emphasis is being placed on the level of education of farmers with respect to running a business. "In short, customers will drive the markets; investing in market intelligence and business planning will be as critical as owning hard assets". (Odyssey Report) The report also encourages farmers operating on a smaller scale to band together to share costly equipment, access to technology, and valuable information. New technology in the agricultural industry is often falsely assumed to be the saviour to operators bearing higher input costs. The report states that, while innovations have helped offset the diminishing profit margins, they often lead to the formation of larger farming organizations. In other words, the only way to combat rising costs of operation is to accommodate large scale production. The Odyssey Report also made a series of suggestions to the government concerning agricultural policy. While the OFA recognizes the benefits of the safety net programs in place, they point out the need for linking these programs. Under current conditions, a farmer is able to apply for crop insurance during natural catastrophes, even when they already have money in their NISA account. The Canadian government never intended for such double withdrawals to occur, but failing to monitor activities in all programs leads to misuse. Overlooking the size of farms involved and participation in other safety net programs is a bad idea. The 'one size fits all approach' should not be used in distributing subsidies; each case should be evaluated on an individual basis.

The Western Canadian Wheat Growers Association (WCWGA), a non-profit organization, is western Canada's largest farming interest group. Their mandate is to advance development of a profitable and sustainable agricultural industry. With thousands of members paying an annual membership fee of $150, the group possesses significant purchasing power, not to mention a heavy influence over government policy. Members get discounts on gas, insurance, equipment, storage, and business software. Yet the main agenda of the organization remains lobbying any and all issues relevant to farmers. Be it marketing, regulation, or taxes, the WCWGA is at the forefront in all aspects of the industry. Their successful lobby efforts include:

- The removal of quotas on canola, flax, and feed grains.
- Quashing a $3.00 per tonne surcharge on grains leaving the west coast.
- Creation of the Pesticide Management Regulatory Policy.
- Helping to develop NISA (Net Income Stabilization Account).
- Represented farmers' concerns over work stoppages in handling grain.

The group continues to move towards independence of government regulation and marketing to keep all profits in farmers' hands.

The National Farmers Union (NFU) is an interest group whose mandate is to promote fair trade policies to benefit farmers and consumers. They are much more concerned with aiding smaller farmers than multinational agricultural corporations. Their issues of concern include funding for public social and educational programs, environmentally-friendly farming practices, and equality for female farmers. The North American Free Trade Agreement, argues the NFU, is responsible for lowering safety standards for food and discouraging farmers from being accountable to the environment. Specifically, they argue that low prices for farm crops force them to choose between dangerous (to the environment, the food supply, and the farmer) shortcuts and feeding their families. And that is no choice any farmer should ever be forced to make, according to NFU. They offer fascinating evidence in their battle against NAFTA:

- Since 1988, agri-food exports have tripled, while farm incomes have remained unchanged.

- Farm debt has nearly doubled since the inception of the Canada-US Free Trade Agreement from $22.5 billion to $44.2 billion. Interest on the debt almost equals Canadian net farm income, so banks are taking as much as farm owners earn.
- While NAFTA was supposed to create jobs in food processing, employment numbers have decreased since its introduction.
- Freight rates in Saskatoon have skyrocketed from $7.15 per tonne to $35.68 per tonne.
- Today, the majority of flour mills and malt plants are owned by American multinational corporations. In 1988, the majority was Canadian owned.
- Prices of fertilizer, transportation, and fuel have skyrocketed since 1988.
- The number of major machine companies has decreased by 50 percent.
- Adjusted for inflation, government agricultural support is at its lowest level in 18 years.

Oxfam is an international development organization supporting community programs in food security, health, and nutrition. Counting primarily on public donations, the organization raises over $350 million annually to fund its lobby efforts. Their long term goal is to eliminate all forms of poverty, but they also have several short term projects. Oxfam fundraisers, petitions, events, and education programs have made considerable progress in closing sweatshops and promoting equal distribution of wealth and social justice. On the Canadian front, Oxfam is involved in lobbying for environmental legislation, fair income for small farmers, and food safety. Since Oxfam Canada's inception in 1966, they have been forefront in providing supplies for schools and developing public policy. Canadian volunteers have also assisted in programming efforts in developing countries. Oxfam recognizes the crucial relationship between farmers and distributing food to those who need it most, and aims to ease the flow of food to the hungry, while allowing farmers to make a fair living. They oppose free trade policies that hinder countries from implementing food safety, farmer sustenance, and anti-poverty programs. They argue that these policies, while easing entry into foreign markets, encourage dumping that puts smaller farmers out of business. Any efforts of rural development have been devastated by accelerated urbanization. With the majority (over 60 percent) of Caribbeans and Latin Americans living in poverty using agriculture as a means to survive, Oxfam is very conscious of the effects of World Trade Organization trade policies: "The economic dictums of the International Monetary Fund and the rules of the World Trade Organization have forced developing countries to eliminate supports for small farmers (such as public credit, price supports and marketing boards) while reducing tariff barriers on agricultural imports. Simultaneously, the World Trade Organization Agreement on Agriculture has allowed industrialized countries to continue their existing systems of agricultural supports". ("Agriculture" — Oxfam Canada)

Oxfam's position is that policies and prices regarding agriculture, particularly for small farmers, are too crucial in eliminating poverty and preserving natural resources to be left for a market to regulate. And with 70 percent of agricultural commodities controlled by six multinational corporations, more

farmer controlled marketing boards, support groups, and organizations are necessary to defend the small farmer. Oxfam's specific public policy suggestions for
improving the state of Agriculture in Central America include:

- Trade rules must not undermine the right of developing countries to implement national agricultural policies that promote food security and sustainable livelihoods. In a fair trade agreement, this could be achieved by
incorporating a food security clause, which would codify the types of interventions that developing countries could make exempt from trade
liberalization commitments.
- All forms of public support for agricultural exports, including direct export subsidies and export credits provided by industrialized countries
should be eliminated.

A fair trade agreement would oblige the United States to re-design its domestic support policies so that they effectively promote social and environmental objectives, and no longer have negative impacts on small producers in Latin
America.

- A fair trade agreement should provide a framework for regulating the
role of multinational corporations in international agricultural trade to allow for greater competition in international agricultural markets.
- Fair trade rules should encourage agricultural diversification and the
public management of commodity supply and production, with the objective of stabilizing prices.

The Saskatchewan Wheat Pool (SWP) is a publicly traded agri-business co-
operative based in Regina. They channel Prairie production to markets worldwide and provide members with supplier discounts and strategic partnerships.
The Saskatchewan Wheat Pool owns a majority share of powerful insurance,
equipment, processing, fertilizer and pesticide companies, and passes significant
savings on to pool members. With over 70,000 farmers holding membership,
they have a great share of the market for all aspects of farming.

The Canada West Equipment Dealers Association (CWEDA), based in
Calgary, deals with government policies regarding the licensing and regulation
of farming equipment. With a steep $450 annual membership fee, the associa-
tion is not for all farmers. But the 403 current members do benefit greatly
from CWEDA's tight relationship with equipment suppliers, as well as insurance and credit companies. The organization also plays the role of a mediator
in contract disputes between dealers and manufacturers. Its lobby efforts include discussions with provincial governments on legislation, licensing requirements and any regulations that affect dealers. CWEDA is also affiliated with
the North America Equipment Dealers Association, one of the largest and most
influential organizations in the world. By creating a Manufacture Relations
Committee, the association keeps peace between suppliers and equipment dealers, all while ensuring fair prices for farmers. It has a close relationship with
such multinational corporations as Deere, Bobcat, Grasshopper and Caterpillar.
In a market where equipment is incredibly expensive and is showing no sign of
getting cheaper, an alliance like this is necessary to ensure farmers, dealers and
suppliers are getting a fair shake.

The Agricultural Sector of the Canadian Federation for Independent Business is by far one of the most powerful players in agricultural policy making. With 7,300 members, the organization is able to pool its funds to get the best professional advice and information. The main areas of concern are "food safety, quality environment, renewal, science and innovation, and business risk management". They meet regularly with the Canadian Wheat Board, Farm Credit Canada, the Bank of Canada, and officials at all levels of government. By regularly surveying farmers' interests and concerns, the CFIB deals only with issues relevant to Canadian farmers. Their lobbying activities of interest include:

- reducing taxes and regulatory burdens
- end ad hoc subsidies and global trade wars
- increased marketing and transportation options
- fighting restrictive labour standards
- increasing farmer RRSP limits.

Government Subsidy Programs

Before analyzing support programs and evaluating their effectiveness, it is important to consider the rationale behind protecting private sectors of the economy. In most cases, market mechanisms and consumer sovereignty are enough to guide business decisions, with the only government involvement being necessary legislation. However, farming, unlike most industries, *must* be protected in order to ensure and secure the safety of our country. As an indigenous industry, farming plays a major role in Canada's culture. It is perhaps the oldest profession in our nation's history, and rural communities define so much of what is Canada. In subsidizing farmers, the government safeguards the food supply of our country, in addition to keeping an enormous portion of the workforce (14 percent in food and beverage) employed. While farming is best treated like any other business in some respects, it is a special entity. Commodity prices on world markets have been extremely unstable, and the climate has been unpredictable as well. Without support in years of drought, declining yields, and decreasing world market prices, tens of thousands would be without jobs. The effects of such unemployment would put our food supply in danger and subject our economy to vicious fluctuations. Moreover, agricultural advances have resulted from investment in new processes and expansion, and without government assistance to minimize risk, investment will dwindle, pulling the plug on the agriculture industry. Farming plays a significant role in foreign trade, and producers have been hurt by other nations' unfair trade policies. Canada must step in, not only to address breaches of free trade agreements, but protect a crucial industry to trade. It is the responsibility of government to be receptive to the needs of citizens, and it is in the best interest of the general public to allocate tax dollars to protecting farming.

Twentieth century economist John Maynard Keynes analyzed the effects of government intervention on business, and argued that the presence of the state in the economy has many advantages. First, market forces are prone to failure because they simply cannot quantify non-commodities such as human and natural resources. While mechanisms are useful in measuring conditions and improving efficiency, they can have irreparable effects on society and the environment. Government intervention, if designed carefully, can simultaneously protect and grow the economy. Public spending can also encourage investment and innovation. Keynes argued that it is necessary to increase the wages of workers at a rate similar to productivity increases to prevent the economy from going into depression. If salaries are not high enough, people will be unable to consume the goods produced, leading to waste and inefficiency. Therefore, government intervention can act to safeguard precious resources and the economy.

Farm Credit Canada (FCC) is a Crown corporation that reports to the Minister of Agriculture. The main goal of the organization is to develop rural Canada by providing business and financial solutions for farm families and agricultural corporations. Their portfolio includes 44,000 farmers borrowing over $7.7 billion. They loan to all types of farmers: small, large, agricorps, full time, and part time. A major part of their organization is promoting value-adding and diversification, and providing business training and market information. FCC has been leading the assistance to farmers who have suffered rock bottom yields this summer due to drought: "We realize that the drought affects producers across a wide range of sectors and in different areas across the country. That's why we have activated our national response program to reach all our customers who might experience cash-flow difficulties due to drought," says John Ryan, FCC President and Chief Executive Officer. (FCC's Drought Response Targets Producers in All Sectors- Farm Credit Canada) By reaching out to clients with donations of hay, delaying loan payments, and restructuring financing programs, the Crown corporation has shown true initiative in offsetting the effects of drought. Farm Credit Canada has donated $80,000 for the transportation of hay and feed to desperate Prairie farmers. Yet Farm Credit Canada maintains that the key to operating a successful farm has as much to do with the climate as it does with the books. They offer a "Performer Loan", where interest rates are lowered when farmers meet targets pertaining to repayment schedules, cash flow, and debt-equity ratio. FCC offers publications, training, and assistance regarding cash flow strategies, environmental upgrades, planning to succeed, and organic farming. All of this information is contained at the FCC website, and is complemented by a toll free number that handles additional queries.

Another popular feature is the Transition Program, which allows retiring farmers to sell their land to those looking to get into the industry. Whereas most loans require 25 percent down for such a purchase, the FCC asks for only 10 percent and guarantees the retiring farmer will get his/her money. This is an extremely effective tool in encouraging young entrepreneurs and university graduates to enter the agriculture industry. The FCC encourages value adding and diversification through its implementation of the Agriculture Value-Added Loan Program. Funded by the FCC, CIBC, and Western Economic Diversification Canada, the program provides $65 million to Prairie companies looking to invest in food processing and non-food agricultural products. The money can only be put towards research and development, commercial development, new production capacity, and market development. This program is only available to small and medium businesses (annual sales of less than $10 million and fewer than 250 employees) that have a commercially viable product but don't have the means to get involved in food processing. In addition to the funding, Farm Credit Canada offers guidance in creating a business plan to support development and production.

The Net Income Stabilization Account (NISA) is a voluntary program developed jointly between producers, the federal government and participating provincial governments. NISA is designed to help farmers achieve long term income stability through matching producer deposits into special accounts and allowing them to withdraw from the funds they've set aside in low income years. The Net Income Stabilization Account has two components: Fund 1 and Fund 2. The first fund, held at a financial institution, contains all deposits (matchable and unmatchable) and withdrawals from this fund are made only if the second fund is depleted. The second fund, a government account, holds contributions and interest earned on both funds, and is where all withdrawals are made until no money remains.

To be eligible for NISA contributions, you must file a Canadian income tax return reporting farming business income, or meet criteria for participating through an entity such as a corporation, cooperative, or communal organization that files a Canadian income tax return reporting farming business income. Income is measured on the basis of qualifying and non-qualifying commodity,

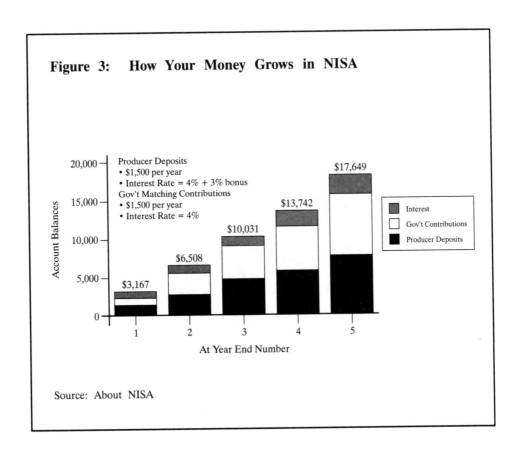

Figure 3: How Your Money Grows in NISA

Source: About NISA

sales, and program payments, as well as income generated from other farm activities, such as agricultural contract work or machine rentals. The maximum contribution a producer can claim is 3 percent of eligible net sales, which are capped at $250,000. (Multimillion dollar agricultural corporations can still apply; their benefits are just maxed at this level.) Eligible net sales are defined by NISA as gross sales of qualifying commodities less purchases of qualifying commodities, including seeds, plants, and livestock purchases.

Agricorp, launched in 1997, is a Crown Corporation that aims to provide affordable crop insurance and consulting services to Ontario's agriculture and food industry. The crop insurance division protects 18,000 producers from reduced yields caused by natural disasters such as droughts, flooding, wind, frost, and insect infestation. Farmers pay half of the cost of premiums, while the federal and provincial governments equally contribute the other half. The plan provides $1.2 billion worth of insurance on 3.5 million acres of land. A Market Revenue Support program protects grain and oilseed growers from income reduction due to low commodity prices. An impressive 22,000 farms are protected in this plan, covering over 85 percent of the eligible acreage in the province. The business services sector of Agricorp offers customized counselling to members in the areas of crop grading and inspection and, in market relations. Membership cost for Agricorp is $160.50 per year.

The problem with Canada's subsidization strategy is that it is too broad; criteria do not exist to exclude farmers who do not require assistance. While intentions of stabilizing income and improving farmers' quality of life are fulfilled, government expenditures are not being put to the best possible use. Since NISA withdrawals and FCC loans are not linked, farmers are able to benefit twice. For example, in a poor harvest year, a farmer can apply for crop insurance payouts from the FCC, even if they have enough money in their NISA account intended to supplement their income. Agricultural corporations, capable of receiving financing from private institutions or not requiring it at all, will apply for assistance because if they do not, their competitor will. The results of farm subsidies are not limited to producers, as spillover effects produce mixed benefits for the rest of society and the economy. In protecting farmers from the unfair trade policies of other countries, Canada only contributes to the problem. Canadian farmers can easily penetrate foreign markets because their exports are subsidized. Much of the poverty in developing nations can be attributed to local growers being unable to compete with foreign farmers dumping subsidized commodities into the market. Even the most efficient farms in the world stand no chance against exports that are 50 percent subsidized. Many Canadian taxpayers are outraged at the idea of having to pay for further support to farmers when they do not receive anything remotely similar to supplement their own income. However, farm income stabilization brings about great advantages to Canadians as well. First, we secure our food supply and have to rely less on trade to feed the country. Second, retailers, consumers, and processors enjoy a steadier industry, as the fluctuations in farm employment, world prices, and farm income can be detrimental to the entire value chain. Furthermore, with sufficient income, farmers are no longer forced to cut corners in food safety and environmental conservation in order to feed their families.

These practices increase the value of Canadian food exports, protect the health of consumers and preserve the land for future generations of Canadian farmers.

The responsiveness of government to distress often rests on the ability of interest groups to communicate member concerns to policy makers. In many cases, government will collaborate with these organizations in the development of assistance programs. Farm Credit Canada can be recognized for their quick response to poor harvesting conditions in their delaying of loan payments due to Prairie farmers who suffered from the drought of 2002. Oftentimes, projected yields by the Canadian Wheat Board are used to prepare subsidies before they are desperately needed.

In many cases, policy makers are compelled to favour large corporations or farming organizations because of their voting power. Much of the assistance granted to producers has come during the months preceding elections and used to silence the angry, starving farmer. The problem continues to be that the starving farmer is not properly using support money to improve the farm, while farming corporations are making the most efficient use of subsidies. In short, those who need the subsidies most are using them worst, while those needing them least are using them best. So, why should the government continue to support those who are not making any effort to help themselves? First, the social and economic effects of immediate elimination of subsidies would be traumatic to the country. Second, farmers must be given the chance to improve their operations, as the idea of farming as a global business is new, while the average farmer is, to put it bluntly, very old. It is in the best interest of the agricultural industry, like any other, to maintain the smaller players who spur innovation, protect their environment, and have the closest contact with the daily operations that define the way the business is run. Those farmers not willing to adapt new methods will be slowly bought out by larger, more efficient corporations, while others will develop into competitive entities.

Public Policy

The majority of provinces operate crop pools and marketing boards to ensure a fair return for farmers' yields. Based in Winnipeg, the Canadian Wheat Board (CWB) is responsible for marketing all wheat and barley grown in western Canada. They have monopoly authority under federal legislation to market Canadian grown wheat and barley. A shared governance corporation, the board consists of five members appointed by government and 10 directors elected by producers. The CWB has over 500 employees, and an annual operating cost of $65.9 million. The board possesses 20 percent of the international market for wheat, making it the largest grain seller in the world. The Wheat Board returns all revenues to farmers, less the cost of administration. Some 85,000 farmers are part of the organization, which has annual revenues of six billion dollars per year. For every tonne of wheat sold by the CWB (as opposed to sold privately), an estimated $13.35 extra is added to the income of Canadian farmers. For those with over 1000 acres of land, this translates into $15,000–$20,000 of additional income per year. They stay ahead of global competitors by ensuring high quality, a reliable supply, and specialized service. Many farmers count on them to buy their harvest at a fair, stable price during global market downturns. The Canadian Wheat Board manages to do this by giving farmers an initial amount based on the grade of the wheat, and pays a certain amount later, based on the price the "pool" of wheat gets on the market. Therefore, the price pooling acts as a stabilizer in times of significant market fluctuations. Farmers sign delivery contract schedules with the board to minimize any cost of storing additional wheat and keep demand for transportation steady. One problem with proposed privatized marketing is that railways and storerooms are beyond capacity during peak periods, as there is no coordination between producers.

The wheat board monopoly keeps prices high, and the specialized information gathered allows them to market wheat and barley to maximize farmer profit. The board bases their decisions on input from weather and crop surveillance, market analysts, risk management, transportation companies, and coordination specialists. In many cases, the data is not possessed by farmers, so aligning with a marketing board is a strategic move.

This saves the small-town farmer from having to make significant decisions regarding technological and business issues that he has no education in. The CWB places a heavy weight on predicted farmer yields, world supply and demand, and price forecasts to develop their sales plan.

The Canadian government in the eighteenth century established the Crow Rate as part of a deal with the Canadian Pacific Railway to build a link between the Crowsnest Pass in the Rockies and into southeastern British Columbia. Government subsidized a portion of the cost of transporting grain within Canada to stabilize farmers' income. By the 1970s, CN and CP railways were complaining about losing hundreds of millions of dollars per year, and many agricultural experts argued that it directed producers away from value-added processing. The United States viewed the Crowsnest Pass Rate as a subsidy that goes against both the North American Free Trade Agreement and World Trade Organization trade agreements. On the other hand, farmers argued that the policy safeguarded them against railways seeking to raise prices excessively, forcing them out of business. After all, they were as essential to the Canadian economy as the railway was, so they should be supported too. On August 1, 1995 the Crow Rate was eliminated and replaced by the Western Grain Transportation Act, which paid railways $658.6 million annually *and* protected farmers from rising freight costs. The Canadian Wheat Board was now being criticized for its role in organizing transportation of grain between farmers and railways. In 1998, the federal government appointed retired Supreme Court Judge Willard Estey to conduct a one year review of grain handling in Canada. The result was the Estey Report, a set of recommendations that were supposed to resolve the freight issue. The conclusions reached in the report included eliminating the wheat board's role in transportation, and removing the cap on rates in exchange for a discount for a long term deal. Transport Minister David Collenette implemented the Estey Report into public policy, minus the CWB condition.

The government failed to consider several other significant findings of the report. Estey suggested that governments begin to spend fuel tax revenues on maintaining rural roads necessary to move grain to market. Many rural highways and streets were in horrible condition due to lack of maintenance and the level of use from enormous trucks constantly transporting the harvest to the Canadian Wheat Board. Many farmers were forced to move commodities using trucks because the cost of using railways was too expensive, or their rural town was so obscure that it was not serviced by a railway. Estey concluded that the government should maintain the Canadian Transportation Agency's mandate to service rural areas and give communities a better chance to purchase branch lines, or at least make the railways pay the money received from closures to the respective communities. One notable finding of the report was that Estey noted that the additional costs of transporting grain to processors was absorbed by the farmer, not by the dealer, the railway, or the consumer.

Many industry experts declare that the Estey Report and similar government subsidies have almost single-handedly put railways out of business due to unfair competition with trucking companies, who have no government restrictions placed upon them. Railways should be allowed to charge what they desire and compete with one another to keep prices fair and provide incentive for servicing rural areas. Farmers feel that grain should be treated like any other commodity, and the red tape and intervention of the Canadian Wheat Board only increases the cost and hassle of handling grain. Recently, the government has lowered hauling charges on a 30 million tonne crop by $178 million per year. A bill was also passed that allows railways to charge more for less-travelled routes in order to meet costs. Railways were given more flexibility to abandon routes, making it easier for short-line operators to acquire lines for local communities and receive compensation. The government has also provided $175 million in funding for roads when rail lines are eliminated.

Agriculture Canada is a government organization that provides information, research, and inspection to ensure the security and safety of the food system. They work with food inspectors in every step of the production process to keep food exports the highest grade and food consumed in Canada safe. The majority of their research is concerned with food testing technologies, genetic screening and developing alternatives to harmful pesticides. They implement policies to protect the environment, reduce greenhouse emissions and prevent soil erosion. Of the one billion dollars Canadians spend on agricultural research annually, Agriculture Canada contributes one-third. The organization is a leader in providing relevant information to allow farmers to make the most of their harvest. The Agrifood Trade Program assists farmers in market access, development and investment, and strategic planning. The program also helps farmers develop alliances with suppliers and other farmers, in addition to informing them of WTO and government regulations and their implications. The Canadian Farm Business Management Program seeks to improve the business management skills of farmers and keep Canadian farms competitive and viable. The Canadian Grain Commission (CGC), under the umbrella of the Minister of Agriculture, is responsible for establishing grading standards for grain to keep Canada's reputation as a premier grain provider. The CGC also licenses primary, process, and terminal elevators. Two Grain Standards Committees meet regularly to discuss necessary changes to grading schemes and quality issues, and is composed of producers, marketers, handlers, and government representatives. Another initiative of the organization is to educate youth about the importance of agriculture to our culture and economy. Touring displays containing all elements of the grain handling system educate and entertain the young and old alike. Another link in the Minister of Agriculture chain includes Farm Credit Canada.

Globalization

The Uruguay Trade Agreement (1995, also known as the World Trade Organization Agreement in Agriculture) was designed to ensure fair competition in the farming industry and eliminate distortion. Trade is "distorted" if prices are higher or lower than they should be, causing quantities produced, bought, and sold to be higher or lower than they would be in a competitive market. Least Developed Countries were exempt from the conditions of the agreement to allow them to secure and stabilize their farming industry. The agreement is based on a restriction of the level of protectionist policies that encourage trade distortion. Governments seek to distort their agricultural market for three reasons. The first is to ensure that enough food is produced. The second is to protect farmers from weather-related catastrophes and world price fluctuations. Finally, the third relates to governments wishing to protect agricultural markets in order to preserve rural society.

The new rules and commitments of the WTO Agreement in Agriculture are based on three areas: Market Access, Domestic Support and Export Subsidies. Market access policies concern any trade restrictions that affect imports. Developed nations are only permitted to use tariffs to protect their markets, as quotas and other non-tariff measures are banned. Tariffication level is limited to the level domestic prices were higher than import prices under previous policies. For example, if, under the previous policy, domestic price levels were 45 percent higher than world prices, the tariff cutoff is 45 percent. Additionally, developed nations are forced to reduce all tariff levels by 36 percent over six years. Domestic Support includes subsidies and programs that raise prices and farmer income. The World Trade Organization criticizes these programs for inciting overproduction, squeezing out imports and encouraging dumping on world markets. Developed nations, under the act, are forced to decrease support levels by 20 percent from the base year by 2001. The act does, however, distinguish research projects, disease control, and food security programs from support programs, and these areas will not be forced to make cuts. Export Subsidies, used to make exports artificially competitive, are also being scrutinized by the WTO. Under the Agreement in Agriculture, the value of export subsidies is being cut by 36 percent and the quantity of them by 21 percent.

The WTO Agreement in Agriculture also contains a section on food safety and licensing, called the Agreement on Application of Sanitary and Phytosanitary Measures. Many trade disputes between nations exist because of a lack of international standard for food safety, allowing countries to block imports by raising their own standards above those of other nations. The new policy still allows countries to set their own standards, but regulations must be across the board and based on scientific reasoning. Any policies must exist to protect humans, animals, or plant life, and cannot be used to discriminate unfairly against global competition. Nations are even allowed to raise their standards above international levels, as long as increases are across the board, and not targeting a specific area.

While many taxpayers would argue that Canadian farmers are over-subsidized, they pale in comparison to their counterparts in other industrialized nations. While nine cents of every dollar of income earned by a Canadian farmer is subsidized directly, the European Union farmers are receiving 56 cents and American farmers receive 45 cents. An astounding 48 percent of the European Union's budget is spent on the Common Agricultural Policy (CAP): this in spite of the fact only 5 percent of the workforce is employed in agriculture.

European Union farmers are fortunate in the sense that the increase in retail prices for food products has kept pace with increasing production costs.

Canadian farmers are seeing their expenses increase at a higher rate than their revenues.

Grants are also given to European farmers who grow their crops organically, a measure that has yet to catch on in North America.

In the United States, the US Farm Bill, released in 2002, is America's latest agricultural policy. The government is increasing spending on the industry to $180 billion, up 70 percent from the previous plan. The extremely complex plan has been harshly criticized for its effects on world markets. American govern-

Table 3: Annual Rate of Change of Agricultural Products

Canada	1995	2000	1995 to 2000	1995	2000	1995 to 2000
	Farms Reporting			Amount		
	Number		% Change	Current $		% Change
All farms in Canada	276,548	245,923	−10.7	...	...	...
Operating expenses	276,548	246,923	−10.7	26,669,926,814	33,213,077,917	24.5
Gross farm receipts[2,3]	276,548	246,923	−10.7	32,230,356,237	38,298,728,817	18.8
Sales of forest products[4]	17,735	13,228	−25.4	180,061,841	117,437,428	−34.8

... Not applicable.
1. Data are reported on Census Day for the preceding or fiscal year.
2. "Gross farm receipts" excludes forest products sold.
3. As in previous censuses, response errors have resulted in an under-reporting of total gross farm receipts. However, the data are comparable with previous censuses.
4. Due to response errors in previous censuses, the sales of forest products may have been overstated. Changes to this question for 2001 limit the comparability of the data to previous censuses.

Source: Statistics Canada, Census of Agriculture

ment seeks to guarantee farm income under *all* conditions (as opposed to Canadian programs that only safeguard farmers from *unavoidable* catastrophes). Therefore, there is no incentive for farmers to follow market trends or operate efficiently, as their income is guaranteed. Such subsidy programs are *counter-cyclical*, in other words, encourage farmers to continue to overproduce in surplus situations. Farmers will attempt to expand production by any means possible in order to increase overall income. Clearly, the US Farm Bill subsidies are geared towards larger producers, as 8% of the farms are eating up 47% of the support funding. Since America exports 25% of its agricultural commodities and 40% of its wheat, the effects of the farm bill on other nations is devastating. The World Trade Organization limit on support programs is $19.1 billion per year, and the United States is expected to grossly exceed this level. Experts are unsure whether the costs of surpassing the limit will be absorbed by the government or lead to reduced support rates. Canada has already started negotiating with the American government over conditions in the farm bill. Canadians want an elimination of agricultural export subsidies, improved market access for all food products, and a reduction in domestic support levels. It is absolutely crucial to the future of Canadian farming that necessary actions be taken to enforce WTO policies.

Canadian farmers and agribusinesses are experiencing difficulty competing with multinational corporations, even in our own country. Despite Canada's efforts to minimize protectionism in agriculture, we are still pressured by other developed nations to eliminate all forms of support — even by the nations mentioned above. Most of Canada's farmers support a decrease in government intervention in order to increase their income and efficiency in the long term; yet, by the time this happens, there will be few small farmers left.

Canadian farmers also suffer from a drastically different market for food, as the North American consumer values speed, convenience, and quantity of food more than quality and variety. This precludes any attempt or measure by farmers to increase their revenues from value-adding or diversification. Consumers in the Western world know what they want to eat, and they clearly do not want to pay any more than they have to for it. Canadians spend just 9.8 percent of their disposable income on food, the lowest rate in the entire world. Yet Canada's quality and safety standards are among the highest in the world. This is another example of how farmers are bearing the costs of improving the finished product, but are not receiving payment for their efforts. So many of the problems with the agricultural industry result from this fallacy. If farmers were compensated for efforts to conserve the environment, not only would they play a more active role in preservation, they would be able to sustain themselves. Billions in tax revenues would no longer be allocated towards subsidization if farmer received the proper price for their harvest. While government intervention in farming is necessary to preserve culture, protect the economy and farmers from violent fluctuations, and ensure food safety, it is only fair to allow the market to determine fair prices for value-added goods, rather than throwing money at farmers whenever a problem arises.

Conclusion/Recommendations
Lifestyle Farmers

While most indicators of current market conditions point to the imminent collapse of lifestyle farmers, much can be done to secure their place in the Canadian economy. Rural development and the educating of youths are necessary to ensure future generations will take over family farms, and be good at running them.

Farm operators should get in the habit of hiring non-relative workers to allow children to finish school and parents to balance risk through off-farm employment. Operators must also be able to get away from the land to continuously upgrade training and business education to ensure efficiency and competitiveness. Farmers cannot expect a full time, stable income if they only work seasonally and make no attempt to educate themselves.

Not only does the tight community farming creates benefit the culture, but it also keeps producers in touch with one another. Lifestyle farmers must develop relationships with suppliers and fellow producers to maximize their ability to control their environment and minimize uncertainty. If an individual farmer is unable to access specialized information or afford new equipment, he must work with other farmers to share in the purchase and benefits of such necessary items. Participation in interest groups is required to educate, motivate, and mobilize farmers to participate in the development of public policy. Lifestyle farmers must also familiarize themselves with computer and internet applications necessary in the record keeping and operations of a business. Furthermore, farmers must plan for highly cyclical and fluctuating conditions through saving in years of good yields for periods of drought and low market prices.

Small Business Farmers

While the number of small business farmers has been decreasing, it is only a sign of their success and ability to expand into multi-million dollar agricultural corporations. Those investing in diversification, undergoing consulting and business training, planning for a violently unstable industry, and spreading risk through off farm income and value adding will continue to be successful. If there is one deserving farming group government must protect, it is the small business farmer: they possess the competitiveness and strategic planning of a corporation, the risk management of a part time farmer, innovativeness and flexibility of a small business, and concern for environment and society of a lifestyle farmer.

Agricultural Corporations

In order to maintain their success, they should continue investing in research, diversification, and value-added processing. Corporations such as Maple Leaf and McCain's maximize their ability to control their environment in a rapidly changing industry through diversifying products and customers, vertical coordination and integration, and development of productivity improving methods of operation. In order to protect their status as global leaders, they must care for the soil they draw so much money out of. A great way to foster consumer loyalty, in Canada and worldwide, is through the environmentally conscious, health and safety regulated production of food.

Government

The Canadian government has an excellent opportunity to secure Canada's position as a leader in agricultural trade for years to come. The regulation, standardization, and licensing of operations and methods are essential to conserving the land for future generations of farmers. Money directed to protecting and developing the agricultural industry is poorly allocated and requires new incentives for new beneficiaries. Rather than throwing subsidy money at flourishing agricultural corporations, government can provide tax incentives for environmentally friendly production and fund socially beneficial research and development of new technologies. Small business farmers would benefit more from expansion-related loans and business counselling than support for income stabilization. Canada would greatly profit from the entry of highly motivated entrepreneurs and university graduates into agriculture. It is up to the government to minimize risk associated with investment and ease entry into the industry. Lifestyle producers are the hardest to influence and intervene on because they are often part of a long lineage of traditional farmers encountering a highly dynamic market. Government programs such as the FCC should continue to place a value on educating and training small farmers to be competitive and responsive to an unstable industry. Rural development is key to sustaining traditional farmers, as communities without schools, high speed internet access, railways, and well maintained highways are not going to accommodate the needs of future generations of producers. If Canadian consumers are unwilling to pay for the processes required to produce quality food, government support is needed. Socially beneficial measures to preserve the environment and meet health safety standards must be funded at least partially by the government or Canadian consumer. Fuel tax revenues should be directed to the maintenance of rural highways so commodity carrying trucks can effectively service rural communities without railways.

Although protectionist measures may conflict with the spirit of free trade agreements, agriculture is a unique industry in the sense that it is naturally unstable and requires intervention to ensure employment and investment. Otherwise, the food supply, foreign trade, health, and society of the nation becomes threatened.

Glossary

Throughout the course of this paper, the following terms alluded to in Statcan statistics are to be defined in the following manner:

Farm
A farm, ranch or agricultural operation that produces at least one of the following products intended for sale: crops, livestock,

poultry, animal products, greenhouse or nursery products, Christmas trees, mushrooms, sod, honey, and maple syrup products.

Farm operator
Persons responsible for day-to-day management decisions made in the operation of the census farm.

Net Farm Income:
Net income (gross receipts from farm sales minus depreciation and cost of operation) received during the 2000 calendar year from the operation of a farm, either on the respondent's own account or in partnership. In the case of partnerships, only the respondent's share of income was reported. Included with gross receipts are cash advances received in 2000, dividends received from cooperatives, rebates and farm-support payments to farmers from federal, provincial, and regional agricultural programs (e.g. milk subsidies and marketing board payments), and the gross insurance proceeds, such as payments from the Net Income Stabilization Account. The value of income "in kind", such as agricultural products produced and consumed on the farm, is excluded.

Net Non-Farm Income From Unincorporated Business and/or Professional Practice
Net income (gross receipts minus expenses of operation, such as wages, rents, and depreciation) received during calendar year 2000 from the respondent's non-farm unincorporated business or professional practice. In the case of partnerships, only the respondent's share was reported. Also included is the net income from persons babysitting in their own homes, persons providing room and board to non-relatives, self-employed fishers, hunters, and trappers, operators of direct distributorships (such as those selling and delivering cosmetics), as well as freelance activities of artists, writers, music teachers, hairdressers, dressmakers, etc.

Rural Farm Population
All persons living in rural areas who are members of the households of farm operators living on their census farms for any length of time during the 12 month period prior to the census.

Rural and Small Town
The population living outside the commuting zone of larger urban centres (LUC's) — specifically, outside Census Metropolitan Areas (CMA's) and Census Agglomerations (CA's). RST includes all municipalities with urban populations of 1,000 to

9,999 and rural areas, where less than 50 percent of the employed individuals commute to the urban core of a CMA/CA.

(Statistics Canada — Catalogue No. 92-378-XIE 2001 Census Dictionary — Internet Version)

References

"About Agriculture and Agri-Food Canada." March 13 2002. Agriculture and Agri-Food Canada. September 12 2002. http://www.agr.gc.ca/aafc_e.phtml

"About Canadian Organic Growers." May 9 2002. Canadian Organic Growers. Sept 12 2002. http://www.cog.ca/aboutcog.htm

"About CCA." 2002. Canadian Cattleman's Association. Sept. 12 2002. http://www.cattle.ca/ABOUT%20CCA/aabout.htm

"About NISA." 29 July 2002. NISA: Net Income Stabilization Account. Nov 27 2002. http://www.agr.gc.ca/nisa/welcome.html

"Agriculture." 2001. Oxfam Canada. 27 Nov 2002. http://www.oxfam.ca/news/Peoples_Summit/Opposes_FTAA.htm#agriculture

"Agriculture: Fairer Markets for Farmers." WTO: Trading Into The Future — agreements — agriculture. November 27 2002. http://www.wto.org/english/thewto_e/whatis_e/tif_e/agrm3_e.htm

Agriculture and Agri-Food Canada, Net Income Stabilization Account. *Program Handbook: A Policy and Administrative Guide for NISA Participants.* Canada: NISA, 2002.

"Annual Rate of Change of...Agricultural Products." European Commission, Eurostat. November 29 2002. http://europa.eu.int/comm/agriculture/agrista/2001/table_en/en334.pdf

"Applications to the Land." May 15 2002. Canadian Statistics. Nov 29 2002. http://www.statcan.ca/english/Pgdb/econ104a.htm

Baumol, Blinder, Scarth. Economics: Principles and Policy. Canada: Harcourt Brace and Company Canada Ltd, 1994.

Boyens, Ingeborg. Another Season's Promise. Toronto: Penguin Group, 2001.

"Budgetary Expenditure on the Common Agricultural Policy." European Commission Directorate General for Agriculture. November 29 2002. http://europa.eu.int/comm/agriculture/agrista/2001/table_en/en341.pdf

Canada. Statistics Canada. *Agricultural and Rural Working Paper Series.* November 14 2002. Catalogue#: 21-601-MIE2002055, 21-601-MIE2001051, 21-601-MIE2001050, 21-601-MIE1999040, 21-601-MIE1998033.

For all papers in the series, visit this site: http://www.statcan.ca/cgi-bin/downpub/listpub.cgi?catno=21-601-MIE

Canada. Statistics Canada. *Agricultural Economic Statistics.* May 2002. Catalogue#: 21-603-UPE.

Canada. Statistics Canada. *Economic Overview of Farm Incomes.* October 23 2002. Catalogue#: 21-005-XIE.

"Canada-US Trade." 2002. The Canadian Embassy Washington, DC. October 29 2002.

www.canadianembassy.org/trade/hark.n-e.asp

"Census Dictionary 2001." Statistics Canada. November 27 2002.
http://www.statcan.ca/english/census2001/dict/appendices/92-378-XIE02002.pdf

"Certified Organic Farming." May 15 2002. Canadian Statistics. 29 Nov 2002.
http://www.statcan.ca/english/Pgdb/econ103a.htm

"CFIB- Agribusiness Index." 11 Sept 2002. CFIB. 19 Sept 2002. http://www.cfib.ca/agri/

Currie, Neil. General Manager, Ontario Federation of Agriculture. Personal interview. 19 November 2002.

"CWB- About Us." 2002. Canadian Wheat Board. Septemberr 12 2002.
http://www.cwb.ca/en/about/

"CWEDA Products and Services Offered by the Association." 4 November 1997. CWEDA. 19 September 2002. http://www.cweda.ca/products.htm

Doern, Hill, Prince, Shutz. Changing the Rules. Toronto: University of Toronto Press, 1999.

"Estey Report." Canada Grain. 25 September 2002.
http://www.grain.gc.ca/english/final.htm

"Employment in Agriculture and in the Other Sectors." European Commission, Eurostat, and OECD. November 29 2002.
http://europa.eu.int/comm/agriculture/agrista/2001/table_en/en3513full.pdf

"Farm Stress Line When You Need Someone To Talk To." 2000. Saskatchewan Agricultural, Food, and Rural Revitalization. November 27 2002.
http://www.agr.gov.sk.ca/docs/about_us/organizational_info/fsf0394.asp

"Farms by Gross Farm Receipts." 15 May 2002. Canadian Statistics. November 29 2002. http://www.statcan.ca/english/Pgdb/econ111a.htm

"FCC-FAC: Corporate Profile." 2002. Farm Credit Canada. Sept 12 2002.
http://www.fcc-fac.ca/english/index.shtml

"FCC's Drought Response Targets Producers in All Sectors." 20 September 2002. FCC-FAC: News Releases. 29 November 2002.
http://www.fcc-fac.ca/english/our_company/media/news_releases/2002_09_20.shtml

"Financial Highlights." 2001. Maple Leaf Investor Zone. November 27 2002.
http://www.mapleleaf.com/investors/financial_highlights.htm

Galbraith, John Kenneth. A Journey Through Economic Time. New York: Houghton Mifflin Company, 1994.

George, Roy E. Understanding the Canadian Economy. Peterborough: Broadview Press, 1988.

"Grain Transportation Review Coverage Index." 29 June 2002. The Western Producer. 19 Sept 2002 http://www.producer.com/standing_editorial/est

"The Green Lane: About Environment Canada." 3 April 2002. Environment Canada. Sept 19 2002 http://www.ec.gc.ca/introec/index_e.htm

"Gross Farm Receipts and Expenses." 15 May 2002. Canadian Statistics. Nov 29 2002.
http://www.statcan.ca/english/Pgdb/econ114a.htm

Grossman, Gene M and Elhanan Helpman. Special Interest Politics. Cambridge: The MIT Press, 2001.

Jurkowski, MacKinnon, Nicholson. Business and Government. North York: Captus Press, 2000.

"McCain World Wide" 2001. McCain.com. November 27 2002.
http://www.mccain.com/McCainWorldWide/

National Farmers Union. *Free Trade: Is It Working For Farmers?* NFU, 2002.

Ontario Federation of Agriculture. *Odyssey Report*. Canada: OFA, 9 Sept 2002.

"Ontario Federation of Agriculture: About" 2002. Ontario Federation of Agriculture. November 27 2002.
http://www.ofa.on.ca/top%20menu/about/_private/default.htm

"Oxfam Canada- About Oxfam." 2001. Oxfam Canada. September 19 2002.
http://www.oxfam.ca/about/index.htm

Presthus, Robert. Elites in the Policy Process. Toronto: The Macmillan Company of Canada Limited, 1974.

Pross, Paul. *Governing Under Pressure: The Special Interest Groups.* Toronto: The Institute of Public Administration Canada, 1982.

Pross, Paul. Pressure Groups. New York: Oxford University Press, 1993.

"Questions and Answers: US Farm Bill." US Farm Bill. November 27 2002.
http://www.eudelindia.org/eu/us_farma_bill.htm

Savoie, Donald J. *The Politics of Public Spending in Canada.* Toronto: University of Toronto Press, 1990.

"Soil Conservation Practices." May 30 2002. Environment Canada. November 27 2002.
http://www.ec.gc.ca/soer-ree/English/SOER/1996report/Doc/1-7-4-4-6-2-2-1.cfm

Stuart, Vaughn. Sales and Market Manager, Royal Bank of Canada, Agriculture and Agribusiness Banking Ontario. Personal Interview. October 2002.

"SWP Agricultural Information." September 03 2002. Saskatchewan Wheat Pool. 19 Sept 2002.   http://www.swp.com/aginfo/

"Take a Positive Stand On.." National Farmers Union. September 19 2002.
http://netsent.com/soyawanna.htm

"Welcome to John Deere." 2002. John Deere. September 19 2002.
http://www.deere.com/en_US/deerecom/sitemap/index.html

"The Western Canadian Wheat Growers Association: About Us. Aug 26 2002. The WCWGA. September 19 2002.   http://www.wcwga.ca/aboutus.html

"What is 4-H Council?" Canada 4-H Council. November 27 2002.
http://www.4-h-canada.ca/index.html

"What is Agricorp?" 1999. Agricorp — Working Together To Strengthen Ontario's Agri-Food Industry. November 27 2002.
http://www.agricorp.com/about.asp

Wilson, Graham K. *Interest Groups.* Oxford: Basil Blackwell Ltd, 1990.

Privatization of Pearson International Airport

Diane Jurkowski

Often associated with privatization is the assumption that government enterprises are dumped at a loss after consuming great amounts of public money. Privatization has not always been properly used to reduce deficits, except by the difference between the sale price and the value at which the assets are carried on government's books. The reasons for privatization have resulted in shaping a number of key policy decisions in the 1990s. In fact, this was the case for the privatization of federal government airports in Montreal's Dorval and Mirabel, the first airports to be privatized, Toronto's Pearson International Airport which is Canada's busiest, Calgary International Airport which is the fourth busiest and Vancouver, which is the second busiest airport in the country.

The Premise for the Privatization of Pearson International Airport

Transport Canada, the federal department responsible for all transportation policies in Canada, had estimated that at a growth rate of 3 percent a year, Pearson International Airport would exceed its 28 million-passenger capacity by 1997 or 1998. However, industry experts disputed this. Industry expert Gordon Sinclair, chair and chief executive of Air Transport Association of Canada, challenged these figures, revealing that air traffic was only 18.5 million passengers in 1991. With the estimated 3 percent growth a year, Pearson International Airport would reach its capacity by 2005. The federal government had problems projecting air traffic growth in the past. In 1970, Transport Canada had tried to justify a new airport in Pickering, northeast of Toronto. It projected that 62 million passengers would require an airport by 2000. This was before deregulation and the price wars that developed and changed these projections. Amid public protest of local residents, the expansion of what at that time was known as Malton Airport, serving 6 million passengers a year, saw the cancelling of the Pickering airport development.

With one of the worst recessions of the century, the Progressive Conservative Minister of Industry, Michael Wilson, was adamant that the debt-laden federal government wanted to avoid incurring any large capital expenses for Pearson International Airport. Protests were voiced believing that the federal government would lose $100 million in annual profits with the privatization of Pearson International Airport.

Controversy began with the announcement by Prime Minister Brian Mulroney that Pearson International Airport was similar to other federal airport facilities and would be expanded and developed by the private sector. The Prime Minister wanted to see the private sector assume job-creating project to assist the economy. He believed that the expansion and development of Pearson International Airport would be such a project. There was also dissension expressed by both provincial and municipal governments that wanted a strategy to develop the region.

The Ontario New Democratic Party Minister Ruth Grier, who was responsible for the Greater Toronto Area, expressed fear that privatization of the re-development and expansion of Pearson International Airport would result in higher charges at the airport. According to her, lucrative international traffic would shift to Montreal. However, this appeared unlikely, given that in 1990, Pearson International Airport handled 22 million passengers, compared with 6.3 million at Dorval and 2.4 million at Mirabel. Of greater interest was the Ontario Ministry of Transport's work on a proposal with regional municipal governments and businesses to establish regional airport authorities that would oversee airports in Buttonville (northeast of Toronto) in Markham, Toronto Island Airport (in downtown Toronto) and the Oshawa Airport which is east of Toronto. By privatizing the terminals at Pearson International Airport before a regional airport authority could be established and operational, the federal government would pre-empt the regional airport authority's ability to shape the development of airline traffic in the Toronto area. As well, Metropolitan Toronto Councillors sought a court injunction to block the privatization of Pearson International Airport. But nothing could stop or prevent the government's decision.

In the summer of 1991, in the grip of one of the worst recessions, Transport Minister Jean Corbeil surprised the development community when he ordered the fast tracking of proposals for privatization of Pearson International Airport. The status of the three terminals indicated that Terminal 1 was operating at about one-third of its capacity and Terminal 3 was operating at 50 percent. Transport Canada was considering whether to invest in extensive renovations or to bulldoze Terminal 1. At the time, Terminal 2, which was not being used to its capacity, had just received $125 million worth of renovations from Air Canada and Transport Canada. In addition, Air Canada was negotiating an alliance with USAir and Canadian Airlines International Ltd. that would see USAir move to Terminal 1.

With the announcement of the privatization of Pearson International Airport, the airline industry advocated that there was no necessity to expand terminal capacity. Gordon Sinclair, chair and chief executive of the Air Transport Association of Canada, stated that there was no immediate urgency to privatize Pearson. Other airline industry people recommended to the Minister of Transport, Jean Corbeil, to wait until mid-1993. By that time, it would be advantageous to project the rate of economic recovery from the recession. Some airport developers argued that an environmental review was required before any decisions be made about the runways. Public hearings were scheduled to begin and a decision about the runways would be made in the summer.

In March 1992, the federal government officially announced a proposal to re-develop and privatize Terminals 1 and 2. Pearson Airport is directly and indirectly responsible for approximately 56,000 jobs. Although revenues declined from $170 million in 1990 to $134 million in 1991 because of the effect of the privately developed Terminal 3 in 1991, the federal government still earned $42 million a year in profits. However, both Air Canada and Canadian Airlines International Ltd. had losses totalling $400 million.

The Road to Privatization

Privatization of Pearson International Airport began in 1987, when Toronto developer Huang and Danczkay Properties Inc. with Lockheed Air Terminal of Canada Ltd., were awarded the development of Terminal 3 at a cost of $520 million. By 1992, there was a growing concern in the airline industry that a repetition of the tactics used by Huang and Danczkay would not be used. It was alleged that Huang and Danczkay gained a monopolistic position in developing the Airport Terminal at the expense of the taxpayers. The current status indicated that the developer was experiencing financial problems. To resolve these, the developer downloaded the debt and cost onto the airline carriers and travelling consumers. For example, the per-passenger costs at Terminal 3 were three times more than at the other Terminals. The airlines feared that privatizing Terminals 1 and 2 would boost everyone's costs to the level of Canada's only private terminal, Terminal 3. The industry's goal was to be more competitive with low-cost carriers.

In October 1990, the federal government announced that it would upgrade Pearson's two older terminals. Developers began to prepare for the project, which was estimated to cost approximately $1 billion. Initially, Paxport Management Inc. was formed through partnerships with 17 companies, most of them linked to the airport or airport development for the specific purpose of responding to the privatization of the two terminals. Transport Canada proposed that those planning, architectural and engineering services of $500 million be awarded to Paxport. However, they were given no notice.

As a former Crown Corporation, Air Canada has always enjoyed good relations with Transport Canada. The airline was not about to give up. Air Canada had been allowed substantial input on the development of facilities when Transport Canada negotiated with the developer of Terminal 3.

On March 12, 1992, Transport Minister Jean Corbeil and Industry Minister Michael Wilson announced the privatization of Pearson's Terminals 1 and 2. Mr. Corbeil stated that in order to avoid future congestion, upgrading of the two terminals was necessary at that time because the process would take five years to complete. Both cabinet ministers stated that they wanted the airport's users, not the taxpayers, to pay for the upgrading and operation of the airport. Developers were to submit their proposals within 90 days to lease, renovate and manage the two terminals. They were to submit two proposals. One would be based on the assumption that no new runways would be built. The other was to be based on the assumption that three runways would be added. When was left unclear was how a non-profit airport authority would function under privatization.

According to Transport Canada policy, airlines cannot own terminals. If the federal government could not finance renovations of Pearson International Airport, the airline carriers were prepared to bear the cost of the airport operations when the time was right. But they did not want to assume unnecessary expenses, particularly after the 1991 losses that totalled nearly $400 million for Air Canada and Canadian Airlines International Ltd. Their main concern was doing business at its most important airports under the control of a privately owned monopoly.

For Air Canada, Terminal 2 is their linchpin and operational centre. Their interest was in an efficiently run facility with minimum costs borne by consumers. The other airline carriers operating out of Terminals 1 and 2 expressed concern about increased costs, as was the case in the development of Terminal 3. Their concern was to ensure that airline carriers would be more competitive with low-cost carriers.

The First Decision

Between July and September 1992, the federal government entertained two major proposals from private sector consortiums. One that seemed to be favoured by senior cabinet ministers was the proposal from Paxport Management, representing a consortium led by Matthews Group Ltd. of Mississauga, Ontario and Agra Industries of Calgary, Alberta and financed by the Canadian Imperial Bank of Commerce. Another proposal was presented by Claridge Properties, Inc., which was a holding company of the Bronfman family. The airline industry continued to be puzzled by the insistence of the federal government's decision to privatize Pearson International Airport, considering that the recently completed $500 million Terminal 3 was showing losses and air passenger traffic was reduced.

Amid criticisms from Opposition Members of Parliament and bureaucrats, the directive from the Prime Minister showed a determination to privatize. The intent was to establish job-creating projects. For example, the Paxport Management proposal estimated 19,000 person-years of employment, perceived necessary in the depressed Toronto construction industry. Federal bureaucrats in Transport Canada opposed the privatization of Pearson. It had been a policy that smaller airports in Canada, such as Corner Brook and Saskatoon, needed Pearson's profits to keep them open. They further pointed out that it would be at least two years before all negotiations would be completed. There was intensive lobbying on behalf of the two bidders, involving lobby groups, senior bureaucrats and powerful cabinet ministers. The Paxport Management proposal was lobbied by former federal Deputy Minister Ray Hession, Hugh Riopelle, who was Air Canada's Ottawa lobbyist and lobbyist William Neville, head of Prime Minister Brian Mulroney's 1984 transition team. Claridge Properties Inc., which took over Terminal 3 from the original developer, Huang and Danczkay, retained the lobbying services of William Fox and Harry Near of Earnscliffe Strategy Group. Both were strategists in the Prime Minister's election campaign and lobbyists for Canadian Airlines International Ltd. and Air Canada.

Prior to announcing the agreement, Paxport Management Ltd. had joined a consortium that owned Terminal 3 to form Pearson Development Corp., which was headed by Don Matthews. This new partnership was 66 percent owned by Terminal 3 Partnership, a company controlled by Charles Bronfman's Claridge Group, 17 percent by the companies owned by Bracknell and Agra companies and another 17 percent by other companies that included Don Matthews.

In December 1992, the decision was made to award the Pearson Development Corporation control over the re-development and management of Pearson International Airport. It is to be noted that during the 1993 federal election campaign the contract to privatize Toronto" Pearson International Airport had been the object of intense debates. Prior to the elections, the Progressive Conservative government insisted on signing the contract during the campaign in October 1993. This provoked insinuations and allegations of wrongdoing. The Liberal leader, Jean Chretien, promised that he would, if elected, cancel the contract.

The privatization deal included what amounted to a 37-year lease to take over Terminals 1 and 2 (with an option to renew for another 20 years) and entitles the Pearson Development Corp. to collect rent from airlines and shopkeepers and fees for parking, and user fees from limousine and taxi drivers. Any pricing changes would require approval from Transport Canada. The agreement restricted Transport Canada from financing improvements or expansions to any airports within a 75 kilometre radius of Pearson International Airport until passenger flow reached 33 million, nearly double the present 19 million.

The federal government would receive $28 million in lease payment for the Terminals in the first year and increased amounts over subsequent years based on gross revenues, compared to approximately $24 million in annual profits that Transport Canada earns from the terminals. However, Transport Canada would defer $33 million over the first three years to allow for development and to prevent airline rental increases. As an added bonus, it was estimated that during the six-year development process the project would employ 1,000 people.

A Reversal in Policy Decision with a Change of Government

Several criticisms about the actual agreement were levied. One was that the process was rushed to accommodate an impending federal election called on

October 25, 1993. Another was that "mega" projects are fiscally irresponsible and unnecessary during a period of recession. Yet, the highly critical and beleaguered Ontario and Toronto municipal governments offered nothing more in the way of a solution than threatening the federal government with a court injunction to prevent the privatization of a federal facility. It could not rally the citizenry to oppose the federal government's intention of privatization.

Against the advice of airline industry officials, Transport Canada's senior public administrators recommended an alternative of a non-profit local airport authority. Private developers faced with an opportunity to gain control of the profitable Pearson International Airport facility hired lobbyists to push for their interests with no mention of a non-profit local airport authority. December 1993 witnessed the formation of the new government of Prime Minister Jean Chretien. The newly elected Prime Minister announced that the Pearson International Airport deal was to be terminated. Although allegations were made of Progressive Conservative patronage, two-thirds of the Pearson Development Corp. were prominent Liberals, including Charles Bronfman's key adviser, Leo Kolber, who is a Liberal fundraiser and a Senator.

To justify Prime Minister Chretien's decision to cancel the Pearson International Airport deal, he appointed Robert Nixon, a former leader of the Ontario Liberal Party, to inquire into the circumstances surrounding the privatization. He produced a report containing only allegations of a very general nature, a bogus report that became the basis of the new Liberal government's cancellation of the contract at great expense to the Canadian taxpayers. The developers and promoters sued the federal government. However, the legislation tabled by the Liberal government to cancel the deal prevented the developers and promoters from taking recourse to the courts. In other words, the developers and promoters could not sue the federal government for the cancellation of the privatization deal. Legal experts were outraged with the government's action. They argued that this was a direct violation of the Canadian Charter of Rights and Freedoms. Neither the Bloc Quebecois nor the Reform Parties opposed it. The Minister of Justice, Allan Rock, defended the indefensible. No one in the public seemed to care. The Canadian Bar Association had denounced it by stating categorically, in writing, that the legislation preventing legal recourse of the developers and promoters affected by the cancelling of their contracts with the government was contrary to the fundamental rights of citizens entrenched in the Charter of Rights and Freedoms. The government was finally forced to back down. It can only be explained by the absence of an Opposition party in the House of Commons.

With the cancellation of the privatization of the Pearson International Airport contract, Cabinet decided to allow Claridge Properties Inc. to begin work immediately on renewing Terminals 1 and 2 and the development of Pearson International Airport in the absence of any clear federal government airport development plan.

The partners of Pearson Development Corp., in turn, launched a $200 million lawsuit to compensate them for $35 million of costs and for $165 million in damages. An additional $445 million lawsuit was filed by contractors and lobbyists who took losses with the cancellation of the agreement. Though the government had only offered $30 million in compensation, an out-of-court set-tlement was finally reached in late 1997 for an estimated $60 million.

In 1994, the federal government released the National Airports Policy (NAP) to provide a framework that defines the federal government's role with airports. Under the National Airports Policy, the federal government would no longer develop or operate airports. Developments were to be undertaken by local interests.

Transport Canada's 1995 Southern Ontario Area Airports Study concluded that future operators of airports in the Greater Toronto Area should plan for a second major airport in time to ensure facilities are available when needed. Otherwise, it could result in significant economic losses in the Greater Toronto Area. This very issue of demand for more airport facilities that was denied by industry people only a few years earlier was only now recognized.

At the March 1997 meeting of the Council of Deputy Ministers Responsible for Transportation and Highway Safety, members agreed to clarify the concept of public-private partnerships. In June 1997, a federal-provincial-territorial task force was established to determine the framework of public-private partnerships in all modes of transportation, especially in highways. In accordance with a National Airport Policy, the Greater Toronto Airports Authority purchased Trillium Terminal 3 at Pearson International Airport for $719.4 million payable over a six-year period. The Greater Toronto Airports Authority purchased twenty-one areas of land to construct runways.

By 1999, Pearson International Airport was the twenty-fifth largest airport in the world, providing direct employment for 115,000 in the Greater Toronto Area and generating $12 to $13 billion in revenues to the local economies.

The Greater Toronto Airports Authority (GTAA)

In December 1993, the Greater Toronto Airports Authority (GTAA) was established. This is a public-private partnership with a 60-year lease. The Greater Toronto Airports Authority was led by the Regional Municipalities of Durham, Halton, Peel, York and the former Metropolitan Toronto, together with the local Boards of Trade and Chambers of Commerce. Under Canada's National Airports Policy, the Greater Toronto Airports Authority was reconstituted in accordance with Canadian Airports Authority guidelines and recognized by the Minister of Transport in November 1994 for the transfer of Toronto Pearson International Airport. The Greater Toronto Airports Authority is a private, not-for-profit corporation. Its fifteen member Board of Directors comprised representatives from the four regional municipalities, the City of Toronto, the Province of Ontario and the Government of Canada. The Board includes members chosen to reflect the interests of the business community, organized labour and consumers. It builds its business upon four cornerstones — safety and security, customer service, environmental sensitivity and financial responsibility. Its mission is to create an airport system that contributes aggressively to economic development.

Diane Jurkowski

Toronto's Pearson International Airport is recognized as a gateway airport. The air travel needed for the region is rapidly growing, with the number of passengers expected to reach 50 million yearly by 2020. The Greater Toronto Airports Authority is fulfilling this need with a comprehensive redevelopment program.

Under the management of the Greater Toronto Airports Authority, a ten year $4.4 billion redevelopment program is under way at Pearson. Initiated in 1998, the Airport Development Program includes a new passenger terminal building to replace the current Terminals 1 and 2, a 12,600 space parking garage, two new runways, an infield cargo area and realigned and expanded roadways.

The last phase of the construction will occur in 2008 with the completion of the fourth stage of the new terminal building. The Airport Development Program represents a vital component of the province's construction industry. From the period 1996 to 2000, the Greater Toronto Airports Authority spent more than $1 billion on development projects. In 2001 alone, expenditures topped $800 million and employed over 2,000 construction workers. The indirect impact of the Greater Toronto Airports Authority's program was felt throughout Toronto and Ontario.

Governments are faced with critical questions in dealing with large infrastructure projects, such as airports. Questions arise about the feasibility of private businesses, and even mega-consortiums having access to the capital investments for such long-term projects. There are still the belief and perception that governments are expected to undertake these types of projects, especially in the establishing of private-public partnerships.

Privatization of Highway 407

Diane Jurkowski

A Historical Overview of Toll Roads in Ontario

The toll road or turnpike was introduced to Upper Canada from England in the early 1800s. The theory was simple: Charge those who used or benefited from the location of a road and use revenue collected for maintenance and payment of construction loans. The first Ontario toll road was established in 1805. These roads did not become popular until after the War of 1812. The success of the Dundas and Waterloo Turnpike Company, incorporated in 1829, encouraged others to try their hand. Before long, the legislature was flooded with applications from people eager to operate toll bridges as well as toll roads.

To take advantage of the highest possible volume of traffic, most toll roads were founded on established main roads. Many improved by planking or macadamization. Toll gates were erected every four or five miles, and manned by a watchful sentry. As there was no standard rate, the toll varied at each booth at the discretion of the operator. At one time, Dundas Street, Yonge Street, Kingston Road, the Lakeshore Road and the Vaughan Road were all toll roads.

At the beginning, the toll road boom resulted in well-maintained roads. However, with time, attractively high revenues caused operators to neglect road maintenance. The high cost of repairs also fuelled their reluctance to spend money on upgrading roads. So, it was predictable that public outrage increased as conditions worsened. In later years, many toll booths were vandalized to protest the high rates and deplorable roads.

To avoid paying the charges of the toll roads, many travellers only used the road part of the way, then turned off and circumnavigated the toll gate. More daring individuals took a more direct approach, simply charging past the toll gate, ignoring the toll booth. This sport was practised by some of the wealthiest and most influential men of the day; many were caught on the return trip.

An Act of 1840 established commissioners in each district of the province with authority to improve macadamized roads. They had the right to alter or sell old thoroughfares, with supervision by engineers, surveyors and collectors to whom the tolls might be given or sold by private tender. Toll roads began to be managed on a uniform basis under a single authority.

The Office of the Commissioner of Roads was dissolved in 1841. A newly established Board of Works that assumed the duties replaced the Office of the Commissioner of Roads. All public works not vested in any other body were given to the Board, which regulated tolls and duties for their use. A provincial highway system was created with the major authority allocated to the province.

In 1849, the Baldwin Act gave municipalities control of the financing and construction of roads within their jurisdictions. Municipal corporations were made responsible for regulating the actions of road construction and determining the levy of tolls. The Act stated that a road must be completed before tolls could be levied. Tolls would be collected for a maximum of twenty-one years. The Act to Authorize Formation of Joint Stock Companies extended the toll system of financing main roads to the municipalities. Municipal corporations could purchase stocks in companies formed under this Act, with the option to buy all stocks twenty-one years after completion of the road at current value. These two Acts were milestones in the history of toll roads, providing for shareholding and ultimate purchase of toll roads by municipalities. A revised schedule of tolls was passed by Parliament in 1849 to regulate tolls to simplify the calculation and collection, to afford public access and to ensure an adequate return from the public works.

Over the years, amendments were made to existing acts, a few of which provided exemptions from tolls or turnpikes. An 1843 amendment decreed that exemptions from tolls would include use of toll roads: by all persons travelling to or from Church on Sunday, or "obligatory holiday"; vehicles carrying manure for agricultural use; vehicles, horses and cattle belonging to the owner of land divided by any turnpike road; and, in 1912, vehicles carrying mail, funeral attendants, officers and soldiers in uniforms and prisoners under military escort.

Despite continual protests, toll roads continued into the twentieth century. However, during the latter half of the nineteenth century, they were absorbed into the growing country road system. The last toll gate in Ontario on Sarnia and Florence Road was removed in 1926. However, the toll road concept was revived in the 1990s with Highway 407. Individual vehicle transponders, video camera surveillance and an electronic account debiting systems replaced the toll gate.

The Problem

The Ontario government, the municipal governments of Toronto and the surrounding Greater Toronto Area face the problem of enormous growth of population and residential, commercial and industrial development. The population is growing at a rate of approximately 90,000 people a year. In twenty years, the number of licensed drivers has doubled and the number of licensed vehicles has more than doubled. The major existing east-west route, Highway 401, is saturated, carrying over 350,000 vehicles per day. Thus, there was the necessity to create another east-west corridor across the Greater Toronto Area. Commuting time became longer, especially with the funnel effect of the single major route available along Highway 401.

The Decision

John Beck, President of Canadian Highways International Corporation, stated that in today's highly competitive world, public infrastructure is key to a country's success. With governments practising fiscal restraint, finding new cost-effective solutions to meet infrastructure needs was a challenge. Governments were finding that the best solution is a public-private partnership. Beck included the following advantages to a public-private partnership:

- Safe roads are being built faster.
- Costs are less than the original forecast.
- Risk is reduced for the public sector.
- The environment is safeguarded.
- New technology and efficiencies are introduced.

The need for the Highway 407 project was recognized in the 1950s. It was conceived as a relief road on the northern outskirts of Toronto. In the 1960s, engineers marked a provisional alignment and engineering studies for the new highway began in 1968. The provincial government began acquiring land for what would become Highway 407. In those days, Toronto's most intensive residential and industrial development was huddled in a linear strip along the shoreline of Lake Ontario and north along Yonge Street. Scattered villages and farms were north of the metropolitan boundary. By the 1980s, urban development had spread north, east and west to form the 7,2000 square kilometre Greater Toronto Area (GTA). It comprises the municipalities of the newly amalgamated city of Toronto and the four surrounding regional municipalities of Durham, Halton, Peel and York, each with their constituent local area municipalities, totalling thirty. Highway 407 was to be a key route connecting these surrounding regional municipalities.

With a population of over 4.5 million, the Greater Toronto Area is one of the largest urban conurbations in North America. Growth forecasts suggest that by the year 2000, Greater Toronto will have more than 5.2 million residents. The Greater Toronto Area is one of the most cosmopolitan of North American city-regions, with a strong multicultural flavour since nearly two out of every five residents are immigrants. The population has doubled in the last two decades and is rising by 3 percent yearly. This has led to a corresponding doubling in the number of registered motor vehicles, mostly in the outer municipalities. Residents often have to travel to work and, in the absence of adequate public transit across the region, car usage has increased, while the average occupancy of vehicles has decreased. Increased car usage is largely due to unbalanced development in the Greater Toronto Area, particularly an imbalance between jobs and population. Some areas, such as Mississauga and Brampton, to the west and northwest, respectively, are attracting many new industries, causing long commutes for workers and extensive criss-crossing of the Greater Toronto Area. Furthermore, although the population is growing more rapidly in the outer areas, the city of Toronto continues to lead in job growth. In the inner municipality, there are over 600 jobs per 1,000 population, versus 500 or less in the outer regions.

For these reasons, car trips in the Greater Toronto Area rose 157 percent between 1964 and 1986, and evening peak periods lengthened from two to at least three hours over the same period. The Greater Toronto Area has paid the price for rapid growth in the form of highly congested roads. Blocked traffic costs businesses in Ontario $2 billion a year in lost time and productivity.

In the early 1970s, the Ontario government approved a 22,000-hectare Parkway Belt along the route of the proposed Highway 407, extending from Markham in the Durham region to the City of Hamilton. The Parkway Belt incorporates the Highway 407 route. It provides utility and transit corridors and creates a green buffer between the different municipalities. With travel demand growing near the corridor, the province increased land acquisitions to install hydro power lines.

The right-of-way for the proposed highway was established at 150 metres. Although the Ministry of Transportation of Ontario (MTO) continued its technical studies, detailed design efforts did not begin in earnest until the mid-1980s, when it was decided that construction should begin. By then, the costs of not building were becoming inescapable. The government feared that continued delay in dealing with the Greater Toronto Area traffic problems could drive away investments.

At that time, the project was a conventional public sector project. It was paid for by the taxpayers and the expense meant that progress was slow. Toronto would not get its new highway by this method unless it was willing to wait until the second or third decade of the new millennium. Globally, major infrastructure projects were routinely built this way in the early 1980s. Between 1997 and 1994, the Ministry of Transportation of Ontario approved 16 contracts worth a total of $240 million for construction work related to the highway. The work involved detours and other advance work on structures and interchanges affecting nine kilometres of the proposed route.

Ontario, like other jurisdictions, built its highways one section at a time, with finance coming from the government's general revenues rather than from any dedicated road or automobile taxes. Highway 407 lagged because of other budgetary priorities. At this rate, the Ministry of Transportation of Ontario could not foresee completing the entire 69-kilometre road for about 25 years.

However, by the end of that decade, the private sector was taking over more responsibility for capital projects. The construction industry terminology grew with new descriptions for different types of private and public-private partnerships. In February 1993, the New Democratic Party government decided to accelerate the development of Highway 407 by using toll financing and involving the private sector.

Three commercial groups presented their proposals. Kiewit's proposal suggested tolling core sections of Toronto's heavily congested Highway 401 as a means of leveraging capital for Highway 407. The government decided that only new highways could be tolled, so the Kiewit submission failed. There were two remaining consortia: the Canadian Highways International Corporation (CHIC) and the Ontario Road Development Corporation. Each was given $1.5 million from the province's job creation fund to develop engineering improvements on Ontario's Ministry of Transportation concepts and designs for Highway 407. Of the two hundred changes and innovations proposed, the Ministry of Transportation of Ontario accepted 60 major ones, resulting in a $200 million reduction from the project's costs.

Ontario endured a global recession from 1991 to 1993. The prospect that the project would create 20,000 jobs directly or indirectly was a tempting proposition, especially in the engineering and construction industries.

Establishing a Crown agency, the Ontario Transportation Capital Corporation, the Ministry of Transportation of Ontario attempted to exploit new financing possibilities presented by the growth of private sector participation. In 1993, through this Crown agency, the Ministry of Transportation of Ontario invited private sector proposals to "develop, design, build, operate and maintain" Highway 407. There were three consortia that responded. While initially revealed that taxpayer funding was not required, it was learned that the Ontario New Democratic Party government decided to retain the financing risk for the highway and awarded the development, design and construction for Highway 407 Central, worth $930 million to Canadian Highway International Corporation. The tolling system contract, worth $72 million was given to Hughes Aircraft of Canada Ltd., Bell Canada, Bell Sygma and Mark IV. Subsequently, in 1996, the Annual Report of the Provincial Auditor stated that significant financial ownership and operation risks associated with Highway 407 remained with the province and a public-private partnership had not been established.

Construction work was completed on the first 36 kilometres of the Central section of the Highway by December 1996. Transpiration Minister Al Palladini requested a safety inspection by the Professional Engineers Ontario, which reported that Highway 407, was as safe as any other North American highway. The Professional Engineers Ontario also recommended twelve further improvements. When these were completed, Highway 407 was opened in May 1997. The Progressive Conservative government announced that Highway 407 would be reviewed under the Ontario Privatization Review Framework. In 1998, the government announced the sale of Highway 407. A year later, in April 1999, the government announced that Highway 407 was sold for $3.1 billion, making it the largest privatization undertaking in Canadian history.

Highway 407 was built twenty years ahead of the government's original plan. Building the highway faster meant jobs and benefits of a modern road were created sooner. Innovations in project management and construction methods were made possible by the partnership approach. Since borrowed money incurs interest, it was desirable to complete the project as quickly as possible. Furthermore, it was in the interest of the builders to produce high-quality results, because they remain responsible for the highway's maintenance. To many people experienced with private-public partnerships in the industry, it was no surprise that the highway cost $300 million less than original government estimates.

Although the financial arrangements were complex and involved interim finance channelled through the public sector, the principle remained that tolls rather than taxes financed the Highway. Therefore, the government also achieved a high level of risk protection for the public by transferring risks associated with construction, costs and deadlines to the private sector. Highway 407 was built with a guaranteed maximum price, defined completion schedules and a provision for liquidated damages if the completion deadlines were not met. The government as a partner shouldered risks, such as those associated with unforeseen environmental difficulty, while Canadian Highways International Corporation was responsible for developing environmental protection plans to safeguard the land and waterways that highways transverse.

The consortium looked for new products and methods to construct the highway and to meet its goals and deadlines. Thus, innovative construction techniques, such as prefabrication, were used on site; bridge beams were manufactured round-the-clock in factory conditions and assembled on-site when the weather permitted; paving machinery produced one kilometre of completed three-lane highway each day as well as paving the highway in concrete rather than less expensive asphalt for durability. Highway 407 is almost certainly best known for its installation of technology in a toll-collection system that allows drivers to pass unhindered along the highway, their charges being calculated automatically. Although this toll-system technology is used in other countries, it is never seen on the scale of kilometres as on Highway 407.

In the case of the privatization of Highway 407, there is evidence for the government's rationale. Given the large capital expenditure that government has incurred for the development and maintenance of infrastructures such as road systems, successive provincial governments sought partnerships with business. This resulted in improved efficiency, reduced government involvement in enterprise decision making, widening of stakeholders' responsibilities and gaining political advantages.

Commercialization of the Liquor Control Board of Ontario

Diane Jurkowski

Crown Corporations

Crown corporations are wholly owned federal or provincial organizations, structured like private or independent enterprises. They are identified by the following characteristics:

- A majority of its ownership must be vested in government;
- Management of its affairs must be relatively independent from government;
- Its primary role must be to provide goods or services to the private sector, not to the government; and
- The prices it sets for these goods and services must reflect the costs of providing them.

Established to carry out regulatory, advisory, administrative, financial or other services or to provide goods and services, Crown corporations generally enjoy greater freedom from direct political control than government departments or ministries. The 1951 federal Financial Administration Act declared that Crown corporations are ultimately accountable, through a Minister to Parliament, for the conduct of their affairs. They are not subject to budgetary systems or direct control of a minister in the same way as government departments. Crown corporations were established because of the unwillingness or inability of private firms to provided important services in a vast, sparsely populate country such as Canada, and not because of a preference for public ownership. This specifically has been cited as the case for establishing Air Canada. Since World War II, federal Crown corporations have emerged as important providers of loans and related financial services to farmers, whose needs were not always met by private financial interests. The Farm Credit Corporation is such an example. The major role for Crown corporations exemplifies the essence of Canada's mixed economy and indicates the central difference between the industrial organization of Canada and that of other countries, such as the United States.

Provincial Crown corporations are also significant, although they differ from their federal counterparts in their roles, economic importance and administration. In most provinces, Crown corporations are responsible for the generation and transmission of electricity, the retail distribution of liquor and the operations of the lottery and gaming industry.

A central rationale of Crown corporations is that the commercial activities of government, to be performed successfully, must be shielded from constant government intervention and legislative oversight. Therefore, Crown corporations enjoy greater administrative freedom than government departments. As government enterprises, their autonomy cannot be absolute and must be tempered by some public control over policy making. The Canadian experience suggests that the imperatives of corporate autonomy, government control and legislative oversight are often conflicting and difficult to reconcile.

The range of controls and influences over federal and, in most cases, of provincial Crown corporations has developed incrementally. But a key element was established in 1951 in the federal Financial Administration Act that established a regime of financial controls over most Crown corporations. This was achieved by organizing them into three "schedules" or types — departmental, agency and proprietary — each of which performed different functions and enjoyed different relationships in government. Proprietary Crown corporations submit capital budgets to the cabinet ministers responsible for the Crown corporations, the Minister of Finance and President or Chair of Management Board. The budgets need the approval of all three cabinet ministers, Cabinet and ultimately, Parliament or the provincial Legislatures. Whether it is the federal Crown corporations or provincial Crown corporations, Parliament or provincial Legislatures must enact Crown corporations' budgets. Legislatures also review the annual reports of Crown corporations, query cabinet ministers during Question Period and discuss corporate performance with Ministers and senior management in the forum of legislative committees.

Cabinet also controls the appointments, remuneration and dismissal of Crown corporations' Boards of Directors and senior officers. Theoretically, Boards of Directors provide the key link between the government and corporate management. However, their effectiveness may be undermined by a lack of precise definitions of the powers, duties and responsibilities of Boards and political patronage in the selection of members.

Two significant events would focus attention on Crown corporations in Canada. The first occurred in the 1970s, when a debate emerged about roles and effectiveness of federal Crown corporations. The debate centred on the view that the scope and economic importance of Crown corporations had outdistanced Ottawa's capacity to control them and that Crown corporations had become too prominent in the economy. Some critics felt that major Crown corporations, particular Canadian National Railway, have escaped political control. Successive Auditor-Generals criticized the financial management of Crown corporations and controversy surrounded the activities of Atomic Energy of Canada Ltd. and Air Canada. Petro Canada's rapid expansion and Via Rail's chronic problems fuelled the discontent. However, there was a deeper problem about the role, nature and purposes of Crown corporations in the Canadian economy. Should Crown corporations use the same criteria as private firms in their decision making? What rules should govern competition between public and private firms? What balance should Crown corporations strike between commercial considerations and accomplishment of political and social goals? In the general sense, is an effective Crown corporation one whose behaviour is similar to, or different from, a comparable private firm? These were questions that required answering.

The second event came with privatization. In privatization, Canadians are presented with a more radical prescription. Proponents of privatization maintain that Canada's political and economic well-being will be enhanced if the assets or shares of Crown corporations are sold to private investors, however, defined in whole or in part. The appeal of privatization, bolstered by the example of the British government's policy, is rooted in the contemporary enthusiasm for more "market driven" policies and reduced economic role for government. Advocates of privatization believe that Crown corporations are inefficient, too sheltered from market forces and simply too numerous. A related proposition is that many Crown corporations have outlived their usefulness as policy instruments and ought to be sold to the private sector. On the other hand, some critics of privatization see it as a short-sighted policy. Critics of the sale of deHavilland Aircraft to Boeing of Seattle question the wisdom of selling of a potentially dynamic Canadian firm to a foreign-owned company. Others worry about the terms and conditions of proposed sales and the possible loss of government control over the economy. Other critics maintain that a partially privatized enterprise embracing a mixture of public as well as private ownership will create an unwieldy organization. The debate over privatization continues as governments endeavour to meet the challenges of their roles under the doctrine of globalization.

The Liquor Control Board of Ontario — Product and Service Management

In Canada, the sale of alcoholic beverages is within the jurisdiction of provincial governments. It is done through liquor control authorities. Between 1923 and 1930, the Conservative Party, under Howard Ferguson, tapped Ontarians' desire to enhanced provincial revenues through the provincially owned Liquor Control Board of Ontario, which was designed to promote temperance as well as revenues. The intent of government was to promote temperance, as stated in the 1929 Annual Report of the Liquor Control Board of Ontario: *"The sin of drunkenness is still with us and probably will remain with the host of other sins and crimes that scourge humanity just so long as human nature is what it is".*

In 1927, the Ontario government replaced prohibition with government control of liquor sales by establishing the Liquor Control Board of Ontario. The Liquor Control Board of Ontario was established by the Liquor Control Act to "control the sale, transportation and delivery" of alcoholic beverages in Ontario. The sale of alcoholic beverages in Canada occurs through various channels. It has been found that approximately 85 percent of alcohol sales in the province are through the Liquor Control Board of Ontario stores, breweries and winery outlets and other legal channels. Smuggling and illegal wine manufacturing account for about 15 percent of alcohol sales in Ontario.

The Liquor Control Board of Ontario purchases spirits, wines and beer from domestic and foreign suppliers for distribution and sale in Ontario to consumers and establishments licensed by the Liquor Control Board of Ontario's companion organization, the Liquor license Board of Ontario, which was established in 1947. The Liquor Control Board of Ontario operates retail stores, oversees private agency stores in small rural communities and regulates The Beer Stores, Ontario winery stores and privately operated duty-free stores. On the other hand, the Liquor Control Board of Ontario regulates the sale of alcohol in more than 15,000 licensed establishments as well as alcohol advertising and promotion.

In its first year of operation, the Liquor Control Board of Ontario opened 86 stores, sales were $12.3 million, and it employed 875 people. The majority of stores was located on back streets and out of sight of the public. The stores often resembled jails rather than retail stores. The era was marked as control-oriented, and product selection was limited. Control was exercised further in the way customers procured their purchases. As customers entered the store, there were lists of products mounted on boards. Each product or brand was assigned a code number. Customers would fill out a form, take the form to a cashier and pay for their purchases. The form was then passed to a store clerk, who would fill the order in the back room of the store. The product was then brought to the customer who stood on the other side of a counter. Customers left the store with their purchases in a brown paper bag. Purchases were very discreet. Further control procedures were exercised, whereby customers were issued permits at a cost of $2 each. All purchases made by customers were recorded.

During 1934, the hotel industry began to flourish. Hotel beverages were license to sell beer while dining rooms were licensed to sell wine and beer, but not spirits. Since 1947, the Liquor license Board of Ontario (now the Alcohol and Gaming Commission of Ontario) took over responsibility for regulating licensed premises from the Liquor Control Board of Ontario.

The practice of customer issued permits continued until 1961, when permits were finally abolished; however, customers were still required to fill out purchase slips when buying alcohol. In 1962, the Liquor Control Board of Ontario established an Agency Store Program that provided retail to beverage alcohol consumers who do not have access to a Liquor Control Board of Ontario store in their community. This program was geared to northern Ontario communities too small to support regular liquor or beer stores. Under the program, the Liquor Control Board of Ontario authorizes independent local retailers, usually grocery stores, general stores or tourist outfitters, to sell beverage alcohol in a corner where other goods are sold. Agency stores sell alcohol to the public at the same price as the Liquor Control Board of Ontario or The Beer Store; however, the operator purchases alcoholic beverages at a discount price. Agency Store appointments are generally awarded for a five-year period although, the Liquor Control Board of Ontario may set a shorter term.

In 1965 and 1968, respectively, Liquor Control of Board of Ontario introduced wine consultants (or product consultants) to selected stores as well as its first two-day wine-tasting seminar at its training centre. They were just more examples of how the Liquor Control Board of Ontario changed into an innovative retailer. However, the most significant change came with the opening of the self-serve stores. Gone were the days where the alcohol products were discreetly hidden in the warehouse at the rear of the store. The first self-serve Liquor Control Board of Ontario store was opened in Weston, a suburb of Toronto. Throughout the province, Liquor Control Board of Ontario stores were either converted to or constructed as self-serve stores. The purpose was to transform the Liquor Control Board of Ontario into a more customer-driven environment. Further changes were made in 1971 with the introduction of 40-ounce bottles and 2-ounce miniature bottles of spirits and 80-ounce wine jugs. The provincial government also changed the age of majority from 21 years of age to 18. It was again changed in 1978 to 19. This permitted younger people to purchase and consume alcohol. In 1972, the Liquor Control Board of Ontario opened the Rare Wines and Spirits store, the forerunner of VINTAGES at its Toronto Warehouse on Freeland Street.

In 1975, the Liquor Control Board of Ontario was incorporated as a Crown corporation. As a Crown corporation, it reports to the Minister of Consumer and Business Services. Today, as a corporate enterprise, the organizational structure consists of a Board, a Chair and Chief Executive Officer, and a President and Chief Operating Officer as well as Vice Presidents for both functional and services responsibilities. In its Annual Report in 2001–02, the mission of the Liquor Control Board of Ontario is to be "customer-intense, performance-driven and profitable retailer of beverage alcohol, supporting the entertaining and responsible use of alcohol products through enthusiastic, courteous and knowledgeable staff".

In an effort to generate more revenues, the Liquor Control Board of Ontario introduced its first merchandising program in 1985. The Innovate, Merchandise and Generate Enthusiasm (IMAGE) program encouraged suppliers to promote products with in-store displays. That same year, the Liquor Control Board of Ontario also opened Durham Logistics Facility, the largest warehouse. The first VINTAGE outlet was opened at the Liquor Control Board of Ontario's Queens Quay Street in Toronto. It was the first Liquor Store to offer product sampling. VINTAGES is the fine wines and premium spirits division of the Liquor Control Board of Ontario. The VINTAGES collection is made available through specialized stores, as well as seven boutiques and approximately 140 corners of regular liquor stores across Ontario. It introduced over 1,750 new and unique products, releasing between 150 and 175 each month into stores. A VINTAGES Classics Catalogue collection, released three times a

Diane Jurkowski

year, provided customers with an additional 900 exceptional products annually in Ontario. Product prices range from $10 to $2,000. These were radical changes that brought customers and products directly together.

In the mid-1980s, for the first time in its history, sales in the liquor stores showed signs of softening. The government was concerned about maintaining the Liquor Control Board of Ontario's transfer dividends to the provincial treasury. In 1988, the Liquor Control Board of Ontario received a new mandate — to be a retailer. Not just a bureaucracy and a distributor, but to be a good retailer. A new team was brought in, led by people with experience in sales, marketing, purchasing, human resources and information technology. According to its Chair and Chief Executive Officer, Andrew S. Brandt, in a speech at the "Mastermind Executive Luncheon Series, Mississauga" on November 14, 2002, said:

> "Our goal was to transform the LCBO from a distributor of wines, spirits and beers to a world-class, leading edge retailer of beverage alcohol... We want customers to visit our stores because they want to. Not because they have to. Unlike other retailers, we can't offer deep price discounts. That would not be socially responsible... Research played a critical role and continues to keep us on track. We looked at what differentiated us in the marketplace. Our competitive advantage was one-stop shopping, backed by helpful, knowledgeable staff and attractive, well-merchandised stores. Market research helped us learn more about customers — who they are and who they are not, what they want from us and what they do not want from us. We went beyond standard demographic research into segmentation studies, where we really learned about who spends the most in our stores and how we can keep them satisfied. We focussed our efforts on growing top three customer segments, outgoing and actives, home entertainers and enthusiasts and moving up or maintaining other two segments of price conscious and homebodies. We have used telephone studies, in-store studies, database mining — everything we can to learn more about what people want in terms of store location, customer service, in-store promotions and production selection.

What do we know about consumers?

> They are more sophisticated, knowledgeable and adventurous than ever before. They want to discover, taste and enjoy what the world has to offer, reflected in the growing popularity of premium offerings in all product categories. They are starved for time and look to the LCBO to help make their buying decisions easier. So, our advertising is designed to involve them in a learning experience that dispels the mystery and takes the risk out of buying wine and other products. It is designed to encourage them to go from in-and-out shopping to spending more time browsing our stores. To give consumers a reason to visit our stores more often, and of course spend more money. We want stores to be the place to plan a dinner or a get-together with friends or to buy a special beverage alcohol gift. It is a place that

takes the intimidation and risk out of buying beverage alcohol and offers entertaining and convenient solutions for the time-starved consumer. Growing the business means promoting consumer choice through education, information and trading up to better quality".

In 1988, following a management study, the Liquor Control Board of Ontario launched a strategy to change from control-based distributor to customer-focussed retailer. In 1989, the new $1.7 million Liquor Control Board of Ontario Quality Assurance laboratory opened to continue the regulatory function of assuring customers tested quality products. Also in 1989, the customer-focussed strategy launched. The Liquor Control Board of Ontario applied retail marketing strategy planning in addressing issues of customer satisfaction. It considered such needs as

- Economic Needs
  - Variety of selection
  - Quality of products
  - Help from salespeople
  - Special services
  - Valued offered
- Emotional of ego and fun shopping
- Product classes in offering convenience of stores in downtown office towers, shopping stores in malls and speciality stores of boutiques and VINTAGES
- Targeting an up-scale population segment

With this in mind, the Liquor Control Board of Ontario, offered the following in customer-focussed services:

- The introduction of a free customer magazine, *LCBO Today*, to provide regular information on products and services. This publication was later revamped and renamed as *Food & Drink* to offer more food and beverage information and responsible hosting tips;
- The establishment of a consignment warehouse to assist agents importing products not available at the Liquor Control Board of Ontario, to be sold to licensed establishments and individuals;
- The launching of a province-wide, bilingual toll free public inquiries telephone number about the Liquor Control Board of Ontario operations and services;
- The appearance of the first Vintners Quality Alliance (VQA) wines in stores, signifying a new era of quality for the domestic wine industry;
- The opening of the first Liquor Control Board of Ontario mini-store at Toronto's First Canadian Place;
- The introduction of refrigerated displays offering chilled products in stores;
- The offering of tutored tastings in selected;
- The presentation of in-store thematic promotions known as Shop the World marketing program;
- The opening of kitchen demonstrations in the Manulife Centre in Toronto, featuring many aspects of "infotainment" offered by the Liquor Control Board;

- The opening of a Liquor Control Board of Ontario ethnic kiosk in Markham serving the Chinese community;
- The introduction of debit and credit card purchases as well as the use of Air Miles;
- The offering of Sunday shopping and extended hours;
- In 1998, the adoption of a whole branding strategy and brand vision known as The Source for Entertaining Ideas;
- The opening of Canada's largest liquor store, in the Bayview Village Mall in Toronto, with 20,000 square feet. The store wins the Best Layout and Design Award from the Retail Council of Canada;
- The opening of the restored Toronto's Store 10 housed in the former North Toronto Station, which is a historic building with grand architectural features. The 21,000 square foot store is now the largest and biggest liquor store in Canada.

The Liquor Control Board of Ontario is the largest single purchaser of beverage alcohol in the world, purchasing fine wines, spirits and beer from more than 60 countries for Ontario consumers and licensees. Through its integrated distribution and retail network, over 6,500 products are available in 600 Liquor Control Board of Ontario stores across Ontario. Staffed by well-trained and knowledgeable Customer Service Representatives and expert Product Consultants, the Liquor Control Board of Ontario's staff assist customers in product information, gift giving and entertaining ideas. Customers are welcomed to spend time browsing and even sampling products. It is a much more inviting environment to shop than its earlier incarnation. The Liquor Control Board of Ontario does not see itself as a monopoly.

The Liquor Control Board of Ontario undertook a customer survey in 1994. Customers rated staff friendliness and helpfulness 9.1 out of 10. The Liquor Control Board of Ontario has won many awards, including:

- In 1995, the *Financial Post Magazine* ranked the Liquor Control Board of Ontario as Canada's most profitable company;
- In 1997 and 1998, the Liquor Control Board of Ontario was named Innovative Retailer of the Year in the large-store category by the Retail Council of Canada. The Innovative Retailer of the Year Award acknowledged overall industry leadership and innovative approaches to customer and employee relations;
- In 1997, it was awarded the Socially Responsible Retailer of the Year Award, recognizing its efforts in promoting responsible use of beverage alcohol.

Sales in the first fiscal year (ending October 31, 1928) amounted to $34 million, yielding a dividend to the province of $7.2 million. The Annual Report 2001–02 reported that with 6,500 staff, sales in fiscal year 2001–02 were just under $3 billion, with a seventh straight record dividend of $905 million, not including taxes. If Provincial Sales Tax, federal excise taxes, custom duties, GST and municipal taxes were remitted to all levels of government, the Liquor Control Board of Ontario total contribution was $1.55 billion, which supports a wide range of government social programs, services and capital projects. Total inventory turns rose from 5.3 in 2000–01 to 5.9 in 2001–02, surpassing the target of 5.5. To further increase inventory efficiencies, all stores are ensured a core assortment of top-selling brands as well as a portfolio of products tailored to local tastes. Another improvement to operations of stores is helping store managers better match staffing levels in retail stores to customer traffic patterns. This is intended to target market segments.

The Liquor Control Board of Ontario takes its role of corporate governance seriously. Its stakeholders include the people of Ontario, the elected officials of Ontario, its employees, its partners and groups that share its concern for public safety. These are accomplished by

- The delivery of quality products and services at competitive prices;
- The distribution of products and services through a variety of retail formats and other sales channels, such as catalogues;
- The promotion of responsible alcohol use;
- The implementation of policies aimed at ensuring that its workplace is safe and free of harassment or discrimination;
- The control of importation, transportation, warehousing and sale of liquor outside of licensed premises, together with quality assurance and pricing, in a fair and impartial manner. Regulatory responsibility for Ontario winery retail stores, Beer Stores, on-site brewery and distillery retail stores and liquor delivery was transferred to the Alcohol and Gaming Commission of Ontario in July 2001.

In its Annual Report 2001–02, corporate governance for the Liquor Control Board of Ontario was stated to mean "the processes and procedures a corporation uses to manage its business and affairs to enhance shareholder value". This includes ensuring the financial viability of the business and the corporation's positive relationships and dealings with stakeholders. Therefore, to fulfil this responsibility to the government and people of Ontario, the Liquor Control Board of Ontario:

- Develops and implements programs and services aimed at deterring the sale of beverage alcohol to persons who cannot provide valid proof of age, who appear intoxicated or who are believed to be buying for either of these parties.
- Maximizes dividends to the government of Ontario.
- Enhances the Liquor Control Board of Ontario's value to the government of Ontario.
- Manages the Liquor Control Board of Ontario's business risks.

The Liquor Control Board of Ontario promotes the moderate consumption of alcohol in the context of entertaining and a balanced lifestyle. Since 1996, the Liquor Control Board of Ontario introduced the BYID or Bring Your Identification photo identification card to make it easier to identify customers of legal drinking age. Under the Check 25 program, Liquor Control Board of Ontario employees ask anyone appearing 25 years or younger for proof of age. In 2001–02, the Liquor Control Board of Ontario reported that 1.2 million would-be customers were challenged because they appeared to under age or were believed to be buying for under age or intoxicated persons. In 1998, the

Liquor Control Board of Ontario raised $227,700 for Canadian Commonwealth Games athletes during its Quest For Glory promotion. In 1999, the Liquor Control Board of Ontario, in partnership with Mothers Against Drunk Driving (MADD) Canada, financially contributed to a responsible drinking advertising campaign that features billboards and other messages. In 2001, the Liquor Control Board of Ontario's Challenge and Refusal programme resulted in more than one million individuals challenged and 80,000 refused service for failing to provide valid proof of age or for appearing to be intoxicated.

The Liquor Control Board of Ontario is committed to showcasing Ontario wines. Through in-store promotions, selections of "craft" wines from smaller producers and enhanced Vintners Quality Alliance displays complement the efforts of the provincial government to increase consumer awareness and appreciation of Ontario's wines as well as domestic beers and spirits.

As a Crown corporation, the Liquor Control Board of Ontario is a policy instrument of government. It regulates the sale, distribution and quality of alcoholic beverage products in the province. The Liquor Control Board of Ontario contributes dividend transfers into the provincial treasury that support social programs, services and public infrastructure projects. As the largest single purchaser of beverage alcohol in the world, the Ontario government uses the Liquor Control Board of Ontario in negotiating trade agreements with other countries. These reasons have been cited for not privatizing the Liquor Control Board of Ontario. Since the transformations of 1988, the Liquor Control Board of Ontario operates not only profitably, but has established a positive image in the community.

Solid Waste Management in Toronto

Diane Jurkowski

The Dilemma of What to do with Toronto's Garbage: Governments Study the Issues of Solid Waste Management

The growing economic prosperity of Ontario in the 1980s was accompanied by increases in the generation of waste requiring disposal. At the same time, landfill and incineration capacity in the province had not kept pace and the difficulty of finding acceptable new sites underscored the importance of seeking solutions to disposal.

In the 1980s and 1990s, both the city of Toronto and the provincial government of Ontario undertook many studies to decide how best both Toronto and the province could resolve the economic and physical issues of waste disposal. One such study conducted by the Ontario government's Ministry of Natural Resources in the early 1990s reported the following:

- Landfill is the method of disposal for most of Ontario's solid waste. Less than two percent of Ontario's solid waste is incinerated. Ontario has three incinerators that accept solid waste, and over 1,400 landfills. Of these, 630 (45 percent) serve communities with populations less than 1,500 and another 350 (25 percent) are operated by the Ministry of Natural Resources.
- One percent of Ontario's solid waste was recycled through residential recycling programs in 1987, and two percent in 1989.

- Forty percent of Ontario's annual landfill capacity will be lost over the next one to three years. Approximately 17 percent of Ontario's landfill capacity will be lost in 1991 with the projected closure of two of the province's largest landfills, Britannia Road (750,000 tonnes/year) and Brock West (964,000 tonnes/year). An additional 23 percent of Ontario's landfill capacity will be lost in 1993 with the projected closure of the province's largest landfill, Keele Valley (2,250,000 tonnes/year) in 2002. Of the province's remaining landfills, an additional 95 are expected to reach capacity in 1991–1993. An estimated 145 will reach capacity between 1994 and 2003 and 10 will extend beyond the year 2004.
- Landfill tipping fees vary through the province, from zero at some landfills to $150 per tonne in the Metropolitan Toronto area. In some cases, tipping fees have increased dramatically in the past few years. Metropolitan Toronto area tipping fees per tonne of waste have increased as follows: $18 (1987), $50 (1988), $85 (1989), $97 (1990) and $150 (1991). Increased tipping fees have encouraged 3R's of an recycling programs, which can now be justified on the economic basis. Smaller communities are reluctant to raise tipping fees because of a concern about illegal dumping of waste.
- Sixty-five hauling companies reported employment for 792 workers. An additional 145 haulage companies employed an estimated 1,977 workers. Total reported sales for haulers was $103 million.
- Residential waste recycling programs had increased dramatically in the last few years. In 1987, the Blue Box Program served 400,000 households. This number increased to 1.8 million households by 1989. At total of 97,000 tonnes of waste generated by the residential sector were recycled in 1987 (2.5 percent of the residential waste stream) and 206,400 tonnes were recycled in 1989 (5.1 percent of the residential waste stream).
- Municipalities spent $10 million on residential waste recycling in 1987, $30 million in 1988 and $42.5 million in 1989. The average operating cost of recycling residential waste in 1989 was $124.83 per tonne.
- The prices paid for recycled material have varied over the past three years and, with the exception of aluminium, have generally decreased. The 1990 price for old newspaper was $7–$12 per tonne. This price was low because of a labour dispute at the only Ontario de-inking mill. Prices for other recycled materials were $60 per tonne for sorted glass, $70 per tonne for loose steel, $90 per tonne for densified steel, $1,400–$2,000 per tonne for baled aluminium, $300 per tonne for baled PET and $125 per tonne for unbaled PET. Aluminium is clearly the most valuable material collected by the Blue Box Program, but accounts for less than 0.5 percent of the residential waste stream.
- In 1987, 98 active recycling programs served 88 municipalities. There were 52 active recyclers employing 287 full- or part-time staff (10 of whom were physically or mentally challenged) and 207 volunteer workers.
- In the early 1990s, the Ontario recycling industry employed 3,400 workers. Annual sales volumes were reported at $590 million. Approximately

30 percent of these companies started operations in the 1980–1989 period.

- There were an additional 31 waste recycling facilities in Ontario that the municipality, the private sector or the third party sector (not-for-profit organizations) operated these facilities, mostly in southern Ontario. Fourteen of these employed 308 full-time and 17 part-time staff.

Possibly driven by a moral vision, in the early 1990s the Ontario New Democratic Party government decision to decree that Toronto and the surrounding municipalities must bury, rather than burn their garbage in their own backyard is seen as a major problem for both municipal and provincial governments. After several years and $80 million, the Ontario provincial agency known as the Interim Waste Authority narrowed the landfill choices to three locations, Caledon, Pickering and Vaughan. After an Ontario provincial election in 1995, the Ontario Progressive Conservative government dismantled the Interim Waste Authority and gave the choice on garbage to the municipalities, with no restrictions. Municipalities could burn it, bury it, ship it or keep it as long as the chosen option met the province's environmental standards.

In January 2001, the city of Toronto created the Waste Diversion Task Force 2010. The Task Force, which was co-chaired by Mayor Mel Lastman and Councillor Betty Disero, was asked to consult with the people of Toronto and develop a comprehensive waste diversion plan by June 2001. The Task Force was to design a "made-in-Toronto" solution for meeting the following targets:

- 30 percent diversion of household waste by 2003
- 60 percent by 2006
- 100 percent by 2010.

The Task Force was a product of sixteen public meetings, 1,116 telephone interviews, seven focus groups and stakeholder discussions with industry representatives, Toronto Youth Cabinet and members of environmental groups.

The Task Force concluded that the city of Toronto could not afford to keep burying garbage in landfills and reaffirmed that the waste that Toronto households produce could be recycled, reused or composted.

For more than fifteen years, the city of Toronto and the province of Ontario have pursued the possibility of creating new landfills. But the closing at the end of 2002 of the city-owned landfill site at Keele Valley ends the option of burying garbage at $12 a tonne. There is nowhere else in Ontario that is willing and able to dispose of, at an affordable cost, the 907,000 tonnes of garbage that Toronto households create in a year. The cost of burying it is estimated to increase from $12 a tonne at the Keele Valley to $52 a tonne in Michigan.

The Task Force proposed a direction that goes beyond landfill to a future where recycling, reusing and composting are seen as the alternatives for both the environment and the economics of the city. The effort proposed producing results of diverting 555,700 tonnes of garbage by 2006 is a better plan than landfilling in Michigan. Some of the Task Force's recommendations involve expanding and improving existing programs, for example collecting overflow recyclable dry material placed in plastic bags, curbside collection of scrap metal, consideration of a new leaf yard waste composting site and reducing bag limits. The most significant opportunity was seen in collecting organics and composting them into a high-quality product that would nourish lawns, parks, fields and forests. These resources, which include all perishable kitchen leftovers and low-grade paper waste, account for 41 percent of what is sent to landfills. Therefore, the Task Force proposed a three-stream separation of garbage from the current two streams — dry recyclables in the Blue and Grey Boxes and garbage and adding a new stream for organic materials. This plan would be phased in for 170,000 single family residence, in 2002, and be fully operational by the end of 2005. The phasing-in of this program is intended to reach the 30 percent target by 2003. To meet the 60 percent target by 2006, there is the requirement of investing in new and emerging technologies. These technologies are offered by the private sector with such companies as Enwave/Toronto Hydro to set up an energy facility. The Task Force also proposed partnering with other Greater Toronto Area regions to explore new and emerging technologies.

Changing habits becomes an important factor in the Task Force's proposals. Residents of Toronto must be encouraged to view leftover household material not as "waste" or garbage, but as a valuable resource that can be used again. Public information and education is a large part of the effort to bring about change. Rather than discussing municipal solid waste, the Task Force refers to it as municipal solid resources. As North America's fifth largest city, Toronto's current residential diversion rate of 27 percent is both impressive and progressive.

The Task Force recommended creating a Resource Diversion Implementation Working Group as a sub-committee of the Works Committee. The Group will: work with City Hall staff on implementing decisions made by City Council; continue to build support with community groups; and deal with follow-up on the implementation of diversion solutions in apartments and condominiums.

The proposed separated organics program is expected to revolutionize the way the public and government deal with garbage in major cities. Organics are materials such as food scraps and low-grade paper resources. Source separation involves residents placing these materials into a separate container (Green Box) from their dry recyclables in their Blue and Grey Boxes and the remaining refuse. The material would then be converted at an anaerobic facility into high-quality compost, which could be used for farmlands or parklands.

There was a great deal of discussion in public meetings about packaging and producer responsibility. Attention was drawn to the creation of a "Take It Back Program" by the private sector in the Ottawa-Carleton Region. Under this voluntary program, residents can drop off certain types of household hazardous resources, such as leftover paint or used oil and needles at hardware stores, gas stations, pharmacies, etc., rather than dispose of the material. The cost of collecting and disposing/recycling is borne by the retailer, except for latex paint, which the city collects from retailers and redistributes through a paint exchange program. Residents find out about participating retailers through a Directory of Take It Back Products, which is distributed free of charge by the *Ottawa Citizen* newspaper. Toronto has a household hazardous waste reuse program. Reusable items received through the program, such as paints, stains, car care products, solvents, aerosols, cleaners and propane tanks, are separated at depots and placed in a location where residents can take material they can use. Toronto also funds the production of a re-use directory published by the Toronto Environmental Alliance. City Hall staff has estimated that the cost to the city of creating a "Take It Back Program" in Toronto would be about $750,000, including staffing costs and advertising. However, discussions with Environmental Non-Governmental Organizations have suggested that they could start such a program for less.

Business representatives were invited to discuss how they could play a bigger role in helping Toronto meet its source diversion targets. In April 2001, the city hosted an open house where representatives of thirty-four companies made presentations illustrating their wide variety of technologies. In particular, Toronto is pursuing investigations with businesses in the building of a facility at its Dufferin Transfer Station that will manage organics using anaerobic digestion technology. This technology manages organics in a closed vessel without the presence of oxygen, which results in the production of bio-gas as a byproduct. The bio-gas can be used as the fuel source for a boiler, which in turn produces steam that can be used to power a generator. Funding for these technologies has come from the Federation of Canadian Municipalities. The city is also actively pursuing the sale of dry goods to the private sector, particularly the emerging plastics management industry. The Task Force also recommended that the city of Toronto pursue discussions with Enwave/Toronto Hydro to consider the use of other energy technologies. This would both increase diversion from landfill and address growing energy and heating/cooling requirements in the downtown core. Also, the city is investigating a lease of land, possibly on the Gulf Oil site or another site on the Port Lands to Enwave/Toronto Hydro for a potential energy facility. City Hall staff is directed to enter into partnership with other Greater Toronto Area regions for the purpose of exploring new and emerging technologies.

The Task Force heard that residents of Toronto were happy with the current Blue and Grey Box Programs, including collection. The only complaint is that when their boxes are full, they have nowhere to store the recyclables. This means residents often throw valuable recyclables into the garbage and they end up in landfills. They would prefer to be able to put their overflow recyclables in a bag that would be picked up along with the Blue and Grey Boxes. The city of Toronto added milk and juice cartons, drink boxes, empty paint cans and empty aerosol cans to the Blue Box, thereby increasing diversion by about 800 tonnes per year. Mandatory recycling for apartments and single-family homes has increased diversion of solid resources management to approximately 5,000 tonnes per year. Hiring students to visit apartments to encourage recycling and producing a Superintendent's Handbook on Recycling have increased diversion by 3,000 tonnes per year. The Task Force also considered increasing Blue and Grey Box collection to once a week, but the extra $2.7 million per year cost could produce better results if spent in other ways. Toronto has established five recycling depots. Materials accepted include tires, drywall, corrugated cardboard, office paper, scrap metal, glass, plastic containers, newspapers and other household papers, used computers, polystyrene and leaf and yard residuals.

Environment Days have also been established at three depots. Three loads per year of collected polystyrene for recycling are sent to the Canadian Polystyrene Association, which gives Toronto $100 a load to cover the city's transportation costs. The Association only takes one load a month from Ontario municipalities for recycling. Unfortunately, the market for polystyrene is very limited and the payloads are very light (less than a tonne per load). Toronto is also considering designing and structuring two city-wide garage sales or giveaways at the Exhibition or Downsview sites, whereby all residents of the city would be invited to participate. A Mayor's proclamation has also been recommended whereby two "Amnesty Days" per year would encourage residents to put their unwanted goods by the curb where they could be picked up by others. A cost-neutral curbside collection method for scrap metal is also proposed. City Hall staff is reviewing the possibilities of an increase of Styrofoam recycling and the possibility of adding it to the Blue Box. They are also reviewing the potential installation of woodbins at transfer stations to allow for the public to deposit used wood.

Residents have mixed feelings about composting. Generally, avid gardeners have the most positive attitude towards composting at home, which reflects their lifestyle and desire to enrich their gardens. Many participants at the public meetings recommended that Toronto continue to support and subsidize the backyard composting program since it allows residents to manage their own kitchen residue on-site and significantly reduce the waste they place at the curbside. Toronto currently subsidizes the price to homeowners, with the composter costing the homeowner $15. Over 170,000 backyard and multi-bin composters have been distributed to residents in Toronto since 1989. This accounts for 17,000 tonnes of waste reduction and is seen as an excellent example of Toronto residents' commitment to reduce waste. Truckload sales of backyard composters at shopping malls have ended because the city stopped subsidizing the cost (promotion and management were relatively expensive). These costs of $10 per unit were in addition to the $15 subsidy. Residents can still buy backyard composters at City Environment Days and from transfer stations at the subsidized rate of $15 per unit.

By the same token, most people are happy that leaf and yard residuals are collected separately from garbage. People enjoy getting compost at Environment Days, but do not like the bits of plastic they find in it. They are also concerned about the plastic bags at the Avondale Composting Facility located near the Keele Valley Landfill Site, which are blown about by the wind and litter the site. The use of kraft bags and rigid open-top containers resolves that problem. Another problem to be resolved is that the Avondale Composting Facility was scheduled to close to new material at the end of 2002. A new replacement site to compost leaf and yard residuals through outdoor windrowing, which is large scale composting by machines is needed. A strategy to replace the Avondale Site is required in the implementation planning of the Task Force's report.

Finally, the Task Force found there was disagreement as to whether bag limits are useful or even needed. There was a consensus that if there is to be a bag limit, people should be given recycling alternatives, including additional management options for their organic residuals, before restrictive bag limits are introduced. This could take the form of a source separated organics program where residents could place their organics at the curbside for collection and processing at a composting plant.

There was an understanding that the Task Force had undertaken a comprehensive study of the current management of solid waste and future solid resource alternatives. The real issue still remained, what the city of Toronto would do about landfills.

The Problems Associated with the Sanitary Landfill Sites

The first method that Toronto, like most municipalities in Ontario, uses to manage solid waste is the sanitary landfill site. Every day, disposable products, unwanted packaging, and discarded items are tossed in the trash and forgotten. These items will be disposed of in a sanitary landfill site. This method of disposal is the safest and least expensive way to deal with the thousands of tonnes of garbage residents and businesses in Toronto produce each year. The existence of sanitary landfill sites is proof of society's ability to generate excessive waste: waste that, if not properly managed, can spread disease and become a home for pests and rodents. A sanitary landfill site is a complex facility that houses state-of-the-art technologies to manage solid waste. It is an engineering method of disposing waste involving the expertise of engineers, hydrologists, geologists and chemists to design and manage the site. It is termed "sanitary" because it is a disposal method that works at keeping air, soil and groundwater free of contaminants. Sanitary landfill sites are not dumps. Unlike dumps, waste disposed of at a sanitary landfill is covered with soil daily to reduce odours, control wind-blown litter and discourage animals. Sanitary landfills are also lined with natural clay to keep liquid run-off, called leachate, in and protect the soil and groundwater beneath it. The liner has collection systems for two natural landfill occurrences: landfill gas and leachate.

Although landfilling is the predominant method of waste disposal in Ontario, it is not without its problems. The majority of the concern focuses on potential environmental hazards, such as contamination of soil and groundwater plus the disruption of the natural environment. The first problem is leachate collection and control. Leachate is a liquid that forms as rainwater and melting snow percolate through the landfill and mix with the decomposing waste. If not contained, it can seep into the soil below the garbage or bleed out of the side slopes of the landfill and lead to contamination of ground and surface water. Therefore, it is important that precautions be taken to ensure that this contamination does not occur. The first precaution that is followed is to ensure that landfill sites are lined with clay on the base and side slopes to stop leachate from escaping. Second, leachate collection systems are installed just above the clay liner to capture leachate so that pressure does not build up on the liner. Third, captured leachate is drained by gravity or by pumps for subsequent treatment and disposal. Fourth, groundwater is tested to ensure that contamination has not taken place. Finally, until the final cover is in place, all storm drainage, that may come in contact with the waste is contained within the lined area of the landfill.

The other problem is landfill gas. Landfill gas collection and control is another problem. According to recent studies conducted by Environment Canada, landfill sites and garbage dumps account for 3.5 percent of Canada's total greenhouse gas emissions. Landfills alone account for nearly one quarter of all methane emitted into the atmosphere. Although carbon dioxide is the most notorious greenhouse gas, methane is much more potent, with 21 times as much global warming effect. Both gases, along with nitrous oxide, are targeted for reduction in the Kyoto Protocol. The purpose of the Protocol is to reduce greenhouse gas emissions in the world's industrialized nations by 2010. Landfill gas is produced when buried waste, in the absence of oxygen, decomposes. It consists of methane (or natural gas) and carbon dioxide. Uncontrolled landfill gas builds up pressure within the landfill until it is either forced into the atmosphere or the ground surrounding the site. Gas that has travelled underground can kill vegetation or prevent growth by displacing oxygen in the soil. (The methane component in the gas when combined with air can form an explosive mixture.) Sanitary landfills control these problems in two ways. The first is passive controls that prevent underground gas migrating through trenches, barriers and vents. This minimizes the migration of landfill gas beyond the site boundaries. Secondly, active controls pump the gas out of the landfill. Vertical and horizontal wells collect the landfill gas through a perforated pipe. Mechanical blowers or compressors attached to the pipe draw the gas to a central location where it is either burned or recovered for its energy potential.

There is also the control of other minor nuisances. Traffic, odour, litter and seagulls are among the minor concerns that some people have with landfill sites. Traffic from the garbage trucks can at times be a bother and contribute to blowing litter and odour. To reduce this problem, trucks must cover their loads and are restricted to only certain access roads to the sites. Landfill crews routinely pick up any litter on the hauling route and high litter fences are built around the site to catch any blowing litter. Seagulls are generally controlled with noisemakers or birds of prey.

The issue of the closure of landfill sites arises. The monitoring of a closed sanitary landfill site may continue for twenty or more years, or for the contaminating life of the site. A closed landfill site is usually converted into "green space" for the community, such as a park, play ground or golf course. A final cover, called a cap, is placed on top of the landfill. The cap consists of several layers of soil and other materials designed to seal the site and must be able to support vegetation.

Sanitary landfills are a good way of disposing of garbage that cannot be reduced, reused or recycled. Since it has become increasingly difficult to find new locations for landfill sites, it is important to extend the use of existing sites.

The closure of the Keele Valley Landfill Site in the city of Vaughan in York Region presents this problem. This site has been in operation since November 1983. More than 22,000,000 tonnes of waste have been deposited there. It was anticipated that the landfill would reach its cubic metric volumetric capacity of 33,125,254 by mid-2002.

In the early 1980s, during environmental hearings regarding the development of the Keele Valley Site, the operational site life was forecast to be 20 years. The 20-year forecast was entered as supporting information in the application for a Certificate of Approval to operate the site. The expectation of a 20-year operational period was subsequently incorporated into the York/Metropolitan Toronto Agreement in May 1983. Through the Agreement, an obligation was made for Toronto to provide York Region with disposal capacity for twenty years (to July 2004) or until the closure of the Keele Valley Site, whichever occurs last. A Supplementary Agreement in June 1996 reinforced the July 2004 disposal obligation of Toronto to York Region.

In the late 1980s the amount of waste disposed at Toronto landfills was significantly higher than at present. In 1989, the total tonnage disposed of at Keele Valley was 3,220,300 tonnes. This higher disposal rate created an expectation in the local community that Keele Valley would be filled by the mid-1990s. In 1991, in recognition that Toronto's landfills were rapidly reaching their capacity and in order to provide additional time to plan for alternate disposal alternatives, the Ontario provincial government directed Toronto to design a vertical "lift" expansion to Keele Valley. Since 1995, forecasting has estimated that Keele Valley would reach capacity by 2002, without the lift at the current rate of receipt of waste. This regular reporting has given the impression that there is finality to the forecasted year of closure.

As a result of settlement and decomposition of waste, the site experiences annual settlement equivalent to the volume that would be occupied by approximately 500,000 tonnes of waste per year. The slower the site is filled up, the more waste can be placed within the approved volumetric capacity. Toronto and York Region can take advantage of this to keep the landfill operating to at least July 2004, which coincides with Toronto's obligation to York Region for provision of disposal capacity. The city of Toronto and York Region were left with three options.

The first was to maintain the status quo. If the status quo was to be maintained, the site would be expected to close in mid-2002. Substantially more expensive private sector disposal capacity would then be required and Toronto would still be obligated to provide disposal capacity for York Region to July 2004.

The second option was Rapid Fill. The solid waste management fee would be reduced which would bring in new revenues from the private sector, but would result in the closure of the site in 2001, resulting in the need to engage private sector disposal capacity earlier than under the status quo option.

The third option was Slow Fill. Revenues from private sector solid waste management fees would decrease, but the service of the site could be extended to mid-2004 due to a reduction in the total annual amount of disposal, the new 3R's program and the settling feature resulting from compaction and organic decomposition. Under the Slow Fill option Toronto would offset the need to purchase substantially more expensive private sector disposal capacity. This would also bring the service of the site to conclusion in accordance with the 20-year expectancy of the site.

Toronto has attempted to use a stop-gap option to extend the use of the Keele Valley Site. However, elected municipal and provincial officials voiced strong opposition to closing the site in 2002. It is their contention that the environment and quality of life of families in neighbouring Maple and Vaughan have suffered enough with Toronto's garbage; Toronto needs to find alternative long-term solutions. A group calling itself the Citizens' Network on Waste Management formed under the rallying cry: "We don't want Toronto's garbage". The group opposed any new landfills and incineration.

The city of Toronto continues to use the Keele Valley Site. It is the largest dump in Canada, sitting next to an immediate population of 25,000 residents. Almost one million tonnes of waste is dumped each year into this landfill site.

Another proposal was considered in Kirkland Lake, Ontario. Toronto planned to dump millions of tonnes of garbage in a lake 600 kilometres north of the city. The lake has formed in the main pit that was once part of Adams iron ore mine. According to the group known as the Against the Adams Mine Campaign, the pit is 55 stories deep and has sunk 300 feet into the water table. The pit is situated in badly fractured rock on the height of land overlooking the rich Temiskaming farming belt. The cost of this plan to Toronto taxpayers was estimated at one billion dollars. The cost to the residents of Temiskaming, in the best case scenario, would mean the contamination of 300 million litres of groundwater every year for one hundred years. This figure represents the yearly amount of groundwater that will have to be pumped from the mine after becoming contaminated with leachate and chemicals. The worse case scenario is based on the assumption that if the experimental design of this pit fails, contaminated groundwater could leach out through the various fractures, resulting in the contamination of groundwater aquifers and wells downstream of the mine.

Thousands of letters have been written protesting the plan. Numerous demonstrations have fought against it. Yet, Toronto City Council continued to push the plan through even though various studies indicated that there are cheaper, less controversial and proven alternatives. Residents of the Temiskaming region feared a number of factors, including:

- The selling of the project began in 1989. The proponents paid for the only real studies over an eight month period in 1995. A follow-up work plan was paid for in 1996.
- The three pits at the Adams Mine are badly fractured. A numbers ground problems exist, such as: unstable rock walls and some cave-ins in excess of two million tonnes of rock plagued the mine.
- The Adams Mine was fast-tracked through a narrowly scoped provincial hearing, which limited the focus of the panel to only one question. The result was a very unclear split decision and yet the project was flagged ahead.
- The dump will be operated by a United States waste giant Waste Management Inc. The company has been dogged by controversy over its waste practices.

In 2000, First Nations residents of north eastern Ontario and environmentally conscious people around the world claimed victory in their struggle to stop the plans to ship Toronto's garbage north by rail and dump it in an abandoned

Kirkland Lake mine. Toronto cancelled the contract at the last minute, after having pushed it though City Council. Protest over the garbage plan had been brewing for months. In early October, demonstrators formed a human blockade that prevented access to the rail line leading to the mine dump site. Members of the Temiskaming First Nation briefly blockaded the railway tracks near Earlton. Toronto's garbage would be sent to existing landfills in Michigan, something Michigan legislators were powerless to prevent due to provisions in the North American Free Trade Agreement that treat garbage as a commodity.

However, the Adams Mine plan is not dead. Secret Crown land sales and negotiations continue with consortiums interested in Toronto's garbage.

In 2003, Toronto began sending its garbage to Michigan. Every day 130 trucks, each carrying 35 tons of rotting Canadian garbage, ends up in a landfill in a township of 12,500 people located southwest of Detroit known as the Carleton Farms landfill, also referred to as Mount Trashmore. A coalition of twenty-one environmental, religious and civic groups launched the "Don't Trash Michigan" campaign with a conference at the Ambassador Bridge, which links Detroit with Windsor. In the 1990s, the United States Supreme Court ruled that states do not have the right to turn down out-of-state garbage, thereby shutting down restrictions on interstate waste shipment. In Congress, Michigan politicians are looking for loopholes in interstate commerce laws. Congressional representatives trying to push through laws prohibiting or limiting the receipt and disposal of out-of-state waste, including the latest iteration of the Solid Waste International Transportation Act, aimed specifically at barring Canadian imports. In the State Legislature in Lansing, two environmental bills have been introduced to stop Canadian garbage. State legislators are concerned about the air quality that the trucks are creating, as well as the structural damage to the road system. Mayors of several cities in southwestern Ontario are trying to arrange a meeting with the Premier of Ontario to discuss their concerns about Toronto's garbage being trucked along Highway 401.

What has not been also is that Michigan exports 53,000 tonnes of hazardous waste to Canada. Michigan was not forced to take Toronto's garbage. Thanks in part to the North American Free Trade Agreement, the state willingly cornered a big chunk of the multi-billion-dollar trash business. The city of Toronto is paying about $42 million Canadian over three years to ship its waste to Michigan. According to the North American Free Trade Agreement, Canadian garbage must be treated like American garbage. Only Virginia and Pennsylvania (being the largest state importer) import more garbage than Michigan. But Michigan has the authority to close the door to Canadian garbage. This was the case in May 2003, when the Alberta government announced one case of Mad Cow Disease. The same day, Michigan closed its border to Toronto garbage fearing that garbage trucks contained contaminated residue. A similar concern was expressed with the outbreak of Severe Acute Respiratory Syndrome. However, if the border between Canada and the United States is closed for 21 days or less the company dealing with the hauling of Toronto's garbage is responsible for arranging another alternative.

Diane Jurkowski

Building Partnerships

In January 1990, Toronto made an official commitment to reduce the city's carbon dioxide emissions by 20 percent, relative to 1988 levels, by the year 2005. In 1999, the newly amalgamated city of Toronto reaffirmed this carbon dioxide reduction goal and remained in full support of this important issue. Toronto undertook the Better Buildings Partnership program to focus on curbing carbon dioxide emission and it would take a lead role in Toronto's overall carbon dioxide reduction commitment. The Better Buildings Partnership programme began in June 1996 and after the Metropolitan wide amalgamation in 1999, the full-scale program was launched to include the entire city. In partnership with Enbridge Consumers Gas, the Toronto Atmospheric Fund, Toronto Hydro and Ontario Hydro Energy Inc., the city of Toronto established the objectives and goals behind the Better Buildings Partnership program. The city also consulted with a broad range of stakeholders, including the International Council for Local Environmental Initiatives, financial institutions, building owners and managers, the environmental community, trade unions, community groups, equipment manufacturers and the construction energy/water efficiency service delivery industries.

Since the program's inception in June 1999, it has become evident that the Better Buildings Partnership program, in co-operation with the building marketplace, has the capacity and momentum to significantly increase the amount of retrofits implemented by 400–800 percent in both dollar value and carbon dioxide emissions per year. The carbon dioxide emission reduction achieved to date represent 4.1 percent of the former city of Toronto's 20 percent target. The full-scale program could potentially achieve over 3 million tonnes of carbon dioxide reduction, a significantly larger portion of the amalgamated city's 20 percent goal.

According to the Waste Diversion Task Force 2010 Report, the city of Toronto is committed to keeping unwanted resources from ending up in landfills. Partnerships must be achieved with the provincial government, federal government, the private sector, the community, city agencies, boards and commissions and schools.

The Task Force called upon the Ontario government to make better and wiser use of its power to regulate reduction of solid resources at their source. The province cannot lag behind in promoting and legislating increased diversion from landfill. Ontario should be a leader. The Blue Box program, though very popular, is expensive. The Ontario government can regulate the private sector to contribute to its costs. A particularly cumbersome component of the Blue Box is containers, both alcoholic and non-alcoholic. They are becoming more difficult to market and municipalities have to subsidize them more heavily. Throughout the Task Force public meetings, people complained about the amount of packaging on everyday household and consumer items. Packaging regulations are a provincial responsibility. So too is the regulation of compost. Ontario municipalities are not on a level playing field with other provinces when it comes to what is an acceptable quality of compost from the processing of organics. The province's guidelines lead to large quantities of compost that would be perfectly acceptable in other provinces being sent to landfill or under-utilized as daily landfill cover.

The federal government also has an important role to play in financially supporting the efforts of municipalities to increase their diversion rates and promote the reduction of greenhouse gas generated by keeping organics out of landfills.

There is a great deal of interest in environmental programs within the private sector. This includes finding opportunities to link corporate names to green programs. The city needs to capitalize on this interest. Also of concern is the need to recover the full cost of managing the private sector's solid resources. Toronto collects nearly 115,000 tonnes of garbage from about 18,650 businesses across Toronto. Most of them, approximately 15,000, are in the former city of Toronto. By the time the Keele Valley Landfill Site closes in 2003, the cost for this practice is expected to be more than $15 million.

Public education and awareness programmes have to be the cornerstone on which efforts to divert are built. The Task Force adopted the slogan: "To involve, we have to inform. To engage, we have to teach". The city has to increase its communication and education efforts on the 3Rs — why they are important and how to carry them out. In this effort, greater use of volunteer Waste Watchers, who can help staff and Councillors answer questions at community meetings, is needed.

If the city of Toronto asks the people of Toronto to make the new source-separated organics program work, it has to lead by example. In 2000, people living in public housing created the city's various agencies, boards, commissions and departments generated over 154,000 tonnes of solid resources, of which 60,000 tonnes. While there are some excellent examples of innovative diversion activities, a great deal more must be done.

Toronto is not required to manage recyclables and dispose of solid resources received from the Toronto District School Board and the Toronto Catholic District School Board. But by continuing to include the School Boards in the city's solid waste management system, students must be encouraged to recycle and compost. The Commissioner of Works and Emergency Services has submitted to the Task Force a series of recommendations linked to the continued provision of solid resource management services to the School Boards, including a full cost recovery program for disposal and no-charge recycling. To reduce the cost of increased diversion in public schools, a number of initiatives have taken place to seek corporate sponsorship of collection containers and provide direct collection of fibre (paper and newsprint).

Privatization of Municipal Services

A history exists of municipal governments and private firms handling municipal solid waste. For decades, municipal governments have pursued privatization for various solid waste services, including recycling, waste collection, landfill management, waste-to-energy facilities and hazardous waste disposal. However, many municipalities had long considered landfills to be a basic function of government. Though some contracted with private firms for landfill management, many municipalities maintained ownership of these facilities. By the 1990s, these operations were increasingly considered to be candidates for full privatization. The dramatic increases in capital and operational costs of solid waste disposal, in part because of regulations, increased the benefits of shifting to larger, regional landfills and accelerated the rate of privatization. For example, over 3,000 municipal solid waste landfills operated in the United States. The average expectancy of these existing landfills is about 16 years. Municipal governments continually chose between closure, expansion and construction of new facilities. Private firms have operations that cut across jurisdictional boundaries. Most private firms operate multiple landfills, offering experience.

A major concern about privatization is the potential effects of consolidation on competition, service quality and costs. The 1980s brought corporate downsizing and a swell of mergers. Almost every industry experienced this trend. As capital markets have grown and technologies have changed, larger firms often offer greater potential efficiencies. The solid waste disposal sector is no different. There are also fears of monopoly pricing, acquisition of competition and competing with capital investment, training and joint-venture partnerships.

There are options available for managing landfills. The first is government ownership and operation of facilities. Some municipal governments opt to privatize either ownership or ongoing operations. Under public ownership and operation, municipal governments enjoy some benefits. They maintain:

- All assets (landfill, equipment);
- Complete control of their own solid waste stream, including the prices they charge or tipping fees;
- Accountability for performance of their own internal systems;
- Control over capacity development and planning;
- Organizational knowledge and continuity without interruption; and
- A long history of actual expenditures, so likely budget needs are well known.

On the other hand, this arrangement has some disadvantages. For example, the municipal government:

- Maintains all operational, environmental, closure, post-closure and other liabilities;
- Maintains all responsibilities for operating costs;
- Remains responsible for all capital needs;
- Continues to grapple directly with not-in-my-backyard and other political pressures;
- May face inertia or slow results from re-engineering efforts; and
- May experience reintroduction of inefficiencies over time in the absence of competition and/or fundamental changes in organizational incentives.

The second option is co-operative agreements between public and private entities. This is a typical form of public-private partnership; landfill operations are separated into different divisions. The municipal government operates some function; the private firm operates other, often capital-intensive functions. For example, private firms may operate compaction, construction and soil top-off, while municipal governments operate scales, groundwater monitoring or methane gas recovery. This type of partnership offers several advantages. Municipal governments

- Maintain all assets;
- Maintain control of their solid waste stream and the prices they charge;
- Share risks and liabilities;
- Maintain organizational knowledge and continuity without interruption; and
- Tap into private sector innovation, experience and knowledge.

On the other hand, this structure also has some disadvantages. Municipal governments:

- Maintain some liabilities;
- Remain responsible for all capital needs;
- Maintain many operational costs;
- May face difficult agreement negotiation processes; and
- Continue to grapple directly with not-in-my-backyard pressures.

The third option is government ownership and private operation of facilities. In the United States, municipal governments use contracting for solid waste services. About 10 percent of publicly owned landfills are managed or operated by private firms. This arrangement offers several advantages. Municipal governments:

- Maintain all assets;
- Maintain complete oversight of the system;
- Maintain or enforce regulatory authority;
- Create a context for running facilities like a business;
- Tap into a breadth of private sector experience and knowledge;
- May specify, in the contract, controls on their solid waste stream and the prices charged;
- Benefit from innovation techniques without having to jump through bureaucratic procurement hoops; and
- Take advantage of competitive opportunities to save money and/or improve services.

There are some disadvantages as well. Municipal governments:

- Maintain some liabilities;
- Remain responsible for most capital needs;
- May face difficulties maintaining operating expertise among their own staff;
- Experience two-pronged costs — contract costs and costs of staff to monitor the contract; and
- May experience lengthy/costly contract negotiation processes.

A fourth option is complete asset divestiture to the private sector. Under divestiture or "service transfer", a service once provided and produced by a government is now provided and produced by someone else. Even though a government no longer provides the service, it is still responsible for monitoring and planning and rarely completely abandons a service. This form of privatization is relatively new in the solid waste disposal sector, though many private firms have built and operated landfills as "merchants". Divestiture has some advantages. Municipal governments:

- Receive an immediate cash flow from asset sales, which can be used to eliminate debt;
- May reduce annual operating costs due to lower fees from private operations and lower staffing requirements (since in-house staff are only needed for planning and monitoring);
- Receive property, income and sales tax revenues; and
- May experience reduced risks and liabilities.

On the other hand, divestiture has some disadvantages. Municipal governments:

- May rely on others to fulfil solid waste management needs;
- May retain some long-term liabilities;
- Lose some institutional knowledge of the service area;
- May face difficulties calculating asset values; and
- May experience legal costs associated with contract negotiations and asset sales.

The fifth option is merchant facilities. Some municipal governments have never been in the solid waste disposal business or have closed their landfills. Instead, they rely on private landfills that simply charge for their use. These municipal governments avoid raising capital or landfill construction; they let the private sector make the initial investment. Especially for small communities, raising the capital to build a modern landfill that complies with all regulations is difficult. The private landfills often are larger and have lower per-unit disposal costs. Using merchant facilities has some advantages. Municipal governments:

- Face no operational or ownership liabilities;
- Do not have to worry about siting and other political issues that accompany landfill ownership and operation;
- Need few solid waste staff;
- Have minimal long-run capacity planning concerns; and
- Can freely choose in both the short- and long-run among landfills and other waste handling options.

There are some disadvantages as well. Municipal governments:

- Must rely on others to fulfil solid waste management needs;
- Must rely on their shopping and negotiating skills to keep costs down; and
- Must start if they want to commence landfill operations in the future.

Why Privatize?

Like all policy decisions, solid waste management decisions involve trade-offs. Solid waste management is a vital public responsibility, but ownership and operation of solid waste facilities are not. Through privatization, public officials are often trying to achieve effective and efficient use of scarce resources. Privatization decisions do not eliminate services. Rather, they create alternative ways of providing those services.

1. Efficiency

Government has two interests. One is the interest in producing public services. The other is delivering these services. Conflict occurs when government executives play dual roles: as policy makers, they are buyers who think about the interests of the taxpayers and consumers; as service providers, they are sellers who think about internal organizational interests. This tension often results in a focus on process, with the consequences that service "price" is determined by cost (or other political considerations that have to be considered to make decisions to subsidize service delivery). But cost itself is determined by process and process is determined by political considerations, rather than cost minimization.

For the private sector, the focus is on product and profit, with firms attempting to receive the highest attainable of their quantity of output. Firms determine the lowest cost at which the desired output can be produced.

To minimize the process focus, government managers can "shop around" for the best "price". But this shopping is possible only when the purchaser and provider functions are split. Through a separation of service-purchaser functions from service-provider functions, policy and regulatory functions are separated from service delivery. The best desired end of this functional split is to free public policy makers from having to choose between the public's best interest and the direct interests of the public agency.

2. Accountability

Opponents of privatization often cite the loss of control or regulatory authority. However, these concerns may be addressed through contract provisions. In the privatization process, governments set service standards, awarding contracts only to producers that meet established goals.

Contractual power may enhance control in another important way. Through explicit and measurable performance standards tied to contractor payments, government managers can hold private providers accountable for their performance. If private firms fail to do their job or to meet performance standards, they can lose revenues or, ultimately, the contract. Such performance-based contracts in competitive markets give governments more control over a contractor than they may have over internal operations and employees.

The process of contracting does not relieve government officials of responsibility. Contract, like any other policy tool, can result in poor outcomes if they are not structured well. From the writing of the request for qualifications to the process of monitoring performance, the contract must incorporate best practices from more experienced jurisdictions as well as technical, financial and legal input from responsible public officials.

3. Debt Elimination

Some government officials see privatization as a tool to reduce debt. Many cities in the United States turned to alternative methods of disposal, such as incineration, to reduce the amount of waste going to landfills and to take advantage of new energy markets by the federal government. They incurred high debt levels to finance these projects, resulting in high debt payments. Privatization may ease the burden of debt payments. Tipping fees are the primary source of revenue for landfills. Fees at privately owned facilities cover all costs. However, tipping fees at publicly owned facilities often do not represent actual capital and operating costs.

4. Access to Capital

Growing interest in privatization is arising from public sector limitations on access to capital. Municipal governments are subject to provincial legislation of mill rate property taxes. Most municipal governments own and operate their own landfill sites. Operations of these sites may not benefit from economies of scale, making costs higher than at larger facilities. Megafills can serve multiple customers and meet regional solid waste management needs.

A summary of privatization motivations bears witness to a number of factors spurring government interest in landfill privatization. The growing portion of waste disposed through government landfills confirms this interest. Every municipal government has a unique mix of reasons that influence privatization decisions. Generally, the most common drivers of privatization are:

- Managing liabilities
- Improving efficiency
- Cutting costs or debt
- Improving access to capital
- Improving accountability

The issue of solid waste/resource management facing the city of Toronto has indicated that Toronto must adopt another plan. The use of landfills has rallied cries, "Not In My Backyard", and rightly so. Burying Toronto's waste in one of Toronto's sites or the one in neighbouring Maple and Vaughan, or shipping it to Temiskaming or Detroit has become an undesirable solution. Privatization offers advantages and disadvantages to both municipal governments and private firms. As many City of Toronto, Greater Toronto Area, Temiskaming and Detroit Councillor as well as Ontario provincial and Michigan State Legislators argue: "Toronto must have a Plan B to deal with its garbage!".

The Stakes of the Canadian Airline Industry

Diane Jurkowski

Background of the Canadian Airline Industry

Canadian government has a history of guardianship. Often, when there were no apparent private sector interest to offer services, government came forward by establishing a Crown corporation for the purpose of delivering a service. This was the case for Trans Canada Airline (renamed Air Canada) and the Bank of Canada. Also in this role of guardianship, government has sought to protect meek and downtrodden industries, often by shielding them from the competition that got them into trouble in the first place, as in the case of the beleaguered fish processing industry in Atlantic Canada. The belief that Canada could not support two large rival airlines prompted the federal government to try fixing the Canadian airlines industry.

The history of Canadian Airlines can be traced to the beginning of Canadian commercial aviation. In 1919, when former World War I pilots returned to Canada with intentions of flying, the first airlines were small operations that served mining communities in northern Canada. In the same year, Canadian Pacific Railway (CPR) charter was extended, allowing it to operate an airline. For the next eleven years, Canadian Pacific Railway did not do anything with its charter. However, other companies started to build an aviation industry in Canada.

James Richardson is known as the father of Canadian commercial aviation. He started his first airline, Western Canadian Airways (WCA), in 1926 with

471

Diane Jurkowski

$200,000 of his own money. His airline flew miners and freight into remote northern mining communities that were only accessible in the summer months. Richardson expanded his business throughout the 1920s buying some eastern airlines and eventually merging them into Canadian Airlines in 1930. Western Canadian Airways had a number of north-south routes in Canada, but did not fly east-west.

In 1930, when the federal government decided to start its own airline, Canadian Pacific Railway and Richardson were asked to take part. Canadian Airways was to be the cornerstone of Canada's national airline. However, the government and Canadian Pacific Railway could not reach an agreement. Some believed that the federal government never intended to share control and, for that reason, Canadian Pacific Railway decided not to take part in the venture. Richardson was disappointed and died after Trans-Canada Air Lines was established. Since Canadian Pacific Railways was determined to be in the aviation business, it bought ten bush airlines in 1942, thus creating Canadian Pacific Airlines. Canadian Pacific Air was formed with the buy out of Richardson.

Grant McConachie managed Canadian Pacific Airlines for twenty years. Under his management, the airline grew quickly, despite being constantly in battle with the government-owned Trans-Canada Airlines (TCA). The airline industry was heavily regulated. Canadian Pacific Air was encouraged to operate bush routes, but when it came to international and transcontinental routes, it lost to Trans-Canada Airlines. Despite this situation, McConachie was able to make Canadian Pacific Air a global airline with flights to Australia, Hong Kong and Amsterdam. Revenues at Canadian Pacific Air grew from $13 million in 1942 to $61 million in 1964.

Canadian airlines' other predecessor, Pacific Western Airlines (PWA), was started in 1945 by a western Canadian bush pilot, Russ Baker. Originally, Baker's airline was called Central British Columbia Airways (CBCA), and had one plane that primarily flew for the British Columbia Forest Service. However, when Alcan began construction of an aluminium smelter in Kitimat, British Columbia, Central British Columbia Airways became responsible for 95 percent of the airlift required to build the site. This allowed Baker to rapidly expand the airline. Over the next six years, Baker bought eight smaller British Columbia-based airlines and, in 1953, the group of companies acquired the name Pacific Western Airlines (PWA).

Pacific Western Airlines and Canadian Pacific Air came together in the late 1950s in an attempt to crack Trans-Canada Airlines' monopoly on transcontinental flights. After a long fight, Canadian Pacific Air was awarded one flight a day from Vancouver to Montreal. Pacific Western Airlines and Canadian Pacific Air competed for the next twenty years, with Canadian Pacific Air agitating for increased competition with Air Canada, the former Trans-Canada Air Lines. Pacific Western Airlines continued to dominate regional travel in western Canada and for nine years was owned by the Alberta government.

In 1979, the federal government announced that it was eliminating fixed transcontinental market shares for Air Canada. Although Canadian Pacific Air had lobbied for this decision from the beginning, it had to spend a billion dollars to expand its fleet and prepare for full-scale competition. Over the next eight years, the Canadian aviation industry was completely restructured. The

472

federal and Alberta governments privatized Air Canada and Pacific Western Airlines, respectively. The two national airlines went on acquisition sprees to establish regional feeder networks. The regulation effectively ended in 1985. Airlines were allowed complete and free access into all domestic markets. Canadian Pacific Air's profits were sporadic. Canadian Pacific Railways enjoyed owning an airline, but in 1986, financial problems resulted in Canadian Pacific Railways selling Canadian Pacific Air.

At the same time, Pacific Western Airlines wanted to expand. It had profits and looked to Air Canada for a possible merger. Air Canada refused Pacific Western Airlines' offer to be its regional feeder in exchange for 33 percent of Air Canada's shares. Pacific Western Airlines bought Canadian Pacific Air for $300 million and agreed to take on its $600 million debt. In April 1987, Pacific Western Airlines announced that the name of the merged airline would be Canadian Airlines International.

In 1989, Canadian Airlines International made a final acquisition by buying Wardair. Many industry analysts believed that this sealed the fate of Canadian Airlines International. Wardair, a national air carrier, was deeply in debt and lacked cash. Canadian Airlines International purchased Wardair for $250 million, thereby eliminating Canada's third airline. However, it added a further $300 million in debt to Canadian Airline International's balance sheet. In three years, Pacific Western Airlines had gone from a powerful regional carrier to a debt-ridden national airline with revenues of nearly $3 billion. Nevertheless, Pacific Western Airlines thought the 1990s would be the opportunity to beat Air Canada at its own game.

Air Canada's Story

The history of Air Canada began in the 1930s with the appointment of C.D. Howe as the first Minister of Transport. The proposed airline was to link Canada from Atlantic to Pacific. It was to be under government control. The intention was for private enterprise to play a role in it, but politics got in the way. In April 1936, Trans-Canada Air Lines (TCA), a federal government-owned airline and subsidiary of Canadian National Railway (CPR), was established as a Crown corporation. Trans-Canada Air Lines began with $5 million in seed money. It bought three airplanes from Canadian Airways, and hired executives from United States airlines such as United Airlines and American Airlines.

In 1942, when Canadian Pacific Railways suggested to the federal government that Canadian Airways, known as Canadian Pacific Airlines, merge with Trans-Canada Air Lines, Prime Minister Mackenzie King refused, and declared Trans-Canada Air Lines to be Canada's only international airline and the only carrier allowed to provide transcontinental service in Canada. This legislation would regulate the aviation industry for the next forty years. King's statement would also become the guiding principle of Air Canada's future into the next millennium. The relationship between Trans-Canada Air Lines and Canadian Pacific Air changed from competitive to combative.

Trans-Canada Air Lines expanded quickly over the next thirty years, adding routes to the United States, Europe, Asia and the Caribbean. The company's name changed to Air Canada in 1965 to reflect that it no longer only flew in Canada, but had an international presence. Canadian Pacific Air was granted an occasional overseas route, but Air Canada always received preferential routes. Its dominance began to wane in the later 1950s, when Canadian Pacific Air was granted one daily flight across Canada. By 1979, with deregulation, there were no controls on domestic competition between the two national airlines. Also, privatization of Air Canada was rumoured in Ottawa circles.

The 1980s were difficult for airlines. Air Canada had increased its debt in order to upgrade its fleet and buy regional airlines that could feed into a national network. It had to deal with a recession early in the decade and incurred a loss of $15 million in 1982. Air Canada fought deregulation, but by 1987, competition was fully established in the skies. As well, Air Canada was for sale. Air Canada was offered for sale through the issuing of company shares. Its shares initially sold for $8.00 each until Pacific Western Airlines bought Wardair in 1989, removing another competitor. Air Canada's goal in the 1990s was to remove one last competitor and to end the 1990s as Canada's only national airline. When Hollis Harris joined Air Canada as its chief executive in 1992, he was given the mandate to eliminate Canadian Airlines International.

Canadian Airlines International Problems

In 1996, Canadian Airlines International was on the verge of collapse for the second time after a four-year restructuring plan that included wage concessions from its 16,000 employees. Its problems could be seen with a fleet of old aircraft, a low Canadian dollar, economic problems in Japan and competition from discount carriers such as WestJet Airlines Limited of Calgary, Alberta. In the strong 1998 economy, it produced a total loss of $137.9 million.

Buzz Hargrove, president of the Canadian Auto Workers Union representing the 4,000 Canadian Airlines International employees, asked Transport Minister David Collenette to help Canadian Airlines International with $300 million in equity over three years. He also recommended eliminating the 25 percent cap on foreign voting shares in Canada's airlines. This would prove to be one of many times when an airline company would petition the Competition Bureau. This was important to Canadian Airlines International, since AMR Corp., the Fort Worth, Texas-based parent of American Airlines Ltd., already had a 33 percent stake in Canadian Airlines International's equity and 25 percent voting shares. Thus, in August 1999, the federal government suspended the Competition Act to let the Canadian airlines industry legally talk about restructuring.

However, returning to the problems that both airlines experienced, it is important to examine events beginning in the 1990s. Both Canadian Airlines International and Air Canada began the decade in a spirit of optimism after the first decade of deregulation. However, a number of problems began in late 1990. First there was the unrest in the Middle East and the anticipation of the Gulf War. This resulted in international travel being reduced and fuels prices increased. With a global recession in the early 1990s, domestic air travel was reduced. These conditions contributed to the overall airline industry problems globally. By 1992, in Canada, both airlines were losing more than a million dollars a day. By 1993, Air Canada and Canadian Airlines International lost more than they had made in all their years of operation.

However, Air Canada was better positioned than Canadian Airlines International because it carried less debt. Air Canada saw an opportunity to merge the two airline carriers in 1991. In 1992, Air Canada offered to buy the international routes of Canadian Airlines International. Although Canadian Airlines International needed a cash infusion, it rejected Air Canada's offer and approached its United States parent company, AMR Corporation. Air Canada successfully lobbied the federal government to disallow AMR Corporation access to the Canadian market. The federal government intervened on behalf of Air Canada. In 1992, when Canadian Airlines International had tentatively agreed to sell three Airbus-310s to the Department of Defence for $150 million, money that Canadian Airlines International needed, the Clerk of the Privy Council told Canadian Airlines International to terminate discussions with AMR Corporation. Canadian Airlines International did and again began merger discussions with Air Canada. Air Canada made a final merger offer in September 1992 that Canadian Airlines International accepted. The impending merger was not greeted enthusiastically by Bay Street analysts, who referred to the merger as "Mapleflot". Air Canada did not think that it could manage a combined debt load of $7.7 billion. Air Canada believed that it could hold off purchasing Canadian Airlines international until after its bankruptcy and then take over Canadian Airlines International's routes for nothing. The merger proposal died and Canadian Airlines International again approached AMR Corporation.

It took two years of legal disputes before Canadian Airlines International received its $246 million cash injection from AMR Corporation. The delays stemmed from the Gemini reservation system that Air Canada and Canadian Airlines International shared. AMR Corporation's condition for cash infusion to Canadian Airlines International was its use of the American Airlines reservation system; otherwise, there was no deal. Air Canada would not release Canadian Airlines International from its Gemini obligation. Until the money was received from AMR Corporation, both the provincial governments of Alberta and British Columbia supported Canadian Airlines International with cash infusions. As well, Canadian Airlines International employees agreed to wage rollbacks and took shares in the company in lieu of pay raises. Canadian Airlines International employees invested $200 million in their company. At the same time when AMR Corporation provided the money, creditors agreed to swap $700 million in debt for shares in the airline. Canadian Airlines International ended 1994 with an improved balance sheet, but it still was not profitable. This did not occur until 1995, when Canadian Airlines International posted a second quarter profit of $2.6 million.

The year 1998 opened with the Asian economic flu causing a decrease in air travel in the Pacific Rim, Canadian Airlines International's most lucrative market. Domestically, Air Canada launched a number of seat sales, trying to press its financial advantage over Canadian Airlines International. At its annual meeting in June 1999, Kevin Benson, the Chief Executive Officer for Canadian

Airlines International, announced that his company and Air Canada should collaborate in sharing under-used routes. Canadian Airlines International was surrendering its 62-year-old battle with Air Canada. In August 1999, the federal government suspended a section of the Competition Act to allow the airlines to discuss restructuring the industry. There was every indication that only a single national air carrier would emerge. On August 20, 1999, Air Canada proposed to buy the international routes of Canadian Airlines International, but the offer was rejected.

Enter Onex Corporation

Then, the Onex Corporation appeared on the horizon. The central character in Onex Corporation is Gerald Schwartz, its Chief Executive Officer, who has built a fortune at Onex by buying underperforming companies cheap and turning them around. The airline industry appeared as an opportunity to do the same. It cost him millions to learn that Air Canada's international partners were deeply committed and would parry every Onex Corporation offer to drive the cost of the offer through the roof.

Gerald Schwartz was interested in repatriating some of Onex Corporation's money with a major Canadian deal. He saw such an opportunity when Onex Corporation made its initial offer on August 24, 1999. Industry experts were surprised. Onex proposed a $5.7 billion offer to buy and merge Air Canada and Canadian Airlines International. The offer involved Onex, backed by American Airlines parent AMR Corporation paying $1.8 million and assuming $3.9 billion in debt. Ownership would be allocated to Onex with 31 percent, American Airlines with 14.9 percent and public shareholders with 54 percent. Gerald Schwartz's plan offered an efficient, financially stronger airline with cheap fares for consumers. It was his contention that the current competition between the two airline carriers only resulted in costly duplication of flights from major cities and poor service in small communities. Canadian Airlines International agreed with the offer and would recommend the $2 per share offer to its shareholders. Onex Corporation's offer to Air Canada was rebuked. Air Canada referred to Onex's offer as unsolicited, stating that the share offer was below market value at $8.70 per share at the time of the offer.

Immediately, Air Canada identified Onex's bid as a hostile takeover and adopted a shareholder rights plan, a poison pill targeted at opposing a takeover. This allowed Air Canada to increase the amount of outstanding shares, effectively doubling the price of any takeover bid not requiring the approval of the Air Canada's Board of Directors. Air Canada's Board then announced that it would convene a special shareholder meeting on January 7, 2000 to consider the proposal. Onex went to court and won a court injunction forcing Air Canada to hold a shareholders' meeting on November 8, 1999.

Public interest focussed on the impact of having only a single national airline. Critics emphasized that ticket prices would increase and regional carriers would be put out of business. There was also concern that if the merger went ahead, Canada's major airline would be controlled by an American company, American Airlines. According to the agreement, American Airlines would be given the right to control the carrier's scheduling, ticket prices and the frequent-flier program. However, Gerald Schwartz was quick to point out that American Airlines would have only two Directors on the merged Board of Directors. He assured that the new Air Canada would remain under domestic control.

There was support from the federal government for Onex Corporation's offer. The federal government worried that it should not be responsible for assisting Canadian Airlines International with bail out money. Minister of Transport David Collenette initially appeared pleased with the Onex offer. However, when Air Canada officials reported in August that the Minister had political ties to Gerald Schwartz, who was a Toronto Liberal fundraiser, Collenette hesitated.

In mid-October, the bidding war began. Air Canada, supported by Lufthansa, United Airlines and the Canadian Imperial Bank of Commerce, presented a $930 million counterbid. The offer amounted to $12 a share for 35 percent of Canadian Airlines International stock. The offer also included a $92 million offer for Canadian Airlines International.

Onex returned with a $13 a share offer. Gerald Schwartz also announced that none of the 5,000 jobs losses expected would be a result of lay-offs. With this announcement, Buzz Hargrove, President of the Canadian Auto Workers union representing unionized workers at Canadian Airlines International supported Onex's bid. Gerald Schwartz further guaranteed that the newly merged airline would eventually be 100 percent Canadian-owned.

Air Canada shot back with an offer of $16 per share. Onex volleyed with $17.50 per share offer three days before Air Canada's shareholders' meeting. Then it was all over.

On November 5, 1999 a Quebec Superior Court judge ruled that the hostile take-over bid by Onex Corporation was illegal. Justice Andre Wery stated that Onex's proposal would violate the law that limits ownership in Air Canada by a single shareholder to 10 percent. It was reported that Schwartz was disappointed, but he accepted the ruling.

The Lobbying Behaviours

There is yet one other perspective of the bidding war between Air Canada and the Onex Corporation that merits consideration. Both companies conducted intensive lobbying campaigns. Lobbyists would liaison between company executives and government officials. Days after Onex Corporation announced its intention to buy Air Canada and merge with Canadian Airlines International, Air Canada's Vice President of Corporate Affairs and Government Relations retained the services of James Crossland, President and Chief Executive Officer of Government Policy Consultants Canada, the country's biggest lobby firm. Air Canada also recruited more support, hiring the airline's former in-house lobbyist, 71 year old Hugh Riopelle. Onex retained two firms with solid Liberal government connections. One was the Earnscliffe Strategy Group and the other was the Capital Hill Group. Gerald Schwartz enlisted the support of his friend, Paul Pellegrini, President of Toronto's Sussex Strategy Group. It was suggested that Onex needed lobbying firms that could provide both analytical ability to describe the issues and executive ability to brief decision-makers in government. Canadian Airlines International relied on two firms that were retained by AMR Corporation. One was the Global Public Affairs, who had the services of the former Liberal Cabinet Minister, David Dingwall, and the other firm was Wallding International Inc.

With the Quebec Superior Court's decision, Air Canada President Robert Milton pressed forward to take over Canadian Airlines International. Canadian Airlines International attempted to make one last appeal to its international partners, but elicited no response. By November 29, 1999 the Board of Directors of Canadian Airlines International accepted Air Canada's $92 million offer. However, the Chief Executive Officer of Canadian Airlines International, Kevin Benson would not give up. He arranged to meet with executives from American Airlines, British Airways, Qantas and Cathay Pacific. American Airlines insisted that it owned 25 percent of Canadian Airlines International through its parent company, AMR Corporation and would not easily relinquish its ownership. No alternative arrangement to Air Canada's take-over could be found. Finally, on December 5, 1999 the Board of Directors of Canadian Airlines International accepted Air Canada's offer. In April 2000, the Board of Directors of Canadian Airlines International approved a reorganization plan for the airline that would protect it from its creditors. The plan would restructure Canadian Airline International, and reduce its debt, and make the airline a wholly-owned subsidiary of Air Canada. In June 2000, amid losses of $100 millions at Canadian Airlines International, Air Canada sent a "cost cutter" to Canadian Airlines International.

Can a Monopoly go Bankrupt?

Since the deregulation of the airline industry in 1987 the federal government has assumed a relatively minor role as the airline industry consolidated rapidly and Canadian Airlines International teetered on bankruptcy. Even before the deregulation of the airline industry, predictions indicated that only one airline would survive. However, in the summer of 1999, there were calls for the federal government to take a stand against the monopolistic Air Canada. In the absence of competition, there were fears that Air Canada would raise fares in excess of the annual rate of inflation or that the travelling consumer would be used as a pawn in any labour-management action. In response, the Minister of Transport David Collenette tabled legislation in February 2000 to prevent price gouging and predatory pricing aimed at reining in Air Canada, the dominant air carrier. A consumer ombudsman's office was awarded sweeping new power to disallow or refund unreasonable fare increases.

In early 2000, Air Canada was financially healthy and was negotiating a restructuring of Canadian Airlines International's $3.4 billion of debt and aircraft lease agreements. The federal government had no intention to change the 25 percent limit on foreign ownership of Canada's airlines. The ownership cap on Air Canada shares was raised to 15 percent from 10 percent. In May, creditors of Canadian Airlines International accused Air Canada's Chief Executive Officer, Robert Milton of forcing Canadian Airlines International into bankruptcy rather than accepting a restructuring of its $3.5 billion debt. In the end, some secured creditors were unhappy with Air Canada's proposal that saw them receive 93 cents on the dollar. The unsecured creditors filed a lawsuit against Canadian Airlines International and Air Canada because the restructuring plan only offered 12 cents on the dollar. As well, British Airways PLC, Air France and Cathay Pacific Airways Ltd., which at one time had agreements with Canadian Airlines International accused Air Canada of abusing its new monopoly position by price gouging.

As for the travelling consumer, confusion was common. Air Canada promised Canadian Airlines International ticket holders that their tickets would be honoured. Canadian Airlines International customers found that flights were overbooked and they were "bumped". Other customers arrived at the airport only to find out there was no record of their flights or their bookings in the computer. Canadian Airlines International customers were not the only ones to complain. Customers who telephoned Air Canada in Toronto encountered busy signals and waits of up to half an hour on hold to speak to an agent. The most problems were encountered at Pearson International Airport where placards in the terminals read, "Check it before you check in!". The posters informed passengers, according to a mind-numbing list of light numbers, which airline they are flying regardless of what their tickets say. Customers and consumer groups were angry at the chaos. These were the precise concerns that the Canadian Consumer Association referred to in its opposition to the merger.

In response to customer complaints, the federal government announced amendments to tough the airline legislation. After appearing before the House of Commons Transport Committee, Robert Milton promised to appoint an ombudsman to deal with customer complaints.

In May 2000, Bill C-26, the new legislation governing Canada's monopoly airline, increased the commissioner of competition's powers to police allegations of anti-competitive behaviour in the airline industry. For the travel consumer, this signalled higher fares. The commissioner made some suggestions, including the removal of restrictions on foreign ownership and cabotage, and making landing slots and membership in Air Canada's frequent flyer plan available to new entrants. Predatory behaviour in the airline industry is a result of lack of enforcement. The Competition Bureau has failed to bring cases against predatory behaviour before the Competition Tribunal. However, Air Canada was poised to be optimistic and ready to expand.

The merger of Canadian Airlines International Ltd. and Air Canada was not a smooth one. But no one could have predicted the events of the next three years. On April 1, 2003, Air Canada announced that it had filed for bankruptcy protection before a Toronto court. According to the Companies' Creditors Arrangement Act, a company can be granted bankruptcy protection for 30 days or longer in order to continue to operate while talking to creditors. On April 25, bankruptcy protection was extended until June 30, 2003.

There were many causes for the decision to file for bankruptcy. Several global problems were identified, including increased competition from low-cost carriers and declining passenger traffic, global economic recession, the impact of the September 11, 2001 terrorist attacks, the war in Iraq, the outbreak of Severe Acute Respiratory Syndrome (SARS) and the increased cost of aviation fuel at $35 per gallon. Air Canada was reported to be losing $3.9 million a day before the start of the war in Iraq. The fear of SARS virus was believed to be causing a decline in international and trans-border passenger traffic. However, the most significant problem rested with Air Canada labouring under heavy debt of $12.9 billion.

Talks with the Minister of Transport David Collenette and Buzz Hargrove, now representing 9,500 Air Canada reservation and airport workers, resulted in lifting a no-layoff clause for 1,060 employees and an immediate agreement to defer a 2.5 percent salary increase. The International Association of Machinists and Aerospace Workers confirmed that it would lose 1,300 jobs in the across-the-board cuts at heavy maintenance centres and airport. This included 600 flight attendant layoffs that were previously announced.

Collenette announced that the federal government would not provide a cash bail out for Air Canada. Business leaders expressed opposition to any such bail out of Air Canada. The Chief Executive Officer of WestJet Airlines, Clive Beddoe, was encouraged that the federal government was determined to make any federal aid conditional on Air Canada first submitting to bankruptcy protection and recognizing Air Canada's business model was flawed. However, Collenette did state that the federal government was ready to help Air Canada with loan guarantees worth between $300 million and $500 million while Air Canada conducted a financial restructuring. However, government assistance proved to be unnecessary.

Air Canada was able to enter into negotiations with General Electric Capital Corporation for a debtor-in-possession loan, which meant that it would be given preference over other lenders in recovering its money. General Electric Capital Corporation offered to loan Air Canada $700 million (US) to help cut costs and restructure its balance sheet. It will charge Air Canada $40 million in fees for the loan. General Electric Capital Corporation gave Air Canada favourable lending rates because it wanted to prevent the airline from returning its aircraft. Air Canada leases 14 Airbus and eight Boeing jets worth a combined $724 million from General Electric Capital Aviation Services Inc. As well, the Canadian Imperial Bank of Commerce proposed to continue to offer its Aerogold Visa credit that gives customers Aeroplan frequent-flier points. The arrangement will give a $350 million prepayment to Air Canada — an asset that would be reduced as it buys points and also more for every mile. The Canadian Imperial Bank of Commerce will take an after-tax charge of between 22 cents and 26 cents a share in the second quarter. The bank will become an unsecured creditor of Air Canada for $181 million, the unamortized amount remaining since it signed an existing contract. However, Bayerische Landesbank Girozentrale, Kreditanstalt fuer Wiederaufbau (KfW) and Deutsche Lufthansa AG have challenged General Electric Capital Corporation's offer. Munich-based Bayerische Landesbank is planning to cut about 700 to 6,300 jobs as part of a restructuring after it lost as much as 1.5 billion euros (or $2.37 billion Canadian) in bad loans in 2002. The state-owned bank has helped raise financing in Europe for new Air Canada planes since 1995 and, along with Lufthansa, helped bankroll Air Canada in 1999 when it fought a hostile take-over from Onex Corporation's Gerald Schwartz.

What will be the future of Air Canada in six months, if all goes well? If Air Canada emerges from bankruptcy protection, industry experts expect that it will offer more frequent and more direct flights both in Canada and into the United States on smaller regional jets and a fleet of newer Airbus planes. The intention is that Air Canada will be sleeker and leaner. Other issues are also raised about the financing arrangements and foreign ownership. Air Canada's future has yet to be determined.

The Canada-US Softwood Lumber Trade Dispute*

Farhan Beg, Steven Fallahzadeh, Alfred Gumiran, Starr Hovius, Kevin C.Y. Liu, Vrindra Misir, Rajiv Ramdeo, James Scott

482 -514

Canada and the US have as part of NAFTA built the world's largest trading co-operative for any two single countries, including Mexico. Trade amongst the three countries is the largest in the world, surpassing even that of the recently formed EU block of countries. This trade union has been historically strong, ranging through all areas of economics from forestry, energy, manufacturing to service employment. In 2001 trade between Canada and the US was valued at $382.6 billion, or 35.3 percent of Canada's entire GDP. This is a staggering amount of money and trust that we, as Canadians, place with one country. The significance of this reliance only begins to be realized when disruptions in our relationship occur. With the change of the last US administration it has become increasingly evident that the trade relationship is very vulnerable. In the following paper we will take a look at the Canada-US softwood lumber dispute and how this has evolved over the past twenty years and what the future holds for both the Canadian lumber industry and various related industries.

---

* Based on a research paper submitted to the School of Liberal and Professional Studies, Atkinson College, York University.

The lumber industry in Canada has historically been a large portion of our international trade and, on a macro level, a great contributor to the Canadian economy. The dispute between Canada and the US is not new; it has been going on for more than twenty years. The value of exports to the US from softwood lumber in 2000 represented in excess of $11.8 billion dollars. Since the inceptions of the prevailing duties in 2001 the exports of lumber has decreased by 7.5%, representing a significant loss in revenues for communities supported by the lumber industry as well as the government revenues that these industries generated in tax dollars.[1] As the dispute continues, the loss of exports and jobs eventually affects every Canadian, and thousands of unemployed workers deplete the resources of the social system. The lumber industry is prevalent throughout all regions of Canada. Some areas have been affected more than others by the duties, given the quantities of exports and species of lumber in each of the provinces.

Below is a brief summary showing the reliance of each region in Canada on softwood lumber. The statistics are based on a full year's worth of exports prior to the expiration of the most recent lumber agreement. Saskatchewan is excluded because of the special treatment the US has given it. Saskatchewan has been exempt from the majority of the existing duties due in part to the limited supply of softwood lumber in the region as well as the domination of forestry in the region by one company. Weyerhaeuser. It is interesting to note that Weyerhaeuser is a US organization and members of the company's board have been instrumental to the US government throughout the dispute.

Atlantic Canada

- The value of Atlantic Canada's exports of softwood lumber averages $950 million annually, or about 8 percent of the national average of $11.8 billion (2000).
- America accounts for almost all (99.6 percent) of the softwood lumber exports from Atlantic Canada. Atlantic Canada has been less affected by the dispute with the US, as the majority of the lumber harvested there comes from private lands. This is the same practice that exists in the US and is the main reason that the duties have not been imposed upon this region.
- Atlantic Canada employment in sawmills is approximately 8,000 jobs. Related logging and forestry activities employ another 11,500, with about 7,500 of those engaged in supplying raw materials to both sawmills and to pulp and paper operations.
- Together, Atlantic Canada's logging and lumber industries represent about 11.5 percent of national employment in these activities, while representing only 2 percent of the region's overall employment.[2]

Quebec Region

- Quebec has about 35,000 direct jobs in forestry and mills. The softwood lumber industry is a major economic engine in Quebec.

483

- Quebec lumber sales to the United States generate revenues of some $3 billion a year: approximately one quarter of Canadian softwood exports to the USA. Quebec is substantially dependent on the US market as almost all Quebec softwood exports — 3.9 billion Mfbm out of 4 billion sold abroad — end up there.
- During the period from May 22 to October 18, 2002, shipments from Quebec plummeted to a mere 73 percent of the volume recorded over the same period in 2001. Quebec thus posted its largest drop in exports to the United States, in terms of both volume and percentages (–54 percent).[3]

Ontario

- The value of Ontario exports of softwood lumber averages $1 billion annually, or about 11 percent of the national average of $11.8 billion (2000).
- The US accounts for almost all (99 percent) of the softwood lumber exports from Ontario.
- Ontario's logging and lumber industries combined represent 12 percent of national employment in these activities, while representing only 0.3 percent of the province's overall employment. Ontario employment in sawmills and planing mills producing both softwood and hardwood lumber is approximately 8000 jobs. Related logging and forestry activities in Ontario employ another 9000 persons.[4]

British Columbia

- The value of British Columbia exports of softwood lumber averages $7 billion annually, or about 60 percent of the national average of $11.8 billion (2000).
- The US accounts for almost 70 percent of the softwood lumber exports from British Columbia. Employment in sawmills and planing mills, both producing softwood lumber, is approximately 25,000 workers. Related logging and forestry activities in BC employ another 33,000 persons. Since the softwood lumber agreement expired, approximately 15,000 people have been laid off throughout the province due to the duties.[5]

Alberta

- In Alberta there are approximately 44 mills employing some 4,575. Alberta exports about 55 percent of its softwood lumber to the United States and accounts for 10 percent of Canadian production.
- Despite the 27 percent duty, Alberta has thus far generally avoided the major layoffs seen in other parts of Canada. Its mills are new or have been modernized, making them cost efficient.[6]

As outlined above, BC has the most to lose and has been the hardest hit by the recent dispute between the two countries. Statistics for layoffs directly related to the lumber industry, although significant, do not include the supporting industries that have been affected by the duties imposed.

As mentioned earlier, the softwood lumber dispute is by any means new. The Americans' main argument is that the system of allocating stumpage rights and the fees that the government charges for those rights equates to an unfair subsidy.

The most significant events were in 1982. The US industry petitioned the softwood exports under the countervailing duty law, claiming the industry unfairly subsidized the Canadian manufacturers. The main focus was the stumpage programs in BC, Alberta, Ontario and Quebec. It was the first of what would be many challenges on the issue. An investigation by the US Department of Commerce determined that the stumpage program did not violate the duty law and that the US could not legally apply export duties against the Canadian companies. Four years later, the US industry originated another petition for duties. This time, a preliminary investigation by the US Department of Commerce ruled against Canada. They contended that the stumpage program, although unchanged from the previous investigation, did in fact confer a weighed average subsidy of 15 percent to the Canadian lumber producers. With this new ruling the Canadian government entered into a Memorandum of Understanding with the US that put in place a 15 percent export tax until a resolution could be reached.[7] British Columbia and Quebec made policy changes to their forestry management systems that, in effect, increased stumpage and provincial charges on softwood lumber production. These changes that were implemented did satisfy the US government and the duty was eliminated for BC and reduced from 15 percent to 3.1 percent for Quebec. The Memorandum of Understanding was terminated between the two governments.

In 1991 the US made another attempt to block the import of Canadian lumber. They imposed a temporary bonding requirement on imports from Canada. This "duty"-like tactic was challenged by Canada. A General Agreement on Tariffs and Trade (GATT) panel determined the bonding of imports contravened an existing GATT subsidies code and the US was again forced to back off. In 1992 the GATT ruling was superseded by the final determination by the US's Department of Commerce ruling that four provinces, BC, Alberta, Ontario and Quebec, once again violated subsidies rules by their method of log export controls. This ruling by the US Department of Commerce imposed a 6.51 percent countervailing duty on exports from four provinces: Saskatchewan, Manitoba, Yukon Territory and Northwest Territories.[8] By this time the Canadian-US Free Trade Agreement had been established which Canada used to challenge the initial ruling and the countervailing duty. The challenge, made as part of the Free Trade Agreement, demanded that if the ruling was in Canada's favour, the duties collected by the US would be returned to the Canadian companies with interest. In August of 1992 an FTA panel, assembled to hear the challenge, ruled twice that the US Department of Commerce did not have enough evidence or legal basis to rule against Canada. After the second ruling came down from the panel, the US government accepted the finding that the log export rules did not act as a countervailing subsidy and terminated the countervailing duty it had previously imposed. The US kept pushing for a victory, claimed that the representatives that sat on the panel to hear the dispute had conflicts of interest, and asked for an extraordinary challenge, as they were permitted to do so under the Free Trade Agreement. The majority of individuals that sat on the extraordinary committee found by a majority in Canada's favour.[9] It was not a unanimous decision but the panel consisted of US representatives as well. Two years later, the US government terminated the countervailing duties and ordered the reimbursement of the monies paid by Canadian companies. Approximately $1 billion was returned. A concerted effort was stimulated on both sides of the border to reach an agreement that would eliminate policies that were, effectively, harassment of an industry.[10]

The two countries finally sat down to work out an agreement. The agreement was established in May 1996, and set out the rules of export for the next five-year period. It established set the limit on the amount of free lumber that could be exported to the US in any given year, and established a fee system in the event that exports rose above those levels. The main provision was for a free export quota per year of 14.7 billion board feet of lumber being manufactured first in BC, Alberta, Ontario and lastly Quebec. In the event that more lumber was exported, a graduated fee basis was established. For the first 650 million board feet above the free 14.7 billion, the fee would be US$50/thousand board feet and anything above 15.35 billion board feet could be exported at a fee of US$100/thousand board feet.[11] All the above fees would be adjusted each year to reflect the level of inflation based on the CPI in Canada and the US. The agreement went further, and built in a trigger price that effectively would also benefit the US. The trigger price reflected a change in the average price per thousand board feet. In any given quarter, if the price of an average thousand board feet equalled or exceeded US$405, or US$410 in any subsequent quarter, Canada could export an additional 92 million board feet of lumber.[12] This was beneficial to the US as it essentially insulated the US consumer from dramatic increases in prices due to short supply. In the supply/demand context, in the event the price rose above $405 additional lumber would flood the market bring the effective price down for consumers.[13] There were also exemptions to benefit Canadian companies. In the event that a company's exports were less than 10 million board feet, no duties were required and, in the event that a company's previous quarter's production was disrupted by a strike, fire or other extraordinary event, no fees would be collected for a period of 60 days following the event. These two somewhat small and extraordinary clauses alludes the understanding that the agreement was mainly to prohibit the large corporations from exporting massive quantities of lumber.

The allocation of the lumber quota per province and the collections of the duties have been left up to the Canadian government. In the first year of the agreement, the quotas were divided among the four provinces based on the average export volumes during a period covering 1994 to 1996. Furthering this process, individual companies were granted quotas based on their historic levels of exports. A portion of the quota was set aside for new entrants into the industry: new entrants or established companies that were undergoing major expansion could apply to receive initial quotas or have their established quotas increased from this pool. The system has actually hurt some companies with high quotas since the expiration of the agreement.[14] Following expiration, the Canadian government initially continued with the company quota system. Companies with high quotas were required to continue operations even when the US forced the 29 percent duty upon exports. If companies discontinued their forest operations, they stood to lose their quota levels in the future when a new agreement was established, putting further hardship on the forest companies.

The agreement in 1996 was for five years and required the Canadian government to maintain statistics on lumber exports to the US. This information would be passed to the US government on a quarterly basis along with any duties that were collected by the Canadian government. It would include the name of the company, the mill in which the lumber was produced and the amount of lumber, in board feet, that was exported for the quarter and calendar year to date.[15] Having the Canadian government ensure the accurate and timely arrival of fees and information added expense to the export system which, in theory, should be passed along to the industry through high stumpage fees that the Canadian government would have to charge. The statistics passed to the US government would be verified against their border check information and any discrepancies about areas of import by companies would be appealed back to the Canadian government, who would have to reconcile the variance and prepare a report. In the event that information could not be reconciled, there were guidelines set up for arbitration to resolve any dispute. At the end of the day, the majority of the paperwork would have to be done by the Canadian government, referring back to the statement regarding the additional cost.

Since the expiry of the aforementioned agreement in April 2001, duties have escalated for Canadian companies. The US is reverting to the argument that Canadian lumber is unfairly subsidized. Various levels of negotiations have demonstrated that nothing is going to satisfy the Americans until the Canadian industry completely adopts their system of open market stumpage fees.

As mentioned above, the US has contended for many years that the Canadian government has provided subsidies to the manufacturers by means of a reduced stumpage fee and the allocation of the lumber available for harvest. In the US, allocation of lumber is by way of an auction. As lands become available, each company can bid for harvesting of a particular plot. There is no mention of where the wood needs to be processed or whether the reforestation of the lands is required. Given the administration of this system, it appears that the trees would go to the highest bidder, thereby driving up the price of the lumber as the quantity of lots for harvest is reduced. The Canadian government, again, allocates lumber based on historic quotas, first on a provincial level and, secondarily, on a company basis. These quotas provide a company with an area they are allowed to harvest but, as already indicated the company is required to harvest the land even in hard economic times. This is where the difference lies. In the US, once a company is granted rights to the land, they can harvest the trees at any time they wish. In the event of an economic decline, there is nothing requiring the US companies to harvest the trees. The Canadian government also requires that companies that are granted plots reforest them as they are cut down, thus providing additional indirect employment in the industry, usually through the use of university and other student help to do the reforesting. It adds to cost of harvesting. The US system does not cover all of these issues. There are rules in Canada for a quota of the raw materials to be made into finished products within the areas the plots are granted. This means that if a company cuts down trees in Canada, the majority of those trees must go to mills within Canada for processing rather than shipping them to the US. Given the above there is not a great amount of difference in the cost lumber for sale in the two countries. It appears that the dispute is more based on the limited supply of available forestry land in the US. Were Canada to adopt the US system for land availability, we would adopt the open market system of bidding for available lumber and reduce the number of restrictions processing now in place. Given the fact the majority of the companies harvesting the forest are already US-based, it would be no surprise that the majority of the land would go to the US in the event of an auction. The American companies have a great advantage when the exchange rate is taken into account. The US firms are also bigger and simply have more funds at their disposal. If the processing restrictions were to be dropped, the amount of raw lumber flowing to the US would be extreme.

The Effect of Interest Groups on the Outcome of the Debate

The dispute between Canadian and US lumber producers is given attention in the mainstream media through the continual efforts of various and often opposing lobby groups. Lobbying groups attempt to raise the profiles of issues through raising public awareness, swaying public opinion and ultimately influencing public policy. It is ironic that, the very trade barriers that were put in place to protect a few lumber producers in the US have proved a great hindrance to other industries and consumers. On one side of the debate, the US government has been accused of placing the interests of a few domestic producers over and above the interests of a much larger consumer group. Pundits in opposition argue the Canadian g8overnment is unfairly subsidizing an industry and thereby promoting export dumping. This section will identify the major interest groups lobbying both sides.

The US Coalition for Fair Lumber Imports

"Canada's lumber subsidies are destroying the US lumber industry, threatening its workers with mounting unemployment, and denying many tree farmers a market for their timber crops".[16] Strong, inflammatory and at times convincing words are the tactics employed by the US Coalition for Fair Lumber Imports (USCFLI), composed of various US-based lumber producers across the spectrum of the industry. They represent sawmill owners and operators and landowners who auction off stumpage rights to forestry companies. They are, in essence, domestic industry protectionists. Their principal argument in the debate is their belief that the Canadian Government subsidizes Canadian producers, thus creating an unfair advantage. Their evidence is the low stumpage fees (the purchase of a right to harvest) charged by the provincial governments. That is, however, the only factor of the operating costs they take into account. In their assessment of the Canadian cost structure, the USCFLI fails to include other operating costs unique to Canadian producers. These costs, covered in more detail in a separate section of this analysis, include reforestation, proof of forestry stewardship through external audits, and the construction and maintenance of roads. In the public eye, the importance of the interests of one group is often mitigated by the interests of other groups.

The National Association of Homebuilders

The National Association of Homebuilders (NAHB), is a US-based consumer protection group whose vision is to create an environment where:

- All Americans have access to the housing of their choice and the opportunity to realize the American dream of home ownership.
- Builders have the freedom to operate as entrepreneurs in an open and competitive environment.
- Housing and those who provide 'it are recognized as the strength of the nation.[17]

The trade restrictions have, in fact, proven to be a great hindrance to American interests, as the NAHB describes them, and do nothing to promote them. The homebuilders and contractors no longer have the "freedom to be entrepreneurs" in their market due to the restrictions. In the interim period where no resolution exists, they are forced to purchase the more expensive, domestically produced building materials and pass the higher costs to homebuyers. Price is not the only factor in choosing Canadian softwood for framing houses. Due to the colder climate in British Columbia, where most of the US supply originates, the trees grow more slowly and are, therefore, stronger. Homebuilders want to be able to use material that is best suited for each application and provide the consumers with affordable quality products. The Softwood Lumber agreement makes this very difficult. The US homebuilders would not be able to meet their housing needs were it not for imports of lumber. The objective of the members of the NAHB range from consumer protection groups to profit seeking individuals and companies.

American Consumers for Affordable Homes (ACAH)

On one hand, there are US lumber producers who advocate protectionism by wishing to continue the trade barriers, while on the other hand, The American Consumers for Affordable Homes is lobbying to bring an end to the trade restrictions and open the market to free trade.

The American Consumers for Affordable Housing represents more than 95 percent of the US softwood lumber consumption. It is an alliance of organizations representing lumber users from across the spectrum of US industries. The Alliance includes homebuilders, lumber dealers, remanufacturers, affordable housing groups, retailers and advocates for free trade. The housing industry in the US produces 4.5 million jobs per year. To put the effects of the lumber dispute in perspective, employees in the major lumber using sectors outnumber the logging and sawmill workers by more than 25 to 1. There are millions more jobs in the US that depend on reasonably priced lumber than there are jobs depending on its domestic lumber production.

Suppliers of Home-building Components and Services

With fewer people able to afford homes, the US workers and businesses suffer. Suppliers lose business and their employees suffer in turn. Businesses that supply the windows and doors for the houses are also affected. The demand for new homes also generates a demand for services of plumbers, electricians, roofers and landscapers, new appliances, furniture, paint manufacturers, furniture manufacturers etc. The trade restrictions on softwood lumber will greatly negatively impact the demand for all these services and products.

Homebuyers

The price of lumber has risen substantially since the beginning of the Softwood dispute back in the early 1980s. The average price of lumber has increased by approximately $50 to $80 per thousand board feet due to the imposition of the trade restrictions. This, in turn, has inflated the cost for homebuyers and

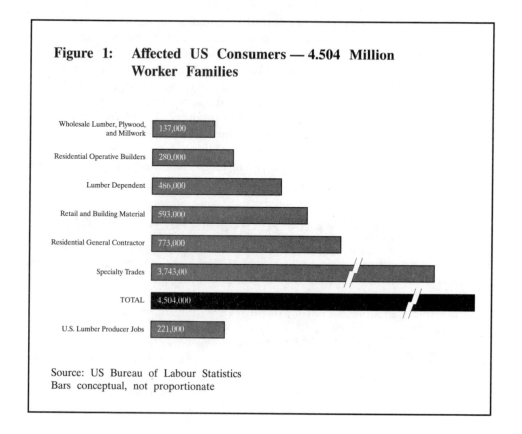

Figure 1:   Affected US Consumers — 4.504 Million Worker Families

Source: US Bureau of Labour Statistics
Bars conceptual, not proportionate

shrunk profits for the lumber users. With approximately 75 percent of softwood lumber in the US being used for home building or structural repairs the housing market has been greatly affected. "The final 27 percent countervailing and antidumping duties on finished lumber for framing homes and remodelling, may increase the average cost of a new home by as much as $1,000. Based on information from the US Census Bureau, that additional $1,000 prevents as many as 300,000 families from qualifying for home mortgages".[18] Many of the homebuyers affected are first-time homebuyers, single parent families, and others with fixed low incomes. The Softwood Lumber Agreement is, therefore, responsible for denying the financially disadvantaged segment of the population from fulfilling the "American Dream" of owning a home.

US Lumber Producers

One third of the US lumber demand is met by Canadian companies. This is not because Canadian lumber is subsidized but because the US lumber industry is unable to meet its domestic demand. In the US, more mills close due to a shortage of timber than close due to the impact of foreign imports.

Native Canadians

Native leaders from BC, Alberta and Ontario are increasing their efforts in pursuing the softwood lumber issue. The Interior Alliance of the BC Indian Nations are arguing that the failure of BC to recognize the Aboriginal title in BC forests as set out by the Supreme Court of Canada in the Delgamuukw decision is equivalent to a subsidy under international law. The Interior Alliance states that the reason for this is that lumber companies are not paying the full price for the timber. The Alliance argues that if timber revenues were shared fairly between Aboriginal and non-Aboriginal people in Canada, the unfair subsidy issue raised by the US would be resolved. By charging a little more and passing on some of the earnings to the Natives, they could probably meet the threshold below which all softwood exports are considered dumping in the US. While the Canadian government argues that its competitive advantage comes from the fact that it has more trees, the Alliance argues that the advantage really comes from the fact that the lumber companies get away with paying small stumpage fees without having to compensate the Natives. The Alliance believes that if the interests of the Natives were to be taken into consideration, there would be a significant impact on the market price for Canadian lumber.

US Proposal to Restructure the Canadian Industry

In hopes of ending the disagreement between nations, the United States Department of Commerce (DOC) has presented to the Canadian government a proposal for the method by which provinces should sell provincial timber to private softwood producing companies within Canada.

The proposal includes two options (which are essentially the same concept), is as follows; the United States feels that if a given province were to repeal all measures that distort the prices at which they sell access to timber on government lands, such as the minimum cut requirements or restrictions on exports of raw logs, and the province were to then sell access to all timber at an auction price reflective of market prices, the countervailing duties imposed by the United States on Canadian softwood lumber companies would be revoked.

The second option states that if a province could eliminate these same "market-distorting measures" and sell a "significant portion" of its standing timber at auction or by other means that provide for free and open competition, the countervailing duties would be revoked.

The US Department of Commerce (DOC) would then judge whether all of the province's timber was actually sold at market rates by a process of comparing the auction price to the provincial administration's set stumpage fee. The term "auction" for the sale of standing timber is used mainly due to the fact that the DOC feels it is the best method to represent what is meant by a market based system of timber sales. In other words, the DOC will enquire whether a province's modified stumpage system produces results consistent with those the province could expect from the sale of all of its standing timber at open auction.[19] Thus, a province will be required to sell a significant portion of its timber at public auction or by some other competitive means, such as competitive log markets. In regards to determining the appropriate price level for the sale of provincially owned timber, the DOC will not rely on the private sale price of timber within a given province as a basis to judge what is considered the market price for the province, unless the private sale proves to be of a sufficient size whereby the DOC feels it occurred independent of the provincial program: in other words, the sale was not influenced in any way by the method employed by the provincial governments for the sale of provincial timber.

To assist in determining a fair market price, a province may submit evidence based on a variety of competitive sales, such as a combination of auction and log markets, or a combination of auction and private sales for independently operating markets. This may establish whether a province is, in fact, receiving adequate compensation for its standing timber, as both the World Trade Organization Agreement on Subsidies and Countervailing Measures and the US countervailing duty law require.[20]

The DOC will employ one of two tests depending on the type of competitive sales, to determine if the competitive sale prices that should be charged for provincial timber are, in fact, the prices the province is charging. These tests include: (1) a standard regression analysis that would make use of market prices gathered from competitive auctions to predict prices for timber on non-auctioned lands; and (2) a residual value calculation that would back out harvesting and hauling costs from competitively sold logs to derive a market price for standing timber. Of the two, given the limitations on the viability of residual value calculations, the DOC has a strong preference for the use of the regression analysis based on properly structured auctions that eliminate the potential for collusion among bidders or other actions that would distort the market.[21]

What is critically important for the DOC is that both the sellers and the buyers in a new Canadian system for the sale of provincial timber are exposed to the same risks inherent in the fluctuation of market prices that would exist with private sales. In short, the provincial fees would respond to the market signals of supply and demand, rather than being insulated from them as they are now. This circumstance in essence is what must prevail in a market-based system of selling provincial timber in order for the DOC to revoke the current countervailing duty.[22]

Hence, the objective of the DOC is to ensure that the sale of Canadian provincial timber is competitive according to US standards for global trade. This objective stems from certain ideologies popular in the American political and economic systems whereby it is felt that the less government involvement the better.

The norm within the United States has always been a product of Adam Smith's, *Wealth of Nations*. Smith felt that competition and the market's invisible hand would always lead to efficient markets. Smith, who said "That government is best which governs less" strongly opposed any government intervention in business affairs, such as trade restrictions, minimum wage laws, and product regulations, which he viewed as detrimental to a nation's economic health. These words of wisdom, which are at the root of pure capitalism, are clearly still evident in the policies of the US today (and as they have been since the nation's conception). Hence, if one were to compare Canada and the US in terms of the extent to which the government's hand extends into business, major differences, such as the provision of health care, would surface. Health care is publicly funded in Canada, while in the US it is still mainly a private sector service. Other examples in Canada include Ontario Hydro and the LCBO, which have government involvement as well. A recent article from the National Post said that "From the US perspective, naturally, the American system is far preferred [over the Canadian]. The United States claims it is relatively free of government intervention, it is transparent and the open market sets the price for timber".[23] It is clearly evident from the American ideology that free markets should set the price of Canadian timber. However, this leads to a problem when one confronts the overall issue. Given that the US supports limited government intervention within the economy, how does one explain why the US is now imposing trade restrictions on Canadian softwood lumber? To answer this question, one needs to examine the recent economic past of the US or, more specifically, the post-Depression period.

In 1936 the economist John Maynard Keynes published *The General Theory of Employment, Interest and Money*, wherein he argued that governments should stimulate the economy in times of need. He noted that an economic slump was not a long-run phenomenon where one should leave the markets to sort themselves out but, rather, a slump short-run problem stemming from a lack of demand. If the private sector was not prepared to spend the required capital to boost demand, then the government should take on this role by, perhaps, running a budget deficit. When the economy turns around and the private sector is spending again, the government can trim its spending and pay off the debts accumulated in the slump. Thanks in part to this theory, known as demand management policy, realized in then US President Franklin D. Roosevelt's "New Deal", the US was able to recover from the effects of the Great Depression and has since employed this theory in its governmental economic policies.

Today, a mix of Smith's and Keynes' ideologies form the dominant theory of US government policy in terms of the economy and, as such, are a major source of conflict between the US and Canada in the softwood lumber issue. But there is another problem. So far the argument can justify the government intervening in the economy when the issue is boosting performance during a slump. In this case, the issue is not a slump in the economy, but rather the US government setting sanctions against another for what it feels to be trade violations. To determine the basis for this argument, one needs to examine the role government has played in the economy since the 1940s.

Starting after World War II and ending in the 1970s. the United States, in experimentation and in hope of bettering its economy, took a lead role in promoting multilateral trade liberalization. The objective was to expand free trade around the world through reduced tariff barriers and foster strong ties among Western countries and non-communist regimes.[24] This process, even though it met its objective for the US, also made it possible for many governments, such as Japan and South Korea, to count on other non-tariff barriers such as subsidies, government procurement policies, or governmental regulations to support business activities. These were behaviours that the US felt were actually damaging fair trade. Thus, the 1970s saw American firms increasingly challenged in domestic and global markets by Japanese and western European manufacturers as their war-devastated economies were revived. By the 1980s, there was a strong rise in economic nationalism in the US due to the effects of a strong dollar that also weakened the competitiveness of American exporters, thus causing huge US trade deficits as imports especially from Japan and other newly industrializing East Asian countries surged. The first and second oil shocks that exploded in the 1970s also negatively influenced the US economy, weakening its position as a dominant world economic power. These global factors led to the highest domestic unemployment and interest rates in recent US history and, thus, forced the US government to begin shifting its attention from free trade to fair trade.[25] The US began making fairer trade policies to defend its domestic manufacturers who were being harmed by foreign manufacturers in the 1980s. Traditionally, to protect domestic industries the US engaged in an import protection strategy where policies and regulations were set to limit what could enter the county. But by the late 1980s, this tendency shifted to promoting US exports, focussing on eliminating foreign barriers, which hindered US exports. The US Government also expanded its definition of what constituted "unfair" trade, as well as its remedies for overcoming unfairness.[26] Currently, the following policies are in place within the US to counter unfair trade:

- Super 301 (*Section 301 of the Tariff Act of 1988*)
  This is essentially a crowbar used to pry open foreign markets that shut out US exports. The saying goes, "If you do not open the market, we close out the market", where the US has the power to investigate and cite instances of foreign restrictions and practices that hamper and discriminate against US exports and impose threats to foreign products.[27]

- Anti-dumping duties
  Dumping is defined as selling an item below full cost or selling a good at one price in one market and at a lower price in another.[28]

- Escape clause provision
  This provides an industry with temporary protection based on article XIX of the GATT, under which a nation is permitted to introduce a temporary tariff to protect an industry when it is judged that imports have caused serious injury to the industry.[29]

The thinking is that, since the US is open to all foreign manufacturers, it has the right to demand market access to all other nations — technically not a protectionist policy. For example, under the super 301 trade provision, when the US confronts trade barriers that discriminate against US exports, it is required to investigate and, sometimes, to punish protectionist nations with retaliatory measures. In the case of softwood lumber, one sees the identical process being applied to imports coming in to the US from Canada.

Initially, the response from Canadian officials to the US proposal on how Canada should handle its sale of provincial timber was somewhat reserved. Sébastien Théberge, a spokesperson for Canada's international trade minister, said Canadian officials would take their time to analyze the paper before they made any "interpretation or speculation" about a potential resolution to the dispute.[30] Soon after, much thought and study, officials in Ottawa publicly rejected the US proposal, saying that "opening Canada's timber auctions would allow large US lumber producers to purchase Canadian logs at a cheap price and then bring them to the United States for processing".[31] This scenario, according to Francois Gendron, Quebec's minister of natural resources, would "destroy" the economy of Canada's forest industry.[32] Others within the nation claim the US proposal is something short of an attack on Canadian independence. Marc Boutin of the Quebec Forest Industry Council said that the choice offered by the proposal, that Canada reform its industry or risk continued duties on its lumber exports is "unacceptable". Such "imposed modifications," said Boutin, "would be an infringement of sovereignty".[33] Thus, Canada has completely rejected the US proposal on grounds of sovereignty. The United States has simply no right to require Canadian provincial governments to act in any manner within the boundaries of Canada. The current process for the sale of provincial timber was developed in the best interests of the given provinces and was in accordance with the Free Trade Agreement. The following question naturally arises: Is Canada practising fair trade? To answer this, one must first examine the basis of, and reasoning for, the Canadian system.

The current Canadian system of forested land tenure, through long-term area-based leases and volume allocations on public lands, has been developed to do two things.

1. Provide the forest industry with a secure long-term wood supply in a situation where forested land is in public ownership.
2. Ensure long-term sustainable forest management of vast areas of publicly owned, forested land through public policy and regulation combined with private enterprise, energy and efficiency in forest management planning and field operations.

The Canadian approach to the sale of provincial timber has focussed on a combination of strong government policy and legislation, coupled with private enterprise efficiency and corporate financial stability. Currently, 70 percent of Canadian timber is harvested from public lands. During the sale, the ownership title is transferred from the public owner (the province) to a private owner at a given stumpage rate set by the provincial government. These stumpage rates are set using an appraisal system that mimics the effect of the free market without actually putting the wood up for sale to all potential buyers on the open market. In many cases the provincial government will periodically set stumpage rates at a level that both reflects the realities of the marketplace and the forest management responsibilities to which the company agrees. This approach includes a factor that ensures the stumpage rate can respond to changes in the market. Under this current system, the provinces have been able to profit from the harvesting of Canadian lumber and in fact reap substantial profits from stumpage rights. Under the proposed US system, there is no guarantee of these profits, as the price of timber may increase beyond levels that do not allow the firms to turn a profit. The result has been much resistance to the United States' offer and one of the major roadblocks in the cross border battle over softwood lumber.

Another aspect of this dilemma is the issue of the erosion of Canadian governmental power. Traditionally, the Canadian political system has been one of equal distribution of power between the federal and provincial governments. The federal government has, therefore, had few opportunities to influence forest resource management, as this is left mainly to the discretion of the provinces. Thus a clash occurs as US authorities attempt to analyze Canadian legislation using criteria of their own federally-legislated responsibilities. The absence of Canadian federal legislation in provincial timberlands leads to charges that its absence provides a de facto subsidy to the Canadian forest industry. Differences have been seen in timber harvested from the Maritimes, which is mostly from private land, similar to that in the United States. The Maritime provinces were, therefore, not governed by the 1996 Softwood Lumber Agreement. In 1996, exempt provinces like Nova Scotia and New Brunswick accounted for about five percent of Canada's lumber production. In the past five years, production in Nova Scotia and New Brunswick has soared 62 percent to more than 1.2 billion board feet. In comparison, Ontario produces 1.5 billion board feet. Ninety percent of New Brunswick's softwood lumber exports go to the United States. The Atlantic provinces are still exempt from the countervailing duties and provincial officials are hoping to win exemption from the antidumping duty. Thus, it would be difficult to establish a solid and complete Canadian policy in terms of the sale of provincial timber that will please all the provinces since each province handles the sale of timber differently. A given measure may be profitable for one province and a financial disaster for another.

Another of Canada's arguments is based on the fact that the nation clearly makes its stand on the basis of free trade. Being a nation blessed with abundant natural resources, it has been able to strategically formulate policies that recognize natural resources as a key to Canadian development, progress and growth. Not surprisingly, the current Canadian national strategy, though incorporated for globalization, has still focussed heavily on natural resources. It advocates against measures that would restrict the availability of foreign capital for development of Canada's natural resources. Canada also stands by its commitment that tariffs should not be imposed that would increase the cost of developed natural resources, as it maintain its purpose of opening foreign markets for the sale of its natural resources and products. Internally, Canada has created and implemented tax laws that favour businesses that develop Canada's natural resources. Canada does not engage in acts that hinder access to the US market for Canadian goods.[34] These policies that make up the nation's overall national strategy express Canada's view of itself in the world today as a global player. Canada has reaffirmed itself through the sale of its natural resources as a nation that is open for international trade and is positioned to foster international trade. The federal and provincial governments are set to play an active role in the economy to ensure the sale of Canada's natural resources to the US and other nations, as this is the best way Canada can sustain its current economic level. Today, Canada must equip its industries with the policies and tools they need to compete on an international basis, and thus feels its policies in terms of softwood lumber are not unfair but, rather, foster the competitive edge needed by Canada and the provinces to compete effectively and fairly.

The BC Government's Stand on the Softwood Lumber Issue

Canada supplies approximately one third of the lumber used in the United States with approximately half of those imports originating in British Columbia.[35] As a result, BC's economy is quite dependent on the forestry industry since it accounts for approximately nine percent of total regional economic output.[36] The government in British Columbia owns approximately 95 percent of the province's forest land and, as a result, the government's responsibilities include managing the forests for the public stakeholders' benefits while simultaneously taking into account environmental, social and economic interests.[37] The relationship between the government and the forest companies in BC is as follows. The BC government owns the forest land and permits forestry companies to harvest on government land in exchange for stumpage fees, which the United States has argued is considerably lower than the market prices of timber which is effectively a subsidy. Additional requirements of the forestry companies are adherence to forest management practices, consultation, planning, reforestation and road-building.[38]

As a result of the expiration of the Softwood Lumber Agreement in March 2001 and allegations that BC softwood lumber producers are subsidized, the government of British Columbia proposed forest policy changes to the US government in December 2001. The proposal was intended to create a "truly competitive market for standing timber, logs and tenure and to expand the role of market forces in the forest sector".[39] The proposal states that forest resources will continue to be government-owned, but the government will focus on the stewardship of the forestry companies involved. The following is a summary of the 2001 proposal made to cover changes in pricing, tenure and mandatory requirements.

The first element of the proposal was that the price of timber would be determined by auctions, with licenses being awarded to the highest bidder.[40] Previously, the allocations of licenses was by bid price, value-added criteria and employment. The purpose was to ensure that 13 percent of the harvest goes to the highest bidder. Another proposal was to price the remaining timber in long-term tenures on the price of standing timber established in competitive auction market for timber sale licenses. Proposal 1. states that timber will not be sold below the cost to the Ministry of Forests.[41] In order to implement this proposal the government has suggested a transparent system of measuring costs and also that the minimum stumpage rate will be set equal to the cost of managing the harvesting process. The last proposal, regarding pricing, was to eliminate the cross-subsidization from higher to lower priced timber to encourage the harvesting of uneconomic timber.[42]

The proposals regarding tenures suggest that timber auctions will be expanded to thirteen percent of BC's harvest up from the current six percent.[43] In essence, an award will be made if the highest bid is equal to or greater than both 70 percent of the market value and the minimum stumpage rate. Proposal 2.2 covering tenures states that new long-term tenures will be granted to the highest bidder however, the government may provide preferential awards to the First Nations.[44] Under the 2001 proposal, companies will also be able to sub-divide and sell tenures unless it is proven by the Chief Forester that sub-division would put forest management at a disadvantage. The final proposal regarding tenures is that tenures will be made freely transferable subject to the discretion of the Minister of Forests that the transfer will not adversely impact competition for timber.[45] Essentially, the Forest Act will also be amended to eliminate the five percent payment of transfer taxes when tenures are transferred.

The Mandatory Requirements proposals include the elimination of annual requirements regarding minimum harvesting levels. Another proposal is to eliminate stipulations for the processing and removing of timber, which essentially means that tenure holders will now be able to make commercial decisions regarding topics such as forest health and forest management.[46] Proposal 3.3 will eliminate the requirement that companies must process timber in company-owned mills or other facilities: which, the BC government argues, will facilitate the ease of entry/exit from the industry. Proposal 3.4 proposes to eliminate provisions related to mill closures, whether they are temporary or permanent.[47] This is an amendment from the previous government policy of reducing a company's timber output when it is determined that a mill closure will occur due to foreseeable market demand conditions. The final proposal is to eliminate company-specific assistance to forest companies, which is provided by the Job Protection Commission, whose objective is to minimize the negative impact on communities of job loss caused by mill closures.[48] Between 2001 and 2003, approximately 20,000 forest sector jobs are expected to be lost as a result of the proposals.[49] The services offered by the Job Protection Commission include facilitating restructuring plans between a company and its creditors and helping them develop economic plans that will allow employment and production to be maintained. Since it can be argued that this program has the characteristics of a subsidy, it will be eliminated in the proposal.

At this point, the United States also submitted a proposal and both governments consulted with stakeholders and talks resumed in February 2002. After weeks of negotiations talks ceased again on March 21, 2002. The United States did not accept Canada's proposal for a binding third-party arbitration and an agreement was not reached on the percentage of harvest to be auctioned in BC, among other topics.

In December 2002, British Columbia proposed that Canada and the United States enter into an agreement that would provide a framework for resolution of the dispute. It would have three main purposes: 1) provide for participating provinces to make policy changes that would lead to a solution in the dispute 2) stabilize the North American softwood lumber market until the agreement has been made, and 3) provide for prevention of future disputes.[50] For provinces agreeing to participate, the agreement will; "define a process for policy change (which deals with handling changes in the agreement), [and] establish new interim measures to replace existing anti-dumping and countervailing duties.[51] In addition, it will define how the existing trade litigation will be addressed and creates a commitment for Canada and the United States to establish a bi-national softwood lumber council".

With respect to the anti-dumping and countervailing duties cases, the government of BC proposed under paragraph 4.1 that the anti-dumping order of softwood lumber exports will be revoked once an agreement has been established. Paragraphs 4.2 and 4.3 state that the countervailing duty will remain in place and will be phased out to zero percent once an agreement has been reached. Paragraph 4.4 permits Canada to pursue Countervailing Duties (CVD) and Anti-Dumping (AD) cases before the World Trade Organization and NAFTA.[52] In addition, the BC government has proposed to refund all cash deposits made as a result of duty assessments to Canadian mills.

In terms of the Interim Measure, the BC government proposes replacing the current AD and reducing the CVD to zero, with export taxes that use the Lumber Reference Price as the average price of lumber over a four-week period. According to Paragraph 2.3 the maximum of 17.5 percent export tax will be levied when the price is less than US$290 per thousand board feet. The tax would then decrease to twelve and a half percent when the lumber reference price is between US$290 and US$320. The seven and a half percent applies when the LRP is between US$320 and US$350 and the two and a half percent applies when the LRP is between US$350 and US$380. Finally, when the LRP is greater than US$380, no export tax is levied.[53] Paragraph 2.4 also proposes to assess only the maximum taxable value of US$500 per thousand board feet. Western red cedar (particularly because US businesses largely rely on this product), white pine, and products of independent manufacturers and mills, which are currently excluded from the CVD, are excluded from the export taxes. Paragraph 2.8 of the proposal states that the exports tax payments will not be refunded to producers of softwood lumber.[54]

British Columbia is Canada's largest lumber producer and is anxious for both sides to arrive at an agreement encompassing each country's requirements and objectives. British Columbia has proposed to make major changes in its forestry practices in response to concerns from the United States government. It appears to be the most willing province due to its ownership interests and is prepared to make concessions with the United States in order to facilitate a smooth transition to a US style, market-based system as the previous discussion has indicated.

Analysis of Provincial Logging Practices and Key Industry Players

Before going on any further, an understanding of how each province deals with their softwood industry is necessary:

Canadian Softwood

Among the things that Canada is famous for, what initially comes to mind is its natural beauty and its vast abundance of natural resources. Forests cover more than half the Canadian landscape — 417.6 million hectares, to be exact.[55] The forestry sector is one of the most dominant features in the Canadian economy. Canadian sawmills employ over 80,000 Canadians and approximately 300 communities are dependent on it.[56] Around 900,000 Canadians are employed either directly or indirectly in the forest products industry.[57] Canada being one of the largest countries with a varying climate, it has the ability to grow several different types of trees. Softwood, for example, is found in British Columbia, Ontario, Quebec and the Maritime provinces. The best softwood is located in the southern parts of the provinces, as the smaller trees are further north. British Columbia is a special case, as the whole province is a great producer of softwood. Most of Canadian forests are publicly owned. Over 71 percent of Canada's forests are Crown land, which is provincially owned land. The federal government owns approximately 23 percent with some managed by, or in co-operation with, the territorial governments. The remaining six percent is privately owned land. The management of public land can be summarized into three different tenures.

1. Long term agreements:
    A company is granted a license to manage a defined area of forested land. These agreements usually range from 15 to 20 years, but they can be longer. The company is responsible for the long-term sustainable forest resource management and is required to carry out and plan the operations in accordance with all regulations. If the company carries out all duties accurately the agreement will be renewed after five years.

2. Long and medium term volume allocation:
    A company is granted a license to obtain a quantity of wood each year from a defined area of forest. Contrary to the long-term agreements, the provincial government is responsible for the long-term sustainable forest resource management. However, the company is responsible for operational planning and must conduct operations in accordance with all the regulations. These licenses are also renewable depending on how the land was managed. Based on the government commitment to social, economic and environmental goals and the industry's desire to secure long

term commitment to wood, companies are usually offered long term tenure. the company must commit to build and operate a major wooded area and/or landfill.

3. Short-term volume based permits:
    These permits are on land that is already under long-term sustainable forest management either by the government or a company. The permits have few planning responsibilities and forest management beyond that of the government or companies. These permits are usually allotted to companies that do not have sawmills, normally last between one and ten years and are usually not renewable.

All Canadian forest product companies have a legal responsibility to ensure a prompt regeneration and harvest. Regulations require the use of either natural regeneration or planting with commercial species that are adapted to the site. The harvested area must be free to grow within a specified period, usually ten years. This means that the young trees must fully occupy the site, and be free of competition from weeds and over-crowding from other young trees. All of these forest management requirements add costs to forestry companies' operations. In 1998, Canada harvested only a quarter of one percent of Canada's forests and planted more trees than were cut down.[58] Due to the slow growth process, Canadian softwood lumber is easy to handle, cut, and nail, and is very popular with building contractors.

Throughout Canada the techniques used for sales, harvesting, extraction of timber and marketing are the same. The government mapped out millions of acres and "sold" a certain percentage to different logging companies using long-term agreements, thereby transferring ownership from public owner to a private owner. These private logging companies in turn went and built their sawmills in the middle of their designated area with only one road that led into the centre of the plot. The thinking behind this was to limit their costs, as they were responsible for the building and maintaining of roads. Each company pays a certain amount per tree that they cut known as a "stumpage rate". This stumpage rate is set using Comparative Value Pricing. They are changed every three months using the price from BC producers.[59] The privately owned lands are bought through auction. The company that bids the highest price usually wins the forest, though their prices are still based on the stumpage fee. The stumpage fees do not include all of the costs associated with logging. There are several other costs, such as transportation fees, building and maintaining roads, land preparation for planting, replanting the trees as well as care and maintenance of the new forests. The provinces differ in how they choose to measure their timber.

There are several different systems of measuring timber throughout North America (see Figure 1). Currently Canada is trying to produce a unified method of measuring lumber. The United States market is very important to Canadians. Approximately 29.5 billion board feet was exported to US in 2002.[60] The Canadian softwood industry needs to be able to trade with Americans.

Exhibit 1:   Provincial Measurement Rules

Quebec — ROY
Ontario — Ontario Log Rule
Maritime Provinces — Maritime Log Rule
British Columbia

Other measurement rules:
International Log Rule
Decimal C Log Rule
Doyle Log Rule (United States)
Scribner Log Rule
Cleveland Log Rule

United States Softwood

In contrast to the Canadian resource distribution, most of the United States' forests, approximately 73 percent, are privately owned.[61] These forests are purchased similar to the way that the privately owned land in Canada is — through an auction. The US stumpage rate is based on market demand and supply. However, their pricing takes into effect all costs, including cutting, maintenance and transportation, as well as subsidization from the government. For the most part they are not responsible for the building and maintenance of roads because forests are already accessible. The private forested lands in the US do not require the same forest management standards as the Canadians lands do. The US National Forests were established to ensure adequate reserves of timber to meet the needs of the nation but most of the National Forests are managed for non-timber purposes. The majority of US softwood lumber is produced in the southeastern region from seeds of fast growing species of pine trees. These trees are heavier, harder and a less stable material than what is grown in Canada because of the fast growth and wood properties. Southern pine is best used for treated lumber, such as outside decks that are constantly exposed to different weather.

Several industries in the United States depend on softwood as well as softwood products. American consumers buy $10 billion worth of Canadian softwood lumber each year. The housing industry and other related industries employ over seven million Americans. The demand for softwood in the United States has surpassed the amount available in their own forests. As much as Canadians are dependent on the US market for sales, the US is equally as dependent on Canadian suppliers.

Who is Affected by this Dispute?

The softwood industry dispute has affected not only the sawmills, but other industries that rely on the softwood as well. To fully understand, a look at the value-chain will show the rippling effects of the high countervailing and anti-dumping duties.

Forestry Value Chain

Trees from woodlots are harvested either manually or through the use of machinery and are then transported by truck, rail, boat, etc. to the sawmills. The sawmills saw the logs into lumber boards or studs and the bark is used for landscape, sawdust for fibre-board and chips for paper. The lumber is then sent to the dry kiln for drying. Once dry, the lumber can go to added value mills for dimension stock, to lumber wholesaler distributors or to furniture/flooring manufacturers. Furniture companies sell to retail outlets for consumers, while the dimension stock gets sold to wholesalers' distributors or end users for furniture/flooring manufacturing and continues down the chain.

The high 27 percent countervailing and anti-dumping duties placed on the sawmills when shipping to the United States have forced sawmills to either find a way to adjust their operations or close their doors. All events in the value-chain after the sawmill will be affected either by higher costs or less supply. As Perrier, an owner of a Quebec logging contractor says, "The softwood tariffs are being felt by the local sawmills. They are selling less lumber, so we, in turn, have less work".[62] Therefore, looking at how sawmills respond to the duty will reflect how the industry as a whole will need to respond.

In Canada there are hundreds of softwood sawmills, all of which are affected by the high duties. The United States market is an important market to Canadian companies, one that many sawmills are very reliant upon. These high duties have created a large barrier that must be overcome in order to survive. At this point it will be useful to briefly detail the profiles of several of the industry's key players.

Canfor Corporation

Canfor Corporation is known as Canada's number one lumber producer. With such high countervailing and anti-dumping duties, would they be able to survive and remain in the number one position? Based in British Columbia with a majority of its woodlands operations and manufacturing facilities in British Columbia and Alberta, Canfor is the leader in integrated forest products. They employ 6,580 people, of whom 5,810 are directly employed and the remaining 770 are employed with affiliated companies.[63] Canfor owns several mills and manufacturing facilities and has joint ventures and partnerships with related companies to help diversify their operations and product offerings. Below is a brief breakdown of Canfor's operating capabilities and their ownership of logging tenures.

Pulp and Paper Manufacturing

Canfor operates two pulp mills and one pulp and paper mill in Prince George. The latter has the capacity to produce over one million tonnes annually of high quality southern kraft pulp and 134,000 tonnes of kraft paper. Canfor has 50 percent ownership of Howe Sound Pulp and Paper Partnership, which produces

---

Exhibit 2: The Amount of Woodlands in Tenures

British Columbia
  A.A.C in Replaceable Tenures: 8,145,465 m3
  A.A.C in Non-replaceable Tenures: 250,478 m3

Alberta
  A.A.C in Replaceable Tenures: 985,425 m3

347,700 tonnes of northern softwood kraft pulp and 210,000 tonnes of newsprint yearly.

Wood Products Manufacturing

Canfor operates 11 sawmills in the northern interior of British Columbia and two in Alberta with total annual production capacity of three billion board feet of lumber. It also operates two finger joint plants: one in the Prince George region and one in Grande Prairie, Alberta. One lumber remanufacturing facility with a capacity of 160 million board feet is operated by the company's US subsidiary. Canfor USA and Canfor also participate in a joint venture remanufacturing facility Kyahwood Forest Products in Moricetown, British Columbia. Two chipping facilities operated in Prince George are capable of producing 325,000 tonnes of oven-dried chips annually. Canfor's Panel and Fibre operation, located in New Westminster, produces a variety of embossed hardwood panels, as well as wood fire production from residual wood. Canfor runs plywood plant in Prince George with an annual capacity of 174,500 msf (3/8') of plywood. Lumber and plywood pressure treating are carried out at the PG Wood Treating Plant.

Canfor's Response to the Tariffs

Canfor first responded to the high tariffs by filing a Notice of Arbitration and Statement of Claim in connection with its action against the US government under Chapter 11 of NAFTA. Canfor had to re-think everything that they were doing. They knew that in order to survive they had to reduce their costs and improve their margins. Their strategy was to design a Cost Reduction/Margin Improvement Program (CRMI). As Mr. Emerson, the President and CEO, said, "We are moving forward into 2003 with a solid foundation for improved results. We have identified the actions required to drive our costs down and improve our margins in all areas of our business. An aggressive timeline for implementation is in place and management incentives are tied directly to achieving these objectives".[64] The CRMI was announced in October of 2002 with the intention of saving $150 million in company-wide structural improvements on an annual basis. The major initiatives are in the business segment:

wood products, pulp and paper group, coastal operations, centralized services and corporate administration.

Following the CRMI requires strict plans on reducing its costs and improving its margins. One of the biggest decisions was the closure of two mills. As David Emerson said, "Decisions about mill closures are never easy but the best thing we can do for shareholders, employees and the communities where we operate is to strengthen our competitive position".[65] Out of the 13 mills, Upper Fraser and Taylor mills had the highest cost/least capacity. With several of their mills not running at full capacity, the closure of these two mills will not impact Canfor's capacity, however it will leave 220 personnel unemployed.[66] Canfor will re-invest in other mills and add a third shift to bring the mills to full capacity and help them become low cost producers. Canfor is investing $40 million in capital projects to upgrade Fort St. John and Prince George sawmills. In committing to the overseas market, Canfor announced, a wholly owned subsidiary of Canadian Forest Products Ltd., and has established an office in Tokyo called Canfor Japan Corporation. This office replaced the Canfor Woodsales and will provide direct customer contact with Canfor and its mills.

Canfor's Financial Results

Throughout all of these ongoing changes and high duties, Canfor has remained a market leader. A survey of Canada's top 30 lumber producers produced jointly by Logging and Sawmilling Journal and WOOD Markets newsletter found that "the Vancouver-based company increased its production last year to 2.81 billion board feet to retain the title for the fourth straight year". According to the news release on February 13, 2003 of the fourth quarter release, Canfor had a net income of $11.5 million, or $0.07 per share for the year of 2002. Though this is down from the previous year, the fact is that they paid $107.6 million in lumber shipments to the United States. The fourth quarter recorded a loss of $58 million, or $0.73 per share; this was the direct results of extremely low prices for both lumber and pulp, and of provisions for termination benefits ($20.4 million, after tax) and mill closure costs ($5.8 million, after tax). Their net sales for the fourth quarter of 2002 were $480.5 million lower than the previous quarter, but $22.9 million higher than the same quarter in 2001. While fourth quarter 2002 sales were lower in all segments, the largest decrease was in the Wood Products group, mainly due to low lumber prices and shipments. Net sales for 2002 were $2,112.3 million, $126.6 million higher than 20012. What this means is that "one out of every ten pieces of lumber in Canada is produced at a Canfor sawmill".[67] Canfor knew that they had to improve their operations if they wanted to remain competitive. They took the challenge and, so far, have succeeded.

With the issue focussed around the countervailing and anti-dumping duties, the question remains about what should be done with the duties that have already been collected. Canfor, like all Canadian companies, wants them returned to Canada and, ultimately, back to the companies that paid them.

Weyerhaeuser

The second leader in the softwood lumber industry is Weyerhaeuser Canada. A leader in forest stewardship, the company began operations in the 1900s in Dallas, and has grown to become the second largest forest products company in western Canada. The company has manufacturing operations in British Columbia, Alberta and Saskatchewan, producing a range of pulp, paper, lumber, engineered panel products, and industrial and consumer chemicals for Canadian and international markets. Weyerhaeuser is the largest producer of softwood lumber for residential and commercial construction. The company's lumber operations are capable of producing 6.8 billion board of dimension lumber a year. More than 8,600 employees in ten states and four provinces work in the company's 43 sawmill operations. Weyerhaeuser Canada's head office is in Kamloops, with corporate offices in Vancouver. The company operates six sawmills in BC's southern interior, three sawmills in Alberta, and one in Saskatchewan. Combined annual capacity of all sawmills exceeds one billion board feet. Distribution and service to retail and industrial customers in Canada is provided through a network of six regional sales centers and four satellites. About 20 percent of Weyerhaeuser Canada's solid wood production is sold in the Canadian market, with the balance exported to the United States and overseas. To assure Canadian customers of a wide selection of quality products, sales outlets supplement their own product lines with material purchased from other manufacturers. The goal of the company is to be the industry leader in stewardship on public forest land. Weyerhaeuser Company is an international forest products company with annual sales of $18.5 billion. The company currently employs about 58,000 people in 18 countries. They are ranked in the Fortune 200 and number one in the industry in social responsibility in *Fortune* magazine's annual corporate reputation survey for seven years. What is Weyerhaeuser's position on the softwood lumber dispute? Weyerhaeuser is working aggressively on both sides of the border to encourage the US and Canadian governments to find a reasonable solution to the issue — one that supports the free trade of forest products, supports the belief that market-based solutions ultimately are the best, and encourages the long-term stewardship of timberland assets.

Weyerhaeuser has suggested that Canada agree to a 25 percent tax, which would decline as lumber prices rise, on all lumber exports to the United States. According to the Weyerhaeuser plan, the United States would then drop its duties in return. the company is optimistic, and expects the border tax proposal to be adopted, although there have been suggestions that the level of the tax will be contentious. Canadian officials have bristled at the 25 percent tax, and suggested a lower tax — 17 percent — in its place. Weyerhaeuser Co. wants the United States to end duties on Canadian softwood lumber imports and Canada to levy a new export tax ,while both countries work with the industry to negotiate an end to their decades-old trade dispute. Weyerhaeuser, called for an end to US import duties on Canadian softwood lumber. Weyerhaeuser began paying duty at a combined rate of 31.18 percent. The duties amount to about $30 million per quarter. Instead, the company wants Canada to adopt its own export tax, with a sliding scale of fees. The Weyerhaeuser plan also calls for the two sides to drop their complaints and appeals to the World Trade Organization and, instead, negotiate a solution that includes restructuring the way Canada values its uncut timber so production costs are equivalent to those in the United States. Weyerhaeuser believes that the history of this issue demonstrates that litigation and tariffs are not the answer and will not solve the problem.

Short-term solutions, such as countervailing and anti-dumping duties, have caused more harm than good because they distort market dynamics and end up being costly and divisive for producers, retailers and, ultimately, customers. Weyerhaeuser's position on both sides of the border gives a perspective shared by no other company. After 20 years of differences, they recognize that the issue can't be solved overnight. However, they strongly believe that a number of confidence-building measures are a good start: First, immediately establish a Canadian border tax on softwood lumber exports; end countervailing and anti-dumping duties; and halt all petitions, litigation and appeals. Second, negotiate changes in Canadian log-pricing practices to more closely mirror those in the United States. For the latter, they support the US Department of Commerce's proposal to let each province reach its own plan for a more market-sensitive system. An equitable distribution of Canadian funds already deposited toward payment of the duties must be an integral part of the solution. Wayerhaeuser is prepared to make concessions to bring the dispute to an end. There's only one way this plan can work. Both sides must be willing to give a little. If everyone gives a little, we can make this work for North America. At Weyerhaeuser, they are willing to do their part, including encouraging structural changes in provincial forest policies, participating in a joint industry/government effort to set realistic policy changes for Canada, and contributing time, energy and information to a joint US/Canada commission that could increase trust and understanding. Unlike many other softwood lumber companies, Weyerhaeuser is not concentrating on anything other than helping as much as possible to resolve the dispute, mainly due to the fact the company, while situated in 18 other countries, has most of its sales in Canada and the US.

Abitibi-Consolodated

Finally, the third largest company is the Quebec-based Abitibi-Consolidated. Abitibi-Consolidated is a global leader in newsprint, uncoated ground wood papers and lumber. They are a team of 16,000 people supplying newspapers, publishers, commercial printers, retailers, cataloguers and builders in more than 70 countries from 27 paper mills, 22 sawmills, 1 engineering wood and 2 remanufacturing facilities in Canada, the US, the UK, South Korea, China and Thailand. They also operate 10 recycling centres. How has the dispute affected the company? All indications are that this company seems to be suffering the most. Abitibi-Consolidated became the first major Canadian lumber producer to announce massive temporary sawmill shutdowns, as a result of the softwood lumber dispute with the US. It is closing 20 sawmills in Quebec and two sawmills in Mackenzie, BC, 170 kilometres north of Prince George, for two to four weeks this summer. Beginning in July, Abitibi is also closing three sawmills in Quebec indefinitely.

Ken Lloyd, Abitibi's general manager in Mackenzie, said the mill's plans have not been changed by the head office announcement. The Mackenzie operation had already planned a four-day shutdown of its two sawmills next week and a two-week shutdown in August. Its two planer mills will continue to operate, producing finished lumber. As a result, about 200 of the Mackenzie operation's 450 workers will be temporarily off the job. Lumber mills in British Columbia and Quebec have also closed in recent weeks due to the US-Canada softwood lumber dispute. Although many companies are still operating, Atco Lumber announced the indefinite closure of its Park Siding division last week. "With the price of lumber where it is, the mills really can't afford to pay an extra 27 percent (tariff)". said IWA Local 1-405 President Bob Matters. In Quebec, Abitibi-Consolidated announced the closure of three mills as well as scheduled down-time this summer in other operations. Operators in northern Ontario and BC have hinted at down-time in the late summer or early fall. On the BC coast, over 4,000 members remain unemployed, about one-quarter of that total due to permanent closures. "Clearly there is a light at the end of the tunnel in the softwood lumber dispute; the problem is that it is a train," said IWA President Dave Haggard. "If the price of lumber drops, which it probably will do by the fall, we are going to see more of this on the BC coast, in Quebec, the BC interior and even Ontario and the prairies. While most lumber producers in Canada are facing combined duties of 27 percent, to put the number in perspective, during 2002, $44 million was paid in total duties, countervailing ($26 million) and anti-dumping ($18 million) duties as a result of the ongoing dispute with the US on softwood lumber. Forest industry consultant Charlie Widman expects that more Quebec sawmills will shut down by the end of the summer, taking out about one billion board feet of lumber production. Abitibi has among the highest combined duties at 31 percent, because it was slapped with an individual anti-dumping duty higher than other companies. Lumber prices dipped after the duties came into effect, although they increased slightly last week to $250 US for the bellwether thousand board feet of two-by-fours. That is still considered below the break-even point, although it varies from mill to mill. What alternatives does the company have in response to the lumber dispute? As with Canfor and Weyerhaeuser, the answer is "Market Diversification and Advocacy".

Both the federal and the BC governments have announced the establishment of wood product marketing initiatives in response to the US softwood lumber duties.

On March 28, 2002, the Minister of Forests announced that the BC government would spend $20 million on forest sector diversification and international marketing.

On May 16, the federal government announced the creation of the $29.7 million Canadian Wood Export Program. This program is intended to expand Canada's wood exports in countries like China, Taiwan, Korea and India.

On May 20, 2002 the government of Canada announced that it would contribute $20 million "to help Canada's softwood lumber industry raise awareness in the US of the impact of punitive US softwood lumber duties on US interests, and to step up Canada's advocacy efforts in the US". Funding of $17 million (over two years) will be provided to the Forest Products Association of

Canada to "undertake a softwood industry-led campaign to raise awareness of the negative impact that softwood lumber duties will have on the US, and to encourage productive negotiations and resolution of the dispute". In addition, $3 million (over two years) will be given to the Canadian Embassy and Consulates in the US to enhance their efforts in this regard.

All the Canadian forest product companies, the federal government and Canadian provincial governments categorically deny the US allegations and strongly disagree with the countervailing and dumping determinations made by the ITC (International Trade Commerce) and DOC (US Department of Commerce). The Canadian government continues to aggressively defend the Canadian industry in this US trade dispute and are appealing the decision of these administrative agencies to the appropriate courts. If the above plan does not work then the Industrial Wood and Allied Workers of Canada have come up with their own seven point plan.

The following is a seven-point action plan to fight the US imposed tariff, which is being supported by the Industrial, Wood and Allied Workers of Canada, CLC (IWA) and other groups:

1. Raise the profile of the issue with American consumers.
2. Raise the profile of the issue with the Prime Minister.
3. Boycott American products and American companies that do not support the Canadian forest industry.
4. Tax all resource products currently being exported to the United States.
5. Provide extended EI and assistance to laid off workers affected by the duties.
6. Seek support from the Canadian workforce to protest the CVD and ADD.
7. Locate and develop alternative markets for Canadian forest products.

The fact remains: North America needs a stable lumber market that reduces uncertainty for mill owners, employees, communities and customers, and encourages long-term investment. Under the current situation, neither side benefits. Canada and the United States have the largest and strongest trading partnership in the world. As strong allies, they owe it to each other to figure out an enduring solution that works. The longer they fight, the more they hurt themselves. It is time for a system that works for everyone; if they do not find a feasible solution, the international markets will benefit from their dispute.

Softwood Companies' Response Trends

It is apparent that all softwood sawmills have to make a decision in response to the high duties or pay the consequences. In order to stay in operation, Canadian softwood sawmills need to export their lumber. They are, therefore, faced with three options:

1. Reduce costs/improve productions
2. Add value
3. Export to other countries

The most obvious response is for the sawmills to reduce their costs to counteract the high duties. Improving their operations will help them in reducing their costs by increasing their efficiencies. Upgrading mills to improve their production seems very costly to companies in the short run, especially when they are trying to reduce their costs. Improving operations can result in anything from eliminating a step in the process to buying new technology. When buying new technology, companies are usually adding value to their productions. They have the ability to diversify their product from the standard dimension. Changing from the standard dimension opens the possibility of entering new markets. Roslyn Kunin from *Logging and Sawmill Journal* points out that "if Western Canada's lumber industry is to diversify their products. Selling 2×4s won't work, as relatively few wood frame houses are built in Asia. However, there are well over a billion Asians hoping for better housing and their apartments will need doors, door frames, window frames, flooring, furnishings and other products that can and often will be made of wood".[68] Depending on the size of the companies and their location, they will need to incorporate one or all three of these options.

Companies have had to take a step back and look at their current operations, educate themselves on other available options and then plan their move. For a lot of the larger companies, like Canfor, who have financial leverage, the best starting move is to upgrade their mills. As Kryzanowski says "While many Canadian softwood lumber producers are feeling the pain of a 27 percent tariff on exports to the United States, the failure to upgrade sawmill facilities in a timely manner — and stay a low cost producer — could eventually prove fatal to a mill".[69] Mill upgrades are what these companies are doing. Buchanan Lumbers' vice-president, Greg Buchanan, says, "After years of making minor upgrades, it was simply time to re-evaluate and replace all the sawmill's major production components in order to remain competitive".[70] Buchanan Lumber invested $11 million in modernization that will result in a 15 percent increase in fibre recovery from its existing wood basket.[71] The company intends to make more random length lumber and metric sized to better serve different markets. They already have been supplying to the Japanese markets and, "believes there is more market opportunity in that part of Asia".[72] Buchanan continues to succeed by seeing opportunities and grabbing them. Miller Western sawmill in Whitecourt, Alberta made a $40 million upgrade. The mill was 20-years-old and had to be completely redesigned from a three-line mill to a single-line mill.[73] The sawmill has achieved a 20 percent improvement in recovery and reduced its need to purchase wood from private sources by 60 percent, while producing the same amount of lumber. The number of employees was also reduced from 137 to 94, reducing labour costs. Interfor's Hammond Cedar Division in Maple Ridge, British Columbia invested $5.3 million in upgrading. They also decided to move their McDonald Cedar value-added operations to Sumas, Washington to reduce the amount paid on the duties. Interfor has had to close a number of coastal mills, including the Fraser Mills in 2002. Tembec in Timmins, Ontario like other companies trying to survive, wanted to get the most out of their logs. At a cost of $8 million to upgrade and with the closure of one of their three mills, the benefit is 25 percent more lumber from the same amount of logs and an increase in the amount of logs per hour.[74] Unfortunately, for the smaller companies spending millions on upgrading operations just is not viable.

Smaller to medium size companies have found that adding value to their operations is the key to their success. "Smaller sawmills are particularly motivated, since they are faced with tight profit margins for commodity dimension lumber and greater competition for a diminishing wood resource from the larger forestry companies",[75] says Keyzanowski. Terry Blair, owner of T. Blair Sawmill in Haliburton, Ontario, demonstrates how smaller sawmills survive by providing value-added wood products. Terry Blair invested in a new machine that allows him to produce dimension lumber, tongue and groove flooring, wood siding, roof sheeting, mouldings, V-joint panelling, wainscotting baseboards, crown mouldings and chair rails.[76] As Blair says, "We can sell the whole package—we've experienced growth through our own efforts with the value-added manufacturing. And we feel we're growing in the right direction".[77] Though Blair reduced his staff to three from five, he has plans to rehire with more diversification.

With all of these companies becoming more efficient, buying new equipment that requires less labour and closing mills down to increase capacity at other locations, hundreds of people are left unemployed. These people and communities that have previously been forestry dependent and left unemployed are opening small companies focussed on value-added products. MacDonald from Logging & Sawmill Journal says, "The real solution for these communities may lie in creating an economic environment for a large number of small and medium companies could be forestry-related — rather than betting the farm on attracting huge industries".[78] In Powell River, BC, Rick Hopper started a company making furniture. He buys wood that supposedly has no value, therefore getting it cheap, and gives it lots of value by the time it leaves the shop. The plant is 5,000 square feet and employs four people. Even though these small businesses may employ under five people, it is still a way of boosting their economy.

The Canadian softwood industry is going through drastic changes. With this dispute the question of how the provinces sell their land is under scrutiny. Companies know that there are going to be more changes. As Pat Macdonald says "An external issue driving efficiency these days at BC's coastal sawmills is pending changes to the tenure system. The liberal provincial government has already said that it wants to see more logs sold on the open market — which would partially satisfy the Americans in the current softwood dispute. With this scenario, companies — whether they be Interfor, Weyerhaeuser or small independents — would have to purchase more of their timber on the open market and rely less on forestry tenures. These changes would make it even more important that sawmills are efficient, since the overall cost of purchasing timber would rise".[79] Canadian softwood companies have to be flexible and learn to continue to deal with the industry changes.

Many of these softwood companies have been successful in becoming more efficient and improving their margins. They have found ways to counteract the hefty US duties. As stated in the Canadian Press, "Despite the duties on softwood exports to the United States and sawmill profits at 16-year lows, lumber output in Canada rose by an estimated one billion board feet in 2002, to hit

29.5 billion board feet".[80] The results also show that geographically, the West was able to increase production by seven to eight percent, while the East struggled to hold volumes to their 2001 levels. In 2002, the ten Canadian companies made it to productions of over one billion board feet. Communities that were dependent on mills and were left unemployed are finding ways through value-added production to boost their economy. Canadian companies are surviving this fight against the United States.

References

1 Statistics Canada, "Annual Report on Canada's State of Trade", www.dfait-maeci.gc.ca, 2001.

2 Statistics Canada, "Annual Report on Canada's State of Trade", www.dfait-maeci.gc.ca, 2001.

3 *Ibid.*

4 *Ibid.*

5 *Ibid.*

6 *Ibid.*

7 Department of Foreign Affairs and International Trade. "North American Free Trade Agreement-Overview", www.dfait-maeci.gc.ca, 2001.

8 International Trade Reporter, May 9 2002, pp. 853–4.

9 World Trade Organization, United States — Preliminary Determinations with respect to Certain Softwood Lumber from Canada, WT/DS236®, September 27 2002.

10 International Trade Reporter, February 21 2002, pp. 298–300; March 14 2002, pp. 460–1; March 21 2002, pp. 504–5; March 28 2002, pp. 522–4;

11 Howlett, Michael. ed. *Canadian Forest Policy: Adapting to Change*, Toronto: University of Toronto Press, 2001.

12 US DOC, ITA, `Notice of preliminary determination of sales at less than fair value and postponement of final determination: certain softwood lumber products from Canada,' 66 Federal Register 56062, 6 November 2001; International Trade Reporter, 1 November 2001, 1749; Inside US Trade, 2 November 2001, 4–5.

13 US ITC, Softwood Lumber from Canada, Pub. no. 3509, May 2002; Canada, News Release No. 46, 2 May 2002; News Release No. 53, 17 May 2002.

14 Ritchie, Gordon. *Wrestling with the Elephant: The Inside Story of the Canada-US Trade Wars,* Toronto: Macfarlane, Walter & Ross, 1997, p. 212.

15 Softwood Lumber Agreement between the Government of Canada and the Government of the United States of America (Canada, Treaty series 1996/16). The SLA was formally signed in May 1996 with application retroactive to 1 April.

16 http://www.fairlumbercoalition.org/index.htm

17 http://www.nahb.org/generic.aspx?sectionID=88

18 http://www.acah.org/Aldonis%20010803.htm

19 http://www.for.gov.bc.ca/HET/Softwood/softwood lumber framework.pdf

20 http://www.for.gov.bc.ca/HET/Softwood/softwood lumber framework.pdf
21 *Ibid.*
22 http://www.for.gov.bc.ca/HET/Softwood/softwood lumber framework.pdf
23 http://www.aacb.com/Softwood/sftwdnews.asp?articleid=710
24 http://gsaps.hanyang.ac.kr/usa/Term/mooney3/
25 http://gsaps.hanyang.ac.kr/usa/Term/mooney3/
26 http://www.freetrade.org/pubs/freetotrade/chapter5.html
27 Ted Walther, The World economy, Chapter 8, The Political Economy of Trade Policy
28 *Ibid.*
29 Ted Walther, The World Economy, Chapter 8, The Political Economy of Trade Policy
30 http://www.safnet.org/archive/0203_canada.htm
31 http://www.safnet.org/archive/0203_canada.htm
32 http://www.safnet.org/archive/0203_canada.htm
33 http://www.safnet.org/archive/0203_canada.htm
34 Gillies & Dickinson. Globalization and Canadian Economic and Industrial Strategy in the Twenty-First Century.
35 http://www.for.gov.bc.ca/HET/Softwood/disputes.htm
36 http://www.for.gov.bc.ca/HET/Softwood/disputes.htm
37 http://www.softwoodlumberissue.com
38 http://www.canada.com/national/features/softwooddispute/
39 *Canada-US Lumber Trade Disputes:* http://www.for.gov.bc.ca.HET/Softwood/disputes.htm
40 A British Columbia Proposal
41 *Ibid.*
42 *Ibid.*
43 *Ibid.*
44 *Ibid.*
45 *Ibid.*
46 *Ibid.*
47 *Ibid.*
48 *Ibid.*
49 *Ibid.*
50 *Ibid.*
51 *Ibid.*
52 *Ibid.*
53 *Ibid.*
54 *Ibid.*
55 http://www.forest.ca/details.php3
56 http://www.dfait-maeci.gc.ca/eicb/softwood/intro-en.asp
57 http://www.cif-ifc.org
58 http://www.cwc.ca/wf_010.html
59 http://www.for.gov.vc.ca/HET/Softwood/topic%20box.pdf
60 http://www.canada.com-"Canfor boosts lumber production despite softwood dispute" March 10, 2003
61 http://www.cbc.ca/cgi-bin/templates/print.cgi?/2002/03/22/woodreax020322 "BC lumber industry braces for even more cuts" March 22, 2003

62   Ednie, Heather. "Proven Formula", *Logging and Sawmill Journal*, February 2003, pp. 27–29.

63   www.canfor.com

64   www.canfor.com/resources/2000/news4q02.pdf

65   www.canfor.com/resources/6000/n030123a.pdf

66   *Ibid.*

67   *Ibid.*

68   Kunin, Roslyn. "Three words lead to success: diversify, diversify, diversify", *Logging and Sawmills Journal.* December 2002/Janruary 2003. p. 62.

69   Kryzanowski, Tony. "Real deals on MILL UPGRADES", *Logging and Sawmill Journal.* February 2003, pp. 22–25.

70   *Ibid.*, pp 18–21

71   *Ibid.*, pp 18–21

72   *Ibid.*, pp 18–21

73   *Ibid.*, pp 22–25

74   Ford, Ray. "SOLID line-up", *Logging and Sawmills Journal.* December 2002/January 2003, pp. 15–17

75   Kryzanowski, Tony. "Making a successful move", Logging and Sawmills Journal. December 2002/January 2003. pp 26–29

76   ibid., pp 26–29

77   ibid., pp 26–29

78   MacDonald, Paul. "A future in furniture", *Logging and Sawmills Journal.* December 2002/January 2003, pp. 34–37.

79   Macdonald, Paul. "To the max", *Logging and Sawmills Journal.* February 2003, pp. 30–33.

80   Macdonald, Paul. "To the max", *Logging and Sawmills Journal.* February 2003, pp. 30–33.

Canadian Provinces, US States and North American Integration

Bench Warmers or Key Players?

Stephen de Boer

Introduction

Much of the recent discussion of further economic integration in the North American context[1] has focussed on issues largely implicating the three federal governments. These range from the facilitation of the cross-border movement of goods to security concerns stemming from more open borders. Looking further ahead, topics have ranged from the possibility of forming a customs union to perhaps the adoption of a common currency throughout North America. These discussions have touched surprisingly little on the role that sub-federal governments — that is, individual states and provinces — might play in any integration efforts. Yet their role in that respect is significant and should be considered.

Existing economic integration mechanisms such as the Canada-US Free Trade Agreement, its successor agreement the North American Free Trade Agreement (NAFTA) and the World Trade Organization (WTO) Agreement necessarily require sub-federal cooperation in order to ensure that countries fully comply with these agreements' provisions. From a Canadian standpoint, these

*   From IRPP, volume 8, number 4, November 2002 (Publication of the Institute for Research in Public Policy). Reproduced with permission of author and publisher.

Stephen de Boer

agreements have expanded beyond the international border into areas within the constitutional jurisdiction of provincial governments: procurement, standards, the removal of non-tariff barriers such as local presence or residency requirements, treatment of investors, services and the regulation of professions, among others.

Although Canada has developed a consultative mechanism with the provinces that is sensitive to the constitutional division of powers in this country, the United States has not done so to the same extent. The subsequent failure of US states to become fully engaged in that nation's trade commitments poses a serious threat to mutually beneficial economic integration in North America, and is indicative of problems that might arise in wider discussions on integration.

In this context, this paper will make suggestions for a more formal and constructive engagement by sub-federal states in the integration agenda, at three distinct levels: that of the respective national processes between federal and sub-federal entities, that of the negotiating processes between federal governments, and that involving sub-national governments directly with each other.

The International Legal Context for Sub-Federal Governments

Neither the US states nor the provinces of Canada are signatories to the NAFTA and WTO [Agreement]. This is logical since, generally, only national governments have the authority to bind their countries in an international context. However, given the breadth of control sub-federal governments have over elements of their respective national economies, signatories to international trade agreements want to ensure that sub-federal governments comply with obligations subscribed to by federal governments. At the same time, the constitutional division of powers within federal states makes it politically difficult if not impossible for national governments to bind state and provincial governments to the provisions of an agreement without their consent.

In order to resolve this issue, international trade agreements make the US and Canadian federal governments responsible for sub-federal compliance. Article 105 of the NAFTA commits both federal governments to "ensure that all necessary measures are taken in order to give effect to the provisions of this Agreement, including their observance, except as otherwise provided in this Agreement, by state and provincial governments." Article 105 is based on Article XXIV:12 of the General Agreement on Tariffs and Trade (GATT), which attempts to achieve a similar result by requiring each signatory to "take such reasonable measures as may be available to it to ensure observance of the provisions of this Agreement by regional and local governments." In the WTO, this language was revised to make member countries "fully responsible"[2] for the observance of the commitments made under the Agreement while also requiring that they take "reasonable measures" to ensure observance of the Agreement by regional and local governments.

The nature of a federal government's obligation to ensure sub-national compliance has been addressed by GATT dispute settlement panel reports. In *United States: Measures Affecting Alcoholic and Malt Beverages*[3] (Beer II), a

GATT panel ruled in 1992, among other things, that certain US state measures which imposed a lower tax or offered tax credits on in-state brewers violated the requirement of national treatment set out in GATT Article III, concerning national treatment on taxation and regulation. In that case, the panel ruled "that because GATT was part of US federal law, which is superior to state law, there is no constitutional impediment to bringing a state into compliance."[4]

In an earlier case, *Canada: Import, Distribution and Sale of Certain Alcoholic Drinks by Provincial Marketing Agencies,*[5] the US argued that Canada could ensure compliance of the provinces to the GATT ruling, which found provincial listing requirements among other things to violate Canada's trade commitments, because the federal parliament had the legal power to discipline provincial liquor boards.[6] In that case, the panel did not define what a reasonable measure would be for the Canadian government to adopt in order to ensure provincial compliance, but the panel did rule that Canada must show that it has made a "serious, persistent, and convincing effort."[7]

Reading these two decisions together suggests that the GATT panellists were cognizant of, and sensitive to, the differences between the federal structures of the United States and Canada. The panels recognized that the US had the legal authority to impose a GATT consistent solution on the states while Canada's legal authority may not be as clear cut. At the same time, Canada could not hide behind its apparent lack of legal authority to ensure compliance. The GATT/WTO system therefore seems to be flexible enough to permit different internal solutions and is cognizant of different internal realities. The aim, however, is the same: sub-national compliance.

Overall, the case for the US federal government binding its sub-federal constituent parts to the provisions of an international trade agreement (or other agreements that enhance economic integration) seems stronger than in the Canadian context. The US government has the legal authority to impose certain measures on its states and is, in fact, required to do so by virtue of GATT Article XXIV:12. The Canadian federal government, on the other hand, does not enjoy the same clear legal authority to bind its sub-federal governments but must, according to the GATT, at least make a "serious, persistent and convincing effort" to ensure that provinces comply with international trade obligations. Theoretically, this should mean that the ability to effectively drive economic-integration efforts in areas of sub-federal jurisdiction is greater in the US. In reality, the US track record is not nearly as favourable. To understand why, one needs to look at the distinctions between the history and practices of the two countries in this area, beginning with Canada.

The Role of Provinces and States in International Trade

The role of sub-federal governments in the Canada-US context is somewhat confused by differing constitutional constraints placed upon the federal and sub-federal governments in both countries. In Canada, it has been noted, with respect to international obligations, that "the federal government holds no trump card over the provinces as a constitutional matter."[8] This view of Canadian constitutional law is derived from the 1937 *Labour Conventions*[9] decision and a rather restrictive court interpretation of the federal government's "trade and commerce" power.

The *Labour Conventions* case essentially determined that the federal government of Canada only had international competence in areas where it enjoyed constitutional jurisdiction. In areas that fell under provincial jurisdiction, as set out in Section 92 of the *Constitution Act, 1867*, the federal government could not assert international competence. In addition, the trade and commerce power bestowed upon the federal government has "never been a strong repository for federal jurisdiction over economic policy."[10] As a consequence, provincial power over property and civil rights has become the default trade power in Canada.[11] Thus, a distinction should be made between the federal power to negotiate and the provincial power, in many cases, to implement.[12]

The court ruling in the *Labour Conventions* case, perhaps coupled with federal and/or provincial fears of losing a challenge that would upset the ruling and the status quo, entails in practice a high level of federal-provincial cooperation for Canada, as a whole, to pursue its trade objectives.[13] This is enhanced by the fact that both levels of government understand the importance of international markets to practically every region of Canada.[14]

Furthermore, in part because of exclusive powers granted to provinces under Section 92, provinces tend to act as sovereign in their sphere and are often treated as such by the federal government. The concept of executive federalism whereby representatives of the national and provincial executive branches of government meet to discuss issues is an implicit recognition of this sovereignty.[15] The Agreement on Internal Trade (AIT) signed by the provincial, territorial and federal governments in 1994 confirms the notion of respective sovereignties. The AIT also reflects the reality that "provincial governments are often the main articulators of regional interests in Canada due to constitutional powers and the weak level of regional representation in federal institutions,"[16] with the noted consequence that "most inter-governmental relations take place between governments rather than within a body such as the Senate."[17]

Some commentators have taken a conciliatory approach when describing the current state of federal-provincial relations, noting that "[o]n balance, Canada's federal arrangements have worked reasonably well in dealing with our trade and investment policy concerns."[18] Others, however, have viewed the current constitutional state of play in negative terms. In one instance, the current situation was described as the "burden of exclusive spheres"[19] and in another as a "disability."[20] Another commentator calls the *Labour Conventions* "an inconvenient precedent"[.][21]Despite these criticisms, it is noteworthy that Canada has not been so "disabled" or "burdened" that it could not commit to the obligations of the GATT, WTO [Agreement], the Canada-US Free Trade Agreement or the NAFTA. In fact, the latter three agreements were all negotiated with significant input from the provinces.

The United States' constitutional structure with respect to international trade is arguably more straightforward than Canada's. A number of constitutional provisions, such as the supremacy clause — according to which federal law trumps conflicting state laws — commerce clause, treaty clause and the president's authority as Commander in Chief, all support the prevalence of federal power over state power in foreign relations.[22] Noted US international-trade-law scholar John Jackson further observes that, in *Missouri v. Holland*, the Supreme Court of the United States ruled that a valid international agreement could extend federal powers beyond "what would be permissible in the absence of such an US agreement."[23]

It seems that the United States federal government has clearer constitutional authority than the Canadian federal government to enter into international undertakings and bind its sub-federal governments in the process. Although this may be true from a strictly legal perspective, it has not always played out in reality. In practice, the US federal government has been reluctant to use its legal powers to bind sub-federal governments to commitments it has made under international trade agreements: "[s]tate and local actions in the international arena are governed more by custom, political practice and intergovernmental comity than by enforcement of constitutional and statutory rules."[24] For example, in some cases, the federal government may be reluctant to challenge individual states because doing so may upset that state's representative in the Senate.

Provincial Involvement in Canadian Trade Policy

Since the commencement of the Tokyo Round of multilateral trade negotiations in the mid-1970s, the Canadian federal government has developed a practice of consulting with the provinces on international trade initiatives. This practice developed out of necessity because the Tokyo Round began to deal with issues that were within the constitutional jurisdiction of the provinces. Subsequent trade negotiations also dealt with provincial issues, so the practice of consulting with the provinces has continued. These consultations have become increasingly important because the focus of international trade negotiations and agreements has "turned overwhelmingly to `inside-the-border' regulatory and expenditure policies that have the potential to distort and impede trade."[25] Services trade, natural resource pricing and agricultural support programs are good examples of provincial policies that fall "inside the border." The nature of these new areas of negotiation has meant that the federal government needs to look to the provinces for information and negotiation support.[26] Furthermore, these federal-provincial consultations are in keeping with Canada's tradition of executive federalism and recognize the lack of constitutional authority permitting the federal government to impose obligations in areas of provincial jurisdiction. This practice of federal-provincial consultations continues in a number of fora, including quarterly meetings of federal and provincial trade officials called C-Trade, meetings between the federal minister of international trade with his or her provincial counterparts, meetings of deputy ministers concerned with trade issues and extensive consultations on trade challenges that implicate provincial measures.

The Canadian system of federal-provincial consultations has developed in a manner that is both consistent with Canada's international trade obligations as set out in the NAFTA and GATT, as well as with the ruling in the Labour

Conventions case. However, the current system presents a number of challenges for the provinces. Problems range from the substantial to the petty, with tensions sometimes erupting over issues as trivial as the number of provincial officials permitted into a meeting room or hearing. Some of the more substantive issues are addressed below.

Fashioning a Canadian Position

The federal government speaks for Canada (including the provinces) in international fora. However, what it says in many cases depends on the positions of the various provinces and on the issues being discussed. Given the differing economic strengths and interests of the provinces, the federal government often finds itself in the unenviable position of attempting to fashion a consensus that it is not at all obvious. For example, Alberta's interest in energy issues is very different from the interests of Ontario or Quebec. British Columbia's interest in softwood lumber trade is markedly different than that of New Brunswick, which has consistently been able to obtain exclusions from US investigations of provincial softwood lumber practices.

The softwood lumber dispute of 1991 and the subsequent Softwood Lumber Agreement (SLA), which limited Canadian exports of lumber to the US from 1996 to 2001, provides an interesting example of how the development of a national position does not always reflect the aspirations of particular provinces. Three of the four largest softwood lumber producing provinces supported the SLA but Ontario did not. Ontario viewed the SLA as an arrangement designed to improve the competitive position of the western producing provinces under the guise of opening up access to a market, the United States, that was not closed at that time. Furthermore, the export restraint agreement was arguably inconsistent with the principles of free trade and in violation of NAFTA and WTO Agreement provisions on export and import controls. This posed a challenge to Ontario, whose position is generally supportive of trade agreements and which defends the benefits of free trade to stakeholders.

The federal-provincial consultative mechanism also suffers because not all provinces have the same capacity to address international trade issues. Although there is no doubt that the provinces collectively are sophisticated on trade issues, the limited capacity of smaller provinces is in stark contrast to the large number of officials that Quebec, Ontario, Alberta and British Columbia can devote to these issues. At the same time, the lack of capacity in some of the smaller provinces is offset by the high level of sophistication of their officials, who may have a narrower set of trade interests upon which to concentrate and know these issues well. No single province, however, has the trade resources, capacity or sophistication of the federal government.

Living With Canada's Trade Obligations

With respect to Canada's trade obligations, it is not always clear for either the federal or provincial governments what these obligations will mean five or ten years in the future. This is a problem for all levels of government, but the degree of uncertainty for sub-federal governments is exacerbated for a number of reasons.

First, the federal government may not expressly design new trade obligations to deal with matters that fall within sub-federal jurisdiction, either because the federal negotiators lack understanding of provincial jurisdiction or fear treading on it. In the case of NAFTA Chapter 11, concerning the protection of foreign investors and their investments, the federal government negotiated a text on the definition and basis for providing compensation for expropriated investments, without any meaningful input from provincial governments. Yet it is provincial governments that are most charged with this issue under the Canadian constitution. As a result, the provinces are left trying to educate the federal government on what expropriation law means at the provincial level as well as trying to revise their thinking on what now constitutes expropriation in the new NAFTA context.

Second, provinces were not at the table during the negotiations, so they may not have a clear understanding of the obligations. As a result, they sometimes maintain measures or introduce new measures that are inconsistent with the new trade obligations.

Third, provincial governments do not have the same resources to deal with trade negotiations and implementation of the subsequent agreements. Although the provinces generally have developed the necessary sophistication on trade matters, they sometimes face problems with respect to capacity and resources; a problem exacerbated by government cut-backs in the 1990s. Consequently, not all provincial issues are adequately flagged for federal negotiators. Even when they are, provincial governments are not always adept at effectively communicating their concerns to federal officials because provincial officials may not have couched them in trade terms or in the language of trade agreements. The lack of provincial sophistication on some of these issues has a political component. Often, provincial ministers concerned with trade restrict their efforts to trade promotion. This limits their engagement with the federal Minister of International Trade and the provision of directions to their own provincial officials concerning the broader question of trade rules-making.

Dealing with Trade Disputes

The need to understand the scope of Canada's trade commitments is most profoundly brought to bear when a foreign government challenges a provincial government's measures as inconsistent with Canada's obligations. Federal and provincial officials consult on trade disputes that implicate provincial measures, as was the case in the US challenge of Ontario beer marketing practices, which included restrictions on private delivery of beer and imposition of minimum prices, before the GATT in the early 1990s (Beer I). Extensive consultations also occur where both federal and provincial measures are threatened by a trade challenge, such as the US challenge, before a NAFTA Chapter 20 dispute settlement panel, of Canada's replacement of import quotas on certain agricultural commodities, subject to provincial marketing boards, by tariffs ("tariffication"). The softwood lumber dispute and a challenge by New Zealand and the US of Canada's dairy export regime are also good examples of instances involving federal-provincial consultations and collaboration. In the latter case, the federal government and the provinces of Quebec and Ontario, in particular, worked together closely in defence of Canada's measures. This included provincial attendance at WTO [Agreement]dispute settlement hearings in Geneva.

Federal-provincial cooperation in these disputes makes sense for a number of reasons. If a foreign government targets a provincial program, the province has the best information on the targeted program and should participate in the defence of the disputed measure. On a more practical level, the federal government needs to share the responsibility for defending the measure because it does not have the personnel and other resources to do it all on its own. Provincial participation also insures greater support for a negotiated settlement to the dispute or compliance with a dispute-settlement panel ruling. Finally, by implicating the province in the process, the federal government is ensuring that it will not have to carry all of the blame if the defence of the measure is ultimately unsuccessful.

In addition, provincial participation in the defence of its own measures has a number of wider positive consequences for Canadian international trade relations. Provincial trade officials develop valuable expertise while participating in trade disputes and begin to understand the dispute settlement process. At the same time, provincial officials also learn some of the consequences of developing non-trade compliant measures, including the cost of defending their measures.

However, not every aspect of federal-provincial relations on international trade issues is positive. It is not always possible to construct a national strategy in a trade dispute that reflects the disparate interests of the various provinces. As well, when only one province's measures are being challenged by another country, there is a risk that the federal government will have a greater interest in seeing the problem go away than in reaching a resolution to the dispute. In addition, larger national concerns can dominate the federal government's agenda in a manner that is insensitive to local issues. The federal government may not realize how politically sensitive the underlying issues are for certain provincial constituencies. From the federal perspective, the dispute may be viewed as little more than an irritant that is undermining Canada's overall trading relationship with the disputing country.

The Context for US States

The most pressing trade problems for provincial governments often involve access to the United States market. Not surprisingly, however, sub-federal governments in the United States often try to undermine such a[c]cess. To better understand why and how this happens, a look at state involvement in international trade negotiations and disputes is instructive.

Problems of Federal-State Consultation

Some commentators assert that "[i]t is not politically desirable for federal officials to appear to be interfering in policies traditionally set at the state level.

Consequently, federal officials often seek to play down the pre-emptive effects of an international trade agreement."[27] Section 102(b)(2) of the *Uruguay Round Agreements Act*, for example, which implemented US WTO commitments in domestic law, makes it clear that the US federal government has the authority to challenge state laws in court if there is a conflict between the state law and the WTO Agreement, but the Act also states that this will only be used as a last resort in cases where a co-operative approach with the state government has not worked.

The Statement of Administrative Action that accompanied the *Uruguay Round Agreements Act* established a consultative mechanism between the federal United States Trade Representative (USTR) and state governments. A similar mechanism exists in the NAFTA implementing legislation. The Office of Intergovernmental Affairs and Public Liaison (IAPL) informs the states about trade-related matters that "directly relate to or that may have a direct effect on them."[28] The IAPL transacts day-to-day communications with a State Single Point of Contact (SPOC) designated by the governor's office in each state.[29] This practice risks limiting the spread of information within state governments by shutting out state legislators or other parts of the executive such as the Attorney General who must deal directly with the impact of trade agreements on state jurisdiction and law-making. The IAPL also facilitates outreach with domestic groups such as the business community as well as agricultural, environmental, labour and consumer organizations.

The nature of both USTR-state consultations and dialogue between USTR and domestic groups creates the impression that the federal government views individual states as just another interest group and not as partners in international trade matters. Furthermore, as noted by John Kincaid, states so viewed are in a disadvantageous position to compete with wealthier groups seeking to influence US trade policy.[30] The IAPL also administers the Intergovernmental Policy Advisory Committee on Trade (IGPAC), containing representatives of governor[']s associations and state and local officials, which provides advice to the USTR on trade policy matters. However, it has been noted that the US federal government has only had sporadic meetings between the USTR and representatives of the National Governors' Association.[31] Moreover, not all state governments have representatives on the IGPAC and, unlike in Canada, some documents, such as draft texts, are only available for viewing in Washington. This latter point alone seriously hampers the ability of state governments to meaningfully assess and convincingly "buy into" US trade liberalization initiatives.

The US federal government, therefore, seems to have made only a half-hearted attempt at establishing something akin to the consultative mechanism that exists between the Canadian government and its provincial counterparts — imperfect as that mechanism is. The US version seems to be missing a number of essential points about the Canadian consultative mechanism, particularly extensive consultations on the text of draft trade agreements.

Arguably, it is not necessary that the US adopt a consultative mechanism similar to Canada's. The federal-provincial consultative mechanism in Canada, which accords a significant role to provincial governments, had been developed in part because of the failure of federal institutions to adequately articulate regional concerns and interests. This is not the case in the US where a strong Senate forcefully expresses the concerns of the various states and regions. However, it is not the Senate that must implement trade agreements at the local level. As such, if a fuller buy-in by the states of federal trade obligations is the objective, there is still a need in the US for a stronger consultative mechanism between the federal and state governments than the existing structure provides.

The USTR's timid consultative mechanism with the states, when added to the US federal government's general reluctance to enforce international trade obligations at the state level and these states' frequent lack of trade sophistication, has serious consequences for economic integration efforts in North America. This will be presently demonstrated with respect to trade negotiations, and the resolution of trade disputes. In fact, it could be argued that there is a relationship between the lack of prior consultation with the states and the federal unwillingness to enforce rulings.

Trade Negotiations Involving US States

One can substantiate state reluctance to participate meaningfully in international trade issues by reviewing the negotiation of the General Agreement on Trade in Services (GATS). These reportedly created a great deal of controversy when the US exempted state measures that did not even need to be exempted, since they did not violate the basic non-discrimination principle of national treatment.[32] This principle generally requires states to treat foreign service providers no less favourably than like domestic service providers. In another example, US sub-federal offers not to discriminate against foreign suppliers for goods and services during the Uruguay Round's renegotiation of the Government Procurement Agreement (GPA) were so meaningless, either because of exemptions or a lack of coverage, that the Canadian government refused to offer provincial commitments to the Agreement.[33]

State reluctance to participate in trade negotiations is not limited to the multilateral context. Between 1994 and 1996, the states and provinces were permitted to list reservations in Annex I of the NAFTA, which was meant to list measures that would otherwise be inconsistent with a number of the commitments in Chapter 11 (Investment) and Chapter 12 (Cross-Border Trade in Services). The idea was that a state or province could reserve and maintain any measure listed in the Annex while any NAFTA-inconsistent measure not listed could be the subject of a legitimate trade challenge. While the Canadian provinces embarked on an exhaustive process to complete this exercise, the US federal government was unable to deliver any meaningful reservation lists from the states. In order to deal with this problem, the NAFTA parties agreed to grandfather, without having to list them, all existing sub-federal measures. This result was a step backward because the exempted measures are not transparent and as such limit the scope of future liberalization.

Ironically, governors supported and actively lobbied Congress to adopt both the NAFTA and WTO implementing legislation.[34] This perhaps had less to do with their interest in overall trade liberalization than it did with developing market opportunities for local firms and creating an attractive economic climate for inbound investment. There is little to suggest that these governors recognized that trade liberalization might also have implications on the development of their own domestic policies, as discussed below.

Trade Disputes Involving US States

The US federal government's inability to deliver meaningful commitments from its states in trade negotiations parallels a sometimes obvious unwillingness to enforce the provisions of agreements that it has already signed and ratified. For example, in the early 1980s, neither the White House nor Congress seemed willing to order state governments to abandon their unitary taxation formulas, which generally tax the income of corporations relative to the degree to which they do business in the state in some cases in violation of international tax treaties. The politicians were loath to face the wrath of state government leaders and their constituents, even though bilateral treaties gave federal officials the right to enforce such treaties.[35] The short-term political price of taking such action seems to have weighed heavier than long-term economic goals as represented by trade commitments.

Washington has not always displayed such reticence. In the early 1970's, Maine attempted to use its regulations for potato marketing to stop imports from Canada, but the US federal government used the court system to quickly overturn the state's actions.[36] Since then, however, the US federal government has shown a reluctance to assert its authority. In 1984, for example, South Dakota banned Canadian imports of pork and live hogs because the producers were using a drug that had been banned by the US Food and Drug Administration. However, the state prohibition lasted a number of months after a similar ban on the drug was instituted in Canada.[37] Nevertheless, in that case, the US federal government declined to take action against South Dakota even [though] it seemed clear that the action was solely designed to keep Canadian imports out.

The beer dispute (Beer II) between Canada and the US provides another example, this time with respect to state laws and regulations governing the distribution and sale of beer. These laws and regulations did not, in general, deny access to Canadian beer but they did discriminate against out-of-state beer (including foreign beer) by providing preferential treatment to in-state beer. In 1992, a GATT panel[38] determined that 62 measures maintained by 39 state governments were in breach of US obligations under the GATT. Since the adoption of that panel report, however, the US federal government and the states have made no effort to remove GATT-inconsistent measures. In fact, the number of such measures has actually increased since the ruling. According to estimates by the Brewers Association of Canada, since the adoption of the 1992 panel report, 50 additional "inconsistent" measures have been introduced in 40 states.[39] In this case, not only has the United States failed to live up to the GATT panel ruling, but the inaction of Washington seems to have allowed an increased level of non-conformity.

Perhaps the most egregious case of state interference with international trade occurred when Massachusetts passed a law in 1996 forbidding state agencies, entities and authorities from doing business with Myanmar (Burma), citing that country's human-rights violations. In addition, however, the law also added a price penalty on bids from foreign companies which were found to have done so. Although legal scholars made a strong case that this action by Massachusetts was unconstitutional,[40] the federal government did not take steps to challenge the state law. The European Union and Japan, whose businesses were adversely affected by the law, were particularly frustrated by the US federal government's inaction and raised this issue at the WTO. The USTR expressed "regret" that the European Union had taken this action and promised to "continue to consult with officials from Massachusetts and the EU in an effort to reach a mutually satisfactory solution."[41] The measure was ultimately ruled to be unconstitutional by the US courts, after a challenge by a US industry group and not the federal government.

The US federal government's preference to use political pressure and negotiated settlements has at times been successful but it has also created uncertainty for Canadian interests. In 1998, South Dakota began to harass Canadian shipments of wheat, cattle and hogs by implementing tougher inspection programs and at one point actually stopped shipments of these Canadian products from entering the state. Other states in the region also participated in a program of increased inspection of these Canadian imports. These actions were widely perceived as a reaction to falling commodity prices, for which rising imports from Canada were blamed, even though allowing greater competition for markets to the advantage of consumers is usually considered to be one of the point of freer trade.

These actions were timed to occur six weeks before mid-term congressional elections and it was speculated that the Democratic US Administration chose not to force the states involved, most of which had Republican governors, to back down because it did not want to create a backlash against Democrats in the upcoming election.[42] Even though Canada sought to have the US federal government overturn the states' actions in the courts, Washington chose instead to negotiate a Record of Understanding (R.O.U.) with Canada aimed at providing a conspicuous response to the political concerns of the states.[43] At the end of the day, Washington was able to resolve the issue, but not before shipments were disrupted and uncertainty was created for Canadian farmers.[44]

While the actions of South Dakota provoked the United States government to eventually take action, the Ontario-Minnesota fish dispute of 1999 demonstrates that relying on the US federal government does not always pay off. The dispute between Ontario and Minnesota arose after the failure of Minnesota to implement recommendations made by a joint Ontario-Minnesota task force on the conservation of sauger and walleye fish stocks in shared boundary waters. Because Minnesota failed to follow the task force recommendations, the Government of Ontario imposed limits on the amount of fish that could be caught and retained by non-resident anglers unless the non-resident angler purchased accommodation services in Ontario (the so-called "overnight stay requirement"). Minnesota subsequently sought the help of USTR to resolve what they saw as a violation of Canada's trade in services commitments. USTR's willingness to become engaged in this dispute, despite the relatively small economic harm suffered as a result of the Ontario measure, is thought to be related to the mid-term congressional elections and the fact that the entire Minnesota Congressional Caucus and the Governor were in support of taking action.

In this dispute, the trade issue was a proxy. The real question was not whether Ontario was acting in a manner consistent with Canada's trade obligations, but how to gain increased access to an Ontario resource, as well as how to resolve conservation issues related to the boundary waters. The problem, in fact, was about conservation and environmental protection and was only disguised as a trade allegation. At the end of the day, Minnesota's characterization of the problem as a trade dispute, and the US Administration's willingness to launch a trade challenge, did not resolve the issue. In fact, the intervention of the federal governments only increased the pressure on Ontario and Minnesota to make the problem go away which, in the end, meant a solution that did little to benefit the aggrieved Minnesota interests. Ontario "solved" the trade problem by removing the overnight stay requirement but lowered catch and retention limits for all non-resident anglers. The international conservation issue has remained largely unresolved. Moreover, support for the NAFTA on the Ontario side of the boundary has been weakened because it is now perceived as a cudgel by which provincial measures can be forcibly modified even in cases where the measure itself was imposed because of intransigence on the US side of the border.

Importantly, in the context of the discussion on further integration between the two countries, this cross-border issue also suggests the broader point that trade agreements are not inherently the proper tool or forum to resolve disputes that are not fundamentally related to trade.

These disputes were counterproductive to the interests of bilateral trade in two ways. First, the states involved did not increase their trade sophistication and, in some cases, were rewarded for their actions or, in the case of beer, inaction. Moreover, behaviour such as that displayed by South Dakota might actually encourage other states to pursue unilateral, trade-inconsistent initiatives to win concessions from Canadian interests — although whether such an action can succeed does seem to depend on the US political climate of the day.

The other, larger problem with this type of behaviour is the broader implications it may have for efforts to deepen economic integration between Canada and the United States. Canadians may begin to doubt the usefulness of formal North American integration if Washington allows states to act in ways that are clearly inimical to Canadian interests.

None of this is to say that provincial policies never run afoul of Canada's international trade obligations or that provincial measures are not also the subject of international trade disputes launched by the United States. Beer I and the Ontario-Minnesota fish dispute are excellent examples of the US targetting a provincial measure. The difference is that once a provincial measure is found not to be in compliance it is, as in the case of Beer I, amended. In contrast, Beer II demonstrates that GATT non-conformity in the US states can, at the limit, actually increase after an adverse panel ruling. Therein lies the irony that, despite the relatively superior powers of Washington over Ottawa to enforce trade decisions, sub-federal non-compliance with international trade obligations is more of a problem in the United States than it is in Canada.

Addressing Canadian Issues

As outlined above, the governments of Canada face a number of challenges with respect to international economic integration efforts. Because of the importance that secure access to US markets has for the Canadian economy, it is this country that must show leadership on this issue. Below I will present three types of initiatives that could be undertaken to address these challenges. They are: 1) improving the existing federal-provincial consultative mechanism; 2) attempting to ensure better sub-federal engagement and compliance within the United States with trade policies set out by Ottawa and Washington; and 3) greater direct provincial engagement of the US states. This section of the paper deals with the first of these, namely identifying and addressing domestic issues.

The Canadian model of federal-provincial cooperation and consultation has minimized, but not eliminated, Canada's exposure to international disputes involving sub-national measures. At the same time, further integration cannot proceed unless the provinces understand the full extent of Canada's international trade obligations. For these reasons, both the federal and provincial governments need to take steps to make the current system better.

One of the biggest problems that provinces face when dealing with Ottawa is their relative lack of trade policy capacity compared to the federal government. The inability to analyse all of the implications of the NAFTA regime for sub-federal governments, for example, has a number of negative consequences for the process of North American economic integration. First, if provincial governments are not living up to the commitments set out in the NAFTA, the process of economic integration cannot proceed at the pace intended. Second, if provinces have not yet fully comprehended the existing integration regime, they may be hesitant to endorse further integration efforts.

To be fair, it should be noted that in some areas within provincial jurisdiction, provincial officials have in-depth expertise that far exceeds the level of sophistication of federal officials. In addition, unlike trade officials in the federal department of Foreign Affairs and International Trade, their provincial counterparts tend to remain in their positions for long periods of time. This means that the latter have greater institutional memory on some trade issues than their federal counterparts, a better ability to develop an expertise in a particular area and more opportunity to develop relationships with officials in other provinces.[45]

These advantages still do not compensate for the relative lack of capacity compared to the federal government. One obvious way to overcome this problem is for the provinces to develop expertise by retaining outside counsel and dedicating more staff to international economic issues. This may be easier said than done, but if provinces want to be players in the game, they must be willing to pay some of the price. The information shared by the federal government will be most meaningful if there are provincial officials to receive and understand it.

Provinces could also mitigate some of these capacity-building costs if they did a better job of cooperating with one another. It is interesting to note that, although the provinces and the federal government meet on a regular basis to discuss international issues, the provinces rarely meet with one another to discuss common provincial concerns. Moreover, because provinces tend to work in isolation, they rarely set the agenda for new international initiatives or approaches and are missing important opportunities to lessen costs and duplication by sharing expertise and dividing up necessary research.

With respect to the current C-Trade consultative mechanism, the provinces have taken different approaches on how this might be modified or improved. In part, these different approaches reflect how the provinces deal with international trade issues within their own jurisdictions. Some provinces treat trade as an intergovernmental matter, while others view it as part of their economic development portfolio. Provinces that place trade matters within the intergovernmental affairs portfolio appear more willing to view interaction between the federal and provincial governments in a broad, intergovernmental context and, consequently, may be more willing to consider a formal federal-provincial structure other than the current C-Trade.

Provinces that participate in C-Trade by sending representatives from their economic development departments generally tend to view the federal-provincial forum in a more narrow economic context and appear less willing to consider modifications to the existing structure. It is therefore difficult to imagine a formal structure that could adequately address these questions and differences in approach to the satisfaction of all governments.

Provinces that wish to have a more formal structure have suggested that the provinces and Ottawa replace the current informal consultative mechanism with a structure that permits provinces to participate in international negotiations and also provides them with a place at the table during international dispute-resolution procedures. It remains unclear, however, how meaningful such provincial participation would be unless provinces are willing to devote more staff and resources to international economic issues. A right to sit at the negotiating table, for example, does not necessarily make good sense if a province does not have an economic interest in the negotiations and/or if it lacks the resources to take its place at the table. Would such a structure recognize the relative importance of trade to some provinces over others? Could it be flexible enough to only involve or accord adequate weight to those provinces that have an economic stake in a particular issue to the exclusion of [un]interested provinces?

Even if a formal structure were devised, there may be no effective way to bind governments to the formal arrangement, because such an intergovernmental agreement would not be enforceable by law. Indeed, such an agreement could not withstand a court reversal of the *Labour Conventions* case and as such could not be used to hem in either level of government should the existing state of the law evolve because of a court decision. Professor Grace Skogstad, Professor of Political Science at the University of Toronto, has noted that this model may be unworkable in practice and might seriously deprive the federal government of its authority by essentially granting the provinces a veto over aspects of international trade negotiations. The current system may therefore be better because the "consultative strategy avoids the joint decision-making traps that shared federal-provincial negotiating authority may create."[46]

Skogstad has reviewed a number of alternatives to the current structure including having the federal government assert its exclusive authority over international trade issues. This may upset the dicta of the *Labour Conventions* case however, which is a risky proposition if the federal government cannot achieve a court ruling that decisively overrules the case in its favour. A diametrically opposed approach would be for the Canadian government to only conclude agreements that fall within the exclusive jurisdiction of the federal government, but this would be out of step with the scope of both existing trade agreements and current trade negotiations.

A final alternative might see the federal government concluding agreements that include areas of provincial jurisdiction, but only fulfilling federal commitments. Provinces would then be given the opportunity to choose whether or not to bind themselves to those commitments that fall within their own purview. This approach was used with respect to adoption of the two NAFTA side agreements on labour and the environment and the federal government practice of seeking the explicit approval of provinces before taking on international commitments in areas of clear provincial jurisdiction, as it did in the Uruguay Round services negotiations. However, it seems unlikely that Canada's trading partners would be content with such an arrangement for all matters.

A survey of alternative mechanisms to the current consultative process would seem to suggest that the status quo, or a modified version of the status quo, is the most useful accommodation of both federal and provincial interests.[47] Canada is not so large and the number of its sub-federal units not so unwieldy that the current structure cannot continue to function, although improvements can and should be made to it. To a certain extent, this is already occurring. Meetings between trade officials from the provinces and federal government now convene quarterly. The federal government has also taken some steps to insure that provincial officials develop further trade expertise by conducting trade seminars and conferences on specific trade issues. Those programs should continue.

The federal government also needs to devote more resources to maintaining its links with provincial trade officials outside of the formal C-Trade mechanism. Although there is a secure web page that permits the federal government to share documents with the provinces, federal officials themselves should be in greater contact with their provincial colleagues. During the C-Trade meetings, Ottawa should allocate more time to the discussion of issues to ensure that these encounters become more of a consultation session and less of a one-way communication.[48] These changes, coupled with improved trade capacity within the provinces, will go a long way toward addressing the domestic challenges to international economic integration issues. In addition to developing better links with trade officials, there needs to be a parallel development of a revitalized federal-provincial ministers' forum. This would be an important tool to assist in provinces' understanding of Canada's trade commitments. Clear ministerial direction would also give more guidance to provincial and federal officials in their consultative process.

Finally, the Canadian government needs to ensure that the provinces have a more realistic understanding of their nation's trading relationships and a more balanced understanding of liberalized trade. Unfortunately the benefits of liberalized free trade are sometimes rather diffuse, while the risks are specific and can have highly visible effects in particular provinces. Discussion of trade initiatives must recognize that trade liberalization will both open up new markets abroad and expose local markets to increased competition.

Greater cooperation and coherence between Canadian governments on international trade issues involving sub-federal measures would mean that stronger Canadian positions could be established on trade and integration issues generally. But the usefulness of such a strengthened East-West mechanism under the aegis of the federal government would still be of limited value in terms of improving access to the US market. As we have seen, such access is often limited by state government measures, and resolving these issues through Ottawa and Washington can very much depend on the good will of Washington to engage the states more deeply on international trade issues. Thus, I will look next at possible ways in which the issue of sub-federal involvement in trade matters could be put on the bilateral agenda. This will include the possibilities for institutional improvements that are more directly North-South or regional in scope, and that would draw the states and provinces more directly together in designing a better cross-border relationship.

Addressing Issues in the US

With respect to the issue of dealing with challenges from the United States, it is useful to review the policies that the Canadian government should not adopt. Because dealing with sub-federal governments generally complicates economic integration efforts, it may be tempting to try to further economic integration without involving this lower level of government. However, meaningful integration must include such things as trade in services, standard setting and the regulation of professions. All of these sectors are regulated at the state and provincial levels and without sub-federal involvement, economic integration will not be comprehensive. Ignoring sub-federal governments is also not risk free. The ability of the US states, in particular, to undermine the goals of its federal government, whether intentional or not, makes indifference towards sub-federal governments an unwise option.

A similar mistake would be to take a "wait-and-see" approach. There is little doubt that, over time, US states will increase their trade sophistication and begin to develop some expertise on economic integration. Although this may be the case, there are a number of problems with such a complacent approach. States may not develop expertise fast enough to keep pace with the demand for further economic integration. A wait-and-see approach also does not address the inherent problems of differences in size and sophistication among sub-federal units, for even if trade sophistication increases over time, it may remain as asymmetrically distributed as it is now. In addition, by doing nothing, the federal government will not be able to discourage the more egregious actions taken by sub-federal states, such as the unilateral policy making evidenced in 1998 by South Dakota. Arguably, a wait-and-see approach is nothing more than passive encouragement of actions that undermine integration efforts.

Perhaps the most serious problem with a "wait-and-see" approach is that it will encourage the US federal government to further develop its consultative mechanism with the states as the only method and forum for dealing with sub-federal governments on international economic issues. The Massachusetts sanctions dispute is perhaps the best example of the US federal government preferring to consult with the states on trade issues rather than flex its constitutional authority. This dispute demonstrated that a consultative mechanism is not always useful if it is not backed up by action that will result in sub-federal compliance.

There are other problems with the suggestion that such a consultative mechanism is the only method and forum for interacting with the states. Like the Canadian federation, there is a great deal of disparity between the size and economic power of the states. However, unlike Canada, which has to deal with 13 sub-federal units, the US must deal with 50 states. The fact that Canada began consulting with the provinces in the 1970s also ensured that there would be a precedent and procedure in place when more comprehensive trade negotiations such as the Uruguay Round and the NAFTA took place. The US model, as set out in the *Uruguay Round Agreements Act*, establishes a mechanism after the fact. It is unclear how the mechanism could be seen as pro-active if states were not consulted during the negotiation of an agreement.

The lack of prior consultations also exacerbates the problem of the lack of trade sophistication among state officials. The mechanism established by the US federal government after the negotiation of the Uruguay Round appears to consist of little more than information sharing and does not address the issue of who gets the information and what is done with it. In other words, consultations and information sharing with uninformed and perhaps unengaged parties do not constitute meaningful consultations.

The consultative mechanism works in Canada because of a clear division of federal and provincial powers, which in turn has encouraged the development of executive federalism and facilitated a means by which the two levels of government can communicate. Also there is no clear separation of legislative and executive power.[49] In almost all cases, the provincial ministers of trade or provincial premiers are capable of speaking on behalf of both the executive and legislative branches of government. In contrast, the US tends to work through a more diffuse political system[50] under which neither the federal executive nor state governors can speak on behalf of their respective governments and represent only one branch of the government. Governors, for example, may see the benefits of liberalized trade but "state representatives, particularly those regulatory officials not responsible for job creation and budgets, are less willing to see state regulatory autonomy, even autonomy used for protectionist purposes, constrained."[51]

Furthermore, because of differences in the constitutional division of powers in both countries and the separation of powers in the US system of government, solutions to [e]nsuring sub-federal involvement and support for economic integration efforts are of necessity country specific. There cannot be a "one size fits all" solution to dealing with sub-federal units, a generic approach that could be prescribed, for example, within international trade agreements. In fact, the language of both the NAFTA and GATT recognizes that different federal systems have different solutions to ensuring compliance with international trade agreements.

Promoting US Sub-Federal Engagement

Certainly, the Canadian government should try to impress upon the US federal government that an assurance of state compliance with commitments that have been made in international trade agreements is a very important matter for Canada. While it would seem unrealistic to seek express assurances from the US that it will enforce its obligations at the sub-federal level in advance of any new integration initiatives, Canada should not hesitate to raise the issue. Canada cannot expect progress on this issue if it is not willing to discuss it. Governments frequently signal to other governments a wide range of issues that they wish to address in the context of trade negotiations including specific commitments they are seeking or more general matters such as increased transparency. There is no reason why a discussion of the role of sub-federal governments in international trade could not be similarly raised.

It seems clear that by raising the issue of sub-federal governments in international trade, Canada will open itself up to an internal discussion of the issue and perhaps criticism from the United States that provinces do not always comply with international trade obligations. Canada should be able to meet these criticisms. In the first place, Canada could make it clear that the different federal structures in the two countries and the language of both the GATT and NAFTA dealing with sub-federal compliance do not require absolute symmetry. Canada could also point out that the current consultative mechanism in Canada is cognizant of its constitutional division of powers but has, nevertheless, proved successful over time. On this last point, Canada should be able to demonstrate that the track record on provincial compliance is stronger than that of the US states. But the key is that, by inviting this criticism, Canada would have underlined the need to explore the issue of sub-federal compliance with its trading partners.

By raising this issue Canada would also be underscoring a key message that a more mutually beneficial integration of the Canadian and US economies will not occur if matters under sub-federal jurisdiction such as services, procurement or investment are subject to little more than the grandfathering of existing measures. Canadian provinces will have little incentive to open their own markets in these areas unless there is a reciprocal benefit for Canadian business. For example, it seems unlikely that Canadian provinces will agree to be bound by the WTO Government Procurement Agreement or the procurement provisions of the NAFTA, unless the US states offer to remove some of the protectionist elements of their local buying preferences.

In any ensuing discussion, Canada could suggest that it might be in the US federal government's interest to improve on the use it makes of its consultative mechanism. In fact, a carefully modified version of the mechanism could be very useful as a tool to further trade liberalization and compliance among the US states. However, the mechanism, in its current form, is no substitute for Washington asserting its authority. Having said that, the exercise of the US federal government's legal powers does not necessarily mean that it should bring on a large number of law suits to enforce sub-federal compliance, if for no other reason than the political heat that this would bring down on Washington.[52] Ideally, the encouragement of voluntary compliance would be best, but not at the expense of abandoning the option of mandatory compliance consistent with the constitutional authority of the US federal government. Washington, therefore, could use the consultative mechanism as a condition precedent to the exercise of its legal authority to impose sub-federal compliance, but not as an alternative.

There are elements of the Canadian model that could be adopted to assist in the goal of voluntary compliance. It has been Canada's experience "that the best way to ensure the involvement of provinces and states in trade policy issues is by involving them often, and in an informed way."[53] This speaks both to the form and content of consultations. However, given the large number of states, it is perhaps impractical to develop a model that requires consultations with all states. Instead, it might make more sense to use institutions already in existence to facilitate consultations. For example, the Council of State Governments could be better utilized as a forum to articulate trade issues with state officials and the federal government could institute a series of regular meetings between the National Governors' Association and USTR. It should also take steps to ensure that states are accorded treatment as another order of government — and not as interest groups. This might involve restructuring of the USTR Office of Intergovernmental Affairs and Public Liaison.

Furthermore, in order to move from a more theoretical discussion of sub-federal compliance of international trade obligations to more practical initiatives, Canada could also propose the creation and institutionalisation of an international joint forum for provinces and states to facilitate discussion of trade issues. For example, during trade negotiations, sub-federal governments could be invited to jointly discuss proposals and draft text. This proposal would not permit a place at the negotiating table for sub-federal governments but could facilitate sub-federal compliance and sophistication on trade issues. Some provinces may criticise the proposal because it may not go far enough to address some of the aspirations of some Canadian provinces. However, it should be viewed by provinces and US states alike as a useful forum to discuss issues of mutual concern and because it explicitly recognizes the sub-federal governments as relevant actors.

The creation of a such a forum creates a valuable "horizontal" bridge between sub-federal governments in addition to the "vertical" relationship that sub-federal governments now have with their central governments. To date, both the states and provinces rely on their respective national governments for information on trade initatives. Rather th[a]n only dealing with their own national governments on issues of international concern, a forum of sub-federal governments from both sides of the border should be encouraged to discuss issues that are unique to their order of government. This is perhaps the most beneficial aspect to this proposal: the forum will facilitate face-to-face meetings of sub-federal officials. These discussions may also result in the formation of common positions amongst sub-federal governments to advocate to their respective federal governments. They could also entice sub-federal governments, particularly the US states, to view trade initiatives as more than simply opportunities for investment attraction or access to new markets abroad, but rather as mutually beneficial exercises in rule-making.

Participation in such a forum should result in an increase of trade sophistication by sub-federal governments, a development of a mutual understanding of the issues facing various jurisdictions and the creation of relationships between trade officials from the various jurisdictions. Specifically, it should be come readily apparent to border states and provinces that some of their regional concerns mean that they have more in common with their US or Canadian counterpart than they do with another sub-federal government in their own country. Ontario and New York, for example, may discover that they have more in common with each other on some issues than they do with their respective western counterparts in British Columbia or California. Indeed, it is likely inevitable that provinces and states will increasingly become directly engaged with each other on matters under their jurisdictions. One recent, but by no means unique, example of this trend is the resolution of the problems that arose from recent New York state measures targeting procurement practices of certain provincial jurisdictions.

Cross-Border Regional Agreements: The Example of Sub-Federal Procurement

In 2000, the New York State Assembly modified existing legislation that allowed the state to designate other US states with discriminatory procurement regimes, for the purpose of restricting access to New York State procurement contracts, to include foreign jurisdictions. In particular, companies from jurisdictions designated under the Act could not bid on contracts with state departments and agencies. After the passage of the legislation, Ontario and Quebec were added to the list of discriminatory jurisdictions, which already included the states of Alaska, Hawaii, Louisiana, Montana, South Carolina and West Virginia.

The New York bill modifying the existing legislation was first introduced in 1999 in response to protests about an Ontario company winning a contract, subsequently terminated, for an "I Love New York" tourism guide. The awarding of the printing contract to an Ontario firm was controversial for a number of reasons. Many viewed the awarding of a contract for governmental tourism promotional material to an out-of-jurisdiction source as illogical while others argued that the low Canadian dollar made the Ontario bid cheaper.[54] It is quite likely, however, that the law was aimed at Ontario's own Canadian preference on procurement purchases and was also a means of applying pressure on Ontario and Quebec to take on international procurement obligations that, to date, they have not undertaken. Because Ontario and Quebec are not subject to international procurement obligations, the US federal government did not have a formal remedy by which to seek recourse against these provinces. In contrast, New York is covered by the WTO Agreement on Government Procurement, which requires them, subject to certain exceptions including Buy American and small business set aside exceptions, to practice open procurement with other signatories. Although New York offered no evidence that local suppliers had difficulty obtaining contracts in Ontario or Quebec, perceptions to that effect may have prompted the state to take action.

In July 2001, Ontario quietly announced it had dropped its Canadian preference policy. For its part, Quebec reached a formal understanding with New York in September of that same year in which it withdrew any limitations on the origin of goods and services procured. As a result, both provinces were removed from the New York list of discriminatory jurisdictions.

Ontario and Quebec-based firms did not, however, get improved access to all New York procurement opportunities, for they continue to be ineligible for New York procurement contracts subject to Buy America restrictions attached to federal funding, including those for steel and transportation projects.

If the resolution seems a bit lopsided, it did result in the creation of a number of mechanisms and potential liberalization opportunities. In particular, the agreement, which resolved the dispute between New York and Quebec established a consultative mechanism to provide early warning on "future measures affecting one another that may reduce access to public procurement."[55] In addition, each government designated a person to assist in the resolution of disputes and as a means to "develop and to favor an increase in the reciprocal opening of their respective public procurements."[56] For its part, Ontario signed an agreement with New York in the same year to develop co-operative mechanisms between the state and province including, among other things, a commitment to collaborate on job creation, promotion of transportation infrastructure improvements, co-operation on joint environmental and natural resource issues, and taking up joint concerns with their respective federal governments.

Toward Deeper State — Provincial Engagement

The progress that remains to be accomplished between the Canadian and the US government[s] on matters involving sub-federal jurisdictions could be complemented and accelerated through a sub-federal forum involving all provinces and states wishing to participate. This being said, it seems clear that in some cases, economic integration will occur on a regional scale before it occurs at a binational level. Indeed, the provinces have begun to develop a series of networks across the Canadian-United States border, as evidenced by provincial membership in US governmental organizations and the signing of memoranda of understanding between state and provincial governments. For example, many provinces have memberships in the Council of State Governments and their regional chapters. Quebec and Ontario are associate members of the Great Lakes Governors' Association while the Atlantic provinces and Quebec participate in the New England Governor[s'] Conference. Alberta is party to a number of regional forums including the Rocky Mountain Trade Corridor, the Can/Am Border Trade Alliance, the Montana-Alberta Bilateral Advisory Council, and several US sectoral and legislative forums.[57] Ontario and Quebec have also participated in summits with New York State to promote regional interests and binational initiatives and, as discussed above, have signed agreements arising out of the New York procurement dispute.

These links, particularly in the past, were used as photo opportunities when provincial premiers and state governors paid visits to each other, and were not designed to bring about substantive actions. But many of these mechanisms could be used to discuss issues of common concern and develop economic integration within each sub-federal unit's constitutional jurisdiction. This might include such things as promoting mutually beneficial economic development aims, road-building initiatives to facilitate border crossings, developing common tourism infrastructure or the harmonization of taxation or environmental measures. Working closely with regional states may also provide an early warning of trade irritants and potential disputes which could prevent these issues from escalating. Provinces and states could then articulate common interests and issues to their national governments.

That said, the respective constitutional powers of the sub-federal governments in each country do limit the scope of these agreements. Neither state nor provincial governments have the legal capacity to enter into anything that might be akin to a binding treaty. Thus, the success of these agreements will depend on the political commitment of the involved state and provincial governments to continue participating in these discussions, as when New York and Quebec made commitments with respect to procurement.

The Agreement on Internal Trade (AIT) signed by the Canadian provinces and federal government provides an interesting example in the Canadian context of how a political agreement can cover a wide range of important issues. Under the AIT, governments have made commitments on matters such as procurement, investment, consumer-related measures and the environment. The AIT also demonstrates that without an ongoing political commitment to the agreement, or without appropriate thought as to how governments might implement it, such a commitment may do nothing more than raise expectations that cannot be met. For example, the AIT chapter on energy has still not been completed despite the conclusion of the rest of the agreement in 1994. Despite its weaknesses, it has been argued that the AIT could "have an important normative or 'legal' effect even if no sovereign body has the power to compel compliance."[58] The same might be said of any cross-border agreements between sub-federal governments provided that they are focussed and capable of achieving measurable results.

In this respect, Ottawa and Washington could envisage a framework accord that would facilitate such broader agreements, on a regional basis, between states and provinces that would consider it mutually beneficial to fast-track improvements in their trading relationship and on other issues of common interest, such as environmental standards. The framework agreement could place such cross-border regional agreements under a common aegis, such as that of the NAFTA Commission, composed of representatives of the governments of the three NAFTA countries, in order to ensure consistency with international accords, and the ultimate role of federal governments in international trade matters.

Finally, provincial governments must guard against becoming complacent in the absence of trade-liberalization initiatives from the US states. Even if the latter decline to offer substantial liberalization in certain sectors, provinces should not be content to let the issue rest. Instead, they should take a pro-active approach and put together their own offers on sub-federal liberalization. As yet, this type of initiative has not been pursued by the provinces.

Conclusion

Some of the most significant steps towards economic integration that have been taken to date, such as tariff elimination and border facilitation issues, fall almost exclusively under the jurisdiction of federal governments. Economic integration in the North American context necessarily implicates sub-federal governments in Canada and the United States because significant sectors of the economy fall within the constitutional competence of the provinces and states. Consequently, there is real potential for sub-federal governments to undermine or reverse economic integration efforts through either deliberate actions designed to limit or harass foreign competition, or failure to share or understand the broader vision of economic integration postulated by central governments.

Until the issue of sub-federal engagement, particularly on the part of US states, is addressed, it is difficult to imagine how meaningful integration initiatives can proceed. In short, if the North American marketplace is to be integrated, the role of sub-federal governments must be recognized and these governments must be encouraged to both implement existing commitments and to contribute effectively to the development of new ones.

Notes

* Senior Policy Advisor and Team Leader, Trade and International Policy Branch, Ministry of Enterprise, Opportunity and Innovation, Government of Ontario. He also teaches business and government at York University. The opinions expressed in this paper are those of the author and do not reflect those of his employer.

1 The focus of the discussion will be on integration between the United States and Canada, principally concerning commercial matters involving the states and provinces. The author wishes to thank Douglas Brown, Peter Morici, Daniel Schwanen and Quebec and Ontario government officials for extensive comments on the first draft of this paper. Thanks also to Armand de Mestral, Patrick Monahan, as well as Alberta and Canadian federal government officials for helpful discussions on specific aspects of subsequent drafts. Responsibility for any remaining errors are those of the author alone.

2 World Trade Organization(1994).

3 GATT (1988*a*).

4 Cooper (1993, p. 155).

5 GATT (1988*b*).

6 Cooper (1993, p. 152).

7 GATT (1988*b*).

8 Fairley (1988, p. 162).

9 *A.-G Can V. A.-G. Ont. et al.* (1937 1 D.L.R. The "Labour Conventions" case).

10 Fairley (1988, p. 107).

11 Monahan (2001, p. 21).

12 McIllroy (1997, p. 433).

13 Fairley (1988, p. 162).
14 Bakvis and Skogstad (2001, p. 15).
15 The negotiations and resulting structure of the Agreement on Internal Trade supports the notion that each level of government considers itself sovereign within its sphere. In particular, it is interesting to note that the language of the AIT replicates, in many cases, the provisions of international trade agreements.
16 Kuchuka (2001, p. 31).
17 Bakvis and Skogstad (2001, p. 7).
18 Anderson (2001*b*, p. 51).
19 Fairley (1988, p. 135).
20 Ziegel (1988, p. 342).
21 McIlroy (1997, p. 438).
22 Jackson (1989, p. 63) Jackson further opines (p. 68) that "with regard to international economic matters, there appears to be no significant constitutional limitation on the powers of the federal government because of state powers. Thus any valid international agreement which has direct application, or any valid federal statute or regulation regarding foreign economic affairs will likely prevail over inconsistent state law."
23 Jackson (1989, p. 68).
24 Kincaid (1999, p. 118).
25 Skogstad (2001, p. 160).
26 Kuchuka (2001, p. 31).
27 Cooper (1993, p. 147).
28 *2002 Trade Policy Agenda and 2001 Annual Report of the President of the United States on the Trade Agreements Program* (p. 225).
29 *2002 Trade Policy Agenda and 2001 Annual Report of the President of the United States on the Trade Agreements Program* (2001, p. 225).
30 Kincaid (1999, p. 125).
31 Fry (1993, p. 130).
32 Schaefer (1999, p. 77).
33 Schaefer (1999, p. 78).
34 Kincaid (1999, p. 124).
35 Fry (1993, p. 131).
36 Gifford (2001, p. 126).
37 Gifford (2001, p. 126).
38 GATT Doc. DS/23/R.
39 Morrison (2001).
40 For example see: Schmahmann and Finch (1997, pp 175–207) who assert that the state enactment is unconstitutionally "infirm" under pre-emption, the foreign commerce clause and the supremacy clause of the US constitution.
41 Press Release from the Office of the United States Trade Representative (1997).
42 *Inside US Trade* (1998, p. 2).
43 Gifford (2001, p. 127).

44 Brosch (2001, p. 115). It is useful to remember that Mexican tomatoes were the target of similar actions by the Florida State officials in response to growing imports from that country.

45 Kuchuka (2001, p. 30).

46 Skogstad (2001, p. 161).

47 Skogstad (2001, p. 163).

48 Kuchuka (2001, p. 24).

49 Anderson (2001*b*, p. 51).

50 Anderson (2001*a*, p. 55 at 58).

51 Schaefer (1999, p. 79).

52 Schaefer (1999, p. 43).

53 Williams (1999).

54 *Memorandum of Understanding on Public Procurement between the Government of the State of New York and the Government of Quebec* (2001, clause 3).

55 *Memorandum of Understanding on Public Procurement between the Government of the State of New York and the Government of Quebec* (2001, clause 4).

56 *Memorandum of Understanding and Cooperation between The Province of Ontario and the State of New York* (2001).

57 Information compiled by International Relations, Alberta International and Intergovernmental Relations, Government of Alberta, July 2000 (www.iir.gov.ab.ca.).

58 Swinton (1995, p. 197).

References

A.-G Can. V. A.-G. Ont. et al., Reference Re Weekly Rest in Industrial Undertakings Act, Minimum Wages Act and Limitation of Hours of Work Act 1 D.L.R. (1937).

Anderson, George. "Discussion Following the Remarks of Mr. Schaefer and Mr. Anderson." *Canada-United States Law Journal*, Vol. 27 (2001*a*): 55–58.

Anderson, George. "Canadian Federalism and Foreign Policy." *Canada-United States Law Journal*, Vol. 27 (2001*b*): 45–53.

Bakvis, Herman and Grace Skogstad. "Canadian Federalism: Performance, Effectiveness and Legitimacy." In *Canadian Federalism: Performance, Effectiveness and Legitimacy*, eds. Herman Bakvis and Grace Skogstad. Toronto: Oxford University Press, 2001.

Brosch, Kevin. "Relative Roles of States/Provinces in Regulation Agriculture and the Resulting Impact on Cross-Border Trade." *Canada-United States Law Journal*, Vol. 27 (2001): 113–121.

Cooper, Kenneth J. "To Compel or Encourage: Seeking Compliance with International Trade Agreements at the State Level." *Minnesota Journal of Global Trade*, Vol. 2, no. 1 (Winter 1993): 143–170.

Fairley, H. Scott. "Jurisdictional Limits on National Purpose: Ottawa, The Provinces and Free Trade with the United States." In *Trade-Offs on Free Trade:*

The Canada-US Free Trade Agreement, eds. Marc Gold and David Leyton-Brown. Toronto: Carswell Co. Ltd., 1988.

Fry, Earl. "The Economic Policies of Subnational Governments in North America: The Potential Impact on NAFTA." In *Beyond NAFTA: An Economic, Political and Sociological Perspective*, eds. A.R. Riggs and Tom Velk. Vancouver: Fraser Institute, 1993.

General Agreement of Trade and Tariffs Secretariat. *United States: Measures Affecting Alcoholic and Malt Beverages*. Document DS/23/R. Washington, D.C.: GATT Secretariat, 1988*a*.

—. *Basic Instruments and Selected Documents*, 35th Supp. 37. Washington, D.C.: GATT Secretariat, 1988*b*.

Gifford, Michael. "Relative Roles of States/Provinces in Regulating Agriculture and the Resulting Impact on Cross-Border Trade: A Canadian Perspective." *Canada-United States Law Journal*, Vol. 27 (2001): 123–128.

Inside US Trade. "Glickman meets with Governors on Border Dispute with Canada." Vol 16, no. 9 (October 2, 1998).

Jackson, John. *The World Trading System: Law and Policy of International Economic Relations*. Cambridge, MA: MIT Press, 1989.

Kincaid, John. "The International Competence of US States and Their Local Governments." In *Paradiplomacy in Action: The Foreign Relations of Subnational Governments*, eds. Francisco Aldecoa and Michael Keating. London: Frank Cass, 1999.

Kuchuka, Christopher. "The Federal Provincial Committee System on International Trade CTRADE: Trigger for Constitutional Change?" Paper prepared for the conference *The Administration of Foreign Affairs: A Renewed Challenge*, November 2, 2001.

McIllroy, James. "NAFTA and the Canadian Provinces: Two Ships Passing in the Night?" *Canada-United States Law Journal*, Vol. 23 (1997): 431–440.

Monahan, Patrick. "Differences Between Canadian and US Federal Systems." *Canada-United States Law Journal*, Vol. 27 (2001): 19–25.

Morrison, R.A. "Memorandum to Stephen de Boer." *Brewers Association of Canada*, November 22, 2001.

New York and Ontario. *Memorandum of Understanding and Cooperation between The Province of Ontario and the State of New York*. Albany and Toronto: Governments of New York and Ontario, 2001.

New York and Quebec. *Memorandum of Understanding on Public Procurement between the Government of the State of New York and the Government of Quebec*. Albany and Quebec: Governments of New York and Quebec, 2001.

Office of the United States Trade Representative. "Ambassador Barshefsky Expresses Regret at European Union's Decision to Request Consultations Regarding Massachusetts' Law Regarding Procurement from Companies Doing Business in Burma." Press release. Washington, D.C.: Office of the United States Trade Representative, 1997.

President of the United States. *2002 Trade Policy Agenda and 2001 Annual Report of the President of the United States on the Trade Agreements Program*. Washington, D.C.: Office of the President of the United States, 2001.

Schaefer, Matthew. "Twenty-First Century Trade Negotiations, the US Constitution, and the Elimination of US State-Level Protectionism." *Journal of International Economic Law*, Vol. 2, no. 2 (June 1999): 71–111.

Schmahmann, David and James S. Finch. "The Unconstitutionality of State and Local Enactments in the United States Restricting Business Ties with Burma (Myanmar)." *Vanderbilt Transnational Law Journal*, Vol. 30, no. 2 (March 1997): 175–207.

Skogstad, Grace. "International Trade Policy and Canadian Federalism: A Constructive Tension." In *Canadian Federalism: Performance, Effectiveness and Legitimacy*, eds. Herman Bakvis and Grace Skogstad. Toronto: Oxford University Press, 2001.

Swinton, Katherine. "Law, Politics, and the Enforcement of the Agreement on Internal Trade." In *Getting There: An Assessment of the Agreement on Internal Trade*, eds. Michael. J. Trebilcock and Daniel Schwanen. Toronto: C.D. Howe Institute, 1995.

Williams, Fred. "New York, Canadian Printers Compete on Uneven Field," *Buffalo News*, February 3, 1999.

World Trade Organization. *Understanding on the Interpretation of Article XXIV of the General Agreement on Tariffs and Trade 1994*. Geneva: World Trade Organization, 1994.

Ziegel, Jacob. "Treaty Making and Implementation Powers in Canada: The Continuing Dilemma." In *Contemporary Problems of International Law: Essays in Honour of Georg Schwarzenberger on his Eightieth Birthday*, eds. B. Cheng and E.D. Brown. Agincourt: Carswell, 1988.